**FOURTH EDITION**

# MICROSOFT®
# VISUAL C#® 2010

## AN INTRODUCTION TO OBJECT-ORIENTED PROGRAMMING

## JOYCE FARRELL

**COURSE TECHNOLOGY**
CENGAGE Learning™

Australia • Brazil • Japan • Korea • Mexico • Singapore • Spain • United Kingdom • United States

## COURSE TECHNOLOGY
### CENGAGE Learning™

**Microsoft® Visual C#® 2010: An Introduction to Object-Oriented Programming, Fourth Edition**
Joyce Farrell

Publisher: Nicole Pinard

Executive Editor: Marie Lee

Acquisitions Editor: Amy Jollymore

Senior Product Manager: Alyssa Pratt

Development Editor: Dan Seiter

Content Project Manager: Lisa Weidenfeld

Manufacturing Buyer: Julio Esperas

Proofreader: Brandy Lilly

Copyeditor: Michael Beckett

Indexer: Sharon Hilgenberg

Art Director: Faith Brosnan

Text Designer: Shawn Girsberger

Cover Photo: iStockphoto.com/Dimitrije

Cover Designer: Bruce Bond

Editorial Assistant: Jacqueline Lacaire

Art Director: Marissa Falco

Marketing Manager: Adam Marsh

Quality Assurance: Chris Scriver and
      Danielle Shaw

Compositor: Integra

For product information and technology assistance, contact us at
**Cengage Learning Customer & Sales Support, 1-800-354-9706**

For permission to use material from this text or product,
submit all requests online at **www.cengage.com/permissions**
Further permissions questions can be e-mailed to
**permissionrequest@cengage.com**

Library of Congress Control Number: 2010930061

ISBN-13: 978-0-538-47951-6

ISBN-10: 0-538-47951-5

**Course Technology**
20 Channel Center Street
Boston, MA 02210
USA

Cengage Learning is a leading provider of customized learning solutions with office locations around the globe, including Singapore, the United Kingdom, Australia, Mexico, Brazil, and Japan. Locate your local office at: **www.cengage.com/global**

Cengage Learning products are represented in Canada by Nelson Education, Ltd.

To learn more about Course Technology, visit **www.cengage.com/coursetechnology**

To learn more about Cengage Learning, visit **www.cengage.com**

Purchase any of our products at your local college store or at our preferred online store **www.cengagebrain.com**

Some of the product names and company names used in this book have been used for identification purposes only and may be trademarks or registered trademarks of their respective manufacturers and sellers.

Any fictional data related to people, companies, or URLs used throughout this book is intended for instructional purposes only. At the time this book was printed, any such data was fictional and not belonging to any real people or companies.

Course Technology, a part of Cengage Learning, reserves the right to revise this publication and make changes from time to time in its content without notice.

The programs in this book are for instructional purposes only. They have been tested with care, but are not guaranteed for any particular intent beyond educational purposes. The author and the publisher do not offer any warranties or representations, nor do they accept any liabilities with respect to the programs.

Printed in the United States of America
1 2 3 4 5 6 7 14 13 12 11 10

# Brief Contents

9 week

7  Internet 2.

# Contents

**CHAPTER 3**  **Using GUI Objects and the Visual Studio IDE** . . . . . . . . . . . . . . . . **103**

**CHAPTER 8**    Advanced Method Concepts. . . . . . . . **315**

xi

xiii

**CHAPTER 14** Files and Streams . . . . . . . . . . **656**

**CHAPTER 15** Using LINQ to Access Data
in C# Programs . . . . . . . . . . . . **708**

# Preface

*Microsoft Visual C# 2010, Fourth edition* provides the beginning programmer with a guide to developing programs in C#. C# is a language developed by the Microsoft Corporation as part of the .NET Framework and Visual Studio platform. The .NET Framework contains a wealth of libraries for developing applications for the Windows family of operating systems. With C#, you can build small, reusable components that are well-suited to Web-based programming applications. Although similar to Java and C++, many features of C# make it easier to learn and ideal for the beginning programmer. You can program in C# using a simple text editor and the command prompt, or you can manipulate program components using Visual Studio's sophisticated Integrated Development Environment. This book provides you with the tools to use both techniques.

This textbook assumes that you have little or no programming experience. The writing is nontechnical and emphasizes good programming practices. The examples are business examples; they do not assume mathematical background beyond high school business math. Additionally, the examples illustrate one or two major points; they do not contain so many features that you become lost following irrelevant and extraneous details. This book provides you with a solid background in good object-oriented programming techniques and introduces you to object-oriented terminology using clear, familiar language.

## Organization and Coverage

*Microsoft Visual C# 2010* presents C# programming concepts, enforcing good style, logical thinking, and the object-oriented paradigm. Chapter 1 introduces you to the language by letting you create working C# programs using both the simple command line and the Visual Studio environment. In Chapter 2 you learn about data and how to input, store, and output data in C#. Chapter 3 provides a quick start to creating GUI applications. You can take two approaches:

- You can cover Chapter 3 and learn about GUI objects so that you can create more visually interesting applications in the subsequent chapters on decision making, looping, and array manipulation. These subsequent chapters confine GUI examples to the end of the chapters, so you can postpone GUI manipulation if you want.

- You can skip Chapter 3 until learning the fundamentals of decision making, looping, and array manipulation, and until studying object-oriented concepts such as classes, objects, polymorphism, inheritance, and exception handling. Then, after Chapter 11, you can return to Chapter 3 and use the built-in GUI component classes with a deeper understanding of how they work.

In Chapters 4, 5, and 6, you learn about the classic programming structures—making decisions, looping, and manipulating arrays—and how to implement them in C#. Chapters 7 and 8 provide a thorough study of methods, including passing parameters into and out of methods and overloading them.

Chapter 9 introduces the object-oriented concepts of classes, objects, data hiding, constructors, and destructors. After completing Chapters 10 and 11, you will be thoroughly grounded in the object-oriented concepts of inheritance and exception handling, and will be able to take advantage of both features in your C# programs. Chapter 12 continues the discussion of GUI objects from Chapter 3. You will learn about controls, how to set their properties, and how to make attractive, useful, graphical, and interactive programs. Chapter 13 takes you further into the intricacies of handling events in your interactive GUI programs. In Chapter 14, you learn to save data to and retrieve data from files. In Chapter 15 you learn how to interact with databases in C# programs—an increasingly valuable skill in the information-driven business world. C# supports LINQ (Language INtegrated Query) statements, which allow you to integrate SQL-like queries into C# programs; Chapter 15 provides you with the fundamentals of this important technology.

## New to this Edition!

*Microsoft Visual C# 2010* is a superior textbook because it also includes the following new features:

**C# 4.0 IN VISUAL STUDIO 2010** This edition is written and tested using the latest edition of C#.

**VIDEO LESSONS** Each chapter includes three or more video lessons produced by the author. These short videos provide instruction, further explanation, or background about a topic covered in the corresponding chapter. These videos are especially useful for online classes, for student review before exams, and for students who are audio learners.

**EARLY GUI APPLICATIONS** Students now can begin to create GUI applications in Chapter 3. The earlier introduction helps engage students who have used GUI applications their entire lives. In subsequent chapters on selections, loops, arrays, and methods, students apply concepts to applications in both console and GUI environments. This keeps some examples simple while increasing the understanding that input, processing, and output are programming universals no matter what interface is used. The book is structured so that students who want to skip Chapter 3 until they understand object-oriented programming can do so with no loss of continuity.

**EXPANDED COVERAGE OF METHODS** Instructions for using methods have been expanded and divided into two chapters. The introductory method chapter covers the basics of calling methods, passing arguments, and returning values. The advanced chapter discusses reference parameters, output parameters, optional parameters, parameter arrays, overloading methods, and avoiding ambiguity. (Optional parameters are a new feature in C# 4.0.)

**MORE ENGAGING EXERCISES ON SPECIFIC TOPICS** Many chapters have additional exercises that employ string manipulation and enumerations. Gaming exercises have been added to many chapters.

## Features of the Text

*Microsoft Visual C# 2010* also includes the following features:

**OBJECTIVES** Each chapter begins with a list of objectives so you know the topics that will be presented in the chapter. In addition to providing a quick reference to topics covered, this feature offers a useful study aid.

 **NOTES** These tips provide additional information—for example, an alternative method of performing a procedure, another term for a concept, background information on a technique, or a common error to avoid.

**FIGURES** Each chapter contains many figures. Code figures are most frequently 25 lines or shorter, illustrating one concept at a time. Frequently placed screen shots show exactly how program output appears. In this edition, all C# keywords that appear in figures are bold to help them stand out from programmer-created identifiers.

**SUMMARIES** Following each chapter is a summary that recaps the programming concepts and techniques covered in the chapter. This feature helps you to recap and check your understanding of the main points in each chapter.

**KEY TERMS** Each chapter includes a list of newly introduced vocabulary, shown in the order of appearance in the text. The list of key terms provides a review of the major concepts in the chapter.

**YOU DO IT** In each chapter, step-by-step exercises help the student create multiple working programs that emphasize the logic a programmer uses in choosing statements. This section enables students to achieve success on their own—even students in online or distance learning classes.

**TWO TRUTHS AND A LIE** This short quiz appears after each main chapter section, with answers provided. This quiz contains three statements—two true and one false—and the student must identify the false one. Over the years, students have requested answers to problems, but we have hesitated to distribute them in case instructors want to use problems as assignments or test questions. These quizzes provide students with immediate feedback as they read, without "giving away" answers to the existing multiple-choice and programming problem questions.

**REVIEW QUESTIONS** Each chapter contains 20 multiple-choice review questions that provide a review of the key concepts in the chapter.

**EXERCISES** Each chapter concludes with meaningful programming exercises that provide additional practice of the skills and concepts you learned in the chapter. These exercises increase in difficulty and allow you to explore logical programming concepts.

**DEBUGGING EXERCISES** Each chapter contains four programs that have syntax and/or logical errors for you to fix. Completing these exercises provides valuable experience in locating errors, interpreting code written by others, and observing how another programmer has approached a problem.

**UP FOR DISCUSSION** Each chapter concludes with a few thought-provoking questions that concern programming in general or C# in particular. The questions can be used to start classroom or online discussions, or to develop and encourage research, writing, and language skills.

**PROGRAM CODE** The downloadable student files provide code for each full program presented in the chapter figures. Providing the code on disk allows students to run it, view the results for themselves, and experiment with multiple input values. Having the code on disk also enables students to experiment with the code without a lot of typing.

**GLOSSARY** A glossary contains definitions for all key terms in the book, presented in alphabetical order.

**QUALITY** Every program example in the book, as well as every exercise, case project, and game solution, was tested by the author and again by a Quality Assurance team using Visual Studio 2010.

# Instructor Resources

The following supplemental materials are available when this book is used in a classroom setting. All of the teaching tools for this book are provided to the instructor on a single CD-ROM, and are also available for download at the companion site for the text (*www.cengage. com/coursetechnology*).

**ELECTRONIC INSTRUCTOR'S MANUAL** The Instructor's Manual that accompanies this textbook includes:

- Additional instructional material to assist in class preparation, including suggestions for lecture topics.

- Solutions to Review Questions, end-of-chapter programming exercises, debugging exercises, and Up For Discussion questions.

**EXAMVIEW**® This textbook is accompanied by ExamView, a powerful testing software package that allows instructors to create and administer printed, computer (LAN-based), and Internet exams. ExamView includes hundreds of questions that correspond to the topics covered in this text, enabling students to generate detailed study guides that include page references for further review. The computer-based and Internet testing components allow students to take exams at their computers, and save the instructor time by grading each exam automatically.

**POWERPOINT PRESENTATIONS** This book comes with Microsoft PowerPoint slides for each chapter. These slides are included as a teaching aid for classroom presentation; teachers can make them available on the network for chapter review or print them for classroom distribution. Instructors can add their own slides for additional topics they introduce to the class.

**SOLUTION FILES** Solutions to all "You Do It" exercises and end-of chapter exercises are provided on the Instructor Resources CD-ROM and on the Course Technology Web site at *www.cengage.com/ coursetechnology*. The solutions are password protected.

**DISTANCE LEARNING** Cengage Learning is proud to present online test banks in WebCT and Blackboard to provide the most complete and dynamic learning experience possible. Instructors are encouraged to make the most of the course, both online and offline. For more information on how to access the online test bank, contact your local Course Technology sales representative.

## Acknowledgments

I would like to thank all of the people who helped to make this book a reality, especially Dan Seiter, the development editor, who once again worked against multiple, aggressive deadlines to make this book into a superior instructional tool. Thanks also to Alyssa Pratt, Senior Product Manager; Amy Jollymore, Acquisitions Editor; and Lisa Weidenfeld, Content Project Manager. I am grateful to be able to work with so many fine people who are dedicated to producing good instructional materials.

I am also grateful to the many reviewers who provided helpful comments and encouragement during this book's development, including Matthew Butcher, Mohave Community College; Dan Guilmette, Cochise College; and Jorge Vallejos, Columbus State Community College.

Thanks, too, to my husband, Geoff, for his constant support and encouragement. Finally, this book is dedicated to Andrea and Forrest, wishing them a lifetime of happiness together.

Joyce Farrell

# Read This Before You Begin

## To the User

To complete the debugging exercises in this book, you will need data files that have been created specifically for the book. Your instructor will provide the data files to you. You also can obtain the files electronically from the Course Technology Web site by connecting to *www.cengage.com/coursetechnology* and then searching for this book title. Note that you can use a computer in your school lab or your own computer to complete the exercises in this book.

The data files for this book are organized such that the examples and exercises are divided into folders named Chapter.*xx*, where *xx* is the chapter number. You can save these files in the same folders unless specifically instructed to do otherwise in the chapter.

### Using Your Own Computer

To use your own computer to complete the steps and exercises, you will need the following:

**SOFTWARE** Microsoft Visual C# 2010, including the Microsoft.NET Framework. If your book came with a copy of the software, you may install it on your computer and use it to complete the material.

**HARDWARE** Minimum requirements identified by Microsoft are a 1.6 GHz CPU, 1024 MB of RAM, 3 GB of available hard disk space, 5400 RPM hard disk drive, DirectX 9-capable video card that runs at 1280×1024 or higher display resolution, and a DVD-ROM drive.

**OPERATING SYSTEM** Windows 7, Vista, or XP.

**DATA FILES** You will not be able to complete the debugging exercises in this book using your own computer unless you have the data files. You can get the data files from your instructor, or you can obtain them electronically from the Course Technology Web site by connecting to *www.cengage.com/coursetechnology* and searching for this book title. Additionally, the data files include code for every example shown in a figure in the book.

## To the Instructor

To complete the debugging exercises and chapters in this book, your users must work with a set of data files. These files are included on the Instructor Resources CD. You can also obtain these files electronically through the Course Technology Web site at *www.cengage.com/ coursetechnology*. Follow the instructions in the Help file to copy the user files to your server or stand-alone computer. You can view the Help file using a text editor such as WordPad or Notepad.

Once the files are copied, you can make copies for the users yourself or tell them where to find the files so they can make their own copies.

### License to Use Data Files

You are granted a license to copy the files that accompany this book to any computer or computer network used by people who have purchased this book.

# CHAPTER 1

# A First Program Using C#

In this chapter you will:

◎ Learn about programming

◎ Learn about procedural and object-oriented programming

◎ Learn about the features of object-oriented programming languages

◎ Learn about the C# programming language

◎ Write a C# program that produces output

◎ Learn how to select identifiers to use within your programs

◎ Improve programs by adding comments and using the System namespace

◎ Write and compile a C# program using the command prompt and using Visual Studio

Programming a computer is an interesting, challenging, fun, and sometimes frustrating task. It requires you to be precise and careful as well as creative. If you are, you will find that learning a new programming language expands your horizons.

C# (pronounced "C Sharp") is a programming language that provides you with a wide range of options and features. As you work through this book, you will master many of them, one step at a time. If this is your first programming experience, you will learn new ways to approach and solve problems and to think logically. If you know how to program but are new to C#, you will be impressed by its capabilities.

In this chapter, you will learn about the background of programming that led to the development of C#, and you will write and execute your first C# programs.

# Programming

A computer **program** is a set of instructions that tell a computer what to do. Programs are also called **software**; software comes in two broad categories:

- **System software** describes the programs that operate the computer. Examples include operating systems such as Microsoft Windows, Mac OSX, and Linux.

- **Application software** describes the programs that allow users to complete tasks such as creating documents, calculating paychecks, and playing games.

The physical devices that make up a computer system are its **hardware**. Internally, computer hardware is constructed from circuitry that consists of small on/off switches; the most basic circuitry-level language that computers use to control the operation of those switches is called **machine language**. Machine language is expressed as a series of 1s and 0s—1s represent switches that are on, and 0s represent switches that are off. If programmers had to write computer programs using machine language, they would have to keep track of the hundreds of thousands of 1s and 0s involved in programming any worthwhile task. Not only would writing a program be a time-consuming and difficult task, but modifying programs, understanding others' programs, and locating errors within programs all would be cumbersome. Additionally, the number and location of switches vary from computer to computer, which means you would need to customize a machine-language program for every type of machine on which the program had to run.

Fortunately, programming has become easier because of the development of high-level programming languages. A **high-level programming**

**language** allows you to use a limited vocabulary of reasonable keywords.
**Keywords** are predefined and reserved identifiers that have special
meaning to the compiler. In other words, high-level language programs
contain words such as "read," "write," or "add" instead of the sequence
of on/off switches that perform these tasks. High-level languages also
allow you to assign reasonable names to areas of computer memory; you
can use names such as hoursWorked or payRate, rather than having to
remember the memory locations (switch numbers) of those values.

Each high-level language has its own **syntax**, or rules of the language.
For example, to produce output, you might use the verb "print" in
one language and "write" in another. All languages have a specific,
limited vocabulary, along with a set of rules for using that vocabulary.
Programmers use a computer program called a **compiler** to translate
their high-level language statements into machine code. The compiler issues an error message each time a programmer commits a
**syntax error**—that is, each time the programmer uses the language
incorrectly. Subsequently, the programmer can correct the error and
attempt another translation by compiling the program again. The program can be completely translated to machine language only when
all syntax errors have been corrected. When you learn a computer
programming language such as C#, C++, Visual Basic, or Java, you are
really learning the vocabulary and syntax rules for that language.

In addition to learning the correct syntax for a particular language, a
programmer must understand computer programming logic. The **logic**
behind any program involves executing the various statements and procedures in the correct order to produce the desired results. For example,
you might be able to execute perfect individual notes on a musical
instrument, but if you do not execute them in the proper order (or
execute a B-flat when an F-sharp was expected), no one will enjoy your
performance. Similarly, you might be able to use a computer language's
syntax correctly, but be unable to obtain correct results because the
program is not logically constructed. Examples of logical errors include
multiplying two values when you should divide them, or attempting to
calculate a paycheck before obtaining the appropriate payroll data.

To achieve a working program that accomplishes its intended tasks,
you must remove all syntax and logical errors from the program. This
process is called **debugging** the program.

In some
languages,
such as
BASIC, the
language
translator is called an
interpreter. In others, such
as assembly language, it
is called an assembler.
These translators operate
in different fashions, but
the ultimate goal of each
is to translate the higher-
level language into
machine language.

Programmers
call some
logical errors
**semantic
errors**. For
example, if you misspell a
programming language
word, you commit a syntax
error, but if you use a
correct word in the wrong
context, you commit a
semantic error, generating
incorrect results.

Since the early days of computer programming, program errors have been
called "bugs." The term is often said to have originated from an actual moth
that was discovered trapped in the circuitry of a computer at Harvard
University in 1945. Actually, the term "bug" was in use prior to 1945 to
mean trouble with any electrical apparatus; even during Thomas Edison's life,
it meant an "industrial defect." In any case, the process of finding and correcting
program errors has come to be known as debugging.

4

# Procedural and Object-Oriented Programming

Two popular approaches to writing computer programs are procedural programming and object-oriented programming.

When you write a **procedural program**, you use your knowledge of a programming language to create and name computer memory locations that can hold values, and you write a series of steps or operations to manipulate those values. The named computer memory locations are called **variables** because they hold values that might vary. In programming languages, a variable is referenced by using a one-word name (an **identifier**) with no embedded spaces. For example, a company's payroll program might contain a variable named payRate. The memory location referenced by the name payRate might contain different values at different times. For instance, an organization's payroll program might use a different value for payRate for each of 100 employees. Additionally, a single employee's payRate variable might contain different values before or after a raise or before or after surpassing 40 work hours in one week. During the execution of the payroll program, each value stored under the name payRate might have many operations performed on it—for example, reading it from an input device, multiplying it by another variable representing hours worked, and printing it on paper.

Examples of procedural programming languages include C and Logo.

**Camel casing** describes the style of identifiers that start with a lowercase letter but contain uppercase letters to identify new words, as in `payRate`. The style is named for the fact that the identifier appears to have a hump in the middle. When programmers adopt the style of capitalizing the first letter of all new words in an identifier, even the first one, as in `PayRate`, they call the style **Pascal casing**. By convention, C# programmers use camel casing when creating variable names.

For convenience, the individual operations used in a computer program often are grouped into logical units called **methods**. For example, a series of four or five comparisons and calculations that together determine an employee's federal tax withholding value might be grouped as a method named `CalculateFederalWithholding()`. A procedural program divides a problem solution into multiple procedures, each with a unique name. The program then **calls** or **invokes** the procedures to input, manipulate, and output the values stored in those locations. A single procedural program often contains hundreds of variables and thousands of procedure calls.

Depending on the programming language, methods are sometimes called *procedures, subroutines,* or *functions.* In C#, the preferred term is *methods.*

In C#, methods conventionally are named using Pascal casing, and all method names are followed by a set of parentheses. When this book refers to a method, the name will be followed with parentheses. This practice helps distinguish method names from variable and class names.

**Object-oriented programming (OOP)** is an extension of procedural programming. OOP uses variables and methods like procedural programs do, but it focuses on objects. An **object** is a concrete entity that has attributes and behaviors. The **attributes of an object** are the features it "has"; the values of an object's attributes constitute the **state of the object**. For example, attributes of a paycheck include its payee and monetary value, and the state of those attributes might be "Alice Nelson" and $400. The **behaviors of an object** are the things it "does"; for example, a paycheck object can be written and cashed, and contains a method to calculate the check amount. Object-oriented programmers might start to design a payroll application by thinking about all the objects needed, such as employees, time cards, and paychecks, and describing their attributes and behaviors.

Programmers use the term *OO,* pronounced "oh oh," as an abbreviation for "object oriented." When discussing object-oriented programming, they use *OOP,* which rhymes with "soup."

Examples of OO languages include C#, Java, Visual Basic, and C++. You can write procedural programs in OO languages, but you cannot write OO programs in procedural languages.

With either approach, procedural or object-oriented, you can produce a correct paycheck, and both techniques employ reusable program modules. The major difference lies in the focus the programmer takes during the earliest planning stages of a project. Taking an **object-oriented approach** to a problem means defining the objects needed to accomplish a task and developing classes that describe the objects so that each object maintains its own data and carries out tasks when another object requests them. The object-oriented approach is said to be "natural"—it is more natural to think of a world of objects and the ways they interact than to consider a world of systems, data items, and the logic required to manipulate them.

Object-oriented programming employs a large vocabulary; you can learn much of this terminology in the chapter called *Using Classes and Objects.*

Originally, object-oriented programming was used most frequently for two major types of applications:

- **Computer simulations**, which attempt to mimic real-world activities so that their processes can be improved or so that users can better understand how the real-world processes operate.

- **Graphical user interfaces**, or **GUIs** (pronounced "gooeys"), which allow users to interact with a program in a graphical environment.

Thinking about objects in these two types of applications makes sense. For example, a city might want to develop a program that simulates traffic patterns to better prevent traffic tie-ups. By creating a model with objects such as cars and pedestrians that contain their own data and rules for behavior, the simulation can be set in motion. For example, each car object has a specific current speed and a procedure for changing that speed. By creating a model of city traffic using objects, a computer can create a simulation of a real city at rush hour.

Creating a GUI environment for users also is a natural use for object orientation. It is easy to think of the components a user manipulates on a computer screen, such as buttons and scroll bars, as similar to real-world objects. Each GUI object contains data—for example, a button on a screen has a specific size and color. Each object also contains behaviors—for example, each button can be clicked and reacts in a specific way when clicked. Some people consider the term *object-oriented programming* to be synonymous with GUI programming, but object-oriented programming means more. Although many GUI programs are object-oriented, one does not imply the other. Modern businesses use object-oriented design techniques when developing all sorts of business applications, whether they are GUI applications or not.

## TWO TRUTHS **&** A LIE

### Procedural and Object-Oriented Programming

1. Procedural programs use variables and tasks that are grouped into methods or procedures.

2. Object-oriented programming languages do not support variables or methods; instead they focus on objects.

3. Object-oriented programs were first used for simulations and GUI programs.

The false statement is #2. Object-oriented programs contain variables and methods just as procedural programs do.

# Features of Object-Oriented Programming Languages

For a language to be considered object-oriented, it must support the following features:

- Classes

- Objects

- Encapsulation and interfaces

- Inheritance

- Polymorphism

A **class** describes potential objects, including their attributes and behaviors. A class is similar to a recipe or a blueprint in that it describes what features objects will have and what they will be able to do after they are created. An object is an **instance of a class**; it is one tangible example of a class.

For example, you might create a class named Automobile. Some of an Automobile's attributes are its make, model, year, and purchase price. All Automobiles possess the same attributes, but not the same values, or states, for those attributes. When you create each specific Automobile object, each can hold unique values for the attributes. Similarly, a Dog has attributes that include its breed, name, age, and shot status (that is, whether its shots are current); the states for a particular dog might be "Labrador retriever", "Murphy", "7", and "yes".

When you understand that an object belongs to a specific class, you know a lot about the object. If your friend purchases an Automobile, you know it has *some* model name; if your friend gets a Dog, you know it has *some* breed. You probably do not know the current state of the Automobile's speed or of the Dog's shots, but you do know that those attributes exist for the Automobile and Dog classes. Similarly, in a GUI operating environment, you expect each window you open to have specific, consistent attributes, such as a menu bar and a title bar, because each window includes these attributes as a member of the general class of GUI windows.

Besides attributes, objects possess methods that they use to accomplish tasks, including changing attributes and discovering the values of attributes. Automobiles, for example, have methods for moving forward and backward. They also can be filled with gasoline or be washed; both are methods that change some of an Automobile's attributes. Methods also exist for determining the status of certain attributes, such as the current speed of an Automobile and the number of gallons of gas in its tank. Similarly, a Dog can walk or run, eat, and

Although procedural and object-oriented programming techniques are somewhat similar, they raise different concerns in the design and development phase that occurs before programs are written.

Programmers also call the values of an object's attributes the **properties** of the object.

By convention, programmers using C# begin their class names with an uppercase letter and use a singular noun. Thus, the class that defines the attributes and methods of an automobile would probably be named Automobile, and the class that contains dogs would probably be named Dog.

get a bath, and there are methods for determining whether it needs a walk, food, or a bath. GUI operating system components, such as windows, can be maximized, minimized, and dragged; depending on the component, they can also have their color or font style altered.

Like procedural programs, object-oriented programs have variables (attributes) and procedures (methods), but the attributes and methods are encapsulated into objects that are then used much like real-world objects. **Encapsulation** is the technique of packaging an object's attributes and methods into a cohesive unit that can be used as an undivided entity. Programmers sometimes refer to encapsulation as using a "**black box**," a device you use without regard for the internal mechanisms. If an object's methods are well written, the user is unaware of the low-level details of how the methods are executed; in such a case, the user must understand only the **interface** or interaction between the method and object. For example, if you can fill your Automobile with gasoline, it is because you understand the interface between the gas pump nozzle and the vehicle's gas tank opening. You do not need to understand how the pump works or where the gas tank is located inside your vehicle. If you can read your speedometer, it does not matter how the display figure is calculated. In fact, if someone produces a new, more accurate speedometer and inserts it into your Automobile, you do not have to know or care how it operates, as long as the interface remains the same as the previous one. The same principles apply to well-constructed objects used in object-oriented programs.

Object-oriented programming languages support two other distinguishing features in addition to organizing objects as members of classes. One feature, **inheritance**, provides the ability to extend a class so as to create a more specific class. The more specific class contains all the attributes and methods of the more general class and usually contains new attributes or methods as well. For example, if you have created a Dog class, you might then create a more specific class named ShowDog. Each instance of the ShowDog class would contain all the attributes and methods of a Dog, along with additional methods or attributes. For example, a ShowDog might require an attribute to hold the number of ribbons won and a method for entering a dog show. The advantage of inheritance is that when you need a class such as ShowDog, you often can extend an existing class, thereby saving a lot of time and work.

The chapters *Using Classes and Objects* and *Introduction to Inheritance* contain much more information on the features of object-oriented programs.

Object-oriented languages also support **polymorphism**, which is the ability to create methods that act appropriately depending on the context. That is, programs written in object-oriented languages can distinguish between methods with the same name based on the type of object that uses them. For example, you are able to "fill" both a Dog and an Automobile, but you do so by very different means. Similarly, the procedure to "fill" a ShowDog might require different food than that for a "plain" Dog. Older, non-object-oriented languages could not make such distinctions, but object-oriented languages can.

Watch the video *Object-Oriented Programming.*

## TWO TRUTHS & A LIE

### Features of Object-Oriented Programming Languages

1. Object-oriented programs contain classes that describe the attributes and methods of objects.

2. Object-oriented programming languages support inheritance, which refers to the packaging of attributes and methods into logical units.

3. Object-oriented programming languages support polymorphism, which is the ability of a method to act appropriately based on the context.

The false statement is #2. Inheritance is the ability to extend classes to make more specific ones. Encapsulation refers to the packaging of attributes and methods.

# The C# Programming Language

The **C# programming language** was developed as an object-oriented and component-oriented language. It is part of Microsoft Visual Studio 2010, a package designed for developing applications that run on Windows computers. Unlike other programming languages, C# allows every piece of data to be treated as an object and to consistently employ the principles of object-oriented programming. C# provides constructs for creating components with properties, methods, and events, making it an ideal language for twenty-first-century programming, where building small, reusable components is more important than building huge, stand-alone applications.

If you have not programmed before, the difference between C# and other languages means little to you. However, experienced programmers will appreciate the thought that the developers of C# put into its features. For example:

- C# contains a GUI interface that makes it similar to Visual Basic, but C# is considered more concise than Visual Basic.

- C# is modeled after the C++ programming language, but is considered easier to learn. Some of the most difficult features to understand in C++ have been eliminated in C#.

You can find Microsoft's C# specifications at *msdn. microsoft. com.* Search for *C# specifications.*

Some differences between C# and C++ are that pointers are not used in C# (except in a mode called unsafe, which is rarely used), object destructors and forward declarations are not needed, and using #include files is not necessary. Multiple inheritance, which causes many C++ programming errors, is not allowed in C#.

The C# programming language was standardized in 2002 by Ecma International. You can read or download this set of standards at *www.ecma-international.org/publications/standards/Ecma-334.htm*.

**10**

- C# is very similar to Java, because Java was also based on C++. However, C# is more truly object-oriented. Unlike in Java, every piece of data in C# is an object, providing all data with increased functionality.

In Java, simple data types are not objects; therefore, they do not work with built-in methods. Additionally, in Java, data can only be passed to and from methods using a copy; C# omits this limitation. You will learn more in two later chapters: *Introduction to Methods* and *Advanced Method Concepts*.

## TWO TRUTHS & A LIE

### The C# Programming Language

1. The C# programming language was developed as an object-oriented and component-oriented language.

2. C# contains several features that make it similar to other languages such as Java and Visual Basic.

3. C# contains many advanced features, so the C++ programming language was created as a simpler version of the language.

The false statement is #3. C# is modeled after the C++ programming language, but some of the most difficult features to understand in C++ have been eliminated in C#.

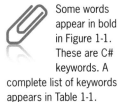

Some words appear in bold in Figure 1-1. These are C# keywords. A complete list of keywords appears in Table 1-1.

# Writing a C# Program That Produces Output

At first glance, even the simplest C# program involves a fair amount of confusing syntax. Consider the simple program in Figure 1-1. This program is written on seven lines, and its only task is to display "This is my first C# program" on the screen.

```csharp
public class FirstClass
{
    public static void Main()
    {
        System.Console.WriteLine("This is my first C# program");
    }
}
```

**Figure 1-1** FirstClass console application

The statement that does the actual work in this program is in the middle of the figure: System.Console.WriteLine("This is my first C# program");

The statement ends with a semicolon because all C# statements do.

The text "This is my first C# program" is a **literal string** of characters—that is, a series of characters that will be used exactly as entered. Any literal string in C# appears between double quotation marks.

The string "This is my first C# program" appears within parentheses because the string is an argument to a method, and arguments to methods always appear within parentheses. **Arguments** represent information that a method needs to perform its task. For example, if making an appointment with a dentist's office was a C# method, you would write the following:

```
MakeAppointment("September 10", "2 p.m.");
```

Accepting and processing a dental appointment is a method that consists of a set of standard procedures. However, each appointment requires different information—the date and time—and this information can be considered the arguments of the MakeAppointment() method. If you make an appointment for September 10 at 2 p.m., you expect different results than if you make one for September 9 at 8 a.m. or December 25 at midnight. Likewise, if you pass the argument "Happy Holidays" to a method, you will expect different results than if you pass the argument "This is my first C# program".

Within the statement System.Console.WriteLine("This is my first C# program");, the method to which you are passing the argument string "This is my first C# program" is named WriteLine(). The **WriteLine() method** displays output on the screen and positions the cursor on the next line, where additional output might be displayed subsequently.

Within the statement System.Console.WriteLine("This is my first C# program");, Console is a class that contains the WriteLine() method. Of course, not all classes have a WriteLine() method (for instance, you can not write a line to a computer's mouse, an Automobile, or a Dog), but the creators of C# assumed that you frequently would want to display output on the screen at your terminal. For this reason, the Console class was created and endowed with the method named WriteLine(). Soon, you will create your own C# classes and endow them with your own methods.

Within the statement System.Console.WriteLine("This is my first C# program");, System is a namespace. A **namespace** is a construct that acts like a container to provide a way to group similar

Although a string can be an argument to a method, not all arguments are strings. In this book, you will see and write methods that accept many other types of data.

The **Write() method** is very similar to the WriteLine() method. With WriteLine(), the cursor is moved to the following line after the message is displayed. With Write(), the cursor does not advance to a new line; it remains on the same line as the output.

The C# programming language is case sensitive. Thus, WriteLine() refers to a completely different method than Writeline().

An advantage to using Visual Studio is that all of its languages use the same namespaces. In other words, everything you learn about any namespace in C# is knowledge you can transfer to Visual C++ and Visual Basic.

classes. To organize your classes, you can (and will) create your own namespaces. The **System namespace**, which is built into your C# compiler, holds commonly used classes.

The dots (periods) in the statement `System.Console.WriteLine("This is my first C# program");` are used to separate the names of the namespace, class, and method. You will use this same namespace-dot-class-dot-method format repeatedly in your C# programs.

In the `FirstClass` class in Figure 1-1, the `WriteLine()` statement appears within a method named `Main()`. Every executable C# application must contain a `Main()` method because that is the starting point for every program. As you continue to learn C# from this book, you will write applications that contain additional methods. You will also create classes that are not programs, and so do not need a `Main()` method.

Every method in C# contains a header and a body. A **method header** includes the method name and information about what will pass into and be returned from a method. A **method body** is contained within a pair of curly braces ({ }) and includes all the instructions executed by the method. The program in Figure 1-1 includes only one statement between the curly braces of the `Main()` method. Soon, you will write methods with many more statements. In Figure 1-1, the `WriteLine()` statement within the `Main()` method is indented within the curly braces. Although the C# compiler does not require such indentation, it is conventional and clearly shows that the `WriteLine()` statement lies within the `Main()` method.

For every opening curly brace ({) in a C# program, there must be a corresponding closing curly brace (}). The precise position of the opening and closing curly braces is not important to the compiler. For example, the method in Figure 1-2 executes exactly the same way as the one shown in Figure 1-1. The only difference is in the amount of whitespace used in the method. In general, whitespace is optional in C#. **Whitespace** is any combination of spaces, tabs, and carriage returns (blank lines). You use whitespace to organize your program code and make it easier to read; it does not affect your program. Usually, vertically aligning each pair of opening and closing curly braces and indenting the contents between them, as in Figure 1-1, makes your code easier to read than the format shown in Figure 1-2.

```
public static void Main(){System.Console.WriteLine
   ("This is my first C# program");}
```

**Figure 1-2** A `Main()` method with little whitespace

The method header for the `Main()` method contains four words. Three of these words are keywords. In the method header `public static void Main()`, the word `public` is an access modifier. When used in a method header, an **access modifier** defines the circumstances under which the method can be accessed. The access modifier **public** indicates that other classes may use this method. On the other hand, the access modifier **private** indicates that other classes cannot use the method; the method is exclusively used for internal purposes within the class where it is defined.

In the English language, the word *static* means "showing little change" or "stationary." In C#, the reserved keyword **static** has a related meaning. It indicates that the `Main()` method will be executed through a class—not by a variety of objects. It means that you do not need to create an object of type `FirstClass` to use the `Main()` method defined within `FirstClass`. In C#, you will create many nonstatic methods within classes that are executed by objects. For example, you might create a `Display()` method in an `Automobile` class that you use to display an `Automobile`'s attributes. If you create 100 `Automobile` objects, the `Display()` method will operate differently and appropriately for each object, displaying different makes, models, and colors of `Automobiles`. (Programmers would say a non-static method is "invoked" by each instance of the object.) However, a `static` method does not require an object to be used to invoke it. You will learn the mechanics of how `static` and nonstatic methods differ later in this book.

In English, the word *void* means empty or having no effect. When the keyword **void** is used in the `Main()` method header, it does not indicate that the `Main()` method is empty, or that it has no effect, but rather that the method does not return any value when called. You will learn more about methods that return values (and do affect other methods) when you study methods in greater detail.

In the method header, the name of the method is `Main()`. `Main()` is not a C# keyword, but all C# applications must include a method named `Main()`, and most C# applications will have additional methods with other names. Recall that when you execute a C# application, the `Main()` method always executes first. Classes that contain a `Main()` method are **application classes**. Classes that do not contain a `Main()` method are **non-application classes**. Non-application classes provide support for other classes.

Applications are executable. Programmers say executable programs that have been translated into machine language are **runnable**. This distinguishes them from classes that are not programs and from files that have not yet been translated into an executable format.

If you do not use an access modifier within a method header, then by default the method is `private`. You will learn more about public and private access modifiers later in this book.

13

Watch the video *The Parts of a C# Program*.

---

## TWO TRUTHS & A LIE

### Writing a C# Program That Produces Output

1. Strings are information that methods need to perform their tasks.

2. The `WriteLine()` method displays output on the screen and positions the cursor on the next line, where additional output might be displayed.

3. Many methods such as `WriteLine()` have been created for you because the creators of C# assumed you would need them frequently.

The false statement is #1. Strings are literal values represented between quotation marks. Arguments represent information that a method needs to perform its task. Although an argument might be a string, not all arguments are strings.

---

## Selecting Identifiers

Every method that you use within a C# program must be part of a class. To create a class, you use a class header and curly braces in much the same way you use a header and braces for a method within a class. When you write `public class FirstClass`, you are defining a class named `FirstClass`. A class name does not have to contain the word "Class" as `FirstClass` does; as a matter of fact, most class names you create will not contain "Class". You can define a C# class using any identifier you need, as long as it meets the following requirements:

 In this book, all identifiers begin with a letter.

- An identifier must begin with an underscore, the "at" sign (@), or a letter. (Letters include foreign-alphabet letters such as Π and Ω, which are contained in the set of characters known as Unicode.)

You will learn more about Unicode in the next chapter.

- An identifier can contain only letters, digits, underscores, and the "at" sign. An identifier cannot contain spaces or any other punctuation or special characters such as #, $, or &.

An identifier with an @ prefix is a **verbatim identifier**.

- An identifier cannot be a C# reserved keyword, such as `public` or `class`. Table 1-1 provides a complete list of reserved keywords. (Actually, you can use a keyword as an identifier if you precede it with an "at" sign, as in `@class`. This feature allows you to use code written in other languages that do not have the same set of reserved keywords. However, when you write original C# programs, you should not use the keywords as identifiers.)

| | | |
|---|---|---|
| abstract | float | return |
| as | for | sbyte |
| base | foreach | sealed |
| bool | goto | short |
| break | if | sizeof |
| byte | implicit | stackalloc |
| case | in | static |
| catch | int | string |
| char | interface | struct |
| checked | internal | switch |
| class | is | this |
| const | lock | throw |
| continue | long | true |
| decimal | namespace | try |
| default | new | typeof |
| delegate | null | uint |
| do | object | ulong |
| double | operator | unchecked |
| else | out | unsafe |
| enum | override | ushort |
| event | params | using |
| explicit | private | virtual |
| extern | protected | void |
| false | public | volatile |
| finally | readonly | while |
| fixed | ref | |

**Table 1-1**   C# reserved keywords

The following identifiers have special meaning in C# but are not keywords: add, alias, get, global, partial, remove, set, value, where, and yield. For clarity, you should avoid using these words as your own identifiers.

A programming standard in C# is to begin class names with an uppercase letter and use other uppercase letters as needed to improve readability. Table 1-2 lists some valid and conventional class names you might use when creating classes in C#. Table 1-3 lists some class names that are valid, but unconventional; Table 1-4 lists some illegal class names.

You should follow established conventions for C# so that other programmers can interpret and follow your programs. This book uses established C# programming conventions.

| Class Name | Description |
|---|---|
| Employee | Begins with an uppercase letter |
| FirstClass | Begins with an uppercase letter, contains no spaces, and has an initial uppercase letter that indicates the start of the second word |
| PushButtonControl | Begins with an uppercase letter, contains no spaces, and has an initial uppercase letter that indicates the start of all subsequent words |
| Budget2012 | Begins with an uppercase letter and contains no spaces |

**Table 1-2**    Some valid and conventional class names in C#

| Class Name | Description |
|---|---|
| employee | Unconventional as a class name because it begins with a lowercase letter |
| First_Class | Although legal, the underscore is not commonly used to indicate new words in class names |
| Pushbuttoncontrol | No uppercase characters are used to indicate the start of a new word, making the name difficult to read |
| BUDGET2013 | Unconventional as a class name because it contains all uppercase letters |
| Public | Although this identifier is legal because it is different from the keyword public, which begins with a lowercase "p," the similarity could cause confusion |

**Table 1-3**    Some unconventional (though legal) class names in C#

| Class Name | Description |
|---|---|
| an employee | Space character is illegal |
| Push Button Control | Space characters are illegal |
| class | "class" is a reserved word |
| 2011Budget | Class names cannot begin with a digit |
| phone# | The # symbol is not allowed; identifiers consist of letters, digits, underscores, or @ |

**Table 1-4**    Some illegal class names in C#

In Figure 1-1, the line `public class FirstClass` contains the keyword `class`, which identifies `FirstClass` as a class. The reserved word `public` is an access modifier. Similar to the way an access modifier describes a method's accessibility, when used with a class, the access modifier defines the circumstances under which the class can be accessed; `public` access is the most liberal type of access.

The simple program shown in Figure 1-1 has many pieces to remember. For now, you can use the program shown in Figure 1-3 as a shell, where you replace the identifier `AnyLegalClassName` with any legal class name, and the line `/*********/` with any statements that you want to execute.

```
public class AnyLegalClassName
{
    public static void Main()
    {
        /*********/;
    }
}
```

**Figure 1-3**  Shell program

Watch the video *C# Identifiers*.

---

### TWO TRUTHS & A LIE

#### Selecting Identifiers

1.  In C#, an identifier must begin with an underscore, the at sign (@), or an uppercase letter.

2.  An identifier can contain only letters, digits, underscores, and the "at" sign, not special characters such as #, $, or &.

3.  An identifier cannot be a C# reserved keyword.

The false statement is #1. In C#, an identifier must begin with an underscore, the at sign (@), or a letter. There is no requirement that the initial letter be capitalized, although in C#, it is a convention that the initial letter of a class name is capitalized.

# Improving Programs by Adding Comments and Using the System Namespace

As you can see, even the simplest C# program takes several lines of code and contains somewhat perplexing syntax. Large programs that perform many tasks include much more code. As you work through this text, you will discover many ways to improve your ability to handle large programs. Two things you can do immediately are to add program comments and use the System namespace.

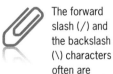

As you work through this book, you should add comments as the first few lines of every program file. The comments should contain your name, the date, and the name of the program. Your instructor might want you to include additional comments.

## Adding Program Comments

As you write longer programs, it becomes increasingly difficult to remember why you included steps and how you intended to use particular variables. **Program comments** are nonexecuting statements that you add to document a program. Programmers use comments to leave notes for themselves and for others who might read their programs in the future.

Comments also can be useful when you are developing a program. If a program is not performing as expected, you can **comment out** various statements and subsequently run the program to observe the effect. When you comment out a statement, you turn it into a comment so that the compiler will ignore it. This approach helps you pinpoint the location of errant statements in malfunctioning programs.

C# offers three types of comments:

- **Line comments** start with two forward slashes (//) and continue to the end of the current line. Line comments can appear on a line by themselves, or at the end of a line following executable code.

- **Block comments** start with a forward slash and an asterisk (/*) and end with an asterisk and a forward slash (*/). Block comments can appear on a line by themselves, on a line before executable code, or after executable code. When a comment is long, block comments can extend across as many lines as needed.

The forward slash (/) and the backslash (\) characters often are confused, but they are distinct characters. You cannot use them interchangeably.

- C# also supports a special type of comment used to create documentation within a program. These comments, called **XML-documentation format comments**, use a special set of tags within angle brackets (< >). (XML stands for Extensible Markup Language.) You will learn more about this type of comment as you continue your study of C#.

Figure 1-4 shows how comments can be used in code. The program covers 10 lines, yet only seven are part of the executable C# program, and the only line that actually *does* anything is the shaded one that displays "Message".

```
/* This program is written to demonstrate
   using comments */
public class ClassWithOneExecutingLine
{
   public static void Main()
   {
      // The next line writes the message
      System.Console.WriteLine("Message");
   } // End of Main
} // End of ClassWithOneExecutingLine
```

**Figure 1-4**   Using comments within a program

## Using the System Namespace

A program can contain as many statements as you need. For example,
the program in Figure 1-5 produces the three lines of output shown
in Figure 1-6. A semicolon separates each program statement.

```
public class ThreeLinesOutput
{
   public static void Main()
   {
      System.Console.WriteLine("Line one");
      System.Console.WriteLine("Line two");
      System.Console.WriteLine("Line three");
   }
}
```

**Figure 1-5**   A program that produces three lines of output

**Figure 1-6**   Output of ThreeLinesOutput program

The program in Figure 1-5 shows a lot of repeated code—the phrase
System.Console.WriteLine appears three times. When you need to
repeatedly use a class from the same namespace, you can shorten the

statements you type by adding a clause that indicates a namespace that contains the class. You indicate a namespace with a **using clause**, or **using directive**, as shown in the shaded statement in the program in Figure 1-7. If you type using System; prior to the class definition, the compiler knows to use the System namespace when it encounters the Console class. The output of the program in Figure 1-7 is identical to that in Figure 1-5, in which System was repeated with each WriteLine() statement.

```
using System;
public class ThreeLinesOutput
{
    public static void Main()
    {
        Console.WriteLine("Line one");
        Console.WriteLine("Line two");
        Console.WriteLine("Line three");
    }
}
```

**Figure 1-7** A program that produces three lines of output with a using System clause

At this point, the clever programmer will say, "I'll shorten my typing tasks even further by typing using System.Console; at the top of my programs, and producing output with statements like WriteLine("Hi");." However, using cannot be used with a class name like System.Console—only with a namespace name like System.

---

### TWO TRUTHS & A LIE

#### Improving Programs by Adding Comments and Using the System Namespace

1. Line comments start with two forward slashes (//) and end with two backslashes (\\).

2. Block comments can extend across as many lines as needed.

3. You use a namespace with a using clause, or using directive, to shorten statements when you need to repeatedly use a class from the same namespace.

The false statement is #1. Line comments start with two forward slashes (//) and continue to the end of the current line.

# Writing and Compiling a C# Program

After you write and save a program, two more steps must be performed before you can view the program output:

1. You must compile the program you wrote (called the **source code**) into **intermediate language (IL)**.

2. The C# **just in time (JIT)** compiler must translate the intermediate code into executable code.

You can perform these steps from the command line in your system or within the Integrated Development Environment that comes with Visual Studio. Both methods produce the same results; the one you use is a matter of preference.

- The **command line** is the line on which you type a command in a system that uses a text interface. The **command prompt** is a request for input that appears at the beginning of the command line. In DOS, the command prompt indicates the disk drive and optional path, and ends with >. You might prefer the simplicity of the command line because you do not work with multiple menus and views. Additionally, if you want to pass command-line arguments to a program, you must compile from the command line.

- The **Integrated Development Environment (IDE)** is a programming environment that allows you to issue commands by selecting choices from menus and clicking buttons. Many programmers prefer using the IDE because it provides features such as color-coded keywords and automatic statement completion.

## Compiling Code from the Command Prompt

To compile your source code from the command line, you first locate the command prompt. For example, in Windows 7 or Vista, you click Start, All Programs, Accessories, and Command Prompt. Then you type csc at the command prompt, followed by the name of the file that contains the source code. The command csc stands for "C Sharp compiler." For example, to compile a file named ThreeLinesOutput.cs, you would type the following and then press the Enter key:

```
csc ThreeLinesOutput.cs
```

One of three outcomes will occur:

- You receive an operating system error message such as "Bad command or file name" or "csc is not recognized as an internal or external command, operable program or batch file". You can

When you compile a C# program, your source code is translated into intermediate language. The JIT compiler converts IL instructions into native code at the last moment, and appropriately for each type of operating system on which the code might eventually be executed. In other words, the same set of IL can be JIT-compiled and executed on any supported architecture.

Some developers say that languages like C# are "semi-compiled." That is, instead of being translated immediately from source code to their final executable versions, programs are compiled into an intermediate version that is later translated into the correct executable statements for the environment in which the program is running.

21

recognize operating system messages because they do not start with the name of the program you are trying to compile.

- You receive one or more program language error messages. You can recognize program language error messages because they start with the name of the program followed by a line number and the position where the error was first noticed.

- You receive no error messages (only a copyright statement from Microsoft), indicating that the program has compiled successfully.

## What to Do if You Receive an Operating System Error Message

If you receive an operating system message such as "csc is not recognized...," or "Source file...could not be found," it may mean that:

- You misspelled the command **csc**.

- You misspelled the filename.

- You forgot to include the extension .cs with the filename.

- You are not within the correct subdirectory or folder on your command line. For example, Figure 1-8 shows the **csc** command typed in the root directory of the C drive. If the ThreeLinesOutput.cs file is stored in a folder on the C drive rather than in the root directory, then the command shown will not work because the C# file cannot be found.

**Figure 1-8** Attempt to compile a program from the root directory at the command line, and error message received

- The C# compiler was not installed properly. If you are working on your own computer, you might need to reinstall C#; if you are working in a school laboratory, you need to notify the system administrator.

- You need to set a path command. To do this, you must locate the C# compiler on your hard disk. To locate the compiler whose name is csc.exe in Windows 7, Vista, or Windows XP, double-click on the following: Computer (or My Computer), the C drive, the Windows folder, the Microsoft.NET folder, the Framework folder, the v4.0 folder, and then confirm that csc.exe is a program listed there. C# should be installed in this location if the program was installed using the default options. If your search fails to find csc.exe, you need to obtain and install a copy of the C# compiler. For more information, visit *http://msdn2.microsoft.com/en-us/vcsharp/default.aspx*.

When you find the csc.exe file, type `path` = at the command line, followed by the complete path name that describes where csc.exe is stored; then try to compile the `ThreeLinesOutput` program again. For example, if C# was stored in the default location, you might type the following:

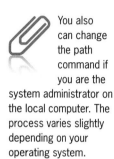

You also can change the path command if you are the system administrator on the local computer. The process varies slightly depending on your operating system.

```
path = c:\Windows\Microsoft.NET\Framework\v4.0
```

Press Enter. Next, type `csc ThreeLinesOutput.cs` and press Enter again.

## What to Do if You Receive a Programming Language Error Message

If you receive a programming language error message, it means that the source code contains one or more syntax errors. A syntax error occurs when you introduce typing errors into your program. Program error messages start with the program name, followed by parentheses that hold the line number and the position in the line where the compiler noticed the error. For example, in Figure 1-9, an error was found in ThreeLinesOutput.cs in line 2, position 1. In this case the message was generated because the first line of the program was typed as "Public" (with an uppercase P). The error message is "`A namespace cannot directly contain members such as fields or methods`". The message is somewhat cryptic, but it means that the compiler does not recognize `ThreeLinesOutput` as a class, so the compiler assumes it must be a field or a method, but all fields and methods must reside within a class. If a problem like this occurs, you must reopen the text file that contains the source code, make the necessary corrections, save the file, and compile it again.

Your folder might not be named v4.0 if you are using a different version of C#.

The C# compiler issues warnings as well as errors. A warning is less serious than an error; it means that the compiler has determined you have done something unusual, but not illegal. If you have purposely introduced a warning situation to test a program, then you can ignore the warning. Usually, however, you should treat a warning message just as you would an error message and attempt to remedy the situation.

**Figure 1-9** Error message generated when "public" is mistyped in the `ThreeLinesOutput` program

## What to Do When the Program Compiles Successfully

If you receive no error messages after compiling the code, then the program compiled successfully and a file with the same name as the source code—but with an .exe extension—is created and saved in the same folder as the program text file. For example, if ThreeLinesOutput.cs compiles successfully, then a file named ThreeLinesOutput.exe is created.

To run the program from the command line, you simply type the program name—for example, `ThreeLinesOutput`. You can also type the full filename, ThreeLinesOutput.exe, but it is not necessary to include the extension.

## Compiling Code within the Visual Studio IDE

As an alternative to using the command line, you can compile and write your program within the Visual Studio IDE. This approach has several advantages:

- Some of the code you need is already created for you.

- The code is displayed in color, so you can more easily identify parts of your program. Reserved words appear in blue, comments in green, and identifiers in black.

- If error messages appear when you compile your program, you can double-click an error message and the cursor will move to the line of code that contains the error.

- Other debugging tools are available. You will become more familiar with these tools as you develop more sophisticated programs.

Figure 1-10 shows a program written in the editor of the Visual Studio IDE. You can see that the environment looks like a word processor, containing menu options such as File, Edit, and Help, and buttons with icons representing options such as Save, Copy, and Paste. You will learn about some of these options later in this chapter and continue to learn about more of them as you work with C# in the IDE.

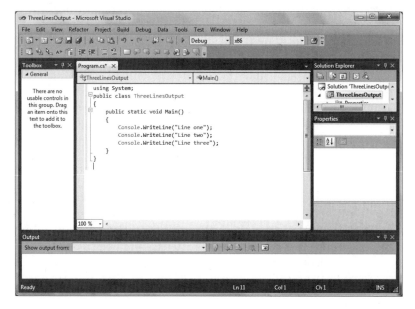

Watch the video *Writing and Compiling a Program.*

**Figure 1-10**  ThreeLinesOutput program as it appears in Visual Studio

---

## TWO TRUTHS & A LIE

### Writing and Compiling a C# Program

1. After you write and save a program, you must compile it into intermediate language and then the C# just in time (JIT) compiler must translate the intermediate code into executable code.

2. You can compile and execute a C# program from the command line or within the Integrated Development Environment (IDE) that comes with Visual Studio.

3. Many programmers prefer to compile their programs from the command line because it provides features such as color-coded keywords and automatic statement completion.

The false statement is #3. Programmers who prefer the command line prefer its simplicity. Programmers who prefer the Visual Studio IDE prefer the color-coded keywords and automatic statement completion.

# You Do It

Now that you understand the basic framework of a program written in C#, you are ready to enter your first C# program into a text editor so you can compile and execute it. It is a tradition among programmers that the first program you write in any language produces "Hello, world!" as its output. You will create such a program now. To create a C# program, you can use the editor that is included as part of the Microsoft Visual Studio IDE. (The C# compiler, other language compilers, and many development tools also are contained in the IDE, which is where you build, test, and debug your C# application.) Alternatively, you can use any text editor. There are advantages to using the C# editor to write your programs, but using a plain text editor is simpler when you are getting started.

## Entering a Program into an Editor

**To write your first C# program:**

1. Start any text editor, such as Notepad, and open a new document, if necessary.

2. Type the `using` statement and the header for the class:

   ```
   using System;
   public class Hello
   ```

3. On the next two lines, type the class-opening and class-closing curly braces: {}. Many programmers type a closing brace as soon as they type the opening one to guarantee that they always type complete pairs.

4. Between the class braces, insert a new line, type three spaces to indent, and write the `Main()` method header:

   ```
   public static void Main()
   ```

5. On the next two lines, type the opening and closing braces for the `Main()` method, indenting them about three spaces.

6. Between the `Main()` method's braces, insert a new line and type six spaces so the next statement will be indented within the braces. Type the one executing statement in this program:

   ```
   Console.WriteLine("Hello, world!");
   ```

   Your code should look like Figure 1-11.

```
using System;
public class Hello
{
    public static void Main()
    {
        Console.WriteLine("Hello, world!");
    }
}
```

**Figure 1-11**   The Hello class

27

Many text editors attach their own filename extension (such as .txt or .doc) to a saved file. Double-check your saved file to ensure that it does not have a double extension (as in Hello.cs.txt). If the file has a double extension, rename it. If you use a word-processing program as your editor, select the option to save the file as a plain text file.

7. Choose a location that is meaningful to you to save your program. For example, you might create a folder named C# on your hard drive. Within that folder, you might create a folder named Chapter.01 in which you will store all the examples and exercises in this chapter. If you are working in a school lab, you might be assigned a storage location on your school's server, or you might prefer to store your examples on a USB drive or other portable storage media. Save the program as **Hello.cs**. It is important that the file extension be .cs, which stands for *C Sharp*. If the file has a different extension, the compiler for C# will not recognize the program as a C# program.

## Compiling and Executing a Program from the Command Line

**To compile and execute your Hello program from the command line:**

1. Go to the command prompt on your system. For example, in Windows 7, Vista, or Windows XP, click **Start**, then click **All Programs**, click **Accessories**, and click **Command Prompt**. Change the current directory to the name of the folder that holds your program.

   If your command prompt indicates a path other than the one you want, you can type **cd\** and then press Enter to return to the root directory. You can then type **cd** to change the path to the one where your program resides. For example, if you stored your program file in a folder named Chapter.01 within a folder named C#, then you can type the following:

   **cd C#\Chapter.01**

   The command **cd** is short for *change directory*.

2. Type the command that compiles your program:

   `csc Hello.cs`

   If you receive no error messages and the prompt returns, it means that the compile operation was successful, that a file named Hello.exe has been created, and that you can execute the program. If you do receive error messages, check every character of the program you typed to make sure it matches Figure 1-11. Remember, C# is case sensitive, so all casing must match exactly. When you have corrected the errors, repeat this step to compile the program again.

3. You can verify that a file named Hello.exe was created in several ways:

   • At the command prompt, type **dir** to view a directory of the files stored in the current folder. Both Hello.cs and Hello.exe should appear in the list. See Figure 1-12.

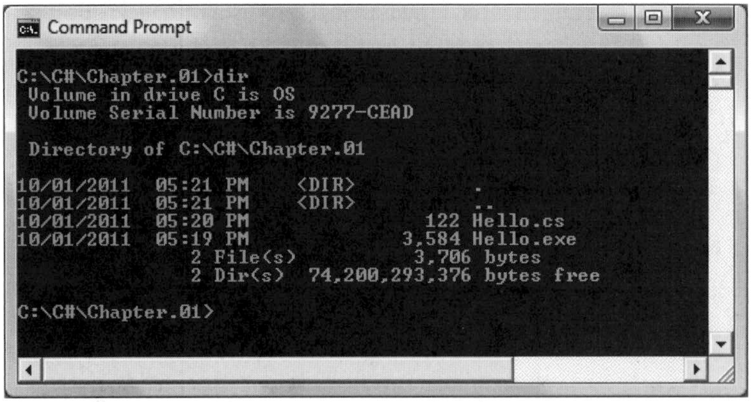

```
C:\C#\Chapter.01>dir
 Volume in drive C is OS
 Volume Serial Number is 9277-CEAD

 Directory of C:\C#\Chapter.01

10/01/2011  05:21 PM    <DIR>          .
10/01/2011  05:21 PM    <DIR>          ..
10/01/2011  05:20 PM               122 Hello.cs
10/01/2011  05:19 PM             3,584 Hello.exe
               2 File(s)          3,706 bytes
               2 Dir(s)  74,200,293,376 bytes free

C:\C#\Chapter.01>
```

**Figure 1-12**  Directory of Chapter.01 folder after compiling Hello.cs

   • Use Windows Explorer to view the contents of the Chapter.01 folder, verifying that two Hello files are listed.

   • Double-click the **My Computer** icon, navigate to and double-click the **Chapter.01** folder, and verify that two Hello files are listed.

4. At the command prompt, type **Hello**, which is the name of the program (the name of the executable file), and then press **Enter**. Alternatively, you can type the full filename **Hello. exe**, but typing the .exe extension is not necessary. The output should look like Figure 1-13.

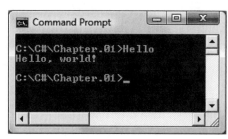

**Figure 1-13** Output of the Hello application

You can use the /out compiler option between the csc command and the name of the .cs file to indicate the name of the output file. For example, if you type csc / out:Hello.exe Hello.cs, you create an output file named Hello. exe. By default, the name of the output file is the same as the name of the .cs file. Usually, this is your intention, so most often you omit the /out option.

29

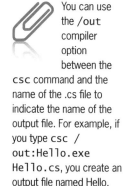

## Compiling and Executing a Program Using the Visual Studio IDE *Make video*

Next, you will use the C# compiler environment to compile and execute the same Hello program you ran from the command line.

**To compile and execute the Hello program in the Visual Studio IDE:**

1. Within the text editor you used to write the Hello program, select the entire program text. In Notepad, for example, you can highlight all the lines of text with your mouse (or press **Ctrl+A**). Next, copy the text to the Clipboard for temporary storage by clicking **Edit** on the menu bar and then clicking **Copy** (or by pressing **Ctrl+C**). You will paste the text in a few steps.

2. Open Visual Studio. If there is a shortcut icon on your desktop, you can double-click it. Alternatively, in Windows 7, Vista, or Windows XP, you can click the **Start** button, click **All Programs**, and then click **Microsoft Visual Studio 2010**.

3. If this is the first time any user has opened Visual Studio, you will be asked to choose your preferred language. As Figure 1-14 shows, choose **Visual C# Development Settings**, and click **Start Visual Studio**. The first time Visual Studio is started, it may take a few minutes to configure the environment for you. When you see the Start Page, click **New Project**, as shown in Figure 1-15.

Depending on your version of Visual Studio, you might see slightly different options than those shown in Figures 1-14 and 1-15.

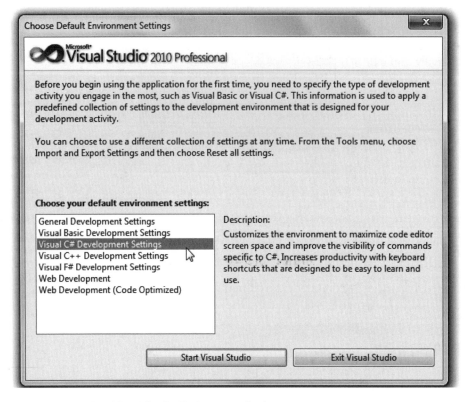

**Figure 1-14**   The Visual Studio Environment Settings screen

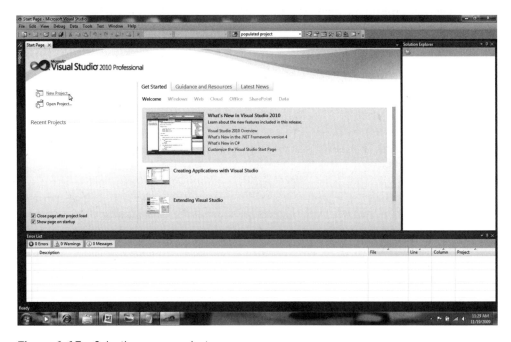

**Figure 1-15**   Selecting a new project

4. In the New Project window, click **Visual C#** and then click **Console Application**. Enter **Hello** as the name for this project and select the path where you want to save the project (see Figure 1-16). Click **OK**. Visual C# creates a new folder for your project named after the project title.

**Figure 1-16** Entering the project name

5. The Hello application editing window appears, as shown in Figure 1-17. A lot of code is already written for you in this window, including some using statements, a namespace named Hello, a class named Program, and a Main() method. You could leave the class header, Main() method header, and other features, and just add the specific statements you need; this would save a lot of typing and prevent typographical errors. But in this case, you have already written a functioning Hello program, so you will replace the prewritten code with your Hello code. Select all the code in the Visual Studio editor window by highlighting it with your mouse (or by pressing **Ctrl+A**). Then press **Delete**. Paste the previously copied Hello program into the editor by pressing **Ctrl+V** (or by clicking **Edit** on the menu bar and then clicking **Paste**).

When you select the code in the editor window, be sure to delete it and not cut it. If you cut it, the same text will be reinserted when you select Paste.

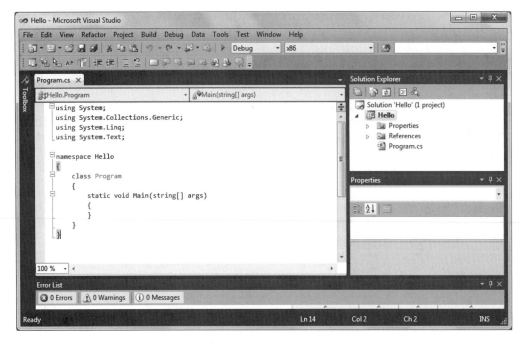

**Figure 1-17**   The Hello application editing window

6. Save the file by clicking **File** on the menu bar and then clicking **Save All**, or by clicking the **Save All** button on the toolbar. Your screen looks like Figure 1-18.

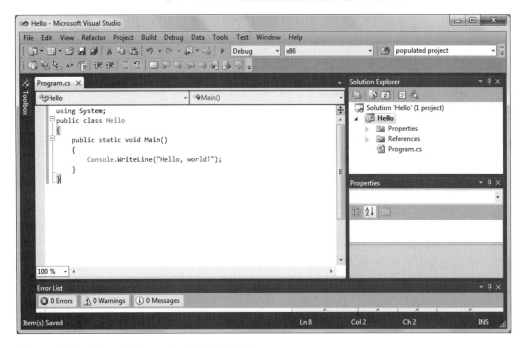

**Figure 1-18**   The Hello application in the IDE

7.  To compile the program, click **Build** on the menu bar and then click **Build Solution**. Alternatively, you can press **F6**. You should receive no error messages, and the words "Build succeeded" should appear near the lower-left edge of the window.

8.  Click **Debug** on the menu bar and then click **Start Without Debugging**. Alternatively, you can press **Ctrl+F5**. Figure 1-19 shows the output; you see "Hello, world!" followed by the message "Press any key to continue". Press any key to close the output screen.

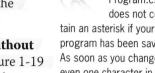

In the IDE, the tab that contains Program.cs does not contain an asterisk if your program has been saved. As soon as you change even one character in the editor, an asterisk appears in the Program. cs tab, indicating that a change has been made but not yet saved.

33

If the output appears but quickly disappears before you can read it, you can add a statement to the program to hold the output screen until you press Enter. After the `Console.WriteLine()` statement, add `Console.ReadLine();`. Then build and start the program again.

**Figure 1-19**   Output of the `Hello` application in Visual Studio

9.  Close Visual Studio by clicking **File** on the menu bar and then clicking **Exit**, or by clicking the **Close** box in the upper-right corner of the Visual Studio window.

10. When you create a C# program using an editor such as Notepad and compiling with the `csc` command, only two files are created—Hello.cs and Hello.exe. When you create a C# program using the Visual Studio editor, many additional files are created. You can view their filenames in several ways:

    - At the command prompt, type **dir** to view a directory of the files stored in the folder where you saved the project (for example, your Chapter.01 folder). Within the folder, a new folder named Hello has been created. Type the command **cd Hello** to change the current path to include this new folder, then type **dir** again. You see another folder named Hello. Type **cd Hello** again, and **dir** again. Figure 1-20 shows the output using this method; it shows several folders and files.

**Figure 1-20** Directory listing for Hello folder

- Double-click the **Computer** icon (or My Computer in Windows XP), find and double-click the correct drive, select the **C#** folder and the **Chapter.01** folder (or the path you are using), double-click the **Hello** folder, and view the contents. Double-click the second **Hello** folder and view the contents there too. Use Windows Explorer to view the contents of the Hello folders within the **Chapter.01** folder. In Windows 7 or Vista, click **Start**, **All Programs**, **Accessories,** and **Windows Explorer**. Then, in the left panel, select **Desktop** and **Computer**. The remaining navigation steps are the same as using **Computer** from the desktop.

If you are using a version of Visual Studio other than 2010, your folder configuration might be slightly different.

Regardless of the technique you use to examine the folders, you will find that the innermost Hello folder contains a bin folder, an obj folder, a Properties folder, and additional files. If you explore further, you will find that the bin folder contains a Debug folder, which includes additional files. Using the Visual Studio editor to compile your programs creates a significant amount of overhead. These additional files become important as you create more sophisticated C# projects. For now, while you learn C# syntax, using the command line to compile programs is simpler.

If you followed the earlier instructions on compiling a program from the command line, and you used the same folder when using the IDE, you will see the additional Hello.cs and Hello.exe files in your folder. These files will have an earlier time stamp than the files you just created. If you were to execute a new program within Visual Studio without saving and executing it from the command line first, you would not see these two additional files.

## Deciding Which Method to Use

When you write, compile, and execute a C# program, you can use either the command line or the Visual Studio IDE. You would never need to use both. You might prefer using an editor with which you are already familiar (such as Notepad) and compiling from the command line because only two files are generated, saving disk space.

On the other hand, the IDE provides many useful features, such as automatic statement completion. For example, if you type System and a dot, then a list of choices is displayed, and you can click Console instead of typing it. Similarly, after the dot that follows Console, a list of choices is displayed from which you can select WriteLine. Additionally, in the IDE, words are displayed using different colors based on their category; for example, one color is used for C#-reserved words and a different color for literal strings. It is also easier to correct many errors using the IDE. When compiler errors or warnings are issued, you can double-click the message, and the cursor jumps to the location in the code where the error was detected. Another advantage to learning the IDE is that if you use another programming language in Visual Studio (C++ or Visual Basic), the environment will already be familiar to you.

The C# language works the same way no matter which method you use to compile your programs. Everything you learn in the next chapters about input, output, decision making, loops, and arrays will work the same way, regardless of the compilation technique you use. You can use just one technique or compile some programs in each environment as the mood strikes you. You can also mix and match techniques if you prefer. For example, you can use an editor you like to compose your programs, then paste them into the IDE to execute them.

Although any program can be written using either compilation technique, when you write GUI applications that use existing objects such as buttons and labels, you will find that the extensive amount of code automatically generated by the IDE is very helpful. The next chapter,

*Using Data*, will continue to focus on console applications to keep things simple, but you will write interactive GUI programs using the IDE in Chapter 3.

## Adding Comments to a Program

**To add comments to your program:**

1. If you prefer compiling programs from the command line, then open the **Hello.cs** file in your text editor. If you prefer compiling programs from Visual Studio, then open Visual Studio, click **File**, point to **Open**, click **Project/Solution**, browse for the correct folder, double-click the **Hello** folder, and then double-click the **Hello** file.

2. Position your cursor at the top of the file, press **Enter** to insert a new line, press the **Up** arrow key to go to that line, and then type the following comments at the top of the file. Press **Enter** after typing each line. Insert your name and today's date where indicated.

   ```
   // Filename Hello.cs
   // Written by <your name>
   // Written on <today's date>
   ```

3. Scroll to the end of the line that reads `public static void Main()` and press **Enter** to start a new line. Then press the **Up** arrow; in the new blank line, aligned with the start of the `Main()` method header, type the following block comment in the program:

   ```
   /* This program demonstrates the use of
   the WriteLine() method to display the
   message Hello, world! */
   ```

4. Save the file, replacing the old Hello.cs file with this new, commented version.

5. If you prefer to compile programs from the command line, type **csc Hello.cs** at the command line. When the program compiles successfully, execute it with the command **Hello**. If you prefer compiling and executing programs from Visual Studio, click **Debug** and **Start Without Debugging**. Adding program comments makes no difference in the execution of the program.

6. If you are working from the command line, you can close the command-line window. If you are working from Visual Studio, you can close the output screen and then close Visual Studio.

# Chapter Summary

- A computer program is a set of instructions that tell a computer what to do. Programmers write their programs, then use a compiler to translate their high-level language statements into intermediate language and machine code. A program works correctly when both its syntax and logic are correct.

- Procedural programming involves creating computer memory locations, called variables, and sets of operations, called methods. In object-oriented programming, you envision program components as objects that are similar to concrete objects in the real world; then you manipulate the objects to achieve a desired result. OOP techniques were first used for simulations and GUIs.

- Objects are instances of classes and are made up of attributes and methods. Object-oriented programming languages support encapsulation, inheritance, and polymorphism.

- The C# programming language was developed as an object-oriented and component-oriented language. It contains many features similar to those in Visual Basic, Java, and C++.

- To write a C# program that produces a line of console output, you must pass a literal string as an argument to the System.Console.WriteLine() method. System is a namespace and Console is a class. Calls to the WriteLine() method can appear within the Main() method of a class you create.

- You can define a C# class or variable by using any name or identifier that begins with an underscore, a letter, or an "at" sign. These names can contain only letters, digits, underscores, and the "at" sign, and cannot be C#-reserved keywords.

- You can improve programs by adding comments, which are nonexecuting statements that you add to document a program or to disable statements when you test a program. The three types of comments in C# are line comments that start with two forward slashes (//) and continue to the end of the current line, block comments that start with a forward slash and an asterisk (/*) and end with an asterisk and a forward slash (*/), and XML-documentation comments. You can also improve programs and shorten the statements you type by using a clause that indicates a namespace where your classes can be found.

- To create a C# program, you can use the Microsoft Visual Studio environment. You can also use any text editor, such as Notepad, WordPad, or any word-processing program. After you write and save a program, you must compile the source code into intermediate and machine language.

# Key Terms

A computer **program** is a set of instructions that tell a computer what to do.

**Software** is computer programs.

**System software** describes the programs that operate the computer.

**Application software** is the programs that allow users to complete tasks.

**Hardware** comprises all the physical devices associated with a computer.

**Machine language** is the most basic circuitry-level language.

A **high-level programming language** allows you to use a vocabulary of keywords instead of the sequence of on/off switches that perform these tasks.

**Keywords** are predefined and reserved identifiers that have special meaning to the compiler.

A language's **syntax** is its set of rules.

A **compiler** is a computer program that translates high-level language statements into machine code.

A **syntax error** is an error that occurs when a programming language is used incorrectly.

The **logic** behind any program involves executing the various statements and methods in the correct order to produce the desired results.

**Semantic errors** are the type of logical errors that occur when you use a correct word in the wrong context, generating incorrect results.

**Debugging** a program is the process of removing all syntax and logical errors from the program.

A **procedural program** is created by writing a series of steps or operations to manipulate values.

**Variables** are named computer memory locations that hold values that might vary.

An **identifier** is the name of a program component such as a variable, class, or method.

**Camel casing** is a style of creating identifiers in which the first letter is not capitalized, but the first letter of each new word is.

**Pascal casing** is a style of creating identifiers in which the first letter of all new words in a name, even the first one, is capitalized.

**Methods** are compartmentalized, named program units that contain instructions that accomplish tasks.

A program **calls** or **invokes** methods.

**Object-oriented programming (OOP)** is a programming technique that features objects, classes, encapsulation, interfaces, polymorphism, and inheritance.

An **object** is a concrete entity that has attributes and behaviors; an object is an instance of a class.

The **attributes of an object** represent its characteristics.

The **state of an object** is the collective value of all its attributes at any point in time.

The **behaviors of an object** are its methods.

Taking an **object-oriented approach** to a problem means defining the objects needed to accomplish a task and developing classes that describe the objects so that each maintains its own data and carries out tasks when another object requests them.

**Computer simulations** are programs that attempt to mimic real-world activities to foster a better understanding of them.

**Graphical user interfaces**, or **GUIs** (pronounced "gooeys"), are program elements that allow users to interact with a program in a graphical environment.

A **class** is a category of objects or a type of object.

An **instance of a class** is an object.

The **properties** of an object are its values.

**Encapsulation** is the technique of packaging an object's attributes and methods into a cohesive unit that can be used as an undivided entity.

A **black box** is a device you use without regard for the internal mechanisms.

An **interface** is the interaction between a method and an object.

**Inheritance** is the ability to extend a class so as to create a more specific class that contains all the attributes and methods of a more general class; the extended class usually contains new attributes or methods as well.

**Polymorphism** is the ability to create methods that act appropriately depending on the context.

The **C# programming language** was developed as an object-oriented and component-oriented language. It exists as part of Visual Studio 2010, a package used for developing applications for the Windows family of operating systems.

A **literal string** of characters is a series of characters enclosed in double quotes that is used exactly as entered.

An **argument** to a method represents information that a method needs to perform its task. An argument is the expression used between parentheses when you call a method.

The **WriteLine() method** displays a line of output on the screen, positions the cursor on the next line, and waits for additional output.

The **Write() method** displays a line of output on the screen, but the cursor does not advance to a new line; it remains on the same line as the output.

A **namespace** is a construct that acts like a container to provide a way to group similar classes.

The **System namespace**, which is built into your C# compiler, holds commonly used classes.

A **method header** includes the method name and information about what will pass into and be returned from a method.

The **method body** of every method is contained within a pair of curly braces ({ }) and includes all the instructions executed by the method.

**Whitespace** is any combination of spaces, tabs, and carriage returns (blank lines). You use whitespace to organize your program code and make it easier to read.

An **access modifier** defines the circumstances under which a method or class can be accessed; **public** access is the most liberal type of access.

In a method header, **public** is an access modifier that indicates other classes may use the method.

In a method header, **private** is an access modifier that indicates other classes may not use the method directly.

The reserved keyword **static** indicates that a method will be executed through a class and not by an object.

In a method header, the keyword **void** indicates that the method does not return any value when called.

**Application classes** contain a Main() method and are executable programs.

**Non-application classes** do not contain a Main() method; they provide support for other classes.

**Runnable** describes files that are executable.

A **verbatim identifier** is an identifier with an @ prefix.

**Program comments** are nonexecuting statements that you add to document a program.

To **comment out** a statement is to make a statement nonexecuting.

**Line comments** start with two forward slashes (//) and continue to the end of the current line. Line comments can appear on a line by themselves, or at the end of a line following executable code.

**Block comments** start with a forward slash and an asterisk (/*) and end with an asterisk and a forward slash (*/). Block comments can appear on a line by themselves, on a line before executable code, or after executable code. They can also extend across as many lines as needed.

**XML-documentation format comments** use a special set of tags within angle brackets to create documentation within a program.

A **using clause** or **using directive** declares a namespace.

**Source code** is the statements you write when you create a program.

**Intermediate language** (**IL**) is the language into which source code statements are compiled.

The C# **just in time** (**JIT**) compiler translates intermediate code into executable code.

The **command line** is the line on which you type a command in a system that uses a text interface.

The **command prompt** is a request for input that appears at the beginning of the command line.

An **Integrated Development Environment (IDE)** is a program development environment that allows you to select options from menus or by clicking buttons. An IDE provides such helpful features as color coding and automatic statement completion.

# Review Questions

1. A computer program written as a series of on and off switches is written in _____.

   a. machine language

   b. a low-level language

   c. a high-level language

   d. a compiled language

2. A program that translates high-level programs into intermediate or machine code is a(n) _____.

   a. mangler

   b. compiler

   c. analyst

   d. logician

3. The grammar and spelling rules of a programming language constitute its _____.

   a. logic

   b. variables

   c. syntax

   d. class

4. Variables are _____.

   a. methods

   b. named memory locations

   c. grammar rules

   d. operations

5. Programs in which you create and use objects that have attributes similar to their real-world counterparts are known as _____ programs.

   a. procedural

   b. logical

   c. authentic

   d. object-oriented

6. Which of the following pairs is an example of a class and an object, in that order?

   a. robin and bird

   b. chair and desk

   c. university and Harvard

   d. oak and tree

7. The technique of packaging an object's attributes into a cohesive unit that can be used as an undivided entity is _____.

   a. inheritance

   b. encapsulation

   c. polymorphism

   d. interfacing

8. Of the following languages, which is least similar to C#?

   a. Java

   b. Visual Basic

   c. C++

   d. COBOL

9. A series of characters that appears within double quotation marks is a(n) _____.

   a. method

   b. interface

   c. argument

   d. literal string

10. The C# method that produces a line of output on the screen and then positions the cursor on the next line is _____.

    a. `WriteLine()`

    b. `PrintLine()`

    c. `DisplayLine()`

    d. `OutLine()`

11. Which of the following is a class?

    a. System

    b. Console

    c. public

    d. WriteLine()

12. In C#, a container that groups similar classes is a(n) _____.

    a. superclass

    b. method

    c. namespace

    d. identifier

13. Every method in C# contains a _____.

    a. header and a body

    b. header and a footer

    c. variable and a class

    d. class and an object

14. Which of the following is a method?

    a. namespace

    b. public

    c. Main()

    d. static

15. Which of the following statements is true?

    a. An identifier must begin with an underscore.

    b. An identifier can contain digits.

    c. An identifier must be no more than 16 characters long.

    d. An identifier can contain only lowercase letters.

16. Which of the following identifiers is not legal in C#?

    a. `per cent increase`

    b. `annualReview`

    c. `HTML`

    d. `alternativetaxcredit`

17. The text of a program you write is called _____.

    a. object code

    b. source code

    c. machine language

    d. executable documentation

18. Programming errors such as using incorrect punctuation or misspelling words are collectively known as _____ errors.

    a. syntax

    b. logical

    c. executable

    d. fatal

19. A comment in the form `/* this is a comment */` is a(n) _____.

    a. XML comment

    b. block comment

    c. executable comment

    d. line comment

20. If a programmer inserts `using System;` at the top of a C# program, which of the following can the programmer use as an alternative to `System.Console.WriteLine("Hello");`?

    a. `System("Hello");`

    b. `WriteLine("Hello");`

    c. `Console.WriteLine("Hello");`

    d. `Console("Hello");`

# Exercises

1. Indicate whether each of the following C# programming language identifiers is legal or illegal.

   a. WeeklySales

   b. last character

   c. class

   d. MathClass

   e. myfirstinitial

   f. phone#

   g. abcdefghijklmnop

   h. 23jordan

   i. my_code

   j. 90210

   k. year2012Budget

   l. abfSorority

2. Name at least three attributes that might be appropriate for each of the following classes:

   a. TelevisionSet

   b. EmployeePaycheck

   c. PatientMedicalRecord

3. Name a class to which each of these objects might belong:

   a. your red bicycle

   b. Albert Einstein

   c. last month's credit card bill

4. Write, compile, and test a program that displays a person's first name on the screen. Save the program as **Name.cs**.

5. Write, compile, and test a program that displays a person's full name, street address, and city and state on three separate lines on the screen. Save the program as **Address.cs**.

6. Write, compile, and test a program that displays your favorite quotation on the screen. Include the name of the person to whom the quote is attributed. Use as many display lines as you feel are appropriate. Save the program as **Quotation.cs**.

7. Write, compile, and test a program that displays a pattern similar to the following on the screen:

```
   X
  XXX
 XXXXX
XXXXXXX
   X
```

Save the program as **Tree.cs**.

8. Write a program that displays your initials in a pattern on the screen. Compose each initial with six lines of smaller initials, as in the following example:

```
     J      FFFFFF
     J      F
     J      FFF
     J      F
 J   J      F
 JJJJJJ     F
```

Save the program as **Initials.cs**.

9. From 1925 through 1963, Burma Shave advertising signs appeared next to highways all across the United States. There were always four or five signs in a row containing pieces of a rhyme, followed by a final sign that read "Burma Shave." For example, one set of signs that has been preserved by the Smithsonian Institution reads as follows:

```
Shaving brushes
You'll soon see 'em
On a shelf
In some museum
Burma Shave
```

Find a classic Burma Shave rhyme on the Web and write a program that displays it. Save the program as **BurmaShave.cs**.

## Debugging Exercises

Each of the following files in the Chapter.01 folder of your downloadable student files has syntax and/or logical errors. In each case, determine the problem and fix the program. After you correct the errors, save each file using the same filename preceded with "Fixed". For example, DebugOne1.cs will become FixedDebugOne1.cs.

a. DebugOne1.cs

b. DebugOne2.cs

c. DebugOne3.cs

d. DebugOne4.cs

## Up For Discussion

1. Using an Internet search engine, find at least three definitions for *object-oriented programming*. (Try searching with and without the hyphen in *object-oriented*.) Compare the definitions and compile them into one "best" definition.

2. What is the difference between a compiler and an interpreter? Which programming languages use each? Under what conditions would you prefer to use one over the other?

3. What is the image of the computer programmer in popular culture? Is the image different in books than in TV shows and movies? Would you like a programmer image for yourself, and if so, which one?

# CHAPTER 2

# Using Data

In this chapter you will:

◎ Learn about declaring variables

◎ Display variable values

◎ Learn about the integral data types

◎ Learn about floating-point data types

◎ Use arithmetic operators

◎ Learn about the `bool` data type

◎ Learn about numeric type conversion

◎ Learn about the `char` data type

◎ Learn about the `string` data type

◎ Define named constants and enumerations

◎ Accept console input

In Chapter 1, you learned about programming in general and the C# programming language in particular. You wrote, compiled, and ran a C# program that produces output. In this chapter, you build on your basic C# programming skills by learning how to manipulate data, including variables, data types, and constants. As you will see, using variables makes writing computer programs worth the effort.

# Declaring Variables

You will learn to create named constants later in this chapter.

You can categorize data as variable or constant. A data item is **constant** when it cannot be changed after a program is compiled—in other words, when it cannot vary. For example, if you use the number 347 within a C# program, then 347 is a constant, and every time you execute the program, the value 347 will be used. You can refer to the number 347 as a **literal constant**, because its value is taken literally at each use.

On the other hand, when you want a data item to be able to change, you can create a variable. A **variable** is a named location in computer memory that can hold different values at different points in time. For example, if you create a variable named heatingBill and include it in a C# program, heatingBill might contain the value 347, or it might contain 200. Different values might be used when the program is executed multiple times, or different values might even be used at different times during the same execution of the program. Because you can use a variable to hold heatingBill within a utility company's billing system, you can write one set of instructions to compute heatingBill, yet use different heatingBill values for thousands of utility customers during one execution of the program.

You learned about the System namespace in Chapter 1.

All of the built-in types except object and string are called **simple types.**

Whether it is a constant or a variable, each data item you use in a C# program has a data type. A **data type** describes the format and size of (amount of memory occupied by) a data item and defines what types of operations can be performed with the item. C# provides for 15 basic or **intrinsic types** of data, as shown in Table 2-1. Of these built-in data types, the ones most commonly used are int, double, decimal, char, string, and bool. Each C# intrinsic type is an **alias**, or other name for, a class in the System namespace.

| Type | System Type | Bytes | Description | Largest Value | Smallest Value |
|------|-------------|-------|-------------|---------------|----------------|
| byte | Byte | 1 | Unsigned byte | 255 | 0 |
| sbyte | Sbyte | 1 | Signed byte | 127 | −128 |
| short | Int16 | 2 | Signed short | 32,767 | −32,768 |
| ushort | UInt16 | 2 | Unsigned short | 65,535 | 0 |
| int | Int32 | 4 | Signed integer | 2,147,483,647 | −2,147,483,648 |
| uint | UInt32 | 4 | Unsigned integer | 4,294,967,295 | 0 |
| long | Int64 | 8 | Signed long integer | Approximately $9 \times 10^{18}$ | Approximately $-9 \times 10^{18}$ |
| ulong | UInt64 | 8 | Unsigned long integer | Approximately $18 \times 10^{18}$ | 0 |
| float | Single | 4 | Floating-point | Approximately $3.4 \times 10^{38}$ | Approximately $-3.4 \times 10^{38}$ |
| double | Double | 8 | Double-precision floating-point | Approximately $1.8 \times 10^{308}$ | Approximately $-1.8 \times 10^{308}$ |
| decimal | Decimal | 16 | Fixed-precision number | Approximately $7.9 \times 10^{28}$ | Approximately $-7.9 \times 10^{28}$ |
| char | Char | 2 | Unicode character | 0xFFFF | 0x0000 |
| bool | Boolean | 1 | Boolean value (true or false) | NA | NA |
| string | String | NA | Unicode string | NA | NA |
| object | Object | NA | Any object | NA | NA |

**Table 2-1**   C# data types

The highest `char` value, 0xFFFF, represents the character in which every bit is turned on. The lowest value, 0x0000, represents the character in which every bit is turned off. Any value that begins with "0x" represents a hexadecimal, or base 16, value.

Although the `Boolean` type has no true maximum or minimum, you can think of `true` as the highest and `false` as the lowest.

For any two `Strings`, the one with the higher Unicode character value in an earlier position is considered higher. For example, "AAB" is higher than "AAA". The `String` type has no true minimum. However, you can think of the empty string " " as being the lowest.

You name variables using the same rules for identifiers as you use for class names. Variable names must start with a letter, cannot include embedded spaces, and cannot be a reserved keyword. By convention, C# variable names start with a lowercase letter.

You must declare all variables you want to use in a program. A **variable declaration** is the statement that names a variable and reserves storage for it. The declaration includes:

You learned the rules for creating identifiers in Chapter 1. The C# reserved keywords are listed in Table 1-1 in Chapter 1.

- The data type that the variable will store

- The variable's name (its identifier)

- An optional assignment operator and assigned value when you want a variable to contain an initial value

- An ending semicolon

For example, the following statement declares a variable of type `int` named `myAge` and assigns it an initial value of 25:

```
int myAge = 25;
```

In other words, the statement reserves four bytes of memory with the name `myAge`, and the value 25 is stored there. The declaration is a complete statement that ends in a semicolon.

The equal sign (=) is the **assignment operator**; any value to the right of the assignment operator is assigned to the identifier to the left. An assignment made when a variable is declared is an **initialization**; an assignment made later is simply an **assignment**. Thus, the following statement initializes `myAge` to 25:

The assignment operator means "is assigned the value of the following expression". In other words, the statement `myAge = 25` can be read as "myAge is assigned the value of the following expression: 25".

```
int myAge = 25;
```

A statement such as the following assigns a new value to the variable:

```
myAge = 42;
```

Notice that the data type is not used again when an assignment is made; it is used only in a declaration.

Also note that the expression `25 = myAge;` is illegal because assignment always takes place from right to left. By definition, a constant cannot be altered, so it is illegal to place one (such as 25) on the left side of an assignment operator.

Instead of using a name from the Type column of Table 2-1, you can use the fully qualified type name from the `System` namespace that is listed in the System Type column. For example, instead of using the type name `int`, you can use the full name `System.Int32`. However, it is better to use the shorter alias `int` for several reasons:

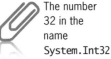

The number 32 in the name `System.Int32` represents the number of bits of storage allowed for the data type. There are 8 bits in a byte, and an `int` occupies 4 bytes.

- The shorter alias is easier to type and read.

- The shorter alias resembles type names used in other languages such as Java and C++.

- Other C# programmers expect the shorter type names.

The variable declaration `int myAge;` declares a variable of type `int` named `myAge`, but no value is assigned at the time of creation. You can make an assignment later in the program, but you cannot use the variable in an arithmetic expression or display the value of the variable until you assign a value to it.

You can declare multiple variables of the same type in separate statements. For example, the following statements declare two variables. The first variable is named `myAge` and its value is 25. The second variable is named `yourAge` and its value is 19.

```
int myAge = 25;
int yourAge = 19;
```

You also can declare multiple variables of the same type in a single statement by using the type once and separating the variable declarations with a comma, as shown in the following statement:

```
int myAge = 25, yourAge = 19;
```

Some programmers prefer to use the data type once and break the declaration across multiple lines, as in the following example:

```
int myAge = 25,
    yourAge = 19;
```

 A statement and a line of code are not synonymous. In C#, a statement might occupy multiple lines or a single line might contain multiple statements. Every statement ends with a semicolon.

 When a statement occupies more than one line, it is easier to read if lines after the first one are indented a few spaces. This book follows that convention.

When you declare multiple variables of the same type, a comma separates the variable names and a single semicolon appears at the end of the declaration statement, no matter how many lines the declaration occupies. However, when declaring variables of different types, you must use a separate statement for each type. The following statements declare two variables of type `int` (`myAge` and `yourAge`) and two variables of type `double` (`mySalary` and `yourSalary`), without assigning initial values to any of them:

```
int myAge, yourAge;
double mySalary, yourSalary;
```

Similarly, the following statements declare two `int`s and two `double`s, assigning values to two of the four named variables:

```
int numCarsIOwn = 2,
    numCarsYouOwn;
double myCarsMpg,
    yourCarsMpg = 31.5;
```

 Watch the video Declaring Variables.

---

## TWO TRUTHS & A LIE

### Declaring Variables

1. A constant value cannot be changed after a program is compiled, but a variable can be changed.

2. A data type describes the format and size of a data item and the types of operations that can be performed with it.

3. A variable declaration requires a data type, name, and assigned value.

The false statement is #3. A variable declaration names a variable and reserves storage for it; it includes the data type that the variable will store, and an identifier. An assignment operator and assigned value can be included, but they are not required.

---

## Displaying Variable Values

You can display variable values by using the variable name within a WriteLine() method call. For example, Figure 2-1 shows a C# program that displays the value of the variable someMoney. Figure 2-2 shows the output of the program.

```
using System;
public class DisplaySomeMoney
{
    public static void Main()
    {
        double someMoney = 39.45;
        Console.WriteLine(someMoney);
    }
}
```

**Figure 2-1** Program that displays a variable value

**Figure 2-2** Output of DisplaySomeMoney program

The output shown in Figure 2-2 is rather stark—just a number with no explanation. The program in Figure 2-3 adds some explanation to the output; the result is shown in Figure 2-4. This program uses the `Write()` method to display the string "The money is $" before displaying the value of `someMoney`. Because the program uses `Write()` instead of `WriteLine()`, the second output appears on the same line as the first output.

```
using System;
public class DisplaySomeMoney2
{
    public static void Main()
    {
        double someMoney = 39.45;
        Console.Write("The money is $");
        Console.WriteLine(someMoney);
    }
}
```

**Figure 2-3**   Program that displays a string and a variable value

**Figure 2-4**   Output of `DisplaySomeMoney2` program

If you want to display several strings and several variables, you can end up with quite a few `Write()` and `WriteLine()` statements. To make producing output easier, you can combine strings and variable values into a single `Write()` or `WriteLine()` statement by using a format string. A **format string** is a string of characters that optionally contains fixed text and contains one or more format items or placeholders for variable values. A **placeholder** consists of a pair of curly braces containing a number that indicates the desired variable's position in a list that follows the string. The first position is always position 0. For example, if you remove the `Write()` and `WriteLine()` statements from the program in Figure 2-3 and replace them with the shaded statement in Figure 2-5, the program produces the output shown in Figure 2-6. The placeholder {0} holds a position into which the value of `someMoney` is inserted. Because `someMoney` is the first variable after the format string (as well as the only variable in this example), its position is 0.

```
using System;
public class DisplaySomeMoney3
{
    public static void Main()
    {
        double someMoney = 39.45;
        Console.WriteLine("The money is ${0} exactly",
            someMoney);
    }
}
```

**Figure 2-5** Using a format string

**Figure 2-6** Output produced using format string

To display two variables within a single call to Write() or WriteLine(), you can use a statement like the following:

```
Console.WriteLine("The money is {0} and my age is {1}",
    someMoney, myAge);
```

The number within the curly braces in the format string must be less than the number of values you list after the format string. In other words, if you list six values to be displayed, valid format position numbers are 0 through 5. You do not have to use the positions in order. For example, you can choose to display the value in position 2, then 1, then 0. You also can display a specific value multiple times. For example, if someMoney has been assigned the value 439.75, the following code produces the output shown in Figure 2-7:

```
Console.WriteLine("I have ${0}. ${0}!! ${0}!!",
    someMoney);
```

When C# program statements become lengthy, you might want to split them into multiple lines in your editor. However, you cannot split a statement in the middle of a string.

**Figure 2-7** Displaying the same value multiple times

When you use a series of `WriteLine()` statements to display a list of variable values, the values are not right-aligned as you normally expect numbers to be. For example, the following code produces the unaligned output shown in Figure 2-8:

```
int num1 = 4, num2 = 56, num3 = 789;
Console.WriteLine("{0}", num1);
Console.WriteLine("{0}", num2);
Console.WriteLine("{0}", num3);
```

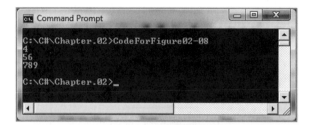

**Figure 2-8**   Displaying values with different numbers of digits without using field sizes

If you use a second number within the curly braces in a format string, you can specify alignment and field size. For example, the following code produces the output shown in Figure 2-9. The output created by each `WriteLine()` statement is right-aligned in a field that is five characters wide.

```
int num1 = 4, num2 = 56, num3 = 789;
Console.WriteLine("{0, 5}", num1);
Console.WriteLine("{0, 5}", num2);
Console.WriteLine("{0, 5}", num3);
```

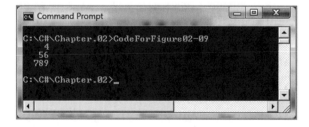

**Figure 2-9**   Displaying values with different numbers of digits using field sizes

By default, numbers are right-aligned in their fields. If you use a negative value for the field size in a `Write()` or `WriteLine()` statement, the value displayed will be left-aligned in the field.

Format strings can become very long. However, when you include any string in a statement in a program, you cannot extend it across multiple lines by pressing Enter. If you do, you will receive an error message: "Newline in constant". Instead, if you want to break a long string into multiple lines of code, you can **concatenate** (join together in a chain) multiple strings into a single entity using a plus sign (+). For example, the following two statements produce identical results. In the second, the format string is broken into two parts and concatenated.

```
Console.WriteLine("I have ${0}. ${0} is a lot.",
    someMoney);
Console.WriteLine("I have ${0}. " +
    "${0} is a lot. ", someMoney);
```

 In the concatenated example, the + could go at the end of the first code line or the beginning of the second one. If the + is placed at the end of the first line, someone reading your code is more likely to notice that the statement is not yet complete. Because of the limitations of this book's page width, you will see examples of concatenation frequently in program code.

---

### TWO TRUTHS **&** A LIE

#### Displaying Variable Values

1. Assuming number and answer are legally declared variables, then the following statement is valid:

   ```
   Console.WriteLine("{1}{2}", number, answer);
   ```

2. Assuming number and answer are legally declared variables, then the following statement is valid:

   ```
   Console.WriteLine("{1}{1}{0}", number, answer);
   ```

3. Assuming number and answer are legally declared variables, then the following statement is valid:

   ```
   Console.WriteLine("{0}{1}{1}{0}", number, answer);
   ```

The false statement is #1. When two values are available for display, the position number between any pair of curly braces in the format string must be 0 or 1. If three values were listed after the format string, the position numbers could be any combination of 0, 1, and 2.

---

## Using the Integral Data Types

In C#, nine data types are considered **integral data types**—that is, types that store whole numbers. The nine types are **byte**, **sbyte**, **short**, **ushort**, **int**, **uint**, **long**, **ulong**, and **char**. The first eight always represent whole numbers, and the ninth type, char, is used for characters like 'A' or 'a'. Actually, you can think of all nine types as numbers because every Unicode character, including the letters of the alphabet and punctuation marks, can be represented as a number. For example, the character 'A' is stored within your computer as a 65. Because you more commonly think of the char type as holding alphabetic characters instead of their numeric equivalents, the char type will be discussed in its own section later in this chapter.

You will learn more about Unicode later in this chapter, and Appendix B contains further information.

The most basic of the other eight integral types is int. You use variables of type int to store (or hold) **integers**, or whole numbers. An int uses four bytes of memory and can hold any whole number value ranging from 2,147,483,647 down to -2,147,483,648. When you type a whole-number constant such as 3 or 589 into a C# program, by default it is an int.

If you want to save memory and know you need only a small value, you can use one of the shorter integer types—byte, sbyte (which stands for signed byte), short (short int), or ushort (unsigned short int). For example, a payroll program might contain a variable named numberOfDependents that is declared as type byte, because numberOfDependents will never need to hold a negative value or a value exceeding 255; for that reason, you can allocate just one byte of storage to hold the value.

When you declare variables, you always make a judgment about which type to use. If you use a type that is too large, you waste storage. If you use a type that is too small, your program will not compile. Many programmers simply use int for most whole numbers.

When you assign a value to any numeric variable, you do not use any commas or other non-numeric characters such as dollar or percent signs; you type only digits. You can also type a plus or minus sign to indicate a positive or negative integer; a value without a sign is assumed to be positive. For example, to initialize a variable named annualSalary, you might write the following without a dollar sign or comma:

```
int annualSalary = 20000;
```

The word *integer* has only one *r*—at the end. Pronouncing it as "in-ter-ger", with an r in the middle, would mark you as unprofessional.

---

## TWO TRUTHS & A LIE

### Using the Integral Data Types

1. C# supports nine integral data types, including the most basic one, int.

2. Every Unicode character, including the letters of the alphabet and punctuation marks, can be represented as a number.

3. When you assign a value to any numeric variable, it is optional to use commas for values in the thousands.

The false statement is #3. When you assign a value to a numeric variable, you do not use commas, but you can type a plus or minus sign to indicate a positive or negative integer.

# Using Floating-Point Data Types

A **floating-point** number is one that contains decimal positions. Floating-point numbers are described as having varying numbers of significant digits. A value's number of **significant digits** specifies the mathematical accuracy of the value. The concept is often used in rounding. For example, in the statement "The population of New York City is 8,000,000," there is just one significant digit—the 8. The zeros serve as placeholders and are meant to approximate the actual value.

C# supports three floating-point data types: float, double, and decimal.

- A **float** data type can hold as many as seven significant digits of accuracy. For example, a float assigned the value 1234.56789 will appear as 1234.568 because it is accurate only to the seventh digit (the third digit to the right of the decimal point).

- A **double** data type can hold 15 or 16 significant digits of accuracy. For example, a double given the value 123456789.987654321 will appear as 123456789.987654 because it is accurate to only the fifteenth digit (the sixth digit to the right of the decimal point).

- Compared to floats and doubles, the **decimal** type has a greater precision and a smaller range, which makes it suitable for financial and monetary calculations. A decimal is significant to 28 or 29 digits. As Table 2-1 shows, a decimal cannot hold as large a value as a double can (the highest value is about $10^{28}$ instead of $10^{308}$), but the decimal will be more accurate to more decimal places.

Because monetary values are extremely important in business applications, many C# developers most frequently use the decimal data type. This book most often uses the double type for floating-point values because floating-point numbers are double by default and do not require a modifying letter after the value. However, you should use the data type preferred by your instructor or boss, or the type that is most appropriate to your application.

Just as an integer constant is an int by default, a floating-point number constant is a double by default. To explicitly store a constant as a float, you place an *F* after the number, as in the following:

```
float pocketChange = 4.87F;
```

You can use either a lowercase or uppercase *F*. You can also place a *D* (or *d*) after a floating-point value to indicate that it is a double; even without the *D*, however, it will be stored as a double by default. To explicitly store a value as a decimal, use an *M* (or *m*) after the number. (*M* stands for monetary; *D* cannot be used for a decimal because it indicates double.)

If you store a value that is too large (or too small) in a floating-point variable, you will see output expressed in **scientific notation**. Values expressed in scientific notation include an *E* (for exponent). For example, if you declare float f = 1234567890f;, the value is output as 1.234568E9, meaning that the numeric constant you used is approximately 1.234568 times 10 to the ninth power, or 1.234568 with the decimal point moved nine positions to the right. When the value that follows the E is negative, it means the value is very small and the decimal point should move to the left. For example, the value 1.234E-07 represents 0.0000001234.

## Formatting Floating-Point Values

By default, C# always displays floating-point numbers in the most concise way it can while maintaining the correct value. For example, if you declare a variable and display it as in the following statements, the output will appear as "The amount is 14".

```
double myMoney = 14.00;
Console.WriteLine("The amount is {0}", myMoney);
```

The two zeros to the right of the decimal point in the value will not appear because they add no mathematical information. To see the decimal places, you can convert the floating-point value to a string using a standard numeric format string.

**Standard numeric format strings** are strings of characters expressed within double quotation marks that indicate a format for output. They take the form *X0*, where *X* is the format specifier and *0* is the precision specifier. The **format specifier** can be one of nine built-in format characters that define the most commonly used numeric format types. The **precision specifier** controls the number of significant digits or zeros to the right of the decimal point. Table 2-2 lists the nine format specifiers.

| Format Character | Description | Default Format (if no precision is given) |
|---|---|---|
| C or c | Currency | $XX,XXX.XX <br> ($XX,XXX.XX) |
| D or d | Decimal | [-]XXXXXXX |
| E or e | Scientific (exponential) | [-]X.XXXXXXE+xxx <br> [-]X.XXXXXXe+xxx <br> [-]X.XXXXXXE-xxx <br> [-]X.XXXXXXe-xxx |
| F or f | Fixed-point | [-]XXXXXXX.XX |
| G or g | General | Variable; either with decimal places or scientific |
| N or n | Number | [-]XX,XXX.XX |
| P or p | Percent | Represents a numeric value as a percentage |
| R or r | Round trip | Ensures that numbers converted to strings will have the same values when they are converted back into numbers |
| X or x | Hexadecimal | Minimum hexadecimal (base 16) representation |

**Table 2-2**    Format specifiers

You can use a format specifier with the `ToString()` method to convert a number into a string that has the desired format. For example, you can use the *F* format specifier to insert a decimal point to the right of a number that does not contain digits to the right of the decimal point, followed by the number of zeros indicated by the precision specifier. (If no precision specifier is supplied, two zeros are inserted.) For example, the first `WriteLine()` statement in the following code produces 123.00, and the second produces 123.000:

You will learn more about strings later in this chapter.

```
double someMoney = 123;
string moneyString;
moneyString = someMoney.ToString("F");
Console.WriteLine(moneyString);
moneyString = someMoney.ToString("F3");
Console.WriteLine(moneyString);
```

You will learn more about creating and using methods in the chapters called *Introduction to Methods* and *Advanced Method Concepts*.

You use *C* as the format specifier when you want to represent a number as a currency value. Currency values appear with a dollar sign and appropriate commas as well as the desired number of decimal places, and negative values appear within parentheses. The integer you use following the *C* indicates the number of decimal places. If you do not provide a value for the number of decimal places, then two digits are shown after the decimal separator by default. For example, both of the following `WriteLine()` statements produce $456,789.00:

```
double moneyValue = 456789;
string conversion;
conversion = moneyValue.ToString("C");
Console.WriteLine(conversion);
conversion = moneyValue.ToString("C2");
Console.WriteLine(conversion);
```

Currency appears with a dollar sign and commas in the English culture. A **culture** is a set of rules that determines how culturally dependent values such as money and dates are formatted. You can change a program's culture by using the `CultureInfoClass`. The .NET framework supports more than 200 culture settings, such as Japanese, French, Urdu, and Sanskrit.

To display a numeric value as a formatted string, you do not have to create a separate string object. You also can make the conversion in a single statement; for example, the following code displays $12,345.00:

```
double payAmount = 12345;
Console.WriteLine(payAmount.ToString("C2"));
```

# Using Arithmetic Operators

Table 2-3 describes the five most commonly used binary arithmetic operators. You use these operators to manipulate values in your programs. The operators are called **binary operators** because you use two arguments with each—one value to the left of the operator and another value to the right of it. The values that operators use in expressions are called **operands**; binary operators are surrounded by two operands.

 Several shortcut arithmetic operators will be discussed in the next section.

| Operator | Description | Example |
|----------|-------------|---------|
| + | Addition | 45 + 2: the result is 47 |
| − | Subtraction | 45 − 2: the result is 43 |
| * | Multiplication | 45 * 2: the result is 90 |
| / | Division | 45 / 2: the result is 22 (not 22.5) |
| % | Remainder (modulus) | 45 % 2: the result is 1 (that is, 45 / 2 = 22 with a remainder of 1) |

**Table 2-3**   Binary arithmetic operators

The operators / and % deserve special consideration. When you divide two numbers and at least one is a floating-point value, the answer is a floating-point value. For example, 45.0 / 2 is 22.5. However, when you divide integers using the / operator, whether they are integer constants or integer variables, the result is an integer; in other words, any fractional part of the result is lost. For example, the result of 45 / 2 is 22, not 22.5.

In older languages, such as assembler, you had to perform division before you could take a remainder. In C#, you do not need to perform a division operation before you can perform a remainder operation. In other words, a remainder operation can stand alone.

When you use the remainder (modulus) operator with two integers, the result is an integer with the value of the remainder after division takes place—so the result of 45 % 2 is 1 because 2 "goes into" 45 twenty-two times with a remainder of 1. However, you cannot perform modulus operations with floating-point numbers. That is because floating-point division results in a floating-point answer, so there is no remainder.

Even though you define a result variable as a floating-point type, integer division still results in an integer. For example, the statement `double d = 7/2;` results in d holding 3, not 3.5, because the expression on the right is evaluated as integer-by-integer division before the assignment takes place. If you want the result to hold 3.5, at least one of the operands in the calculation must be a floating-point number, or else you must perform a cast. You will learn about casting later in this chapter.

When you combine mathematical operations in a single statement, you must understand **operator precedence**, or the rules that determine the order in which parts of a mathematical expression are evaluated. Multiplication, division, and remainder always take place prior to addition or subtraction in an expression. For example, the following expression results in 14:

```
int result = 2 + 3 * 4;
```

The result is 14 because the multiplication operation (3 * 4) occurs before adding 2. You can override normal operator precedence by putting the operation that should be performed first in parentheses. The following statement results in 20 because the addition within parentheses takes place first:

```
int result = (2 + 3) * 4;
```

In this statement, an intermediate result (5) is calculated before it is multiplied by 4.

Operator precedence is also called **order of operation**. A closely linked term is **associativity**, which specifies the order in which a sequence of operations with the same precedence are evaluated. Appendix A contains a chart that describes the precedence and associativity of every C# operator.

You can use parentheses in an arithmetic expression even if they do not alter the default order of operation. You can do so to make your intentions clearer to other programmers who read your programs, and so they do not have to rely on their memory of operator precedence.

In summary, the order of operations for arithmetic operators is:

- Parentheses—Evaluate expressions within parentheses first.

- Multiplication, division, remainder—Evaluate these operations next from left to right.

- Addition, subtraction—Evaluate these operations next from left to right.

## Using Shortcut Arithmetic Operators

Increasing the value held in a variable is a common programming task. Assume that you have declared a variable named `counter` that counts the number of times an event has occurred. Each time the event occurs, you want to execute a statement such as the following:

```
counter = counter + 1;
```

This type of statement looks incorrect to an algebra student, but the equal sign (=) is not used to compare values in C#; it is used to assign values. The statement `counter = counter + 1;` says "Take the value of `counter`, add 1 to it, and assign the result to `counter`."

Because increasing the value of a variable is such a common task, C# provides several shortcut ways to count and accumulate. The following two statements are identical in meaning:

```
counter += 1;
counter = counter + 1;
```

The += operator is the **add and assign operator**; it adds the operand on the right to the operand on the left and assigns the result to the operand on the left in one step. Similarly, the following statement increases `bankBal` by a rate stored in `interestRate`:

```
bankBal += bankBal * interestRate;
```

Besides the shortcut operator +=, you can use −=, *=, and /=. Each of these operators is used to perform an operation and assign the result in one step. For example:

- `balanceDue -= payment` subtracts a payment from `balanceDue` and assigns the result to `balanceDue`.

- `rate *= 100` multiplies `rate` by 100 and assigns the result to `rate`. For example, it converts a fractional value stored in `rate`, such as 0.27, to a whole number, such as 27.

- `payment /= 12` changes a payment value from an annual amount to a monthly amount due.

 You cannot place spaces between the two symbols used in any of the shortcut arithmetic operators. Spaces surrounding the operators are optional.

When you want to increase a variable's value by exactly 1, you can use either of two other shortcut operators—the **prefix increment operator** and the **postfix increment operator**. To use a prefix increment operator, you type two plus signs before the variable name. For example, these statements result in `someValue` holding 7:

```
int someValue = 6;
++someValue;
```

The variable someValue holds 1 more than it held before the ++ operator was applied. To use a postfix ++, you type two plus signs just after a variable name. Executing the following statements results in anotherValue holding 57:

```
int anotherValue = 56;
anotherValue++;
```

You can use the prefix ++ and postfix ++ with variables, but not with constants. An expression such as ++84 is illegal because 84 is constant and must always remain as 84. However, you can create a variable as in int val = 84;, and then write ++val or val++ to increase the variable's value to 85.

The prefix and postfix increment operators are **unary operators** because you use them with one operand. Most arithmetic operators, like those used for addition and multiplication, are binary operators that operate on two operands.

When you only want to increase a variable's value by 1, there is no apparent difference between using the prefix and postfix increment operators. However, these operators function differently. When you use the prefix ++, the result is calculated and stored, and then the variable is used. For example, in the following code, both b and c end up holding 5. The WriteLine() statement displays "5 5". In this example, 4 is assigned to b, then b becomes 5, and then 5 is assigned to c.

```
b = 4;
c = ++b;
Console.WriteLine("{0} {1}", b, c);
```

In contrast, when you use the postfix ++, the variable is used, and then the result is calculated and stored. For example, in the second line of the following code, 4 is assigned to c; then, *after* the assignment, b is increased and takes the value 5.

```
b = 4;
c = b++;
Console.WriteLine("{0} {1}", b, c);
```

This last WriteLine() statement displays "5 4". In other words, if b = 4, then the value of b++ is also 4, and that value is assigned to c. However, after the 4 is assigned to c, b is increased to 5.

Watch the video *Using Shortcut Arithmetic Operators.*

Besides the prefix and postfix increment operators, you can use a prefix or postfix **decrement operator** (--) that reduces a variable's value by 1. For example, if s and t are both assigned the value 34, then the expression --s has the value 33 and the expression t-- has the value 34, but t then becomes 33.

**TWO TRUTHS & A LIE**

### Using Arithmetic Operators

1. The value of 26 % 4 * 3 is 18.

2. The value of 4 / 3 + 2 is 3.

3. If price is 4 and tax is 5, then the value of price - tax++ is –1.

26. Then 2 * 3 is 6.
of the expression, 26 % 4, is 2, because 2 is the remainder when 4 is divided into
The false statement is #1. The value of 26 % 4 * 3 is 6. The value of the first part

## Using the bool Data Type

Boolean logic is based on true-or-false comparisons. An int variable can hold millions of different values at different times, but a **Boolean variable** can hold only one of two values—true or false. You declare a Boolean variable by using type **bool**. The following statements declare and assign appropriate values to two bool variables:

```
bool isItMonday = false;
bool areYouTired = true;
```

 If you begin a bool variable name with a form of the verb "to be" or "to do," such as "is" or "are," then you can more easily recognize the identifiers as Boolean variables when you encounter them within your programs.

 When you use "Boolean" as an adjective, as in "Boolean variable," you usually begin with an uppercase B because the data type is named for Sir George Boole, the founder of symbolic logic, who lived from 1815 to 1864. The C# data type bool, however, begins with a lowercase "b."

You also can assign values based on the result of comparisons to Boolean variables. A **comparison operator** compares two items; an expression containing a comparison operator has a Boolean value. Table 2-4 describes the six comparison operators that C# supports.

| Operator | Description | true Example | false Example |
|---|---|---|---|
| < | Less than | 3 < 8 | 8 < 3 |
| > | Greater than | 4 > 2 | 2 > 4 |
| == | Equal to | 7 == 7 | 3 == 9 |
| <= | Less than or equal to | 5 <=5 | 8 <= 6 |
| >= | Greater than or equal to | 7 >= 3 | 1 >= 2 |
| != | Not equal to | 5 != 6 | 3 != 3 |

**Table 2-4**   Comparison operators

When you use any of the operators that require two keystrokes (==, <=, >=, or !=), you cannot place any whitespace between the two symbols.

Legal (but somewhat useless) declaration statements might include the following, which compare two values directly:

```
bool isSixBigger = 6 > 5; // Value stored would be true
bool isSevenSmallerOrEqual = 7 <= 4;
    // Value stored would be false
```

Using Boolean values is more meaningful when you use variables (that have been assigned values) rather than constants in the comparisons, as in the following examples:

```
bool doesEmployeeReceiveOvertime = hoursWorked > 40;
bool isEmployeeInHighTaxBracket = annualIncome > 100000;
```

In the first statement, the `hoursWorked` variable is compared to a constant value of 40. If the `hoursWorked` variable holds a value less than or equal to 40, then the expression is evaluated as false. In the second statement, the `annualIncome` variable value must be greater than 100000 for the expression to be true.

 Boolean variables become more useful after you learn to make decisions within C# programs in the chapter called *Making Decisions*.

 When you display a `bool` variable's value with `Console.WriteLine()`, the displayed value is capitalized as `True` or `False`. However, the values within your programs are `true` and `false`.

---

## TWO TRUTHS **&** A LIE

### Using the bool Data Type

1. If `rate` is 7.5 and `min` is 7, then the value of `rate >= min` is false.

2. If `rate` is 7.5 and `min` is 7, then the value of `rate < min` is false.

3. If `rate` is 7.5 and `min` is 7, then the value of `rate == min` is false.

The false statement is #1. If `rate` is 7.5 and `min` is 7, then the value of `rate >= min` is true.

---

# Understanding Numeric Type Conversion

When you perform arithmetic with variables or constants of the same type, the result of the arithmetic retains the same type. For example, when you divide two `int`s, the result is an `int`; when you subtract two `double`s, the result is a `double`. Often, however, you need to perform mathematical operations on different types. For example, in the following code, you multiply an `int` by a `double`:

```
int hoursWorked = 36;
double payRate = 12.35;
double grossPay = hoursWorked * payRate;
```

When you perform arithmetic operations with operands of dissimilar types, C# chooses a **unifying type** for the result and **implicitly** (or automatically) converts nonconforming operands to the unifying type, which is the type with the higher **type precedence**. The conversion is called an **implicit conversion** or an **implicit cast**—the automatic transformation that occurs when a value is assigned to a type with higher precedence.

For example, if you multiply an int and a double, the result is implicitly a double. This requirement means the result must be stored in a double; if you attempt to assign the result to an int, you will receive a compiler error message like the one shown in Figure 2-10.

**Figure 2-10** Error message received when trying to compile a program that attempts to store a double in an int

The implicit numeric conversions are:

- From sbyte to short, int, long, float, double, or decimal

- From byte to short, ushort, int, uint, long, ulong, float, double, or decimal

- From short to int, long, float, double, or decimal

- From ushort to int, uint, long, ulong, float, double, or decimal

- From int to long, float, double, or decimal

- From uint to long, ulong, float, double, or decimal

- From long to float, double, or decimal

- From ulong to float, double, or decimal

- From char to ushort, int, uint, long, ulong, float, double, or decimal

- From float to double

A constant expression of type int, such as 25, can be converted to sbyte, byte, short, ushort, uint, or ulong. For example, sbyte age = 19; is legal. However, you must make sure that the value of the constant expression is within the range of the destination type, or the program will not compile.

Implicit conversions are not always the result of arithmetic calculations; simple assignments often result in implicit conversions. For example, if money is declared as a double, then the following statement implicitly converts the integer 15 to a double:

money = 15;

Conversions from int, uint, or long to float and from long to double may cause a loss of precision, but will not cause a loss of magnitude.

The error message in Figure 2-10 asks "are you missing a cast?". You may **explicitly** (or purposefully) override the unifying type imposed by C# by performing an explicit cast. An **explicit cast** involves placing the desired result type in parentheses followed by the variable or constant to be cast. For example, two explicit casts are performed in the following code:

```
double bankBalance = 189.66;
float weeklyBudget = (float) bankBalance / 4;
    // weeklyBudget is 47.415, one-fourth of bankBalance
int dollars = (int) weeklyBudget;
    // dollars is 47, the integer part of weeklyBudget
```

The value of bankBalance / 4 is implicitly a double because a double divided by an int produces a double. The double result is then converted to a float before it is stored in weeklyBudget, and the float value weeklyBudget is converted to an int before it is stored in dollars. When the float value is converted to an int, the decimal-place values are lost.

It is easy to lose data when performing a cast. For example, the largest byte value is 255, and the largest int value is 2,147,483,647, so the following statements produce distorted results:

```
int anOkayInt = 345;
byte aBadByte = (byte)anOkayInt;
```

Watch the video *Numeric Type Conversion.*

If you attempt to store 256 in a byte, you will receive an error message unless you place the statement in a section of code preceded by the keyword unchecked, which tells the compiler not to check for invalid data. If you use the unchecked mode and store 256 in a byte, the results will look the same as storing 0; if you store 257, the result will appear as 1. You will see 89 when you store 345 in a byte variable and display the results, because the value 89 is exactly 256 less than 345.

---

## TWO TRUTHS **&** A LIE

### Understanding Numeric Type Conversion

1. If deptNum is an int with a value of 10, then double answer = deptNum is a valid statement.

2. If deptNum is an int with a value of 10, and answer is a double with a value of 4, then deptNum = answer is a valid statement.

3. If deptNum is an int with a value of 10, and answer is a double with a value of 4, then double answer = (int)value is a valid statement.

The false statement is #2. If deptNum is an int with a value of 10, and answer is a double with a value of 4, then deptNum = answer is invalid because a double cannot be implicitly converted to an int.

# Using the char Data Type

You use the **char** data type to hold any single character. You place constant character values within single quotation marks because the computer stores characters and integers differently. For example, the following statements are both legal:

```
char aCharValue = '9';
int aNumValue = 9;
```

However, the following statements are both illegal:

```
char aCharValue = 9;
int aNumValue = '9';
```

A number can be a character, in which case it must be enclosed in single quotation marks and declared as a char type. An alphabetic letter, however, cannot be stored in a numeric type variable. The following code shows how you can store several characters using the char data type:

```
char myInitial = 'J';
char percentSign = '%';
char numThatIsAChar = '9';
```

A variable of type char can hold only one character. To store a string of characters, such as a person's name, you must use a string. You will learn about strings later in this chapter.

You can store any character—including nonprinting characters such as a backspace or a tab—in a char variable. To store these characters, you use two symbols in an **escape sequence**, which always begins with a backslash. The pair of symbols represents a single character. For example, the following code stores a backspace character and a tab character in the char variables aBackspaceChar and aTabChar, respectively:

```
char aBackspaceChar = '\b';
char aTabChar = '\t';
```

In the preceding code, the escape sequence indicates a unique value for each character—a backspace or tab instead of the letter *b* or *t*. Table 2-5 describes some common escape sequences that are used in C#.

| Escape Sequence | Character Name |
|---|---|
| \' | Single quotation mark |
| \" | Double quotation mark |
| \\ | Backslash |
| \0 | Null |
| \a | Alert |
| \b | Backspace |
| \f | Form feed |
| \n | Newline |
| \r | Carriage return |
| \t | Horizontal tab |
| \v | Vertical tab |

**Table 2-5**    Common escape sequences

The characters used in C# are represented in **Unicode**, which is a 16-bit coding scheme for characters. For example, the letter *A* actually is stored in computer memory as a set of 16 zeros and ones—namely, 0000 0000 0100 0001. (The spaces are inserted here after every set of four digits for readability.) Because 16-bit numbers are difficult to read, programmers often use a shorthand notation called **hexadecimal**, or **base 16**. In hexadecimal shorthand, 0000 becomes 0, 0100 becomes 4, and 0001 becomes 1. Thus, the letter *A* is represented in hexadecimal as 0041. You tell the compiler to treat the four-digit hexadecimal 0041 as a single character by preceding it with the \u escape sequence. Therefore, there are two ways to store the character *A*:

For more information about Unicode, see Appendix B.

```
char letter = 'A';
char letter = '\u0041';
```

The second option, using hexadecimal, obviously is more difficult and confusing than the first option, so it is not recommended that you store letters of the alphabet using the hexadecimal method. However, you can produce some interesting values using the Unicode format. For example, letters from foreign alphabets that use characters instead of letters (Greek, Hebrew, Chinese, and so on) and other special symbols (foreign currency symbols, mathematical symbols, geometric shapes, and so on) are not available on a standard keyboard, but they are available in Unicode.

---

## TWO TRUTHS **&** A LIE

### Using the `char` Data Type

1. The following statement is legal in C#:

   ```
   char department = '5';
   ```

2. The following statement is legal in C#:

   ```
   char department = '\f';
   ```

3. The following statement is legal in C#:

   ```
   char department = '32';
   ```

The false statement is #3. Only a single character can appear between single quotes, with the exception of escape sequence characters such as `'\t'`, and `'\f'`. In these cases, a single character is created using two symbols.

---

# Using the `string` Data Type

In C#, you use the **string** data type to hold a series of characters. The value of a `string` is expressed within double quotation marks. For example, the following statement declares a `string` named firstName and assigns "Jane" to it:

```
string firstName = "Jane";
```

When you assign a literal (such as "Jane") to a `string`, you can compare the `string` to another `string` using the == and != operators in the same ways that you compare numeric or character variables. For example, the program in Figure 2-11 declares three `string` variables. Figure 2-12 shows the results: `strings` that contain "Amy" and "Amy" are considered equal, but `strings` that contain "Amy" and "Matthew" are not.

You can also initialize a string with a character array. The *Using Arrays* chapter explains more.

```
using System;
public class CompareNames1
{
    public static void Main()
    {
        string name1 = "Amy";
        string name2 = "Amy";
        string name3 = "Matthew";
        Console.WriteLine("compare {0} to {1}: {2}",
            name1, name2, name1 == name2);
        Console.WriteLine("compare {0} to {1}: {2}",
            name1, name3, name1 == name3);
    }
}
```

**Figure 2-11**   Program that compares two strings using == operator (not recommended)

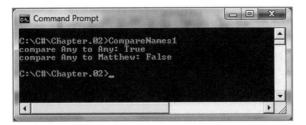

**Figure 2-12**   Output of CompareNames1 program

Later in this chapter, you learn how to allow a user to enter data into a program from the keyboard.

Besides the == comparison operator, you can use several prewritten methods to compare strings. The advantage to using these other methods is that they have standard names; when you use most other C# classes written by others, they will use methods with the same names to compare their objects. You can compare strings with any of the following methods: Equals(), Compare(), and CompareTo().

The String class **Equals() method** requires two string arguments that you place within its parentheses, separated by a comma. As when you use the == operator, the Equals() method returns true or false.

The String class **Compare() method** also requires two string arguments, but it returns an integer. When it returns 0, the two strings are equivalent; when it returns a positive number, the first string is greater than the second; and when it returns a negative value, the first string is less than the second. A string is considered equal to, greater than, or less than another string **lexically**, which in the case of letter values means alphabetically. That is, when you compare two strings, you compare each character in turn from left to right. If each Unicode value is the same, then the strings are equivalent. If any corresponding character values are different, the `string` that has the greater Unicode value earlier in the string is considered greater.

The **CompareTo() method** also compares two `strings`. However, one `string` is used before the dot and method name, and the second `string` is placed within the method's parentheses as an argument. Like the `Compare()` method, the `CompareTo()` method returns a 0 when the compared `strings` are equal, a negative number if the first `string` is less, and a positive number if the second `string` (the one in parentheses) is less. Figure 2-13 shows a program that makes several comparisons using the three methods; in each case the method name is shaded. Figure 2-14 shows the program's output.

Methods like Compare() that are not preceded with an object and a dot when they are called are *static methods*. Methods like CompareTo() that are preceded with an object and a dot are *nonstatic* and are called *instance methods*. The *Advanced Method Concepts* chapter explains more.

The comparisons made by the Equals(), Compare(), and CompareTo() methods are case sensitive. In other words, "Amy" does not equal "amy". In Unicode, the decimal value of each uppercase letter is exactly 32 less than its lowercase equivalent. For example, the decimal value of a Unicode 'a' is 97 and the value of 'A' is 65.

```
using System;
public class CompareTwoNames
{
    public static void Main()
    {
        string name1 = "Amy";
        string name2 = "Amy";
        string name3 = "Matthew";
        Console.WriteLine("Using Equals() method");
        Console.WriteLine("compare {0} to {1}: {2}",
            name1, name2, String.Equals(name1, name2));
        Console.WriteLine("compare {0} to {1}: {2}",
            name1, name3, String.Equals(name1, name3));
        Console.WriteLine("Using Compare() method");
        Console.WriteLine("compare {0} to {1}: {2}",
            name1, name2, String.Compare(name1, name2));
        Console.WriteLine("compare {0} to {1}: {2}",
            name1, name3, String.Compare(name1, name3));
        Console.WriteLine("Using CompareTo() method");
        Console.WriteLine("compare {0} to {1}: {2}",
            name1, name2, name1.CompareTo(name2));
        Console.WriteLine("compare {0} to {1}: {2}",
            name1, name3, name1.CompareTo(name3)); }
}
```

**Figure 2-13** Program that compares two strings using three methods

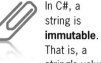

In C#, a string is **immutable**. That is, a string's value is not actually modified when you assign a new value to it. For example, when you write
`name = "Amy";`
followed by
`name = "Donald";`,
the first literal string of characters "Amy" still exists in computer memory, but the `name` variable no longer refers to the string's memory address. The situation is different than with numbers; when you assign a new value to a numeric variable, the value at the named memory address actually changes.

**76**

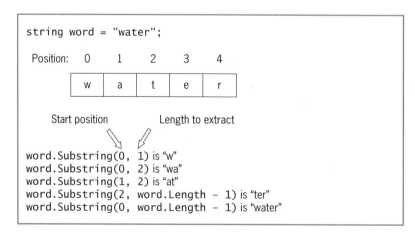

**Figure 2-14**  Output of CompareTwoNames program

You can use the **Length property** of a string to determine its length. For example, suppose you declare a string as follows:

```
string word = "water";
```

The value of `word.Length` is 5.

The **Substring() method** can be used to extract a portion of a string from a starting point for a specific length. For example, Figure 2-15 shows a string that contains the word "water". The first character in a string is at position 0, and the last character is at position `Length - 1`. Therefore, after you declare `word = "water"`, each of the statements in the figure is true.

```
string word = "water";

Position:   0   1   2   3   4

          | w | a | t | e | r |

    Start position      Length to extract

word.Substring(0, 1) is "w"
word.Substring(0, 2) is "wa"
word.Substring(1, 2) is "at"
word.Substring(2, word.Length - 1) is "ter"
word.Substring(0, word.Length - 1) is "water"
```

**Figure 2-15**  Using the Substring() method

Another useful string method is the **StartsWith() method**. In the example that defines word as "water", the expression `word.StartsWith("wa")` is true.

# Defining Named Constants

By definition, a variable's value can vary, or change. Sometimes you want to create a **named constant** (often called simply a constant), an identifier for a memory location whose contents cannot change. You create a named constant by adding the keyword `const` before the data type in a declaration. Although there is no requirement to do so, programmers usually name constants using all uppercase letters, inserting underscores for readability. This convention makes constant names stand out so that a reader is less likely to confuse them with variable names. For example, the following declares a constant named TAX_RATE that is initialized to 0.06:

```
const double TAX_RATE = 0.06;
```

You must assign a value to a constant when you create it. You can use a constant just as you would use a variable of the same type—for example, display it or use it in a mathematical equation—but you cannot assign any new value to it.

It is good programming practice to use named constants for any values that should never change; doing so makes your programs clearer. For example, when you declare a constant `const int INCHES_IN_A_FOOT = 12;` within a program, then you can use a statement such as the following:

```
lengthInInches = lengthInFeet * INCHES_IN_A_FOOT;
```

This statement is **self-documenting**; that is, even without a program comment, it is easy for someone reading your program to tell why you performed the calculation in the way you did.

# Working with Enumerations

An **enumeration** is a set of constants represented by identifiers. You place an enumeration in a class outside of any methods. You create an enumeration using the keyword enum and an identifier, followed by a comma-separated list of constants between curly braces. By convention, the enumerator identifier begins with an uppercase letter. For example, the following is an enumeration called DayOfWeek:

```
enum DayOfWeek
{
    SUNDAY, MONDAY, TUESDAY, WEDNESDAY,
        THURSDAY, FRIDAY, SATURDAY
}
```

By default, enumeration values are integers. You could also declare an enum's type to be byte, sbyte, short, ushort, uint, long, or ulong by including a colon and the type after the enumeration name and before the opening curly brace of the assignment list.

Frequently, the identifiers in an enumeration are meant to hold consecutive values. When you do not supply values for the items in an enum list, they start with 0 and are automatically increased by 1. For example, in the DayOfWeek enumeration, SUNDAY is 0, MONDAY is 1, and so on.

 As is the convention with other constants, you might prefer to name enum constants using all uppercase letters and underscores for readability, as shown in the DayOfWeek enumeration here. This helps distinguish enumeration names from variables. However, the developers of C# frequently violate this convention in both their online documentation and in built-in enumerations in the language. For example, the built-in FontStyle enumeration contains constants with mixed-case names such as Bold and Italic. When you create enumerations, you should follow the convention your instructor or supervisor prefers.

 Another convention is to use a singular noun or noun phrase as the enum identifier. In other words, DayOfWeek is better than DaysOfWeek.

If you want the first enum constant in the list to have a value other than 0, you can assign one, as in the following:

```
enum DayOfWeek
{
    SUNDAY = 1, MONDAY, TUESDAY, WEDNESDAY,
        THURSDAY, FRIDAY, SATURDAY
}
```

In this case, SUNDAY is 1, MONDAY is 2, TUESDAY is 3, and so on.

As another option, you can assign values to each enumeration, as in the following:

```
enum SpeedLimit
{
    SCHOOL_ZONE_SPEED = 20,
    CITY_STREET_SPEED = 30,
    HIGHWAY_SPEED = 55
}
```

The names used within an enum must be unique, but the values assigned do not have to be.

When you create an enumeration, you clearly identify what values are valid for an item. You also make your code more self-documenting. You should consider creating an enumeration any time you have a fixed number of integral values allowed for a variable.

After you have created an enumeration, you can declare variables of the enumeration type, and you can assign enumeration values to them. For example, you can use the following statements to declare orderDay as data type DayOfWeek, and assign a value to it.

```
DayOfWeek orderDay;
orderDay = DayOfWeek.TUESDAY;
```

In the chapter called *Using Classes and Objects*, you will learn to create many additional data types that are more complex than the built-in data types.

This discussion is meant to be a brief introduction to enumerations. At this point in your study of C#, the advantages to using enumerations are limited. Enumerations are particularly useful with switch statements, which you will learn about in the *Making Decisions* chapter.

You can convert an enum value to another data type or an integral type to an enum value by using a cast. For example, the following are valid statements:

```
int shipDay;
DayOfWeek deliverDay;
shipDay = (int)DayOfWeek.THURSDAY;
deliverDay = (DayOfWeek) shipDay;
```

## TWO TRUTHS & A LIE

### Defining Named Constants

1. The following is a valid C# constant:

   ```
   const string FIRST_HEADING = "Progress Report";
   ```

2. The following is a valid C# constant:

   ```
   const double COMMISSION_RATE;
   ```

3. By default, enumeration values are integers.

The false statement is #2. A constant must be assigned a value when it is declared.

The Console.Read() method is similar to the Console.ReadLine() method. Console.Read() reads just one character from the input stream, whereas Console.ReadLine() reads every character in the input stream until the user presses the Enter key.

In the program in Figure 2-16, the angle brackets at the end of the prompt are not required; they are merely cosmetic. You might prefer other punctuation such as a colon, ellipsis, or hyphen to indicate that input is required.

# Accepting Console Input

A program that allows user input is an **interactive program**. You can use the **Console.ReadLine() method** to create an interactive program that accepts user input from the keyboard. This method accepts all of the characters entered by a user until the user presses Enter. The characters can be assigned to a string. For example, the following statement accepts a user's input and stores it in the variable myString:

```
myString = Console.ReadLine();
```

If you want to use the input value as a type other than string, then you must use a conversion method to change the input string to the proper type.

Figure 2-16 shows an interactive program that prompts the user for a price and calculates a six percent sales tax. The program displays "Enter the price of an item" on the screen. Such an instruction to the user is a **prompt**. Notice that the program uses a Write() statement for the prompt instead of a WriteLine() statement so that the user's input appears on the screen on the same line as the prompt. Also notice that the prompt contains a space just before the closing quote so that the prompt does not crowd the user's input on the screen. After the prompt appears, the Console.ReadLine() statement accepts a string of characters and assigns them to the variable itemPriceAsString. Before the tax can be calculated, this value must be converted to a number. This conversion is accomplished in the shaded statement. Figure 2-17 shows a typical execution of the program in which the user typed 28.77 as the input value.

```
using System;
public class InteractiveSalesTax
{
    public static void Main()
    {
        const double TAX_RATE = 0.06;
        string itemPriceAsString;
        double itemPrice;
        double total;
        Console.Write("Enter the price of an item >> ");
        itemPriceAsString = Console.ReadLine();
        itemPrice = Convert.ToDouble(itemPriceAsString);
        total = itemPrice * TAX_RATE;
        Console.WriteLine("With a tax rate of {0}, a {1} item " +
            "costs {2} more.", TAX_RATE, itemPrice.ToString("C"),
            total.ToString("C"));
    }
}
```

**Figure 2-16**   InteractiveSalesTax program

**Figure 2-17**  Typical execution of InteractiveSalesTax program

As a shortcut, you can avoid declaring and using the
string itemPriceAsString in the program in Figure 2-16. Instead,
you can accept and convert the input string in one step by nesting the
ReadLine() and ToDouble() method calls, as in the following:

itemPrice = Convert.ToDouble(Console.ReadLine());

Table 2-6 shows Convert class methods you can use to change
strings into additional useful data types. The methods use the
class types (also called run-time types) in their names. For example,
recall from Table 2-1 that the "formal" name for an int is Int32,
so the method you use to convert a string to an int is named
Convert.ToInt32().

| Method | Description |
|---|---|
| ToBoolean() | Converts a specified value to an equivalent Boolean value |
| ToByte() | Converts a specified value to an 8-bit unsigned integer |
| ToChar() | Converts a specified value to a Unicode character |
| ToDecimal() | Converts a specified value to a decimal number |
| ToDouble() | Converts a specified value to a double-precision floating-point number |
| ToInt16() | Converts a specified value to a 16-bit signed integer |
| ToInt32() | Converts a specified value to a 32-bit signed integer |
| ToInt64() | Converts a specified value to a 64-bit signed integer |
| ToSByte() | Converts a specified value to an 8-bit signed integer |
| ToSingle() | Converts a specified value to a single-precision floating-point number |
| ToString() | Converts the specified value to its equivalent String representation |
| ToUInt16() | Converts a specified value to a 16-bit unsigned integer |
| ToUInt32() | Converts a specified value to a 32-bit unsigned integer |
| ToUInt64() | Converts a specified value to a 64-bit unsigned integer |

**Table 2-6**  Selected Convert class methods

# You Do It

## Declaring and Using Variables

In the following steps, you will write a program that declares several integral variables, assigns values to them, and displays the results.

**To write a program with integral variables:**

1. Open a new file in the text editor you are using to write your C# programs. Create the beginning of a program that will demonstrate variable use. Use the System namespace, name the class **DemoVariables**, and type the class-opening curly brace.

   ```
   using System;
   public class DemoVariables
   {
   ```

2. In the Main() method, declare two variables (an integer and an unsigned integer) and assign values to them.

   ```
   public static void Main()
   {
       int anInt = -123;
       uint anUnsignedInt = 567;
   ```

3. Add a statement to display the two values.

   ```
   Console.WriteLine ("The int is {0} and the unsigned int
       is {1}.", anInt, anUnsignedInt);
   ```

4. Add two closing curly braces—one that closes the `Main()` method and one that closes the `DemoVariables` class. Align each closing curly brace vertically with the opening brace that is its partner. In other words, the first closing brace aligns with the brace that opens `Main()`, and the second aligns with the brace that opens `DemoVariables`.

5. Save the program as **DemoVariables.cs** and compile it. If you receive any error messages, correct the errors and compile the program again. When the file is error-free, execute the program. The output should look like Figure 2-18.

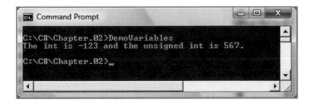

**Figure 2-18**  Output of `DemoVariables` program

6. Experiment with the program by introducing invalid values for the named variables. For example, change the value of `anUnsignedInt` to **−567** by typing a minus sign in front of the constant value. Compile the program. You receive the following error message:

*Constant value '−567' cannot be converted to a 'uint'.*

7. Correct the error either by removing the minus sign or by changing the data type of the variable to **int**, and compile the program again. You should not receive any error messages. Remember to save your program file after you make each change and before you compile.

8. Change the value of `anInt` from −123 to **−123456789000**. When you compile the program, the following error message appears:

*Cannot implicitly convert type 'long' to 'int'.*

The value is a `long` because it is greater than the highest allowed `int` value. Correct the error either by using a lower value or by changing the variable type to **long**, and compile the program again. You should not receive any error messages.

9. Experiment with other changes to the variables. Include some variables of type `short`, `ushort`, `byte`, and `sbyte`, and experiment with their values.

# Performing Arithmetic

In the following steps, you will add some arithmetic statements to a program.

**To use arithmetic statements in a program:**

1. Open a new C# program file and enter the following statements to start a program that demonstrates arithmetic operations:

```
using System;
public class DemoVariables2
{
    public static void Main()
    {
```

2. Write a statement that will declare seven integer variables. You will assign initial values to two of the variables; the values for the other five variables will be calculated. Because all of these variables are the same type, you can use a single statement to declare all seven integers. Recall that to do this, you insert commas between variable names and place a single semicolon at the end. You can place line breaks wherever you want for readability. (Alternatively, you could use as many as seven separate declarations.)

Instead of declaring the variables sum, `diff`, product, quotient, and remainder and assigning values later, you could declare and assign all of them at once, as in `int sum = value1 + value2;`. The only requirement is that `value1` and `value2` must be assigned values before you can use them in a calculation.

```
int value1 = 43, value2 = 10,
    sum, diff, product, quotient, remainder;
```

3. Write the arithmetic statements that calculate the sum of, difference between, product of, quotient of, and remainder of the two assigned variables.

```
sum = value1 + value2;
diff = value1 - value2;
product = value1 * value2;
quotient = value1 / value2;
remainder = value1 % value2;
```

4. Include five `WriteLine()` statements to display the results.

```
Console.WriteLine("The sum of {0} and {1} is {2}",
    value1, value2, sum);
Console.WriteLine("The difference between {0} and {1}" +
    " is {2}", value1, value2, diff);
Console.WriteLine("The product of {0} and {1} is {2}",
    value1, value2, product);
Console.WriteLine("{0} divided by {1} is {2}", value1,
    value2, quotient);
Console.WriteLine("and the remainder is {0}", remainder);
```

5. Add two closing curly braces—one for the `Main()` method and the other for the `DemoVariables2` class.

6. Save the file as **DemoVariables2.cs**. Compile and execute the program. The output should look like Figure 2-19.

```
C:\C#\Chapter.02>DemoVariables2
The sum of 43 and 10 is 53
The difference between 43 and 10 is 33
The product of 43 and 10 is 430
43 divided by 10 is 4
and the remainder is 3

C:\C#\Chapter.02>_
```

**Figure 2-19**   Output of DemoVariables2 program

7. Change the values of the value1 and value2 variables, save the program, and compile and run it again. Repeat this process several times. After each execution, analyze the output to make sure you understand the results of the arithmetic operations.

## Working with Boolean Variables

Next, you will write a program that demonstrates how Boolean variables operate.

**To write a program that uses Boolean variables:**

1. Open a new file in your editor and name it **DemoVariables3.cs**.

2. Enter the following code. In the Main() method, you declare an integer value, then assign different values to a Boolean variable. Notice that when you declare value and isSixMore, you assign types. When you reassign values to these variables later in the program, you do not redeclare them by using a type name. Instead, you simply assign new values to the already declared variables.

```
using System;
public class DemoVariables3
{
    public static void Main()
    {
        int value = 4;
        bool isSixMore = 6 > value;
        Console.WriteLine("When value is {0}" +
            "isSixMore is {1}", value, isSixMore);
        value = 35;
        isSixMore = 6 > value;
        Console.WriteLine("When value is {0}" +
            "isSixMore is {1}", value, isSixMore);
    }
}
```

3. Save, compile, and run the program. The output looks like Figure 2-20.

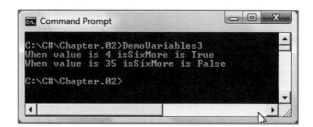

**Figure 2-20** Output of DemoVariables3 program

4. Change the value of the variable named value and try to predict the outcome. Run the program to confirm your prediction.

## Using Escape Sequences

Next, you will write a short program to demonstrate the use of escape sequences.

**To write a program using escape sequences:**

1. Open a new file in your text editor and name it **DemoEscapeSequences**.

2. Enter the following code. The three WriteLine() statements demonstrate using escape sequences for tabs, a newline, and alerts.

```
using System;
public class DemoEscapeSequences
{
   public static void Main()
   {
      Console.WriteLine("This line\tcontains two\ttabs");
      Console.WriteLine
         ("This statement\ncontains a new line");
      Console.WriteLine("This statement sounds " +
         " three alerts\a\a\a");
   }
}
```

3. Save the program as **DemoEscapeSequences.cs**. Compile and test the program. Your output should look like Figure 2-21. Additionally, if your system has speakers and they are on, you should hear three "beep" sounds caused by the three alert characters: '\a'.

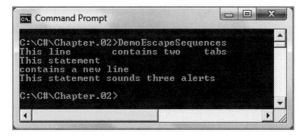

**Figure 2-21**  Output of DemoEscapeSequences program

# Writing a Program that Accepts User Input

In the next steps, you will write an interactive program that allows the user to enter two integer values. The program then calculates and displays their sum.

**To write the interactive addition program:**

1. Open a new file in your editor. Type the first few lines needed for the Main() method of an InteractiveAddition class:

```
using System;
public class InteractiveAddition
{
    public static void Main()
    {
```

2. Add variable declarations for two strings that will accept the user's input values. Also, declare three integers for the numeric equivalents of the string input values and their sum.

```
string name, firstString, secondString;
int first, second, sum;
```

3. Prompt the user for his or her name, accept it into the name string, and then display a personalized greeting to the user, along with the prompt for the first integer value.

```
Console.Write("Enter your name...");
name = Console.ReadLine();
Console.Write("Hello {0}! Enter the first integer...", name);
```

4. Accept the user's input as a string, and then convert the input string to an integer.

```
firstString = Console.ReadLine();
first = Convert.ToInt32(firstString);
```

5. Add statements that prompt for and accept the second string and convert it to an integer.

```
Console.Write("Enter the second integer...");
secondString = Console.ReadLine();
second = Convert.ToInt32(secondString);
```

6. Assign the sum of the two integers to the sum variable and display all of the values. Add the closing curly brace for the Main() method and the closing curly brace for the class.

```
sum = first + second;
Console.WriteLine("{0}, the sum of {1} and {2} is {3}",
    name, first, second, sum);
    }
}
```

7. Save the file as **InteractiveAddition.cs**. Compile and run the program. When prompted, supply your name and any integers you want, and confirm that the result appears correctly. Figure 2-22 shows a typical run of the program.

**Figure 2-22**  Typical execution of InteractiveAddition program

## Chapter Summary

- A constant is a data value that cannot be changed after a program is compiled; a value in a variable can change. C# provides for 15 basic built-in types of data. A variable declaration includes a data type, an identifier, an optional assigned value, and a semicolon.

- You can display variable values by using the variable name within a WriteLine() or Write() method call. To make producing output easier, you can combine strings and variable values into a single Write() or WriteLine() statement by using a format string.

- In C#, nine data types are considered integral data types—byte, sbyte, short, ushort, int, uint, long, ulong, and char.

- C# supports three floating-point data types: float, double, and decimal. You can use format and precision specifiers to display floating-point data to a specified number of decimal places.

- You use the binary arithmetic operators +, −, *, /, and % to manipulate values in your programs. Multiplication, division, and remainder always take place prior to addition or subtraction in an expression, unless you use parentheses to override the normal precedence. C# provides you with several shortcut arithmetic operators, including the binary operators +=, −=, *=, /=, and the unary prefix and postfix increment (++) and decrement (−−) operators.

- A bool variable can hold only one of two values—true or false. C# supports six comparison operators: >, <, >=, <=, ==, and !=. An expression containing a comparison operator has a Boolean value.

- When you perform arithmetic with variables or constants of the same type, the result of the arithmetic retains the same type. When you perform arithmetic operations with operands of different types, C# chooses a unifying type for the result and implicitly converts nonconforming operands to the unifying type. You may explicitly override the unifying type imposed by C# by performing a cast.

- You use the char data type to hold any single character. You place constant character values within single quotation marks. You can store any character—including nonprinting characters such as a backspace or a tab—in a char variable. To store these characters, you must use an escape sequence, which always begins with a backslash.

- In C#, you use the string data type to hold a series of characters. The value of a string is expressed within double quotation marks. Although the == and != comparison operators can be used with strings that are assigned literal values, you also can use the Equals(), Compare(), CompareTo(), and Substring() methods and the Length property that belong to the String class.

- Named constants are program identifiers whose values cannot change. Conventionally, their identifiers are all uppercase, with underscores inserted for readability. Enumerations are lists of named constants. The constants are integers by default, and frequently the list holds consecutive values.

- You can use the Console.ReadLine() method to accept user input. Often you must use a Convert class method to change the input string into a usable data type.

# Key Terms

**Constant** describes data items whose values are fixed; constants can be unnamed literals or named.

A **literal constant** is a value that is taken literally at each use.

A **variable** is a named location in computer memory that can hold different values at different points in time.

A **data type** describes the format and size of a data item and defines what types of operations can be performed with the item.

**Intrinsic types** of data are basic types; C# provides 15 intrinsic types.

An **alias** is another name for something.

A **simple type** is one of the following in C#: byte, sbyte, short, ushort, int, uint, long, ulong, float, double, decimal, char, and bool.

A **variable declaration** is the statement that names a variable; it includes the data type that the variable will store, an identifier that is the variable's name, an optional assignment operator and assigned value when you want a variable to contain an initial value, and an ending semicolon.

The **assignment operator** is the equal sign (=); any value to the right of the assignment operator is assigned to, or taken on by, the variable to the left.

An **initialization** is an assignment made when a variable is declared.

An **assignment** is a statement that provides a variable with a value.

A **format string** is a string of characters that contains one or more placeholders for variable values.

A **placeholder** in a format string consists of a pair of curly braces containing a number that indicates the desired variable's position in a list that follows the string.

To **concatenate** strings is to join them together in a chain.

**Integral data types** are those that store whole numbers.

The nine integral types are **byte, sbyte, short, ushort, int, uint, long, ulong,** and **char.** The first eight always represent whole numbers, and the ninth type, char, is used for characters like 'A' or 'a'.

**Integers** are whole numbers.

A **floating-point** number is one that contains decimal positions.

A value's number of **significant digits** specifies the mathematical accuracy of the value.

A **float** data type can hold a floating-point number with as many as seven significant digits of accuracy.

A **double** data type can hold a floating-point number with 15 or 16 significant digits of accuracy.

The **decimal** data type is a floating-point type that has a greater precision and a smaller range than a **float or double**, which makes it suitable for financial and monetary calculations.

**Scientific notation** is a means of expressing very large and small numbers using an exponent.

**Standard numeric format strings** are strings of characters expressed within double quotation marks that indicate a format for output.

The **format specifier** in a format string can be one of nine built-in format characters that define the most commonly used numeric format types.

The **precision specifier** in a format string controls the number of significant digits or zeros to the right of the decimal point.

A **culture** is a set of rules that determines how culturally dependent values such as money and dates are formatted.

**Binary operators** use two arguments—one value to the left of the operator and another value to the right of it.

**Operands** are the values that operators use in expressions.

**Operator precedence** determines the order in which parts of a mathematical expression are evaluated.

Operator precedence is also called **order of operation**.

**Associativity** specifies the order in which a sequence of operations with the same precedence are evaluated.

The **add and assign operator** (+=) adds the operand on the right to the operand on the left and assigns the result to the operand on the left in one step.

The **prefix increment operator** (++ before a variable) increases the variable's value by 1 and then evaluates it.

The **postfix increment operator** (++ after a variable) evaluates a variable and then adds 1 to it.

**Unary operators** are operators used with one operand.

The **decrement operator** (– –) reduces a variable's value by 1. There is a prefix and a postfix version.

A **Boolean variable** can hold only one of two values—true or false.

The **bool** data type holds a Boolean value.

A **comparison operator** compares two items; an expression containing a comparison operator has a Boolean value.

A **unifying type** is the type chosen for an arithmetic result when operands are of dissimilar types.

**Implicitly** means automatically.

**Type precedence** is a hierarchy of data types used to determine the unifying type in arithmetic expressions containing dissimilar data types.

An **implicit conversion** or **implicit cast** is the automatic transformation that occurs when a value is assigned to a type with higher precedence.

**Explicitly** means purposefully.

An **explicit cast** purposefully assigns a value to a different data type; it involves placing the desired result type in parentheses followed by the variable or constant to be cast.

The **char** data type can hold any single character.

An **escape sequence** is two symbols beginning with a backslash that represent a nonprinting character such as a tab.

**Unicode** is a 16-bit coding scheme for characters.

**Hexadecimal**, or **base 16**, is a mathematical system that uses 16 symbols to represent numbers.

The **string** data type is used to hold a series of characters.

The String class **Equals() method** determines if two strings have the same value; it requires two **string** arguments that you place within its parentheses, separated by a comma.

The **Compare() method** requires two **string** arguments. When it returns 0, the two **strings** are equivalent; when it returns a positive number, the first **string** is greater than the second; and when it returns a negative value, the first **string** is less than the second.

**Lexically** means alphabetically.

The **CompareTo() method** uses a **string**, a dot, and the method name. When it returns 0, the two **strings** are equivalent; when it returns a positive number, the first **string** is greater than the second; and when it returns a negative value, the first **string** is less than the second.

In C#, a string is **immutable**, or unchangeable. That is, a string's value is not actually modified when you assign a new value to it; instead, the string refers to a new memory location.

The **Length property** contains a string's length.

The **Substring() method** can be used to extract a portion of a string from a starting point for a specific length.

The **StartsWith() method** is used with a string and a dot, and its parentheses contain another string. It returns true if the first string starts with the characters contained in the second string.

A **named constant** (often called simply a constant) is an identifier whose value must be assigned upon declaration and whose contents cannot change.

A **self-documenting** program element is one that is self-explanatory.

An **enumeration** is a set of constants represented by identifiers.

An **interactive program** is one that allows user input.

The **Console.ReadLine() method** accepts user input from the keyboard.

A **prompt** is an instruction to the user to enter data.

# Review Questions

1. When you use a number such as 45 in a C# program, the number is a _____.

    a. literal constant

    b. figurative constant

    c. literal variable

    d. figurative variable

2. A variable declaration must contain all of the following *except* a(n) _____.

    a. data type

    b. identifier

    c. assigned value

    d. ending semicolon

3. Which of the following is true of variable declarations?

    a. Two variables of the same type can be declared in the same statement.

    b. Two variables of different types can be declared in the same statement.

    c. Two variables of the same type must be declared in the same statement.

    d. Two variables of the same type cannot coexist in a program.

4. Assume you have two variables declared as int var1 = 3; and int var2 = 8;. Which of the following would display *838*?

    a. `Console.WriteLine("{0}{1}{2}", var1, var2);`

    b. `Console.WriteLine("{0}{1}{0}", var1, var2);`

    c. `Console.WriteLine("{0}{1}{2}", var2, var1);`

    d. `Console.WriteLine("{0}{1}{0}", var2, var1);`

5. Assume you have a variable declared as int var1 = 3;. Which of the following would display *X 3X*?

    a. `Console.WriteLine("X{0}X", var1);`

    b. `Console.WriteLine("X{0,2}X", var1);`

    c. `Console.WriteLine("X{2,0}X", var1);`

    d. `Console.WriteLine("X{0}{2}", var1);`

6. Assume you have a variable declared as int var1 = 3;. What is the value of 22 % var1?

    a. 0

    b. 1

    c. 7

    d. 21

7. Assume you have a variable declared as int var1 = 3;. What is the value of 22 / var1?

    a. 1

    b. 7

    c. 7.333

    d. 21

8. What is the value of the expression 4 + 2 * 3?

    a.  0

    b.  10

    c.  18

    d.  36

9. Assume you have a variable declared as `int var1 = 3;`. If `var2 = ++var1`, what is the value of `var2`?

    a.  2

    b.  3

    c.  4

    d.  5

10. Assume you have a variable declared as `int var1 = 3;`. If `var2 = var1++`, what is the value of `var2`?

    a.  2

    b.  3

    c.  4

    d.  5

11. A variable that can hold the two values `true` and `false` is of type _____.

    a.  `int`

    b.  `bool`

    c.  `char`

    d.  `double`

12. Which of the following is *not* a C# comparison operator?

    a.  `=>`

    b.  `!=`

    c.  `==`

    d.  `<`

13. What is the value of the expression 6 >= 7?

    a. 0

    b. 1

    c. true

    d. false

14. Which of the following C# types *cannot* contain floating-point numbers?

    a. float

    b. double

    c. decimal

    d. int

15. Assume you have declared a variable as double hourly = 13.00;. What will the statement Console.WriteLine(hourly); display?

    a. 13

    b. 13.0

    c. 13.00

    d. 13.000000

16. Assume you have declared a variable as double salary = 45000.00;. Which of the following will display *$45,000*?

    a. Console.WriteLine(salary.ToString("c"));

    b. Console.WriteLine(salary.ToString("c0"));

    c. Console.WriteLine(salary);

    d. two of these

17. When you perform arithmetic operations with operands of different types, such as adding an int and a float, _____.

    a. C# chooses a unifying type for the result

    b. you must choose a unifying type for the result

    c. you must provide a cast

    d. you receive an error message

18. Unicode is _____.

    a. an object-oriented language

    b. a subset of the C# language

    c. a 16-bit coding scheme

    d. another term for hexadecimal

19. Which of the following declares a variable that can hold the word *computer*?

    a. `string device = 'computer';`

    b. `string device = "computer";`

    c. `char device = 'computer';`

    d. `char device = "computer";`

20. Which of the following compares two string variables named `string1` and `string2` to determine if their contents are equal?

    a. `string1 = string2`

    b. `string1 == string2`

    c. `Equals.String(string1,string2)`

    d. two of the above

## Exercises

1. What is the numeric value of each of the following expressions, as evaluated by the C# programming language?

    a. 4 + 2 * 3

    b. 6 / 4 * 7

    c. 16 / 2 + 14 / 2

    d. 18 / 2

    e. 17 / 2

    f. 32 / 5

    g. 14 % 2

    h. 15 % 2

    i. 28 % 5

j. 28 % 4 * 3 + 1

k. (2 + 6) * 4

l. 20 / (4 + 1)

2. What is the value of each of the following Boolean expressions?

   a. 5 > 2

   b. 6 <= 18

   c. 49 >= 49

   d. 2 == 3

   e. 2 + 6 == 7

   f. 3 + 7 <= 10

   g. 3 != 9

   h. 12 != 12

   i. −2 != 2

   j. 2 + 5 * 3 ==21

3. Are any of the following expressions illegal? For the legal expressions, what is the numeric value of each statement, as evaluated by the C# programming language?

   a. 2.2 * 1.4

   b. 6.78 – 2

   c. 24.0 / 6.0

   d. 7.0 % 3.0

   e. 9 % 2.0

4. Choose the best data type for each of the following, so that no memory storage is wasted. Give an example of a typical value that would be held by the variable and explain why you chose the type you did.

   a. your age

   b. the U.S. national debt

   c. your shoe size

   d. your middle initial

5. In this chapter, you learned that although a `double` and a `decimal` both hold floating-point numbers, a `double` can hold a larger value. Write a C# program that declares two variables—a `double` and a `decimal`. Experiment by assigning the same constant value to each variable so that the assignment to the `double` is legal but the assignment to the `decimal` is not. In other words, when you leave the `decimal` assignment statement in the program, an error message should be generated that indicates the value is outside the range of the type `decimal`, but when you comment out the `decimal` assignment, the program should compile correctly. Save the program as **DoubleDecimalTest.cs**.

6. Write a C# program that declares variables to represent the length and width of a room in feet. Assign appropriate values to the variables, such as `length = 15` and `width = 25`. Compute and display the floor space of the room in square feet (area = length * width). As output, do not display only a value; instead, display explanatory text with the value, such as *The floor space is 375 square feet.* Save the program as **Room.cs**.

7. Write a C# program that declares variables to represent the length and width of a room in feet and the price of carpeting *per square foot* in dollars and cents. Assign appropriate values to the variables. Compute and display, with explanatory text, the cost of carpeting the room. Save the program as **Carpet.cs**.

8. Write a program that declares variables to represent the length and width of a room in feet and the price of carpeting *per square yard* in dollars and cents. Assign the value 25 to the `length` variable and the value 42 to the `width` variable. Compute and display the cost of carpeting the room. (*Hint:* There are nine square feet in one square yard.) Save the program as **Yards.cs**.

9. Write a program that declares a `minutes` variable to represent minutes worked on a job, and assign a value to it. Display the value in hours and minutes. For example, 197 minutes becomes 3 hours and 17 minutes. Save the program as **HoursAndMinutes.cs**.

10. Write a program that declares four variables to hold the number of eggs produced in a month by each of four chickens, and assign a value to each variable. Sum the eggs, then display the total in dozens and eggs. For example, a total of 127 eggs is 10 dozen and 7 eggs. Save the program as **Eggs.cs**.

11. Modify the Eggs program in Exercise 10 so it prompts the user for and accepts a number of eggs for each chicken. Save the program as **EggsInteractive.cs**.

12. Write a program that declares five variables to hold scores for five tests you have taken, and assign a value to each variable. Display the average of the test scores to two decimal places. Save the program as **Tests.cs**.

13. Modify the Tests program in Exercise 12 so it accepts five test scores from a user. Save the program as **TestsInteractive.cs**.

14. Write a program that declares two variables to hold the names of two of your friends, and assign a value to each variable. Display the result of using the String.Compare() method with your friends' names. Save the program as **TwoFriends.cs**.

15. Modify the TwoFriends program in Exercise 14 so it accepts your friends' names from the keyboard. Save the program as **TwoFriendsInteractive.cs**.

16. Write a program that prompts the user for a name, Social Security number, hourly pay rate, and number of hours worked. In an attractive format (similar to Figure 2-23), display all the input data as well as the following:

    - Gross pay, defined as hourly pay rate times hours worked
    - Federal withholding tax, defined as 15% of the gross pay
    - State withholding tax, defined as 5% of the gross pay
    - Net pay, defined as gross pay minus taxes

    Save the program as **Payroll.cs**.

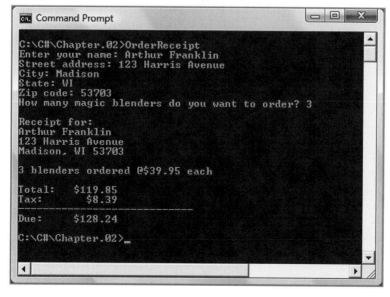

**Figure 2-23** Typical execution of `Payroll` program

17. Write a program for the Magic Blender Company. The program prompts the user for a name, street address, city, state, zip code, and quantity of blenders ordered at $39.95 each. In an attractive format (similar to Figure 2-24), display all the input data as well as the following:

   - Amount due before tax, defined as number ordered times price each

   - Sales tax, defined as 7% of the amount due

   - Net due, defined as amount due before tax, plus tax

   Save the program as **OrderReceipt.cs**.

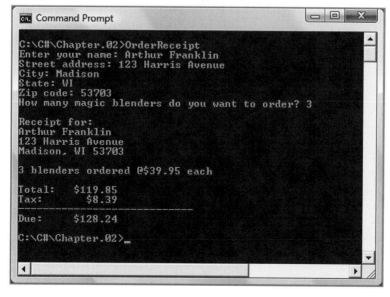

**Figure 2-24** Typical execution of `OrderReceipt` program

18. Create an enumeration named Month that holds values for the months of the year, starting with JANUARY equal to 1. Prompt the user for a month integer. Convert the user's entry to a Month value and display it. Save the file as **MonthNames.cs**.

19. Pig Latin is a nonsense language. To create a word in pig Latin, you remove the first letter and then add the first letter and "ay" at the end of the word. For example, "dog" becomes "ogday" and "cat" becomes "atcay". Write a program that allows the user to enter a word. Output the pig Latin version. Save the file as **PigLatin.cs**.

## Debugging Exercises

Each of the following files in the Chapter.02 folder of your downloadable student files has syntax and/or logical errors. In each case, determine the problem and fix the program. After you correct the errors, save each file using the same filename preceded with "Fixed". For example, DebugTwo1.cs will become FixedDebugTwo1.cs.

    a.  DebugTwo1.cs

    b.  DebugTwo2.cs

    c.  DebugTwo3.cs

    d.  DebugTwo4.cs

## Up For Discussion

1. What advantages are there to requiring variables to have a data type?

2. Some programmers use a system called Hungarian notation when naming their variables. What is Hungarian notation, and why do many object-oriented programmers feel it is not a valuable style to use?

3. Computers can perform millions of arithmetic calculations in an hour. How can we possibly know the results are correct?

# CHAPTER 3

# Using GUI Objects and the Visual Studio IDE

In this chapter you will:

◎ Create a Form in the Visual Studio IDE

◎ Use the Toolbox to add a Button to a Form

◎ Add Labels and TextBoxes to a Form

◎ Name Forms and controls

◎ Correct errors

◎ Decide which interface to use

You first learned about GUIs in Chapter 1.

In Visual Studio versions before .NET, each language such as C++ and Visual Basic had its own IDE, so you had to learn about a new environment with each language you studied. Now, you can use one IDE to create projects in all the supported languages.

You have learned to write simple C# programs that accept input from a user at the console and produce output at the command line. The environment the user sees is a program's **interface**; unfortunately, the interfaces in the applications you have written so far look dull. Most modern applications, and certainly most programs you have used on the Internet, use visually pleasing graphic objects to interact with users. These graphical user interface (GUI) objects include the labels, buttons, and text boxes you control with a mouse when interacting with Windows-type programs.

When you write a console application, you can use a simple text editor such as Notepad or you can use the Visual Studio integrated development environment (IDE). Technically, you have the same options when you write a GUI program. However, so much code is needed to create even the simplest of GUI programs that it is far more practical to develop the user interface visually in the IDE. This approach allows the IDE to automatically generate much of the code you need to develop appealing and attention-grabbing GUI programs.

## Creating a Form in the IDE

You should almost always provide a more meaningful name for applications than the default name suggested. The default names for most options are retained for the first examples in this chapter to minimize the number of changes you need to make if you want to replicate these steps on your computer.

**Forms** are GUI objects that provide an interface for collecting, displaying, and delivering information. You can use a Form to represent any window you want to display within an application. Although they are not required, Forms almost always include **controls**, which are devices such as labels, text boxes, and buttons that users can manipulate to interact with a program.

To create a Form visually using the IDE, you select New Project after starting Visual Studio and then choose Windows Forms Application, as shown in Figure 3-1. By default, Visual Studio names your first Forms application in a folder WindowsFormsApplication1. You can change the name if you want, and you can browse to choose a location to save the application.

**Figure 3-1** Choosing Windows Forms Application in the New Project window

After you click OK in the New Project window, you see the IDE main window, as shown in Figure 3-2. The main window contains several smaller windows, each of which can be resized, relocated, or closed. If a window is not currently visible, you can select it from the View menu in the main menu bar. Some key features in Visual C# include:

- The name of the application shown in three places: the title bar, the Solution Explorer, and the Properties window. In Figure 3-2, the application has the default name `WindowsFormsApplication1`.

- The **main menu**, which lies horizontally across the top of the window, and includes a File menu from which you open, close, and save projects. It also contains submenus for editing, debugging, and help tasks, among others.

- The **Toolbox tab**, which provides lists of controls you can drag onto a `Form` so that you can develop programs visually, using a mouse.

- The **Form Designer**, which appears in the center of the screen. This is where you design applications visually.

- The **Solution Explorer**, for viewing and managing project files and settings.

As you work through any project, you should choose Save All frequently. You can select this action from the File menu or click the Save All button, which has an icon that looks like a stack of disks.

105

If some of these features are not visible after you start a project in the IDE, you can select them from the View menu.

- The **Properties window**, for configuring properties and events on controls in your user interface. For example, you can use this window to set the Size property of a Button or the Text property of a Form.

- The **error list**, which displays messages about compiler errors in your code.

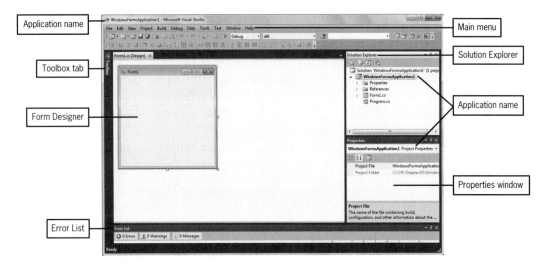

**Figure 3-2** The IDE main window

The Solution Explorer file list shows the files that are part of the current project. The Program.cs file contains the automatically generated Main() method of the application. The Form1.cs file contains other automatically generated code, and is where you write code that describes what tasks you will assign to the controls in your application. If you expand the Form1.cs node by clicking the small triangle to its left, you see a file named Form1.Designer.cs. The Windows Form Designer automatically writes code in the Designer.cs file; the code created there implements all the actions that are performed when you drag and drop controls from the Toolbox. When your applications become more sophisticated and hold resources such as images and audio clips, you will see an additional file named Form1.resx.

The text on the folder in the Form Designer window is Form1.cs [Design]*. The word *Design* means that you are viewing the visual design environment instead of the code. The asterisk means that your current work has not yet been saved. If no changes have been made since an application was last saved, then no asterisk appears on the folder.

When you create a Windows Forms project, Visual C# adds a form to the project and calls it Form1. You can see Form1 in the following locations in Figure 3-3:

- On the folder tab at the top of the Form Designer area

- In the title bar of the form in the Form Designer area

- In the Solution Explorer file list (with a .cs extension)

When you click the Form in the Form Designer area, you will see its name in a fourth location: in the Properties window in the lower-right corner, as shown in Figure 3-3. You can change the appearance, size, color, and window management features of a Form by setting its properties. The Form class contains approximately 100 properties; Table 3-1 lists a few to give you an idea of the Form features you can change. For example, setting the Text property allows you to specify the caption of the Form in the title bar, and setting the Size, BackColor, and ForeColor allow you to further customize the Form.

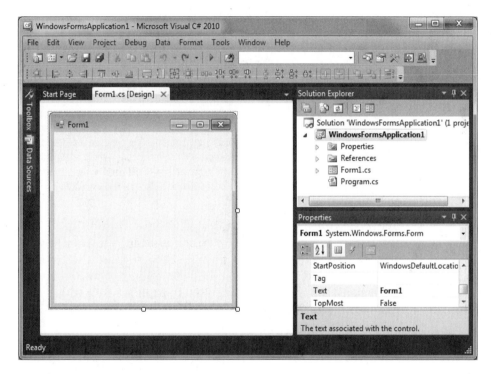

**Figure 3-3** Displaying the properties of Form1

 If you click a property, a brief description of it appears at the bottom of the Properties window. Not every property that can be used with a Form appears in the Properties window in the Visual Studio IDE—only the most frequently used are listed.

 Two buttons on the far left in the Properties list allow you to organize properties by category or alphabetically. The properties in Figure 3-3 are in alphabetical order.

| Property Name | Description |
|---|---|
| AcceptButton | Gets or sets the button on the form that is clicked when the user presses the Enter key |
| BackColor | Gets or sets the background color of the Form |
| CancelButton | Gets or sets the button control that is clicked when the user presses the Esc key |
| ForeColor | Gets or sets the foreground color of the Form |
| Name | Gets or sets the name of the Form |
| Size | Gets or sets the size of the Form |
| Text | Gets or sets the text associated with the control |
| Visible | Gets or sets a value indicating whether the control is visible |

**Table 3-1**    Selected properties of Forms

 A **node** is an icon that appears beside a list or a section of code and that can be expanded or condensed. In Visual Studio 2010, the nodes look like small triangles. When a triangle points straight to the right, you see a condensed view. Clicking the triangle reveals hidden items or code—the triangle will point diagonally down and to the right, and you see all the items in the list (or all the hidden code). Clicking the triangle again collapses the list so you can work with a condensed view.

 An opening parenthesis has a lower Unicode value than any alphabetic letter. Appendix B contains information on Unicode.

The property names generally appear in alphabetical order in the Properties window. A notable exception is the Name entry. Name appears in parentheses, so that when the Properties list is sorted in alphabetical order, it will be near the top and easy to find. For most professional applications, you will want to provide a Form with a reasonable identifier that is more descriptive than Form1.

Do not confuse a Form's Name with its Text property. If you change a Form's Name, you will not notice any difference in the visual design, but all references to the form will be changed in the code. Therefore, a Form's Name property is an identifier and it must follow the rules for variable names. This means, for example, that a Form's Name cannot contain spaces and cannot start with a digit. However, a Form's Text is what appears in its title bar, and it can be any string. (Although a Form's Text is a string, you do not type containing quotes when you enter a value for the Text property in the Properties list.) For example, in an accounting application, you might name a Form BudgetForm, but assign "2011 Budget Calculator" as its Text.

 Watch the video *The Visual Studio IDE.*

> **TWO TRUTHS & A LIE**
>
> ### Creating a Form in the IDE
>
> 1. The Visual Studio IDE allows you to use a visual environment for designing `Form`s.
>
> 2. Some key features in Visual C# include the Toolbox, Form Designer, and Solution Explorer.
>
> 3. When you create a first Windows Forms project in any folder, Visual C# names the project `MyFirstForm` by default.
>
> The false statement is #3. When you create a first Windows Forms project in any folder, Visual C# names the project `WindowsFormsApplication1` by default.

# Using the Toolbox to Add a **Button** to a Form

When you open the IDE, the left border displays a Toolbox tab. (If you do not see the tab, you can select View and then Toolbox from the IDE's main menu.) When you open the Toolbox, a list of tool groups is displayed. The list will automatically close when you move your mouse off the list, or you can pin the Toolbox to the screen by clicking the pushpin icon at the top of the list. See Figure 3-4. When you pin the Toolbox, the `Form` moves to the right to remain fully visible. Selecting All Windows Forms at the top of the Toolbox displays a complete list of available tools; selecting Common Controls displays a smaller list that is a subset of the original one. As shown in Figure 3-4, this list contains many controls: the GUI objects a user can click or manipulate. The list includes controls you probably have seen when using Windows applications—for example, `Button`, `CheckBox`, and `Label`. You can drag these controls onto the `Form`.

 This chapter features only three controls from the Toolbox— `Label`, `Button`, and `TextBox`. You will learn about many of the other controls in the chapter called *Using Controls*.

 All windows in Visual C# can be made dockable or floating, hidden or visible, or can be moved to new locations. To change the behavior of a window, click the down arrow or pushpin icon on the title bar and select from the available options. You can customize many aspects of the IDE by clicking the Tools menu, then clicking Options.

**Figure 3-4** Pinning the Toolbox

You can drag controls onto a Form where you think they will be most useful. After a control is on a Form, you can relocate it by dragging it, or delete the control by selecting it and pressing the Del key on your keyboard. You also can delete it by right-clicking the control and selecting Delete.

A **Button** is a clickable object that allows a user to interact with a GUI program. In Figure 3-5, the programmer has dragged a button onto the Form. By default, its name is button1. (You might guess that if you drag a second Button onto a Form, its Name will automatically be button2.) In a professional application, you would probably want to change the Name property of the Button to a unique and memorable identifier.

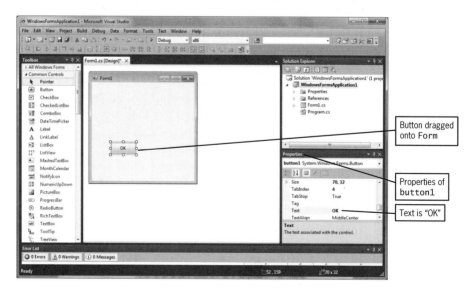

**Figure 3-5** A Button dragged onto a Form

In Figure 3-5, the programmer has clicked button1, so the Properties window shows the properties for button1. (If you click the Form, the Properties window changes to show Form properties instead of Button properties.) The Text property of button1 has been changed to "OK", and the button on the Form has handles that can be used to resize it. You can scroll through the Properties list and examine other properties you can alter for the Button. For example, you can change its BackColor, ForeColor, Font, and Size. Table 3-2 describes a few of the properties available for Button objects.

This chapter discusses only a few properties of each control. You can learn about other properties in the chapter called *Using Controls*.

| Property Name | Description |
|---|---|
| BackColor | Gets or sets the background color for the control |
| Enabled | Gets or sets whether the control is enabled |
| Font | Gets or sets the current font for the control |
| ForeColor | Gets or sets the foreground color of the control |
| Name | Gets or sets the name of the control |
| Size | Gets or sets the size of the control |
| Text | Gets or sets the text associated with the control |
| Visible | Gets or sets a value indicating whether the control is visible |

**Table 3-2**    Selected properties of Buttons

Instead of clicking a control to display its Properties list in the Properties window, you can click the arrow next to any other control name in the Properties list and select the desired control to view from a drop-down list.

## Adding Functionality to a **Button** on a **Form**

Adding functionality to a Button is easy when you use the IDE. After you have dragged a Button onto a Form, you can double-click it to create a method that executes when the user clicks the Button. For example, if you have dragged a Button onto a Form and have not changed its default name from button1, code is automatically generated, as shown in Figure 3-6. You can view the code by selecting View and then Code from the main menu. As you create GUI applications, you frequently will switch back and forth between the visual environment and the code. You can use the tabs, or click View on the main menu and then Code or Designer for the desired view. Pressing F7 and Shift-F7 on the keyboard also switches the views back and forth.

Instead of automatically generating the method that executes when a user clicks a Button, you could write the method. However, you would have to know more about both methods and event handlers. You will learn about these topics in later chapters.

111

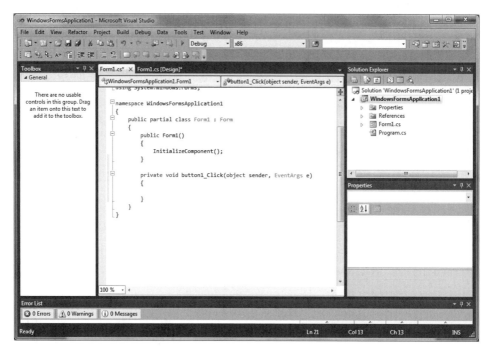

**Figure 3-6** The automatically generated code after clicking `button1`

If you scroll through the exposed code, you will see many generated statements, some of which are confusing. However, to make a `Button` perform an action, you can ignore most of the statements. You only need to write code between the curly braces of the method with the following header:

```
private void button1_Click(object sender, EventArgs e)
```

The method where you have written code in console applications has the following header:

```
public static void Main()
```

Both of these headers use the `void` return type, but they differ in the following ways:

- The `button1_Click()` method has a `private` access specifier, whereas the `Main()` method is `public`. The GUI application also contains a `public Main()` method that is created automatically; you can see it by opening the Program.cs file that is part of the application. The `button1_Click()` method is private because it is meant to be called only from the class you are currently developing. If you changed the `button1_Click()` method's access specifier to `public`, you would not notice a difference in how your program executes.

- The `Main()` method is `static`, whereas the `button1_Click()` method is not. A `static` method executes without an object. The `button1_Click()` method cannot be `static` because it needs an object, which is the `Form` in which it is running. The chapter called *Using Classes and Objects* provides more detail about the keyword `static`.

- The `button1_Click()` method contains parameters between its parentheses. These represent values about the event (the user clicking the button) that causes execution of the method. When a user interacts with a GUI object, an **event** is generated that causes the program to perform a task. When a user clicks a `Button`, the action fires a **click event**, which causes the `Button`'s `Click()` method to execute.

This chapter discusses only click events. You can learn about other events in the *Event Handling* chapter.

If you change the `Name` property of the `button1` object in the IDE, the name of its subsequently created `Click()` method will also change automatically. For example, if you rename `button1` to `okButton`, then double-click it, the name of the generated method is:

`okButton_Click()`

If you change a `Button`'s `Name` from `button1` and then place a second button on the `Form`, the new `Button` is named `button1`. If you leave the first `Button`'s default name as `button1`, then the second `Button` you place on the `Form` is named `button2`, and its default `Click()` method is named `button2_Click()`. C# automatically creates a method name based on its associated object's name.

Later in this chapter you will learn what to do if you create the event method first and change the control's name later.

You are not required to create a `Click()` method for a `Button`. If, for some reason, you did not want to take any action when a user clicked a `Button`, you simply would not include the method in your program. Alternatively, you could create an empty method that contains no statements between its curly braces and thus does nothing. However, these choices would be unusual and a poor programming practice—you usually place a `Button` on a `Form` because you expect it to be clicked at some point. You will frustrate users if you do not allow your controls to act in expected ways.

You can write any statements you want between the curly braces of the `button1_Click()` method. For example, you can declare variables, perform arithmetic statements, and produce output. The next sections include several statements added to a `Click()` method.

Watch the video *Creating a Functional Button.*

## TWO TRUTHS & A LIE

### Using the Toolbox to Add a Button to a Form

1. When a user clicks a Button, the action fires a click event that causes the Button's Click() method to execute.

2. If a Button's identifier is reportButton, then the name of its Click() method is reportButton.Click().

3. You can write any statements you want between the curly braces of a Button's Click() method.

The false statement is #2. If a Button's identifier is reportButton, then the name of its Click() method is reportButton_Click().

# Adding Labels and TextBoxes to a Form

Suppose you want to create an interactive GUI program that accepts two numbers from a user and outputs their sum when the user clicks a Button. To provide prompts for the user and to display output, you will need to add Labels to a Form, and to get input from a user, you will need to provide TextBoxes.

Labels are controls that you use to display text to communicate with an application's user. Just like a Button, you can drag a Label onto a Form, as shown in Figure 3-7. By default, the first Label you drag onto a Form is named label1. You can change its Text property to display any string of text; depending on the amount of text you enter, you might need to change the size of the Label by dragging its resizing handles or altering its Size property. If you want to create multiple lines of text on a Label, use the arrow to the right of the Text property to open an editor and type the needed text in separate lines. In Figure 3-7, "Enter a number" has been assigned to label1's Text property.

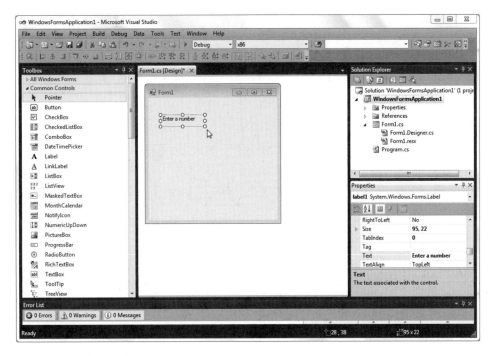

**Figure 3-7** A Label on a Form

**TextBoxes** are controls through which a user can enter input data in a GUI application. Figure 3-8 shows a TextBox dragged onto a Form. If a user is supposed to enter data in a TextBox, you frequently want to start with its Text property empty.

When a user types a value into a TextBox in an executing program, it becomes the value for the Text property of the TextBox. Because a user might type any value, the value in a TextBox is a string by default. When you write an application in which the user is supposed to enter a number, you must convert the entered string into a number. You are familiar with this process because it's exactly the same action you must take when a user enters data in response to a Console.ReadLine() statement. So, for example, to convert a user's entry in a TextBox named textBox1 to an int and a user's entry in a TextBox named moneyTextBox to a double, you can make statements similar to the following:

```
int num1 = Convert.ToInt32(textBox1.Text);
double money = Convert.ToDouble(moneyTextBox.Text);
```

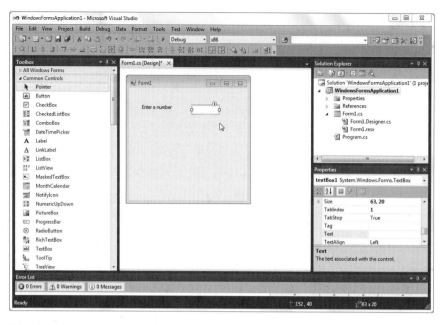

**Figure 3-8**   A Label and TextBox on a form

Figure 3-9 shows a Form with three Labels, two TextBoxes, and a Button. The third Label has not yet been provided with text, so it still contains "label3". You can delete the Text value in the Properties window if you want the Label to be empty at first.

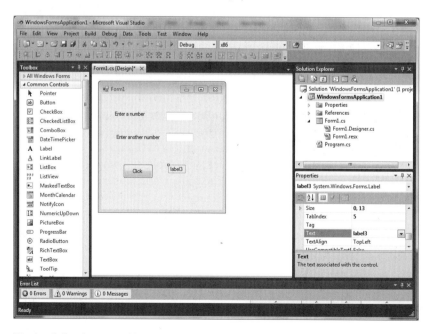

**Figure 3-9**   A Form with several controls

When a user runs the program that displays the Form in Figure 3-9, the intention is for the user to enter two numbers in the TextBoxes. When the user clicks the Button, the sum of the two numbers will be displayed in label3. To create the code that does this, you must write code for the Button. In the Form Designer, you can double-click the Button to expose the prewritten shell of the button1_Click() method, as shown in Figure 3-10.

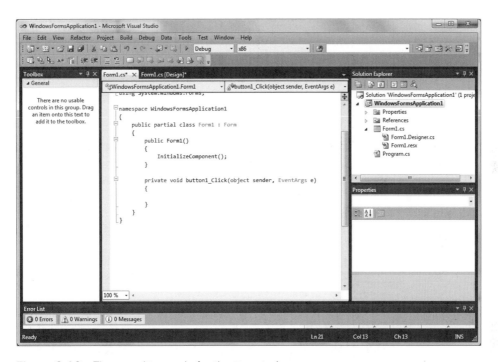

**Figure 3-10** The prewritten code for the Form1 class

Figure 3-11 shows the code you can write within the button1_Click() method. You declare three integers, then assign the first two values converted from a user's string TextBox entries. You perform the addition operation, and then assign a string and the concatenated sum to the Text property of the Label that displays the output.

```
private void button1_Click(object sender, EventArgs e)
{
    int num1;
    int num2;
    int sum;
    num1 = Convert.ToInt32(textBox1.Text);
    num2 = Convert.ToInt32(textBox2.Text);
    sum = num1 + num2;
    label3.Text = "Sum is " + sum;
}
```

**Figure 3-11** The button1_Click() method that calculates the sum of the entries in two TextBoxes

You can execute a program from the IDE by selecting Debug from the main menu and then Start Without Debugging. Figure 3-12 shows how the Form appears when the program executes, and Figure 3-13 shows the result after the user has entered numbers and clicked the Button.

**Figure 3-12** The Form when it first appears

**Figure 3-13** The Form after a user has entered two integers and clicked the Button

Watch the video *Visual Studio's Automatically Generated Code.*

You can change the values in either or both of the TextBoxes in the Form and click the Button to see a new result. When you finish using the application, you can close it by clicking the Close button in the upper-right corner of the Form.

## Formatting Data in GUI Applications

In Chapter 2, you learned about format strings that can be used to make numeric data align appropriately and display the desired number of decimal places. You can use the same format strings in your GUI applications. For example, suppose you have retrieved a double from a TextBox with a statement similar to the following:

```
double money = Convert.ToDouble(textBox1.Text);
```

You can display the value on a label with explanatory text and as currency with two decimal places with a statement similar to the following:

```
label1.Text = String.Format("The money value is {0}",
    money.ToString("C2"));
```

If necessary, you also can use escape characters in strings that are assigned to controls such as labels. For example, a two-line label might be created using the following code:

```
Label1.text = "Hello\nthere";
```

---

### TWO TRUTHS & A LIE

#### Adding Labels and TextBoxes to a Form

1. A Label and a TextBox both have a Text property.

2. When a user types a value on a Label in an executing program, it becomes the value for the Text property of the Label.

3. You can display the value on a Label using a format string.

The false statement is #2. A user does not type on a Label. When a user types a value into a TextBox in an executing program, it becomes the value for the Text property of the TextBox.

---

# Naming Forms and Controls

Usually, you want to provide reasonable Name property values for all the controls you place on a Form. Although any identifier that starts with a letter is legal, note the following conventions:

- Start control names with a lowercase letter and use camel casing as appropriate.

- Start Form names with an uppercase letter and use camel casing as appropriate. A Form is a class and, by convention, C# class names start with an uppercase letter.

- Use the type of object in the name. For example, use names such as okButton, firstValueTextBox, or ArithmeticForm.

- Professional programmers usually do not retain the default names for Forms and controls. An exception is sometimes made for Labels that never change. For example, if three labels provide directions or explanations to the user and are never altered during a program's execution, many programmers would approve of retaining their names as label1, label2, and label3.

Most often, you will want to name controls as soon as you add them to a Form. If you rename a control after you have created an event for it, the event code will generate errors. For example, assume you have created a button named button1 and you have double-clicked it, creating a method named button1_Click(). Then suppose you decide to change the Name property of the Button to sumButton. Afterward, when you look at the program code, the Click() method is still named button1_Click(). To fix this, you must refactor the code. **Code refactoring** is the process of changing a program's internal structure without changing the way the program works. After you change the name of the control using the Designer, switch to view the code. Then right-click the name of the method button1_Click(). From the menu that appears, point to Refactor and then click Rename, as shown in Figure 3-14.

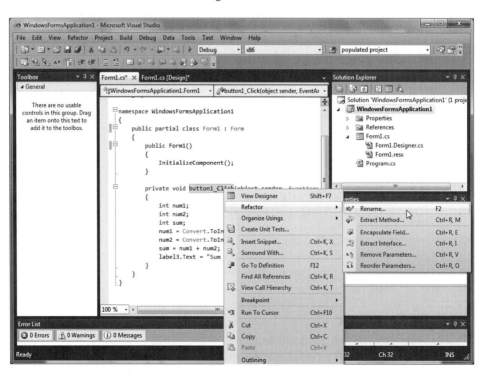

**Figure 3-14**   Choosing the Refactor option

When you click Rename, a dialog box opens, as shown in
Figure 3-15. Type the new method name; for example, you can enter
sumButton_Click using the button's Name, an underscore, and Click,
but not adding the parentheses that appear in the method header.
When you finish, click OK. A Preview Changes dialog box will highlight the change. You can confirm the change by clicking Apply.

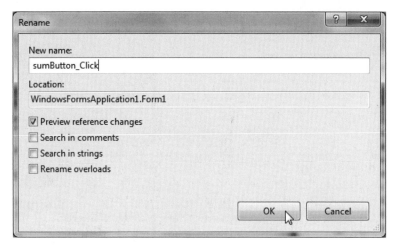

**Figure 3-15**   The Rename dialog box

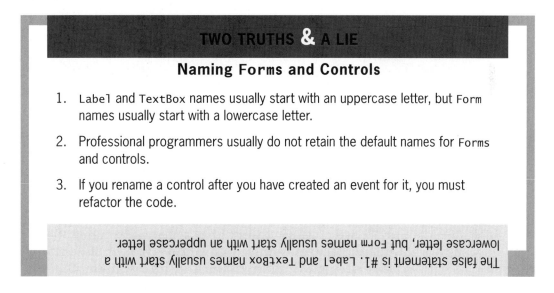

TWO TRUTHS & A LIE

**Naming Forms and Controls**

1.  Label and TextBox names usually start with an uppercase letter, but Form
    names usually start with a lowercase letter.

2.  Professional programmers usually do not retain the default names for Forms
    and controls.

3.  If you rename a control after you have created an event for it, you must
    refactor the code.

The false statement is #1. Label and TextBox names usually start with a
lowercase letter, but Form names usually start with an uppercase letter.

# Correcting Errors

Just like in console-based programs, you will often generate syntax
errors when you use the visual developer to create GUI applications.
If you build or run a program that contains a syntax error, you see
"Build failed" in the lower-left corner of the IDE. You also see an

error dialog box like the one shown in Figure 3-16. You should always click No in response to "Would you like to continue and run the last successful build?" Clicking Yes will run the previous version of the program you created before inserting the mistake that caused the dialog box to appear.

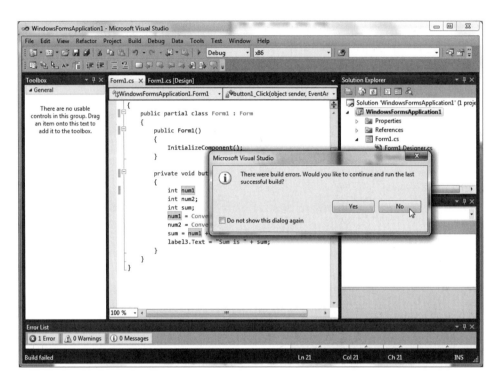

**Figure 3-16** Error dialog box

Errors will be listed in the error list at the lower-left corner of the screen. If you do not see error messages, you can click View from the IDE's main menu and then click Error List. If the list is hidden, you can drag up on the divider between the development window and the error list and click the Error tab. For example, Figure 3-17 shows a single error, "; expected". The error list also shows the file, line, position in the line, and project in which the error occurred. If you double-click the error message, the cursor is placed at the location in the code where the error was found. In this case, a semicolon is missing at the end of a statement. You can fix the error and attempt another compilation.

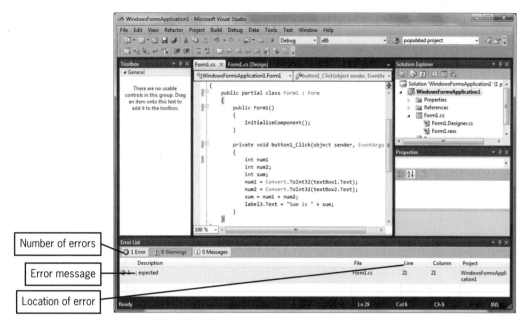

**Figure 3-17** Displaying the error list at the bottom of the screen

As with console-based programs, GUI applications might compile successfully but contain logical errors. For example, you might type a minus sign instead of a plus sign in the statement that calculates the sum of the two input numbers. You should be prepared to execute a program multiple times and carefully examine the output to discover any logical errors.

## Deleting an Unwanted Event-Handling Method

When you are working in the Form Designer in the IDE, it is easy to inadvertently double-click a control and automatically create an event-handling method that you do not want. For example, you might double-click a Label named label1 by mistake and generate a method named label1_Click(). You can leave the automatically created method empty so that no actions result, but in a professional program you typically would not include empty methods. You cannot just delete the method because, behind the scenes, other code will have been created that refers to the method, and the program will not compile. Instead of deleting the method code, you should click the control with the unwanted method so it appears in the Properties window, then click the Events button, which looks like a lightning bolt. Select the event you want to eliminate, and delete the name of the method (see Figure 3-18). This eliminates all the references to the method, and your program can again run successfully.

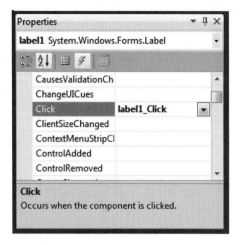

**Figure 3-18** Deleting an event from the Properties window

## Failing to Close a Form Before Attempting to Reexecute a Program

Often you will execute a GUI application and notice something you want to correct in the program. For example, you might want to reword the Text on a Label, or reposition a Button on the Form. In your haste to make the improvement, you might forget to close the application that is still running. If you make a change to the program and then try to rerun it, you get an error message that starts with the words "Unable to copy file...". The solution is simply to close the previous execution of the application and then try again.

## Using Visual Studio Help

When working with a class that is new to you, such as Button or Form, no book can answer all of your questions. The ultimate authority on C# classes is the Visual Studio Help documentation. You should use this tool often as you continue to learn about C# in particular and the Visual Studio products in general. The Help documentation for Visual Studio is in the MSDN Library, which you can install locally on your own computer. It is also available at *http://msdn.microsoft.com*.

Two popular ways to find help include the following:

- *F1 Search*—In the Code Editor, you can position the cursor on or just after a keyword or class member and press F1. The Help provided is context-sensitive, which means the screen you see depends on where your cursor is located.

- *Search*—On the main menu, you can click Help, click View Help, and enter a topic.

The first time you press F1, you are asked to choose whether you want to use the Internet to find help or to use help stored locally on your computer.

---

**TWO TRUTHS & A LIE**

### Correcting Errors

1. When a program in Visual Studio has a syntax error, you see an error dialog box that asks if you want to continue with the last successful build. You should always respond Yes.

2. In the Visual Studio IDE, any displayed syntax errors include the file, line, position in the line, and project in which the error occurred.

3. If you inadvertently create a `Click()` method in Visual Studio, you should not delete its code. You should select the event in the Properties window and delete it there.

The false statement is #1. When a program in Visual Studio has a syntax error, you see an error dialog box that asks if you want to continue with the last successful build. You should always respond No.

---

# Deciding Which Interface to Use

You have learned to create console applications in which most of the action occurs in a `Main()` method and the `WriteLine()` and `ReadLine()` methods are used for input and output. You also have learned to create GUI applications in which most of the action occurs within an event-handling method such as a `Click()` method, and `Label`s and `TextBox`es are used for input and output. Both types of applications can use declared variables and constants, and, as you will learn in the next few chapters, both types of programs can contain the basic building blocks of applications—decisions, loops, arrays, and calls to other methods. When you want to write a program that displays a greeting or sums some integers, you can do so using either type of interface and using the same logic to get the same results. So, should you develop programs using a GUI interface or a console interface?

Designing aesthetically pleasing, functional, and user-friendly Forms is an art; entire books are devoted to the topic.

- GUI applications look "snazzier." It is easy to add colors and fonts to them, and they contain controls that a user can manipulate with a mouse. Also, users are accustomed to GUI applications from their experiences on the Web. However, GUI programs usually take longer to develop than their console counterparts because you can spend a lot of time setting up the controls, placing them on a Form, and adjusting their sizes and relative positions before you write the code that does the actual work of the program. GUI applications created in the IDE also require much more disk space to store.

- Console applications look duller, but they can often be developed more quickly because you do not spend much time setting up objects for a user to manipulate. When you are learning programming concepts like decision-making and looping, you might prefer to keep the interface simple so that you can better concentrate on the new logical constructs being presented.

In short, it does not matter which interface you use to develop programs while learning the intricacies of the C# programming language. In the You Do It section next, you will develop an application that is similar to the one you developed at the console in Chapter 1. In the programming exercises at the end of this chapter, you will develop programs that are identical in purpose to programs written using the console in the chapter called *Using Data*. Throughout the next several chapters on decisions, looping, and arrays, many concepts will be illustrated in console applications, because the programs are shorter and the development is simpler. However, you also will occasionally see the same concept illustrated in a program that uses a GUI interface, to remind you that the program logic is the same no matter which interface is used. After you cover the chapters *Using Classes and Objects*, *Using Controls*, and *Handling Events*, you will be able to write even more sophisticated GUI applications.

When writing your own programs, you will use the interface you prefer or the one that your instructor or boss requires. If time permits, you might even want to develop programs both ways in future chapter exercises.

# You Do It

## Working With the Visual Studio IDE

In the next steps, you will use the IDE to create a Form with a Button and a Label. Your first console application in Chapter 1's You Do It section displayed "Hello, World!" at the command prompt. This application will display "Hello, Visual World!" on a Form.

**To use the IDE:**

1. Open Microsoft Visual C#. You might have a desktop shortcut you can double-click, or you might click **Start** on the taskbar, point to **All Programs**, and then click **Microsoft Visual Studio 2010** and **Microsoft Visual Studio 2010 – ENU**. If you are using a school network, you might be able to select Visual Studio from the school's computing menu.

Your steps might differ slightly from the ones listed here if you are using a version of C# other than the one in Visual Studio 2010.

2. Select **New Project** and then **Windows Forms Application**. Make the name of the project **HelloVisualWorld**, as shown in Figure 3-19. Then click **OK**.

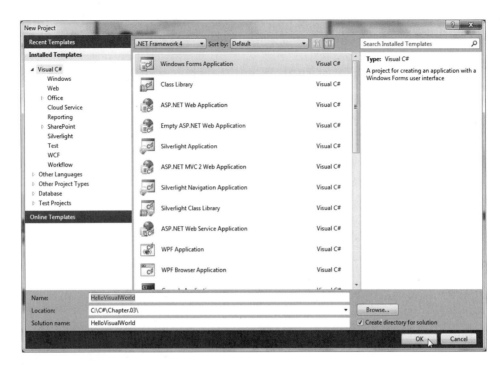

**Figure 3-19** Opening a new project

3. The HelloVisualWorld design environment opens. The text in the title bar of the blank Form contains the default name Form1. If you click the Form, its Properties window appears in the lower-right portion of the screen, and you can see that the Text property for the Form is set to Form1. Take a moment to scroll through the list in the Properties window, examining the values of other properties of the Form. For example, the value of the Size property is 300, 300.

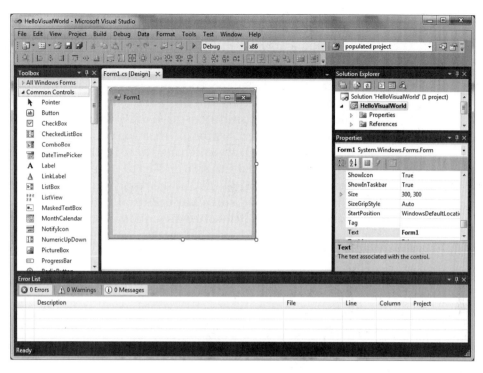

**Figure 3-20** Starting the HelloVisualWorld project

 If you do not see the error list at the bottom of the screen, as in Figure 3-20, select View from the main menu and then select Error List. You might have to drag up on the divider that separates the error list from the window above it.

 If you do not see the Properties window in the lower-right corner of your screen, click the title bar on the Form. Alternatively, click View in the main menu and click Properties Window.

4. In the Properties window, change the Name of the Form to **HelloForm**. Then change the Text of the Form to **Hello Visual World**. Press **Enter**; the title of the Form in the center of the screen changes to "Hello Visual World". See Figure 3-21.

**Figure 3-21** Form with new Text

 If you do not see the Toolbox shown in Figure 3-20, click the Toolbox tab at the left side of the screen, and then click the pushpin near the top to pin the Toolbox to the screen. Alternatively, click View from the main menu and then click Toolbox.

5. Examine the Toolbox on the left side of the screen. Select **Common Controls** if it is not already selected. In the Toolbox, click **Button**. As you move your mouse off the Toolbox and onto the form, the mouse pointer changes so that it appears to carry a Button. Position your mouse anywhere on the form, then click and drag down and to the right. When you release the mouse button, the Button appears on the Form and contains the text "button1". When you click the Button, it displays handles that you can drag to resize the Button. When you click off the Button on the Form, the handles disappear. Click the Button to display the properties for button1. Change its Name to **displayOutputButton**, and change its Text property to **Click here**. As soon as you press Enter on the keyboard or click anywhere on the Form, the text of the Button on the Form changes to "Click here". See Figure 3-22.

**Figure 3-22**    A Button with changed Text

6. Scroll through the other button1 properties. The Button's Location is 90, 175. Your Location property might be different, depending on where you released the Button when you dragged it onto the Form. Drag the Button across the Form to a new position. Each time you release your mouse button, the value of the Form Button's Location property is updated to reflect the new location. Try to drag the Button to Location 90, 175. Alternatively, delete the contents of the Location property field and type **90, 175**. The Button moves to the requested location on the Form.

7. Save your form by clicking **File** on the menu bar, then clicking **Save All**. Alternatively, you can click the **Save All** button on the toolbar; its icon is a stack of diskettes.

8. Although your Form does not do much yet, you can execute the program anyway. Click **Debug** on the menu bar and then click **Start Without Debugging**, or press **Ctrl+F5**. The Form appears. You can drag, minimize, and restore it, and you can click its Button. The Button has not yet been programmed to do anything, but it appears to be pressed when you click it. Click the Form's **Close** button to dismiss the Form.

9. Exit Visual Studio by clicking the **Close** button in the upper-right corner of the screen, or by clicking **File** on the menu bar and then clicking **Exit**. If you have made more changes since the last time you saved, you will be prompted to save again. When you choose **Yes**, the program closes.

## Providing Functionality for a Button

In the next steps, you will make the Button on the HelloVisualWorld Form functional; it will display a message when the user clicks it.

**To make a Button functional:**

1. Start Visual Studio. On the Start screen, select **HelloVisualWorld** from the recent Projects list.

2. When the Form appears, drag a Label from the Toolbox to the Form. Change its Name to **helloLabel** and its Text property to **Hello, Visual World!** If you want your Form to match Figure 3-23 exactly, change the Label's Location property to 90, 75.

**Figure 3-23** The helloLabel on the Form

3. Scroll through the Properties list for the Label and change its Visible property from True to **False**. You can still see the Label in the Designer, but the Label will be invisible when you execute the program.

4. Double-click the Button on the Form. A new window that contains program code is displayed, revealing a newly created displayOutputButton_Click() method with no statements. Between the curly braces, type the following:

   **helloLabel.Visible = true;**

   This will cause the Label to appear when the user clicks the Button on the Form.

5. Save the file, then run the program by clicking **Debug** on the menu bar and clicking **Start Without Debugging**, or by pressing **Ctrl+F5**. When the Form appears, click the **Click here** button to reveal the greeting.

6. If you want, experiment with values for some of the Label properties, such as Font, BackColor, and ForeColor.

## Adding a Second Button to a Form

In the next steps, you will add a second Button to the Form in the HelloVisualWorld project.

1. Drag a second button onto the Form below the first Button. Change the new Button's Name property to changeOutputButton and change its Text to **Click me last**.

2. Double-click the changeOutputButton to expose the changeOutputButton_Click() method.

3. Between the curly braces of the method, add the following code:

   **helloLabel.Text = "Goodbye";**

4. Save the project, then execute the program. Click the displayOutputButton to reveal "Hello, Visual World!". Then click the changeOutputButton to reveal "Goodbye".

5. Execute the program again. This time, click the second Button first. No message appears because the Label with the message has not been made visible. When you click the displayOutputButton, the Label becomes visible, but it displays "Goodbye" because the changeOutputButton's Click() method has already changed the Label's Text.

6. Return to the Form1.cs [Design] tab. Click the changeOutputButton and change its Enabled property to **False**. Now, when the program executes, the user will not be immediately able to click the second Button.

7. Double-click the displayOutputButton and add a new statement to the method so that the changeOutputButton becomes enabled when the displayOutputButton is clicked:

   **changeOutputButton.Enabled = true;**

8. Save the project, then execute the program. When the Form appears, the changeOutputButton is dimmed and not clickable because it is not enabled. Click the enabled displayOutputButton to reveal the "Hello, Visual World!" message and to enable the second Button. Then click the changeOutputButton to expose the "Goodbye" message.

9. Dismiss the Form and close Visual Studio.

## Chapter Summary

- Forms are GUI objects that provide an interface for collecting, displaying, and delivering information. Forms almost always include controls such as labels, text boxes, and buttons that users can manipulate to interact with a program. Every Form and control on a Form has multiple properties you can set using the IDE.

- The Toolbox displays a list of available controls you can add to a Form. The list includes Button, CheckBox, and Label. From the Toolbox, you can drag controls onto a Form where they will be most useful. After you have dragged a Button onto a Form, you can double-click it to create the method that executes when a user clicks the Button, and you can write any statements you want between the curly braces of the Click() method.

- Labels are controls that you use to display text to communicate with an application's user. TextBoxes are controls through which a user can enter input data in a GUI application. Both have a Text property; frequently an application starts with the Text empty for TextBoxes. Because a user might type any value, the value in a TextBox is a string by default.

- Usually, you want to provide reasonable Name property values for all the controls you place on a Form. Although any identifier that starts with a letter is legal, by convention you should start control names with a lowercase letter and use camel casing as appropriate, start Form names with an uppercase letter and use camel casing as appropriate, and use the type of object in the name.

- If you build or run a program that contains a syntax error, you see "Build failed" in the lower-left corner of the IDE and an error dialog box. Other errors also will be shown in the error list at the lower-left corner of the screen. The error list shows the file, line, position in the line, and project in which the error occurred. If you double-click the error message, the cursor is placed at the location in the code where the error was found. If you inadvertently create an event-handling method that you do not want, you should eliminate the event using the Properties window in the IDE. The ultimate authority on C# classes is the Visual Studio Help documentation.

- Both console and GUI applications can contain variables and constants, decisions, loops, arrays, and calls to other methods. GUI applications look "snazzier," and they contain controls that a user can manipulate with a mouse. However, GUI programs usually take longer to develop than their console counterparts. When writing your own programs, you will use the interface you prefer or the one that your instructor or boss requires.

# Key Terms

The **interface** is the environment a user sees when a program executes.

**Forms** are GUI objects that provide an interface for collecting, displaying, and delivering information.

**Controls** are devices such as labels, text boxes, and buttons that users can manipulate to communicate with a GUI program.

The **main menu** in the IDE lies horizontally across the top of the window, and includes submenus that list additional options.

The **Toolbox tab** in the IDE provides lists of controls that can be dragged onto a Form so that you can develop programs visually, using a mouse.

The **Form Designer** in the IDE is the area where you design applications visually.

The **Solution Explorer** in the IDE provides the means to view and manage project files and settings.

The **Properties window** in the IDE provides the means to configure properties and events on controls in your user interface.

The **error list** in the IDE displays messages about compiler errors in your code.

A **node** is an icon that appears beside a list or a section of code and that can be expanded or condensed.

A **Button** is a clickable object that allows a user to interact with a GUI program.

An **event** causes a program to perform a task.

A **click event** is the event generated when a user clicks a control in a GUI program.

**Labels** are controls that you use to display text to communicate with an application's user.

**TextBoxes** are controls through which a user can enter input data in a GUI application.

**Code refactoring** is the process of changing a program's internal structure without changing the way the program works.

## Review Questions

1. Which of the following is a GUI object that provides an interface for collecting, displaying, and delivering information, and that contains other controls?

   a. Form

   b. Button

   c. TextBox

   d. Label

2. In the Visual Studio IDE main window, where does the main menu lie?

   a. vertically along the left border

   b. vertically along the right border

   c. horizontally across the top of the window

   d. horizontally across the bottom of the window

3. In the IDE, the area where you visually construct a Form is the _____.

   a. Toolbox

   b. Palette

   c. Easel

   d. Form Designer

4. When you create a new Windows Forms project, by default the first Form you see is named _____.

   a. Form

   b. Form1

   c. FormA

   d. FormAlpha

5. The Form class has _____ properties.

   a. three

   b. ten

   c. about 100

   d. about 1000

6. Which of the following is not a Form property?

   a. BackColor

   b. ProjectName

   c. Size

   d. Text

7. Which of the following is a legal Form Name property?

   a. Payroll Form

   b. PayrollForm

   c. either of the above

   d. none of the above

8. Which of the following is a legal Form Text property?

   a. Payroll Form

   b. PayrollForm

   c. either of the above

   d. none of the above

9. Which of the following does not appear in the IDE's Toolbox list?

   a. Text

   b. Button

   c. Label

   d. TextBox

10. After you have dragged a Button onto a Form in the IDE, you can double-click it to _____.

   a. delete it

   b. view its properties

   c. create a method that executes when a user clicks the Button

   d. execute a method when a user clicks the Button

11. The button1_Click() method that is generated by the IDE _____.

   a. has a private access specifier

   b. is nonstatic

   c. contains parameters between its parentheses

   d. all of the above

12. A(n) _____ is generated when a user interacts with a GUI object.

   a. event

   b. occasion

   c. method

   d. error

13. If you create a Button named yesButton, the name of the method that responds to clicks on it is _____.

   a. button1_Click()

   b. yesButton_Method()

   c. click_YesButton()

   d. yesButton_Click()

14. Statements allowed in a `Click()` method include _____.

    a. variable declarations

    b. arithmetic statements

    c. both of the above

    d. none of the above

15. _____ are controls through which a user can enter input data in a GUI application.

    a. `Labels`

    b. `Tags`

    c. `Tickets`

    d. `TextBoxes`

16. The value in a `TextBox` is _____.

    a. an `int`

    b. a `double`

    c. a `string`

    d. It might be any of the above.

17. Which of the following is a legal and conventional name for a `TextBox`?

    a. `Salary TextBox`

    b. `salaryTextBox`

    c. both of the above

    d. none of the above

18. The process of changing a program's internal structure without changing the way the program works is _____.

    a. compiling

    b. debugging

    c. code refactoring

    d. systems analysis

19. If you inadvertently create a `Click()` method for a control that should not generate a click event, you can successfully eliminate the method by _____.

    a. deleting the method code from the Form1.cs file

    b. eliminating the method from the event list in the Properties window

    c. adding the method to the Discard window

    d. making the method a comment by placing two forward slashes at the start of each line

20. Of the following, the most significant difference between many console applications and GUI applications is _____.

    a. their appearance

    b. their ability to accept input

    c. their ability to perform calculations

    d. their ability to be created using C#

## Exercises

1. Write a GUI program that allows a user to input the number of eggs produced in a month by each of five chickens. Sum the eggs, then display the total in dozens and eggs. For example, a total of 127 eggs is 10 dozen and 7 eggs. Save the project as **EggsInteractiveGUI**. Figure 3-24 shows a typical execution.

The exercises in this section should look familiar to you. Each is similar to an exercise in Chapter 2, where you created solutions using console input and output.

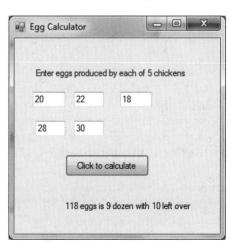

**Figure 3-24**  An EggsInteractiveGUI application

2. Write a GUI program that allows a user to enter scores for five tests he has taken. Display the average of the test scores to two decimal places. Save the project as **TestsInteractiveGUI**.

3. Write a GUI program that accepts the names of two of your friends. Display the result of using the String.Compare() method with your friends' names. Save the project as **TwoFriendsInteractiveGUI**.

4. Write a GUI program that prompts the user for a name, Social Security number, hourly pay rate, and number of hours worked. In an attractive format, display all the input data as well as the following:

   • Gross pay, defined as hourly pay rate times hours worked

   • Federal withholding tax, defined as 15% of the gross pay

   • State withholding tax, defined as 5% of the gross pay

   • Net pay, defined as gross pay minus taxes

   Save the project as **PayrollGUI**.

5. Write a GUI program for the Magic Blender Company. The program prompts the user for a name, street address, city, state, zip code, and quantity of blenders ordered at $39.95 each. Display all the input data as well as the following:

   • Amount due before tax, defined as number ordered times price each

   • Sales tax, defined as 7% of the amount due

   • Net due, defined as amount due before tax, plus tax

   Save the project as **OrderReceiptGUI**.

6. Create an enumeration named Month that holds values for the months of the year, starting with JANUARY equal to 1. (Recall that an enumeration must be placed within a class but outside of any method.) Using a GUI interface, prompt the user for a month integer. Convert the user's entry to a Month value and display it. Save the project as **MonthNamesGUI**.

7. Pig Latin is a nonsense language. To create a word in pig Latin, you remove the first letter and then add the first letter and "ay" at the end of the word. For example, "dog" becomes "ogday" and "cat" becomes "atcay". Write a GUI program that allows the user to enter a word. Output the pig Latin version. Save the project as **PigLatinGUI**.

Debugging Exercises

Each of the following projects in the Chapter.03 folder of your down-loadable student files has syntax and/or logical errors. In each case, immediately save a copy of the project with its new name, determine the problem, and fix the program. The new project should be pre-ceded with *Fixed*. For example, the project folder for DebugThree1 will become FixedDebugThree1.

 Immediately save the project folders with their new names before you correct their errors.

 141

    a.   DebugThree1

    b.   DebugThree2

    c.   DebugThree3

    d.   DebugThree4

 Up For Discussion

1. Think of some practice or position to which you are opposed. For example, you might have objections to organizations on the far right or left politically. Suppose that such an organiza-tion offered you twice your annual salary to create Web sites for them. Would you do it? If not, is there a price at which you would do it? What if the organization was not so extreme, but featured products you found distasteful? What if the Web site was not objectionable, but the parent company's policies were? For example, if you are opposed to smoking, would you design a Web site for a tobacco company? At what price? What if the site just displayed sports scores without promot-ing smoking directly?

2. Suppose you have learned a lot about programming from your employer. Is it ethical for you to use this knowledge to start your own home-based programming business on the side? Does it matter whether you are in competition for the same clients as your employer? Does it matter whether you use just your programming expertise or whether you also use information about clients' preferences and needs gathered from your regular job?

# CHAPTER 4

# Making Decisions

In this chapter you will:

◎  Understand logic-planning tools and decision making

◎  Learn how to make decisions using the `if` statement

◎  Learn how to make decisions using the `if-else` statement

◎  Use compound expressions in `if` statements

◎  Make decisions using the `switch` statement

◎  Use the conditional operator

◎  Use the NOT operator

◎  Learn to avoid common errors when making decisions

◎  Learn about decision-making issues in GUI programs

Computer programs are powerful because of their ability to make decisions. Programs that decide which travel route will offer the best weather conditions, which Web site will provide the closest match to search criteria, or which recommended medical treatment has the highest probability of success all rely on a program's decision making. In this chapter you will learn to make decisions in C# programs.

143

## Understanding Logic-Planning Tools and Decision Making

When computer programmers write programs, they rarely just sit down at a keyboard and begin typing. Programmers must plan the complex portions of programs using paper and pencil. Programmers often use **pseudocode,** a tool that helps them plan a program's logic by writing plain English statements. Using pseudocode requires that you write down the steps needed to accomplish a given task. You write pseudocode in everyday language, not the syntax used in a programming language. In fact, a task you write in pseudocode does not have to be computer-related. If you have ever written a list of directions to your house—for example, (1) go west on Algonquin Road, (2) turn left on Roselle Road, (3) enter expressway heading east, and so on—you have written pseudocode. A **flowchart** is similar to pseudocode, but you write the steps in diagram form, as a series of shapes connected by arrows.

 You learned the difference between a program's logic and its syntax in Chapter 1.

Some programmers use a variety of shapes to represent different tasks in their flowcharts, but you can draw simple flowcharts that express very complex situations using just rectangles and diamonds. You use a rectangle to represent any unconditional step and a diamond to represent any decision. For example, Figure 4-1 shows a flowchart and pseudocode describing driving directions to a friend's house. Notice how the actions illustrated in the flowchart and the pseudocode statements correspond. The logic in Figure 4-1 is an example of a logical structure called a **sequence structure**—one step follows another unconditionally. A sequence structure might contain any number of steps, but when one task follows another with no chance to branch away or skip a step, you are using a sequence.

144

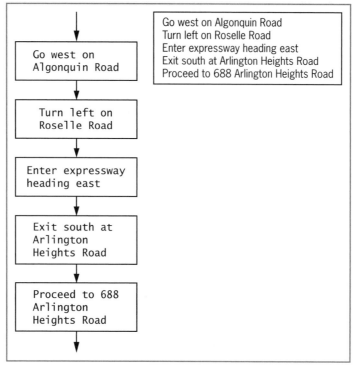

**Figure 4-1**  Flowchart and pseudocode for a series of sequential steps

Sometimes, logical steps do not follow in an unconditional sequence—some tasks might or might not occur based on decisions you make. Flowchart creators use diamond shapes to indicate alternative courses of action, which are drawn starting from the sides of the diamonds. Figure 4-2 shows a flowchart describing directions in which the execution of some steps depends on decisions.

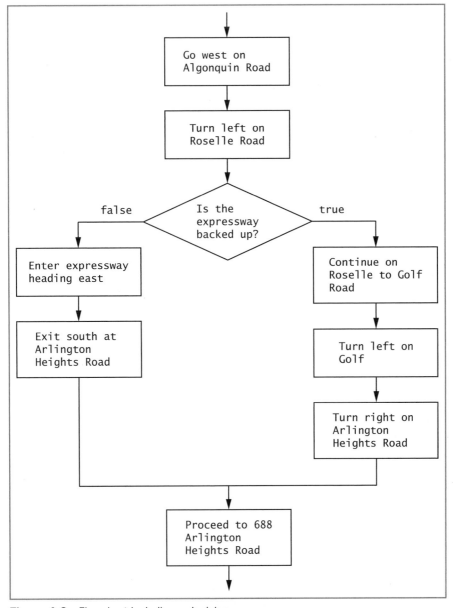

**Figure 4-2**  Flowchart including a decision

Figure 4-2 shows a **decision structure**—one that involves choosing between alternative courses of action based on some value within a program. When reduced to their most basic form, all computer decisions are true-or-false decisions. This is because computer circuitry consists of millions of tiny switches that are either "on" or "off," and the result of every decision sets one of these switches in memory. The values `true` and `false` are Boolean values; every computer decision results in a Boolean value. Thus, internally, a program you write never asks, for example, "What number did the user enter?" Instead, the decisions might be "Did the user enter a 1?" "If not, did the user enter a 2?" "If not, did the user enter a 3?"

---

### TWO TRUTHS **&** A LIE

#### Understanding Logic-Planning Tools and Decision Making

1. A sequence structure has three or more alternative logical paths.

2. A decision structure involves choosing between alternative courses of action based on some value within a program.

3. When reduced to their most basic form, all computer decisions are yes-or-no decisions.

The false statement is #1. In a sequence structure, one step follows another unconditionally.

---

# Making Decisions Using the if Statement

You learned about Boolean expressions and the bool data type in Chapter 2. Table 2-4 summarizes how you use the comparison operators.

The if and if-else statements are the two most commonly used decision-making statements in C#. You use an **if statement** to make a single-alternative decision. In other words, you use an if statement to determine whether an action will occur. The if statement takes the following form:

```
if(testedExpression)
    statement;
```

where *testedExpression* represents any C# expression that can be evaluated as true or false and *statement* represents the action that will take place if the expression evaluates as true. You must place the if statement's evaluated expression between parentheses.

In the chapter *Introduction to Methods*, you will learn to write methods that return values. A method call that returns a Boolean value also can be used as the tested expression in an if statement.

Usable expressions in an if statement include Boolean expressions such as amount > 5 and month == "May" as well as the value of bool variables such as isValidIDNumber. If the expression evaluates as true, then the statement executes. Whether the expression evaluates as true or false, the program continues with the next statement following the complete if statement.

In some programming languages, such as C++, nonzero numbers evaluate as `true` and 0 evaluates as `false`. However, in C#, only Boolean expressions evaluate as `true` and `false`.

For example, the code segment written and diagrammed in Figure 4-3 displays "A" and "B" when `number` holds a value less than 5. The expression `number < 5` evaluates as `true`, so the statement that displays "A" executes. Then the independent statement that displays "B" executes.

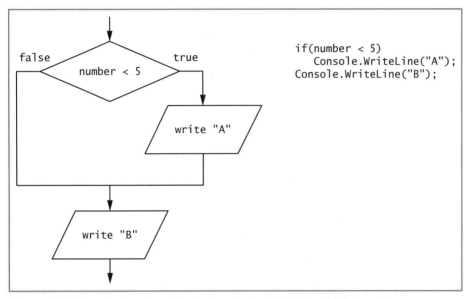

```
if(number < 5)
    Console.WriteLine("A");
Console.WriteLine("B");
```

**Figure 4-3**  Flowchart and code including a typical `if` statement followed by a separate statement

 You can leave a space between the keyword `if` and the opening parenthesis if you think that format is easier to read.

When an evaluated expression is `false`, the rest of the statement does not execute. For example, when `number` is 5 or greater in Figure 4-3, only "B" is displayed. Because the expression `number < 5` is `false`, the statement that displays "A" never executes.

In Figure 4-3, notice there is no semicolon at the end of the line that contains `if(number < 5)`. The statement does not end at that point; it ends after `Console.WriteLine("A");`. If you incorrectly insert a semicolon at the end of `if(number < 5)`, then the statement says, "If `number` is less than 5, do nothing; then, no matter what the value of number is, the next independent statement displays "A". Figure 4-4 shows the flowchart logic that matches the code when a semicolon is placed at the end of the if expression.

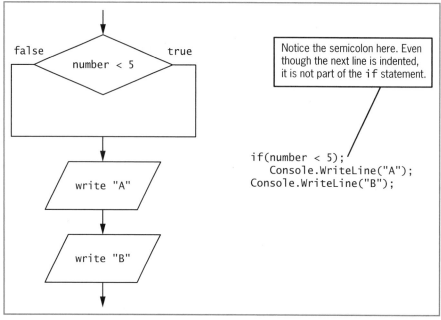

**Figure 4-4**    Flowchart and code including an if statement with a semicolon following the if expression

Although it is customary, and good style, to indent any statement that executes when an if Boolean expression evaluates as true, the C# compiler does not pay any attention to the indentation. Each of the following if statements displays "A" when number is less than 5. The first shows an if written on a single line; the second shows an if on two lines but with no indentation. The third uses conventional indentation.

Although these first two formats work for if statements, they are not conventional and using them makes a program harder to understand.

```
if(number < 5) Console.WriteLine("A");
if(number < 5)
Console.WriteLine("A");
if(number < 5)
    Console.WriteLine("A");
```

When you want to execute two or more statements conditionally, you must place the statements within a block. A **block** is a collection of one or more statements contained within a pair of curly braces. For example, the code segment written and diagrammed in Figure 4-5 displays both "C" and "D" when number is less than 5, and it displays neither when number is not less than 5.

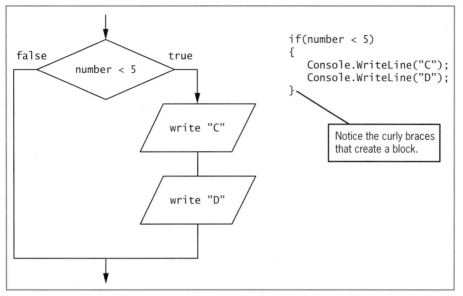

```
if(number < 5)
{
    Console.WriteLine("C");
    Console.WriteLine("D");
}
```

Notice the curly braces that create a block.

149

**Figure 4-5** Flowchart and code including a typical if statement containing a block

Indenting alone does not cause multiple statements to depend on the evaluation of a Boolean expression in an if. For multiple statements to depend on an if, they must be blocked with braces. For example, Figure 4-6 shows two statements that are indented below an if expression. When you glance at the code, it might first appear that both statements depend on the if; in fact, however, only the first one does, as shown in the flowchart, because the statements are not blocked.

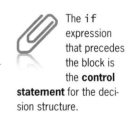

The if expression that precedes the block is the **control statement** for the decision structure.

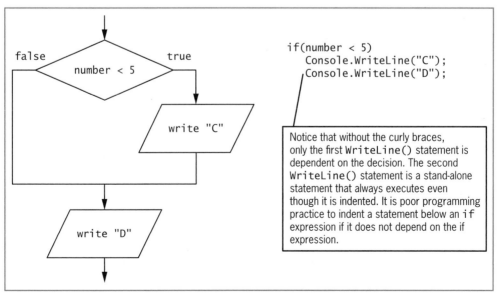

```
if(number < 5)
    Console.WriteLine("C");
    Console.WriteLine("D");
```

Notice that without the curly braces, only the first WriteLine() statement is dependent on the decision. The second WriteLine() statement is a stand-alone statement that always executes even though it is indented. It is poor programming practice to indent a statement below an if expression if it does not depend on the if expression.

**Figure 4-6** Flowchart and code including an if statement that is missing curly braces or that has inappropriate indenting

In C#, it is customary to align opening and closing braces in a block. Some programmers prefer to place the opening brace on the same line as the `if` expression instead of giving the brace its own line. This style is called the **K & R style**, named for Brian Kernighan and Dennis Ritchie, who wrote the first book on the C programming language.

150

When you create a block using curly braces, you do not have to place multiple statements within it. It is perfectly legal to block a single statement. Blocking a single statement can be a useful technique to help prevent future errors. When a program later is modified to include multiple statements that depend on the `if`, it is easy to forget to add curly braces. You will naturally place the additional statements within the block if the braces are already in place. It also is legal to create a block that contains no statements. You usually do so only when starting to write a program, as a reminder to yourself to add statements later.

You can place any number of statements within the block contained by the curly braces, including other `if` statements. Of course, if a second `if` statement is the only statement that depends on the first `if`, then no braces are required. Figure 4-7 shows the logic for a **nested if** statement—one in which one decision structure is contained within another. With a nested `if` statement, a second `if`'s Boolean expression is tested only when the first `if`'s Boolean expression evaluates as **true**.

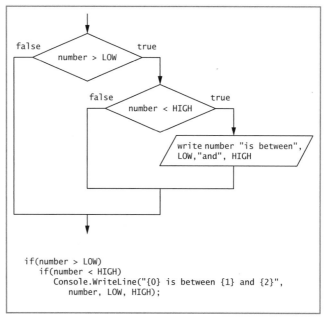

```
if(number > LOW)
    if(number < HIGH)
        Console.WriteLine("{0} is between {1} and {2}",
            number, LOW, HIGH);
```

**Figure 4-7** Flowchart and code showing the logic of a nested `if`

Figure 4-8 shows a program that contains the logic. When a user enters a number greater than 5 in the program in Figure 4-8, the first `if` expression evaluates as **true** and the `if` statement that tests whether the number is less than 10 executes. When the second `if` evaluates as **true**, the `Console.WriteLine()` statement executes. However, if the second `if` is **false**, no output occurs. When the user enters a number less than or equal to 5, the first if expression is false and the second if expression is never tested, and again no output occurs. Figure 4-9 shows the output after the program is executed three times using three different input values. Notice that when the value input by the user is not between 5 and 10, no output message appears; the message is displayed only when both if expressions are true.

```
using System;
public class NestedDecision
{
    public static void Main()
    {
        const int HIGH = 10, LOW = 5;
        string numberString;
        int number;
        Console.Write("Enter an integer ");
        numberString = Console.ReadLine();
        number = Convert.ToInt32(numberString);
          if(number > LOW)
            if(number < HIGH)
              Console.WriteLine("{0} is between {1} and {2}",
                 number, LOW, HIGH);
    }
}
```

**Figure 4-8** Program using nested if

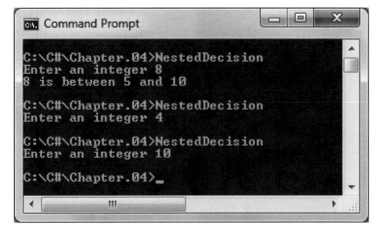

**Figure 4-9** Output of three executions of the NestedDecision program

## A Note on Equivalency Comparisons

Often, programmers mistakenly use a single equal sign rather than the double equal sign when attempting to determine equivalency. For example, the following expression does not compare `number` to `HIGH`:

```
number = HIGH
```

Instead, it attempts to assign the value `HIGH` to the variable `number`. When it is part of an `if` statement, this assignment is illegal.

The only condition under which the assignment operator would work as part of the tested expression in an `if` statement is when the assignment is made to a `bool` variable. For example, suppose a payroll program contains a `bool` variable named `doesEmployeeHaveDependents`, and then uses the following statement:

```
if(doesEmployeeHaveDependents = numDependents > 0)...
```

In this case, `numDependents` would be compared to 0, and the result, `true` or `false`, would be assigned to `doesEmployeeHaveDependents`. Then the decision would be made based on the result.

### TWO TRUTHS & A LIE

#### Making Decisions Using the `if` Statement

1. In C#, you must place an `if` statement's evaluated expression between parentheses.

2. In C#, for multiple statements to depend on an `if`, they must be indented.

3. In C#, you can place one `if` statement within a block that depends on another `if` statement.

The false statement is #2. Indenting alone does not cause multiple statements to depend on the evaluation of a Boolean expression in an `if`. For multiple statements to depend on an `if`, they must be blocked with braces.

## Making Decisions Using the `if-else` Statement

Some decisions you make are **dual-alternative decisions**; they have two possible resulting actions. If you want to perform one action when a Boolean expression evaluates as `true` and an alternate action when it evaluates as false, you can use an **if-else statement**. The if-else statement takes the following form:

```
if(expression)
    statement1;
else
    statement2;
```

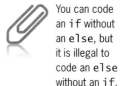

You can code an if without an else, but it is illegal to code an else without an if.

153

Just as you can block several statements so they all execute when an expression within an if is true, you can block multiple statements after an else so that they will all execute when the evaluated expression is false.

For example, Figure 4-10 shows the logic for an if-else statement, and Figure 4-11 shows a program that contains the statement. With every execution of the program, one or the other of the two WriteLine() statements executes. Figure 4-12 shows two executions of the program.

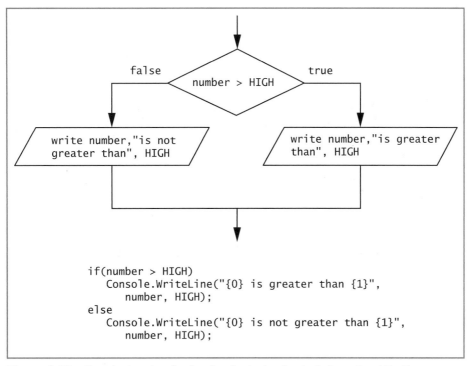

**Figure 4-10** Flowchart and code showing the logic of a dual-alternative if-else statement

```
using System;
public class IfElseDecision
{
    public static void Main()
    {
        const int HIGH = 10;
        string numberString;
        int number;
        Console.Write("Enter an integer ");
        numberString = Console.ReadLine();
        number = Convert.ToInt32(numberString);
        if(number > HIGH)
            Console.WriteLine("{0} is greater than {1}",
                number, HIGH);
        else
            Console.WriteLine("{0} is not greater than {1}",
                number, HIGH);
    }
}
```

The indentation shown in the if-else example in Figure 4-11 is not required, but is standard. You vertically align the keyword if with the keyword else, and then indent the action statements that depend on the evaluation.

**Figure 4-11** Program with a dual-alternative if-else statement

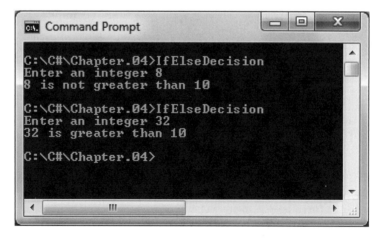

**Figure 4-12** Output of two executions of the IfElseDecision program

When if-else statements are nested, each else always is paired with the most recent unpaired if. For example, in the following code, the else is paired with the second if.

```
if(saleAmount > 1000)
    if(saleAmount < 2000)
        bonus = 100;
    else
        bonus = 50;
```

In this example, the following bonuses are assigned:

- If saleAmount is between $1000 and $2000, bonus is $100 because both evaluated expressions are true.

- If saleAmount is $2000 or more, bonus is $50 because the first evaluated expression is true and the second one is false.

- If saleAmount is $1000 or less, bonus is unassigned because the first evaluated expression is false and there is no corresponding else.

155

---

**TWO TRUTHS & A LIE**

### Making Decisions Using the if-else Statement

1. Dual-alternative decisions have two possible outcomes.

2. In an if-else statement, a semicolon is always the last character typed before the else.

3. When if-else statements are nested, the first if always is paired with the first else.

The false statement is #3. When if-else statements are nested, each else always is paired with the most recent unpaired if.

---

# Using Compound Expressions in if Statements

In many programming situations you encounter, you need to make multiple decisions before taking action. For example, suppose a specific college scholarship is available:

- If your high school class rank is higher than 75 percent

- And if your grade-point average is higher than 3.0

- And if you are a state resident

- Or if you are a resident of a cooperating state

- Or if you have participated in at least five extracurricular activities and held a part-time job

No matter how many decisions must be made, you can decide on the scholarship eligibility for any student by using a series of if statements to test the appropriate variables. For convenience and clarity, however, you can combine multiple decisions into a single if statement using a combination of conditional AND and OR operators to create compound Boolean expressions.

## Using the Conditional AND Operator

As an alternative to nested if statements, you can use the **conditional AND operator** (or simply the **AND operator**) to create a compound Boolean expression. The conditional AND operator is written as two ampersands (&&).

A tool that can help you understand the && operator is a truth table. **Truth tables** are diagrams used in mathematics and logic to help describe the truth of an entire expression based on the truth of its parts. Table 4-1 shows a truth table that lists all the possibilities with compound Boolean expressions. For any two expressions x and y, the expression x && y is true only if both x and y are individually true. If either x or y alone is false, or if both are false, then the expression x && y is false.

| x | y | x && y |
|---|---|--------|
| True | True | True |
| True | False | False |
| False | True | False |
| False | False | False |

**Table 4-1** Truth table for the conditional && operator

For example, the two code samples shown in Figure 4-13 work exactly the same way. The age variable is tested, and if it is greater than or equal to 0 and less than 120, a message is displayed to explain that the value is valid.

```
// using &&
   if(age >= 0 && age < 120)
      Console.WriteLine("Age is valid");
// using nested ifs
   if(age >= 0)
      if(age < 120)
        Console.WriteLine("Age is valid");
```

**Figure 4-13** Comparison of the && operator and nested if statements

Using the && operator is never required, because nested if statements achieve the same result, but using the && operator often makes your code more concise, less error-prone, and easier to understand.

It is important to note that when you use the && operator, you must include a complete Boolean expression on each side of the operator. If you want to set a bonus to $400 when a saleAmount is both over $1000 and under $5000, the correct statement is as follows:

```
if(saleAmount > 1000 && saleAmount < 5000)
   bonus = 400;
```

The following statement is incorrect and will not compile:

```
if(saleAmount > 1000 && < 5000)
   bonus = 400;
```

> 5000 is not a Boolean expression (it is a numeric constant), so this statement is invalid.

For clarity, many programmers prefer to surround each Boolean expression that is part of a compound Boolean expression with its own set of parentheses. For example:

```
if((saleAmount > 1000) && (saleAmount < 5000))
   bonus = 400;
```

Use this format if it is clearer to you.

The expressions in each part of a compound Boolean expression are evaluated only as much as necessary to determine whether the entire expression is true or false. This feature is called **short-circuit evaluation.** With the && operator, both Boolean expressions must be true before the action in the statement can occur. If the first expression is false, the second expression is never evaluated, because its value does not matter. For example, if a is not greater than LIMIT in the following if statement, then the evaluation is complete because there is no need to evaluate whether b is greater than LIMIT.

```
if(a > LIMIT && b > LIMIT)
   Console.WriteLine("Both are greater than LIMIT");
```

## Using the Conditional OR Operator

You can use the **conditional OR operator** (or simply the **OR operator**) when you want some action to occur even if only one of two conditions is true. The OR operator is written as ||. When you use the || operator, only one of the listed conditions must be met for the resulting action to take place. Table 4-2 shows the truth table for the || operator. As you can see, the entire expression x || y is false only when x and y each are false individually.

| x | y | x || y |
|---|---|---|
| True | True | True |
| True | False | True |
| False | True | True |
| False | False | False |

**Table 4-2**   Truth table for the conditional || operator

You create the conditional OR operator by using two vertical pipes. On most keyboards, the pipe is found above the backslash key; typing it requires that you also hold down the Shift key.

For example, if you want to display a message indicating an invalid age when the variable is less than 0 or is 120 or greater, you can use either code sample in Figure 4-14.

```
// using ||
  if(age < 0 || age >= 120)
    Console.WriteLine("Age is not valid");
// using nested ifs
  if(age < 0)
    Console.WriteLine("Age is not valid");
  else
    if(age >= 120)
      Console.WriteLine("Age is not valid");
```

**Figure 4-14** Comparison of the || operator and nested if statements

A common use of the || operator is to decide to take action whether a character variable is uppercase or lowercase. For example, in the following decision, any subsequent action occurs whether the selection variable holds an uppercase or lowercase 'A':

```
if(selection == 'A' || selection == 'a')...
```

When the || operator is used in an if statement, only one of the two Boolean expressions in the tested expression needs to be true for the resulting action to occur. As with the && operator, this feature is called short-circuit evaluation. When you use the || operator and the first Boolean expression is true, the second expression is never evaluated, because it does not matter whether it is true or false.

Watch the video *Using the AND and OR Operators*.

## Using the Logical AND and OR Operators

The **Boolean logical AND operator** (&) and **Boolean logical inclusive OR operator** (|) work just like their && and || (*conditional* AND and OR) counterparts, except they do not support short-circuit evaluation. That is, they always evaluate both sides of the expression, no matter what the first evaluation is. This can lead to a **side effect**, or unintended consequence. For example, in the following statement that uses &&, if salesAmountForYear is not at least 10,000, the first half of the expression is false, so the second half of the Boolean expression is never evaluated and yearsOfService is not increased.

```
if(salesAmountForYear >= 10000 && ++yearsOfService > 10)
    bonus = 200;
```

On the other hand, when a single & is used and salesAmountForYear is not at least 10,000, then even though the first half of the expression is `false`, the second half is still evaluated, and `yearsOfService` is increased:

```
if(salesAmountForYear >= 10000 & ++yearsOfService > 10)
    bonus = 200;
```

Because the first half of the expression is `false`, the entire evaluation is `false`, and, as with `&&`, `bonus` is still not set to 200. However, a side effect has occurred: `yearsOfService` is incremented.

In general, you should avoid writing expressions that contain side effects. If you want `yearsOfService` to increase no matter what the `salesAmountForYear` is, then you should increase it in a stand-alone statement before the decision is made, and if you want it increased only when the sales amount exceeds 10,000, then you should increase it in a statement that depends on that decision.

The `&` and `|` operators are Boolean logical operators when they are placed between Boolean expressions. When the same operators are used between integer expressions, they are **bitwise operators** that are used to manipulate the individual bits of values.

## Combining AND and OR Operators

You can combine as many AND and OR operators in an expression as you need. For example, when three conditions must be `true` before performing an action, you can use an expression such as `if(a && b && c)`. When you combine `&&` and `||` operators within the same Boolean expression, the `&&` operators take precedence, meaning their Boolean values are evaluated first.

For example, consider a program that determines whether a movie theater patron can purchase a discounted ticket. Assume discounts are allowed for children (age 12 and younger) and for senior citizens (age 65 and older) who attend G-rated movies. The following code looks reasonable, but it produces incorrect results because the `&&` evaluates before the `||`.

To keep the comparisons simple, this example assumes that movie ratings are always a single character.

```
if(age <= 12 || age >= 65 && rating == 'G')
    Console.WriteLine("Discount applies");
```

For example, assume a movie patron is 10 years old and the movie rating is 'R'. The patron should not receive a discount (or be allowed to see the movie!). However, within the `if` statement above, the compound expression `age >= 65 && rating == 'G'` evaluates first. It is `false`, so the `if` becomes the equivalent of `if(age <= 12 || false)`. Because `age <= 12` is `true`, the `if` becomes the equivalent of `if(true || false)`, which evaluates as `true`, and the statement "Discount applies" incorrectly displays.

You can use parentheses to correct the logic and force the expression `age <= 12 || age >= 65` to evaluate first, as shown in the following code.

```
if((age <= 12 || age >= 65) && rating == 'G')
    Console.WriteLine("Discount applies");
```

With the added parentheses, if age is 12 or less OR 65 or greater, the expression is evaluated as if(true && rating == 'G'). When the age value qualifies a patron for a discount, then the rating value must also be acceptable. Figure 4-15 shows the if within a complete program; note that the discount age limits now are represented as named constants. Figure 4-16 shows the execution before the parentheses were added to the if statement, and Figure 4-17 shows the output after the inclusion of the parentheses.

```
using System;
public class MovieDiscount
{
    public static void Main()
    {
        int age = 10;
        char rating = 'R';
        const int CHILD_AGE = 12;
        const int SENIOR_AGE = 65;
        Console.WriteLine("When age is {0} and rating is {1}",
          age, rating);
        if((age <= CHILD_AGE || age >= SENIOR_AGE) &&
          rating == 'G')
          Console.WriteLine("Discount applies");
        else
          Console.WriteLine("Full price");
    }
}
```

**Figure 4-15**   Movie ticket discount program using parentheses to alter precedence of Boolean evaluations

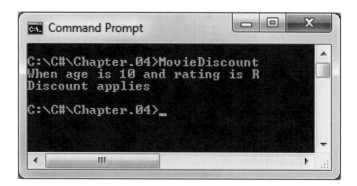

**Figure 4-16**   Incorrect results when MovieDiscount program is executed without added parentheses

You can use parentheses for clarity even when they are not required. For example, the following expressions both evaluate a && b first:

```
a && b || c
(a && b) || c
```

If the version with parentheses makes your intentions clearer, you should use it.

161

**Figure 4-17** Correct results when parentheses are added to MovieDiscount program

In Chapter 2, you controlled arithmetic operator precedence by using parentheses. Appendix A describes the precedence of every C# operator. For example, in Appendix A you can see that the comparison operators <= and >= have higher precedence than both && and ||.

Watch the video *Combining AND and OR Operations.*

---

## TWO TRUTHS & A LIE

### Using Compound Expressions in `if` Statements

1. If a is `true` and b and c are `false`, then the value of b && c || a is `true`.

2. If d is `true` and e and f are `false`, then the value of e || d && f is `true`.

3. If g is `true` and h and i are `false`, then the value of g || h && i is `true`.

The false statement is #2. If d is true and e and f are false, then the value of e || d && f is false. Because you evaluate && before ||, first d && f is evaluated and found to be false, then e || false is evaluated and found to be false.

---

# Making Decisions Using the `switch` Statement

By nesting a series of `if` and `else` statements, you can choose from any number of alternatives. For example, suppose you want to display different strings based on a student's class year. Figure 4-18 shows the logic using nested if statements. The program segment tests the year variable four times and executes one of four statements, or displays an error message.

```
if(year == 1)
    Console.WriteLine("Freshman");
else
    if(year == 2)
        Console.WriteLine("Sophomore");
    else
        if(year == 3)
            Console.WriteLine("Junior");
        else
            if(year == 4)
                Console.WriteLine("Senior");
            else
                Console.WriteLine("Invalid year");
```

**Figure 4-18** Executing multiple alternatives using a series of if statements

An alternative to the series of nested if statements in Figure 4-18 is to use the switch structure (see Figure 4-19). The **switch structure** tests a single variable against a series of exact matches. The switch structure in Figure 4-19 is easier to read and interpret than the series of nested if statements in Figure 4-18. The if statements would become harder to read if additional choices were required and if multiple statements had to execute in each case. These additional choices and statements might also make it easier to make mistakes.

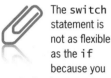

The switch statement is not as flexible as the if because you can test only one variable, and it must be tested for equality.

```
switch(year)
{
    case 1:
        Console.WriteLine("Freshman");
        break;
    case 2:
        Console.WriteLine("Sophomore");
        break;
    case 3:
        Console.WriteLine("Junior");
        break;
    case 4:
        Console.WriteLine("Senior");
        break;
    default:
        Console.WriteLine("Invalid year");
        break;
}
```

You are not required to list the case label values in ascending order, as shown in Figure 4-19. However, doing so can make the statement easier for a reader to follow. From the computer's perspective, it is most efficient to list the most common case first; often, the default case is the most common.

**Figure 4-19** Executing multiple alternatives using a switch statement

The `switch` structure uses four new keywords:

- The keyword **switch** starts the structure and is followed immediately by a test expression (called the **switch expression**) enclosed in parentheses.

- The keyword **case** is followed by one of the possible values that might equal the `switch` expression. A colon follows the value. The entire expression—for example, `case 1:`—is a `case` label. A **case label** identifies a course of action in a `switch` structure. Most `switch` structures contain several `case` labels.

- The keyword **break** usually terminates a `switch` structure at the end of each `case`. Although other statements can end a `case`, `break` is the most commonly used.

- The keyword **default** optionally is used prior to any action that should occur if the test expression does not match any `case`.

The `switch` structure shown in Figure 4-19 begins by evaluating the year variable. If year is equal to the first `case` label value, which is 1, then the statement that displays `"Freshman"` executes. The `break` statement causes a bypass of the rest of the `switch` structure, and execution continues with any statement after the closing curly brace of the `switch` structure.

If the year variable is not equivalent to the first `case` label value of 1, then the next `case` label value is compared, and so on. If the year variable does not contain the same value as any of the `case` label expressions, then the `default` statement or statements execute.

In C#, an error occurs if you reach the end point of the statement list of a `switch` section. For example, the following code is not allowed because when the year value is 1, `"Freshman"` is displayed, and the code reaches the end of the `case`.

```
switch(year)
{
   case 1:
      Console.WriteLine("Freshman");
   case 2:
      Console.WriteLine("Sophomore");
      break;
}
```

This code is invalid because the end of the case is reached after "Freshman" is displayed.

Not allowing code to reach the end of a `case` is known as the "no fall through rule." In several other programming languages, such as Java and C++, when year equals 1, both `"Freshman"` and `"Sophomore"` would be displayed. However, falling through to the next `case` is not allowed in C#.

A `switch` structure does not need to contain a `default` case. If the test expression in a `switch` does not match any of the `case` label values,

Instead of `break`, you can use a `return` statement or a `throw` statement to end a `case`. You learn about `return` statements in the chapter *Introduction to Methods* and `throw` statements in the chapter *Exception Handling*.

The **governing type** of a `switch` statement is established by the `switch` expression. The governing type can be `sbyte`, `byte`, `short`, `ushort`, `int`, `uint`, `long`, `ulong`, `char`, `string`, or an `enum` type. You learned about `enum` types in Chapter 2.

and there is no `default` value, then the program simply continues with the next executable statement. However, it is good programming practice to include a `default` label in a `switch` structure; that way, you provide for actions when your data does not match any case. The `default` label does not have to appear last, although usually it does.

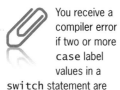
You receive a compiler error if two or more `case` label values in a `switch` statement are the same.

You can use multiple labels to govern a list of statements. For example, in the code in Figure 4-20, `"Upperclass"` is displayed whether the year value is 3 or 4.

```
switch(year)
{
    case 1:
        Console.WriteLine("Freshman");
        break;
    case 2:
        Console.WriteLine("Sophomore");
        break;                                    ┌─────────────┐
    case 3:  ─────────────────────────────────────│ Cases 3 and │
    case 4:                                        │ 4 are both  │
        Console.WriteLine("Upperclass");           │ "Upperclass".│
        break;                                    └─────────────┘
    default:
        Console.WriteLine("Invalid year");
        break;
}
```

**Figure 4-20** Example `switch` structure using multiple labels to execute a single statement block

Using a `switch` structure is never required; you can always achieve the same results with nested `if` statements. The `switch` structure is simply a convenience you can use when there are several alternative courses of action depending on a match with a variable. Additionally, it makes sense to use a `switch` only when there are a reasonable number of specific matching values to be tested. For example, if every sale amount from $1 to $500 requires a 5% commission, it is not reasonable to test every possible dollar amount using the following code:

```
switch(saleAmount)
{
    case 1:
        commRate = .05;
        break;
    case 2:
        commRate = .05;
        break;
    case 3:
        commRate = .05;
        break;
//...and so on for several hundred more cases
```

## Using an Enumeration with a `switch` Statement

Using an enumeration with a `switch` structure can often be convenient. Recall from Chapter 2 that an enumeration allows you to apply values to a list of constants. For example, Figure 4-21 shows a program that uses an enumeration to represent major courses of study at a college. Suppose that students who are Accounting, CIS, or Marketing majors are in the Business Division of the college, and English or Math majors are in the Humanities Division. The program shows how the enumeration values can be used in a `switch` structure. In the shaded `switch` control statement, notice how the input integer is cast to an enumeration value. Figure 4-22 shows a typical execution of the program.

 In the enumeration list in Figure 4-21, ACCOUNTING is assigned 1, so the other values in the list are 2, 3, 4, and 5 in order.

```
using System;
public class DivisionBasedOnMajor
{
    enum Major
    {
        ACCOUNTING = 1, CIS, ENGLISH, MATH, MARKETING
    }
    public static void Main()
    {
        int major;
        Console.Write("Enter major code >> ");
        major = Convert.ToInt32(Console.ReadLine());
        switch ((Major) major)
        {
          case Major.ACCOUNTING:
          case Major.CIS:
          case Major.MARKETING:
            Console.WriteLine("Major is in the Business Division");
            break;
          case Major.ENGLISH:
          case Major.MATH:
            Console.WriteLine("Major is in the Humanities Division");
            break;
          default:
            Console.WriteLine("Department number is invalid");
            break;
        }
    }
}
```

**Figure 4-21**   The `DivisionBasedOnMajor` class

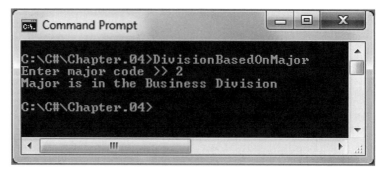

**Figure 4-22** Typical execution of the DivisionBasedOnMajor program

---

**TWO TRUTHS & A LIE**

### Making Decisions Using the switch Statement

1. In a switch statement, the keyword case is followed by one of the possible values that might equal the switch expression, and a colon follows the value.

2. The keyword break always terminates a switch structure at the end of each case.

3. A switch statement does not need to contain a default case.

The false statement is #2. The keyword break usually terminates a switch structure at the end of each case, but other statements can end a case.

---

## Using the Conditional Operator

Unary operators use one operand; binary operators use two. The conditional operator ?: is **ternary** because it requires three arguments: a test expression and true and false result expressions. The conditional operator is the only ternary operator in C#.

The **conditional operator** is used as an abbreviated version of the if-else statement; it requires three expressions separated with a question mark and a colon. Like the switch structure, using the conditional operator is never required. Rather, it is simply a convenient shortcut, especially when you want to use the result immediately as an expression. The syntax of the conditional operator is:

```
testExpression ? trueResult : falseResult;
```

The first expression, testExpression, is evaluated as true or false. If it is true, then the entire conditional expression takes on the value of the expression following the question mark (trueResult). If the value of the testExpression is false, then the entire expression takes on the value of falseResult. For example, consider the following statement:

```
biggerNum = (a > b) ? a : b;
```

This statement evaluates a > b. If a is greater than b, then the entire conditional expression takes the value of a, which then is assigned to biggerNum. If a is not greater than b, then the expression assumes the value of b, and b is assigned to biggerNum.

The conditional operator is most often used when you want to use the result as an expression without creating an intermediate variable. For example, a conditional operator can be used directly in an output statement such as the following:

```
Console.WriteLine((testScore >= 60) ? "Pass" : "Fail");
```

Conditional expressions are frequently more difficult to read than if-else statements, but they can be used in places where if-else statements cannot.

---

### TWO TRUTHS & A LIE

### Using the Conditional Operator

1.  If j = 2 and k = 3, then the value of the following expression is 2:

    ```
    int m = j < k ? j : k;
    ```

2.  If j = 2 and k = 3, then the value of the following expression is "yes":

    ```
    string ans = j < k ? "yes" : "no";
    ```

3.  If j = 2 and k = 3, then the value of the following expression is 5:

    ```
    int n = j > k? j + k : j * k;
    ```

The false statement is #3. If j = 2 and k = 3, then the value of the expression int n = j > k? j + k : j * k; is 6 because j is not greater than k and the false result is j * k, which is 2 * 3.

---

# Using the NOT Operator

You use the **NOT operator**, which is written as an exclamation point (!), to negate the result of any Boolean expression. Any expression that evaluates as true becomes false when preceded by the ! operator, and any false expression preceded by the ! operator becomes true.

In Chapter 2, you learned that an exclamation point and equal sign together form the "not equal to" operator.

For example, suppose a monthly car insurance premium is $200 if the driver is younger than age 26 and $125 if the driver is age 26 or older. Each of the following if statements (which have been placed on single lines for convenience) correctly assigns the premium values.

```
if(age < 26) premium = 200; else premium = 125;
if(!(age < 26)) premium = 125; else premium = 200;
if(age >= 26) premium = 125; else premium = 200;
if(!(age>= 26)) premium = 200; else premium = 125;
```

The statements with the ! operator are somewhat more difficult to read, particularly because they require the double set of parentheses, but the result is the same in each case. Using the ! operator is clearer when the value of a Boolean variable is tested. For example, a variable initialized as bool oldEnough = (age >= 25); can become part of the relatively easy-to-read expression if(!oldEnough)....

The ! operator has higher precedence than the && and || operators. For example, suppose you have declared two Boolean variables named ageOverMinimum and ticketsUnderMinimum. The following expressions are evaluated in the same way:

```
ageOverMinimum && !ticketsUnderMinimum
ageOverMinimum && (!ticketsUnderMinimum)
```

Augustus de Morgan was a 19ᵗʰ-century mathematician who originally observed the following:

```
!(a && b) is equivalent to !a || !b
!(a || b) is equivalent to !(a && b)
```

## TWO TRUTHS & A LIE

### Using the NOT Operator

1. Assume p, q, and r are all Boolean variables that have been assigned the value true. After the following statement executes, the value of p is still true.

    p = !q || r;

2. Assume p, q, and r are all Boolean variables that have been assigned the value true. After the following statement executes, the value of p is still true.

    p = !(!q && !r);

3. Assume p, q, and r are all Boolean variables that have been assigned the value true. After the following statement executes, the value of p is still true.

    p = !(q || !r);

The false statement is #3. If p, q, and r are all Boolean variables that have been assigned the value true, then after p = !(q || !r); executes, the value of p is false. First q is evaluated as true, so the entire expression within the parentheses is true. The leading NOT operator reverses that result to false and assigns it to p.

# Avoiding Common Errors When Making Decisions

New programmers frequently make errors when they first learn to make decisions. As you have seen, the most frequent errors include the following:

- Using the assignment operator (=) instead of the comparison operator (==) when testing for equality

- Inserting a semicolon after the Boolean expression in an if statement instead of using it after the entire statement is completed

- Failing to block a set of statements with curly braces when several statements depend on the if or the else statement

- Failing to include a complete Boolean expression on each side of an && or || operator in an if statement

In this section, you will learn to avoid other types of errors with if statements. Programmers often make errors at the following times:

- When performing a range check incorrectly or inefficiently

- When using the wrong operator with && and ||

- Using ! incorrectly

## Performing Accurate and Efficient Range Checks

When new programmers must make a range check, they often introduce incorrect or inefficient code into their programs. A **range check** is a series of if statements that determine whether a value falls within a specified range. Consider a situation in which salespeople can receive one of three possible commission rates based on their sales. For example, a sale totaling $1000 or more earns the salesperson an 8% commission, a sale totaling $500 through $999 earns 6% of the sale amount, and any sale totaling $499 or less earns 5%. Using three separate if statements to test single Boolean expressions might result in some incorrect commission assignments. For example, examine the following code:

```
if(saleAmount >= 1000)
    commissionRate = 0.08;
if(saleAmount >= 500)
    commissionRate = 0.06;
if(saleAmount <= 499)
    commissionRate = 0.05;
```

> Although it was not the programmer's intention, both of the first two if statements are true for any saleAmount greater than or equal to 1000.

In this example, saleAmount is assumed to be an integer. As long as you are dealing with whole dollar amounts, the expression if(saleAmount >= 1000) can be expressed just as well as if(saleAmount > 999). If saleAmount was a floating-point variable, the preceding code would fail to assign a commission rate for sales from $499.01 through $499.99.

Using this code, if a saleAmount is $5000, the first if statement executes. The Boolean expression (saleAmount >= 1000) evaluates as true, and 0.08 is correctly assigned to commissionRate. However, the next if expression, (saleAmount >= 500), also evaluates as true, so the commissionRate, which was 8%, is incorrectly reset to 6%.

A partial solution to this problem is to use an else statement following the if(saleAmount >= 1000) expression:

```
if(saleAmount >= 1000)
    commissionRate = 0.08;
else if(saleAmount >= 500)
    commissionRate = 0.06;
else if(saleAmount <= 499)
    commissionRate = 0.05;
```

> If the logic reaches this point, the expression is always true, so it is a waste of time to make this decision.

The last two logical tests in this code are sometimes called else-if statements because each else and its subsequent if are placed on the same line. When the else-if format is used to test multiple cases, programmers frequently forego the traditional indentation and align each else-if with the others.

With this code, when the saleAmount is $5000, the expression (saleAmount >= 1000) is true and the commissionRate becomes 8%; then the entire if structure ends. When the saleAmount is not greater than or equal to $1000 (for example, $800), the first if expression is false and the else statement executes and correctly sets the commissionRate to 6%.

This version of the code works, but it is somewhat inefficient. When the saleAmount is any amount that is at least $500, either the first if sets commissionRate to 8% for amounts of at least $1000, or its else sets commissionRate to 6% for amounts of at least $500. In either of these two cases, the Boolean value tested in the next statement, if(saleAmount <= 499), is always false. After you know that the saleAmount is not at least $500, rather than asking if(saleAmount <= 499), it is easier and more efficient to use an else. If the saleAmount is not at least $1000 and is also not at least $500, it must by default be less than or equal to $499. The improved code is as follows:

```
if(saleAmount >= 1000)
    commissionRate = 0.08;
else if(saleAmount >= 500)
    commissionRate = 0.06;
else commissionRate = 0.05;
```

In other words, because this example uses three commission rates, two boundaries should be checked. If there were four rates, there would be three boundaries to check, and so on.

Within a nested if-else, it is most efficient to first ask the question that is most likely to be true. In other words, if you know that a large number of saleAmount values are over $1000, compare saleAmount to that value first. That way, you frequently avoid asking multiple questions. If, however, you know that most saleAmounts are small, you should ask if(saleAmount < 500) first.

## Using && and || Appropriately

Beginning programmers often use the && operator when they mean to use ||, and often use || when they should use &&. Part of the problem lies in the way we use the English language. For example, your boss might request, "Display an error message when an employee's hourly pay rate is under $5.65 and when an employee's hourly pay rate is over $60." Because your boss used the word "and" in the request, you might be tempted to write a program statement like the following:

```
if(payRate < 5.65 && payRate > 60)
    Console.WriteLine("Error in pay rate");
```
— This expression can never be true.

However, as a single variable, no payRate value can ever be both below 5.65 and over 60 at the same time, so the output statement can never execute, no matter what value the payRate has. In this case, you must write the following statement to display the error message under the correct circumstances:

```
if(payRate < 5.65 || payRate > 60)
    Console.WriteLine("Error in pay rate");
```

Similarly, your boss might request, "Output the names of those employees in departments 1 and 2." Because the boss used the word "and" in the request, you might be tempted to write the following:

```
if(department == 1 && department == 2)
    Console.WriteLine("Name is: {0}", name);
```
— This expression can never be true.

However, the variable department can never contain both a 1 and a 2 at the same time, so no employee name will ever be output, no matter what department the employee is in.

The correct statement is:

```
if(department == 1 || department == 2)
    Console.WriteLine("Name is: {0}", name);
```

## Using the ! Operator Correctly

Whenever you use negatives, it is easy to make logical mistakes. For example, suppose your boss says, "Make sure if the sales code is not 'A' or 'B', the customer gets a 10% discount." You might be tempted to code the following:

```
if(salesCode != 'A' || salesCode != 'B')
    discount = 0.10;
```
— This expression can never be true.

However, this logic will result in every customer receiving the 10% discount because every `salesCode` is either not 'A' or not 'B'. For example, a `salesCode` of 'A' is not 'B'. The statement above is always `true`. The correct statement is either one of the following:

```
if(salesCode != 'A' && salesCode != 'B')
    discount = 0.10;
if(!(salesCode == 'A' || salesCode == 'B'))
    discount = 0.10;
```

In the first example, if the `salesCode` is not 'A' and it also is not 'B', then the discount is applied correctly. In the second example, if the `salesCode` is 'A' or 'B', the inner Boolean expression is `true`, and the NOT operator (!) changes the evaluation to `false`, not applying the discount for 'A' or 'B' sales. You also could avoid the confusing negative situation by asking questions in a positive way, as in the following:

Watch the video *Avoiding Common Decision Errors.*

```
if(salesCode == 'A' || salesCode == 'B')
    discount = 0;
else
    discount = 0.10;
```

## TWO TRUTHS & A LIE

### Avoiding Common Errors When Making Decisions

1.  If you want to display "OK" when `userEntry` is 12 and when it is 13, then the following is a usable C# statement:

    ```
    if(userEntry == 12 && userEntry == 13)
        Console.WriteLine("OK");
    ```

2.  If you want to display "OK" when `userEntry` is 20 or when `highestScore` is at least 70, then the following is a usable C# statement:

    ```
    if(userEntry == 20 || highestScore >= 70)
        Console.WriteLine("OK");
    ```

3.  If you want to display "OK" when `userEntry` is anything other than 99 or 100, then the following is a usable C# statement:

    ```
    if(userEntry != 99 && userEntry != 100)
        Console.WriteLine("OK");
    ```

The false statement is #1. If you want to display "OK" when userEntry is 12 and when it is 13, then you want to display it when it is either 12 or 13 because it cannot be both simultaneously. The expression userEntry == 12 && userEntry == 13 can never be true. The correct Boolean expression is userEntry == 12 || userEntry == 13.

# Decision-Making Issues in GUI Programs

Making a decision within a method in a GUI application is no different from making one in a console application; you can use `if`, `if...else`, and `switch` statements in the same ways. For example, Figure 4-23 shows a GUI `Form` that determines a movie patron discount as described in a program earlier in this chapter. Patrons who are under 12 or over 65 and are seeing a G-rated movie receive a discount, and any other combination pays full price. Figure 4-24 contains the `Click()` method that makes the discount determination based on age and rating after a user clicks the Determine Discount button. The Boolean expression tested in the `if` statement in this method is identical to the one in the console version of the program in Figure 4-15.

**Figure 4-23**  The Movie Discount `Form`

```
private void discountButton_Click(object sender, EventArgs e)
{
    int age;
    char rating;
    const int CHILD_AGE = 12;
    const int SENIOR_AGE = 65;
    age = Convert.ToInt32(textBox1.Text);
    rating = Convert.ToChar(textBox2.Text);
    outputLabel.Text = String.Format("When age is {0} and rating is {1}",
        age, rating);
    if ((age <= CHILD_AGE || age >= SENIOR_AGE) && rating == 'G')
        outputLabel.Text += "\nDiscount applies";
    else
        outputLabel.Text += "\nFull price";
}
```

**Figure 4-24** The `discountButton_Click()` method for the `Form` in Figure 4-23

Programmers say that decisions that occur when a program is running occur **at runtime**.

Event-driven programs often require fewer coded decisions than console applications. That is because in event-driven programs, some events are determined by the user's actions when the program is running, rather than by the programmer's coding beforehand. You might say that in many situations, a console-based application must act, but an event-driven application has to *react*.

Suppose you want to write a program in which the user must select whether to receive instructions in English or Spanish. In a console application, you would issue a prompt such as the following:

```
Which language do you prefer? Enter 1 for English or
2 for Spanish >>
```

The program would accept the user's entry, make a decision about it, and take appropriate action. However, in a GUI application, you are more likely to place controls on a `Form` to get a user's response. For example, you might use two `Buttons`—one for English and one for Spanish. The user clicks a `Button` and an appropriate method executes. No decision is written in the program because a different event is fired from each `Button`, causing execution of a different `Click()` method. The interactive environment decides which method is called, so the programmer does not have to. (Of course, you might alternately place a `TextBox` on a `Form` and ask a user to enter a 1 or a 2. In that case, the decision-making process would be identical to that in the console-based program.)

An additional benefit to having the user click a button to select an option is that the user cannot enter an invalid value. For example, if the user enters a letter in response to a prompt for an integer, the program will fail unless you write additional code to handle the mistake. However, if the user has a limited selection of buttons to click, no invalid entry can be made.

---

**TWO TRUTHS & A LIE**

### Decision-Making Issues in GUI Programs

1.  Event-driven programs can contain `if`, `if...else`, and `switch` statements.

2.  Event-driven programs often require fewer coded decisions than console applications.

3.  Event-driven programs always contain more automatic decisions determined by user-initiated events than programmer-coded decisions.

The false statement is #3. Event-driven programs might have any number of event-caused or programmer-caused decisions. However, event-driven programs can contain user-initiated events.

---

# You Do It

## Using `if-else` Statements

In the next steps, you will write a program that requires using multiple, nested `if-else` statements to accomplish its goal—determining whether any of the three integers entered by a user are equal.

**To create a program that uses nested `if-else` statements:**

1.  Open a new text file and write the first lines necessary for a CompareThreeNumbers class:

    ```
    using System;
    public class CompareThreeNumbers
    {
    ```

2.  Begin a `Main()` method by declaring a string for input and three integers that will hold the input values.

    ```
    public static void Main()
    {
       string numberString;
       int num1, num2, num3;
    ```

3.  Add the statements that retrieve the three integers from the user and assign them to the appropriate variables.

In the chapter *Introduction to Methods*, you will learn to write methods, avoiding repetitive code like that shown here.

```
Console.Write("Enter an integer ");
numberString = Console.ReadLine();
num1 = Convert.ToInt32(numberString);
Console.Write("Enter an integer ");
numberString = Console.ReadLine();
num2 = Convert.ToInt32(numberString);
Console.Write("Enter an integer ");
numberString = Console.ReadLine();
num3 = Convert.ToInt32(numberString);
```

4. If the first number and the second number are equal, there are two possibilities: either the first is also equal to the third, in which case all three numbers are equal, or the first is not equal to the third, in which case only the first two numbers are equal. Insert the following code:

```
if(num1 == num2)
   if(num1 == num3)
      Console.WriteLine("All three numbers are equal");
   else
      Console.WriteLine("First two are equal");
```

5. If the first two numbers are not equal, but the first and third are equal, display an appropriate message. For clarity, the else should vertically align under if(num1 == num2).

```
else
   if(num1 == num3)
      Console.WriteLine("First and last are equal");
```

6. When num1 and num2 are not equal, and num1 and num3 are not equal, but num2 and num3 are equal, display an appropriate message. For clarity, the else should vertically align under if(num1 == num3).

```
else
   if(num2 == num3)
      Console.WriteLine("Last two are equal");
```

7. Finally, if none of the pairs (num1 and num2, num1 and num3, or num2 and num3) are equal, display an appropriate message. For clarity, the else should vertically align under if(num2 == num3).

```
else
   Console.WriteLine
      ("No two numbers are equal");
```

8. Add a closing curly brace for the Main() method and a closing curly brace for the class.

9. Save the file as **CompareThreeNumbers.cs**. Compile the program, then execute it several times, providing different combinations of equal and nonequal integers when prompted. Figure 4-25 shows several executions of the program.

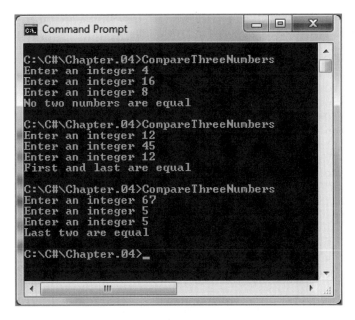

**Figure 4-25** Several executions of the `CompareThreeNumbers` program

## Using AND and OR Logic

In the next steps, you will create an interactive program that allows you to test AND and OR logic for yourself. The program decides whether a delivery charge applies to a shipment. If the customer lives in Zone 1 or Zone 2, then shipping is free, as long as the order contains fewer than ten boxes. If the customer lives in another zone or if the order is too large, then a delivery charge applies. First, you will create a program with incorrect logic; then you will fix it to demonstrate correct use of parentheses when combining ANDs and ORs.

**To create the delivery charge program:**

1. Open a new file in your text editor and enter the first few lines of the program. Define constants for ZONE1, ZONE2, and the LOWQUANTITY limit as well as variables to hold the customer's input string, which will be converted to the zone and number of boxes in the shipment.

```
using System;
public class DemoORAndANDWrongLogic
{
    public static void Main()
    {
        const int ZONE1 = 1, ZONE2 = 2;
        const int LOWQUANTITY = 10;
        string inputString;
        int quantity;
        int deliveryZone;
```

2. Enter statements that describe the delivery charge criteria to the user and accept keyboard values for the customer's delivery zone and shipment size.

```
Console.WriteLine("Delivery is free for zone {0} or {1}",
    ZONE1, ZONE2);
Console.WriteLine("when the number of boxes is less than {0}",
    LOWQUANTITY);
Console.WriteLine("Enter delivery zone ");
inputString = Console.ReadLine();
deliveryZone = Convert.ToInt32(inputString);
Console.WriteLine
    ("Enter the number of boxes in the shipment");
inputString = Console.ReadLine();
quantity = Convert.ToInt32(inputString);
```

3. Write a compound if statement that appears to test whether the customer lives in Zone 1 or 2 and has a shipment consisting of fewer than ten boxes.

```
if(deliveryZone == ZONE1 || deliveryZone == ZONE2 &&
    quantity < LOWQUANTITY)
        Console.WriteLine("Delivery is free");
else
        Console.WriteLine("A delivery charge applies");
```

4. Add closing curly braces for the Main() method and for the class, and save the file as **DemoORAndANDWrongLogic.cs**. Compile and execute the program. Enter values for the zone and shipment size. The program appears to run correctly until you enter a shipment for Zone 1 that exceeds nine boxes. Such a shipment should not be free, but the output indicates that it is. Figure 4-26 shows the output.

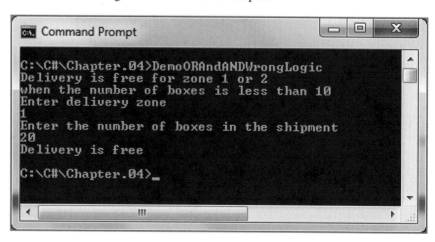

**Figure 4-26** Sample execution of DemoORAndANDWrongLogic program

5. To remedy the problem, insert parentheses around the expression `deliveryZone == ZONE1 || deliveryZone == ZONE2` within the `if` statement in the `Main()` method. Change the class name to DemoORAndAND (removing *WrongLogic*). Save the new version of the program as **DemoORAndAND.cs**. When you compile and execute this version of the program, every combination of zone and quantity values should work correctly. Figure 4-27 shows the output for a Zone 1 delivery of 20 boxes.

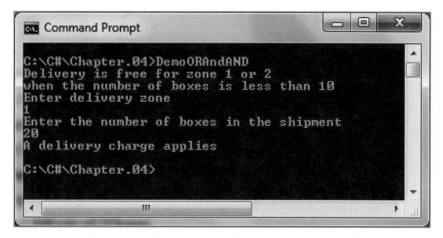

**Figure 4-27** Output of DemoORAndAND program when user enters 1 and 20

# Chapter Summary

- A flowchart is a pictorial tool that helps you understand a program's logic. A decision structure is one that involves choosing between alternative courses of action based on some value within a program.

- You use an `if` statement to make a single-alternative decision. The `if` statement takes the following form:

```
if(expression)
    statement;
```

When you want to execute multiple statements conditionally, you can place the statements within a block defined by curly braces.

- When you make a dual-alternative decision, you can use an if-else statement. The if-else statement takes the following form:

```
if(expression)
    statement1;
else
    statement2;
```

Just as you can block several statements so they all execute when an expression within an if is true, you can block multiple statements after an else so they all execute when the evaluated expression is false.

- You can use the conditional AND operator (or simply the AND operator) within a Boolean expression to determine whether two expressions are both true. The AND operator is written as two ampersands (&&).

- You can use the conditional OR operator (or simply the OR operator) when you want some action to occur when at least one of two conditions is true. The OR operator is written as ||.

- When you combine && and || operators within the same Boolean expression without parentheses, the && operators take precedence, meaning their Boolean values are evaluated first.

- The switch statement tests a single variable against a series of exact matches.

- The conditional operator is used as an abbreviated version of the if-else statement. It requires three expressions separated with a question mark and a colon.

- You use the NOT operator, which is written as an exclamation point (!), to negate the result of any Boolean expression.

- Common errors when making decisions include using the assignment operator instead of the comparison operator, inserting a semicolon after the Boolean expression in an if statement, failing to block a set of statements when they should be blocked, and performing a range check incorrectly or inefficiently.

- Making a decision within a method in a GUI application is no different from making one in a console application; you can use if, if...else, and switch statements in the same ways. However, event-driven programs often require fewer coded decisions than console applications because some events are determined by the user's actions when the program is running, rather than by the programmer's coding beforehand.

# Key Terms

**Pseudocode** is a tool that helps programmers plan a program's logic by writing plain English statements.

A **flowchart** is a tool that helps programmers plan a program's logic by writing program steps in diagram form, as a series of shapes connected by arrows.

A **sequence structure** is a unit of program logic in which one step follows another unconditionally.

A **decision structure** is a unit of program logic that involves choosing between alternative courses of action based on some value.

An **if statement** is used to make a single-alternative decision.

A **block** is a collection of one or more statements contained within a pair of curly braces.

A **control statement** is the part of a structure that determines whether the subsequent block of statements executes.

**K & R style** is a way of writing code so that the opening curly brace of a structure is on the same line as the control statement; it is named for Brian Kernighan and Dennis Ritchie, who wrote the first book on the C programming language.

A **nested if** statement is one in which one decision structure is contained within another.

**Dual-alternative decisions** have two possible outcomes.

An **if-else statement** performs a dual-alternative decision.

The **conditional AND operator** (or simply the **AND operator**) determines whether two expressions are both true; it is written using two ampersands (&&).

**Truth tables** are diagrams used in mathematics and logic to help describe the truth of an entire expression based on the truth of its parts.

**Short-circuit evaluation** is the C# feature in which parts of an AND or OR expression are evaluated only as far as necessary to determine whether the entire expression is true or false.

The **conditional OR operator** (or simply the **OR operator**) determines whether at least one of two conditions is true; it is written using two pipes (||).

The **Boolean logical AND operator** determines whether two expressions are both true; it is written using a single ampersand (&). Unlike the conditional AND operator, it does not use short-circuit evaluation.

The **Boolean logical inclusive OR operator** determines whether at least one of two conditions is `true`; it is written using a single pipe (`|`). Unlike the conditional OR operator, it does not use short-circuit evaluation.

A **side effect** is an unintended consequence.

**Bitwise operators** are used to manipulate the individual bits of values.

The `switch` **structure** tests a single variable against a series of exact matches.

The keyword `switch` starts a `switch` structure.

The `switch` **expression** is a condition in a `switch` statement enclosed in parentheses.

The keyword `case` in a `switch` structure is followed by one of the possible values that might equal the `switch` expression.

A **case label** identifies a course of action in a `switch` structure.

The keyword `break` optionally terminates a `switch` structure at the end of each `case`.

The keyword `default` optionally is used prior to any action that should occur if the test expression in a `case` structure does not match any `case`.

The **governing type** of a `switch` statement is established by the `switch` expression. The governing type can be `sbyte`, `byte`, `short`, `ushort`, `int`, `uint`, `long`, `ulong`, `char`, `string`, or `enum`.

The **conditional operator** is used as an abbreviated version of the `if-else` statement; it requires three expressions separated by a question mark and a colon.

A **ternary** operator requires three arguments.

The **NOT operator** (`!`) negates the result of any Boolean expression.

A **range check** is a series of `if` statements that determine whether a value falls within a specified range.

"**At runtime**" is a phrase that means "during the time a program is running."

# Review Questions

1. What is the output of the following code segment?

   ```
   int a = 3, b = 4;
   if(a == b)
      Console.Write("Black ");
      Console.WriteLine("White");
   ```

   a. Black

   b. White

   c. Black White

   d. nothing

2. What is the output of the following code segment?

   ```
   int a = 3, b = 4;
   if(a < b)
   {
      Console.Write("Black ");
      Console.WriteLine("White");
   }
   ```

   a. Black

   b. White

   c. Black White

   d. nothing

3. What is the output of the following code segment?

   ```
   int a = 3, b = 4;
   if(a > b)
      Console.Write("Black ");
   else
      Console.WriteLine("White");
   ```

   a. Black

   b. White

   c. Black White

   d. nothing

4. If the following code segment compiles correctly, what do you know about the variable x?

```
if(x) Console.WriteLine("OK");
```

   a. x is an integer variable

   b. x is a Boolean variable

   c. x is greater than 0

   d. none of these

5. What is the output of the following code segment?

```
int c = 6, d = 12;
if(c > d);
    Console.Write("Green ");
    Console.WriteLine("Yellow");
```

   a. Green

   b. Yellow

   c. Green Yellow

   d. nothing

6. What is the output of the following code segment?

```
int c = 6, d = 12;
if(c < d)
    if(c > 8)
        Console.Write("Green");
    else
        Console.Write("Yellow");
    else
        Console.Write("Blue");
```

   a. Green

   b. Yellow

   c. Blue

   d. nothing

7. What is the output of the following code segment?

```
int e = 5, f = 10;
if(e < f && f < 0)
    Console.Write("Red ");
else
    Console.Write("Orange");
```

   a. Red

   b. Orange

   c. Red Orange

   d. nothing

8. What is the output of the following code segment?

```
int e = 5, f = 10;
if(e < f || f < 0)
    Console.Write("Red ");
else
    Console.Write("Orange");
```

   a. Red

   b. Orange

   c. Red Orange

   d. nothing

9. Which of the following expressions is equivalent to the following code segment?

```
if(g > h)
    if(g < k)
        Console.Write("Brown");
```

   a. if(g > h && g < k) Console.Write("Brown");

   b. if(g > h && < k) Console.Write("Brown");

   c. if(g > h || g < k) Console.Write("Brown");

   d. two of these

10. Which of the following expressions assigns `true` to a Boolean variable named `isIDValid` when the `idNumber` is greater than 1000, less than or equal to 9999, or equal to 123456?

    a. `isIDValid = (idNumber > 1000 && idNumber <= 9999 && idNumber == 123456)`

    b. `isIDValid = (idNumber > 1000 && idNumber <= 9999 || idNumber == 123456)`

    c. `isIDValid = ((idNumber > 1000 && idNumber <= 9999) || idNumber == 123456)`

    d. two of these

11. Which of the following expressions is equivalent to `a || b && c || d`?

    a. `a && b || c && d`

    b. `(a || b) && (c || d)`

    c. `a || (b && c) || d`

    d. two of these

12. How many `case` labels would a `switch` statement require to be equivalent to the following `if` statement?

```
if(v == 1)
    Console.WriteLine("one");
else
    Console.WriteLine("two");
```

    a. zero

    b. one

    c. two

    d. impossible to tell

13. Falling through a `switch case` is most often prevented by using the _____.

    a. `break` statement

    b. `default` statement

    c. `case` statement

    d. `end` statement

14. If the test expression in a `switch` does not match any of the `case` values, and there is no `default` value, then _____.

   a. a compiler error occurs

   b. a run-time error occurs

   c. the program continues with the next executable statement

   d. the expression is incremented and the `case` values are tested again

15. Which of the following is equivalent to the statement
`if(m == 0) d = 0 ; else d = 1;?`

   a. `? m == 0 : d = 0, d = 1;`

   b. `m? d = 0; d = 1;`

   c. `m == 0 ; d = 0; d = 1?`

   d. `m == 0 ? d = 0 : d = 1;`

16. Which of the following C# expressions is equivalent to
`a < b && b < c?`

   a. `c > b > a`

   b. `a < b && c >= b`

   c. `!(b <= a) && b < c`

   d. two of these

17. Which of the following C# expressions means, "If `itemNumber` is not 8 or 9, add TAX to `price`"?

   a. `if(itemNumber != 8 || itemNumber != 9)`
      `price = price + TAX;`

   b. `if(itemNumber != 8 && itemNumber != 9)`
      `price = price + TAX;`

   c. `if(itemNumber != 8 && != 9)`
      `price = price + TAX;`

   d. two of these

18. Which of the following C# expressions means, "If itemNumber is 1 or 2 and quantity is 12 or more, add TAX to price"?

    a.  ```
        if(itemNumber = 1 || itemNumber = 2 &&
           quantity >= 12)
           price = price + TAX;
        ```

    b.  ```
        if(itemNumber == 1 || itemNumber == 2 ||
           quantity >= 12)
           price = price + TAX;
        ```

    c.  ```
        if(itemNumber == 1 && itemNumber == 2 &&
           quantity >= 12)
           price = price + TAX;
        ```

    d.  none of these

19. Which of the following C# expressions means, "If itemNumber is 5 and zone is 1 or 3, add TAX to price"?

    a.  ```
        if(itemNumber == 5 && zone == 1 || zone == 3)
           price = price + TAX;
        ```

    b.  ```
        if(itemNumber == 5 && (zone == 1 || zone == 3))
           price = price + TAX;
        ```

    c.  ```
        if(itemNumber == 5 && (zone == 1 || 3))
           price = price + TAX;
        ```

    d.  two of these

20. Which of the following C# expressions means, "If itemNumber is not 100, add TAX to price"?

    a.  ```
        if(itemNumber != 100)
           price = price + TAX;
        ```

    b.  ```
        if(!(itemNumber == 100))
           price = price + TAX;
        ```

    c.  ```
        if((itemNumber <100) || (itemNumber > 100))
           price = price + TAX;
        ```

    d.  all of these

## Exercises

1.  a.  Write a console-based program that prompts the user for an hourly pay rate. If the value entered is less than $7.50, display an error message. Save the program as **CheckLowRate.cs**.
        ```

    b. Create a GUI application that allows the user to enter an hourly pay rate in a TextBox. When the user clicks a button and the value in the TextBox is less than $7.50, display an error message. Save the project as **CheckLowRateGUI**.

2. a. Write a console-based program that prompts a user for an hourly pay rate. If the value entered is less than $7.50 or greater than $49.99, display an error message; otherwise, display a message indicating that the rate is okay. Save the program as **CheckLowAndHighRate.cs**.

    b. Create a GUI application that allows the user to enter an hourly pay rate in a TextBox. When the user clicks a button and the value in the TextBox is less than $7.50 or greater than $49.99, display an error message; otherwise, display a message indicating that the rate is okay. Save the project as **CheckLowAndHighRateGUI**.

3. a. Write a console-based program that prompts a user for an hourly pay rate. If the user enters values less than $7.50 or greater than $49.99, prompt the user again. If the user enters an invalid value again, display an appropriate error message. If the user enters a valid value on either the first or second attempt, display the pay rate as well as the weekly rate, which is calculated as 40 times the hourly rate. Save the program as **SecondChancePayRate.cs**.

    b. Create a GUI application similar to the one described in Exercise 3a. Allow the user to click a button to submit a rate. After the user has made a valid entry, or after two invalid entries, make the button invisible. Save the project as **SecondChancePayRateGUI**.

4. a. Write a console-based program that accepts a user's message and determines whether it is short enough for a social networking service that does not accept messages of more than 140 characters. Save the program as **Twitter.cs**.

    b. Create a GUI application similar to Exercise 4a. Save the project as **TwitterGUI**.

5. a. Write a console-based program for a college's admissions office. The user enters a numeric high school grade point average (for example, 3.2) and an admission test score.

Display the message "Accept" if the student meets either of the following requirements:

- A grade point average of 3.0 or higher and an admission test score of at least 60

- A grade point average of less than 3.0 and an admission test score of at least 80

If the student does not meet either of the qualification criteria, display "Reject". Save the program as **Admission.cs**.

  b. Create a GUI application for the college admissions office described in Exercise 5a. Save the project as **AdmissionGUI**.

6.   a. Write a console-based program that prompts the user for an hourly pay rate and hours worked. Compute gross pay (hours times pay rate), withholding tax, and net pay (gross pay minus withholding tax). Withholding tax is computed as a percentage of gross pay based on the following:

To align numbers vertically on a Label using a format string, choose a monospaced font such as Courier New. In a monospaced font, each character occupies the same amount of horizontal space.

| Gross Pay | Withholding Percentage |
|---|---|
| Up to and including 300.00 | 10% |
| 300.01 and up | 12% |

Save the program as **Payroll.cs**.

  b. Create a GUI application that performs the same payroll calculations described in Exercise 6a. Save the project as **PayrollGUI**.

7.   a. Write a console-based program for a lawn-mowing service. The lawn-mowing season lasts 20 weeks. The weekly fee for mowing a lot under 400 square feet is $25. The fee for a lot that is 400 square feet or more, but under 600 square feet, is $35 per week. The fee for a lot that is 600 square feet or over is $50 per week. Prompt the user for the length and width of a lawn, and then display the weekly mowing fee, as well as the total fee for the 20-week season. Save the file as **Lawn.cs**.

  b. Create a GUI application that performs the same functions as those described in Exercise 7a. Save the project as **LawnGUI**.

  c. To the Lawn application you created in Exercise 7a, add a prompt that asks the user whether the customer wants to pay (1) once, (2) twice, or (3) 20 times per season. If the user enters 1 for once, the fee for the season is simply the seasonal total. If the customer requests two payments, each payment is half the seasonal fee plus a $5 service charge. If the user requests 20 separate payments, add a $3 service charge per week. Display the number of payments the customer must make, each payment amount, and the total for the season. Save the file as **Lawn2.cs**.

8. Write a console-based application that asks a user to enter an IQ score. If the score is a number less than 0 or greater than 200, issue an error message; otherwise, issue an "above average", "average", or "below average" message for scores over, at, or under 100, respectively. Save the file as **IQ.cs**.

9. a. You can create a random number that is at least min but less than max using the following statements:

```
Random ranNumberGenerator = new Random();
int randomNumber;
randomNumber = ranNumberGenerator.Next(min, max);
```

Write a console-based program that generates a random number between 1 and 10. (In other words, min is 1 and max is 11.) Ask a user to guess the random number, then display the random number and a message indicating whether the user's guess was too high, too low, or correct. Save the file as **GuessingGame.cs**.

b. Create a GUI application that performs the same tasks as the program in Exercise 9a. Save the project as **GuessingGameGUI**.

10. a. In the game Rock Paper Scissors, two players simultaneously choose one of three options: rock, paper, or scissors. If both players choose the same option, then the result is a tie. However, if they choose differently, the winner is determined as follows:

   • Rock beats scissors, because a rock can break a pair of scissors.

   • Scissors beats paper, because scissors can cut paper.

   • Paper beats rock, because a piece of paper can cover a rock.

   Create a console-based game in which the computer randomly chooses rock, paper, or scissors. Let the user enter a character, 'r', 'p', or 's', each representing one of the three choices. Then, determine the winner. Save the application as **RockPaperScissors.cs**.

b. Create a GUI application in which the user can play Rock, Paper, Scissors by clicking one of three buttons. Save the project as **RockPaperScissorsGUI**.

11. a. Create a console-based lottery game application. Generate three random numbers, each between 1 and 4. Allow the user to guess three numbers. Compare each of the user's guesses to the three random numbers and display a message that includes the user's guess, the randomly determined three-digit number, and the amount of money the user has won as follows:

| Matching Numbers | Award ($) |
|---|---|
| Any one matching | 10 |
| Two matching | 100 |
| Three matching, not in order | 1000 |
| Three matching in exact order | 10,000 |
| No matches | 0 |

Make certain that your application accommodates repeating digits. For example, if a user guesses 1, 2, and 3, and the randomly generated digits are 1, 1, and 1, do not give the user credit for three correct guesses—just one. Save the file as **Lottery.cs**.

b. Create a GUI application that lets the user play the Lottery game described in Exercise 11a. Save the project as **LotteryGUI**.

 *Debugging Exercises*

Each of the following files in the Chapter.04 folder of the downloadable student files has syntax and/or logical errors. In each case, determine the problem and fix the program. After you correct the errors, save each file using the same filename preceded with *Fixed*. For example, save DebugFour1.cs as **FixedDebugFour1.cs**.

a. DebugFour1.cs

b. DebugFour2.cs

c. DebugFour3.cs

d. DebugFour4.cs

## Up For Discussion

1. In this chapter, you learned how computer programs make decisions. Insurance companies use programs to make decisions about your insurability as well as the rates you will be charged for health and life insurance policies. For example, certain preexisting conditions may raise your insurance premiums considerably. Is it ethical for insurance companies to access your health records and then make insurance decisions about you?

2. Job applications are sometimes screened by software that makes decisions about a candidate's suitability based on keywords in the applications. For example, when a help-wanted ad lists "management experience," the presence of those exact words might determine which résumés are chosen for further scrutiny. Is such screening fair to applicants?

3. Medical facilities often have more patients waiting for organ transplants than there are available organs. Suppose you have been asked to write a computer program that selects which of several candidates should receive an available organ. What data would you want on file to use in your program, and what decisions would you make based on the data? What data do you think others might use that you would not use?

# Looping

In this chapter you will:

◎ Learn how to create loops using the `while` statement

◎ Learn how to create loops using the `for` statement

◎ Learn how to create loops using the `do` statement

◎ Use nested loops

◎ Accumulate totals

◎ Understand how to improve loop performance

◎ Learn about looping issues in GUI programs

In the last chapter, you learned how computers make decisions by evaluating Boolean expressions. Looping allows a program to repeat tasks based on the value of a Boolean expression. For example, programs that produce thousands of paychecks or invoices rely on the ability to loop to repeat instructions. Likewise, programs that repeatedly prompt you for a valid credit card number or for the correct answer to a tutorial question require the ability to loop to do their jobs efficiently. In this chapter, you will learn to create loops in C# programs.

## Using the `while` Loop

If making decisions is what makes programs seem smart, looping is what makes programs seem powerful. A **loop** is a structure that allows repeated execution of a block of statements. Within a looping structure, a Boolean expression is evaluated. If it is `true`, a block of statements called the **loop body** executes, and the Boolean expression is evaluated again. As long as the expression is `true`, the statements in the loop body continue to execute and the loop-controlling Boolean expression continues to be reevaluated. When the Boolean evaluation is `false`, the loop ends. Figure 5-1 shows a diagram of the logic of a loop.

One execution of any loop is called an **iteration**.

Recall from the chapter *Making Decisions* that a block of statements might be a single statement with or without curly braces, or it might be multiple statements with curly braces.

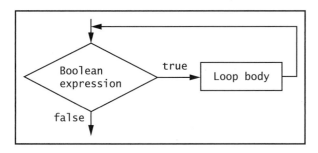

**Figure 5-1** Flowchart of a loop structure

You can use a **while loop** to execute a body of statements continuously as long as the loop's test condition continues to be `true`. A `while` loop consists of the keyword `while`, followed by a Boolean expression within parentheses, followed by the body of the loop. The body can be a single statement or a block of statements surrounded by curly braces.

The evaluated Boolean expression in a `while` statement can be a compound expression that uses ANDs and ORs (just as within an `if` statement).

For example, the following code shows an integer declaration followed by a loop that causes the message "Hello" to display (theoretically) forever because there is no code to end the loop. A loop that never ends is called an **infinite loop**.

```
int number = 1;
while (number > 0)
    Console.WriteLine("Hello");
```

An infinite loop does not actually execute infinitely. All programs run with the help of computer memory and hardware, both of which have finite capacities.

It is always a bad idea to write an infinite loop, although even experienced programmers write them by accident. If you ever find yourself in the midst of an infinite loop in a console application, you can break out by holding down the Ctrl key and pressing the C key or the Break (Pause) key. In a GUI program, you can simply close the Frame that is hosting the application.

In this loop, the expression number > 0 evaluates as true, and "Hello" is displayed. The expression number > 0 evaluates as true again and "Hello" is displayed again. Because nothing ever alters the value of number, the loop runs forever, evaluating the same Boolean expression and repeatedly displaying "Hello" (as long as computer memory and hardware allow).

To make a while loop end correctly, three separate actions should occur:

- A variable, the **loop control variable**, is initialized (before entering the loop).

- The loop control variable is tested in the while expression.

- The body of the while statement must take some action that alters the value of the loop control variable (so that the while expression eventually evaluates as false).

For example, Figure 5-2 shows the logic for a loop that displays "Hello" four times. The variable number is initialized to 1 and a constant, LIMIT, is initialized to 5. The variable is less than LIMIT, and so the loop body executes. The loop body shown in Figure 5-2 contains two statements. The first displays "Hello" and the second adds 1 to number. The next time number is evaluated, its value is 2, which is still less than LIMIT, so the loop body executes again. "Hello" displays a third time and the number becomes 4, then "Hello" displays a fourth time and the number becomes 5. Now when the expression number < LIMIT evaluates, it is false, so the loop ends. If there were any subsequent statements following the while loop's closing curly brace, they would execute after the loop was finished.

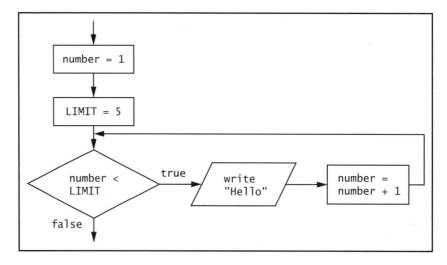

**Figure 5-2** Flowchart for the logic of a while loop whose body executes four times

Figure 5-3 shows a C# program that uses the same logic as diagrammed in Figure 5-2. After the declarations, the shaded `while` expression compares `number` to `LIMIT`. The two statements that execute each time the Boolean expression is `true` are blocked using a pair of curly braces. Figure 5-4 shows the output.

```csharp
using System;
public class FourHellos
{
    public static void Main()
    {
        int number = 1;
        const int LIMIT = 5;
        while(number < LIMIT)
        {
            Console.WriteLine("Hello");
            number = number + 1;
        }
    }
}
```

**Figure 5-3** A program that contains a `while` loop whose body executes four times

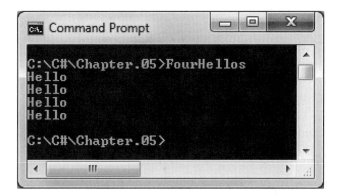

**Figure 5-4** Output of `FourHellos` program

Recall from Chapter 2 that you also can use a shortcut operator to increase the value of a variable by 1. Instead of `number = number + 1`, you could achieve the same final result by writing `number++`, `++number`, or `number += 1`. Because counting is such a common feature of loops, you might want to review the difference between the prefix and postfix increment operators. Chapter 2 contains a video called *Using Shortcut Arithmetic Operators*.

The curly braces surrounding the body of the `while` loop in Figure 5-3 are important. If they are omitted, the `while` loop ends at the end of the "Hello" statement. Adding 1 to `number` would no longer be part of the loop body, so an infinite loop would be created. Even if the statement `number = number + 1;` was indented under the `while` statement, it would not be part of the loop without the surrounding curly braces. Figure 5-5 shows the incorrect logic that would result from omitting the curly braces.

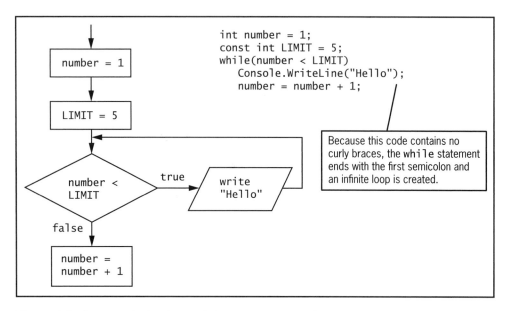

**Figure 5-5**  Incorrect logic when curly braces are omitted from the loop in the `FourHellos` program

Also, if a semicolon is mistakenly placed at the end of the partial statement, as in Figure 5-6, then the loop is also infinite. This loop has an **empty body**, or a body with no statements in it. In this case, `number` is initialized to 1, the Boolean expression `number < LIMIT` evaluates, and because it is `true`, the loop body is entered. Because the loop body is empty, ending at the semicolon, no action takes place, and the Boolean expression evaluates again. It is still `true` (nothing has changed), so the empty body is entered again, and the infinite loop continues. The program can never progress to either the statement that displays "Hello" or the statement that increases the value of `number`. The fact that these two statements are blocked using curly braces has no effect because of the incorrectly placed semicolon.

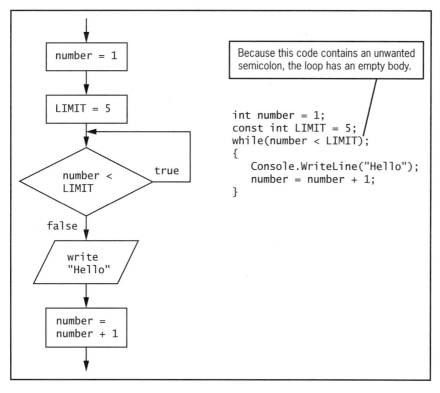

**Figure 5-6** Incorrect logic when an unwanted semicolon is mistakenly added to the loop in the `FourHellos` program

Within a correctly functioning loop's body, you can change the value of the loop control variable in a number of ways. Many loop control variable values are altered by **incrementing**, or adding to them, as in Figures 5-2 and 5-3. Other loops are controlled by reducing, or **decrementing**, a variable and testing whether the value remains greater than some benchmark value. A loop for which the number of iterations is predetermined is called a **definite loop** or **counted loop**. Often, the value of a loop control variable is not altered by arithmetic, but instead is altered by user input. For example, perhaps you want to continue performing some task while the user indicates a desire to continue. In that case, you do not know when you write the program whether the loop will be executed two times, 200 times, or not at all. This type of loop is an **indefinite loop**.

Consider a program that displays a bank balance and asks if the user wants to see what the balance will be after one year of interest has accumulated. Each time the user indicates she wants to continue, an increased balance appears. When the user finally indicates she has had enough, the program ends. The program appears in Figure 5-7, and a typical execution appears in Figure 5-8.

```
using System;
public class LoopingBankBal
{
    public static void Main()
    {
        double bankBal = 1000;
        const double INT_RATE = 0.04;
        string inputString;
        char response;
        Console.Write("Do you want to see your balance? Y or N ...");
        inputString = Console.ReadLine();
        response = Convert.ToChar(inputString);
        while(response == 'Y')
        {
            Console.WriteLine("Bank balance is {0}", bankBal.ToString("C"));
            bankBal = bankBal + bankBal * INT_RATE;
            Console.Write("Do you want to see next year's balance? Y or N ...");
            inputString = Console.ReadLine();
            response = Convert.ToChar(inputString);
        }
        Console.WriteLine("Have a nice day!");
    }
}
```

**Figure 5-7** LoopingBankBal program

The program shown in Figure 5-7 continues to display bank balances while the response is Y. It could also be written to display while the response is not N, as in `while (response != 'N')`.... A value such as 'Y' or 'N' that a user must supply to stop a loop is called a **sentinel value**.

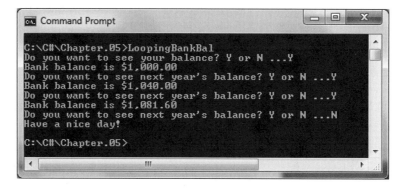

**Figure 5-8** Typical execution of the LoopingBankBal program

In the program shown in Figure 5-7, the loop control variable is response. It is initialized by the first input and tested with `while(response == 'Y')`. If the user types any response other than *Y*, then the loop body never executes; instead, the next statement to execute displays "Have a nice day!". However, if the user enters *Y*, then all five statements within the loop body execute. The current balance is displayed, and the program increases the balance by the interest rate value; this value will not be displayed unless the user requests another loop repetition. Within the loop, the program prompts the user and reads in a new value for `response`. This is the statement that potentially alters the loop control variable. The loop ends with a closing curly brace, and program control returns to the top of the loop, where the Boolean expression is tested again. If the user typed *Y* at the last prompt, then the loop is reentered and the increased `bankBal` value that was calculated during the last loop cycle is displayed.

In C#, character data is case sensitive. If a program tests `response == 'Y'`, a user response of *y* will result in a `false` evaluation. Beware of the pitfall of writing a loop similar to `while(response != 'Y' || response != 'y')`... to test both for uppercase and lowercase versions of the response. Every character is either not 'Y' or not 'y', even 'Y' and 'y'. A correct loop might begin with the following:

`while(response != 'Y' && response != 'y')`...

Watch the video *Using the `while` Loop*.

---

## TWO TRUTHS & A LIE

### Using the `while` Loop

1. To make a `while` loop that executes correctly, a loop control variable is initialized before entering the loop.

2. To make a `while` loop that executes correctly, the loop control variable is tested in the `while` expression.

3. To make a `while` loop that executes correctly, the body of the `while` statement must never alter the value of the loop control variable.

The false statement is #3. To make a `while` loop that executes correctly, the body of the `while` statement must take some action that alters the value of the loop control variable.

---

# Using the `for` Loop

Each time the `LoopingBankBal` program in Figure 5-7 executes, the user might continue the loop a different number of times, which makes it an indefinite loop. You can use a `while` loop for either definite or indefinite loops. To write either type of `while` loop, you initialize a loop control variable, and as long as its test expression is `true`, you continue to execute the body of the `while` loop. To avoid an infinite loop, the body of the `while` loop must contain a statement that alters the loop control variable.

Because you need definite loops so frequently when you write programs, C# provides a shorthand way to create such a loop. This shorthand structure is called a **for loop**. With a for loop, you can indicate the starting value for the loop control variable, the test condition that controls loop entry, and the expression that alters the loop control variable, all in one convenient place.

You begin a for statement with the keyword for followed by a set of parentheses. Within the parentheses are three sections separated by exactly two semicolons. The three sections are usually used for:

- Initializing the loop control variable
- Testing the loop control variable
- Updating the loop control variable

As with an if or a while statement, you can use a single statement as the body of a for loop, or you can use a block of statements enclosed in curly braces. The while and for statements shown in Figure 5-9 produce the same output—the integers 1 through 10.

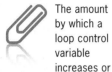

The amount by which a loop control variable increases or decreases on each cycle through the loop is often called the **step value**. That is because in the BASIC programming language, the keyword STEP was actually used in for loops.

```
// Declare loop control variable and limit
int x;
const int LIMIT = 10
// Using a while loop to display 1 through 10
x = 1;
while(x <= LIMIT)
{
    Console.WriteLine(x);
    ++x;
}
// Using a for loop to display 1 through 10
for(x = 1; x <= LIMIT; ++x)
    Console.WriteLine(x);
```

**Figure 5-9**  Displaying integers 1 through 10 with while and for loops

Within the parentheses of the for statement shown in Figure 5-9, the initialization section prior to the first semicolon sets a variable named x to 1. The program will execute this statement once, no matter how many times the body of the for loop eventually executes.

After the initialization expression executes, program control passes to the middle, or test, section of the for statement. If the Boolean expression found there evaluates to true, then the body of the for loop is entered. In the program segment shown in Figure 5-9, x is initialized to 1, so when x <= LIMIT is tested, it evaluates to true and the loop body outputs the value of x.

202

After the loop body executes, the final one-third of the for expression (the update section) executes, and x increases to 2. Following the third section, program control returns to the second (test) section, where x is compared to LIMIT a second time. Because the value of x is 2, it is still less than or equal to LIMIT, so the body of the for loop executes and the value of x is displayed. Then the third, altering portion of the for statement executes again. The variable x increases to 3, and the for loop continues.

Eventually, when x is *not* less than or equal to LIMIT (after 1 through 10 have been output), the for loop ends, and the program continues with any statements that follow the for loop.

Although the three sections of the for loop are most commonly used for initializing, testing, and incrementing, you can also perform other tasks:

- You can initialize more than one variable by placing commas between the separate statements, as in the following:
  ```
  for(g = 0, h = 1; g < 6; ++g)
  ```

- You can declare a new variable, as in the following:
  ```
  for(int k = 0; k < 5; ++k)
  ```

  In this example, k is declared to be an int and is initialized to 0. This technique is used frequently when the variable exists only to control the loop and for no other purpose. When a variable is declared inside a loop, as k is in this example, it can be referenced only for the duration of the loop body; then it is **out of scope**, which means it is not usable because it has ceased to exist.

- You can perform more than one test by evaluating compound conditions, as in the following:
  ```
  for(g = 0; g < 3 && h > 1; ++g)
  ```

- You can decrement or perform some other task at the end of the loop's execution, as in:
  ```
  for(g = 5; g >= 1; --g)
  ```

- You can perform multiple tasks at the end of the loop's execution, as in:
  ```
  for(g = 0; g < 5; ++g, ++h)
  ```

- You can leave one or more portions of the for expression empty, although the two semicolons are still required as placeholders to separate the three sections.

Generally, you should use the for loop for its intended purpose, which is a shorthand way of programming a definite loop.

You will learn about a similar loop, the foreach loop, when you study arrays in the next chapter.

Just as with a decision or a while loop, statements in a for loop body can be blocked. For example, the following loop displays "Hello" and "Goodbye" four times each:

```
const int TIMES = 4;
for(int var = 0; var < TIMES; ++var)
{
    Console.WriteLine("Hello");
    Console.WriteLine("Goodbye");
}
```

 Watch the video *Using the for Loop.*

Without the curly braces in this code, the for loop would end after the statement that displays "Hello". In other words, "Hello" would be displayed four times, but "Goodbye" would be displayed only once.

---

### TWO TRUTHS & A LIE

### Using the for Loop

1.  The following statement displays the numbers 3 through 6:

    ```
    for(int x = 3; x <= 6; ++x)
        Console.WriteLine(x);
    ```

2.  The following statement displays the numbers 4 through 9:

    ```
    for(int x = 3; x < 9; ++x)
        Console.WriteLine(x + 1);
    ```

3.  The following statement displays the numbers 5 through 12:

    ```
    for(int x = 5; x < 12; ++x)
        Console.WriteLine(x);
    ```

The false statement is #3. That loop only displays the numbers 5 through 11, because when x is 12, the loop body is not entered.

---

## Using the do Loop

With each of the loop statements you have learned about so far, the loop body might execute many times, but it is also possible that the loop will not execute at all. For example, recall the bank balance program that displays compound interest, part of which is shown in Figure 5-10. The loop begins at the shaded line by testing the value of response. If the user has not entered *Y*, the loop body never executes. The while loop checks a value at the "top" of the loop.

```
Console.Write("Do you want to see your balance? Y or N ...");
inputString = Console.ReadLine();
response = Convert.ToChar(inputString);
while(response == 'Y')
{
    Console.WriteLine("Bank balance is {0}", bankBal.ToString("C"));
    bankBal = bankBal + bankBal * INT_RATE;
    Console.Write("Do you want to see next year's balance? Y or N ...");
    inputString = Console.ReadLine();
    response = Convert.ToChar(inputString);
}
```

**Figure 5-10**  Part of the bank balance program using a while loop

Sometimes you might need a loop body to execute at least one time.
If so, you want to write a loop that checks at the "bottom" of the
loop after the first iteration. The **do loop** checks the loop-controlling
Boolean expression at the bottom of the loop after one repetition has
occurred. Figure 5-11 shows a diagram of the structure of a do loop.

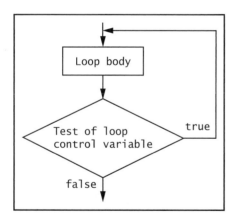

**Figure 5-11**  Flowchart of a do loop

Figure 5-12 shows the logic for a do loop in a bank balance program,
along with the C# code. The loop starts with the keyword do. The
body of the loop follows and is contained within curly braces. Within
the loop, the next balance is calculated and the user is prompted
for a response. The Boolean expression that controls loop execution is written using a while statement, placed after the loop body.
The bankBal variable is output the first time before the user has any
option of responding. At the end of the loop, the user is prompted,
"Do you want to see next year's balance? Y or N ...." Now the user has
the option of seeing more balances, but the first view of the balance
was unavoidable. The user's response is checked at the bottom of the
loop. If it is *Y*, then the loop repeats.

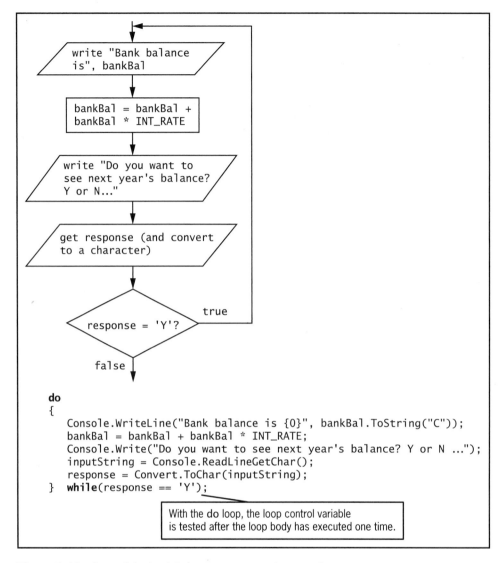

Figure 5-12  Part of the bank balance program using a do loop

 In a do loop, as a matter of style, many programmers prefer to align the while expression with the do keyword that starts the loop. Others feel that placing the while expression on its own line increases the chances that readers might misinterpret the line as the start of its own while statement instead of marking the end of a do statement.

In any situation where you want to loop, you never are required to use a do loop. Within the bank balance example, you could unconditionally display the bank balance once, prompt the user, and then start a while loop that might not be entered. However, when you know you want to perform some task at least one time, the do loop is convenient.

A while loop is a **pretest loop**—one in which the loop control variable is tested before the loop body executes. The do . . . while loop is a **posttest loop**—one in which the loop control variable is tested after the loop body executes.

## TWO TRUTHS & A LIE

### Using the do Loop

1.  In a do loop, a loop-controlling expression is evaluated after one repetition has occurred.

2.  The Boolean expression that controls do loop execution is written using a do statement, placed after the loop body.

3.  You never are required to use a do loop; you can always substitute one execution of the body statements followed by a while loop.

The false statement is #2. The Boolean expression that controls do loop execution is written using a while statement, placed after the loop body.

# Using Nested Loops

Like if statements, loop statements also can be nested. You can place a while loop within a while loop, a for loop within a for loop, a while loop within a for loop, or any other combination. When loops are nested, each pair contains an **inner loop** and an **outer loop**. The inner loop must be entirely contained within the outer loop; loops can never overlap. Figure 5-13 shows a diagram in which the shaded loop is nested within another loop; the shaded area is the inner loop as well as the body of the outer loop.

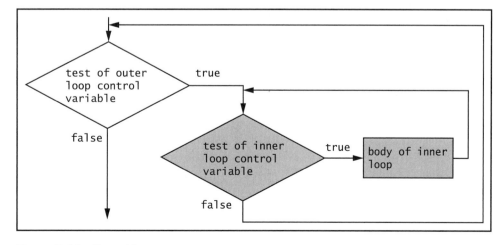

**Figure 5-13** Nested loops

Suppose you want to display future bank balances for different years at a variety of interest rates. Figure 5-14 shows an application that contains an outer loop controlled by interest rates (starting with the first shaded statement in the figure) and an inner loop controlled by years (starting with the second shaded statement). The application displays annually compounded interest on $1000 at 4%, 6%, and 8% interest rates for 1 through 5 years. Figure 5-15 shows the output.

```
using System;
public class LoopingBankBal2
{
    public static void Main()
    {
        double bankBal;
        double rate;
        int year;
        const double START_BAL = 1000;
        const double START_INT = 0.04;
        const double INT_INCREASE = 0.02;
        const double LAST_INT = 0.08;
        const int END_YEAR = 5;
        for(rate = START_INT; rate <= LAST_INT; rate += INT_INCREASE)
        {
            bankBal = START_BAL;
            Console.WriteLine("Starting bank balance is {0}",
                bankBal.ToString("C"));
            Console.WriteLine(" Interest Rate: {0}",
                rate.ToString("P"));
            for(year = 1; year <= END_YEAR; ++year)
            {
                bankBal = bankBal + bankBal * rate;
                Console.WriteLine(" After year {0}, bank balance is {1}",
                    year, bankBal.ToString("C"));
            }
        }
    }
}
```

**Figure 5-14** The LoopingBankBal2 program

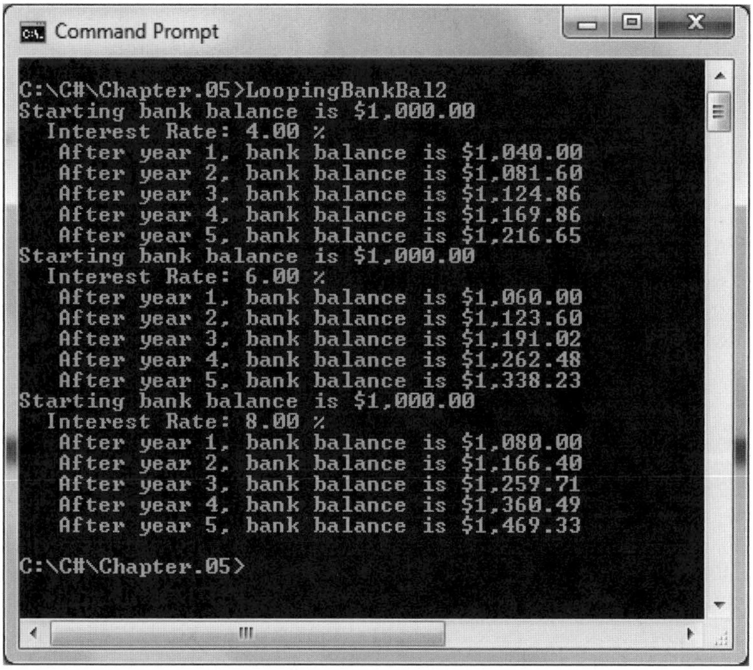

**Figure 5-15** Output of the `LoopingBankBal2` program

When you use a loop within a loop, you should always think of the outer loop as the all-encompassing loop. When you describe the task at hand, you often use the word "each" to refer to the inner loop. For example, if you wanted to output balances for different interest rates each year for ten years, you could appropriately initialize some constants as follows:

```
const double RATE1 = 0.03;
const double RATE2= 0.07
const double RATE_INCREASE = 0.01
const int END_YEAR = 10;
```

Then you could use the following nested for loops:

```
for(rate = RATE1; rate <= RATE2; rate += RATE_INCREASE)
   for(year = 1; year <= END_YEAR; ++year)
      Console.WriteLine(bankBal + bankBal * rate);
```

However, if you wanted to display balances for years 1 through 10 for each possible interest rate, you would use the following:

```
for(year = 1; year <= END_YEAR; ++year)
   for(rate = RATE1; rate <= RATE2; rate += RATE_INCREASE)
      Console.WriteLine(bankBal + bankBal * rate);
```

In both of these examples, the same 50 values would be displayed— five different interest rates for ten years. However, in the first example,

Watch the video *Using Nested Loops*.

balances for years 1 through 10 would display "within" each interest rate, and in the second example, each balance for each interest rate would display "within" each year, 1 through 10. In other words, in the first example, the first 10 amounts to display would be annual values using a rate of 0.03, and in the second example, the first five amounts to display would be based on different interest values in the first year.

---

## TWO TRUTHS & A LIE

### Using Nested Loops

1. The body of the following loop executes six times:

   ```
   for(a = 1; a < 4; ++a)
       for(b = 2; b < 3; ++b)
   ```

2. The body of the following loop executes four times:

   ```
   for(c = 1; c < 3; ++c)
       for(d = 1; d < 3; ++d)
   ```

3. The body of the following loop executes 15 times:

   ```
   for(e = 1; e <= 5; ++e)
       for(f = 2; f <= 4; ++f)
   ```

The false statement is #1. That loop executes only three times. First, a = 1, and it is less than 4, so the inner loop executes. In the inner loop, b is 2 and it is less than 3, so the loop body executes a first time. Then b becomes 3 and the inner loop ends. Then a becomes 2, and the inner loop executes a second time. Finally a becomes 3 and the inner loop executes a third time.

---

## Accumulating Totals

Many computer programs display totals. When you receive a credit card or telephone service bill, you are usually provided with individual transaction details, but you are most interested in the total bill. Similarly, some programs total the number of credit hours generated by college students, the gross payroll for all employees of a company, or the total accounts receivable value for an organization. These totals are **accumulated**—that is, they are summed one at a time in a loop.

Figure 5-16 shows an example of an interactive program that accumulates the user's total purchases. The program prompts the user to enter a purchase price or 0 to quit. While the user continues to enter nonzero values, the amounts are added to a total. With each pass through the loop, the total is calculated to be its current amount plus the new purchase amount. After the user enters the loop-terminating 0, the accumulated total can be displayed. Figure 5-17 shows a typical program execution.

```csharp
using System;
public class TotalPurchase
{
    public static void Main()
    {
        double purchase;
        double total = 0;
        string inputString;
        const double QUIT = 0;
        Console.WriteLine("Enter purchase amount ");
        inputString = Console.ReadLine();
        purchase = Convert.ToDouble(inputString);
        while(purchase != QUIT)
        {
            total += purchase;
            Console.WriteLine("Enter next purchase amount, or " +
                QUIT + " to quit ");
            inputString = Console.ReadLine();
            purchase = Convert.ToDouble(inputString);
        }
        Console.WriteLine("Your total is {0}", total.ToString("C"));
    }
}
```

**Figure 5-16**   An application that accumulates total purchases entered by the user

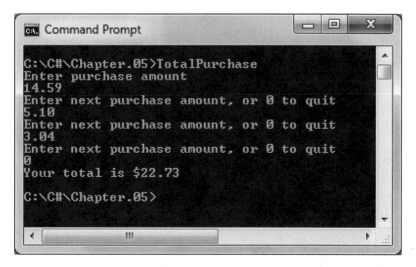

**Figure 5-17**   Typical execution of the `TotalPurchase` program

Recall from Chapter 2 that the expression `total += purchase` uses the shortcut add and assign operator, and that it is equivalent to `total = total + purchase`. The add and assign operator is most frequently used when a running total is kept.

In the application in Figure 5-16, it is very important that the `total` variable used for accumulation is set to 0 before the loop begins. When it is not, the program will not compile. When `total` is not initialized, it might hold any value. The value could be 0 by chance, but it also could be any other value that happens to be located at the memory address of `total`. (For example, by chance, it could hold 1000 and your total would end up $1000 too high.) An unknown value is known as **garbage**. The C# compiler prevents you from seeing an incorrect total by requiring you to provide a starting value; C# will not use the garbage value that happens to be stored at an uninitialized memory location.

In the application in Figure 5-16, the `total` variable must be initialized to 0, but the `purchase` variable is uninitialized. Many programmers would say it makes no sense to initialize this variable because no matter what starting value you provide, the value can be changed by the first input statement before the variable is ever used. As a matter of style, this book will not initialize a variable if the initialization value is never used; doing so might mislead you into thinking the starting value had some purpose.

## TWO TRUTHS & A LIE

### Accumulating Totals

1. When totals are accumulated, 1 is added to a variable that represents the total.

2. A variable used to hold a total must be set to 0 before it is used to accumulate a total.

3. The C# compiler will not allow you to accumulate totals in an uninitialized variable.

The false statement is #1. When totals are accumulated, any value might be added to a variable that represents the total. For example, if you total 10 test scores, then each score is added. If you add only 1 to a total variable on each cycle through a loop, then you are counting rather than accumulating a total.

# Improving Loop Performance

Whether you decide to use a `while`, `for`, or `do...while` loop in an application, you can improve loop performance by making sure the loop does not include unnecessary operations or statements. For example, suppose a loop should execute while x is less than the sum of two integers, a and b. The loop could be written as:

```
while(x < a + b)
    // loop body
```

If this loop executes 1000 times, then the expression a + b is calculated 1000 times. Instead, if you use the following code, the results are the same, but the arithmetic is performed only once:

```
int sum = a + b;
while(x < sum)
    // loop body
```

Of course, if a or b is altered in the loop body, then a new sum must be calculated with every loop iteration. However, if the sum of a and b is fixed prior to the start of the loop, then writing the code the second way is far more efficient.

As another example, suppose you need a temporary variable within a loop to use for some calculation. The loop could be written as follows:

```
while(x < LIMIT)
{
    int tempTotal = a + b;
    // more statements here
}
```

When you declare a variable like `tempTotal` within a loop, it exists only for the duration of the loop; that is, it exists only until the loop's closing brace. Each time the loop executes, the variable is re-created. A more efficient solution is to declare the variable outside of the loop, as follows:

```
int tempTotal;
while(x < LIMIT)
{
    tempTotal = a + b;
    // more statements here
}
```

> It is more efficient to declare this variable outside the loop than to redeclare it on every loop iteration.

As you continue to study programming, you will discover many situations in which you can make your programs more efficient. You should always be on the lookout for ways to improve program performance.

Some programmers use break and continue statements to leave a loop. A break statement exits the nearest enclosing switch, while, do, for, or foreach statement. A continue statement starts a new iteration of the loop contained in the nearest enclosing while, do, for, or foreach statement. Collectively, break and continue are **jump statements**, because they cause program logic to "jump" out of the normal flow of control in a logical structure. Using jump statements (except in a switch structure) almost always makes your programs more confusing, and their use is not recommended. However, you might see jump statements in programs written by others.

---

### TWO TRUTHS **&** A LIE

#### Improving Loop Performance

1. You can improve loop performance by making sure the loop does not include unnecessary operations or statements.

2. You can improve loop performance by declaring temporary variables outside of a loop instead of continuously redeclaring them.

3. You can improve loop performance by omitting the initialization of the loop control variable.

The false statement is #3. A loop control variable must be initialized for every loop.

---

## Looping Issues in GUI Programs

Using a loop within a method in a GUI application is no different from using one in a console application; you can use while, for, and do . . . while statements in the same ways in both types of programs. For example, Figure 5-18 shows a GUI Form that prompts a user to enter a number and then displays "Hello" the corresponding number of times. The image on the left shows the Form when the program starts, and the image on the right shows the output after the user enters a value and clicks the button. Figure 5-19 shows the code in the greetingsButton_Click() method. When a user clicks the greetingsButton, an integer is extracted from the TextBox on the Form. Then a for loop appends "Hello" and a newline character to the Text property of the outputLabel the correct number of times.

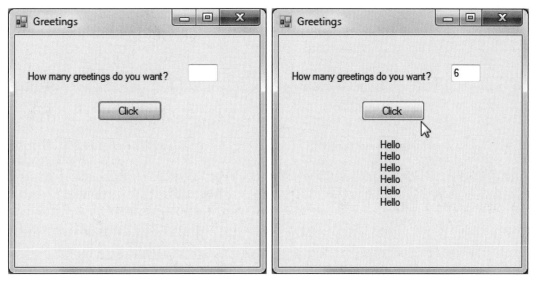

**Figure 5-18** The Greetings Form when it starts and after the user enters a number and clicks the button

```
private void greetingsButton_Click(object sender, EventArgs e)
{
    int numGreetings = Convert.ToInt32(greetingsTextBox.Text);
    int count;
    for (count = 0; count < numGreetings; ++count)
        outputLabel.Text += "Hello\n";
}
```

**Figure 5-19** The greetingsButton_Click() method in the ManyHellosGUI application

Event-driven programs sometimes require fewer coded loops than their counterpart console applications, because in event-driven programs some events are determined by the user's actions when the program is running, rather than by the programmer's coding beforehand. You can write an event-driven program so that an action continues as long as the user continues to make an appropriate selection. Depending on the application, the sentinel value for this sort of implicit loop might occur when the user clicks a button that indicates "quit," or clicks the close button on the Form that hosts the application.

For example, Figure 5-20 shows a Form that controls a bank balance application similar to the one shown earlier in this chapter in Figure 5-7. The left side of the figure shows the Form when the application starts, and the right side shows the Form after the user has clicked the Yes button three times. Figure 5-21 shows the significant Form class code.

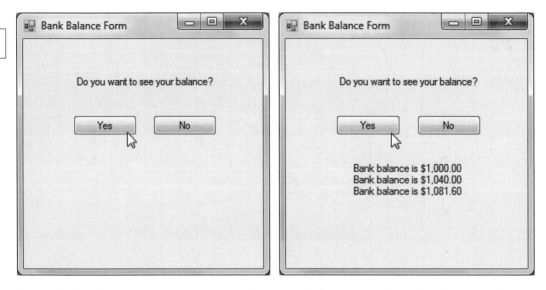

**Figure 5-20** The BankBalance Form when it starts and after the user has clicked Yes three times

```
namespace LoopingBankBalGUI
{
    public partial class Form1 : Form
    {
        double bankBal = 1000;
        const double INT_RATE = 0.04;
        private void yesButton_Click(object sender, EventArgs e)
        {
            outputLabel.Text += String.Format("Bank balance is {0}\n",
                bankBal.ToString("C"));
            bankBal = bankBal + bankBal * INT_RATE;
        }
        private void noButton_Click(object sender, EventArgs e)
        {
            outputLabel.Text = "Have a nice day!";
        }
    }
}
```

**Figure 5-21** Code for the LoopingBankBalGUI program

 In the LoopingBankBalGUI program, you might also choose to disable the Yes button or make it invisible so that the user cannot select it again after clicking No.

No loop is written in the code in Figure 5-21 because a loop body execution is caused automatically each time a user clicks the Yes button on the Form. Whenever yesButton_Click() executes, the Text of the outputLabel is appended to include a new line that displays the bank balance, and then the bank balance is increased by the interest rate. It is important that the bankBal variable is initialized outside the yesButton_Click() method; if it was initialized within the method, the balance would be reset to the original value of $1000 with each new button click. In the application in Figure 5-21, the balances in the outputLabel are replaced with "Have a nice day!" when the user indicates no more balances are needed.

## You Do It

### Using a while Loop

In the next steps, you will write a program that continuously prompts the user for a valid ID number until the user enters one. For this application, assume that a valid ID number must be between 1000 and 9999 inclusive.

**To create an application that verifies an ID number:**

1. Open a new file in your text editor and enter the beginning of the program. It begins by declaring variables for an ID number, the user's input, and constant values for the highest and lowest acceptable ID numbers.

```
using System;
public class ValidID
{
    public static void Main()
    {
        int idNum;
        string input;
        const int LOW = 1000;
        const int HIGH = 9999;
```

2. Add code to prompt the user for an ID number and to then convert it to an integer.

```
Console.Write("Enter an ID number: ");
input = Console.ReadLine();
idNum = Convert.ToInt32(input);
```

3. Create a loop that continues while the entered ID number is out of range. While the number is invalid, explain valid ID parameters and reprompt the user, converting the input to an integer.

```
while(idNum < LOW || idNum > HIGH)
{
    Console.WriteLine("{0} is an invalid ID number",
        idNum);
    Console.Write("ID numbers must be ");
    Console.WriteLine("between {0} and {1} inclusive",
        LOW, HIGH);
    Console.Write("Enter an ID number: ");
    input = Console.ReadLine();
    idNum = Convert.ToInt32(input);
}
```

4. When the user eventually enters a valid ID number, the loop ends. Display a message and add closing curly braces for the Main() method and for the class.

```
        Console.WriteLine("ID number {0} is valid", idNum);
    }
}
```

5. Save the file as **ValidID.cs**. Compile and execute the program. A typical execution during which the user makes several invalid entries is shown in Figure 5-22.

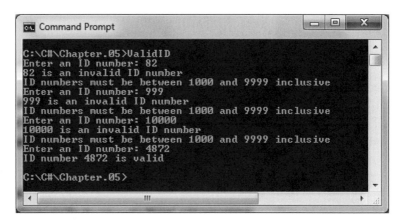

**Figure 5-22** Typical execution of ValidID program

## Using for Loops

In the next steps, you will write a program that creates a tipping table. Restaurant patrons can use this table to approximate the correct tip for meal prices from $10 to $100, at tipping percentage rates from 10% to 25%. The program uses several loops.

## To create the tipping table:

1.  Open a new file in your text editor and enter the beginning of the program. It begins by declaring variables to use for the price of a dinner, a tip percentage rate, and the amount of the tip.

```
using System;
public class TippingTable
{
    public static void Main()
    {
        double dinnerPrice = 10.00;
        double tipRate;
        double tip;
```

2.  Next, create some constants. Every tip from 10% through 25% will be computed in 5% intervals, so declare those values as LOWRATE, MAXRATE, and TIPSTEP. Tips will be calculated on dinner prices up to $100.00 in $10.00 intervals, so declare those constants too.

```
        const double LOWRATE = 0.10;
        const double MAXRATE = 0.25;
        const double TIPSTEP = 0.05;
        const double MAXDINNER = 100.00;
        const double DINNERSTEP = 10.00;
```

3.  To create a heading for the table, display "Price". (For alignment, insert three spaces after the quotes and before the *P* in *Price*.) On the same line, use a loop that displays every tip rate from LOWRATE through MAXRATE in increments of TIPSTEP. In other words, the tip rates are 0.10, 0.15, 0.20, and 0.25. Complete the heading for the table using a WriteLine() statement that advances the cursor to the next line of output and a WriteLine() statement that displays a dashed line.

```
Console.Write("   Price");
for(tipRate = LOWRATE; tipRate <= MAXRATE;
  tipRate += TIPSTEP)
    Console.Write("{0, 8}",tipRate.ToString("F"));
Console.WriteLine();
Console.WriteLine
("----------------------------------------");
```

Recall that within a for loop, the expression before the first semicolon executes once, the middle expression is tested, the loop body executes, and then the expression to the right of the second semicolon executes. In other words, TIPSTEP is not added to tipRate until after the tipRate displays on each cycle through the loop.

As an alternative to typing 40 dashes in the WriteLine() statement, you could use the following loop to display a single dash 40 times. When the 40 dashes were completed, you could use WriteLine() to advance the cursor to a new line.

```
const int NUM_DASHES = 40;
for(int x = 0; x < NUM_DASHES; ++x)
    Console.Write("-");
Console.WriteLine();
```

4. Reset `tipRate` to 0.10. You must reset the rate because after the last loop, the rate will have been increased to greater than 0.25.

   ```
   tipRate = LOWRATE;
   ```

5. Create a nested loop that continues while the `dinnerPrice` remains 100.00 (`MAXDINNER`) or less. Each iteration of this loop displays one row of the tip table. Within this loop, display the `dinnerPrice`, then loop to display four tips while the `tipRate` varies from 0.10 through 0.25. At the end of the loop, increase the `dinnerPrice` by 10.00, reset the `tipRate` to 0.10 so it is ready for the next row, and write a new line to advance the cursor.

   ```
   while(dinnerPrice <= MAXDINNER)
   {
       Console.Write("{0, 8}", dinnerPrice.ToString("C"));
       while(tipRate <= MAXRATE)
       {
           tip = dinnerPrice * tipRate;
           Console.Write("{0, 8}",tip.ToString("F"));
           tipRate += 0.05;
       }
       dinnerPrice += DINNERSTEP;
       tipRate = LOWRATE;
       Console.WriteLine();
   }
   ```

Recall that the {0, 8} format string in the `Write()` statements displays the first argument in fields that are eight characters wide. You learned about format strings in Chapter 2.

6. Add two closing curly braces—one for the `Main()` method and one for the class.

7. Save the file as **TippingTable.cs**. Compile and execute the program. The output looks like Figure 5-23.

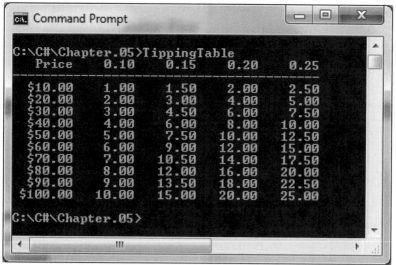

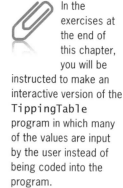

In the exercises at the end of this chapter, you will be instructed to make an interactive version of the TippingTable program in which many of the values are input by the user instead of being coded into the program.

221

**Figure 5-23** Output of TippingTable program

## Chapter Summary

- You can use a while loop to execute a body of statements continuously while a condition continues to be true. A while loop consists of the keyword while, followed by a Boolean expression within parentheses, followed by the body of the loop, which can be a single statement or a block of statements surrounded by curly braces.

- When you use a for statement, you can indicate the starting value for the loop control variable, the test condition that controls loop entry, and the expression that alters the loop control variable, all in one convenient place. You begin a for statement with the keyword for, followed by a set of parentheses. Within the parentheses are three sections that are separated by exactly two semicolons. The three sections are typically used to initialize, test, and update the loop control variable.

- The do loop checks the loop-controlling Boolean expression at the bottom of the loop after one repetition has occurred.

- You can nest any combination of loops to achieve desired results.

- In computer programs, totals frequently are accumulated—that is, summed one at a time in a loop.

- You can improve loop performance by making sure the loop does not include unnecessary operations or statements.

- You can use `while`, `for`, and `do...while` statements in the same ways in console and GUI programs. However, event-driven programs sometimes require fewer coded loops than console applications because some events are determined by the user's actions when the program is running, rather than by the programmer's coding beforehand.

# Key Terms

A **loop** is a structure that allows repeated execution of a block of statements.

A **loop body** is the block of statements executed in a loop.

An **iteration** is one execution of any loop.

A `while` **loop** executes a body of statements continuously while a test condition continues to be `true`; it uses the keyword `while`.

An **infinite loop** is one that (theoretically) never ends.

A **loop control variable** determines whether loop execution will continue.

An **empty body** has no statements in it.

**Incrementing** a variable means adding a value to it. (Specifically, the term often means to add 1 to a variable.)

**Decrementing** a variable means subtracting a value from it. (Specifically, the term often means to subtract 1 from a variable.)

In a **definite loop**, the number of iterations is predetermined.

A **counted loop** is a definite loop.

In an **indefinite loop**, the number of iterations is not predetermined.

A **sentinel value** is one that a user must supply to stop a loop.

A `for` **loop** contains the starting value for the loop control variable, the test condition that controls loop entry, and the expression that alters the loop control variable, all in one statement.

A **step value** is the amount by which a loop control variable is altered, especially in a `for` loop.

**Out of scope** describes a program component that is not usable because it has ceased to exist.

The **do loop** checks the loop-controlling Boolean expression at the bottom of the loop after one repetition has occurred.

In a **pretest loop**, the loop control variable is tested before the loop body executes.

In a **posttest loop**, the loop control variable is tested after the loop body executes.

An **inner loop** is the loop in a pair of nested loops that is entirely contained within another loop.

An **outer loop** is the loop in a pair of nested loops that contains another loop.

**Accumulated** totals are computed by adding values one at a time in a loop.

**Garbage** is a term used to describe an unknown memory value.

**Jump statements** cause program logic to "jump" out of the normal flow in a control structure. Jump statements include `break` and `continue`.

## Review Questions

1. A structure that allows repeated execution of a block of statements is a(n) _____.

   a. selection

   b. loop

   c. sequence

   d. array

2. The body of a `while` loop can consist of _____.

   a. a single statement

   b. a block of statements within curly braces

   c. either a or b

   d. neither a nor b

3. A loop that never ends is called a(n) _____ loop.

   a. `while`

   b. `for`

   c. counted

   d. infinite

4. Which of the following is not required of a loop control variable in a correctly working loop?

   a. It is initialized before the loop starts.

   b. It is tested.

   c. It is reset to its initial value before the loop ends.

   d. It is altered in the loop body.

5. A while loop with an empty body contains no _____.

   a. loop control variable

   b. statements

   c. curly braces

   d. test within the parentheses of the while statement

6. A loop for which you do not know the number of iterations is a(n) _____.

   a. definite loop

   b. indefinite loop

   c. counted loop

   d. for loop

7. What is the major advantage of using a for loop instead of a while loop?

   a. With a for loop, it is impossible to create an infinite loop.

   b. It is the only way to achieve an indefinite loop.

   c. Unlike with a while loop, the execution of multiple statements can depend on the test condition.

   d. The loop control variable is initialized, tested, and altered all in one place.

8. A for loop statement must contain _____.

   a. two semicolons

   b. three commas

   c. four dots

   d. five pipes

9. In a for statement, the section before the first semicolon executes _____.

   a. once

   b. once prior to each loop iteration

   c. once after each loop iteration

   d. one less time than the initial loop control variable value

10. The three sections of the for loop are most commonly used for _____ the loop control variable.

   a. testing, outputting, and incrementing

   b. initializing, testing, and incrementing

   c. incrementing, selecting, and testing

   d. initializing, converting, and outputting

11. Which loop is most convenient to use if the loop body must always execute at least once?

   a. a do loop

   b. a while loop

   c. a for loop

   d. an if loop

12. The loop control variable is checked at the bottom of which kind of loop?

   a. a while loop

   b. a do loop

   c. a for loop

   d. all of the above

13. A for loop is an example of a(n) _____ loop.

   a. untested

   b. pretest

   c. posttest

   d. infinite

225

14. A while loop is an example of a(n) _____ loop.

   a. untested

   b. pretest

   c. posttest

   d. infinite

15. When a loop is placed within another loop, the loops are said to be _____.

   a. infinite

   b. bubbled

   c. nested

   d. overlapping

16. What does the following code segment display?

```
a = 1;
while (a < 5);
{
    Console.Write("{0} ", a);
    ++a;
}
```

   a. 1 2 3 4

   b. 1

   c. 4

   d. nothing

17. What is the output of the following code segment?

```
s = 1;
while (s < 4)
    ++s;
    Console.Write(" {0}", s);
```

   a. 1

   b. 4

   c. 1 2 3 4

   d. 2 3 4

18. What is the output of the following code segment?

```
j = 5;
while(j > 0)
{
    Console.Write("{0} ", j);
    j--;
}
```

a. 0

b. 5

c. 5 4 3 2 1

d. 5 4 3 2 1 0

19. What does the following code segment display?

```
for(f = 0; f < 3; ++f);
    Console.Write("{0} ", f);
```

a. 0

b. 0 1 2

c. 3

d. nothing

20. What does the following code segment display?

```
for(t = 0; t < 3; ++t)
    Console.Write("{0} ", t);
```

a. 0

b. 0 1

c. 0 1 2

d. 0 1 2 3

## Exercises

1. Write a console-based application that allows the user to enter any number of integer values continuously (in any order) until the user enters 999. Display the sum of the values entered, not including 999. Save the file as **Sum.cs**.

2. Write a console-based application that asks the user to type a vowel from the keyboard. If the character entered is a vowel, display "OK"; if it is not a vowel, display an error message.

Be sure to allow both uppercase and lowercase vowels. The program continues until the user types '!'. Save the file as **GetVowel.cs**.

3. Write a console-based application that prompts a user for an hourly pay rate. While the user enters values less than $5.65 or greater than $49.99, continue to prompt the user. Before the program ends, display the valid pay rate. Save the program as **EnsureValidPayRateLoop.cs**.

4. Three salespeople work at Sunshine Hot Tubs—Andrea, Brittany, and Eric. Write a console-based application that prompts the user for a salesperson's initial ('A', 'B', or 'E'). While the user does not type 'Z', continue by prompting for the amount of a sale the salesperson made. Calculate the salesperson's commission as 10% of the sale amount, and add the commission to a running total for that salesperson. After the user types 'Z' for an initial, display each salesperson's total commission earned. Save the file as **TubSales.cs**.

5. a. Write a console-based application that displays a multiplication table of the product of every integer from 1 through 10 multiplied by every integer from 1 through 10. Save the file as **DisplayMultiplicationTable.cs**.

   b. Create a GUI application that displays the multiplication table when the user clicks a button. Save the project as **DisplayMultiplicationTableGUI**.

6. a. Write a console-based application that displays all even numbers from 2 to 100, inclusive. Save the file as **EvenNums.cs**.

   b. Create a GUI application that displays all the even numbers from 2 to 100 inclusive when the user clicks a button. Save the project as **EvenNumsGUI**.

7. a. Write a console-based application that displays every integer value from 1 to 20, along with its squared value. Save the file as **TableOfSquares.cs**.

   b. Create a GUI application that displays every integer from 1 to 20, along with its squared value when the user clicks a button. Save the project as **TableOfSquaresGUI**.

8. a. Write a console-based application that sums the integers from 1 to 50. Save the file as **Sum50.cs**.

   b. Create a GUI application that sums the integers from 1 to 50. Display the sum when the user clicks a button. Save the project as **Sum50GUI**.

9. a. Write a console-based application that displays every perfect number from 1 through 1000. A number is perfect if it equals the sum of all the smaller positive integers that divide evenly into it. For example, 6 is perfect because 1, 2, and 3 divide evenly into it and their sum is 6. Save the file as **Perfect.cs**.

   b. Create a GUI application that displays every perfect number from 1 through 1000 when the user clicks a button. Save the project as **PerfectGUI**.

10. a. In the "You Do It" section of this chapter, you created a tipping table for patrons to use when analyzing their restaurant bills. Modify the program so that each of the following values is obtained from user input:

   • The lowest tipping percentage

   • The highest tipping percentage

   • The lowest possible restaurant bill

   • The highest restaurant bill

   Save the file as **TippingTable2.cs**.

   b. Create a GUI application that creates a tipping table after the user clicks a button. Get the lowest and highest tipping percentages and the lowest and highest restaurant bills from TextBox entries. The application should look similar to Figure 5-24. Save the project as **TippingTable2GUI**.

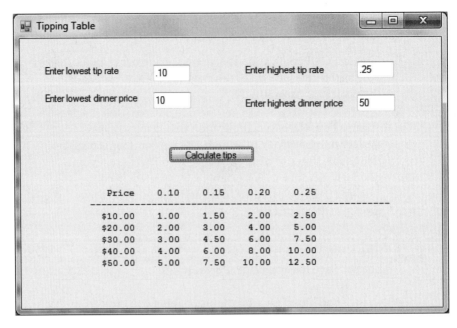

**Figure 5-24** Typical execution of TippingTable2GUI program

11. a. Write a console-based program that asks a user for a business name. Suggest a good Web address by adding "www." to the front of the name, removing all spaces from the name, and adding ".com" to the end of the name. For example, a good Web address for "Acme Plumbing and Supply" is www.AcmePlumbingandSupply.com. Save the file as **WebAddress.cs**.

   b. Create a GUI application that creates a Web address name from a business name, as described in Exercise 11a. Save the project as **WebAddressGUI**.

12. a. Write a console-based program that accepts a phrase from the user and counts the number of vowels in the phrase. For this exercise, count both uppercase and lowercase vowels, but do not consider "y" to be a vowel. Save the file as **CountVowels.cs**.

   b. Create a GUI application that does the same thing as Exercise 12a. Save the project as **CountVowelsGUI**.

13. a. In the chapter *Making Decisions*, you created a console-based program that generates a random number, allows a user to guess it, and displays a message indicating whether the guess is too low, too high, or correct. Now modify that program so that the user can continue to enter values

until the correct guess is made. After the user guesses correctly, display the number of guesses made. Save the file as **GuessingGame2.cs**.

Recall that you can generate a random number between min and max using the following statements:
```
Random ranNumberGenerator = new Random();
int randomNumber;
randomNumber = ranNumberGenerator.Next(min, max);
```

b. Modify the GuessingGame2 program so that the player is criticized for making a "dumb" guess. For example, if the player guesses that the random number is 4 and is told that the guess is too low, and then the player subsequently makes a guess lower than 4, display a message that the user should have known not to make such a low guess. Save the file as **GuessingGame3.cs**.

## Debugging Exercises

Each of the following files in the Chapter.05 folder of your downloadable student files has syntax and/or logical errors. In each case, determine the problem and fix the program. After you correct the errors, save each file using the same filename preceded with *Fixed*. For example, save DebugFive1.cs as **FixedDebugFive1.cs**.

    a. DebugFive1.cs

    b. DebugFive2.cs

    c. DebugFive3.cs

    d. DebugFive4.cs

## Up For Discussion

1. Suppose you wrote a program that you suspect is in an infinite loop because it keeps running for several minutes with no output and without ending. What would you add to your program to help you discover the origin of the problem?

2. Suppose that every employee in your organization has a seven-digit logon ID number for retrieving personal information, some of which might be sensitive in nature. For example, each employee has access to his own salary data and insurance claim information, but not to the information of others. Writing a loop would be useful to guess every combination of seven digits in an ID. Are there any circumstances in which you should try to guess another employee's ID number?

# Using Arrays

In this chapter you will:

◎ Declare an array and assign values to array elements

◎ Access array elements

◎ Search an array using a loop

◎ Use the `BinarySearch()`, `Sort()`, and `Reverse()` methods

◎ Use multidimensional arrays

◎ Learn about array issues in GUI programs

Storing values in variables provides programs with flexibility—a program that uses variables to replace constants can manipulate different values each time the program executes. When you add loops to your programs, the same variable can hold different values during successive cycles through the loop within the same program execution. This ability makes the program even more flexible. Learning to use the data structure known as an array offers further flexibility—you can store multiple values in adjacent memory locations and access them by varying a value that indicates which of the stored values to use. In this chapter, you will learn to create and manage C# arrays.

# Declaring an Array and Assigning Values to Array Elements

Sometimes, storing just one value in memory at a time is not adequate. For example, a sales manager who supervises 20 employees might want to determine whether each employee has produced sales above or below the average amount. When you enter the first employee's sales figure into a program, you cannot determine whether it is above or below average because you will not know the average until you have entered all 20 figures. You might plan to assign 20 sales figures to 20 separate variables, each with a unique name, then sum and average them. That process is awkward and unwieldy, however—you need 20 prompts, 20 input statements using 20 separate storage locations (in other words, 20 separate variable names), and 20 addition statements. This method might work for 20 salespeople, but what if you have 30, 40, or 10,000 salespeople?

A superior approach is to assign the sales value to the same variable in 20 successive iterations through a loop that contains one prompt, one input statement, and one addition statement. Unfortunately, when you enter the sales value for the second employee, that data item replaces the figure for the first employee, and the first employee's value is no longer available to compare to the average of all 20 values. With this approach, when the data-entry loop finishes, the only sales value left in memory is the last one entered.

The best solution to this problem is to create an array. An **array** is a list of data items that all have the same data type and the same name. Each object in an array is an **array element**. You can distinguish each element from the others in an array with a subscript. A **subscript** (also called an **index**) is an integer contained within square brackets that indicates the position of one of an array's elements.

You declare an array variable with a data type, a pair of square brackets, and an identifier. For example, to declare an array of `double` values to hold sales figures for salespeople, you write the following:

```
double[] sales;
```

In some programming languages, such as C++ and Java, you also can declare an array variable by placing the square brackets after the array name, as in `double sales[];`. This format is illegal in C#.

You can change the size of an array associated with an identifier, if necessary. For example, if you declare `int[] array;`, you can assign five elements later with `array = new int[5];;` later in the program, you might alter the array size to 100 with `array = new int[100];`. Still later, you could alter it again to be either larger or smaller. Most other programming languages do not provide this capability. If you resize an array in C#, the same identifier refers to a new array in memory and all the values are set to 0.

In C#, an array subscript must be an integer. For example, no array contains an element with a subscript of 1.5. A subscript can be an integer constant or variable or an expression that evaluates to an integer.

The first element in an array is sometimes called the "zeroth element."

After you create an array variable, you still need to create the actual array. Declaring an array and actually reserving memory space for it are two distinct processes. To reserve memory locations for 20 `sales` objects, you declare the array variable with the following two statements:

```
double[] sales;
sales = new double[20];
```

The keyword **new** is also known as the **new operator**; it is used to create objects. In this case, it creates 20 separate `sales`. You also can declare and create an array in one statement, such as the following:

```
double[] sales = new double[20];
```

The statement `double[] sales = new double[20];` reserves 20 memory locations. In C#, an array's elements are numbered beginning with 0, so if an array has 20 elements, you can use any subscript from 0 through 19. In other words, the first `sales` array element is `sales[0]` and the last `sales` element is `sales[19]`. Figure 6-1 shows how the array of 20 sales figures appears in computer memory. The figure assumes that the array begins at memory address 20000. Because a `double` takes eight bytes of storage, each element of the array is stored in succession at an address that is eight bytes higher than the previous one.

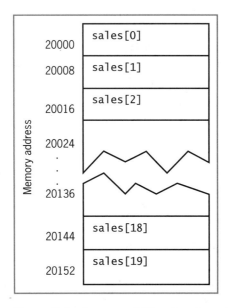

**Figure 6-1** An array of 20 `sales` items in memory

When you instantiate an array, you cannot choose its location in memory any more than you can choose the location of any other variable. However, you do know that after the first array element, the subsequent elements will follow immediately.

Some other languages, such as COBOL, BASIC, and Visual Basic, use parentheses rather than square brackets to refer to individual array elements. By using brackets, the creators of C# made it easier for you to distinguish arrays from methods. Like C#, C++ and Java also use brackets surrounding array subscripts.

A common mistake is to forget that the first element in an array is element 0, especially if you know another programming language in which the first array element is element 1. Making this mistake means you will be "off by one" in your use of any array. If you are "off by one" but still using a valid subscript when accessing an array element, your program will produce incorrect output. If you are "off by one" so that your subscript becomes larger than the highest value allowed, you will cause a program error.

When you work with any individual array element, you treat it no differently than you treat a single variable of the same type. For example, to assign a value to the first `sales` in an array, you use a simple assignment statement, such as the following:

```
sales[0] = 2100.00;
```

To output the value of the last `sales` in a 20-element array, you write:

```
Console.WriteLine(sales[19]);
```

## Initializing an Array

In C#, arrays are objects. When you instantiate an array, you are creating a specific instance of a class that derives from, or builds upon, the built-in class named `System.Array`. When you declare arrays or any other objects, the following are default values:

- Numeric fields are set to 0.

- Character fields are set to '\u0000' or `null`.

- `bool` fields are set to `false`.

For example, when you declare an array of five `int`s, each of the elements is initialized to 0.

You can assign nondefault values to array elements upon creation by declaring a comma-separated list of values enclosed within curly braces. For example, if you want to create an array named `myScores` and store five test scores within the array, you can use any of the following declarations:

```
int[] myScores = new int[5] {100, 76, 88, 100, 90};
int[] myScores = new int[] {100, 76, 88, 100, 90};
int[] myScores = {100, 76, 88, 100, 90};
```

To remember that array elements begin with element 0, it might be helpful to think of the first array element as being "zero elements away from" the beginning of the array, the second element as being "one element away from" the beginning of the array, and so on.

235

An array subscript can be an expression, as long as the expression evaluates to an integer. For example, if x and y are integers and their sum is at least 0 but less than the size of an array named `array`, then it is legal to refer to `array[x + y]`.

Watch the video *Declaring Arrays.*

You learned about the notation '\u0000' in Chapter 2.

In the chapter *Introduction to Inheritance* you will learn more about deriving classes.

You first learned the term *instance* to refer to an object in Chapter 1. You will understand instances more thoroughly after you complete the chapter *Using Classes and Objects*.

When you use curly braces at the end of a block of code, you do not follow the closing curly brace with a semicolon. However, when you use curly braces to enclose a list of array values, you must complete the statement with a semicolon.

The list of values provided for an array is an **initializer list**. When you initialize an array by providing a size and an initializer list, as in the first example, the stated size and number of list elements must match. However, when you initialize an array with values, you are not required to give the array a size, as shown in the second example; in that case, the size is assigned based on the number of values in the initializing list. The third example shows that when you initialize an array, you do not need to use the keyword **new** and repeat the type; instead, memory is assigned based on the stated array type and the length of the list of provided values. Of these three examples, the first is most explicit, but it requires two changes if the number of elements is altered. The third example requires the least typing, but might not clarify that a new object is being created. Use the form of array initialization that is clearest to you or that is conventional in your organization.

Programmers who have used other languages such as C++ and Java might expect that when an initialization list is shorter than the number of declared array elements, the "extra" elements will be set to default values. This is not the case in C#; if you declare a size, then you must list a value for each element.

An array of characters can be assigned to a string. For example, you can write the following:

```
char[] arrayOfLetters = {'h', 'e', 'l', 'l', 'o'};
string word = new string(arrayOfLetters);
```

## TWO TRUTHS & A LIE

### Declaring an Array and Assigning Values to Array Elements

1. To reserve memory locations for ten `testScore` objects, you can use the following statement:

   ```
   int[] testScore = new int[9];
   ```

2. To assign 60 to the last element in a 10-element array named `testScore`, you can use the following statement:

   ```
   testScore[9] = 60;
   ```

3. The following statement creates an array named `purchases` and stores four values within the array:

   ```
   double[] purchases = new double[] {23.55, 99.20, 4.67, 9.99};
   ```

The false statement is #1. To reserve memory locations for ten `testScore` objects, you must use ten within the second set of square braces. The ten elements will use the subscripts 0 through 9.

236

## Accessing Array Elements

If you treat each array element as an individual entity, declaring an array does not offer much of an advantage over declaring individual variables. The power of arrays becomes apparent when you use subscripts that are variables rather than constant values.

For example, when you declare an array of five integers, such as the following, you often want to perform the same operation on each array element:

```
int[] myScores = {100, 76, 88, 100, 90};
```

To increase each array element by 3, for example, you can write the following five statements:

```
myScores[0] += 3;
myScores[1] += 3;
myScores[2] += 3;
myScores[3] += 3;
myScores[4] += 3;
```

You can shorten the task by using a variable as a subscript. Then you can use a loop to perform arithmetic on each element in the array. For example, you can use a `while` loop, as follows:

```
int sub = 0;
while(sub < 5)
{
    myScores[sub] += 3;
    ++sub;
}
```

You also can use a `for` loop, as follows:

```
for(int sub = 0; sub < 5; ++sub)
    myScores[sub] += 3;
```

In both examples, the variable `sub` is declared and initialized to 0, then compared to 5. Because it is less than 5, the loop executes and `myScores[0]` increases by 3. The variable `sub` is incremented and becomes 1, which is still less than 5, so when the loop executes again, `myScores[1]` increases by 3, and so on. If the array had 100 elements, individually increasing the array values by 3 would require 95 additional statements, but the only change required using either loop would be to change the limiting value for `sub` from 5 to 100.

New array users sometimes think there is a permanent connection between a variable used as a subscript and the array with which it is used, but that is not the case. For example, if you vary `sub` from 0 to 10 to fill an array, you do not need to use `sub` later when displaying the array elements—either the same variable or a different variable can be used as a subscript elsewhere in the program.

## Using the Length Property

When you work with array elements, you must ensure that the subscript you use remains in the range of 0 through one less than the array's length. If you declare an array with five elements and use a subscript that is negative or more than 4, you will receive the error message "IndexOutOfRangeException" when you run the program. This message means the index, or subscript, does not hold a value that legally can access an array element. For example, if you declare an array of five integers, you can display them as follows:

```
int[] myScores = {100, 75, 88, 100, 90};
for(int sub = 0; sub < 5; ++sub)
    Console.WriteLine("{0} ", myScores[sub]);
```

 You will learn about the `IndexOutOfRangeException` in the chapter *Exception Handling*.

 An array's `Length` is a read-only property—you cannot assign it a new value. It is capitalized, like all property identifiers. You will create property identifiers for your own classes in the chapter *Using Classes and Objects*.

 In C#, every string also has a built-in `Length` property. For example, if you declare `string firstName = "Chloe"`, then `firstName.Length` is 5.

If you modify your program to change the size of the array, you must remember to change the comparison in the `for` loop as well as every other reference to the array size within the program. Many text editors have a "find and replace" feature that lets you change (for example) all of the 5s in a file, either simultaneously or one by one. However, you must be careful not to change 5s that have nothing to do with the array; for example, do not change the 5 in the score 75 inadvertently—it is the second listed value in the `myScores` array and has nothing to do with the array size.

A better approach is to use a value that is automatically altered when you declare an array. Because every array automatically derives from the class **System.Array**, you can use the fields and methods that are part of the System.Array class with any array you create. The **Length property** is a member of the System.Array class that automatically holds an array's length and is always updated to reflect any changes you make to an array's size. The following segment of code displays "Array size is 5" and subsequently displays the array's contents:

```
int[] myScores = {100, 76, 88, 100, 90};
Console.WriteLine("Array size is {0}", myScores.Length);
for(int x = 0; x < myScores.Length; ++x)
    Console.WriteLine(myScores[x]);
```

## Using `foreach`

You can easily navigate through arrays using a `for` or `while` loop that varies a subscript from 0 through `Array.Length` - 1. C# also supports a **foreach statement** that you can use to cycle through every array element without using a subscript. With the `foreach` statement, you provide a temporary **iteration variable** that automatically holds each array value in turn.

For example, the following code displays each element in the `payRate` array in sequence:

```
double[] payRate = {6.00, 7.35, 8.12, 12.45, 22.22};
foreach(double money in payRate)
   Console.WriteLine("{0}", money.ToString("C"));
```

The variable money is declared as a double within the foreach statement. During the execution of the loop, money holds each payRate
value in turn—first, payRate[0], then payRate[1], and so on. As a
simple variable, money does not require a subscript, making it easier
to work with.

The foreach statement is used only under certain circumstances:

- You typically use foreach only when you want to access every
  array element; to access only selected array elements, you must
  manipulate subscripts using some other technique—for example,
  using a for loop or while loop.

- The foreach iteration variable is read-only—that is, you cannot
  assign a value to it. If you want to assign a value to array elements,
  you must use a different type of loop.

## Using foreach with Enumerations

The foreach statement can provide a convenient way to display
enumeration values. For example, Figure 6-2 shows a program that
contains an enumeration for days of the week, and Figure 6-3 shows
the output. The foreach block in the Main() method gets and displays
each string in the enumeration using the GetNames() method that is
built into the Enum class. You will learn more about built-in classes and
methods in the coming chapters, but for now you can use the format
shown in Figure 6-2 to conveniently work with enumeration values.

```
using System;
public class DemoForEachWithEnum
{
   enum Day
   {
      SUNDAY, MONDAY, TUESDAY, WEDNESDAY,
         THURSDAY, FRIDAY, SATURDAY
   }
   public static void Main()
   {
      foreach(string day in Enum.GetNames(typeof(Day)))
         Console.WriteLine(day);
   }
}
```

**Figure 6-2**   DemoForEachWithEnum program

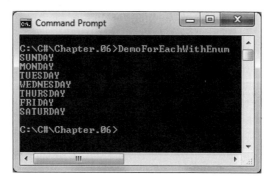

**Figure 6-3**  Output of DemoForEachWithEnum program

## TWO TRUTHS & A LIE

### Accessing Array Elements

1.  Assume you have declared an array of six doubles named balances. The following statement displays all the elements:

    ```
    for(int index = 0; index < 6; ++index)
        Console.WriteLine(balances[index]);
    ```

2.  Assume you have declared an array of eight doubles named prices. The following statement subtracts 2 from each element:

    ```
    for(double pr = 0; pr < 8; ++pr)
        prices[pr] -= 2;
    ```

3.  The following code displays 3:

    ```
    int[] array = {1, 2, 3};
    Console.WriteLine(array.Length);
    ```

The false statement is #2. You can only use an int as the subscript to an array, and this example attempts to use a double.

## Searching an Array Using a Loop

When you want to determine whether a variable holds one of many possible valid values, one option is to use if statements to compare the variable to valid values. For example, suppose that a company manufactures ten items. When a customer places an order for an item, you need to determine whether the item number is valid. If valid item numbers are sequential, say 101 through 110, then the following simple if statement that uses a logical AND operator can verify the order number and set a Boolean field to true:

```
if(itemOrdered >= 101 && itemOrdered <= 110)
   isValidItem = true;
```

If the valid item numbers are nonsequential, however—for example, 101, 108, 201, 213, 266, 304, and so on—you must code the following deeply nested if statement or a lengthy OR comparison to determine the validity of an item number:

```
if(itemOrdered == 101)
   isValidItem = true;
else if(itemOrdered == 108)
   isValidItem = true;
else if(itemOrdered == 201)
   isValidItem = true;
// and so on
```

## Using a `for` Loop to Search an Array

Instead of creating a long series of if statements, a more elegant solution is to compare the itemOrdered variable to a list of values in an array. You can initialize the array with the valid values by using the following statement:

```
int[] validValues = {101, 108, 201, 213, 266, 304, 311,
   409, 411, 412};
```

Next, you can use a for statement to loop through the array and set a Boolean variable to true when a match is found:

```
for(int x = 0; x < validValues.Length; ++x)
   if(itemOrdered == validValues[x])
      isValidItem = true;
```

This simple for loop replaces the long series of if statements. What's more, if a company carries 1000 items instead of ten, then the list of valid items in the array must be altered, but the for statement does not change at all. As an added bonus, if you set up another array as a **parallel array** with the same number of elements and corresponding data, you can use the same subscript to access additional information. For example, if the ten items your company carries have ten different prices, then you can set up an array to hold those prices as follows:

```
double[] prices = {0.89, 1.23, 3.50, 0.69...}; // and so on
```

The prices must appear in the same order as their corresponding item numbers in the validValues array. Now the same for loop that finds the valid item number also finds the price, as shown in the program in Figure 6-4. In other words, if the item number is found in the second position in the validValues array, then you can find the correct price in the second position in the prices array. In the program in Figure 6-4, the variable used as a subscript, x, is set to 0 and

You might prefer to declare the validValues array as a constant because, presumably, the valid item numbers should not change during program execution. In C#, you must use the keywords static and readonly prior to the constant declaration. To keep these examples simple, all arrays in this chapter are declared as variable arrays.

In place of the for loop, you could use a foreach loop. You also could use a while loop, but for and foreach loops are used more commonly with arrays.

This type of search is called a **sequential search** because each array element is examined in sequence.

If you initialize parallel arrays, it is convenient to use spacing so that the corresponding values visually align on the screen or printed page.

the Boolean variable isValidItem is false. In the shaded portion of the figure, while the subscript remains smaller than the length of the array of valid item numbers, the subscript is continuously increased so that subsequent array values can be tested. When a match is found between the user's item and an item in the array, isValidItem is set to true and the price of the item is stored in itemPrice. Figure 6-5 shows two typical program executions.

In the fourth statement of the Main() method in Figure 6-4, itemPrice is set to 0. Setting this variable is required because its value is later altered only if an item number match is found in the validValues array. When C# determines that a variable's value is only set depending on an if statement, C# will not allow you to display the variable, because the compiler assumes the variable might not have been set to a valid value.

```csharp
using System;
public class FindPriceWithForLoop
{
    public static void Main()
    {
        int[] validValues = {101, 108, 201, 213, 266,
            304, 311, 409, 411, 412};
        double[] prices = {0.89, 1.23, 3.50, 0.69, 5.79,
            3.19, 0.99, 0.89, 1.26, 8.00};
        int itemOrdered;
        double itemPrice = 0;
        bool isValidItem = false;
        Console.Write("Please enter an item ");
        itemOrdered = Convert.ToInt32(Console.ReadLine());
        for(int x = 0; x < validValues.Length; ++x)
        {
            if(itemOrdered == validValues[x])
            {
                isValidItem = true;
                itemPrice = prices[x];
            }
        }
        if(isValidItem)
            Console.WriteLine("Price is {0}", itemPrice);
        else
            Console.WriteLine("Sorry - item not found");
    }
}
```

**Figure 6-4** The FindPriceWithForLoop program

In an array with many possible matches to a search value, the most efficient strategy is to place the most common items first so they are matched right away. For example, if item 311 is ordered most often, place 311 first in the validValues array and its price ($0.99) first in the prices array.

**Figure 6-5** Two typical executions of the FindPriceWithForLoop program

Within the code shown in Figure 6-4, you compare every
itemOrdered with each of the ten validValues. Even when an
itemOrdered is equivalent to the first value in the validValues array
(101), you always make nine additional cycles through the array. On
each of these nine additional iterations, the comparison between
itemOrdered and validValues[x] is always false. As soon as a
match for an itemOrdered is found, the most efficient action is to
break out of the for loop early. An easy way to accomplish this task is
to set x to a high value within the block of statements executed when
a match is found. Then, after a match, the for loop will not execute
again because the limiting comparison (x < validValues.Length)
will have been surpassed. The following code shows this approach.

```
for(int x = 0; x < validValues.Length; ++x)
{
    if(itemOrdered == validValues[x])
    {
        isValidItem = true;
        itemPrice = prices[x];
        x = validValues.Length;
            // break out of loop when you find a match
    }
}
```

Instead of the statement that sets x to validValues.Length when
a match is found, you could remove that statement and change
the comparison in the middle section of the for statement to a
compound statement, as follows:

```
for(int x = 0; x < validValues.Length && !isValidItem; ++x)...
```

As another alternative, you could remove the statement that sets x to
validValues.Length and place a break statement within the loop in
its place. Some programmers disapprove of exiting a for loop early,
whether by setting a variable's value or by using a break statement.
They argue that programs are easier to debug and maintain if each
program segment has only one entry and one exit point. If you (or
your instructor) agree with this philosophy, then you can select an
approach that uses a while statement, as described next.

Although
parallel arrays
can be very
useful, they
also can
increase the likelihood of
mistakes. Any time you
make a change to one
array, you must
remember to make the
corresponding change in
its parallel array. As you
continue to study C#, you
will learn superior ways
to correlate data items.
For example, in the
chapter *Using Classes
and Objects* you will learn
that you can encapsulate
corresponding data items
in objects and create
arrays of objects.

## Using a while Loop to Search an Array

As an alternative to using a for or foreach loop to search an array,
you can use a while loop to search for a match. Using this approach,
you set a subscript to 0 and, while the itemOrdered is not equal to a
value in the array, increase the subscript and keep looking. You search
only while the subscript remains lower than the number of elements
in the array. If the subscript increases to match validValues.Length,
then you never found a match in the ten-element array. If the loop

ends before the subscript reaches validValues.Length, then you found a match and the correct price can be assigned to the itemPrice variable. Figure 6-6 shows a program that uses this approach.

```
using System;
public class FindPriceWithWhileLoop
{
    public static void Main()
    {
        int x;
        string inputString;
        int itemOrdered;
        double itemPrice = 0;
        bool isValidItem = false;
        int[] validValues = {101, 108, 201, 213, 266,
            304, 311, 409, 411, 412};
        double[] prices = {0.89, 1.23, 3.50, 0.69, 5.79,
            3.19, 0.99, 0.89, 1.26, 8.00};
        Console.Write("Enter item number ");
        inputString = Console.ReadLine();
        itemOrdered = Convert.ToInt32(inputString);
        x = 0;
        while(x < validValues.Length &&
            itemOrdered != validValues[x])
              ++x;
        if(x != validValues.Length)
        {
            isValidItem = true;
            itemPrice = prices[x];
        }
        if(isValidItem)
            Console.WriteLine("Item {0} sells for {1}",
                itemOrdered, itemPrice.ToString("C"));
        else
            Console.WriteLine("No such item as {0}",
                itemOrdered);
    }
}
```

**Figure 6-6** The FindPriceWithWhileLoop program that searches with a while loop

In the application in Figure 6-6, the variable used as a subscript, x, is set to 0 and the Boolean variable isValidItem is false. In the shaded portion of the figure, while the subscript remains smaller than the length of the array of valid item numbers, and while the user's requested item does not match a valid item, the subscript is increased so that subsequent array values can be tested. The while loop ends when a match is found or the array tests have been exhausted, which-ever comes first. When the loop ends, if x is not equal to the size of the array, then a valid item has been found and its price can be retrieved from the prices array. Figure 6-7 shows two executions of the program. In the first execution, a match is found; in the second, an invalid item number is entered, so no match is found.

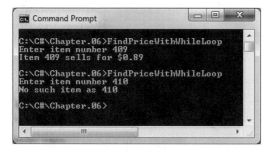

```
C:\C#\Chapter.06>FindPriceWithWhileLoop
Enter item number 409
Item 409 sells for $0.89

C:\C#\Chapter.06>FindPriceWithWhileLoop
Enter item number 410
No such item as 410

C:\C#\Chapter.06>
```

**Figure 6-7**    Two executions of the FindPriceWithWhileLoop application

Watch the video *Searching an Array.*

## Searching an Array for a Range Match

Searching an array for an exact match is not always practical. For example, suppose your mail-order company gives customer discounts based on the quantity of items ordered. Perhaps no discount is given for any order of up to a dozen items, but increasing discounts are available for orders of increasing quantities, as shown in Figure 6-8.

| Total Quantity Ordered | Discount (%) |
|---|---|
| 1 to 12 | None |
| 13 to 49 | 10 |
| 50 to 99 | 14 |
| 100 to 199 | 18 |
| 200 or more | 20 |

**Figure 6-8**    Discount table for a mail-order company

One awkward, impractical option is to create a single array to store the discount rates. You could use a variable named numOfItems as a subscript to the array, but the array would need hundreds of entries, such as the following:

```
double[] discount = {0, 0, 0, 0, 0, 0, 0, 0, 0, 0,
    0, 0, 0, 0.10, 0.10, 0.10 ...}; // and so on
```

When numOfItems is 3, for example, then discount[numOfItems] or discount[3] is 0. When numOfItems is 14, then discount[numOfItems] or discount[14] is 0.10. Because a customer might order thousands of items, the array would need to be ridiculously large.

Notice that 13 zeroes are listed in the discount array in this example. The first array element has a 0 subscript (and a 0 discount for 0 items). The next 12 discounts (1 through 12 items) also have 0 discounts.

A better option is to create parallel arrays. One array will hold the five discount rates, and the other array will hold five discount range limits. Then you can perform a **range match** by determining the pair of limiting values between which a customer's order falls. The Total Quantity Ordered column in Figure 6-8 shows five ranges. If you use only the first figure in each range, then you can create an array that holds five low limits:

```
int[] discountRangeLowLimit = {1, 13, 50, 100, 200};
```

A parallel array will hold the five discount rates:

```
double[] discount = {0, 0.10, 0.14, 0.18, 0.20};
```

Then, starting at the last discountRangeLowLimit array element, for any numOfItems greater than or equal to discountRangeLowLimit[4], the appropriate discount is discount[4]. In other words, for any numOfItems less than discountRangeLowLimit[4], you should decrement the subscript and look in a lower range. Figure 6-9 shows the code.

In the search in Figure 6-9, one less than the Length property of either array could have been used to initialize sub.

```
// assume numOfItems is a declared integer for which a user
// has input a value
int[] discountRangeLowLimit = {1, 13, 50, 100, 200};
double[] discount =            {0, 0.10, 0.14, 0.18, 0.20};
double customerDiscount;
int sub = discountRangeLowLimit.Length - 1;
while(sub >= 0 && numOfItems < discountRangeLowLimit[sub])
    --sub;
customerDiscount = discount[sub];
```

**Figure 6-9**    Searching an array of range limits

As an alternate approach to the range-checking logic in Figure 6-9, you can choose to create an array that contains the upper limit of each range, such as the following:

```
int[] discountRangeUpperLimit = {12, 49, 99, 199, 9999999};
```

Then the logic can be written to compare numOfItems to each range limit until the correct range is located, as follows:

```
int sub = 0;
while(sub < discountRangeUpperLimit.Length && numOfItems >
    discountRangeUpperLimit[sub])
    ++sub;
customerDiscount = discount[sub];
```

In this example, sub is initialized to 0. While it remains within array bounds, and while numOfItems is more than each upper-range limit, sub is increased. In other words, if numOfItems is 3, the while expression is false on the first loop iteration, the loop ends, sub remains 0, and the customer discount is the first discount. However, if numOfItems is 30, then the while expression is true on the first loop iteration, sub becomes 1, the while expression is false on the second iteration, and the second discount is used. In this example, the last discountRangeUpperLimit array value is 9999999. This very high value was used with the assumption that no numOfItems would ever exceed it. As with many issues in programming, multiple correct approaches frequently exist for the same problem.

---

## TWO TRUTHS & A LIE

### Searching an Array Using a Loop

1. A parallel array has the same number of elements as another array, and corresponding data.

2. When you search an array for an exact match in a parallel array, you must perform a loop as many times as there are elements in the arrays.

3. One practical solution to creating an array with which to perform a range check is to design the array to hold the lowest value in each range.

The false statement is #2. When you search an array for an exact match in a parallel array, you can perform a loop as many times as there are elements in the arrays, but once a match is found, the additional loop iterations are unnecessary. It is most efficient to terminate the loop cycles as soon as a match is found.

---

# Using the BinarySearch(), Sort(), and Reverse() Methods

You have already learned that because every array in C# is derived from the System.Array class, you can use the Length property. Additionally, the System.Array class contains a variety of useful, built-in methods that can search, sort, and manipulate array elements.

You already have used many built-in C# methods such as WriteLine() and ReadLine(). You will learn to write your own methods in the next chapter.

## Using the BinarySearch() Method

The **BinarySearch() method** finds a requested value in a sorted array. Instead of employing the logic you used to find a match in the last section, you can take advantage of this built-in method to locate a value within an array, as long as the array items are organized in ascending order.

A binary search is one in which a sorted list of objects is split in half repeatedly as the search gets closer and closer to a match. Perhaps you have played a guessing game, trying to guess a number from 1 to 100. If you asked, "Is it less than 50?," then continued to narrow your guesses upon hearing each subsequent answer, you have performed a binary search.

Figure 6-10 shows a program that declares an array of integer idNumbers arranged in ascending order. The program prompts a user for a value, converts it to an integer, and, rather than using a loop to examine each array element and compare it to the entered value, simply passes the array and the entered value to the BinarySearch() method in the shaded statement. The method returns −1 if the value is not found in the array; otherwise, it returns the array position of the sought value. Figure 6-11 shows two executions of this program.

The BinarySearch() method takes two arguments—the array name and the value for which to search. In Chapter 1, you learned that arguments represent information that a method needs to perform its task. When methods require multiple arguments, they are separated by commas. For example, when you have used the Console.WriteLine() method, you have passed a format string and values to be displayed, all separated by commas.

```
using System;
public class BinarySearchDemo
{
    public static void Main()
    {
        int[] idNumbers = {122, 167, 204, 219, 345};
        int x;
        string entryString;
        int entryId;
        Console.Write("Enter an Employee ID ");
        entryString = Console.ReadLine();
        entryId = Convert.ToInt32(entryString);
        x = Array.BinarySearch(idNumbers, entryId);
        if(x < 0)
            Console.WriteLine("ID {0} not found", entryId);
        else
            Console.WriteLine("ID {0} found at position {1} ",
                entryId, x);
    }
}
```
These values must be sorted in ascending order for the BinarySearch() method to work correctly.

Figure 6-10   BinarySearchDemo program

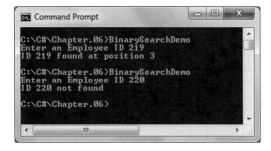

Figure 6-11   Two executions of the BinarySearchDemo program

When you use the following statement, you send a string to the
`Write()` method:

```
Console.Write("Enter an Employee ID ");
```

When you use the following statement, you get a value back from the
`ReadLine()` method:

```
entryString = Console.ReadLine();
```

In Figure 6-10, the following single statement both sends a value to a
method and gets a value back:

```
x = Array.BinarySearch(idNumbers, entryId);
```

The statement calls the method that performs the search, returning a −1 or the position where `entryId` was found; that value is then
stored in x. This single line of code is easier to write, less prone to
error, and easier to understand than writing a loop to cycle through
the `idNumbers` array looking for a match. Still, it is worthwhile to
understand how to perform the search without the `BinarySearch()`
method, as you learned while studying parallel arrays. You will need
to use that technique under the following conditions, when the
`BinarySearch()` method proves inadequate:

- If your array items are not arranged in ascending order, the
  `BinarySearch()` method does not work correctly.

- If your array holds duplicate values and you want to find all of
  them, the `BinarySearch()` method does not work—it can return
  only one value, so it returns the position of the first matching value
  it finds (which is not necessarily the first instance of the value in
  the array).

- If you want to find a range match rather than an exact match, the
  `BinarySearch()` method does not work.

## Using the `Sort()` Method

The **`Sort()` method** arranges array items in ascending order.
Ascending order is lowest to highest; it works numerically for number types and alphabetically for characters and strings. To use the
method, you pass the array name to `Array.Sort()`, and the element
positions within the array are rearranged appropriately. Figure 6-12
shows a program that sorts an array of strings; Figure 6-13 shows
its execution.

```
using System;
public class SortArray
{
    public static void Main()
    {
        string[] names = {"Olive", "Patty",
            "Richard", "Ned", "Mindy"};
        int x;
        Array.Sort(names);
        for(x = 0; x < names.Length; ++x)
            Console.WriteLine(names[x]);
    }
}
```

**Figure 6-12** SortArray program

The Array.Sort() method provides a good example of encapsulation—you can use the method without understanding how it works internally. The method actually uses an algorithm named Quicksort. You will learn how to implement this algorithm yourself as you continue to study programming.

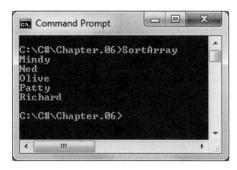

**Figure 6-13** Execution of SortArray program

Because the BinarySearch() method requires that array elements be sorted in order, the Sort() method is often used in conjunction with it.

## Using the Reverse() Method

The **Reverse() method** reverses the order of items in an array. In other words, for any array, the element that starts in position 0 is relocated to position Length – 1, the element that starts in position 1 is relocated to position Length – 2, and so on until the element that starts in position Length – 1 is relocated to position 0. You call the Reverse() method the same way you call the Sort() method—you simply pass the array name to the method. Figure 6-14 shows a program that uses Reverse() with an array of strings, and Figure 6-15 shows its execution.

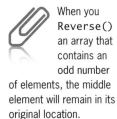

When you Reverse() an array that contains an odd number of elements, the middle element will remain in its original location.

```
using System;
public class ReverseArray
{
    public static void Main()
    {
        string[] names = {"Zach", "Rose", "Wendy", "Marcia"};
        int x;
        Array.Reverse(names);
        for(x = 0; x < names.Length; ++x)
            Console.WriteLine(names[x]);
    }
}
```

The `Reverse()` method does not sort array elements; it only rearranges their positions to the opposite order.

251

**Figure 6-14**  ReverseArray program

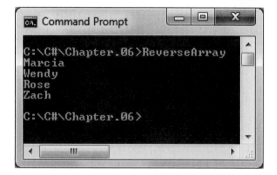

```
Command Prompt

C:\C#\Chapter.06>ReverseArray
Marcia
Wendy
Rose
Zach

C:\C#\Chapter.06>
```

**Figure 6-15**  Execution of ReverseArray program

## TWO TRUTHS & A LIE

### Using the BinarySearch(), Sort(), and Reverse() Methods

1.  When you use the `BinarySearch()` method with an array, the array items must first be organized in ascending order.

2.  The `Array.Sort()` and `Array.Reverse()` methods are similar in that both require a single argument.

3.  The `Array.Sort()` and `Array.Reverse()` methods are different in that one places items in ascending order and the other places them in descending order.

The false statement is #3. The Array.Sort() method places items in ascending order, but the Array.Reverse() method simply reverses the existing order of any array whether it was presorted or not.

# Using Multidimensional Arrays

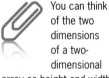

You can think of the single dimension of a single-dimensional array as the height of the array.

When you declare an array such as double[] sales = new double[20];, you can envision the declared integers as a column of numbers in memory, as shown at the beginning of this chapter in Figure 6-1. In other words, you can picture the 20 declared numbers stacked one on top of the next. An array that you can picture as a column of values, and whose elements you can access using a single subscript, is a **one-dimensional** or **single-dimensional array**.

C# also supports **multidimensional arrays**—those that require multiple subscripts to access the array elements. The most commonly used multidimensional arrays are two-dimensional arrays that are rectangular. **Two-dimensional arrays** have two or more columns of values for each row, as shown in Figure 6-16. In a **rectangular array**, each row has the same number of columns. You must use two subscripts when you access an element in a two-dimensional array. When mathematicians use a two-dimensional array, they often call it a **matrix** or a **table**; you might have used a two-dimensional array called a spreadsheet.

| sales[0, 0] | sales[0, 1] | sales[0, 2] | sales[0, 3] |
| sales[1, 0] | sales[1, 1] | sales[1, 2] | sales[1, 3] |
| sales[2, 0] | sales[2, 1] | sales[2, 2] | sales[2, 3] |

**Figure 6-16** View of a rectangular, two-dimensional array in memory

You can think of the two dimensions of a two-dimensional array as height and width.

A sales array with two dimensions, as shown in Figure 6-16, could have several uses. For example, each row could represent a category of items sold and each column could represent a salesperson who sold them.

When you declare a one-dimensional array, you type a single, empty set of square brackets after the array type, and you use a single subscript in a set of square brackets when reserving memory. To declare a two-dimensional array, you type a comma in the square brackets after the array type, and you use two subscripts, separated by a comma in brackets, when reserving memory. For example, the array in Figure 6-16 can be declared as the following, creating an array named sales that holds three rows and four columns:

When you declare a two-dimensional array, spaces surrounding the comma within the square brackets are optional.

double[ , ]sales = new double[3, 4];

Just as with a one-dimensional array, if you do not provide values for the elements in a two-dimensional numerical array, the values are set to the default value for the data type (zero for numeric data). You can assign other values to the array elements later. For example, the following statement assigns the value 14.00 to the element of the `sales` array that is in the first column of the first row:

```
sales[0, 0] = 14.00;
```

Alternatively, you can initialize a two-dimensional array with values when it is created. For example, the following code assigns values to `sales` when it is created:

```
double[ , ] sales = {{14.00, 15.00, 16.00, 17.00},
                     {21.99, 34.55, 67.88, 31.99},
                     {12.03, 55.55, 32.89, 1.17}};
```

The `sales` array contains three rows and four columns. You contain the entire set of values within a pair of curly braces. The first row of the array holds the four `doubles` 14.00, 15.00, 16.00, and 17.00. Notice that these four values are placed within their own inner set of curly braces to indicate that they constitute one row, or the first row, which is row 0. Similarly, the next four values make up the second row (row 1), which you reference with the subscript 1. The value of `sales[0, 0]` is 14.00. The value of `sales[0, 1]` is 15.00. The value of `sales[2, 3]` is 1.17. The first value within the brackets following the array name always refers to the row; the second value, after the comma, refers to the column.

You do not need to place each row of values that initializes a two-dimensional array on its own line. However, doing so makes the positions of values easier to understand.

As an example of how useful two-dimensional arrays can be, assume you own an apartment building with four floors—a basement, which you refer to as floor zero, and three other floors numbered one, two, and three. In addition, each of the floors has studio (with no bedroom), one-, and two-bedroom apartments. The monthly rent for each type of apartment is different, and the rent is higher for apartments with more bedrooms. Figure 6-17 shows the rental amounts.

| Floor | Zero Bedrooms | One Bedroom | Two Bedrooms |
| --- | --- | --- | --- |
| 0 | 400 | 450 | 510 |
| 1 | 500 | 560 | 630 |
| 2 | 625 | 676 | 740 |
| 3 | 1000 | 1250 | 1600 |

**Figure 6-17**  Rents charged (in dollars)

To determine a tenant's rent, you need to know two pieces of information: the floor on which the tenant rents an apartment and the number of bedrooms in the apartment. Within a C# program, you can declare an array of rents using the following code:

```
int[ , ] rents = { {400, 450, 510},
                   {500, 560, 630},
                   {625, 676, 740},
                   {1000, 1250, 1600} };
```

Assume you declare two integers to hold the floor number and bedroom count, as in the following statement:

```
int floor, bedrooms;
```

Then any tenant's rent can be referred to as `rents[floor, bedrooms]`.

Figure 6-18 shows a complete program that uses a rectangular, two-dimensional array to hold rent values. Figure 6-19 shows a typical execution.

```
using System;
public class RentFinder
{
    public static void Main()
    {
        int[ , ] rents = { {400, 450, 510},
                           {500, 560, 630},
                           {625, 676, 740},
                           {1000, 1250, 1600} };
        int floor;
        int bedrooms;
        string inputString;
        Console.Write("Enter the floor on which you want to live ");
        inputString = Console.ReadLine();
        floor = Convert.ToInt32(inputString);
        Console.Write("Enter the number of bedrooms you need ");
        inputString = Console.ReadLine();
        bedrooms = Convert.ToInt32(inputString);
        Console.WriteLine("The rent is {0}",
            rents[floor, bedrooms]);
    }
}
```

**Figure 6-18**   The RentFinder program

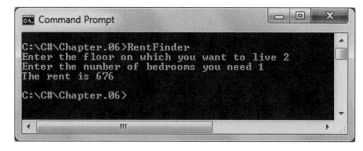

 Watch the video *Using a Two-Dimensional Array.*

**Figure 6-19**   Typical execution of the RentFinder program

C# supports arrays with more than two dimensions. For example, if you own a multistory apartment building with different numbers of bedrooms available in apartments on each floor, you can use a two-dimensional array to store the rental fees. If you own several apartment buildings, you might want to employ a third dimension to store the building number. Suppose you want to store rents for four buildings that have three floors each and that each hold two types of apartments. Figure 6-20 shows how you might define such an array.

```
int[ , , ] rents = { { {400, 500}, {450, 550}, {500, 550}},
                     { {510, 610}, {710, 810}, {910, 1010}},
                     { {525, 625}, {725, 825}, {925, 1025}},
                     { {850, 950}, {1050, 1150}, {1250, 1350}}};
```

**Figure 6-20** A three-dimensional array definition

The empty brackets that follow the data type contain two commas, showing that the array supports three dimensions. A set of curly braces surrounds all the data. Four inner sets of braces surround the data for each floor. In this example, each row of values represents a building (0 through 3). Then 12 sets of innermost brackets surround the values for each floor—first a zero-bedroom apartment and then a one-bedroom apartment.

Using the three-dimensional array in Figure 6-20, an expression such as rents[building, floor, bedrooms] refers to a specific rent figure for a building whose number is stored in the building variable and whose floor and bedroom numbers are stored in the floor and bedrooms variables. Specifically, rents[3, 1, 0] refers to a studio (zero-bedroom) apartment on the first floor of building 3 ($1050 in Figure 6-20). When you are programming in C#, you can use four, five, or more dimensions in an array. As long as you can keep track of the order of the variables needed as subscripts, and as long as you do not exhaust your computer's memory, C# lets you create arrays of any size.

C# also supports jagged arrays. A **jagged array** is a one-dimensional array in which each element is another array. The major difference between jagged and rectangular arrays is that in jagged arrays, each row can be a different length.

For example, consider an application in which you want to store train ticket prices for each stop along five different routes. Suppose some of the routes have as many as ten stops and others have as few as two. Each of the five routes could be represented by a row in a multidimensional array. Then you would have two logical choices for the columns:

- You could create a rectangular, two-dimensional array, allowing ten columns for each row. In some of the rows, as many as eight of the columns would be empty, because some routes have only two stops.

- You could create a jagged two-dimensional array, allowing a different number of columns for each row. Figure 6-21 shows how you could implement this option.

```
double[][] tickets = {
   new double[] {5.50, 6.75, 7.95, 9.00, 12.00,
      13.00, 14.50, 17.00, 19.00, 20.25},
   new double[] {5.00, 6.00},
   new double[] {7.50, 9.00, 9.95, 12.00, 13.00, 14.00},
   new double[] {3.50, 6.45, 9.95, 10.00, 12.75},
   new double[] {15.00, 16.00} };
```

**Figure 6-21**   A jagged, two-dimensional array

Two square brackets are used following the data type of the array in Figure 6-21. This notation declares a jagged array, which is composed of five separate one-dimensional arrays. Within the jagged array, each row needs its own **new** operator and data type. To refer to a jagged array element, you use two sets of brackets after the array name— for example, tickets[route][stop]. In Figure 6-21, the value of tickets[0][0] is 5.50, the value of tickets[0][1] is 6.75, and the value of tickets[0][2] is 7.95. The value of tickets[1][0] is 5.00, and the value of tickets[1][1] is 6.00. Referring to tickets[1][2] is invalid because there is no column 2 in the second row (that is, there are only two stops, not three, on the second train route).

## TWO TRUTHS & A LIE

### Using Multidimensional Arrays

1.  A rectangular array has the same number of columns as rows.

2.  The following array contains two rows and three columns:

    ```
    int[ , ] departments = {{12, 54, 16},
                            {22, 44, 47}};
    ```

3.  A jagged array is a one-dimensional array in which each element is another array.

The false statement is #1. In a rectangular array, each row has the same number of columns, but the numbers of rows and columns are not required to be the same.

# Array Issues In GUI Programs

The major unusual consideration when using an array in a GUI program is that if the array values change based on user input, the array must be stored outside any method that reacts to the user's event. For example, consider an application that accumulates contribution totals for a fund-raising drive competition between four departments in a company. The left side of Figure 6-22 shows a Form into which a user types a department number and a contribution amount. The user clicks OK, then enters the next contribution amount. When the user clicks the Done button, a summary of contributions appears, as in the right half of Figure 6-22.

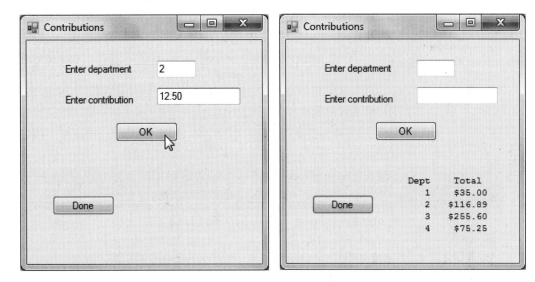

**Figure 6-22** The Form for the CountContributions program as the user enters values and after the user clicks Done

Figure 6-23 shows the code needed to implement the application. An array named total is declared outside of any methods. The okButton_Click() method accepts a department number and contribution amount from the user. It then adds the contribution into the array element that corresponds to the department and clears the text boxes so they are empty prior to the next entry. The total array must be declared outside of the okButton_Click() method; if it was inside the method, it would be redeclared and all its elements would be reset to 0 with each button click. The doneButton_Click() method displays the array's contents.

```
double[] total = { 0, 0, 0, 0 };
private void okButton_Click(object sender, EventArgs e)
{
    int dept;
    double contribution;
    dept = Convert.ToInt32(deptTextbox.Text);
    contribution = Convert.ToDouble(contributionTextbox.Text);
    --dept;
    total[dept] += contribution;
    deptTextbox.Text = "";
    contributionTextbox.Text = "";
}

private void doneButton_Click(object sender, EventArgs e)
{
    outputLabel.Text = "Dept     Total";
    for (int x = 0; x < total.Length; ++x)
        outputLabel.Text +=
            String.Format("\n {0}{1, 10}", x + 1, total[x].ToString("C"));
}
```

**Figure 6-23** Code that declares array and two methods needed for the CountContributions application

## TWO TRUTHS & A LIE

### Array Issues in GUI Programs

1. A GUI program can contain declarations for any number of arrays of any data type.

2. If a method reacts to a user-initiated event, it cannot contain an array declaration.

3. If a method reacts to a user-initiated event and the method contains an array declaration, the array will be redeclared with each event occurrence.

The false statement is #2. If a method reacts to a user-initiated event, it can contain an array. The only problem is that the array will be redeclared with each new event, so it cannot store data that must persist over a number of events.

# You Do It

## Creating and Using an Array

In the next steps, you will create a small array to see how they are used. The array will hold salaries for four categories of employees.

**To create a program that uses an array:**

1. Open a new text file in your text editor.

2. Begin the class that will demonstrate array use by typing the following:

```
using System;
public class ArrayDemo1
{
    public static void Main()
    {
```

3. Declare and create an array that holds four `double` values by typing:

```
double[] payRate = {6.00, 7.35, 8.12, 12.45};
```

4. To confirm that the four values have been assigned, display them using the following code:

```
for(int x = 0; x < payRate.Length; ++x)
    Console.WriteLine("Pay rate {0} is {1}",
        x, payRate[x].ToString("C"));
```

5. Add the two closing curly brackets that end the `Main()` method and the `ArrayDemo1` class.

6. Save the program as **ArrayDemo1.cs**.

7. Compile and run the program. The program's output appears in Figure 6-24.

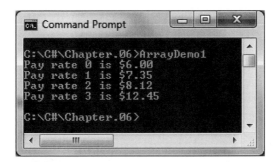

**Figure 6-24** Output of `ArrayDemo1` program

## Using the `Sort()` and `Reverse()` Methods

In the next steps, you will create an array of integers and use the `Sort()` and `Reverse()` methods to manipulate it.

**To use the `Sort()` and `Reverse()` methods:**

1. Open a new file in your text editor.

2. Type the beginning of a class named `ArrayDemo2` that includes an array of eight integer test scores, an integer you will use as a subscript, and a string that will hold user-entered data.

```
using System;
public class ArrayDemo2
{
    public static void Main()
    {
        int[] scores = new int[8];
        int x;
        string inputString;
```

The program displays `x + 1` with each `score[x]` because, although array elements are numbered starting with 0, people usually count items starting with 1.

3. Add a loop that prompts the user, accepts a test score, converts the score to an integer, and stores it as the appropriate element of the `scores` array.

```
for(x = 0; x < scores.Length; ++x)
{
    Console.Write("Enter your score on test {0} ", x + 1);
    inputString = Console.ReadLine();
    scores[x] = Convert.ToInt32(inputString);
}
```

4. Add a statement that creates a dashed line to visually separate the input from the output. Display "Scores in original order:", then use a loop to display each score in a field that is six characters wide.

You learned to set display field sizes when you learned about format strings in Chapter 2.

```
Console.WriteLine("\n--------------------------------");
Console.WriteLine("Scores in original order:");
for(x = 0; x < scores.Length; ++x)
    Console.Write("{0, 6}", scores[x]);
```

5. Add another dashed line for visual separation, then pass the `scores` array to the `Array.Sort()` method. Display "Scores in sorted order:", then use a loop to display each of the newly sorted scores.

```
Console.WriteLine("\n--------------------------------");
Array.Sort(scores);
Console.WriteLine("Scores in sorted order:");
for(x = 0; x < scores.Length; ++x)
    Console.Write("{0, 6}", scores[x]);
```

6. Add one more dashed line, reverse the array elements by passing scores to the Array.Reverse() method, display "Scores in reverse order:", and show the rearranged scores.

```
Console.WriteLine("\n--------------------------------");
Array.Reverse(scores);
Console.WriteLine("Scores in reverse order:");
for(x = 0; x < scores.Length; ++x)
    Console.Write("{0, 6}", scores[x]);
```

7. Add two closing curly braces—one for the Main() method and one for the class. Save the file as **ArrayDemo2.cs**. Compile and execute the program. Figure 6-25 shows a typical execution of the program. The user-entered scores are not in order, but after the call to the Sort() method, they appear in ascending order. After the call to the Reverse() method, they appear in descending order.

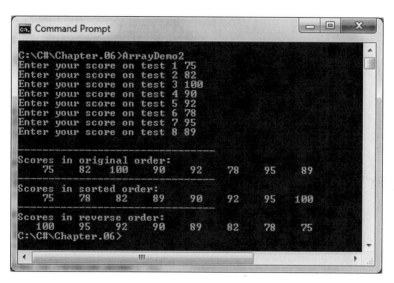

**Figure 6-25** Typical execution of ArrayDemo2 program

# Chapter Summary

• An array is a list of data items, all of which have the same type and the same name, but are distinguished from each other using a subscript or index. You declare an array variable by inserting a pair of square brackets after the type, and reserve memory for an array by using the keyword new. Any array's elements are numbered 0 through one less than the array's length. In C#, arrays are objects that derive from a class named System.Array. An array's fields are initialized to default values. To initialize an array to nondefault values, you use a list of values that are separated by commas and enclosed within curly braces.

- The power of arrays becomes apparent when you begin to use subscripts that are variables rather than constant values, and when you use loops to process array elements. When you work with array elements, you must ensure that the subscript you use remains in the range of 0 through length - 1. You can use the Length property, which is a member of the System.Array class, to automatically hold an array's length. You can use the foreach statement to cycle through every array element without using subscripts. With the foreach statement, you provide a temporary variable that automatically holds each array value in turn.

- When you want to determine whether a variable holds one of many possible valid values, you can compare the variable to a list of values in an array. If you set up a parallel array with the same number of elements and corresponding data, you can use the same subscript to access additional information. You can create parallel arrays to more easily perform a range match.

- The BinarySearch() method finds a requested value in a sorted array. The method returns −1 if the value is not found in the array; otherwise, it returns the array position of the sought value. You cannot use the BinarySearch() method if your array items are not arranged in ascending order, if the array holds duplicate values and you want to find all of them, or if you want to find a range match rather than an exact match. The Sort() method arranges array items in ascending order. The Reverse() method reverses the order of items in an array.

- C# supports multidimensional arrays—those that require multiple subscripts to access the array elements. The most commonly used multidimensional arrays are two-dimensional arrays that are rectangular. Two-dimensional arrays have two or more columns of values for each row. In a rectangular array, each row has the same number of columns. C# also supports jagged arrays, which are arrays of arrays.

- The major unusual consideration when using an array in a GUI program is that if the array values change based on user input, the array must be stored outside any method that reacts to the user's event.

# Key Terms

An **array** is a list of data items that all have the same data type and the same name, but are distinguished from each other by a subscript or index.

Each object in an array is an **array element**.

A **subscript** (also called an **index**) is an integer contained within square brackets that indicates the position of one of an array's elements.

The keyword **new** is also known as the **new operator**; it is used to create objects.

An **initializer list** is the list of values provided for an array.

The class **System.Array** defines fields and methods that belong to every array.

The **Length property** is a member of the System.Array class that automatically holds an array's length.

The **foreach statement** is used to cycle through every array element without using a subscript.

A temporary **iteration variable** holds each array value in turn in a foreach statement.

A **sequential search** is conducted by examining a list in sequence.

A **parallel array** has the same number of elements as another array and corresponding data.

A **range match** determines the pair of limiting values between which a value falls.

The **BinarySearch() method** finds a requested value in a sorted array.

The **Sort() method** arranges array items in ascending order.

The **Reverse() method** reverses the order of items in an array.

A **one-dimensional** or **single-dimensional array** is an array whose elements you can access using a single subscript.

**Multidimensional arrays** require multiple subscripts to access the array elements.

**Two-dimensional arrays** have two or more columns of values for each row.

In a **rectangular array,** each row has the same number of columns.

When mathematicians use a two-dimensional array, they often call it a **matrix** or a **table**.

A **jagged array** is a one-dimensional array in which each element is another array.

# Review Questions

1. In an array, every element has the same _____.

   a. subscript

   b. data type

   c. memory location

   d. all of the above

2. The operator used to create objects is _____.

   a. `=`

   b. `+=`

   c. `new`

   d. `create`

3. Which of the following correctly declares an array of four integers?

   a. `int array[4];`

   b. `int[] array = 4;`

   c. `int[4] array;`

   d. `int[] array = new int[4];`

4. The value placed within square brackets after an array name is _____.

   a. a subscript

   b. an index

   c. always an integer

   d. all of these

5. If you define an array to contain seven elements, then the highest array subscript you can use is _____.

   a. 5

   b. 6

   c. 7

   d. 8

6. Initializing an array is _____ in C#.

   a. required

   b. optional

   c. difficult

   d. prohibited

7. When you declare an array of six `double` elements but provide no initialization values, the value of the first element is _____.

   a. 0.0

   b. 1.0

   c. 5.0

   d. unknown

8. Which of the following correctly declares an array of four integers?

   a. `int[] ages = new int[4] {20, 30, 40, 50};`

   b. `int[] ages = new int[] {20, 30, 40, 50};`

   c. `int[] ages = {20, 30, 40, 50};`

   d. all of these

9. When an `ages` array is correctly initialized using the values `{20, 30, 40, 50}`, as in Question 8, then the value of `ages[1]` is _____.

   a. 0

   b. 20

   c. 30

   d. undefined

10. When an **ages** array is correctly initialized using the values {20, 30, 40, 50}, as in Question 8, then the value of ages[4] is _____.

    a. 0

    b. 4

    c. 50

    d. undefined

11. When you declare an array as int[] temperature = {0, 32, 50, 90, 212, 451};, the value of temperature.Length is _____.

    a. 5

    b. 6

    c. 7

    d. unknown

12. Which of the following doubles every value in a ten-element integer array named amount?

    a. for(int x = 9; x >= 0; --x) amount[x] *= 2;

    b. foreach(int number in amount) number *= 2;

    c. both of these

    d. neither of these

13. Which of the following adds 10 to every value in a 16-element integer array named points?

    a. for(int sub = 0; sub > 15; ++sub) points[sub] += 10;

    b. foreach(int sub in points) points += 10;

    c. both of these

    d. neither of these

14. Two arrays that store related information in corresponding element positions are _____.

    a. analogous arrays

    b. polymorphic arrays

    c. relative arrays

    d. parallel arrays

15. Assume an array is defined as `int[] nums = {2, 3, 4, 5};`. Which of the following would display the values in the array in reverse?

    a. `for(int x = 4; x > 0; --x) Console.Write(nums[x]);`

    b. `for(int x = 3; x >= 0; --x) Console.Write(nums[x]);`

    c. `for(int x = 3; x > 0; --x) Console.Write(nums[x]);`

    d. `for(int x = 4; x >= 0; --x) Console.Write(nums[x]);`

16. Assume an array is defined as `int[] nums = {7, 15, 23, 5};`. Which of the following would place the values in the array in descending numeric order?

    a. `Array.Sort(nums);`

    b. `Array.Reverse(nums);`

    c. `Array.Sort(nums); Array.Reverse(nums);`

    d. `Array.Reverse(nums); Array.Sort(nums);`

17. Which of the following traits do the `BinarySearch()` and `Sort()` methods have in common?

    a. Both methods take a single argument that must be an array.

    b. Both methods belong to the `System.Array` class.

    c. The array that each method uses must be in ascending order.

    d. They both operate on arrays made up of simple data types but not class objects.

18. If you use the `BinarySearch()` method and the object you seek is not found in the array, _____.

    a. an error message is displayed

    b. a zero is returned

    c. the value `false` is returned

    d. a negative value is returned

19. The `BinarySearch()` method is inadequate when _____ .

   a. array items are in ascending order

   b. the array holds duplicate values and you want to find them all

   c. you want to find an exact match for a value

   d. array items are not numeric

20. Which of the following declares an integer array that contains eight rows and five columns?

   a. `int[8, 5] num = new int[ , ];`

   b. `int [8][5] num = new int[];`

   c. `int [ , ] num = new int[5, 8];`

   d. `int [ , ] num = new int[8, 5];`

## Exercises

Although each sample program name in this section ends with a .cs extension, indicating a console-based application, you can create these programs as console-based or GUI applications. Your instructor might require one or both types.

1. Write a program containing an array that holds five integers. Assign values to the integers. Display the integers from first to last, and then display them from last to first. Save the program as **IntegerList.cs**.

2. Write a program for a package delivery service. The program contains an array that holds the ten zip codes to which the company delivers packages. Prompt a user to enter a zip code and display a message indicating whether the zip code is one to which the company delivers. Save the program as **CheckZips.cs**.

3. Write another program for the package delivery service in Exercise 2. The program should again use an array that holds the ten zip codes to which the company delivers packages. Create a parallel array containing ten delivery charges that differ for each zip code. Prompt a user to enter a zip code and then display either a message indicating the price of delivery to that zip code or a message indicating that the company does not deliver to the requested zip code. Save the program as **DeliveryCharges.cs**.

4. The Chat-A-While phone company provides service to six area codes and charges the per-minute rates for phone calls shown in the accompanying table.

| Area Code | Per-Minute Rate ($) |
|-----------|---------------------|
| 262 | 0.07 |
| 414 | 0.10 |
| 608 | 0.05 |
| 715 | 0.16 |
| 815 | 0.24 |
| 920 | 0.14 |

Write a program that allows a user to enter an area code and the length of time for a call in minutes, then display the total cost of the call. Save the program as **ChatAWhile.cs**.

5. The Whippet Bus Company charges prices for tickets based on distance traveled, as shown in the accompanying table.

| Distance (miles) | Ticket Price ($) |
|------------------|------------------|
| 0 – 99 | 25.00 |
| 100 – 299 | 40.00 |
| 300 – 499 | 55.00 |
| 500 and farther | 70.00 |

Write a program that allows a user to enter a trip distance. The output is the ticket price. Save the program as **WhippetBus.cs**.

6. a. Write a program that prompts the user to make a choice for a pizza size—S, M, L, or X—and then displays the price as $6.99, $8.99, $12.50, or $15.00, respectively. Save the program as **PizzaPrices.cs**.

   b. Modify the `PizzaPrices` program so that the following discounts apply: no discount for one pizza, 10% for two pizzas, 15% for three or four pizzas, and 20% for five or more pizzas. Display a full accounting of the transaction, similar to that shown in Figure 6-26. Save the program as **PizzaPrices2.cs**.

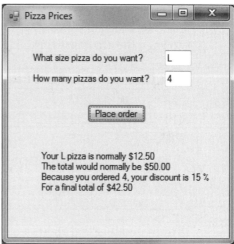

**Figure 6-26** Typical execution of `PizzaPrices2` program as a command-line application and as a GUI application

7. Write a program that computes commissions for automobile salespeople based on the value of the car. Salespeople receive 5% of the sale price for any car sold for up to and including $15,000; 7% for any car over $15,000 up to and including $24,000; and 10% of the sale price of any car over $24,000. Write a program that allows a user to enter a car price. The output is the salesperson's commission. Save the program as **Commission.cs**.

8. Create an array that stores 20 prices. Prompt a user to enter 20 values, then display the sum of the values. Next, display all values of less than $5.00. Finally, calculate the average of the prices, and display all values that are higher than the calculated average. Save the program as **Prices.cs**.

9. The Tiny Tots Tee-Ball league has 12 players who have jersey numbers 0 through 11. The coach wants a program into which he can type a player's number and the number of bases the player got in a turn at bat (a number 0 through 4). Write a program that allows the coach to continually enter the values until 99 is entered. Store the statistics in a two-dimensional array. At the end of a data-entry session, display each player's number and the number of 0-base, 1-base, 2-base, 3-base, and 4-base turns the player had. Display a separate count of the number of data-entry errors the coach makes (a player number greater than 11 or a number of bases greater than 4). Save the program as **TeeBall.cs**.

10. Create a game similar to Hangman in which a player guesses letters to try to replicate a hidden word. Store at least eight words in an array, and randomly select one to be the hidden word. (The statements needed to generate a random number are shown in the Exercises in the *Decision Making* and *Looping* chapters.) Initially, display the hidden word using asterisks to represent each letter. Allow the user to guess letters to replace the asterisks in the hidden word until the user completes the entire word. If the user guesses a letter that is not in the hidden word, display an appropriate message. If the user guesses a letter that appears multiple times in the hidden word, make sure that each correct letter is placed. Figure 6-27 shows typical games in progress in a console-based application and in a GUI application. Save the file as **GuessAWord.cs**. *Hint:* If you create the GUI version of the game, you might want to include a Start button that selects the random word and performs other start-up tasks before you reveal the game interface. After the start-up tasks are complete, you can remove the Start button from the form.

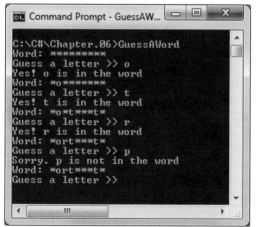 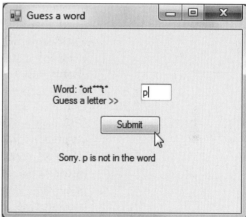

**Figure 6-27** Typical executions of console-based and GUI `GuessAWord` programs

 *Debugging Exercises*

Each of the following files in the Chapter.06 folder of your downloadable student files has syntax and/or logical errors. In each case, determine the problem and fix the program. After you correct the errors, save each file using the same filename preceded with *Fixed*. For example, DebugSix01.cs will become FixedDebugSix01.cs.

a.   DebugSix01.cs

b.   DebugSix02.cs

c.   DebugSix03.cs

d.   DebugSix04.cs

 *Up For Discussion*

1.   A train schedule is an everyday, real-life example of an array. Think of at least four more.

2.   This chapter discusses sorting data. Suppose you are hired by a large hospital to write a program that displays lists of potential organ recipients. The hospital's doctors will consult this list if they have an organ that can be transplanted. You are instructed to sort potential recipients by last name and display them sequentially in alphabetical order. If more than ten patients are waiting for a particular organ, the first ten patients are displayed; the user can either select one of these or move on to view the next set of ten patients. You worry that this system gives an unfair advantage to patients with last names that start with A, B, C, and D. Should you write and install the program? If you do not, many transplant opportunities will be missed while the hospital searches for another programmer to write the program.

3.   This chapter discusses sorting data. Suppose your supervisor asks you to create a report that lists all employees sorted by salary. Suppose you also know that your employer will use this report to lay off the highest-paid employee in each department. Would you agree to write the program? Instead, what if the report's purpose was to list the worst performer in each department in terms of sales? What if the report grouped employees by gender? What if the report grouped employees by race? Suppose your supervisor asks you to sort employees by the dollar value of medical insurance claims they have in a year, and you fear the employer will use the report to eliminate workers who are driving up the organization's medical insurance costs. Do you agree to write the program even if you know that the purpose of the report is to eliminate workers?

# Using Methods

In this chapter you will:

◎ Learn about methods and implementation hiding

◎ Write methods with no parameters and no return value

◎ Write methods that require a single argument

◎ Write methods that require multiple arguments

◎ Write a method that returns a value

◎ Pass an array to a method

◎ Learn some alternate ways to write a `Main()` method header

◎ Learn about issues using methods in GUI programs

In the first chapters of this book, you learned to create C# programs containing `Main()` methods that declare variables, accept input, perform arithmetic, and produce output. You learned to add decisions, loops, and arrays to your programs. As your programs grow in complexity, their `Main()` methods will contain many additional statements. Rather than creating increasingly long `Main()` methods, most programmers prefer to modularize their programs, placing instructions in additional methods that the `Main()` method can access. In this chapter, you learn to create many types of C# methods. You will understand how to send data to these methods and receive information back from them.

## Understanding Methods and Implementation Hiding

A **method** is an encapsulated series of statements that carry out a task. Any class can contain an unlimited number of methods. So far, you have written console-based applications that contain a `Main()` method, but no others. You also have created GUI applications with a `Click()` method. Frequently, the methods you have written have **invoked**, or **called**, other methods; that is, your program used a method's name and the method executed to perform a task for the class. For example, you have created many programs that call the `WriteLine()` and `ReadLine()` methods. These methods are prewritten; you only had to call them to have them work.

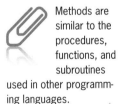

You first learned the term "argument" in Chapter 1. An argument is the data that appears between the parentheses in a method call.

Methods are similar to the procedures, functions, and subroutines used in other programming languages.

For example, consider the simple `HelloClass` program shown in Figure 7-1. The `Main()` method contains a statement that calls the `Console.WriteLine()` method. You can identify method names because they always are followed by a set of parentheses. Depending on the method, there might be an argument within the parentheses. The call to the `WriteLine()` method within the `HelloClass` program in Figure 7-1 contains the string argument "Hello". The simplest methods you can invoke do not require any arguments.

In the `HelloClass` program in Figure 7-1, `Main()` is a **calling method**—one that calls another. The `WriteLine()` method is a **called method**.

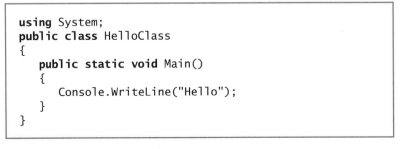

```
using System;
public class HelloClass
{
    public static void Main()
    {
        Console.WriteLine("Hello");
    }
}
```

**Figure 7-1** The `HelloClass` program

# Understanding Implementation Hiding

When you call the WriteLine() method within the HelloClass program in Figure 7-1, you use a method that has already been created for you. Because the creators of C# knew you would often want to write a message to the output screen, they created a method you could call to accomplish that task. This method takes care of all the hardware details of producing a message on the output device; you simply call the method and pass the desired message to it. The WriteLine() method provides an example of **implementation hiding**, which means keeping the details of a method's operations hidden. For example, when you make a dental appointment, you do not need to know how the appointment is actually recorded at the dental office—perhaps it is written in a book, marked on a large chalkboard, or entered into a computerized database. The implementation details are of no concern to you as a client, and if the dental office changes its methods from one year to the next, the change does not affect your use of the appointment method. Your only concern is the way you **interface** or interact with the dental office, not how the office records appointments. Similarly, if you use a thermostat to control the temperature in your apartment or house, you do not need to know whether the heat is generated by natural gas, electricity, solar energy, or a hamster on a wheel. As long as you receive heat, the implementation details can remain hidden.

Hidden implementation methods often are said to exist in a black box. A **black box** is any device you can use without knowing how it works internally.

The same is true with well-written program methods; the invoking program or method must know the name of the method it is using (and what type of information to send it), but the program does not need to know how the method works. Later, you might substitute a new, improved method for the old one, and if the interface to the method does not change, you will not need to make any changes in programs that invoke the method.

A method that uses another is called a **client** of the method it uses.

The creators of C# were able to anticipate many of the methods that would be necessary for your programs; you will continue to use many of these methods throughout this book. However, your programs often will require custom methods that the creators of C# could not have expected. In this chapter, you will learn to write your own custom methods.

To more easily incorporate methods into a program, it is common practice to store methods (or groups of associated methods) in their own classes and files. Then you can add the methods into any application that uses them. The resulting compound program is called a **multifile assembly**. As you learn more about C#, you might prefer to take this approach with your own programs. For simplicity, example methods in this book are contained in the same file as any other methods that use them.

276

**Understanding Methods and Implementation Hiding**

1. A method is an encapsulated series of statements that carry out a task.

2. Any class can contain an unlimited number of methods.

3. All the methods your programs will use have been written for you and stored in files.

The false statement is #3. As you write programs, you will want to write many of your own custom methods.

# Writing Methods with No Parameters and No Return Value

The output of the program in Figure 7-1 is simply the word "Hello". Suppose you want to add three more lines of output to display a standard welcoming message when users execute your program. Of course, you can add three new WriteLine() statements to the existing program, but you also can create a method to display the three new lines.

Creating a method instead of adding three lines to the existing program is useful for two major reasons:

- If you add a method call instead of three new lines, the Main() method will remain short and easy to follow. The Main() method will contain just one new statement that calls a method rather than three separate WriteLine() statements.

- More importantly, a method is easily *reusable*. After you create the welcoming method, you can use it in any program, and you can allow other programmers to use it in their programs. In other words, you do the work once, and then you can use the method many times.

In C#, a method must include:

- A **method declaration**, which is also known as a **method header** or **method definition**

- An opening curly brace

- A **method body**, which is a block of statements that carry out the method's work

- A closing curly brace

 When you place code in a callable method instead of repeating the same code at several points in a program, you are avoiding **code bloat**—a colorful term that describes unnecessarily long or repetitive statements.

The method declaration defines the rules for using the method. It contains:

- Optional declared accessibility

- An optional `static` modifier

- The return type for the method

- The method name, or identifier

- An opening parenthesis

- An optional list of method parameters (separated with commas if there is more than one parameter)

- A closing parenthesis

## Understanding Accessibility

The optional declared **accessibility** for a method sets limits as to how other methods can use your method; accessibility can be any of the levels described in Table 7-1. The two levels you will use most frequently are:

- **Public access**, which you select by including a `public` modifier in the member declaration. This modifier allows unlimited access to a method.

- **Private access**, which you select by including a `private` modifier in the member declaration. This modifier limits method access to the class that contains the method.

| Declared accessibility | Containing classes | Derived classes | Containing programs | All classes |
|---|---|---|---|---|
| `public` | Yes | Yes | Yes | Yes |
| `protected internal` | Yes | Yes | Yes | No |
| `protected` | Yes | Yes | No | No |
| `internal` | Yes | No | Yes | No |
| `private` | Yes | No | No | No |

**Table 7-1**   Summary of method accessibility

If you do not provide an accessibility modifier for a method, it is `private` by default. As you study C#, deciding which access modifier to choose will become clearer. For example, when you begin to create your own class objects, you usually will provide them with `public` methods, but sometimes you will make methods `private`. For now, as long as the `Main()` method in your console applications is `public`, you can create workable programs using any access modifier.

You will learn about protected access and what it means to derive types in the chapter *Introduction to Inheritance*.

## Understanding the Optional `static` Modifier

Additionally, you can declare a method to be **static** or **nonstatic**. If you use the keyword modifier `static`, you indicate that a method can be called without referring to an object. Instead, you refer to the class. For example, if you have a class named `PayrollApplication` that contains a static method named `DeductUnionDues()`, you can call the method using the class name, a dot, and the method name, as in the following:

`PayrollApplication.DeductUnionDues();`

If you call the method from another method in the same class, you can use the class name as a prefix, although this is not required.

If you do not indicate that a method is `static`, it is nonstatic by default and can only be used in conjunction with an object. Static methods cannot call nonstatic methods. (However, nonstatic methods can call static ones.) When you begin to create your own class objects in the chapter *Using Classes and Objects*, you will write many nonstatic methods and your understanding of the use of these terms will become clearer. Although `static` and nonstatic methods (and data) can be combined in a class, for now this book will follow two rules:

- All methods you create in console-based applications will be `static`.

- Later in this chapter, you will learn that the methods you create in GUI applications in a `Form` class will be nonstatic.

## Understanding the Return Type

Every method has a **return type**, indicating what kind of value the method will return to any other method that calls it. If a method does not return a value, its return type is `void`. A method's return type is known more succinctly as a **method's type**. Later in this chapter, you will create methods that return values; for now, the methods will be `void` methods.

 When a method's return type is `void`, most C# programmers do not end the method with a `return` statement. However, you can end a `void` method with the following statement that indicates nothing is returned:

`return:`

 You have used a return value from the `ReadLine()` method when you have written a statement such as `inputString = Console.ReadLine();`. The fact that the `ReadLine()` method call can be assigned to a string means that its return type is `string`.

# Understanding the Method Identifier

Every method has a name that must be a legal C# identifier; that is, it must not contain spaces and must begin with a letter of the alphabet or an underscore. By convention, many programmers start method names with a verb because methods cause actions. Examples of conventional method names include DeductTax() and DisplayNetPay().

Every method name is followed by a set of parentheses. Sometimes these parentheses contain parameters, but in the simplest methods, the parentheses are empty. A **parameter to a method** is a variable that holds data passed to a method when it is called. The terms *argument* and *parameter* are closely related. An argument is data in a method call and a parameter receives an argument's value when the method executes.

# Creating a Simple Method

In summary, the first methods you write in console-based applications will be public, static, and void and will have empty parameter lists. Therefore, you can write the ShowWelcomeMessage() method as it is shown in Figure 7-2. According to its declaration, the method is public and static. It returns nothing, so the return type is void. Its identifier is ShowWelcomeMessage, and it receives nothing, so the parentheses are empty. The method body, consisting of three WriteLine() statements, appears within curly braces.

```
public static void ShowWelcomeMessage()
{
   Console.WriteLine("Welcome");
   Console.WriteLine("It's a pleasure to serve you");
   Console.WriteLine("Enjoy the program");
}
```

**Figure 7-2**  The ShowWelcomeMessage() method

You can place any statements you want within a method body, and you can declare variables within a method. When a variable is declared within a method, it is known only from that point to the end of the method; the variable is not known to other methods in the same class. A program element's **scope** is the segment of code in which it can be used.

You can place a method in its own file, as you will learn in the next section. You also can place a method within the file of a program that will use it, but you cannot place a method within any other method. Figure 7-3 shows the two locations where you can place the

ShowWelcomeMessage() method within the HelloClass program file—before the Main() method header or after the Main() method's closing brace.

```
using System;
public class HelloClass
{
    // The ShowWelcomeMessage() method could go here
    public static void Main()
    {
        Console.WriteLine("Hello");
    }
    // Alternatively, the ShowWelcomeMessage() method could go here
    // But it cannot go in both places
}
```

**Figure 7-3** Placement of methods

If a Main() method calls the ShowWelcomeMessage() method, then you simply use the ShowWelcomeMessage() method's name as a statement within the body of the Main() method. Figure 7-4 shows the complete program with the method call shaded, and Figure 7-5 shows the output.

```
using System;
public class HelloClass
{
    public static void Main()
    {
        ShowWelcomeMessage();
        Console.WriteLine("Hello");
    }
    public static void ShowWelcomeMessage()
    {
        Console.WriteLine("Welcome");
        Console.WriteLine("It's a pleasure to serve you");
        Console.WriteLine("Enjoy the program");
    }
}
```

**Figure 7-4** HelloClass program with Main() method calling the ShowWelcomeMessage() method

The ShowWelcomeMessage() method must be static because it is called from Main(), which is also static, and no object is created to use the ShowWelcomeMessage() method.

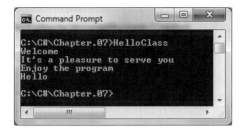

**Figure 7-5** Output of `HelloClass` program

When the `Main()` method executes, it calls the `ShowWelcomeMessage()` method, and then it displays "Hello". Because the `Main()` method calls the `ShowWelcomeMessage()` method before it displays "Hello", the three lines that make up the welcome message appear first in the output.

 Each of two different classes can have its own method named `ShowWelcomeMessage()`. Such a method in the second class would be entirely distinct from the identically named method in the first class.

 Watch the video *Using Methods.*

---

**TWO TRUTHS & A LIE**

### Writing Methods with No Parameters and No Return Value

1.  A method header must contain declared accessibility.

2.  A method header must contain a return type.

3.  A method header must contain an identifier.

The false statement is #1. Declaring accessibility in a method header is optional. If you do not use an access modifier, the method is private by default.

---

281

# Writing Methods That Require a Single Argument

Some methods require additional information. If a method could not receive arguments, then you would have to write an infinite number of methods to cover every possible situation. For example, when you make a dental appointment, you do not need to employ a different method for every date of the year at every possible time of day. Rather, you can supply the date and time as information to the method, and no matter what date and time you supply, the method is carried out correctly. If you design a method to triple numeric values, it makes sense that you can supply the Triple() method with an argument representing the value to be tripled, rather than having to develop a Triple1() method, a Triple2() method, and so on.

 You already have used a method to which you supplied a wide variety of parameters. At any call, the System.WriteLine() method can receive any one of an infinite number of strings as a parameter—"Hello", "Goodbye", and so on. No matter what message you send to the WriteLine() method, the message will be displayed correctly.

When you write the declaration for a method that accepts a parameter, you need to include the following items within the method declaration parentheses:

- The type of the parameter
- A local identifier (name) for the parameter

For example, consider a public method named DisplaySalesTax(), which multiplies a selling price by 7% and displays the result. The method header for a usable DisplaySalesTax() method could be the following:

```
public static void DisplaySalesTax(double saleAmount)
```

You can think of the parentheses in a method declaration as a funnel into the method—data parameters listed there are "dropping in" to the method.

The parameter double saleAmount within the parentheses indicates that the DisplaySalesTax() method will receive a value of type double. Within the method, the value will be known as saleAmount. Figure 7-6 shows a complete method.

```
public static void DisplaySalesTax(double saleAmount)
{
    double tax;
    const double RATE = 0.07;
    tax = saleAmount * RATE;
    Console.WriteLine("The tax on {0} is {1}",
        saleAmount.ToString("C"), tax.ToString("C"));
}
```

**Figure 7-6**   The DisplaySalesTax() method

Within the `DisplaySalesTax()` method, you must use the format string and `ToString()` method if you want figures to display to exactly two decimal positions. You learned how to display values to a fixed number of decimal places in Chapter 2; recall that using the fixed format with no number defaults to two decimal places.

You create the `DisplaySalesTax()` method as a `void` method (has a `void` return type) because you do not need it to return any value to any method that uses it—its only function is to receive the `saleAmount` value, multiply it by 0.07, and then display the result. You create it as a `static` method because you do not want to create an object with which to use it and you want the static `Main()` method to be able to call it.

Within a program, you can call the `DisplaySalesTax()` method by using the method's name, and, within parentheses, an argument that is either a constant value or a variable. Thus, both of the following calls to the `DisplaySalesTax()` method invoke it correctly:

```
double myPurchase = 12.99;
DisplaySalesTax(12.99);
DisplaySalesTax(myPurchase);
```

A variable is local to a method when it is declared within that method.

You can call the `DisplaySalesTax()` method any number of times, with a different constant or variable argument each time. The value of each of these arguments becomes known as `saleAmount` within the method. The identifier `saleAmount` holds any `double` value passed into the method. Interestingly, if the argument in the method call is a variable, it might possess the same identifier as `saleAmount` or a different one, such as `myPurchase`. The identifier `saleAmount` is simply the name the value "goes by" while being used within the method, no matter what name it goes by in the calling program. That is, the variable `saleAmount` is a **local variable** to the `DisplaySalesTax()` method. The variable `saleAmount` is also an example of a **formal parameter**, a parameter within a method header that accepts a value. In contrast, arguments within a method *call* often are referred to as **actual parameters**.

The variable `saleAmount` is also an example of a value parameter, or a parameter that receives a copy of the value passed to it. You will learn more about value parameters and other types of parameters in the next chapter.

The `DisplaySalesTax()` method employs implementation hiding. That is, if a programmer changes the way in which the tax value is calculated—for example, by coding one of the following—programs that use the `DisplaySalesTax()` method will not be affected and will not need to be modified:

```
tax = saleAmount * 7 / 100;
tax = 0.07 * saleAmount;
tax = RATE * saleAmount;
```

Each of these statements computes `tax` as 7% of `saleAmount`. No matter how the tax is calculated, a calling program passes a value into the DisplaySalesTax() method, and a calculated result appears on the screen.

Figure 7-7 shows a complete program called UseTaxMethod. It uses the DisplaySalesTax() method twice: first with a variable argument and then with a constant argument. The program's output appears in Figure 7-8.

```csharp
using System;
public class UseTaxMethod
{
    public static void Main()
    {
        double myPurchase = 12.99;
        DisplaySalesTax(myPurchase);
        DisplaySalesTax(35.67);
    }
    public static void DisplaySalesTax(double saleAmount)
    {
        double tax;
        const double RATE = 0.07;
        tax = saleAmount * RATE;
        Console.WriteLine("The tax on {0} is {1}",
            saleAmount.ToString("C"), tax.ToString("C"));
    }
}
```

**Figure 7-7** Complete program using the DisplaySalesTax() method two times

**Figure 7-8** Output of the UseTaxMethod program

 Watch the video *Arguments and Parameters.*

 Now that you have seen how to write methods that accept an argument, you might guess that when you write Console.WriteLine("Hello");, the header for the called method is similar to public void WriteLine(string s). You might not know the parameter name the creators of C# have chosen, but you do know the method's return type, name, and parameter type. (If you use the IntelliSense feature of Visual Studio, you can discover the parameter name. See Appendix C for more details.)

---

**TWO TRUTHS & A LIE**

## Writing Methods That Require a Single Argument

1. When you write the declaration for a method that accepts a parameter, you need to include the parameter's data type within the method header.

2. When you write the declaration for a method that accepts a parameter, you need to include the identifier of the argument that will be sent to the method within the method header.

3. When you write the declaration for a method that accepts a parameter, you need to include a local identifier for the parameter within the method header.

The false statement is #2. When you write the definition for a method, you include the data type and a local parameter name within the parentheses of the method header, but you do not include the name of any argument that will be sent from a calling method. After all, the method might be invoked any number of times with any number of different arguments.

---

# Writing Methods That Require Multiple Arguments

A method can require more than one argument. You can pass multiple arguments to a method by listing the arguments within the call to the method and separating them with commas. For example, rather than creating a `DisplaySalesTax()` method that multiplies an amount by 0.07, you might prefer to create a more flexible method to which you can pass two values—the value on which the tax is calculated and the tax percentage by which it should be multiplied. Figure 7-9 shows a method that uses two such arguments.

```
public static void DisplaySalesTax(double saleAmount, double taxRate)
{
    double tax;
    tax = saleAmount * taxRate;
    Console.WriteLine("The tax on {0} at {1} is {2}",
        saleAmount.ToString("C"),
        taxRate.ToString("P"), tax.ToString("C"));
}
```

**Figure 7-9** The `DisplaySalesTax()` method that takes two arguments

286

A declaration for a method that receives two or more arguments must list the type for each parameter separately, even if the parameters have the *same* type.

If two method parameters are of the same type— for example, two doubles—passing arguments to a method in the wrong order results in a logical error. If a method expects parameters of diverse types, then passing arguments in reverse order constitutes a syntax error.

In Figure 7-9, two parameters (saleAmount and taxRate) appear within the parentheses in the method header. A comma separates the parameters, and each parameter requires its own named type (in this case, both parameters are of type double) and an identifier. When you pass values to the method in a statement such as DisplaySalesTax(myPurchase, localRate);, the first value passed will be referenced as saleAmount within the method, and the second value passed will be referenced as taxRate. Therefore, it is very important that arguments be passed to a method in the correct order. The following call results in output stating that "The tax on $200.00 at 10.00% is $20.00":

```
DisplaySalesTax(200.00, 0.10);
```

However, the following call results in output stating that "The tax on $0.10 at 20,000.00% is $20.00", which is clearly incorrect.

```
DisplaySalesTax(0.10, 200.00);
```

You can write a method to take any number of parameters in any order. When you call the method, however, the arguments you send to it must match (in both number and type) the parameters listed in the method declaration. Thus, a method to compute an automobile salesperson's commission might require arguments such as an integer value of a sold car, a double percentage commission rate, and a character code for the vehicle type. The correct method will execute only when three arguments of the correct types are sent in the correct order.

## TWO TRUTHS & A LIE

### Writing Methods That Require Multiple Arguments

1. The following is a usable C# method header:

   ```
   public static void MyMethod(double amt, sum)
   ```

2. The following is a usable C# method header:

   ```
   private void MyMethod2(int x, double y)
   ```

3. The following is a usable C# method header:

   ```
   static void MyMethod3(int id, string name, double rate)
   ```

The false statement is #1. In a method header, each parameter must have a data type, even if the data types for all the parameters are the same. The header in #2 does not contain the keyword static, but that that is optional. Likewise, the header in #3 does not contain an accessibility indicator, but that is optional as well.

# Writing a Method That Returns a Value

A method can return, at most, one value to a method that calls it. The return type for a method can be any type used in the C# programming language, which includes the basic built-in types int, double, char, and so on, as well as class types (including class types you create). Of course, a method also can return nothing, in which case the return type is void.

In addition to the primitive types, a method can return a class type. If a class named BankLoan exists, a method might return a BankLoan, as in public BankLoan ApprovalProcess(). In other words, a method can return anything from a simple int to a complicated BankLoan object that contains 20 data fields. You will create classes like BankLoan in the chapter *Using Classes and Objects*. You also will learn that when an object such as BankLoan is returned, its memory address is returned.

For example, a method that returns true or false depending on whether an employee worked overtime hours might be defined as:

```
public bool IsOvertimeEarned()
```

This method is public and returns a bool value; in other words, the method's type is bool.

Suppose you want to create a method to accept the hours an employee worked and the hourly pay rate, and to return a calculated gross pay value. The header for this method could be:

```
public static double CalcPay(double hours, double rate)
```

Figure 7-10 shows this method.

```
public static double CalcPay(double hours, double rate)
{
    double gross;
    gross = hours * rate;
    return gross;
}
```

**Figure 7-10**   The CalcPay() method

Notice the return type double that precedes the method name in the method header. Also notice the return statement, which is the last statement within the method. A **return statement** causes a value to be sent back to the calling method; in the CalcPay() method, the value stored in gross is sent back to any method that calls the CalcPay()

method. The data type used in a method's `return` statement must be the same as the return type declared in the method's header.

If a method returns a value and you call the method, you typically will want to use the returned value, although you are not required to use it. For example, when you invoke the `CalcPay()` method, you might want to assign the value to a `double` variable named `grossPay`, as in the following statement:

```
grossPay = CalcPay(myHours, myRate);
```

The `CalcPay()` method returns a `double`, so it is appropriate to assign the returned value to a `double` variable. Figure 7-11 shows a program that uses the `CalcPay()` method in the shaded statement, and Figure 7-12 shows the output.

```
using System;
public class UseCalcPay
{
   public static void Main()
   {
      double myHours = 37.5;
      double myRate = 12.75;
      double grossPay;
      grossPay = CalcPay(myHours, myRate);
      Console.WriteLine("I worked {0} hours at {1} per hour",
         myHours, myRate);
      Console.WriteLine("My gross pay is {0}",
         grossPay.ToString("C"));
   }
   public static double CalcPay(double hours, double rate)
   {
      double gross;
      gross = hours * rate;
      return gross;
   }
}
```

**Figure 7-11**  Program using the `CalcPay()` method

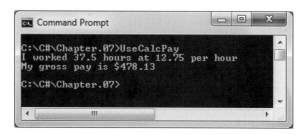

**Figure 7-12**  Output of `UseCalcPay` program

Instead of storing a method's returned value in a variable, you can use it directly, as in either of the following statements:

```
Console.WriteLine("My gross pay is {0}",
    CalcPay(myHours, myRate).ToString("C"));

double tax = CalcPay(myHours, myRate) * TAX_RATE;
```

In the first statement, the call to the `CalcPay()` method is made within the `WriteLine()` method call. In the second, `CalcPay()`'s returned value is used in an arithmetic statement. Because `CalcPay()` returns a `double`, you can use the method call `CalcPay()` in the same way you would use any `double` value. The method call `CalcPay()` has a `double` value in the same way a `double` variable has a `double` value.

As an additional example, suppose you have a method named `GetPrice()` whose header is as follows:

```
double GetPrice(int itemNumber)
```

The method accepts an integer item number and returns its price. Further suppose that you want to ask the user to enter an item number from the keyboard so you can pass it to the `GetPrice()` method. You can get the value from the user, store it in a string, convert the string to an integer, pass the integer to the `GetPrice()` method, and store the returned value in a variable named `price` in four or five separate statements. Or, you can write the following:

```
price = GetPrice(Convert.ToInt32(Console.ReadLine()));
```

This statement contains a method call to `ReadLine()` within a method call to `Convert.ToInt32()`, within a method call to `GetPrice()`. When method calls are placed inside other method calls, the calls are **nested method calls**. When you write a statement with three nested method calls like the previous statement, the innermost method executes first. Its return value is then used as an argument to the intermediate method, and its return value is used as an argument to the outer method. There is no limit to how "deep" you can go with nested method calls.

Now that you have seen how to write methods that accept arguments, you might guess that the method header for the `Console.ReadLine()` method is `public static string ReadLine()`. You know the method returns a `string`, and you know it takes no parameters.

## Writing a Method that Returns a Boolean Value

When a method returns a value that is type `bool`, the method call can be used anywhere you can use a Boolean expression. For example, suppose you have written a method named `isPreferredCustomer()` that returns a Boolean value indicating whether a customer is a preferred customer who qualifies for a discount. Then you can write an `if` statement such as the following:

```
if(isPreferredCustomer())
    price = price - DISCOUNT;
```

In Chapter 4, you learned about side effects and how they affect compound Boolean expressions. When you use Boolean methods, you must be especially careful not to cause unintended side effects. For example, consider the following if statement, in which the intention is to set a delivery fee to 0 if both the isPreferredCustomer() and isLocalCustomer() methods return true:

```
if(isPreferredCustomer() && isLocalCustomer())
    deliveryFee = 0;
```

If the isLocalCustomer() method should perform a desired task—for example, displaying a message about the customer's status—then you might not see the desired output. Because of short-circuit evaluation, if the isPreferredCustomer() method returns false, the isLocalCustomer() method never executes. If that is your intention, then using methods in this way is fine, but always consider any unintended side effects.

## TWO TRUTHS & A LIE

### Writing a Method That Returns a Value

1. A method can return, at most, one value to a method that calls it.

2. The data type used in a method's return statement must be the same as the return type declared in the method's header.

3. If a method returns a value and you call the method, you must store the value in a variable that has the same data type as the method's parameter.

The false statement is #3. If a method returns a value and you call the method, you typically will want to use the returned value, but you are not required to use it. Furthermore, if you do store the returned value in a variable, that variable must be the same data type as the method's return value, not its parameter's value.

## Passing an Array to a Method

In the chapter *Using Arrays*, you learned that you can declare an array to create a list of elements, and that you can use any individual array element in the same manner as you would use any single variable of the same type. That is, suppose you declare an integer array as follows:

```
int[] someNums = new int[12];
```

You can subsequently output someNums[0] or add 1 to someNums[1], just as you would for any integer. Similarly, you can pass a single array element to a method in exactly the same manner as you would pass a variable.

Consider the program shown in Figure 7-13. This program creates and uses an array of four integers. Figure 7-14 shows the program's execution.

```csharp
using System;
public class PassArrayElement
{
    public static void Main()
    {
        int[] someNums = {10, 12, 22, 35};
        int x;
        Console.Write("\nAt beginning of Main() method...");
        for(x = 0; x < someNums.Length; ++x)
            Console.Write("{0,6}", someNums[x]);
        Console.WriteLine();
        for(x = 0; x < someNums.Length; ++x)
            MethodGetsOneInt(someNums[x]);
        Console.Write("At end of Main() method..........");
        for(x = 0; x < someNums.Length; ++x)
            Console.Write("{0,6}", someNums[x]);
    }
    public static void MethodGetsOneInt(int oneVal)
    {
        Console.Write("In MethodGetsOneInt() {0}", oneVal);
        oneVal = 999;
        Console.WriteLine("     After change {0}", oneVal);
    }
}
```

**Figure 7-13**  PassArrayElement program

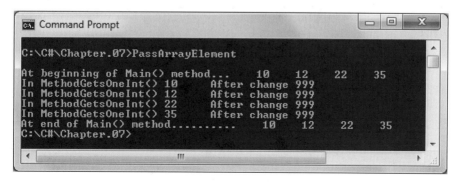

**Figure 7-14**  Output of PassArrayElement program

As you can see in Figure 7-14, the program displays the four original values, then passes each to the `MethodGetsOneInt()` method, where it is displayed and then changed to 999. After the method executes four times, the `Main()` method displays the four values again, showing that they are unchanged by the assignments within `MethodGetsOneInt()`. The `oneVal` variable is local to the `MethodGetsOneInt()` method; therefore, any changes to variables passed into the method are not permanent and are not reflected in the array declared in the `Main()` program. Each time the `MethodGetsOneInt()` method executes, its `oneVal` parameter holds only a copy of the array element passed into the method, and the `oneVal` variable exists only while the `MethodGetsOneInt()` method is executing.

You already have seen that methods can alter arrays passed to them. When you use the `Sort()` and `Reverse()` methods, the methods change the array contents.

Instead of passing a single array element to a method, you can pass an entire array. You indicate that a method parameter must be an array by placing square brackets after the data type in the method's parameter list. When you pass an array to a method, changes you make to array elements within the method are permanent; they are reflected in the original array that was sent to the method. Arrays, like all objects but unlike built-in types, are **passed by reference**; in other words, the method receives the actual memory address of the array and has access to the actual values in the array elements.

You can create and pass an unnamed array to a method in a single step. For example, you can write the following:

```
MethodThatAcceptsArray(new int[] {45, 67, 89});
```

The program shown in Figure 7-15 creates an array of four integers. After the integers are displayed, the entire array is passed to a method named `MethodGetsArray()` in the shaded statement. Within the method header, the parameter is declared as an array by using square brackets after the parameter data type. Within the method, the numbers are output, which shows that they retain their values from `Main()` upon entering the method, but then the value 888 is assigned to each number. Even though `MethodGetsArray()` is a void method (meaning that nothing is returned to the `Main()` method), when the program displays the array for the second time within the `Main()` method, all of the values have been changed to 888, as you can see in Figure 7-16. Because arrays are passed by reference, the `MethodGetsArray()` method "knows" the address of the array declared in `Main()` and makes its changes directly to the original array that was declared in the `Main()` method.

```
using System;
public class PassEntireArray
{
   public static void Main()
   {
      int[] someNums = {10, 12, 22, 35};
      int x;
      Console.Write("\nAt beginning of Main() method...");
      for(x = 0; x < someNums.Length; ++x)
         Console.Write("{0, 6}", someNums[x]);
      Console.WriteLine();
      MethodGetsArray(someNums);
      Console.Write("At end of Main() method.........");
      for(x = 0; x < someNums.Length; ++x)
         Console.Write("{0, 6}", someNums[x]);
   }
   public static void MethodGetsArray(int[] vals)
   {
      int x;
      Console.Write("In MethodGetsArray() ");
      for(x = 0; x < vals.Length; ++x)
         Console.Write(" {0}", vals[x]);
      Console.WriteLine();
      for(x = 0; x < vals.Length; ++x)
         vals[x] = 888;
      Console.Write("After change");
      for(x = 0; x < vals.Length; ++x)
         Console.Write(" {0}", vals[x]);
      Console.WriteLine();
   }
}
```

**Figure 7-15**   PassEntireArray program

**Figure 7-16**   Output of the PassEntireArray program

You can pass a multidimensional array to a method by indicating the appropriate number of dimensions after the data type in the method header. For example, the following method headers accept two-dimensional arrays of ints and doubles, respectively:

```
public static void displayScores(int[,]scoresArray)
```

```
public static boolean areAllPricesHigh(double[,] prices)
```

With jagged arrays, you can insert the appropriate number of square brackets after the data type in the method header. For example, the following method headers accept jagged arrays of ints and doubles, respectively:

```
public static void displayIDs(int[][] idArray)
public static double computeTotal(double[][] prices)
```

In each case, notice that the brackets that define the array in the method header are empty. Inserting numbers into the brackets is not necessary because each passed array name is a starting memory address. The way you manipulate subscripts within the method determines how rows and columns are accessed.

Watch the video *Passing Arrays to Methods.*

The size of each dimension of a multidimensional array can be accessed using the GetLength() method. For example, scoresArray.GetLength(0) returns the value of the first dimension of scoresArray.

---

## TWO TRUTHS **&** A LIE

### Passing an Array to a Method

1.  You indicate that a method parameter can be an array element by placing a data type and identifier in the method's parameter list.

2.  You indicate that a method parameter must be an array by placing parentheses after the data type in the method's parameter list.

3.  Arrays are passed by reference; that is, the method receives the actual memory address of the array and has access to the actual values in the array elements.

The false statement is #2. You indicate that a method parameter must be an array by placing square brackets after the data type in the method's parameter list.

# Alternate Ways to Write a Main() Method Header

Throughout this book, you have written Main() methods with the following header:

```
public static void Main()
```

Using the return type void and listing nothing between the parentheses that follow Main is just one way to write a Main() method header in a program. However, it is the first way listed in the C# documentation, and it is the convention used in this book.

You might see different Main() method headers in other books or in programs written by others. An alternate way to write a Main() method header is as follows:

```
public static void Main(string[] args)
```

The phrase string[] args is a parameter to the Main() method. The variable args represents an array of strings that you can pass to Main(). Although you can use any identifier, args is conventional. Use this format for the Main() method header if you need to access command-line arguments passed in to your application. For example, the program in Figure 7-17 displays an args array that is a parameter to its Main() method. Figure 7-18 shows how a program might be executed from the command line using arguments to Main().

```
using System;
public class DisplayArgs
{
    public static void Main(string[] args)
    {
        for(int x = 0; x < args.Length; ++ x)
            Console.WriteLine("Argument {0} is {1}", x, args[x]);
    }
}
```

**Figure 7-17**  A Main() method with a string[] args parameter

In particular, Java programmers might prefer the version of Main() that includes the string[] args parameter because conventionally they write their main methods with the same parameter.

**Figure 7-18**   Executing the DisplayArgs program with arguments

Even if you do not need access to command-line arguments, you can still use the version of the Main() method header that references them. You should use this version if your instructor or supervisor indicates you should follow this convention.

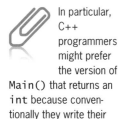

In particular, C++ programmers might prefer the version of Main() that returns an int because conventionally they write their main methods with an int return type.

Some programmers prefer to write Main() method headers that have a return type of int instead of void. If you use this form, the last statement in the Main() method must be a return statement that returns an integer. By convention, a return value of 0 means that an application ended without error. The value might be used by your operating system or another program that uses your program.

Even if you do not need to use a return value from a Main() method, you can still use the version of the Main() method header that uses a return value. You should use this version if your instructor or supervisor indicates you should follow this convention.

---

## TWO TRUTHS **&** A LIE

### Alternate Ways to Write a Main() Method Header

1.  In C#, a Main() method header can be written public static void Main().

2.  In C#, a Main() method header can be written public static void Main(string[] args).

3.  In C#, a Main() method header can be written public static int main(string args).

The false statement is #3. In C#, a Main() method header can be written as shown in either of the first two examples, or as public static int Main(string[] args). That is, Main() must be capitalized and string must be followed by a pair of square brackets.

# Issues Using Methods in GUI Programs

You can call methods from other methods in a GUI application in the same way you can in a console application. Some special considerations when creating GUI applications are:

- Understanding methods that are automatically generated in the visual environment

- Appreciating scope in a GUI program

- Creating methods to be nonstatic when associated with a `Form`

## Understanding Methods that are Automatically Generated in the Visual Environment

When you create GUI applications using the IDE, many methods are generated automatically. For example, when you place a `Button` named `okButton` on a `Form` in the IDE and double-click it, a method is generated with the following header:

```
private void okButton_Click(object sender, EventArgs e)
```

The method is `private`, which means it can only be used within its class, and it is `void`, meaning it does not return a value. The parameters it receives arrive automatically when a user clicks the `okButton`. The parameter `sender` is the object that generated the event that caused the method to execute, and the parameter `e` contains information about the type of event. Figure 7-19 shows a `Click()` method in a GUI application that displays the `ToString()` values of these two parameters.

```
private void okButton_Click(object sender, EventArgs e)
{
    label1.Text = sender.ToString();
    label2.Text = e.ToString();
}
```

**Figure 7-19**   The `okButton_Click()` method in the `ClickParameterDemo` program

Figure 7-20 shows the output after the button is clicked. The object that generated the event is the button that contains the text "OK" and the type of event was generated by a mouse. You have seen many `Click()` methods in earlier chapters that had the same parameters, but you did not use them. As with any other method, you never are required to use the parameters passed in.

**Figure 7-20**  Output generated by the `okButton_Click()` method in Figure 7-19

## Appreciating Scope in A GUI Program

When you create event-handling methods in a GUI application, you must constantly be aware of which variables and constants are needed by multiple methods. When you declare a variable or constant within a method, it is local to that method. If a variable or constant is needed by multiple event-handling methods—for example, by two different `Click()` methods—then the variables or constants in question must be defined outside the methods (but within the `Form` class) so that both `Click()` methods have access to them. When you write other methods, you can decide what arguments to pass in, but automatically generated event-handling methods have predefined sets of parameters, so you cannot be as flexible in using them as you can with other methods you write.

## Creating Methods to be Nonstatic when Associated with a `Form`

You might have noticed that automatically generated event-handling methods in your GUI programs are `private` by default. You also might want to make your called methods `private` instead of `public`, although this is not required to make a working program.

In Chapter 1, you learned that the keyword `static` is used with `Main()` methods in console applications because the method is associated with its containing class and not with an object. When you create a GUI application and generate a method, such as a `Click()` method associated with a `Button` on a `Form`, the keyword `static` does not appear in the method header because the method is associated with an object—the `Form` from which the method-invoking events are sent. Nonstatic methods can only call other methods that also are nonstatic. In the chapter *Using Classes and Objects*, you will learn much more about the differences between static and nonstatic methods. For now, omit the word `static` when you create methods that are intended to be called by other nonstatic methods in your GUI applications.

# You Do It

## Calling a Method

**To write a program in which a Main() method calls another method that displays a company's logo:**

1.  Open a new file in your text editor. Enter the statement that uses the System namespace, then type the class header for the DemoLogo class and type the class-opening curly brace.

    ```
    using System;
    public class DemoLogo
    {
    ```

2.  Type the Main() method for the DemoLogo class. This method displays a line, then calls the DisplayCompanyLogo() method.

    ```
    public static void Main()
    {
       Console.Write("Our company is ");
       DisplayCompanyLogo();
    }
    ```

3. Add a method that displays a two-line logo for a company.

```
public static void DisplayCompanyLogo()
{
    Console.WriteLine("See Sharp Optical");
    Console.WriteLine("We prize your eyes");
}
```

4. Add the closing curly brace for the class ( } ), then save the file as **DemoLogo.cs**.

5. Compile and execute the program. The output should look like Figure 7-21.

**Figure 7-21**  Output of the DemoLogo program

## Writing a Method that Receives Parameters and Returns a Value

Next, you will write a method named CalcPhoneCallPrice() that both receives parameters and returns a value. The purpose of the method is to take the length of a phone call in minutes and the rate charged per minute, and to then calculate the price of a call, assuming each call includes a 25-cent connection charge in addition to the per-minute charge. After writing the CalcPhoneCallPrice() method, you will write a Main() method that calls the CalcPhoneCallPrice() method using four different sets of data as arguments.

**To create a class containing a method that receives two parameters and returns a value:**

1. Open your text editor and type the **using System;** statement.

2. Add the class header for **public class PhoneCall** and an opening curly brace.

3. Type the following CalcPhoneCallPrice() method. It receives an integer and a double as parameters. The fee for a call is calculated as 0.25 plus the minutes times the rate per minute. The method returns the phone call fee to the calling method.

```
public static double CalcPhoneCallPrice(int minutes,
   double rate)
{
   const double BASE_FEE = 0.25;
   double callFee;
   callFee = BASE_FEE + minutes * rate;
   return callFee;
}
```

4. Add the `Main()` method header for the `PhoneCall` class. Begin the method by declaring two arrays; one contains two call lengths and the other contains two rates. You will use all the possible combinations of call lengths and rates to test the `CalcPhoneCallPrice()` method. Also, declare a `double` named `priceOfCall` that will hold the result of a calculated call price.

```
public static void Main()
{
   int[] callLength = {2, 5};
   double[] rate = { 0.03, 0.12};
   double priceOfCall;
```

5. Add a statement that displays column headings under which you can list combinations of call lengths, rates, and prices. The three column headings are right-aligned, each in a field ten characters wide.

```
Console.WriteLine("{0, 10}{1, 10}{2, 10}",
   "Minutes", "Rate", "Price");
```

6. Add a pair of nested loops that, in turn, passes each `callLength` and each `rate` to the `CalcPhoneCallPrice()` method. As each pair is passed, the result is stored in the `priceOfCall` variable, and the details are displayed. Using the nested loops allows you to pass each combination of call time and rate so that multiple possibilities for the values can be tested conveniently.

```
for(int x = 0; x < callLength.Length; ++x)
   for(int y = 0; y < rate.Length; ++y)
   {
      priceOfCall = CalcPhoneCallPrice(callLength[x],
         rate[y]);
      Console.WriteLine("{0, 10}{1, 10}{2, 10}",
         callLength[x], rate[y],
         priceOfCall.ToString("C"));
   }
```

7. Add a closing curly brace for the `Main()` method and another for the `PhoneCall` class.

8. Save the file as **PhoneCall.cs**. Compile and run the program. The output looks like Figure 7-22. It shows how a single method can produce a variety of results when you use different values for the arguments.

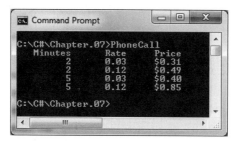

**Figure 7-22**  Output of the PhoneCall program

# Chapter Summary

- A method is a series of statements that carry out a task. Any class can contain an unlimited number of methods. Object-oriented programs hide their methods' implementations; a client method uses an interface to work with the method.

- You write methods to make programs easier to understand and so that you can easily reuse them. In C#, a method must include a method declaration, an opening curly brace, a method body, and a closing curly brace. The method declaration defines the rules for using the method; it contains an optional declared accessibility, an optional static modifier, a return type for the method, an identifier, and an optional list of method parameters between parentheses.

- Some methods require passed-in information. The data items sent in method calls are arguments. The items received by a method are parameters. When you write the declaration for a method that can receive a parameter, you need to include the type of parameter and a local identifier for it within the method declaration parentheses. A variable declared in a method header is a formal parameter, and an argument within a method call is an actual parameter.

- You can pass multiple arguments to a method by listing the arguments within the parentheses in the call to the method and separating them with commas. You can write a method to take any number of parameters in any order. When you call the method, however, the arguments you send to it must match (in both number and type) the parameters listed in the method declaration.

- The return type for a method defines the type of value sent back to the calling method. It can be any type used in the C# programming language, which includes the basic built-in types int, double, char, and so on, as well as class types (including class types you create). A method also can return nothing, in which case the return type is void.

- You can pass an array as a parameter to a method. You indicate that a method parameter is an array by placing square brackets after the data type in the method's parameter list. Arrays, like all objects but unlike built-in types, are passed by reference; that is, the method receives the actual memory address of the array and has access to the actual values in the array elements.

- You might see different Main() method headers in other books or in programs written by others. Some programmers include an array of strings as a parameter to Main(), and some programmers return an int from the Main() method.

- Special considerations exist for methods when you create GUI applications. You must understand the automatically generated methods in the visual environment, appreciate the differences in scope in GUI programs, and understand that many methods must be nonstatic when associated with a Form.

## Key Terms

A **method** is an encapsulated series of statements that carry out a task.

Methods are **invoked**, or **called**, by other methods.

**Implementation hiding** means keeping the details of a method's operations hidden.

To **interface** with a system is to interact with it.

A **black box** is any device you can use without knowing how it works internally.

A **client** is a method that uses another method.

A **calling method** calls another method.

A method invoked by another is a **called method**.

A **multifile assembly** is a group of files containing methods that work together to create an application.

**Code bloat** is a term that describes unnecessarily long or repetitive program statements.

A **method declaration** is a **method header** or **method definition**.

A **method body** is a block of statements that carry out a method's work.

**Accessibility** for a method is a declaration that sets limits as to whether and how other methods can use the method.

**Public access** is a level of method accessibility that allows unlimited access to a method.

**Private access** is a level of method accessibility that limits method access to the containing class.

A **static** method can be called without referring to an object. It can be called using its class name, a dot, and the method name. Within its class, a static method can be called by just using its name.

A **nonstatic** method requires an object reference.

A **return type** indicates what kind of value a method will return to any other method that calls it.

A **method's type** is its return type.

A **parameter to a method** is a variable that holds data passed to a method when it is called.

A variable's **scope** is the segment of program code where it can be used.

A **local variable** is one that is declared in the current method.

A **formal parameter** is a parameter within a method header that accepts a value.

**Actual parameters** are arguments within a method call.

A **return statement** causes a value to be sent back from a method to its calling method.

**Nested method calls** are method calls placed inside other method calls.

When data is **passed by reference** to a method, the method receives the memory address of the argument passed to it.

# Review Questions

1. At most, a class can contain _____ method(s).

   a. 0

   b. 1

   c. 2

   d. any number of

2. What is the most important reason for creating methods within a program?

   a. Methods are easily reusable.

   b. Because all methods must be stored in the same class, they are easy to find.

   c. The `Main()` method becomes more detailed.

   d. All of these are true.

3. In C#, a method must include all of the following *except* a _____.

   a. return type

   b. parameter list

   c. body

   d. closing curly brace

4. A method declaration might contain _____.

   a. declared accessibility

   b. a nonstatic modifier

   c. multiple return types

   d. parameters separated by dots

5. A method declaration must contain _____.

   a. a statement of purpose

   b. declared accessibility

   c. the static modifier

   d. a return type

6. If you want to create a method that other methods can access without limitations, you declare the method to be _____.

   a. unlimited

   b. public

   c. shared

   d. unrestricted

7. If you use the keyword modifier static in a method header, you indicate that the method _____.

   a. can be called without referring to an object

   b. cannot be copied

   c. can be called only once

   d. cannot require parameters

8. A method's type is also its _____.

   a. accessibility

   b. parameter type

   c. return type

   d. scope

9. When you use a method, you do not need to know how it operates internally. This feature is called _____.

   a. scope management

   b. selective ignorance

   c. privacy

   d. implementation hiding

10. When you write the method declaration for a method that can receive a parameter, you need to include all of the following items *except* _____.

   a. a pair of parentheses

   b. the type of the parameter

   c. a local name for the parameter

   d. an initial value for the parameter

11. Suppose you have declared a variable as `int myAge = 21;`.
    Which of the following is a legal call to a method with the
    declaration `public static void AMethod(int num)`?

    a. `AMethod(int 55);`

    b. `AMethod(myAge);`

    c. `AMethod(int myAge);`

    d. `AMethod();`

12. Suppose you have declared a method named `public`
    `static void CalculatePay(double rate)`. When a
    method calls the `CalculatePay()` method, the calling
    method _____.

    a. must contain a declared `double` named `rate`

    b. might contain a declared `double` named `rate`

    c. cannot contain a declared `double` named `rate`

    d. cannot contain any declared `double` variables

13. In the method call `PrintTheData(double salary);`, `salary`
    is the _____ parameter.

    a. formal

    b. actual

    c. proposed

    d. preferred

14. A program contains the method call `PrintTheData(salary);`.
    In the method definition, the name of the formal parameter
    must be _____.

    a. `salary`

    b. any legal identifier other than `salary`

    c. any legal identifier

    d. omitted

15. What is a correct declaration for a method that receives two `double` arguments and calculates and displays the difference between them?

    a. `public static void CalcDifference(double price1, price2)`

    b. `public static void CalcDifference(double price1, double price2)`

    c. Both of these are correct.

    d. None of these are correct.

16. What is a correct declaration for a method that receives two `double` arguments and sums them?

    a. `public static void CalcSum(double firstValue, double secondValue)`

    b. `public static void CalcSum(double price1, double price2)`

    c. Both of these are correct.

    d. None of these are correct.

17. A method is declared as `public static double CalcPay(int hoursWorked)`. Suppose you write a `Main()` method in the same class that contains the declarations `int hours = 35;` and `double pay;`. Which of the following represents a correct way to call the `CalcPay()` method from the `Main()` method?

    a. `hours = CalcPay();`

    b. `hours = Main.CalcPay();`

    c. `pay = CalcPay(hoursWorked);`

    d. `pay = CalcPay(hours);`

18. Suppose the value of `isRateOK()` is `true` and the value of `isQuantityOK()` is `false`. When you evaluate the expression `isRateOK() || isQuantityOK()`, which of the following is true?

    a. Only the method `isRateOK()` executes.

    b. Only the method `isQuantityOK()` executes.

    c. Both methods execute.

    d. Neither method executes.

19. Suppose the value of isRateOK() is true and the value of isQuantityOK() is false. When you evaluate the expression isRateOK() && isQuantityOK(), which of the following is true?

    a. Only the method isRateOK() executes.

    b. Only the method isQuantityOK() executes.

    c. Both methods execute.

    d. Neither method executes.

20. When an array is passed to a method, the method has access to the array's memory address. This means an array is passed by _____.

    a. reference

    b. value

    c. alias

    d. orientation

# Exercises

1. Create a C# statement that uses each of the following built-in methods you have used in previous chapters, then make an intelligent guess about the return type and parameter list for the method used in each statement you created.

    a. Console.WriteLine()

    b. String.Equals()

    c. String.Compare()

    d. Convert.ToInt32()

    e. Convert.ToChar()

    f. Array.Sort()

2. a. Create a console-based program whose Main() method uses several WriteLine() calls to display a memo to your boss. Use the company name "C# Software Developers" at least three times in the memo. Each time you want to display the company name, call a method named DisplayCompanyName() that displays the name as part of the memo. Save the file as **Memo.cs**.

b. Create a GUI version of the Memo program. When the user clicks a button, display the memo, getting the company name from the DisplayCompanyName() method. Save the project as **MemoGUI**.

3. a. Create a console-based program whose Main() method holds two integer variables. Assign values to the variables. Within the class, create two methods, Sum() and Difference(), that compute the sum of and difference between the values of the two variables, respectively. Each method should perform the computation and display the results. In turn, call each of the two methods from Main(), passing the values of the two integer variables. Save the program as **Numbers.cs**.

b. Add a method named Product() to the Numbers class. This method should compute the multiplication product of two integers, but not display the answer. Instead, it should return the answer to the calling Main() method, which displays the answer. Save the program as **Numbers2.cs**.

c. Create a GUI application that contains the methods described in Exercises 3a and 3b. When the user clicks a button, display the results. Save the project as **Numbers2GUI**.

4. a. Create a console-based application whose Main() method holds an integer variable named inches, and prompt the user for a value. Create a method to which you pass inches. The method converts the value to feet and inches and displays the result. For example, 67 inches is 5 feet 7 inches. Save the program as **InchesToFeet.cs**.

b. Add a second method to the InchesToFeet class. This method displays a passed argument as yards, feet, and inches. For example, 67 inches is 1 yard, 2 feet, and 7 inches. Add a statement to the Main() method so that after it calls the method to convert inches to feet and inches, it passes the same variable to the new method to convert the same value to yards, feet, and inches and then displays the result. Save the program as **InchesToYards.cs**.

c. Create a GUI application in which the user enters a value for inches. When the user clicks a button, convert the value to feet and inches and to yards, feet, and inches, using separate methods for the calculations described in Exercises 4a and 4b. Save the project as **InchesConversionsGUI**.

5. a. Create a console-based program whose Main() method contains six character variables that hold your first, middle, and last initials, and a friend's first, middle, and last initials, respectively. Create a method named DisplayMonogram() to which you pass three initials. The method displays the initials surrounded by two asterisks on each side and with periods following each initial, as shown in the following example:

   ** J. M. F. **

   Within the Main() method, call the DisplayMonogram() method twice—once using your initials and once using your friend's initials. Save the program as **Monogram.cs**.

   b. Create a GUI application that allows a user to enter three initials into three TextBoxes. After the user clicks a button, pass the initials to the DisplayMonogram() method described in Exercise 5a. (For a more interesting application, you might want to increase the font size of the output Label.) Save the project as **MonogramGUI**.

6. a. Create a console-based application whose Main() method asks the user to input an integer and then calls a method named MultiplicationTable(), which displays the results of multiplying the integer by each of the numbers 2 through 10. Save the file as **Multiplication.cs**.

   b. Create a GUI application that calls the MultiplicationTable() method described in Exercise 6a after the user enters an integer into a TextBox and clicks a Button. Save the project as **MultiplicationGUI**.

7. a. Create a console-based program named Commission. Its Main() method calls two other methods. The first called method should ask a salesperson for the dollar value of daily sales and return the entered value to the Main() method. (Assume all sales are in whole dollars.) The second called method should calculate the salesperson's commission based on the rates in the accompanying table.

| Sales | Commission |
| --- | --- |
| 0–999 | 3% |
| 1000–2999 | 4% |
| 3000–up | 5% |

The dollar value of the calculated commission should be returned to the Main() method, which then displays the value. Save the file as **Commission.cs**.

b. Create a GUI version of the class described in Exercise 7a. Save the project as **CommissionGUI**.

8. a. Create a console-based program whose Main() method prompts the user for an integer value and, in turn, passes the value to a method that squares the number and to a method that cubes the number. The Cube() method should call the Square() method. The Main() method displays the results returned from each of the other methods. Save the program as **Exponent.cs**.

b. Create a GUI application that accomplishes the same tasks as Exercise 8a. Save the project as **ExponentGUI**.

9. a. Create a console-based application that computes the price of a desk and whose Main() method calls four other methods:

- A method to accept the number of drawers in the desk as input from the keyboard. This method returns the number of drawers to the Main() method.

- A method to accept as input and return the type of wood—'m' for mahogany, 'o' for oak, or 'p' for pine.

- A method that accepts the number of drawers and wood type, and calculates the cost of the desk based on the following:

  - Pine desks are $100.

  - Oak desks are $140.

  - All other woods are $180.

  - A $30 surcharge is added for each drawer.

  - This method returns the cost to the Main() method.

- A method to display all the details and the final price.

Save the file as **Desks.cs**.

b. Create a GUI application that accepts desk order data from TextBoxes and whose button's Click() method calls all the methods described in Exercise 9a. Save the project as **DesksGUI**.

10. a. Create a console-based application whose `Main()` method accepts ten integer values from the user at the keyboard and stores them in an array. Pass the array to a method that determines and displays the smallest and largest of the ten values. Save the file as **SmallAndLarge.cs**.

    b. Create a GUI application whose button's `Click()` method accepts ten integer values from a `TextBox` and stores them in an array that is declared above the `Click()` method. After ten entries have been made, call a method that determines and displays the smallest and largest of the ten values. Save the project as **SmallAndLargeGUI**.

11. Create either a console-based or GUI program that declares at least three integer arrays of different sizes. In turn, pass each array to a method that displays all the integers in each array and their sum. Save the file as **FlexibleArrayMethod.cs** or the project as **FlexibleArrayMethodGUI**.

 ## Debugging Exercises

Each of the following files in the Chapter.07 folder of your down-loadable student files has syntax and/or logical errors. In each case, determine the problem and fix the program. After you correct the errors, save each file using the same filename preceded with *Fixed*. For example, DebugSeven1.cs will become FixedDebugSeven1.cs.

   a. DebugSeven1.cs

   b. DebugSeven2.cs

   c. DebugSeven3.cs

   d. DebugSeven4.cs

 ## Up For Discussion

1. In this chapter, you learned that hidden implementations are often said to exist in a black box. What are the advantages to this approach in both programming and real life? Are there any disadvantages?

2.  Software developers employ black box testing and white box testing of their programs. First, try to guess what the terms mean. Then, find out what they actually mean. If you could only use one approach, which would it be?

3.  In this chapter you learned how to use command-line arguments with a `Main()` method. Describe at least three situations in which using this approach would provide a practical benefit.

# Advanced Method Concepts

In this chapter you will:

◎ Learn about parameter types: `ref` parameters, `out` parameters, and parameter arrays

◎ Overload methods

◎ Learn how to avoid ambiguous methods

◎ Use optional parameters

In the last chapter, you learned to call methods, pass arguments to them, and receive values from them. In this chapter, you will expand your method-handling skills to include some more sophisticated techniques, including using reference, output, and optional parameters and overloading methods. Understanding how to manipulate methods is crucial when you are working on large, professional, real-world projects. With methods, you can coordinate your work with that of other programmers.

# Understanding Parameter Types

In C#, you can write methods with several kinds of formal parameters listed within the parentheses in the method header. Parameters can be mandatory or optional. When you use a **mandatory parameter,** an argument for it is required in every method call.

The four types of mandatory parameters are:

- Value parameters when they are declared without default values

- Reference parameters, which are declared with the `ref` modifier

- Output parameters, which are declared with the `out` modifier

- Parameter arrays, which are declared with the `params` modifier

C# supports only one type of optional parameter:

- Value parameters when they are declared with default values

## Using Mandatory Value Parameters

So far, all of the method parameters you have created have been mandatory, and all except arrays have been value parameters. When you use a **value parameter** in a method header, you indicate the parameter's type and name, and the method receives a copy of the value passed to it.

A popular advertising campaign declares, "What happens in Vegas, stays in Vegas." The same is true of value parameters within a method—changes to them do not persist outside the method.

The value of a method's value parameter is stored at a different memory address than the variable that was used as the argument in the method call. In other words, the actual parameter (the argument in the calling method) and the formal parameter (the parameter in the method header) refer to two separate memory locations, and the called method receives a copy of the sent value. Changes to value parameters never affect the original arguments in calling methods.

Figure 8-1 shows a program that declares a variable named `quantity`, assigns 4 to it, displays the variable, and passes it to a method that accepts a value parameter. The method assigns a new value, 777, to the passed parameter and displays it. When control returns to the Main() method, the value of quantity remains 4. Changing the value of quantity within the DisplayValueParameter() method has no effect on quantity in Main(). Even though both methods contain a variable named quantity, they represent two separate variables, each with its own memory location. Figure 8-2 shows the output.

```csharp
using System;
public class ParameterDemo1
{
    public static void Main()
    {
        int quantity = 4;
        Console.WriteLine("In Main quantity is {0}", quantity);
        DisplayValueParameter(quantity);
        Console.WriteLine("In Main quantity is {0}", quantity);
    }
    public static void DisplayValueParameter(int quantity)
    {
        quantity = 777;
        Console.WriteLine("In DisplayValueParameter(), quantity is {0}",
            quantity);
    }
}
```

**Figure 8-1** Program calling method with a value parameter

**Figure 8-2** Output of ParameterDemo1 program

 Programmers say that a value parameter is used for "in" parameter passing—that is, values for these parameters go into a method, but modifications to them do not come "out."

 A variable that is used as an argument to a method with a value parameter must have a value assigned to it. If it does not, the program will not compile.

In the program in Figure 8-1, it makes no difference whether you use the name quantity as the Main() method's actual parameter or use some other name. In either case, the parameter received by the DisplayValueParameter() method occupies a separate memory location.

318

## Using Reference and Output Parameters

On occasion, you might want a method to be able to alter a value you pass to it. In that case, you can use a reference parameter or an output parameter. Both **reference parameters** and **output parameters** represent memory addresses that are passed to a method, allowing the method to alter the original variables. Reference and output parameters differ as follows:

- When you declare a reference parameter in a method header, the argument used to call the method must have been assigned a value.

- When you use an output parameter, the argument used in the call need not contain an original, assigned value. However, an output parameter must be assigned a value before the method ends.

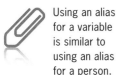

Using an alias for a variable is similar to using an alias for a person. Jane Doe might be known as "Ms. Doe" at work but "Sissy" at home. Both names refer to the same person.

Neither reference nor output parameters occupy their own memory locations. Rather, both reference and output parameters act as **aliases**, or pseudonyms (other names), for the same memory location occupied by the original passed variable. You use the keyword ref as a modifier to indicate a reference parameter and the keyword out as a modifier to indicate an output parameter.

Figure 8-3 shows a Main() method that calls a DisplayReferenceParameter() method. The Main() method declares a variable, displays its value, and then passes the variable to the DisplayReferenceParameter() method in the shaded statement. The modifier ref precedes both the variable name in the method call and the parameter declaration in the method header. The method's parameter number refers to the memory address of quantity, making number an alias for quantity. When DisplayReferenceParameter() changes the value of number, the change persists in the quantity variable within Main(). Figure 8-4 shows the output of the program.

```
using System;
public class ParameterDemo2
{
    public static void Main()
    {
        int quantity = 4;
        Console.WriteLine("In Main quantity is {0}", quantity);
        DisplayReferenceParameter(ref quantity); // notice use of ref
        Console.WriteLine("In Main quantity is {0}", quantity);
    }
    public static void DisplayReferenceParameter(ref int number)
        // notice use of ref
    {
        number = 888;
        Console.WriteLine("In DisplayReferenceParameter(), number is {0}",
            number);
    }
}
```

**Figure 8-3**  Program calling method with a reference parameter

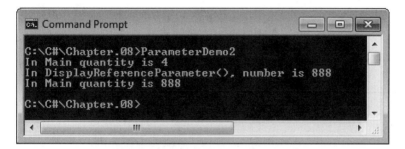

**Figure 8-4**  Output of `ParameterDemo2` program

In the header for the `DisplayReferenceParameter()` method, it makes no difference whether you use the same name as the `Main()` method's passed variable (`quantity`) or some other name, such as `number`. In either case, the passed and received variables occupy the same memory location—the address of one is the address of the other.

When you use a reference parameter, any passed variable must have an assigned value. Using an output parameter is convenient when the passed variable does not have a value yet. For example, the program in Figure 8-5 uses `InputMethod()` to obtain values for two parameters. The arguments that are sent in the shaded statement get their values from the method, so it makes sense to provide them with no values going in. Instead, they acquire values in the method and retain the values coming out. Figure 8-6 shows a typical execution of the program.

```
using System;
public class InputMethodDemo
{
    public static void Main()
    {
        int first, second;
        InputMethod(out first, out second); // notice use of out
        Console.WriteLine("After InputMethod first is {0}", first);
        Console.WriteLine("and second is {0}", second);
    }
    public static void InputMethod(out int one, out int two)
        // notice use of out
    {
        string s1, s2;
        Console.Write("Enter first integer ");
        s1 = Console.ReadLine();
        Console.Write("Enter second integer ");
        s2 = Console.ReadLine();
        one = Convert.ToInt32(s1);
        two = Convert.ToInt32(s2);
    }
}
```

**Figure 8-5** InputMethodDemo program

**Figure 8-6** Output of InputMethodDemo program

In summary, when you need a method to alter a single value, you have two options:

- You can send an argument to a method that accepts a value parameter, alter the local version of the variable within the method, return the altered value, and assign the return value to the original variable back in the calling method.

- You can send an argument to a method that accepts a reference or output parameter and alter the value at the original memory location within the method.

A major advantage to using reference or output parameters exists when you want a method to change multiple variables. A method can have only a single return type and can return only one value at most. By using reference or output parameters to a method, you can change multiple values.

However, a major disadvantage to using reference and output parameters is that they allow multiple methods to have access to the same data, weakening the "black box" paradigm that is so important to object-oriented methodology. You should never use ref or out parameters to avoid having to return a value, but you should understand them so you can use them if required.

Watch the video *Using* ref *and* out *Parameters*.

As with simple parameters, you can use out or ref when passing an array to a method. You do so when you want to declare the array in the calling method, but use the new operator to allocate memory for it in the called method.

## Using Parameter Arrays

When you do not know how many arguments of the same data type you might eventually send to a method, you can declare a **parameter array**—a local array declared within the method header by using the keyword **params**. Such a method accepts any number of arguments that are all the same type.

For example, a method with the following header accepts an array of strings:

```
public static void DisplayStrings(params string[] people)
```

In the call to this method, you can use one, two, or any other number of strings as actual parameters; within the method, they will be treated as an array. Figure 8-7 shows a program that calls `DisplayStrings()` three times—once with one string argument, once with three string arguments, and once with an array of strings. In each case, the method works correctly, treating the passed strings as an array and displaying them appropriately. Figure 8-8 shows the output.

```
using System;
public class ParamsDemo
{
    public static void Main()
    {
        string[] names = {"Mark", "Paulette", "Carol", "James"};
        DisplayStrings("Ginger");
        DisplayStrings("George", "Maria", "Thomas");
        DisplayStrings(names);
    }
    public static void DisplayStrings(params string[] people)
    {
        foreach(string person in people)
            Console.Write("{0} ", person);
        Console.WriteLine("\n----------------");
    }
}
```

**Figure 8-7** ParamsDemo program

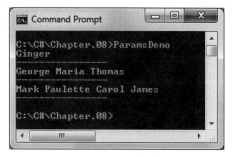

**Figure 8-8** Output of `ParamsDemo` program

You could create an even more flexible method by using a method header such as `Display(params Object[] things)`. Then the passed parameters could be any type—strings, integers, other classes, and so on. The method could be implemented as follows:

```
public static void Display(params Object[] things)
{
    foreach(Object obj in things)
        Console.Write("{0} ", obj);
    Console.WriteLine("\n---------------")
}
```

All data types are `Object`s; you will learn more about the `Object` class in the chapters *Using Classes and Objects* and *Introduction to Inheritance*.

When a method header uses the `params` keyword, the following two restrictions apply:

- Only one `params` keyword is permitted in a method declaration.

- If a method declares multiple parameters, the `params`-qualified parameter must be the last one in the list.

## TWO TRUTHS & A LIE

### Understanding Parameter Types

1. Both reference and output parameters represent memory addresses that are passed to a method, allowing the method to alter the original variables.

2. When you declare a reference parameter in a method header, the parameter must not have been assigned a value.

3. When you use an output parameter, it need not contain an original, assigned value when the method is called, but it must receive a value before the method ends.

The false statement is #2. When you declare a reference parameter in a method header, the parameter must have been assigned a value.

# Overloading Methods

**Overloading** involves using one term to indicate diverse meanings. When you use the English language, you frequently overload words. When you say "open the door," "open your eyes," and "open a computer file," you describe three very different actions that use different methods and produce different results. However, anyone who speaks English fluently has no trouble comprehending your meaning because the verb "open" is understood in the context of the noun that follows it.

Some C# operators are overloaded. For example, a + between two values indicates addition, but a single + to the left of a value means the value is positive. The + sign has different meanings based on the arguments used with it. In the chapter *Using Classes and Objects,* you will learn how to overload operators to make them mean what you want with your own classes.

When you overload a C# method, you write multiple methods with a shared name but different parameter lists. A method's name and parameter list constitute the method's **signature**.

The compiler understands which method to use based on the arguments you use in a method call. For example, suppose you create a method to display a string surrounded by a border. The method receives a string and uses the string Length property to determine how many asterisks to use to construct a border around the string. Figure 8-9 shows a program that contains the method.

Recall that arrays and strings both automatically have a Length property.

```
using System;
public class BorderDemo1
{
    public static void Main()
    {
        DisplayWithBorder("Ed");
        DisplayWithBorder("Theodore");
        DisplayWithBorder("Jennifer Ann");
    }
    public static void DisplayWithBorder(string word)
    {
        const int EXTRA_STARS = 4;
        const string SYMBOL = "*";
        int size = word.Length + EXTRA_STARS;
        int x;
        for(x = 0; x < size; ++x)
            Console.Write(SYMBOL);
        Console.WriteLine();
        Console.WriteLine(SYMBOL + " " + word + " " + SYMBOL);
        for(x = 0; x < size; ++x)
            Console.Write(SYMBOL);
        Console.WriteLine("\n\n");
    }
}
```

**Figure 8-9**   The BorderDemo1 program

When the Main() method calls the DisplayWithBorder() method
in the program in Figure 8-9 and passes a string value, the method
calculates a size as the length of the string plus 4, and then draws that
many symbols on a single line. The method then displays a symbol,
a space, the string, another space, and another symbol on the next
line. The method ends by again displaying a row of symbols and some
blank lines. Figure 8-10 shows the output.

**Figure 8-10** Output of the `BorderDemo1` program

Suppose you are so pleased with the output of the `DisplayWithBorder()` method that you want to use something similar to display your company's weekly sales goal figure. The problem is that the weekly sales goal amount is stored as an integer, and so it cannot be passed to the existing method. You can take one of several approaches:

- You can convert the integer sales goal to a `string` and use the existing method. This is an acceptable approach, but it requires that you remember to write an extra step in any program in which you display an integer using the border.

- You can create a new method with a unique name such as `DisplayWithBorderUsingInt()` and use it to accept an integer parameter. The drawback to this approach is that you must remember different method names when you use different data types.

- You can overload the `DisplayWithBorder()` method. Overloading methods involves writing multiple methods with the same name, but with different parameter types. For example, in addition to the `DisplayWithBorder()` method shown in Figure 8-9, you could use the method shown in Figure 8-11.

```
public static void DisplayWithBorder(int number)
{
    const int EXTRA_STARS = 4;
    const string SYMBOL = "*";
    int size   = EXTRA_STARS + 1;
    int leftOver = number;
    int x;
    while(leftOver >= 10)
    {
        leftOver = leftOver / 10;
        ++size;
    }
    for(x = 0; x < size; ++x)
        Console.Write(SYMBOL);
    Console.WriteLine();
    Console.WriteLine(SYMBOL + " " + number + " " + SYMBOL);
    for(x = 0; x < size; ++x)
        Console.Write(SYMBOL);
    Console.WriteLine("\n\n");
}
```

**Figure 8-11** The DisplayWithBorder() method with an integer parameter

In the version of the DisplayWithBorder() method in Figure 8-11, the parameter is an int. The method used to determine how many asterisks to display is to discover the number of digits in the parameter by repeatedly dividing by 10. For example, when the argument to the method is 456, leftOver is initialized to 456. Because it is at least 10, it is divided by 10, giving 45, and size is increased to 2. Then 45 is divided by 10, giving 4, and size is increased to 3. Because 4 is not at least 10, the loop ends, and the program has determined that the parameter contains three digits. The rest of the method executes like the original version that accepts a string parameter.

The DisplayWithBorder() method does not quite work correctly if a negative integer is passed to it because the negative sign occupies an additional display space. To rectify the problem, you could modify the method to add an extra symbol to the border when a negative argument is passed in, or you could force all negative numbers to be their positive equivalent.

If both versions of DisplayWithBorder() are included in a program and you call the method using a string, as in DisplayWithBorder("Ed"), the first version of the method shown in Figure 8-9 executes. If you use an integer as the argument in the call to DisplayWithBorder(), as in DisplayWithBorder(456), then the method shown in Figure 8-11 executes. Figure 8-12 shows a program that demonstrates several method calls, and Figure 8-13 shows the output.

```
using System;
public class BorderDemo2
{
   public static void Main()
   {
      DisplayWithBorder("Ed");
      DisplayWithBorder(3);
      DisplayWithBorder(456);
      DisplayWithBorder(897654);
      DisplayWithBorder("Veronica");
   }
   public static void DisplayWithBorder(string word)
   {
      const int EXTRA_STARS = 4;
      const string SYMBOL = "*";
      int size = word.Length + EXTRA_STARS;
      int x;
      for(x = 0; x < size; ++x)
         Console.Write(SYMBOL);
      Console.WriteLine();
      Console.WriteLine(SYMBOL + " " + word + " " + SYMBOL);
      for(x = 0; x < size; ++x)
         Console.Write(SYMBOL);
      Console.WriteLine("\n\n");
   }
   public static void DisplayWithBorder(int number)
   {
      const int EXTRA_STARS = 4;
      const string SYMBOL = "*";
      int size  = EXTRA_STARS + 1;
      int leftOver = number;
      int x;
      while(leftOver >= 10)
      {
         leftOver = leftOver / 10;
         ++size;
      }
      for(x = 0; x < size; ++x)
         Console.Write(SYMBOL);
      Console.WriteLine();
      Console.WriteLine(SYMBOL + " " + number + " " + SYMBOL);
      for(x = 0; x < size; ++x)
         Console.Write(SYMBOL);
      Console.WriteLine("\n\n");
   }
}
```

**Figure 8-12**   The BorderDemo2 program

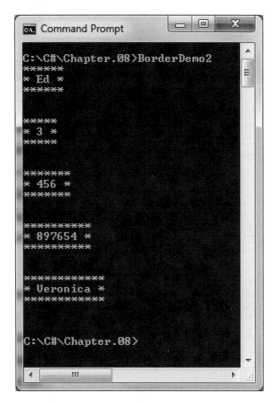

**Figure 8-13**   Output of the BorderDemo2 program

Methods are overloaded correctly when they have the same identifier but their parameter lists are different. Parameter lists differ when the number and order of types within the lists are unique. For example, you could write several methods with the same identifier and one method could accept an int, another two ints, and another three ints. A fourth overloaded method could accept an int followed by a double, and another could accept a double followed by an int. Yet another version could accept no parameters. The parameter identifiers in overloaded methods do not matter, and neither do the return types of the method. Only the method identifier and parameter list types cause a method to be overloaded.

Instead of overloading methods, you can choose to use methods with different names to accept the diverse data types, and you can place a decision within your program to determine which version of the method to call. However, it is more convenient to use one method name and then let the compiler determine which method to use. Overloading a method also makes it more convenient for other programmers to use your method in the future. Frequently, you create overloaded methods in your classes not because you need them immediately, but because you know client programs might need multiple versions in the future, and it is easier for programmers to remember one reasonable name for tasks that are functionally identical except for parameter types.

Usually you do not create overloaded methods so that a single program can use all the versions. More often, you create overloaded methods so different programs can use the version most appropriate to the task at hand.

**329**

In this book you have seen the `Console.WriteLine()` method used with a string parameter, a numeric parameter, and with no parameter. You have also seen it used with several parameters when you use a format string along with several variables. Therefore, you know `Console.WriteLine()` is an overloaded method.

## Understanding Overload Resolution

When a method call could execute multiple overloaded method versions, C# determines which method to execute using a process called **overload resolution**. For example, suppose you create a method with the following declaration:

```
public static void MyMethod(double d)
```

You can call this method using a `double` argument, as in the following:

```
MyMethod(2.5);
```

You can also call this method using an `int` argument, as in the following:

```
MyMethod(4);
```

The call that uses the `int` argument works because an `int` can automatically be promoted to a `double`.

In Chapter 2, you learned that when an `int` is promoted to a `double`, the process is called an *implicit conversion* or *implicit cast*.

Suppose you create overloaded methods with the following declarations:

```
public static void MyMethod(double d)
public static void MyMethod(int i)
```

If you then call `MyMethod()` using an integer argument, both methods are **applicable methods**. That means either method on its own could accept a call that uses an `int`. However, if both methods exist in the same class (making them overloaded), the second version will execute because it is a better match for the method call. The rules that determine which method version to call are known as **betterness rules**.

Betterness rules are similar to the implicit conversion rules you learned in Chapter 2. For example, although an `int` could be accepted by a method that accepts an `int`, a `float`, or a `double`, an `int` is the best match. If no method version with an `int` parameter exists, then a `float` is a better match than a `double`. Table 8-1 shows the betterness rules for several data types.

| Data type | Conversions are better in this order |
|-----------|--------------------------------------|
| byte | short, ushort, int, uint, long, ulong, float, double, decimal |
| sbyte | short, int, long, float, double, decimal |
| short | int, long, float, double, decimal |
| ushort | int, uint, long, ulong, float, double, decimal |
| int | long, float, double, decimal |
| uint | long, ulong, float, double, decimal |
| long | float, double, decimal |
| ulong | float, double, decimal |
| float | double |
| char | ushort, int, uint, long, ulong, float, double, decimal |

**Table 8-1**   Betterness rules for data type conversion

## Understanding Built-In Overloaded Methods

When you use the IDE to create programs, Visual Studio's IntelliSense features provide information about methods you are using. For example, Figure 8-14 shows the IDE while the programmer is typing a reference to the `Convert.ToInt32()` method to accept an integer from a `TextBox`. Notice the drop-down list that indicates `Convert.ToInt32(bool value)` is just 1 of 19 overloaded versions of the method. When retrieving an entry from a `TextBox` on a `Form`, your intention is to use the `Convert.ToInt32(string value)` version of the method, but many overloaded versions are available for your convenience. C# could have included multiple methods with different names such as `ConvertBool.ToInt32()` and `ConvertString.ToInt32()`, but having a single method with the name `Convert.ToInt32()` that takes many different argument types makes it easier for you to remember the method name and to use it. As you work with the IDE, you will examine many such methods.

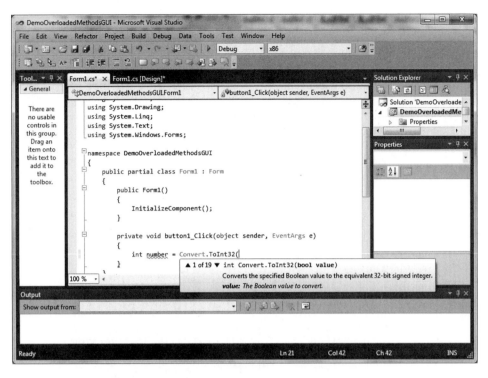

**Figure 8-14** Examining the overloaded versions of Convert.ToInt32()

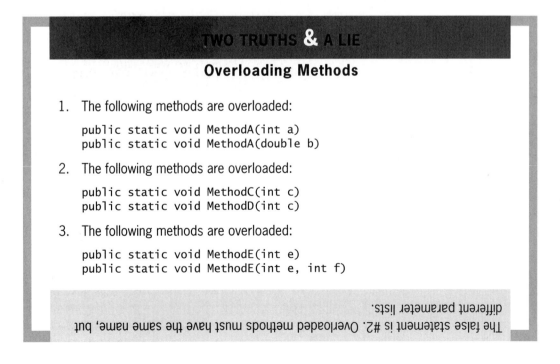

TWO TRUTHS **&** A LIE

## Overloading Methods

1. The following methods are overloaded:

   ```
   public static void MethodA(int a)
   public static void MethodA(double b)
   ```

2. The following methods are overloaded:

   ```
   public static void MethodC(int c)
   public static void MethodD(int c)
   ```

3. The following methods are overloaded:

   ```
   public static void MethodE(int e)
   public static void MethodE(int e, int f)
   ```

The false statement is #2. Overloaded methods must have the same name, but different parameter lists.

# Avoiding Ambiguous Methods

When you overload a method, you run the risk of creating **ambiguous** methods—a situation in which the compiler cannot determine which method to use. Every time you call a method, the compiler decides whether a suitable method exists; if so, the method executes, and if not, you receive an error message.

For example, suppose you write two versions of a simple method, as in the program in Figure 8-15. The class contains two versions of a method named SimpleMethod()—one that takes a double and an int, and one that takes an int and a double.

```
using System;
public class AmbiguousMethods
{
    public static void Main()
    {
        int iNum = 20;
        double dNum = 4.5;
        SimpleMethod(iNum, dNum);   // calls first version
        SimpleMethod(dNum, iNum);   // calls second version
        SimpleMethod(iNum, iNum);   // error! Call is ambiguous.
    }
    public static void SimpleMethod(int i, double d)
    {
        Console.WriteLine("Method receives int and double");
    }
    public static void SimpleMethod(double d, int i)
    {
        Console.WriteLine("Method receives double and int");
    }
}
```

**Figure 8-15**　Program containing ambiguous method call

In the Main() method in Figure 8-15, a call to SimpleMethod() with an integer argument first and a double argument second executes the first version of the method, and a call to SimpleMethod() with a double argument first and an integer argument second executes the second version of the method. With each of these calls, the compiler can find an exact match for the arguments you send. However, if you call SimpleMethod() using two integer arguments, as in the shaded statement, an ambiguous situation arises because there is no exact match for the method call. Because the first integer could be promoted to a double (matching the second version of the overloaded method), or the second integer could be promoted to a double (matching the first version), the compiler does not know which version of SimpleMethod() to use, and the program will not compile or execute. Figure 8-16 shows the error message that is generated.

```
C:\C#\Chapter.08>csc Ambiguousmethods.cs
Microsoft (R) Visual C# 2010 Compiler version 4.0.21006.1
Copyright (C) Microsoft Corporation. All rights reserved.

AmbiguousMethods.cs(10,7): error CS0121: The call is ambiguous between the
        following methods or properties: 'AmbiguousMethods.SimpleMethod(int,
        double)' and 'AmbiguousMethods.SimpleMethod(double, int)'

C:\C#\Chapter.08>
```

**Figure 8-16**  Error message generated by ambiguous method call

 If you remove one of the versions of SimpleMethod() from the program in Figure 8-15, then the method call that uses two integer arguments would work, because one of the integers could be promoted to a double.

 An overloaded method is not ambiguous on its own—it becomes ambiguous only if you create an ambiguous situation. A program with potentially ambiguous methods will run without problems if you make no ambiguous method calls. For example, if you remove the SimpleMethod() call that contains two integers from the program in Figure 8-15, the program runs as expected.

Methods can be overloaded correctly by providing different parameter lists for methods with the same name. Methods with identical names that have identical parameter lists but different return types are not overloaded—they are illegal. For example, the following two methods cannot coexist within a class:

```
public static int AMethod(int x)
public static void AMethod(int x)
```

The compiler determines which of several versions of a method to call based on parameter lists. When the method call AMethod(17); is made, the compiler will not know which method to execute because both possibilities take an integer argument. Similarly, the following method could not coexist with either of the previous versions:

```
public static void AMethod(int someNumber)
```

Even though this method uses a different local identifier for the passed value, its parameter list—a single integer—is still the same to the compiler.

 Watch the video *Overloading Methods.*

> **TWO TRUTHS & A LIE**
>
> ## Avoiding Ambiguous Methods
>
> 1. The following methods are potentially ambiguous:
>
> ```
> public static int Method1(int g)
> public static int Method1(int g, int h)
> ```
>
> 2. The following methods are potentially ambiguous:
>
> ```
> public static double Method2(int j)
> public static void Method2(int k)
> ```
>
> 3. The following methods are potentially ambiguous:
>
> ```
> public static void Method3(string m)
> public static string Method3(string n)
> ```

The false statement is #1. Those methods are not ambiguous because they have different parameter lists. Their matching return types do not cause ambiguity.

# Using Optional Parameters

Sometimes it is useful to create a method that allows one or more arguments to be omitted from the method call. An **optional parameter** to a method is one for which a default value is automatically supplied if you do not explicitly send one as an argument. You make a parameter optional by providing a value for it in the method declaration. Only value parameters can be given default values; ref, out, and array parameters cannot have default values. Any optional parameters in a parameter list must follow all mandatory parameters.

For example, suppose you write a method that calculates either the area of a square or the volume of a cube, depending on whether two or three arguments are sent to it. Figure 8-17 shows such a method; notice the shaded default value provided for the third parameter. When you want a cube's volume, you can pass three arguments to the method: length, width, and height. When you want a square's area, you pass only two parameters, and a default value of 1 is used for the height. In this example, the height is a default parameter and is optional; the length and width, which are not provided with default values, are mandatory parameters. That is, at least two arguments must be sent to the DisplaySize() method, but three can be sent. In the program in Figure 8-17, calling DisplaySize(4, 6) has the same effect as calling DisplaySize(4, 6, 1). Figure 8-18 shows the execution of the OptionalParameterDemo program.

```
using System;
public class OptionalParameterDemo
{
    public static void Main()
    {
        Console.Write("Using 2 arguments: ");
        DisplaySize(4, 6);
        Console.Write("Using 3 arguments: ");
        DisplaySize(4, 6, 8);
    }
    public static void DisplaySize(int length, int width, int height = 1)
    {
        int area = length * width * height;
        Console.WriteLine("Size is {0}", area);
    }
}
```

**Figure 8-17**  The OptionalParameterDemo class

**Figure 8-18**  Execution of the OptionalParameterDemo program

If you assign a default value to any variable in a method's parameter list, then all parameters to the right of that parameter must also have default values. Table 8-2 shows some examples of valid and invalid method declarations.

| Method declaration | Explanation |
| --- | --- |
| public static void M1(int a, int b, int c, int d = 10) | Valid. The first three parameters are mandatory and the last one is optional. |
| public static void M2(int a, int b = 3, int c) | Invalid. Because b has a default value, c must also have one. |
| public static void M3(int a = 3, int b = 4, int c = 5) | Valid. All parameters are optional. |
| public static void M4(int a, int b, int c) | Valid. All parameters are mandatory. |
| public static void M5(int a = 4, int b, int c = 8) | Invalid. Because a has a default value, both b and c must have default values. |

**Table 8-2**  Examples of valid and invalid optional parameter method declarations

When you call a method that contains default parameters, you can always choose to write a method call that provides a value for every parameter. However, if you omit an argument when you call a method that has default parameters, then you must do one of the following:

- You must leave out all unnamed arguments to the right of the last argument you use.

- You can name arguments.

## Leaving Out Unnamed Arguments

When you call a method with optional parameters (and you are using unnamed arguments), you must leave out any arguments to the right of the last one you use. In other words, as soon as you leave out an argument, you must leave out all the arguments that would otherwise follow.

For example, assume you have declared a method as follows:

```
public static void Method1(int a, char b, int c = 22,
    double d = 33.2)
```

Table 8-3 shows some legal and illegal calls to this method.

| Call to Method1() | Explanation |
| --- | --- |
| Method1(1, 'A', 3, 4.4); | Valid. The four arguments are assigned to the four parameters. |
| Method1(1, 'K', 9); | Valid. The three arguments are assigned to a, b, and c in the method, and the default value of 33.2 is used for d. |
| Method1(5, 'D'); | Valid. The two arguments are assigned to a and b in the method, and the default values of 22 and 33.2 are used for c and d, respectively. |
| Method1(1); | Invalid. Method1() requires at least two arguments. |
| Method1(); | Invalid. Method1() requires at least two arguments. |
| Method1(3, 18.5); | Invalid. The first argument, 3, can be assigned to a, but the second argument must be type char. |
| Method1(4, 'R', 55.5); | Invalid. The first argument, 4, can be assigned to a, and the second argument, 'R', can be assigned to b, but the third argument must be type int. You cannot "skip" parameter c, use its default value, and assign 55.5 to parameter d. |

**Table 8-3**    Examples of legal and illegal calls to Method1()

# Using Named Arguments

In C# 4.0, you can leave out optional arguments in a method call if you pass the remaining arguments by name. Named arguments can appear in any order, but they must appear after all the unnamed arguments have been listed. You name an argument using its parameter name and a colon before the value.

For example, assume you have declared a method as follows:

```
public static void Method2(int a, char b, int c = 22,
    double d = 33.2)
```

Table 8-4 shows some legal and illegal calls to this method.

| Call to Method2() | Explanation |
| --- | --- |
| Method2(1, 'A'); | Valid. The two arguments are assigned to a and b in the method, and the default values of 22 and 33.2 are used for c and d, respectively. |
| Method2(2, 'E', 3); | Valid. The three arguments are assigned to a, b, and c. The default value 33.2 is used for d. |
| Method2(2, 'E', c : 3); | Valid. This call is identical to the one above. |
| Method2(1, 'K', d : 88.8); | Valid. The first two arguments are assigned to a and b. The default value 22 is used for c. The named value 88.8 is used for d. |
| Method2(5, 'S', d : 7.4, c: 9); | Valid. The first two arguments are assigned to a and b. Even though the values for c and d are not listed in order, they are assigned correctly. (Note that parameter values can be expressions instead of constants. In this method call, then, it might be important to realize that the value of d would be evaluated before the value of c.) |
| Method2(d : 11.1, 6, 'P'); | Invalid. Named arguments must appear after all unnamed arguments. |

**Table 8-4**    Examples of legal and illegal calls to Method2()

Optional parameters can provide a convenient shortcut to writing multiple overloaded versions of a method. For example, suppose you want to create a method that adds your signature to business letters. Usually, you want the signature to be "Sincerely, James O'Hara". However, occasionally you want to change the name to a more casual "Jim". You could write two method versions, as shown on the top in Figure 8-19, or you could write one version, as shown on the bottom. With both versions, you can call Closing() with or without an argument. The version with the optional parameter is less work when you write the method. It is also less work if you later want to modify the method—for example, to change "Sincerely," to "Best wishes," or some other closing.

```
// Overloaded implementations of Closing()
public static void Closing()
{
    Console.WriteLine("Sincerely,");
    Console.WriteLine("James O'Hara");
}
public static void Closing(string name)
{
    Console.WriteLine("Sincerely,");
    Console.WriteLine(name);
}

// Single implementation of Closing() with optional parameter
public static void Closing(string name = "James O'Hara")
{
    Console.WriteLine("Sincerely,");
    Console.WriteLine(name);
}
```

**Figure 8-19** Two ways to implement Closing() to accept a name parameter or not

A disadvantage to using named arguments is that the calling method becomes linked to details within the method. This means that an important principle of programming—method implementation hiding—is compromised. If the parameter name in the called method is changed in the future, the client method also will have to change.

## Overload Resolution with Named and Optional Arguments

Named and optional arguments affect overload resolution. The rules for betterness on argument conversions are applied only for arguments that are given explicitly; in other words, omitted optional arguments are ignored for betterness purposes. For example, suppose you have the following methods:

```
public static void AMethod(int a, double b = 2.2)
public static void AMethod(int a, char b = 'H')
```

Both are applicable methods; in other words, if either method existed alone, the call AMethod(12) would work. When the two methods coexist, however, neither is "better." Because C# cannot determine which one is better, the code will not compile.

If two signatures are equally good, the one that does not omit optional parameters is considered better. For example, suppose you have two methods as follows:

```
public static void BMethod(int a)
public static void BMethod(int a, char b = 'B')
```

If either method existed alone, the call BMethod(12) would work, but when the two coexist, the first version is better because no optional parameters are omitted in the call.

Watch the video *Using Optional Method Parameters*.

---

**TWO TRUTHS & A LIE**

### Using Optional Parameters

1.  An optional parameter to a method is one for which an argument can be a value parameter, a ref parameter, or an out parameter.

2.  You make a parameter optional by providing a value for it in the method declaration.

3.  If you assign a default value to any variable in a method's parameter list, then all parameters to the right of that parameter must also have default values.

The false statement is #1. An optional parameter to a method is one for which a default value is automatically supplied if you do not explicitly send one as an argument.

---

# You Do It

## Using Reference Parameters

You use reference parameters when you want a method to have access to the memory address of arguments in a calling method. For example, suppose you have two values and you want to exchange them (or swap them), making each equal to the value of the other. Because you want to change two values, a method that accepts copies of arguments will not work—a method can return one value at most. Therefore, you can use reference parameters to provide your method with the actual addresses of the values you want to change.

340

**To write a program that uses a method to swap two values:**

1. Open your editor and begin the SwapProgram as follows:

```
using System;
public class SwapProgram
{
    public static void Main()
    {
```

2. Declare two integers and display their values. Call the Swap() method and pass in the addresses of the two variables to swap. Because the parameters already have assigned values, and because you want to alter those values in Main(), you can use reference parameters. After the method call, display the two values again. Add the closing curly brace for the Main() method.

```
int first = 34, second = 712;
Console.Write("Before swap first is {0}", first);
Console.WriteLine(" and second is {0}", second);
Swap(ref first, ref second);
Console.Write("After swap first is {0}", first);
Console.WriteLine(" and second is {0}", second);
}
```

3. Create the Swap() method as shown. You can swap two values by storing the first value in a temporary variable, then assigning the second value to the first variable. At this point, both variables hold the value originally held by the second variable. When you assign the temporary variable's value to the second variable, the two values are reversed.

```
public static void Swap(ref int one, ref int two)
{
    int temp;
    temp = one;
    one = two;
    two = temp;
}
```

4. Add the closing curly brace for the class. Save the file as **SwapProgram.cs**. Compile and execute the program. Figure 8-20 shows the output.

Before swap first is 34 and second is 712
After swap first is 712 and second is 34

```
C:\C#\Chapter.08>SwapProgram
Before swap first is 34 and second is 712
After swap first is 712 and second is 34

C:\C#\Chapter.08>
```

**Figure 8-20** Output of SwapProgram program

You might want to use a module like Swap() as part of a larger program in which you verify, for example, that a higher value is displayed before a lower one; you would include the call to Swap() as part of a decision whose body executes only when a first value is less than a second one.

**341**

## Overloading Methods

In the next steps, you will overload a method that correctly triples an integer or a string, depending on how you call the method.

1.  Open a new file in your text editor. Create a method that triples and displays an integer parameter as follows:

    ```
    public static void Triple(int num)
    {
        const int MULT_FACTOR = 3;
        Console.WriteLine("{0} times {1} is {2}\n",
            num, MULT_FACTOR, num * MULT_FACTOR);
    }
    ```

2.  Create a second method with the same name that takes a string parameter. Assume you want to define tripling a message as displaying it three times, separated by tabs.

    ```
    public static void Triple(string message)
    {
        Console.WriteLine("{0}\t{0}\t{0}\n", message);
    }
    ```

3.  Position your cursor at the top of the file and add a `using` statement, class header, and opening curly brace so the overloaded `Triple()` methods will be contained in a class named `OverloadedTriples`.

    ```
    using System;
    public class OverloadedTriples
    {
    ```

4.  Position your cursor at the bottom of the file and add the closing curly brace for the `OverloadedTriples` class.

5.  Position your cursor after the opening curly brace for the class. On a new line, insert a `Main()` method that declares an integer and a string and, in turn, passes each to the appropriate `Triple()` method.

```
public static void Main()
{
    int num = 20;
    string message = "Go team!";
    Triple(num);
    Triple(message);
}
```

6. Save the file as **OverloadedTriples.cs**. Compile and execute the program. Figure 8-21 shows the output. Even though the same method name is used in the two method calls, the appropriate overloaded method executes each time.

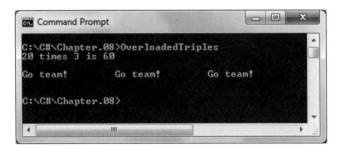

**Figure 8-21**   Output of OverloadedTriples program

# Chapter Summary

- Method parameters can be mandatory or optional. The mandatory parameters are reference parameters, which are declared with the `ref` modifier; output parameters, which are declared with the `out` modifier; and parameter arrays, which are declared with the `params` modifier. Value parameters can be mandatory or optional.

- When you overload a C# method, you write multiple methods with a shared name but different parameter lists. The compiler understands your meaning based on the combination of arguments you use with the method. When a method call could execute multiple overloaded method versions, C# determines which method to execute using a process called overload resolution.

- When you overload a method, you run the risk of creating an ambiguous situation—one in which the compiler cannot determine which method to use. Methods can be overloaded correctly by providing different parameter lists for methods with the same name.

- An optional parameter to a method is one for which a default value is automatically supplied if you do not explicitly send one as an argument. You make a parameter optional by providing a value for it in the method declaration. When you call a method with optional parameters, you must leave out all unnamed arguments to the right of the last argument you use, or you can name arguments.

# Key Terms

**Mandatory parameters** are method parameters for which an argument is required in every method call.

A **value parameter** in a method header receives a copy of the value passed to it; a value parameter is declared using the parameter's type and an identifier.

A **reference parameter** in a method header must have been assigned a value before it is used in the method call; the method receives the parameter's address.

An **output parameter** in a method header need not contain an original value; the method receives the parameter's address.

**Aliases** are alternate names or pseudonyms.

A **parameter array** is a local array declared within a method header.

The keyword **params** is used to declare a local array in a method so the method can receive any number of arguments.

**Overloading** involves using one term to indicate diverse meanings. When you overload a C# method, you write multiple methods with the same name but different parameter lists.

A method's **signature** is composed of its name and parameter list.

**Overload resolution** is the process of determining which of multiple applicable methods is the best match for a method call.

**Applicable methods** are all the methods that could be used by a method call if the method was not overloaded.

**Betterness rules** are the rules that determine the best overloaded method to execute based on the arguments in a method call.

**Ambiguous** methods are overloaded methods from which the compiler cannot determine which one to use.

An **optional parameter** to a method is one for which a default value is automatically supplied if you do not explicitly send one as an argument; a parameter is optional when it is given a value in the method declaration.

# Review Questions

1. A mandatory parameter _____.

    a. is any argument sent to a method

    b. is preceded by the keyword `man`

    c. requires an argument to be sent from a method call

    d. All of the above are true.

2. Which is *not* a type of method parameter in C#?

    a. value

    b. reference

    c. forensic

    d. output

3. Which type of method parameter receives the address of the variable passed in?

    a. a value parameter

    b. a reference parameter

    c. an output parameter

    d. two of the above

4. When you declare a value parameter, you precede its name with _____.

    a. nothing

    b. a data type

    c. the keyword `val` and a data type

    d. the keyword `ref` and its data type

5. Assume you declare a variable as `int x = 100;` and correctly pass it to a method with the declaration `public static void IncreaseValue(ref int x)`. There is a single statement within the `IncreaseValue()` method: `x = x + 25;`. Back in the `Main()` method, after the method call, what is the value of x?

    a. 100

    b. 125

c. It is impossible to tell.

d. The program will not run.

6. Assume you declare a variable as `int x = 100;` and correctly pass it to a method with the declaration `public static void IncreaseValue(int x)`. There is a single statement within the `IncreaseValue()` method: `x = x + 25;`. Back in the `Main()` method, after the method call, what is the value of `x`?

   a. 100

   b. 125

   c. It is impossible to tell.

   d. The program will not run.

7. What is the difference between a reference parameter and an output parameter?

   a. A reference parameter receives a memory address; an output parameter does not.

   b. A reference parameter occupies a unique memory address; an output parameter does not.

   c. A reference parameter must have an initial value; an output parameter need not.

   d. A reference parameter need not have an initial value; an output parameter must.

8. A parameter array _____.

   a. is declared using the keyword `params`

   b. can accept any number of arguments of the same data type

   c. Both of these are true.

   d. None of these are true.

9. Assume you have declared a method with the following header:

   `public static void DisplayScores(params int[] scores)`

   Which of the following method calls is valid?

   a. `DisplayScores(20);`

   b. `DisplayScores(20, 33);`

   c. `DisplayScores(20, 30, 90);`

   d. All of the above are valid.

10. Correctly overloaded methods must have the same _____.

    a. return type

    b. identifier

    c. parameter list

    d. All of the above.

11. Methods are ambiguous when they _____.

    a. are overloaded

    b. are written in a confusing manner

    c. are indistinguishable to the compiler

    d. have the same parameter type as their return type

12. Which of the following pairs of method declarations represent correctly overloaded methods?

    a. `public static void MethodA(int a)`
       `public static void MethodA(int b, double c)`

    b. `public static void MethodB(double d)`
       `public static void MethodB()`

    c. `public static double MethodC(int e)`
       `public static double MethodD(int f)`

    d. Two of these are correctly overloaded methods.

13. Which of the following pairs of method declarations represent correctly overloaded methods?

    a. `public static void Method(int a)`
       `public static void Method(int b)`

    b. `public static void Method(double d)`
       `public static int Method()`

    c. `public static double Method(int e)`
       `public static int Method(int f)`

    d. Two of these are correctly overloaded methods.

14. The process of determining which overloaded version of a method to execute is overload _____.

    a. confusion

    b. infusion

    c. revolution

    d. resolution

15. When one of a method's parameters is optional, it means that _____.

    a. no arguments are required in a call to the method

    b. a default value will be assigned to the parameter if no argument is sent for it

    c. a default value will override any argument value sent to it

    d. you are not required to use the parameter within the method body

16. Which of the following is an illegal method declaration?

    a. `public static void CreateStatement(int acctNum,`
       `   double balance = 0.0)`

    b. `public static void CreateStatement(int acctNum`
       `   = 0, double balance)`

    c. `public static void CreateStatement(int acctNum`
       `   = 0, balance = 0)`

    d. All of these are legal.

17. Assume you have declared a method as follows:

    ```
    public static double ComputeBill(int
    acct, double price, double discount = 0)
    ```

    Which of the following is a legal method call?

    a. `ComputeBill();`

    b. `ComputeBill(1001);`

    c. `ComputeBill(1001, 200.00);`

    d. None of the above are legal.

18. Assume you have declared a method as follows:

    ```
    public static double CalculateDiscount(int acct = 0,
        double price = 0, double discount = 0)
    ```

    Which of the following is a legal method call?

    a. `CalculateDiscount();`

    b. `CalculateDiscount(200.00);`

    c. `CalculateDiscount(3000.00. 0.02);`

    d. None of the above are legal.

19. Assume you have declared a method as follows:

    ```
    public static double DisplayData(string name = "XX",
        double amount = 10.0)
    ```

    Which of the following is an illegal method call?

    a. `DisplayData(name : "Albert");`

    b. `DisplayData(amount : 200, name : "Albert");`

    c. `DisplayData(amount : 900.00);`

    d. All of these are legal.

20. Suppose you have declared an integer array named `scores` and you make the following method call:

    ```
    TotalScores(scores, num : 1);
    ```

    Of the following overloaded method definitions, which would execute?

    a. `TotalScores(int[] scores)`

    b. `TotalScores(int[] scores, int num)`

c.  `TotalScores(int[] scores, int num = 10,`
    `int code = 10)`

d.  The program would not compile.

# Exercises

1.  a.  Create a console-based program whose `Main()` method declares three integers named `firstInt`, `middleInt`, and `lastInt`. Assign values to the variables, display them, and then pass them to a method that accepts them as reference variables, places the first value in the `lastInt` variable, and places the last value in the `firstInt` variable. In the `Main()` method, display the three variables again, demonstrating that their positions have been reversed. Save the program as **Reverse3.cs**.

    b.  Create a new program named `Reverse4`, which contains a method that reverses the positions of four variables. Write a `Main()` method that demonstrates the method works correctly. Save the program as **Reverse4.cs**.

    c.  Create a GUI application that accepts four integers from a user. When the user clicks a button, the application calls a method that reverses the positions of the variables. Save the project as **Reverse4GUI**.

2.  a.  Create a console-based application whose `Main()` method declares an array of eight integers. Call a method to interactively fill the array with any number of values up to eight. Call a second method that accepts `out` parameters for the arithmetic average and the sum of the values in the array. Display the array values, the number of entered elements, and their average and sum in the `Main()` method. Save the program as **ArrayManagement.cs**.

    b.  Create a GUI application with eight text boxes. Allow the user to enter any number of integers up to eight. When the user clicks a button, call a method to store the entered numbers in an array. Then call a second method that accepts `out` parameters for the arithmetic average and the sum of the values in the array. Display the array values, the number of entered elements, and their average and sum. Save the project as **ArrayManagementGUI**.

3. a. Create a console-based application named `Area`. Include three overloaded methods that compute the area of a rectangle when two dimensions are passed to it. One method takes two integers as parameters, one takes two `doubles`, and the third takes an integer and a `double`. Write a `Main()` method that demonstrates each method works correctly. Save the program as **Area.cs**.

   b. Create a GUI application that demonstrates the same methods as Exercise 3a when the user clicks a button. Save the project as **AreaGUI**.

4. a. Create a console-based application named `ComputeWeeklySalary`. Include two overloaded methods—one that accepts an annual salary as an integer and one that accepts an annual salary as a `double`. Each method should calculate and display a weekly salary, assuming 52 weeks in a year. Include a `Main()` method that demonstrates both overloaded methods work correctly. Save the program as **ComputeWeeklySalary.cs**.

   b. Create a GUI application that demonstrates the methods described in Exercise 4a when the user clicks a button. Save the project as **ComputeWeeklySalaryGUI**.

5. a. Create a console-based application named `TaxCalculation`. Include two overloaded methods—one that accepts a price and a tax rate expressed as `doubles` (for example, 79.95 and 0.06, where 0.06 represents 6%), and one that accepts a price as a `double` and a tax rate as an integer (for example, 79.95 and 6, where 6 also represents 6%). Include a `Main()` method that demonstrates each method calculates the same tax amount appropriately. Save the program as **TaxCalculation.cs**.

   b. Create a GUI application that demonstrates the methods described in Exercise 5a when a user clicks a button. Save the project as **TaxCalculationGUI**.

6. The `InputMethod()` in the `InputMethodDemo` program in Figure 8-5 contains repetitive code that prompts the user and retrieves integer values. Rewrite the program so the `InputMethod()` calls another method to do the work. The rewritten `InputMethod()` will need to contain only two statements:

```
one = DataEntry("first");
two = DataEntry("second");
```

Save the new program as **InputMethodDemo2.cs**.

7. Create a method named Sum() that accepts any number of integer parameters and displays their sum. Write a Main() method that demonstrates the Sum() method works correctly when passed one, three, or five integers, or an array of ten integers. Save the program as **UsingSum.cs**.

8. Rewrite the Desks program you created in Chapter 7 so that all the methods are void methods and receive ref or out parameters as appropriate. Save the file as **Desks2.cs**.

9. a. Write a method named CustomerCreditLimit() that accepts a double as a parameter and displays the value as the amount of credit granted to a customer. Provide a default value for the method so that if a program calls the method without using an argument, the credit limit displays $500. Write a console-based program with a Main() method that proves the credit limit method works correctly whether it is called with an argument or not. Save the file as **Credit.cs**.

   b. Create a GUI application that calls the methods described in Exercise 9a when the user clicks a button. Save the project as **CreditGUI**.

10. a. Write a method that accepts and displays two parameters: a string name of a movie and an integer running time in minutes. Provide a default value for the minutes so that if you call the method without an integer argument, minutes is set to 90. Write a console-based program with a Main() method that proves you can call the movie method with only a string argument as well as with a string and an integer. Save the file as **Movie.cs**.

    b. Write a GUI application that demonstrates the methods described in Exercise 10a when the user clicks a button. Save the project as **MovieGUI**.

11. a. In the card game War, a deck of playing cards is divided between two players. Each player exposes a card; the player whose card has the higher value wins possession of both exposed cards. Create a computerized game of War in which a standard 52-card deck is randomly divided

between two players, one of which is the computer. Reveal one card for the computer and one card for the player at a time. Award two points for the player whose card has the higher value. (For this game the king is the highest card, followed by the queen and jack, then the numbers 10 down to 2, and finally the ace.) If the computer and player expose cards with equal values in the same turn, award one point to each. At the end of the game, all 52 cards should have been played only once, and the sum of the player's and computer's score will be 52.

Use an array of 52 integers to store unique values for each card. Write a method named `FillDeck()` that places 52 unique values into this array. Write another method named `SelectCard()` that you call twice on each deal to select a unique card for each player, with no repetition of cards in 26 deals.

The left side of Figure 8-22 shows the start of a typical program execution.

Save the program as **WarCardGame.cs**. (Caution: This is a difficult exercise!)

> To pause the play between each dealt hand, use a call to `ReadLine()`.

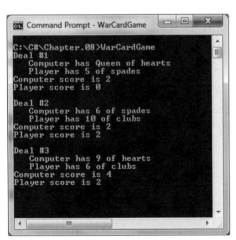
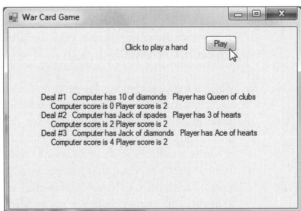

**Figure 8-22** Start of typical execution of console-based and GUI `WarCardGame` programs

b. Create a GUI version of the War card game described in Exercise 11a. Let the user click a button to deal the cards, then make that button invisible and expose a Play button. Each time the user clicks Play, a pair of cards is revealed. To keep the `Frame` size reasonable, you might want to erase the output label's contents every four hands or so. The right side of Figure 8-22 shows a typical game in progress.

*Debugging Exercises*

Each of the following files in the Chapter.08 folder of your download-able student files has syntax and/or logical errors. In each case, determine the problem and fix the program. After you correct the errors, save each file using the same filename preceded with *Fixed*. For example, DebugEight1.cs will become FixedDebugEight1.cs.

    a.  DebugEight1.cs

    b.  DebugEight2.cs

    c.  DebugEight3.cs

    d.  DebugEight4.cs

 *Up For Discussion*

1.   One of the advantages to writing a program that is subdivided into methods is that such a structure allows different programmers to write separate methods, thus dividing the work. Would you prefer to write a large program by yourself, or to work on a team in which each programmer produces one or more modules? Why?

2.   Suppose you could use only one type of parameter: value, ref, or out. Which would you choose? Why?

3.   Suppose your organization asks you to develop a code of ethics for the Information Technology Department. What would you include?

# Using Classes and Objects

In this chapter you will:

◎ Learn about class concepts

◎ Create classes from which objects can be instantiated

◎ Create objects

◎ Create properties, including auto-implemented properties

◎ Learn more about using `public` and `private` access modifiers

◎ Learn about the `this` reference

◎ Write constructors and use them

◎ Use object initializers

◎ Overload operators

◎ Declare an array of objects and use the `Sort()` and `BinarySearch()` methods with them

◎ Write destructors

◎ Understand GUI application objects

Much of your understanding of the world comes from your ability to categorize objects and events into classes. As a young child, you learned the concept of "animal" long before you knew the word. Your first encounter with an animal might have been with the family dog, a neighbor's cat, or a goat at a petting zoo. As you developed speech, you might have used the same term for all of these creatures, gleefully shouting "Doggie!" as your parents pointed out cows, horses, and sheep in picture books or along the roadside on drives in the country. As you grew more sophisticated, you learned to distinguish dogs from cows; still later, you learned to distinguish breeds. Your understanding of the class "animal" helps you see the similarities between dogs and cows, and your understanding of the class "dog" helps you see the similarities between a Great Dane and a Chihuahua. Understanding classes gives you a framework for categorizing new experiences. You might not know the term "okapi," but when you learn it is an animal, you begin to develop a concept of what an okapi might be like.

Classes are also the basic building blocks of object-oriented programming. You already understand that differences exist among the `Double`, `Int32`, and `Float` classes, yet you also know items that are members of these classes possess similarities—they are all data types, you can perform arithmetic with all of them, they all can be converted to strings, and so on. Understanding classes enables you to see similarities in objects and increases your understanding of the programming process. In this chapter, you will discover how C# handles classes, learn to create your own classes, and learn to construct objects that are members of those classes.

## Understanding Class Concepts

When you write programs in C#, you create two distinct types of classes:

- Classes that are only application programs with a `Main()` method. These classes can contain other methods that the `Main()` method calls.

- Classes from which you instantiate objects. These classes can contain a `Main()` method, but it is not required.

When you think in an object-oriented manner, everything is an object, and every object is an instance or example of a class. You can think of any inanimate physical item as an object—your desk, your computer, and your house are all called "objects" in everyday

Every object is an instance of a more general class. Your desk is a specific instance of the class that includes all desks, and your pet fish is an instance of the class that contains all fish. An object is an **instantiation** of a class; it is one tangible example of a class.

conversation. You can think of living things as objects, too—your houseplant, your pet fish, and your sister are objects. Events also are objects—for example, the stock purchase you made, the mortgage closing you attended, or a graduation party in your honor.

In part, the concept of a class is useful because it provides you with knowledge about objects. Objects receive their attributes from classes, so, for example, if you invite me to a graduation party, I automatically know many things about the object. I assume there will be a starting time, a number of guests, and some refreshments. I understand your party because of my previous knowledge of the Party class. I do not necessarily know the number of guests or the date or time of this particular party, but I understand that because all parties have a date and time, then this one must as well. Similarly, even though every stock purchase is unique, each must have a dollar amount and a number of shares. All objects have predictable attributes because they are instances of certain classes.

The data components of a class that differ for each object are stored in **instance variables**. Also, object attributes often are called **fields** to help distinguish them from other variables you might use. The set of contents of an object's instance variables also are known as its **state**. For example, the current state of a particular party is 8 p.m. and Friday; the state of a particular stock purchase is $10 and five shares.

In addition to their attributes, objects have methods associated with them, and every object that is an instance of the same class possesses the same methods. Methods associated with objects are **instance methods**. For example, two Party objects might possess the identifiers myGraduationParty and yourAnniversaryParty that both have access to an IssueInvitations() method. The method might operate in the same way for both Party objects, but use data appropriate to the specific object. When you program in C#, you frequently create classes from which objects will be instantiated (or other programmers create them for you). You also write applications to use the objects, along with their data and methods. Often, you will write programs that use classes created by others, as you have used the Console class; similarly, you might create a class that other programmers will use to instantiate objects within their own programs. A program or class that instantiates objects of another prewritten class is a **class client** or **class user**.

# Creating a Class from Which Objects Can Be Instantiated

When you create a class, you must assign a name to it and determine what data and methods will be part of the class. For example, suppose you decide to create a class named Employee. One instance variable of Employee might be an employee number, and one necessary method might display a welcome message to new employees. To begin, you create a **class header** or **class definition** that starts the class. It contains three parts:

1. An optional access modifier

2. The keyword class

3. Any legal identifier you choose for the name of your class; because each class represents a type of object, class names are usually singular nouns.

You will learn other optional components you can add to a class definition as you continue to study C#.

For example, a header for an Employee class is internal class Employee. The keyword internal is an example of a **class access modifier**. You can declare a class using any of the modifiers in Table 9-1.

| Class Access Modifier | Description |
|---|---|
| public | Access to the class is not limited. |
| protected | Access to the class is limited to the class and to any classes derived from the class. |
| internal | Access is limited to the assembly to which the class belongs. |
| private | Access is limited to another class to which the class belongs. In other words, a class can be private if it is contained within another class, and only the containing class should have access to the private class. |

**Table 9-1**   Class access modifiers

You will learn about deriving classes in the chapter *Introduction to Inheritance*.

When you declare a class using a namespace, you only can declare it to be public or internal.

**358**

An **assembly** is a group of code modules compiled together to create an executable program. The .exe files you create after compiling a C# program are assemblies.

For now, you will use either the public or internal modifier with your classes. If you do not explicitly include an access specifier, class access is internal by default. Because most classes you create will have internal access, typing an access specifier is often unnecessary.

By convention, this book will declare application program classes that test or demonstrate other class instantiations to be public so they can be accessed from other assemblies, but this book will declare classes used to instantiate objects to be internal.

In addition to the class header, classes you create must have a class body enclosed between curly braces. Figure 9-1 shows a shell for an Employee class.

```
class Employee
{
    // Instance variables and methods go here
}
```

**Figure 9-1**   Employee class shell

## Creating Instance Variables and Methods

When you create a class, you define both its attributes and its methods. You declare the class's instance variables within the curly braces using the same syntax you use to declare other variables—you provide a type and an identifier. For example, within the Employee class, you can declare an integer ID number, and when you create Employee objects, each will have its own idNumber. You can define the ID number simply as int idNumber;. However, programmers frequently include an access modifier for each of the class fields and declare the idNumber as private int idNumber;. Figure 9-2 shows an Employee class that contains the private idNumber field.

```
class Employee
{
    private int idNumber;
}
```

**Figure 9-2**   Employee class containing idNumber field

The allowable field modifiers are `new`, `public`, `protected`, `internal`, `private`, `static`, `readonly`, and `volatile`. If you do not provide an access specifier for a class field, its access is `private` by default. Most class fields are nonstatic and `private`, which means that no other class can access the field's values, and only nonstatic methods of the same class will be allowed to set, get, or otherwise use the field. Using `private` fields within classes is an example of **information hiding**, a feature found in all object-oriented languages. You see cases of information hiding in real-life objects every day. For instance, you cannot see into your automobile's gas tank to determine how full it is. Instead, you use a gauge on the dashboard to provide you with the necessary information. Similarly, data fields are frequently `private` in object-oriented programming, but their contents are accessed through `public` methods. The `private` data of a class should be changed or manipulated only by its own methods, not by methods that belong to other classes.

In contrast to a class's `private` data fields, most instance methods are not usually `private`; they are `public`. The resulting `private` data/`public` method arrangement provides a means to control outside access to your data—only a class's nonprivate methods can be used to access a class's `private` data. The situation is similar to having a "public" receptionist who controls the messages passed in and out of your private office. The way in which the nonprivate methods are written controls how you will use the `private` data.

For example, an `Employee` class that contains an `idNumber` might need a method to display the employee's welcoming message to company clients. A reasonable name for this method is `WelcomeMessage()`, and its declaration is `public void WelcomeMessage()`, because it will have `public` access and return nothing. Figure 9-3 shows the `Employee` class with the addition of the `WelcomeMessage()` method.

A benefit of information hiding is the ability to validate data. A method that sets a variable's value can ensure that the value falls within a specified range. For example, an `Employee`'s salary should not be below the federal minimum wage, or perhaps a department number should not be negative or greater than 10.

```
class Employee
{
    private int idNumber;
    public void WelcomeMessage()
    {
        Console.WriteLine("Welcome from Employee #{0}", idNumber);
        Console.WriteLine("How can I help you?");
    }
}
```

**Figure 9-3**  `Employee` class with `idNumber` field and `WelcomeMessage()` method

You can call class (static) methods without creating an instance of the class. Instance methods require an instantiated object; class methods do not.

Notice that the WelcomeMessage() method does not employ the static modifier, unlike many other methods you have created. The keyword static is used for class-wide methods, but not for instance methods that "belong" to objects. If you are creating a program with a Main() method that you will execute to perform some task, then many of your methods will be static. You can call the static methods from Main() without creating an object. However, if you are creating a class from which objects will be instantiated, most methods will probably be nonstatic, as you will be associating the methods with individual objects and their data. Each time the WelcomeMessage() instance method is used in the class in Figure 9-3, it will display an idNumber for a specific object. In other words, the method will work appropriately for each object instance.

The Employee class in Figure 9-3 is not a program that will run; it contains no Main() method. Rather, it simply describes what Employee objects will have (an idNumber) and be able to do (display a greeting) when you write a program that contains one or more Employee objects.

Watch the video *Creating a Class*.

A class can contain fields that are objects of other classes. For example, you might create a class named Date that contains a month, day, and year, and add two Date fields to an Employee class to hold the Employee's birth date and hire date. Using an object within another object is known as **composition**. The relationship created is also called a **has-a relationship** because one class "has an" instance of another.

## TWO TRUTHS **&** A LIE

### Creating a Class from Which Objects Can Be Instantiated

1. A class header always contains the keyword class.

2. When you create a class, you define both its attributes and its methods.

3. Most class fields and methods are private.

The false statement is #3. Most class fields are private, but most class methods are public.

# Creating Objects

Declaring a class does not create any actual objects. A class is just an abstract description of what an object will be like if any objects are ever actually instantiated. Just as you might understand all the characteristics of an item you intend to manufacture long before the first item rolls off the assembly line, you can create a class with fields and methods before you instantiate any objects that are occurrences of that class.

A two-step process creates an object that is an instance of a class. First, you supply a type and an identifier, just as when you declare any variable. Second, you create the object, which includes allocating computer memory for it. For example, you might define an integer as `int someValue;` and you might define an `Employee` as `Employee myAssistant;`, where `myAssistant` could be any legal identifier you choose to represent an `Employee`.

When you declare an integer as `int myInteger;`, you notify the compiler that an integer named `myInteger` will exist, and computer memory automatically is reserved for it at the same time—the exact amount of computer memory depends on the declared data type. When you declare the `myAssistant` instance of the `Employee` class, you are notifying the compiler that you will use the identifier `myAssistant`. However, you are not yet setting aside computer memory in which the `Employee` named `myAssistant` can be stored—that is done only for the built-in, predefined types. To allocate the needed memory and instantiate the object, you must use the `new` operator.

Defining an `Employee` object named `myAssistant` requires two steps—you must declare a reference to the object and then you must use the statement that actually sets aside enough memory to hold `myAssistant`:

```
Employee myAssistant;
myAssistant = new Employee();
```

You also can declare and reserve memory for `myAssistant` in one statement, as in the following:

```
Employee myAssistant = new Employee();
```

In this statement, `Employee` is the object's type (as well as its class), and `myAssistant` is the name of the object. The equal sign is the assignment operator, so a value is being assigned to `myAssistant`. The `new` operator is allocating a new, unused portion of computer memory for `myAssistant`. The value being assigned to `myAssistant` is a memory address at which the value will be located. You need not be concerned with the actual memory address—when you refer to `myAssistant`, the compiler will locate it at the appropriate address for you.

You can think of a class declaration as similar to a blueprint for building a new house or a recipe for baking a cake. In other words, it is a plan that exists before any objects are created.

Every object name is a reference— that is, it holds a computer memory location where the fields for the object reside. The memory location holds the values for the object.

You used the new operator earlier in this book when you learned to set aside memory for an array.

You also can use the **new** operator for simple data types. For example, to declare an integer variable x, you can write the following:

```
int x = new int();
```

However, programmers usually use the simpler form:

```
int x;
```

With the first form, x is initialized to 0. With the second form, x holds no usable starting value.

Because the identifiers for objects are references to their memory addresses, you can call any class a **reference type**—in other words, a type that refers to a specific memory location. A reference type is a type that holds an address, as opposed to the predefined types such as int, double, and char, which are **value types**.

Later in this chapter you will learn that the automatically generated constructor for a class is a *default constructor*, which means it takes no parameters. Programmers sometimes erroneously equate the terms *automatically generated* and *default*. The automatically created constructor for a class is an *example* of a default constructor, but you also can explicitly create your own default constructor.

In the statement Employee myAssistant = new Employee();, the last portion of the statement after the **new** operator, Employee(), looks suspiciously like a method name with its parentheses. In fact, it is the name of a method that constructs an Employee object. Employee() is a constructor. You will write your own constructors later in this chapter. For now, note that when you do not write a constructor for a class, C# writes one for you, and the name of the constructor is always the same as the name of the class whose objects it constructs.

After an object has been instantiated, its nonstatic public members (usually its methods) can be accessed using the object's identifier, a dot, and a method call. For example, if you declare an Employee named myAssistant, you can access myAssistant's WelcomeMessage() method with the following statement:

```
myAssistant.WelcomeMessage();
```

The statement myAssistant.WelcomeMessage() would be illegal if WelcomeMessage() was a static method. The method can be used with an Employee object only because it is nonstatic.

No class client can access myAssistant's idNumber directly; the only way a client can access the private data is by using one of the object's public methods. Because the WelcomeMessage() method is part of the same class as idNumber, and because WelcomeMessage() is public, a client (for example, a Main() method in a program) can use the method. Figure 9-4 shows a class named CreateEmployee whose Main() method declares an Employee and displays the Employee's welcome message. Figure 9-5 shows the execution of the program.

```
using System;
public class CreateEmployee
{
    public static void Main()
    {
        Employee myAssistant = new Employee();
        myAssistant.WelcomeMessage();
    }
}
```

**Figure 9-4**  The CreateEmployee program

**Figure 9-5**  Output of the CreateEmployee program

In the output in Figure 9-5, the Employee's ID number is 0. By default, all unassigned numeric fields in an object are initialized to 0. When you compile the program in Figure 9-4, you receive a warning message:

```
Field 'Employee.idNumber' is never assigned to, and will always have its default value 0.
```

Of course, usually you want to provide a different value for each Employee's idNumber field. One way to accomplish this is to create properties, which you will do later in this chapter.

## Passing Objects to Methods

A class represents a data type, and you can pass objects to methods just as you can pass simple data types. For example, the program in Figure 9-6 shows how string and Employee objects can be passed to a DisplayEmployeeData() method. Each Employee is assigned to the emp parameter within the method. Figure 9-7 shows the program's output.

```
using System;
public class CreateTwoEmployees
{
    public static void Main()
    {
        Employee aWorker = new Employee();
        Employee anotherWorker = new Employee();
        DisplayEmployeeData("First", aWorker);
        DisplayEmployeeData("Second", anotherWorker);
    }
    internal static void DisplayEmployeeData(string order, Employee emp)
    {
        Console.WriteLine("\n{0} employee's message:", order);
        emp.WelcomeMessage();
    }
}
```

**Figure 9-6**   CreateTwoEmployees program

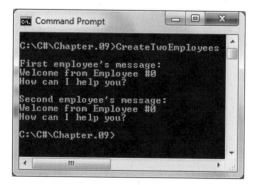

**Figure 9-7**   Output of CreateTwoEmployees program

When you pass an object to a method, you pass a reference. Therefore, any change made to an object parameter in a method also affects the object used as an argument in the calling method.

In Figure 9-6, notice that the DisplayEmployeeData() method is internal. Because the method accepts an Employee parameter, it must be no more accessible than the Employee class, which is also internal. This restriction preserves the security provided for the Employee class's nonpublic members. The program would also work if you made both the DisplayEmployeeData() method and the Employee class public.

# Creating Properties

Frequently, methods you call with an object are used to alter the states of its fields. For example, you might want to set or change the date or time of a party. In the Employee class, you could write a method such as SetIdNumber() to set an employee's idNumber field as follows:

```
public void SetIdNumber(int number)
{
    idNumber = number;
}
```

Then, after you instantiate an Employee object named myAssistant, you could call the method with a statement like the following:

```
myAssistant.SetIdNumber(785);
```

Although this technique would work, and might be used in other programming languages, C# programmers more often create properties to perform similar tasks. A **property** is a member of a class that provides access to a field of a class; properties define how fields will be set and retrieved. Properties are a combination of the best features of private fields and public methods:

- Like public methods, they protect private data from outside access.

- Like fields, their names are used in the same way simple variable names are used. When you create properties, the syntax in your client programs becomes more natural and easier to understand.

C# programmers refer to properties as "smart fields."

Properties have **accessors** that specify the statements that execute when a class's fields are accessed. Specifically, properties contain **set accessors** for setting an object's fields and **get accessors** for retrieving the stored values.

When a property has a set accessor, programmers say the property can be "written to." When it has a get accessor, programmers say the property can be "read from." When a property has only a get accessor (and not a set accessor), it is a **read-only property**.

In C#, the get and set accessors often are called the **getter** and the **setter**, respectively.

Figure 9-8 shows an Employee class in which a property named IdNumber has been defined in the shaded area. A property declaration resembles a variable declaration; it contains an access modifier, a data type, and an identifier. It also resembles a method in that it is followed by curly braces that contain statements. By convention, a property identifier is the same as the field it manipulates, except the first letter is capitalized. Following the property identifier, you define accessors between curly braces. The IdNumber property in Figure 9-8 contains both get and set accessors; a property declaration can contain a get accessor, a set accessor, or both.

```csharp
class Employee
{
    private int idNumber;
    public int IdNumber
    {
        get
        {
            return idNumber;
        }
        set
        {
            idNumber = value;
        }
    }
    public void WelcomeMessage()
    {
        Console.WriteLine("Welcome from Employee #{0}", IdNumber);
        Console.WriteLine("How can I help you?");
    }
}
```

**Figure 9-8** Employee class with defined property

Be careful with capitalization of properties. For example, within a get accessor for IdNumber, if you return IdNumber instead of idNumber, you initiate an infinite loop—the property continuously accesses itself.

In the `WelcomeMessage()` method in Figure 9-8, the `IdNumber` property is displayed. Alternately, this method could continue to use the `idNumber` field (as in Figure 9-3) because the method is a member of the same class as the field. Programmers are divided on whether a method of a class should use a field or a property to access its own methods. One popular position is that if `get` and `set` accessors are well-designed, they should be used everywhere, even within the class. Sometimes, you want a field to be read-only, so you do not create a `set` accessor. In such a case, you can use the field (with the lowercase initial by convention) within class methods.

Throughout this book you have seen keywords displayed in boldface in the program figures. The words `get` and `set` are not C# keywords—for example, you could declare a variable named `get` within a C# program. However, within a property, `get` and `set` have special meanings and are not allowed to be declared as identifiers there. In the Visual Studio Integrated Development Environment, the words `get` and `set` appear in blue within properties, but in black elsewhere. Although the word "value" has special meaning in properties, it does not appear in color in the Visual Studio IDE, so it is not shown in boldface in this book.

Identifiers that act like keywords in specific circumstances are **contextual keywords**. C# has six contextual keywords: `get`, `set`, `value`, `partial`, `where`, and `yield`.

Each accessor in a property looks like a method, except no parentheses are included in the identifier. A `set` accessor acts like a method that accepts a parameter and assigns it to a variable. However, it is not a method and you do not use parentheses with it. A `get` accessor returns the value of the field associated with the property, but you do not code a `return` type; the `return` type of a `get` accessor is implicitly the type of the property in which it is contained.

When you use `set` and `get` accessors in a method, you do not use the words "set" or "get." Instead, to set a value, you use the assignment operator (=), and to get a value, you simply use the property name. For example, if you declare an `Employee` named `myChef`, you can assign an `IdNumber` as simply as you would a variable, as in the following:

```
Employee myChef = new Employee();
myChef.IdNumber = 2345;
```

In the second statement, the `IdNumber` property is set to 2345. The value to the right of the equal sign is sent to the `set` accessor as an implicit parameter named `value`. (An **implicit parameter** is one that is undeclared and that gets its value automatically.) In the statement `myChef.IdNumber = 2345;`, the constant 2345 is sent to the `set` accessor, where it becomes the value of value. Within the set accessor, value is assigned to the class field idNumber. The idNumber field could not have been set directly from Main() because it is private; however, the IdNumber property can be set through its set accessor because the property is public.

Writing a get accessor allows you to use a property like you would a simple variable. For example, a declared Employee's ID number can be displayed with the following:

```
Console.WriteLine("ID number is {0}", myChef.IdNumber);
```

The expression myChef.idNumber (using the field name that starts with a lowercase *i*) would not be allowed in a client program because idNumber is private; however, the public get accessor of the property allows myChef.IdNumber to be displayed. Figure 9-9 shows a complete application that uses the Employee class with accessors defined in Figure 9-8. Figure 9-10 shows the output.

```
using System;
public class CreateEmployee2
{
    public static void Main()
    {
        Employee myChef = new Employee();
        myChef.IdNumber = 2345;
        Console.WriteLine("ID number is {0}",
            myChef.IdNumber);
        myChef.WelcomeMessage();
    }
}
```

**Figure 9-9**   The CreateEmployee2 application that uses the Employee class containing a property

**Figure 9-10**   Output of the CreateEmployee2 application

At this point, declaring get and set accessors that do nothing except retrieve a value from a field or assign a value to one might seem like a lot of work for very little payoff. After all, if a class field was public instead of private, you would just use it directly and avoid the work of creating the property. However, it is conventional (and consistent with object-oriented principles) to make class fields private and allow accessors to manipulate them only as you deem appropriate. Keeping data hidden is an important feature of object-oriented programming, as is controlling how data values are set and used. Additionally, you can customize accessors to suit the restrictions you want to impose on how some class fields are retrieved and accessed. For example, you could write a set accessor that restricts ID numbers within the Employee class as follows:

```
set
{
    if(value < 500)
        idNumber = value;
    else
        idNumber = 500;
}
```

This set accessor would ensure that an Employee idNumber would never be greater than 500. If clients had direct access to a private idNumber field, you could not control what values could be assigned there, but when you write a custom set accessor for your class, you gain full control over the allowed data values.

## Using Auto-Implemented Properties

Although you can include any number of custom statements within the get and set accessors in a property, the most frequent scenario is that a set accessor simply assigns a value to the appropriate class field, and the get accessor simply returns the field value. Because the code in get and set accessors frequently is standard as well as brief, programmers sometimes take one of several shorthand approaches to writing properties.

For example, instead of writing an IdNumber property using 11 code lines as in Figure 9-8, a programmer might write the property on five lines, as follows:

```
public int IdNumber
{
    get{return idNumber;}
    set{idNumber = value;}
}
```

This format does not eliminate any of the characters typed in the original version of the property; it only eliminates some of the white space, placing each accessor on a single line.

Other programmers choose an even more condensed form and write the entire property on one line as:

```
public int IdNumber {get{return idNumber;} set{idNumber = value;}}
```

An even more concise format was introduced in C# 3.0. In this and newer versions of C#, you can write a property as follows:

```
public int IdNumber {get; set;}
```

Auto-implemented properties are sometimes called **automatic properties**.

A property written in this format is an **auto-implemented property**. The property's implementation (its set of working statements) is created for you automatically with the assumptions that the set accessor should simply assign a value to the appropriate field and the get accessor should simply return the field. You cannot use an auto-implemented property if you need to include customized statements within one of your accessors (such as placing restrictions on an assigned value), and you can only declare an auto-implemented property when you use both get and set.

The instruction not to code corresponding fields applies only to auto-implemented properties. When you code a property that is not auto-implemented, you can continue to code the corresponding fields.

When you use an auto-implemented property, you should not declare the field that corresponds to the property. The corresponding field is generated by the compiler and has an internal name that would not match the field's name if you had coded the field yourself. If you also declare a field for the property, your field and the property's field refer to separate memory addresses, leading to potential confusion and errors.

For example, Figure 9-11 shows an Employee class in which no specialized code is needed for the properties associated with the ID number and salary. In this class, the fields are not declared explicitly; only auto-implemented properties are declared. The figure also contains a short program that uses the class, and Figure 9-12 shows the output. Auto-implemented properties provide a convenient shortcut when you need both get and set abilities without specialized statements.

The field that supports a property is its **backing field**. You code the field when you create properties, but not when you create auto-implemented properties.

```
using System;
public class CreateEmployee3
{
    public static void Main()
    {
        Employee aWorker = new Employee();
        aWorker.IdNumber = 3872;
        aWorker.Salary = 22.11;
        Console.WriteLine("Employee #{0} makes {1}",
            aWorker.IdNumber, aWorker.Salary.ToString("C"));
    }
}
class Employee
{
    public int IdNumber {get; set;}
    public double Salary {get; set;}
}
```

**Figure 9-11**   An `Employee` class with no declared fields and auto-implemented properties, and a program that uses them

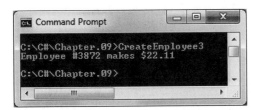

**Figure 9-12**   Output of the `CreateEmployee3` application

If you want to create a read-only property using auto-implemented accessors, you can make the `set` accessor private, as in the following:

```
public int IdNumber {get; private set;}
```

Using this technique, the `IdNumber` property cannot be set by any statement in another class. However, it could be assigned a value by methods within its own class. Less frequently, you might want to create a property that outside classes could set but not retrieve, as follows:

```
public int IdNumber {private get; set;}
```

Watch the video *Creating Properties.*

**TWO TRUTHS & A LIE**

**Creating Properties**

1. A property is a member of a class that defines how fields will be set and retrieved.

2. Properties contain set accessors for retrieving an object's fields and get accessors for setting the stored values.

3. You can create auto-implemented properties when you want a field's set accessor to assign a value to the appropriate class field, and a field's get accessor simply to return the field value.

The false statement is #2. Properties contain set accessors for setting an object's fields and get accessors for retrieving the stored values.

# More About public and private Access Modifiers

Most of the time, class data fields are private and class methods are public. This technique ensures that data will be used and changed only in the ways provided in your accessors. Novice programmers might make a data field public to avoid having to create a property containing get and set accessors. However, doing so violates a basic principle of object-oriented programming. Data should be hidden when at all possible, and access to it should be controlled by well-designed accessors.

Although private fields and public methods and accessors are the norm, occasionally you need to create public fields or private methods. Consider the Carpet class shown in Figure 9-13. Although it contains several private data fields, this class also contains one public constant field (shaded). Following the three public property declarations, one private method is defined (also shaded).

```
class Carpet
{
    public const string MOTTO = "Our carpets are quality-made";
    private int length;
    private int width;
    private int area;
    public int Length
    {
        get
        {
            return length;
        }
        set
        {
            length = value;
            CalcArea();
        }
    }
    public int Width
    {
        get
        {
            return width;
        }
        set
        {
            width = value;
            CalcArea();
        }
    }
    public int Area
    {
        get
        {
            return area;
        }
    }
    private void CalcArea()
    {
        area = Length * Width;
    }
}
```

**Figure 9-13** The Carpet class

 In the Carpet class, the Area property does not contain a set accessor because no outside program is allowed to set the area. Instead, it is calculated whenever width or length changes.

For example, you can create a public field when you want all objects of a class to contain the same value. When you create Carpet objects from the class in Figure 9-13, each Carpet will have its own length, width, and area, but all Carpet objects will have the same MOTTO. The field MOTTO is preceded by the keyword const, meaning MOTTO is constant. That is, no program can change its value. Making a constant public does not violate information hiding in the way that making an object's data fields public would, because programs that use this class cannot change the constant's value.

Some built-in C# classes contain useful named constants, such as Math.PI, which contains the value of pi. You do not create a Math object to use PI; therefore, you know it is static.

When you define a named constant within a class, it is always static, even though you cannot use the keyword static as a modifier. In other words, the field belongs to the entire class, not to any particular instance of the class. When you create a static field, only one copy is stored for the entire class, no matter how many objects you instantiate. When you use a constant field in a client class, you use the class name and a dot rather than an object name, as in Carpet.MOTTO.

Throughout this book, you have been using static to describe the Main() method of a class. You do not need to create an object of any class that contains a Main() method to be able to use Main().

Figure 9-14 shows a program that instantiates and uses a Carpet object, and Figure 9-15 shows the results when the program executes. Notice that, although the output statements require an object to use the Width, Length, and Area properties, MOTTO is referenced using the class name only.

```csharp
using System;
public class TestCarpet
{
    public static void Main()
    {
        Carpet aRug = new Carpet();
        aRug.Width = 12;
        aRug.Length = 14;
        Console.Write("The {0} X {1} carpet ", aRug.Width, aRug.Length);
        Console.WriteLine("has an area of {0}", aRug.Area);
        Console.WriteLine("Our motto is: {0}", Carpet.MOTTO);
    }
}
```

**Figure 9-14** The TestCarpet class

**Figure 9-15** Output of the TestCarpet program

The `Carpet` class contains one private method named `CalcArea()`. As you examine the code in the `TestCarpet` class in Figure 9-14, notice that `Width` and `Length` are set using an assignment operator, but `Area` is not. The `TestCarpet` class can make assignments to `Width` and `Length` because these properties are `public`. However, you would not want a client program to assign a value to `Area` because the assigned value might not agree with the `Width` and `Length` values. Therefore, the `Area` property is a read-only property—it does not contain a `set` accessor, and no assignments by clients are allowed. Instead, whenever the `Width` or `Length` properties are set, the `private` `CalcArea()` method is called from the accessor. The `CalcArea()` method is defined as `private` because there is no reason for a client class like `TestCarpet` to call `CalcArea()`. The `Carpet` class's own accessors should call `CalcArea()` only after a valid value has been assigned to the `length` or `width` field. You create a method to be `private` when it should be called only by other methods or accessors within the class and not by outside classes.

 Programmers probably create `private` methods more frequently than they create `public` data fields. Some programmers feel that the best style is to use `public` methods that are nothing but a list of method calls with descriptive names. Then, the methods that actually do the work are all `private`.

## TWO TRUTHS & A LIE

### More About `public` and `private` Access Modifiers

1. Good object-oriented techniques require that data should usually be hidden and access to it should be controlled by well-designed accessors.

2. Although `private` fields, methods, and accessors are the norm, occasionally you need to create `public` versions of them.

3. When you define a named constant within a class, it is always `static`; that is, the field belongs to the entire class, not to any particular instance of the class.

The false statement is #2. Although `private` fields and methods and `public` fields and methods are the norm, occasionally you need to create `public` fields or `private` methods.

# Understanding the `this` Reference

When you create a class, only one copy of the class code is stored in computer memory. However, you might eventually create thousands of objects from the class. When you create each object, you provide storage for each of the object's instance variables. For example, Figure 9-16 shows part of a Book class that contains only three fields, a property for the title field, and an advertising message method. When you declare several Book objects, as in the following statements, each Book object requires separate memory locations for its `title`, `numPages`, and `price`:

```
Book myBook = new Book();
Book yourBook = new Book();
```

```csharp
class Book
{
    private string title;
    private int numPages;
    private double price;
    public string Title
    {
        get
        {
            return title;
        }
        set
        {
            title = value;
        }
    }
    public void AdvertisingMessage()
    {
        Console.WriteLine("Buy it now: {0}", Title);
    }
}
```

**Figure 9-16** Partially developed Book class

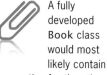 A fully developed Book class would most likely contain properties for the other data fields. This version excludes those properties to keep the example short.

 When you compile the Book class, you receive warnings that the numPages and price fields are never used. The omission was purposeful for this demonstration program.

 An object's nonstatic fields are "instance variables" because there is a stored version for each object instance.

Storing a single Book object requires allocating storage space for three separate fields; the storage requirements for Book objects used by a library or retail bookstore would be far more considerable, but necessary—each Book must be able to "hold" its own data, including publisher, date published, author, ISBN, and so on. If each Book object also required its own copy of each property and method contained in the class, the storage requirements would multiply. It makes sense that each Book needs space to store its unique title and other data, but because every Book uses the same methods, storing multiple copies is wasteful and unnecessary.

Fortunately, each Book object does not need to store its own copy of each property and method. Whether you make the method call myBook.AdvertisingMessage() or yourBook.AdvertisingMessage(), you access the same AdvertisingMessage() method. However, there must be a difference between the two method calls, because each displays a different title in its message. The difference lies in an implicit, or invisible, reference that is passed to every instance method and property accessor. The implicitly passed reference is the **this reference**. The `this` reference is the address of the object to which the method applies. When you call the method myBook. AdvertisingMessage(), you automatically pass the `this` reference to the method so the method knows which instance of Book to use.

You can explicitly refer to the `this` reference within an instance method or property, as shown in Figure 9-17. When you refer to Title (or title) within a Book class method or accessor, you are referring to the title field of "this" Book—the Book whose name you used in the method call—perhaps myBook or yourBook. Using the shaded keywords in Figure 9-17 is not required; the version of the methods shown in Figure 9-16 (where `this` was implied but not written explicitly) works just as well. Figure 9-18 shows an application that uses the Book class, and Figure 9-19 shows the output.

 Only nonstatic methods receive a `this` reference. Nonstatic methods are instance methods—they can work differently and appropriately for each object—so it makes sense that they receive a `this` reference.

 The `this` reference is aptly named. When you execute a nonstatic method such as myBook.AdvertisingMessage(), you might ask yourself which object's data will be used in the method. The answer is "*This* object's (myBook's) data."

```csharp
class Book
{
    private string title;
    private int numPages;
    private double price;
    public string Title
    {
        get
        {
            return this.title;
        }
        set
        {
            this.title = value;
        }
    }
    public void AdvertisingMessage()
    {
        Console.WriteLine("Buy it now: {0}", this.Title);
    }
}
```

**Figure 9-17**  Book class with methods explicitly using `this` references

```
using System;
public class CreateTwoBooks
{
    public static void Main()
    {
        Book myBook = new Book();
        Book yourBook = new Book();
        myBook.Title = "Silas Marner";
        yourBook.Title = "The Time Traveler's Wife";
        myBook.AdvertisingMessage();
        yourBook.AdvertisingMessage();
    }
}
```

**Figure 9-18** Program that declares two Book objects

**Figure 9-19** Output of CreateTwoBooks program

The Book class in Figure 9-17 worked without adding the explicit references to this. However, you should be aware that the this reference is always there, working behind the scenes, even if you do not code it. Sometimes, you may want to include the this reference within a method for clarity, so the reader has no doubt when you are referring to a class instance variable.

Watch the video *The this* Reference.

On occasion, you might need to explicitly code the this reference. For example, consider the abbreviated Book class in Figure 9-20. The programmer has chosen the same identifier for a field and a parameter to a method that uses the field. To distinguish between the two, the field must be referenced as this.price. All references to price (without using this) in the SetPriceAndTax() method in Figure 9-20 are references to the local parameter. If the method included the statement price = price;, the parameter's value would be assigned to itself and the class's field would never be set.

```
                    class Book
                    {
                        private double price;
                        private double tax;
                        public void SetPriceAndTax(double price)
                        {
                            const double TAX = 0.07;
                            this.price = price;
                            tax = price * TAXRATE;
                        }
                    }
```

this.price refers to the object's price. In other words, it refers to the price field in the class.

price refers to the method parameter.

**Figure 9-20** Book class that must explicitly use the this reference

## TWO TRUTHS & A LIE

### Understanding the this Reference

1. An implicit, or invisible, this reference is passed to every instance method and property accessor in a class; instance methods and properties are nonstatic.

2. You can explicitly refer to the this reference within an instance method or property.

3. Although the this reference exists in every instance method, you can never refer to it within a method.

The false statement is #3. Sometimes, you may want to include the this reference within a method for clarity, so the reader has no doubt when you are referring to a class instance variable.

# Understanding Constructors

When you create a class such as Employee and instantiate an object with a statement such as Employee aWorker = new Employee();, you are actually calling a method named Employee() that is provided by C#. A **constructor** is a method that instantiates (creates an instance of) an object. If you do not write a constructor for a class, then each class you create is automatically supplied with a public constructor with no parameters. A constructor without parameters is a class's **default constructor**. The automatically created constructor named Employee() establishes one Employee with the identifier aWorker, and provides the following initial values to the Employee's data fields:

You will learn to create constructors with parameters in the next section of this chapter.

The value of an object initialized with a default constructor is known as the **default value of the object**.

The term *default constructor* is not just used for a class's automatically supplied constructor; it is used for any constructor that takes no parameters.

If you create a class in which one or more fields are never assigned a value, the compiler will issue a warning that the fields in question will hold default values.

- Numeric fields are set to 0 (zero).

- Character fields are set to '\0'.

- Boolean fields are set to `false`.

- References, such as `string` fields or any other object fields, are set to `null` (or empty).

If you do not want an `Employee`'s fields to hold these default values, or if you want to perform additional tasks when you create an `Employee`, you can write your own constructor to replace the automatically supplied version. Any constructor you write must have the same name as its class, and constructors cannot have a return type. For example, if you create an `Employee` class that contains a `Salary` property, and you want every new `Employee` object to have a salary of 300.00, you could write the constructor for the `Employee` class as follows:

```
Employee()
{
    Salary = 300.00;
}
```

Assuming a `Salary` property has been defined for the `salary` field, any instantiated `Employee` will have a default `salary` value of 300.00.

You can write any statement in a constructor. For example, you can perform arithmetic or display a message. However, the most common constructor task is to initialize fields.

## Passing Parameters to Constructors

You can create a constructor to ensure that all objects of a class are initialized with the same values in their data fields. Alternatively, you might create objects initialized with unique field values by writing constructors to which you pass one or more parameters. You then can use the parameter values to set properties or fields for individual object instantiations.

For example, consider an `Employee` class with two data fields, a constructor, and an auto-implemented property, as shown in Figure 9-21. Its constructor assigns 9.99 to each potentially instantiated `Employee`'s `PayRate`. Any time an `Employee` object is created using a statement such as `Employee partTimeWorker = new Employee();`, even if no other data-assigning methods are ever used, you are ensured that the `Employee`'s `PayRate` holds a default value.

```
class Employee
{
    private int idNumber;
    private string name;
    public Employee()
    {
        PayRate = 9.99;
    }
    public double PayRate {get; set;}
    // Other class members can go here
}
```

**Figure 9-21**   Employee class with a parameterless constructor

The constructor in Figure 9-21 is a **parameterless constructor**—one that takes no arguments. In other words, it is a default constructor. As an alternative, you might choose to create Employees with different initial PayRate values for each Employee. To accomplish this task, you can pass a pay rate to the constructor. Figure 9-22 shows an Employee constructor that receives a parameter. An integer is passed to the constructor using a statement such as the following:

```
Employee partTimeWorker = new Employee(12.50);
```

When the constructor executes, the double used as the actual parameter within the method call is passed to Employee() and assigned to the Employee's PayRate.

A class can contain only one parameterless constructor: the default constructor. If you wrote multiple parameterless constructors, they would be ambiguous.

```
public Employee(double rate)
{
    PayRate = rate;
}
```

**Figure 9-22**   Employee constructor with parameter

## Overloading Constructors

C# automatically provides a default constructor for your classes. As soon as you create your own constructor, whether it has parameters or not, you no longer have access to the automatically created version. However, if you want a class to have both parameter and parameterless versions of a constructor, you can create them. Like any other C# methods, constructors can be overloaded. You can write as many constructors for a class as you want, as long as their parameter lists do not cause ambiguity. For example, the Employee class in Figure 9-23 contains four constructors. The Main() method within the CreateSomeEmployees class in Figure 9-24 shows how different types of Employees might be instantiated. Notice that one version of the Employee constructor—the one that supports a character parameter—does not even use the parameter; sometimes you might create a constructor with a specific parameter type simply to force that constructor to be the version that executes. The output of the CreateSomeEmployees program is shown in Figure 9-25.

 If you create class constructors but do not create a parameterless version, then the class does not have a default constructor.

```
class Employee
{
    public int IdNumber {get; set;}
    public double Salary {get; set;}

    public Employee()
    {
        IdNumber = 999;
        Salary = 0;
    }
    public Employee(int empId)
    {
        IdNumber = empId;
        Salary = 0;
    }
    public Employee(int empId, double sal)
    {
        IdNumber = empId;
        Salary = sal;
    }
    public Employee(char code)
    {
        IdNumber = 111;
        Salary = 100000;
    }
}
```

> This parameterless constructor is the class's default constructor.

**Figure 9-23** Employee class with four constructors

```
using System;
public class CreateSomeEmployees
{
    public static void Main()
    {
        Employee aWorker = new Employee();
        Employee anotherWorker = new Employee(234);
        Employee theBoss = new Employee('A');
        Console.WriteLine("{0,4}{1,14}", aWorker.IdNumber,
            aWorker.Salary.ToString("C"));
        Console.WriteLine("{0,4} {1,14}", anotherWorker.IdNumber,
            anotherWorker.Salary.ToString("C"));
        Console.WriteLine("{0,4}{1,14}", theBoss.IdNumber,
            theBoss.Salary.ToString("C"));
    }
}
```

**Figure 9-24**   CreateSomeEmployees program

**Figure 9-25**   Output of CreateSomeEmployees program

Most likely, a single application would not use all four constructors of the Employee class. More likely, each application that uses the class would use only one or two constructors. You create a class with multiple constructors to provide flexibility for your clients. For example, some clients might choose to construct Employee objects with just ID numbers, and others might prefer to construct them with ID numbers and salaries.

## Using Constructor Initializers

The Employee class in Figure 9-23 contains four constructors, and each constructor initializes the same two fields. In a fully developed class used by a company, many more fields would be initialized, creating a lot of duplicated code. Besides the original extra work of writing the repetitive statements in these constructors, even more extra work will be required when the class is modified in the future.

For example, if your organization institutes a new employee ID number format that requires a specific number of digits, then each constructor will have to be modified, which will require extra work. In addition, one or more of the constructor versions that must be modified might be overlooked, introducing errors into the programs that are clients of the class.

As an alternative to repeating code in the constructors, you can use a constructor initializer. A **constructor initializer** is a clause that indicates another instance of a class constructor should be executed before any statements in the current constructor body. Figure 9-26 shows a new version of the Employee class using constructor initializers in three of the four overloaded constructor versions.

```
class Employee
{
    public int IdNumber {get; set;}
    public double Salary {get; set;}
    public Employee() : this(999, 0)
    {
    }
    public Employee(int empId) : this(empId, 0)
    {
    }
    public Employee(int empId, double sal)
    {
        IdNumber = empId;
        Salary = sal;
    }
    public Employee(char code) : this(111, 100000)
    {
    }
}
```

**Figure 9-26**  Employee class with constructor initializers

In the three shaded clauses in Figure 9-26, the this reference is used to mean "the constructor for this object being constructed." For example, when a client calls the parameterless Employee constructor, 999 and 0 are passed to the two-parameter constructor. There, they become empId and sal, parameters that are assigned to the IdNumber and Salary properties. If statements were written within the parameterless constructor, they would then execute; however, in this class, additional statements are not necessary. Similarly, if a client uses the constructor version that accepts only an ID number, that parameter and a 0 for salary are passed to the two-parameter constructor. The only time just one version of the constructor executes is when a client uses both an ID number and a salary as constructor arguments. In the future, if additional statements needed to be added to the class (for example, a decision that ensures an ID number was at least five digits at construction), the decision would be added only to the two-parameter version of the constructor, and all the other versions could use it.

---

### TWO TRUTHS & A LIE

#### Understanding Constructors

1. Every class you create is automatically supplied with a `public` constructor with no parameters.

2. If you write a constructor for a class, you do not have a default constructor for the class.

3. Any constructor you write must have the same name as its class, and constructors cannot have a return type.

The false statement is #2. If you write a parameterless constructor for a class, it becomes the default constructor, and you lose the automatically supplied version. If you write only constructors that require parameters, then the class no longer contains a default constructor.

---

# Using Object Initializers

An **object initializer** allows you to assign values to any accessible members or properties of a class at the time of instantiation without calling a constructor with parameters. For example, assuming an `Employee` class has been created with a public `IdNumber` property and a parameterless constructor, you can write an object initializer as follows:

```
Employee aWorker = new Employee {IdNumber = 101};
```

In this statement, 101 is assigned to the aWorker object's `IdNumber` property. The assignment is made within a pair of curly braces; no parentheses are used with the class name. When this statement executes, the parameterless, default constructor for the class is executed first, and then the object initializer assignment is made.

For example, Figure 9-27 shows an `Employee` class that contains properties for `IdNumber` and `Salary` and a default constructor that assigns a value to Salary. For demonstration purposes, the constructor displays the current object's ID number and salary. The figure also shows a program that instantiates one Employee object and displays its value, and Figure 9-28 shows the output. When the object is created in the shaded statement, the constructor executes, assigns 99.99 to Salary, and displays the first line of output, showing IdNumber is still 0. After the object is constructed in the Main() method, the next output line is displayed, showing that the assignment of the ID number occurred after construction.

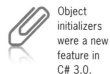

Object initializers were a new feature in C# 3.0.

```
using System;
public class DemoObjectInitializer
{
    public static void Main()
    {
        Employee aWorker = new Employee {IdNumber = 101};
        Console.WriteLine("Employee #{0} exists. Salary is {1}.",
            aWorker.IdNumber, aWorker.Salary);
    }
}
class Employee
{
    public int IdNumber {get; set;}
    public double Salary {get; set;}
    public Employee()
    {
        Salary = 99.99;
        Console.WriteLine("Employee #{0} created. Salary is {1}.",
            IdNumber, Salary);
    }
}
```

**Figure 9-27**    DemoObjectInitializer program

**Figure 9-28**    Output of DemoObjectInitializer program

For you to use object initializers, a class must have a default constructor. That is, you either must not create any constructors or you must create one that requires no parameters.

Multiple assignments can be made with an object initializer by separating them with commas, as in the following:

```
Employee myAssistant = new Employee {IdNumber = 202,
   Salary = 25.00};
```

This single code line has the same results as the following three statements:

```
Employee myAssistant = new Employee();
myAssistant.IdNumber = 202;
myAssistant.Salary = 25.00;
```

Using object initializers allows you to create multiple objects with different initial assignments without having to provide multiple constructors to cover every possible situation. Additionally, using object initializers allows you to create objects with different starting values for different properties of the same data type. For example, consider a class like the Box class in Figure 9-29 that contains multiple properties of the same type. The constructor sets the Height, Width, and Depth properties to 1. You could write a constructor that accepts an integer parameter to be assigned to Height (using the default value 1 for the other dimensions), but then you could not write an additional over-loaded constructor that accepts an integer parameter to be assigned to Width because the constructors would be ambiguous. However, by using object initializers, you can create objects to which you assign the properties you want. Figure 9-30 shows a program that declares three Box objects, each with a different assigned dimension, and Figure 9-31 shows the output, which demonstrates that each property was assigned appropriately.

Object initializers have additional uses in LINQ statements. You will learn about LINQ in the chapter *Data Queries and LINQ*.

```
class Box
{
   public int Height {get; set;}
   public int Width {get; set;}
   public int Depth {get; set;}
   public Box()
   {
      Height = 1;
      Width = 1;
      Depth = 1;
   }
}
```

**Figure 9-29** The Box class

```
using System;
public class DemoObjectInitializer2
{
    public static void Main()
    {
        Box box1 = new Box {Height = 3};
        Box box2 = new Box {Width = 15};
        Box box3 = new Box {Depth = 268};
        DisplayDimensions(1, box1);
        DisplayDimensions(2, box2);
        DisplayDimensions(3, box3);
    }
    internal static void DisplayDimensions(int num, Box box)
    {
        Console.WriteLine("Box {0}: Height: {1} Width: {2} Depth: {3}",
            num, box.Height, box.Width, box.Depth);
    }
}
```

**Figure 9-30**   The DemoObjectInitializer2 program

**Figure 9-31**   Output of the DemoObjectInitializer2 program

## TWO TRUTHS & A LIE

### Using Object Initializers

Assume a working program contains the following object initializer:

Invoice oneBill = new Invoice {Amount = 0};

1.  You know that the Invoice class contains a default constructor.

2.  You know that Amount is public.

3.  You know that the Invoice class contains a single property.

The false statement is #3. The Invoice class might have any number of properties. However, only one is being initialized in this statement.

# Overloading Operators

C# operators are the symbols you use to perform operations on objects. You have used many operators, including arithmetic operators (such as + and -) and logical operators (such as == and <). Separate actions can result from what seems to be the same operation or command. This occurs frequently in all computer programming languages, not just object-oriented languages. For example, in most programming languages and applications such as spreadsheets and databases, the + operator has a variety of meanings. A few of them include:

- Alone before a value (called unary form), + indicates a positive value, as in the expression +7.

- Between two integers (called binary form), + indicates integer addition, as in the expression 5 + 9.

- Between two floating-point numbers (also called binary form), + indicates floating-point addition, as in the expression 6.4 + 2.1.

You have learned that when a language feature such as the plus sign has multiple meanings depending on the context, it is overloaded.

Expressing a value as positive is a different operation from using the + operator to perform arithmetic, so + is overloaded several times in that it can take one or two arguments and have a different meaning in each case. It also can take different operand types—you use a + to add two ints, two doubles, an int and a double, and a variety of other combinations. Each use results in different actions behind the scenes.

In addition to overloading, compilers often need to perform coercion, or implicit casting, when the + symbol is used with mixed arithmetic. For example, when an integer and floating-point number are added in C#, the integer is coerced into a floating-point number before the appropriate addition code executes. You learned about casting in Chapter 2.

Just as it is convenient to use a + between both integers and doubles to add them, it also can be convenient to use a + between objects, such as Employees or Books, to add them. To be able to use arithmetic symbols with your own objects, you must overload the symbols.

C# operators are classified as unary or binary, depending on whether they take one or two arguments, respectively. The rules for overloading are shown in the following list.

Although `true` and `false` are not used explicitly as operators in expressions, they are considered operators in Boolean expressions and in expressions involving the conditional operator and conditional logical operators.

You are already familiar with about half of these operators. You will learn more about the rest as you continue to study C#.

When you overload `==`, you also receive warnings about methods in the `Object` class. You will learn about this class in the chapter *Introduction to Inheritance*; you should not attempt to overload `==` until you have studied that chapter.

- The overloadable unary operators are:

  `+ - ! ~ ++ -- true false`

- The overloadable binary operators are:

  `+ - * / % & | ^ == != > < >= <=`

- You cannot overload the following operators:

  `= && || ?? ?: checked unchecked new typeof as is`

- You cannot overload an operator for a built-in data type. For example, you cannot change the meaning of + between two `int`s.

- When a binary operator is overloaded and it has a corresponding assignment operator, it is also overloaded. For example, if you overload +, then += is automatically overloaded too.

- Some operators must be overloaded in pairs. For example, when you overload ==, you also must overload !=, and when you overload >, you also must overload <.

You have used many of the operators listed above. If you want to include these operators in your own classes, you must decide what the operator will mean in your class. When you do, you write statements in a method to carry out your meaning. The method has a return type and arguments just like other methods, but its identifier is required to be followed by the operator being overloaded—for example, `operator+()` or `operator*()`.

For an overloaded unary operator, the method has the following format:
*type* `operator` *overloadable-operator* (*type identifier*)
For an overloaded binary operator, the method has the following format:
*type* `operator` *overloadable-opewrator* (*type identifier, type operand*)

For example, suppose you create a `Book` class in which each object has a title, number of pages, and a price. Further assume that, as a publisher, you have decided to "add" `Book`s together. That is, you want to take two existing `Book`s and combine them into one. Assume you want the new book to have the following characteristics:

- The new title is a combination of the old titles, joined by the word "and."

- The number of pages in the new book is equal to the sum of the pages in the original `Book`s.

- Instead of charging twice as much for a new Book, you have decided to charge the price of the more expensive of the two original Books, plus $10.

A different publisher might have decided that "adding Books" means something different—for example, an added Book might have a fixed new price of $29.99. The statements you write in your operator+() method depend on how you define adding for your class. You could write an ordinary method to perform these tasks, but you could also overload the + operator to mean "add two Books." Figure 9-32 shows a Book class that has properties for each field and a shaded operator+() method.

```
class Book
{
    public Book(string title, int pages, double price)
    {
        Title = title;
        NumPages = pages;
        Price = price;
    }
    public static Book operator+(Book first, Book second)
    {
        const double EXTRA = 10.00;
        string newTitle = first.Title + " and " +
            second.Title;
        int newPages = first.NumPages + second.NumPages;
        double newPrice;
        if(first.Price > second.Price)
            newPrice = first.Price + EXTRA;
        else
            newPrice = second.Price + EXTRA;
        return(new Book(newTitle, newPages, newPrice));
    }
    public string Title {get; set;}
    public int NumPages {get; set;}
    public double Price {get; set;}
}
```

**Figure 9-32**   Book class with overloaded + operator

The operator+() method in Figure 9-32 is declared to be public (so that class clients can use it) and static, which is required. The method is static because it does not receive a this reference to any object; instead, the two objects to be added are both parameters to the method.

The return type is Book because the addition of two Books is defined to be a new Book with different values from either of the originals.

You could overload the + operator so that when two Books are added they return some other type, but it is most common to make the addition of two objects result in an "answer" of the same type.

The two parameters in the operator+() method in the Book class are both Books. Therefore, when you eventually call this method, the data types on both sides of the + sign will be Books. For example, you could write other methods that add a Book and an Employee, or a Book and a double.

Within the operator+() method, the statements perform the following tasks:

- A constant is declared to hold the extra price used in creating a new Book from two existing ones.

Notice that the + between the strings in creating the new Book title is itself an overloaded operator; concatenating strings is a different operation from adding ints or doubles.

- A new string is created and assigned the first parameter Book's title, plus the string "and", plus the second parameter Book's title.

- A new integer is declared and assigned the sum of the number of pages in each of the parameter Books.

- A new double is declared and assigned the value of the more expensive original Book plus $10.00.

- Within the return statement, a new anonymous Book is created (an anonymous object has no identifier) using the new title, page number, and price, and is returned to the calling method. (Instead of an anonymous Book, it would have been perfectly acceptable to use two statements—the first one creating a named Book with the same arguments, and the second one returning the named Book.)

It is possible to rewrite the operator + () method in the Book class in Figure 9-32 so that all the work is done in the return statement. For example:

```
public static Book operator+(Book first, Book second)
{
    const double EXTRA = 10.00;
    return(new Book(first.Title + " and " + second.Title,
        first.NumPages + second.NumPages,
        first.Price > second.Price ? first.Price + EXTRA :
            second.Price + EXTRA));
}
```

Figure 9-33 shows a client program that can use the + operator in the Book class. It first declares three Books, then adds two Books together and assigns the result to the third. When book1 and book2 are added, the operator+() method is called. The returned Book is assigned to book3, which is then displayed. Figure 9-34 shows the results.

```
using System;
public class AddBooks
{
    public static void Main()
    {
        Book book1 = new Book("Silas Marner", 350, 15.95);
        Book book2 = new Book("Moby Dick", 250, 16.00);
        Book book3;
        book3 = book1 + book2;
        Console.WriteLine("The new book is \"{0}\"",
            book3.Title);
        Console.WriteLine("It has {0} pages and costs {1}",
            book3.NumPages, book3.Price.ToString("C"));
    }
}
```

**Figure 9-33**   The AddBooks program

**Figure 9-34**   Output of the AddBooks program

 Because each addition operation returns a Book, it is possible to chain addition in a statement such as `collection = book1 + book2 + book3;` (assuming all the variables have been declared to be Book objects). In this example, book1 and book2 would be added, returning a temporary Book. Then the temporary Book and book3 would be added, returning a different temporary Book that would be assigned to `collection`.

In the Book class, it took many statements to overload the operator; however, in the client class, just typing a + between objects allows a programmer to use the objects and operator intuitively. You could write any statements you wanted within the operator method. However, for clarity, you should write statements that intuitively have the same meaning as the common use of the operator. For example, although you could overload the operator*() method to display a Book's title and price instead of performing multiplication, it would be a bad programming technique.

 Watch the video *Overloading Operators.*

 When you overload an operator, at least one argument to the method must be a member of the containing class. In other words, within the Book class, you can overload operator*() to multiply a Book by an integer, but you cannot overload operator*() to multiply a double by an integer.

---

**TWO TRUTHS & A LIE**

### Overloading Operators

1.  All C# operators can be overloaded for a class.

2.  You cannot overload an operator for a built-in data type.

3.  Some operators must be overloaded in pairs.

The false statement is #1. You cannot overload the following operators: = && || ?? ?: checked unchecked new typeof as is

---

# Declaring an Array of Objects

Just as you can declare arrays of integers or doubles, you can declare arrays that hold elements of any type, including objects. Remember that object names are references. For example, you can create an array of references to seven Employee objects as follows:

```
Employee[] empArray = new Employee[7];
```

This statement reserves enough computer memory for the references to seven Employee objects named empArray[0] through empArray[6]. It does not actually construct those Employees; all the references are initialized to null. To create objects for the array, you must call the Employee() constructor seven times.

If the Employee class contains a default constructor, you can use the following loop to call the constructor seven times:

```
for(int x = 0; x < empArray.Length; ++x)
    empArray[x] = new Employee();
```

As x varies from 0 through 6, each of the seven empArray objects is constructed.

 When you create an array from a value type, such as int or char, the array holds the actual values. When you create an array from a reference type, such as a class you create, then the array holds the memory addresses of the objects. In other words, the array "refers to" the objects instead of containing the objects.

If you want to use a nondefault constructor, you must provide appropriate arguments. For example, if the Employee class contains a constructor with an int parameter, you can write the following:

```
Employee[] empArray = {new Employee(123),
    new Employee(234), new Employee(345)};
```

To use a method that belongs to an object that is part of an array, you insert the appropriate subscript notation after the array name and before the dot-method. For example, to set all seven `Employee` `IdNumber` properties to 999, you can write the following:

```
for(int x = 0; x < empArray.Length; ++x)
    empArray[x].IdNum = 999;
```

## Using the `Sort()` and `BinarySearch()` Methods with Arrays of Objects

In the chapter *Using Arrays*, you learned about using the `System.Array` class's built-in `BinarySearch()` and `Sort()` methods with simple data types such as `int`, `double`, and `string`. The `Sort()` method accepts an array parameter and arranges its elements in descending order. The `BinarySearch()` method accepts a sorted array and a value that it attempts to match in the array.

A complication arises when you consider searching or sorting arrays of objects you create. When you create and sort an array of simple data items, there is only one type of value to consider, and the order is based on the Unicode value of that item. The classes that support simple data items each contain a method named **CompareTo()**, which provides the details of how the basic data types compare to each other. In other words, they define comparisons such as "2 is more than 1" and "B is more than A." The `Sort()` and `BinarySearch()` methods use the `CompareTo()` method for the current type of data being sorted. In other words, `Sort()` uses the `Int32` version of `CompareTo()` when sorting integers and the `Char` version of `CompareTo()` when sorting characters.

You learned about the built-in data type class names in Chapter 2; they are summarized in Table 2-1.

When you create a class in which comparisons will be made between objects, you must tell the compiler which field to use when making those comparisons. For example, you logically might sort an organization's `Employee` objects by ID number, salary, department number, last name, hire date, or any field contained in the class. To tell C# which field to use for placing `Employee` objects in order, you must create an interface.

You have been using the `String` class (and its `string` alias) throughout this book. The class also contains a `CompareTo()` method that you first used in Chapter 2.

An **interface** is a data type, like a class. It is a collection of abstract methods (and perhaps other members) that can be used by any class, as long as the class provides a definition to override the interface's do-nothing, or abstract, method definitions. Unlike a class, an interface cannot contain instance fields, and you cannot create objects from them.

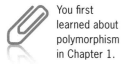

You first learned about polymorphism in Chapter 1.

A class that implements an interface must override the interface's methods. When a method **overrides** another, it takes precedence over the method, hiding the original version. In other words, the methods in an interface are empty, and any class that uses them must contain a new version that provides the details. Interfaces define named behaviors that classes must implement, so that all classes can use the same method names but use them appropriately for the class. In this way, interfaces provide for polymorphism—the ability of different objects to use the same method names but act appropriately based on the context.

When a method overrides another, it has the same signature as the method it overrides. When methods are overloaded, they have different signatures. You will learn more about overriding methods and abstract methods and classes in the next chapter.

C# supports many interfaces. You can identify an interface name by its initial letter I.

C# contains an **IComparable interface**, which contains the definition for the CompareTo() method that compares one object to another and returns an integer. Figure 9-35 shows the definition of IComparable. The CompareTo() method accepts a parameter Object, but does not contain any statements; you must provide an implementation for this method in classes you create if you want the objects to be comparable. In other words, you must determine the meanings of *greater than*, *less than*, and *equal to* for the class.

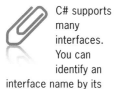

Object is a class—the most generic of all classes. Every Employee object you create is not only an Employee, but also an Object. (This concept is similar to "every banana is a fruit" or "every collie is a dog.") By using the type Object as a parameter, the CompareTo() method can accept anything. You will learn more about the Object class in the next chapter.

```
interface IComparable
{
    int CompareTo(Object o);
}
```

**Figure 9-35**　The IComparable interface

When you create a class whose instances will likely be compared by clients:

- You must include a single colon and the interface name IComparable after the class name.

- You must write a method that contains the following header:

    ```
    int IComparable.CompareTo(Object o)
    ```

To work correctly in methods such as BinarySearch() and Sort(), the CompareTo() method you create for your class must return an integer value. Table 9-2 shows the return values that every version of CompareTo() should provide.

| Return Value | Meaning |
| --- | --- |
| Negative | This instance is less than the compared object. |
| Zero | This instance is equal to the compared object. |
| Positive | This instance is greater than the compared object. |

**Table 9-2**   Return values of `IComparable.CompareTo()` method

When you create a class that contains an `IComparable.CompareTo()` method, the method is an instance method and receives a `this` reference to the object used to call it. A second object is passed to the method; within the method, you first must convert, or cast, the passed object to the same type as the calling object's class, and then compare the corresponding fields you want from the `this` object and the passed object. For example, Figure 9-36 shows an `Employee` class that contains a shaded `CompareTo()` method and compares `Employee` objects based on the contents of their `idNumber` fields.

You first learned about casting in Chapter 2.

```
class Employee : IComparable
{
    public int IdNumber {get; set;}
    public double Salary {get; set;}

    int IComparable.CompareTo(Object o)
    {
        int returnVal;
        Employee temp = (Employee)o;
        if(this.IdNumber > temp.IdNumber)
            returnVal = 1;
        else
            if(this.IdNumber < temp.IdNumber)
                returnVal = -1;
            else
                returnVal = 0;
        return returnVal;
    }
}
```

**Figure 9-36**   `Employee` class using `IComparable` interface

The `Employee` class in Figure 9-36 uses a colon and `IComparable` in its class header to indicate an interface. The shaded method is an instance method; that is, it "belongs" to an `Employee` object. When another `Employee` is passed in as `Object o`, it is cast as an `Employee` and stored in the `temp` variable. The `idNumber` values of the `this` Employee and the passed `Employee` are compared, and one of three integer values is returned.

For example, if you declare two `Employee` objects named `worker1` and `worker2`, you can use the following statement:

```
int answer = worker1.CompareTo(worker2);
```

The controlling "`this`" object in an instance method is the **invoking object**.

Within the `CompareTo()` method in the `Employee` class, `worker1` would be "`this`" Employee—the controlling `Employee` in the method. The `temp` Employee would be `worker2`. If, for example, `worker1` had a higher ID number than `worker2`, the value of `answer` would be 1.

Figure 9-37 shows a program that uses the `Employee` class. The program declares an array of five `Employee` objects with different ID numbers and salaries; the ID numbers are purposely out of order to demonstrate that the `Sort()` method works correctly. The program also declares a `seekEmp` object with an ID number of 222. The program sorts the array, displays the sorted elements, then finds the array element that matches the `seekEmp` object. Figure 9-38 shows the program execution.

```
using System;
public class ComparableEmployeeArray
{
    public static void Main()
    {
        Employee[] empArray = new Employee[5];
        int x;
        for(x = 0; x < empArray.Length; ++x)
            empArray[x] = new Employee();
        empArray[0].IdNumber = 333;
        empArray[1].IdNumber = 444;
        empArray[2].IdNumber = 555;
        empArray[3].IdNumber = 111;
        empArray[4].IdNumber = 222;
        Employee seekEmp = new Employee();
        seekEmp.IdNumber = 222;
        Array.Sort(empArray);
        Console.WriteLine("Sorted employees:");
        for(x = 0; x < empArray.Length; ++x)
            Console.WriteLine("Employee #{0}: {1} {2}",
                x, empArray[x].IdNumber,
                empArray[x].Salary.ToString("C"));
        x = Array.BinarySearch(empArray, seekEmp);
        Console.WriteLine("Employee #{0} was found at position {1}",
            seekEmp.IdNumber, x);
    }
}
```

**Figure 9-37** ComparableEmployeeArray program

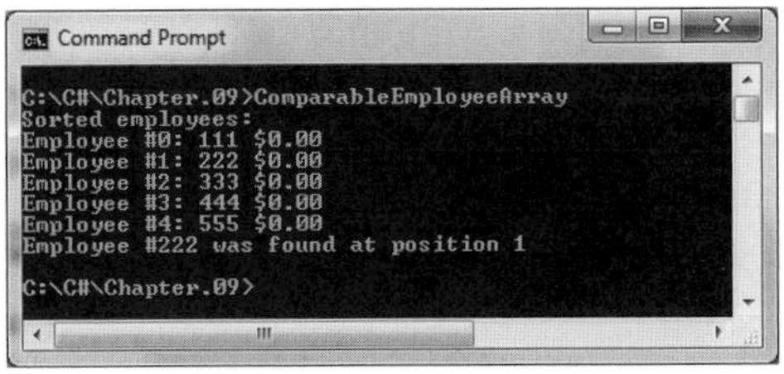

**Figure 9-38** Output of `ComparableEmployeeArray` program

Notice that the `seekEmp` object matches the `Employee` in the second array position based on the `idNumber` only—not the salary—because the `CompareTo()` method in the `Employee` class uses only `idNumber` values and not salaries to make comparisons. You *could* have written code that requires both the `idNumber` and `salary` values to match before returning a positive number.

---

## TWO TRUTHS & A LIE

### Declaring an Array of Objects

Assume a working program contains the following array declaration:

`BankAccount[] acctArray = new BankAccount[500];`

1.  This statement reserves enough computer memory for 500 `BankAccount` objects.

2.  This statement constructs 500 `BankAccount` objects.

3.  The valid subscripts for `acctArray` are 0 through 499.

The false statement is #2. This statement declares 500 BankAccount objects but does not actually construct those objects; to do so, you must call the 500 individual constructors.

---

# Understanding Destructors

A **destructor** contains the actions you require when an instance of a class is destroyed. Most often, an instance of a class is destroyed when it goes out of scope. As with constructors, if you do not explicitly create a destructor for a class, C# automatically provides one.

To explicitly declare a destructor, you use an identifier that consists of a tilde (~) followed by the class name. You cannot provide any parameters to a destructor; it must have an empty argument list. As a consequence, destructors cannot be overloaded; a class can have one destructor at most. Like a constructor, a destructor has no return type.

Figure 9-39 shows an `Employee` class that contains only one field (`idNumber`), a property, a constructor, and a (shaded) destructor. When you execute the `Main()` method in the `DemoEmployeeDestructor` class in Figure 9-40, you instantiate two `Employee` objects, each with its own `idNumber` value. When the `Main()` method ends, the two `Employee` objects go out of scope, and the destructor for each object is called. Figure 9-41 shows the output.

```
class Employee
{
    public int idNumber {get; set;}
    public Employee(int empID)
    {
        IdNumber = empID;
        Console.WriteLine("Employee object {0} created", IdNumber);
    }
    ~Employee()
    {
        Console.WriteLine("Employee object {0} destroyed!", IdNumber);
    }
}
```

**Figure 9-39** Employee class with destructor

```
using System;
public class DemoEmployeeDestructor
{
    public static void Main()
    {
        Employee aWorker = new Employee(101);
        Employee anotherWorker = new Employee(202);
    }
}
```

**Figure 9-40** DemoEmployeeDestructor program

```
Command Prompt

C:\C#\Chapter.09>DemoEmployeeDestructor
Employee object 101 created
Employee object 202 created
Employee object 202 destroyed!
Employee object 101 destroyed!

C:\C#\Chapter.09>
```

**Figure 9-41** Output of `DemoEmployeeDestructor` program

The program in Figure 9-40 never explicitly calls the `Employee` class destructor, yet you can see from the output that the destructor executes twice. Destructors are invoked automatically; you cannot explicitly call one. Interestingly, the last object created is the first object destroyed; the same relationship would hold true no matter how many objects the program instantiated.

For now, you have little reason to create a destructor except to demonstrate how it is called automatically. Later, when you write more sophisticated C# programs that work with files, databases, or large quantities of computer memory, you might want to perform specific clean-up or close-down tasks when an object goes out of scope. Then you will place appropriate instructions within a destructor.

An instance of a class becomes eligible for destruction when it is no longer possible for any code to use it—that is, when it goes out of scope. The actual execution of an object's destructor might occur at any time after the object becomes eligible for destruction.

## TWO TRUTHS & A LIE

### Understanding Destructors

1. To explicitly declare a destructor, you use an identifier that consists of a tilde (~) followed by the class name.

2. You cannot provide any parameters to a destructor; it must have an empty argument list.

3. The return type for a destructor is always `void`.

The false statement is #3. Like a constructor, a destructor has no return type.

## Understanding GUI Application Objects

The objects you have been using in GUI applications, such as Forms, Buttons, and Labels, are objects just like others you have studied in this chapter. That is, they encapsulate properties and methods. When you start a Windows Forms application in the IDE and drag a Button onto a Form, a statement is automatically created to instantiate a Button object.

Figure 9-42 shows a new GUI application that a programmer started simply by dragging one Button onto a Form.

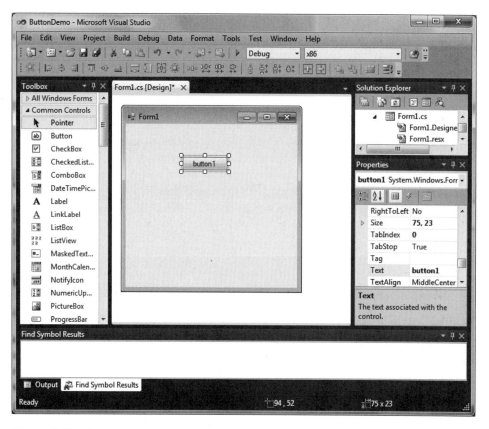

**Figure 9-42** A Button on a Form

If you click on Form1.Designer.cs in the Solution Explorer, you can display the code where the Button is declared. See Figure 9-43.

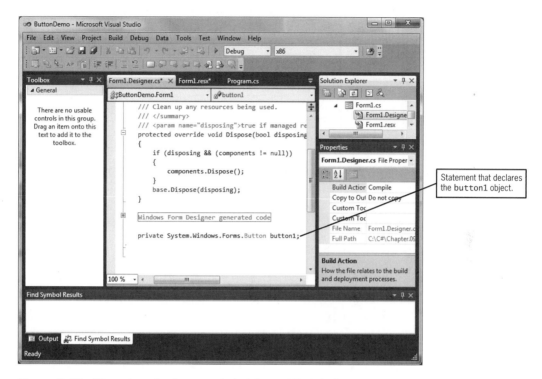

Statement that declares the button1 object.

**Figure 9-43** The automatically generated statement that declares button1

If you right-click button1 in the code and select Find All References from the menu that appears, a list of every reference to button1 in the project is displayed in the Find Symbol Results area at the bottom of the IDE. You can double-click each entry in the list in turn to locate all the places where code has been generated for button1. For example, the first instance is in a method named InitializeComponent(), as shown in Figure 9-44. This first reference to button1 calls its constructor. You can also see how the Button's Name, Location, Size, and other properties are set. You could have written these statements yourself, especially now that you know more about objects and how they are constructed, but it is easier to develop an application visually by dragging a Button onto a Form and allowing the IDE to create these statements for you.

Now that you understand how to create properties in your own classes, you can understand the properties of GUI objects and how they were created for your use.

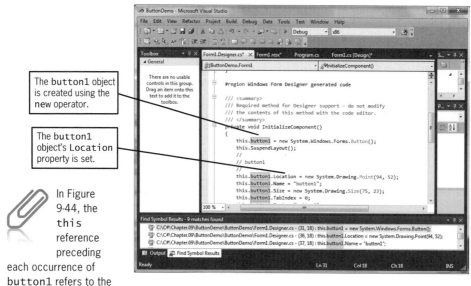

The button1 object is created using the new operator.

The button1 object's Location property is set.

In Figure 9-44, the this reference preceding each occurrence of button1 refers to the class (Form1) that contains these statements.

**Figure 9-44** Some automatically generated button1 references in the IDE

# You Do It

## Creating a Class and Objects

In this section, you will create a Student class and instantiate objects from it. This class contains an ID number, last name, and grade point average for the Student. It also contains properties that get and set each of these fields. You will also pass each Student object to a method.

**To create a Student class:**

1. Open a new file in your text editor. Begin the Student class by declaring the class name, inserting an opening curly brace, and declaring three private fields that will hold an ID number, last name, and grade point average, as follows:

```
class Student
{
    private int idNumber;
    private string lastName;
    private double gradePointAverage;
```

2. Add two constants that represent the highest and lowest possible values for a grade point average.

```
public const double HIGHEST_GPA = 4.0;
public const double LOWEST_GPA = 0.0;
```

Because you do not provide an access modifier for the Student class, its access is internal.

3. Add two properties that get and set idNumber and lastName. By convention, properties have an identifier that is the same as the field they service, except they start with a capital letter.

```
public int IdNumber
{
   get
   {
      return idNumber;
   }
   set
   {
      idNumber = value;
   }
}
public string LastName
{
   get
   {
      return lastName;
   }
   set
   {
      lastName = value;
   }
}
```

4. Add the following set accessor in the property for the gradePointAverage field. It sets limits on the value assigned, assigning 0 if the value is out of range.

```
public double GradePointAverage
{
   get
   {
      return gradePointAverage;
   }
   set
   {
      if(value >= LOWEST_GPA && value <= HIGHEST_GPA)
         gradePointAverage = value;
      else
         gradePointAverage = LOWEST_GPA;
   }
}
```

5. Add a closing curly brace for the class. Save the file as **CreateStudents.cs**.

6. At the top of the file, begin a program that creates two
Student objects, assigns some values, and displays
the Students.

```
using System;
public class CreateStudents
{
```

7. Add a Main() method that declares two Students. Assign
field values, including one "illegal" value—a grade point
average that is too high.

```
public static void Main()
{
    Student first = new Student();
    Student second = new Student();
    first.IdNumber = 123;
    first.LastName = "Anderson";
    first.GradePointAverage = 3.5;
    second.IdNumber = 789;
    second.LastName = "Daniels";
    second.GradePointAverage = 4.1;
```

8. Instead of creating similar WriteLine() statements to display
the two Students, call a method with each Student. You will
create the method to accept a Student argument in the next
step. Add a closing curly brace for the Main() method.

```
    Display(first);
    Display(second);
}
```

Recall that
field contents
are left
aligned when
you use a
minus sign before the
field size. Also recall
that the "F1" argument
to the ToString()
method causes the value
to be displayed to one
decimal place.

9. Write the Display() method so that the passed-in Student's
IdNumber, LastName, and GradePointAverage are displayed
and aligned. The method is internal so that it can access
the internal Student class. Add a closing curly brace for the
class.

```
internal static void Display(Student stu)
{
    Console.WriteLine("{0,5} {1,-10}{2,6}",
        stu.IdNumber, stu.LastName,
        stu.GradePointAverage.ToString("F1"));
}
}
```

10. Save the file, then compile and execute the program. Figure
9-45 shows the output. Each Student has unique data values
and uses the same Display() method. Notice how the second Student's grade point average was forced to 0 by the set
accessor in the property for the field.

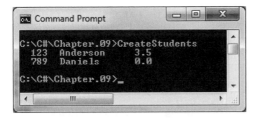

**Figure 9-45** Output of CreateStudents program

## Using Auto-Implemented Properties

When a property's get accessor simply returns the corresponding field's value, and its set accessor simply assigns a value to the appropriate field, you can reduce the code in your classes by using auto-implemented properties. In the Student class, both IdNumber and LastName are candidates for this shortcut, so you can replace the full versions of these properties with their auto-implemented versions. The GradePointAverage property cannot take advantage of auto-implementation because additional code is required for the property to fulfill its intended function.

**To include auto-implemented properties in the Student class:**

1. Open the file that contains the Student class if it is not still open on your screen. Remove the properties for IdNumber and LastName and replace them with these auto-implemented versions:

```
public int IdNumber {get; set;}
public string LastName {get; set;}
```

2. Remove the declarations for the fields idNumber and lastName.

3. Save the file, then recompile and execute it. The output is the same as when the program used the original version of the Student class in Figure 9-45.

## Adding Overloaded Constructors To a Class

Frequently, you create constructors for a class so that fields will hold initial values when objects are instantiated. You can overload constructors by writing multiple versions with different parameter lists; you often want to do this so that different clients can use your class in the way that suits them best.

**To add overloaded constructors to the Student class:**

1. Open the file that contains the Student class if it is not still open on your screen. Just before the closing curly brace for the Student class, add the following constructor. It takes three parameters and assigns them to the appropriate fields:

```
public Student(int id, string name, double gpa)
{
    IdNumber = id;
    LastName = name;
    GradePointAverage = gpa;
}
```

2. Add a second parameterless constructor. It calls the first constructor, passing 0 for the ID number, "XXX" for the name, and 0.0 for the grade point average. Its body is empty.

```
public Student() : this(0, "XXX", 0.0)
{
}
```

3. Change the name of the CreateStudents class to CreateStudents2.

4. After the existing declarations of the Student objects, add two more declarations. With one, use three arguments, but with the other, do not use any.

```
Student third = new Student(456, "Marco", 2.4);
Student fourth = new Student();
```

5. At the end of the Main() method, just after the two existing calls to the Display() method, add two more calls using the new objects:

```
Display(third);
Display(fourth);
```

6. Save the file, then compile and execute it. The output looks like Figure 9-46. All four objects are displayed. The first two have had values assigned to them after declaration, but the third and fourth ones obtained their values from their constructors.

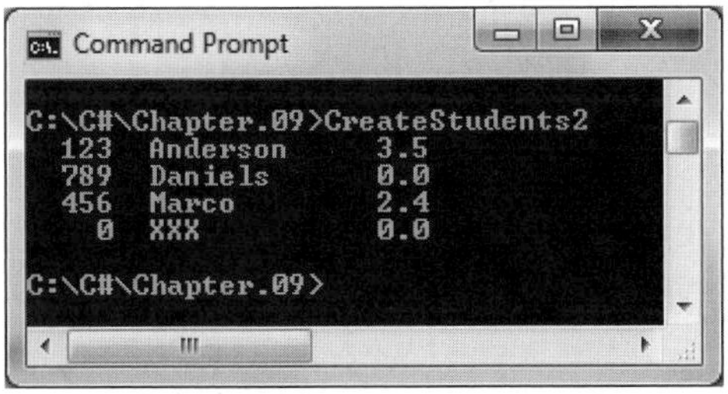

**Figure 9-46** Output of `CreateStudents2` program

## Creating an Array of Objects

Just like variables of the built-in, primitive data types, objects you create can be stored in arrays. In the next steps, you will create an array of `Student` objects. You will prompt the user for data to fill the array, and you will sort the array by student ID number before displaying all the data.

**To create and use an array of objects:**

1. Open the **CreateStudents2.cs** file and immediately save it as **CreateStudents3.cs**. Change the class name to **CreateStudents3**.

2. Delete all the existing statements in the `Main()` method, leaving the opening and closing curly braces. Between the braces, declare an array of eight `Student` objects. Also declare a variable to use as an array subscript and declare three variables that will temporarily hold a user's input data before `Student` objects are constructed.

```
Student[] student = new Student[8];
int x;
int id;
string name;
double gpa;
```

3. In a loop, call a `GetData()` method (which you will write shortly); send it `out` arguments so that you can retrieve values for variables that will hold an ID number, name, and grade point average. Then, in turn, send these three values to the `Student` constructor for each of the eight `Student` objects.

```
for(x = 0; x < student.Length; ++x)
{
   GetData(out id, out name, out gpa);
   student[x] = new Student(id, name, gpa);
}
```

4. Call the `Array.Sort()` method, sending it the student array. Then, one object at a time in a loop, call the `Display()` method that you wrote in the last set of steps.

```
Array.Sort(student);
Console.WriteLine("Sorted List:");
for(x = 0; x < student.Length; ++x)
    Display(student[x]);
```

5. Write the `GetData()` method. Its parameters are out parameters so that their values will be known to the calling method. The method simply prompts the user for each data item, reads it, and converts it to the appropriate type, if necessary.

```
internal static void GetData(out int id, out string name,
    out double gpa)
    {
        string inString;
        Console.Write("Please enter student ID number ");
        inString = Console.ReadLine();
        id = Convert.ToInt32(inString);
        Console.Write("Please enter last name for " +
            "student {0} ", id);
        name = Console.ReadLine();
        Console.Write("Please enter grade point average ");
        inString = Console.ReadLine();
        gpa = Convert.ToDouble(inString);
    }
```

6. After the header for the `Student` class, add a colon and `IComparable` so that objects of the class can be sorted:

```
public class Student : IComparable
```

7. Just before the closing curly brace for the `Student` class, add the `IComparable.CompareTo()` method that is required for the objects of the class to be sortable. The method will sort `Student` objects based on their ID numbers, so it returns 1, −1, or 0 based on `IdNumber` property comparisons. The method accepts an object that is cast to a `Student` object. If the `IdNumber` of the controlling `Student` object is greater than the argument's `IdNumber`, then the return value is set to 1. If the `IdNumber` of the controlling `Student` object is less than the argument's `IdNumber`, then the return value is −1. Otherwise, the return value is 0.

```
int IComparable.CompareTo(Object o)
{
    int returnVal;
    Student temp = (Student)o;
    if(this.IdNumber > temp.IdNumber)
        returnVal = 1;
    else
        if(this.IdNumber < temp.IdNumber)
```

```
            returnVal = -1;
        else
            returnVal = 0;
    return returnVal;
}
```

8.  Save the file (as CreateStudents3.cs) and compile and execute it. When prompted, enter any student IDs, names, and grade point averages you choose. The objects will be sorted and displayed in idNumber order. Figure 9-47 shows a typical execution.

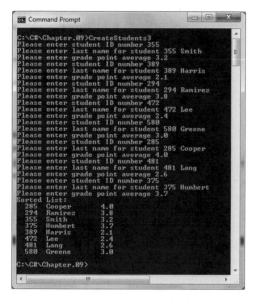

**Figure 9-47**  Typical execution of CreateStudents3 program

# Chapter Summary

- When you write programs in C#, you create application classes that contain a Main() method and that are programs. You also can create classes from which you instantiate objects. The data components of a class are its instance variables (or fields) and methods. A program or class that instantiates objects of another prewritten class is a class client or class user.

- When you create a class, you must assign a name to it and determine what data and methods will be part of the class. A class header or class definition contains an optional access modifier, the keyword `class`, and any legal identifier you choose. A class body is enclosed between curly braces. When you create a class, you define both its attributes and its methods. You usually declare instance variables to be `private` and instance methods to be `public`.

- When you create an object that is an instance of a class, you supply a type and an identifier, and you allocate computer memory for that object using the `new` operator. After an object has been instantiated, its `public` methods can be accessed using the object's identifier, a dot, and a method call. You can pass objects to methods just as you can pass simple data types.

- A property is a member of a class that provides access to a field of a class. Properties have `set` accessors for setting an object's fields and `get` accessors for retrieving the stored values. As a shortcut, you can create an auto-implemented property when a field's `set` accessor should simply assign a value to the appropriate field, and when its `get` accessor should simply return the field.

- In most classes, fields are `private` and methods are `public`. This technique ensures that data will be used and changed only in the ways provided in the class's accessors. Occasionally, however, you need to create `public` fields or `private` methods.

- The `this` reference is passed to every instance method and property accessor in a class. You can explicitly refer to the `this` reference within an instance method or property, but usually you are not required to do so.

- A constructor is a method that instantiates (creates an instance of) an object. If you do not write a constructor, then each class is automatically supplied with a `public` constructor with no parameters. You can write your own constructor to replace the automatically supplied version. Any constructor you write must have the same name as its class, and constructors cannot have a return type. You can overload constructors and pass arguments to a constructor. Frequently you do so to initialize fields.

- An object initializer allows you to assign values to any accessible members or properties of a class at the time of instantiation without calling a constructor with parameters. Using object initializers allows you to create multiple objects with different initial assignments without having to provide multiple constructors to cover every possible situation. Additionally, using object initializers allows you to create objects with different starting values for different properties of the same data type.

- You can overload an operator to use with objects by writing a method whose identifier is `operator`, followed by the operator being overloaded—for example, `operator+()` or `operator*()`. When you overload an operator, you should write statements that intuitively have the same meaning as the common use of the operator.

- You can declare arrays of references to objects. After doing so, you must call a constructor to instantiate each object. To use a method that belongs to an object that is part of an array, you insert the appropriate subscript notation after the array name and before the dot-method. The `IComparable` interface contains the definition for the `CompareTo()` method; you override this method to tell the compiler how to compare objects.

- A destructor contains the actions you require when an instance of a class is destroyed. If you do not explicitly create a destructor for a class, C# automatically provides one. To explicitly declare a destructor, you use an identifier that consists of a tilde ($\sim$) followed by the class name. You cannot provide any parameters to a destructor; a class can have one destructor at most.

- GUI objects such as `Forms`, `Buttons`, and `Labels` are typical C# objects that encapsulate properties and methods. When you start a Windows Forms application and drag a `Button` onto a `Form`, a statement is automatically created by the IDE to instantiate a `Button` object.

## Key Terms

An **instantiation** of a class is a created object.

The **instance variables** of a class are the data components that exist separately for each instantiation.

**Fields** are instance variables within a class.

An object's **state** is the set of contents of its fields.

**Instance methods** are methods that are used with object instantiations.

A **class client** or **class user** is a program or class that instantiates objects of another prewritten class.

A **class header** or **class definition** describes a `class`; it contains an optional access modifier, the keyword `class`, and any legal identifier for the name of the class.

A **class access modifier** describes access to a class.

The **public** class access modifier means access to the class is not limited.

The **protected** class access modifier means access to the class is limited to the class and to any classes derived from the class.

The **internal** class access modifier means access is limited to the assembly to which the class belongs.

The **private** class access modifier means access is limited to another class to which the class belongs. In other words, a class can be private if it is contained within another class, and only the containing class should have access to the private class.

An **assembly** is a group of code modules compiled together to create an executable program.

**Information hiding** is a feature found in all object-oriented languages, in which a class's data is private and changed or manipulated only by its own methods.

**Composition** is the technique of using an object within another object.

The relationship created using composition is called a **has-a relationship** because one class "has an" instance of another.

A **reference type** is a type that holds a memory address.

**Value types** hold a value; they are predefined types such as int, double, and char.

A **property** is a member of a class that provides access to a field of a class; properties define how fields will be set and retrieved.

**Accessors** in properties specify how a class's fields are accessed.

An object's fields are assigned by **set accessors** that allow use of the assignment operator with a property name.

An object's fields are accessed by **get accessors** that allow retrieval of a field value by using a property name.

A **read-only property** has only a get accessor, and not a set accessor.

The **getter** is another term for a class property's get accessor.

The **setter** is another term for a class property's set accessor.

**Contextual keywords** are identifiers that act like keywords in specific circumstances.

An **implicit parameter** is undeclared and gets its value automatically.

An **auto-implemented property** is one in which the code within the accessors is created automatically. The only action in the `set` accessor is to assign a value to the associated field, and the only action in the `get` accessor is to return the associated field value.

**Automatic properties** are auto-implemented properties.

A **backing field** is a field that has a property coded for it.

The **`this` reference** is the reference to an object that is implicitly passed to an instance method of its class.

A **constructor** is a method that instantiates (creates an instance of) an object.

A **default constructor** is a parameterless constructor.

The **default value of an object** is the value initialized with a default constructor.

A **parameterless constructor** is one that takes no arguments.

A **constructor initializer** is a clause that indicates another instance of a class constructor should be executed before any statements in the current constructor body.

An **object initializer** allows you to assign values to any accessible members or properties of a class at the time of instantiation without calling a constructor with parameters.

The **`CompareTo()`** method of the `IComparable` interface compares one object to another and returns an integer.

An **interface** is a collection of abstract methods (and perhaps other members) that can be used by any class, as long as the class provides a definition to override the interface's do-nothing, or abstract, method definitions.

When a method **overrides** another, it takes precedence over the method, hiding the original version.

The **`IComparable` interface** contains the definition for the `CompareTo()` method.

An instance method's **invoking object** is the object referenced by `this`.

A **destructor** contains the actions you require when an instance of a class is destroyed.

# Review Questions

1. An object is a(n) _____ of a class.

   a. child

   b. institution

   c. instantiation

   d. relative

2. A class header or class definition can contain all of the following *except* _____.

   a. an optional access modifier

   b. the keyword `class`

   c. an identifier

   d. initial field values

3. Most fields in a class are created with the _____ modifier.

   a. `public`

   b. `protected`

   c. `new`

   d. `private`

4. Most methods in a class are created with the _____ modifier.

   a. `public`

   b. `protected`

   c. `new`

   d. `private`

5. Instance methods that belong to individual objects are _____ `static` methods.

   a. always

   b. usually

   c. occasionally

   d. never

6. To allocate memory for an object instantiation, you must use the _____ operator.

   a. `mem`

   b. `alloc`

   c. `new`

   d. `instant`

7. Assume you have created a class named `MyClass`. The header of the `MyClass` constructor can be _____.

   a. `public void MyClass()`

   b. `public MyClassConstructor()`

   c. Either of these can be the constructor header.

   d. Neither of these can be the constructor header.

8. Assume you have created a class named `MyClass`. The header of the `MyClass` constructor can be _____.

   a. `public MyClass()`

   b. `public MyClass (double d)`

   c. Either of these can be the constructor header.

   d. Neither of these can be the constructor header.

9. Assume you have created a class named `DemoCar`. Within the `Main()` method of this class, you instantiate a `Car` object named `myCar` and the following statement executes correctly:

   ```
   Console.WriteLine("The Car gets {0} miles per gallon",
      myCar.ComputeMpg());
   ```

   Within the `Car` class, the `ComputeMpg()` method can be _____.

   a. `public` and `static`

   b. `public` and nonstatic

   c. `private` and `static`

   d. `private` and nonstatic

10. Assume you have created a class named TermPaper that contains a character field named letterGrade. You also have created a property for the field. Which of the following cannot be true?

   a. The property name is letterGrade.

   b. The property is read-only.

   c. The property contains a set accessor that does not allow a grade lower than 'C'.

   d. The property does not contain a get accessor.

11. A this reference is _____.

   a. implicitly passed to nonstatic methods

   b. implicitly passed to static methods

   c. explicitly passed to nonstatic methods

   d. explicitly passed to static methods

12. When you use an instance variable within a class's nonstatic methods, you _____ explicitly refer to the method's this reference.

   a. must

   b. can

   c. cannot

   d. should (even though it is not required)

13. A class's default constructor _____.

   a. sets numeric fields to 0

   b. is parameterless

   c. both of these

   d. none of these

14. Assume you have created a class named Chair with a constructor defined as Chair(int height). Which of the following overloaded constructors could coexist with the Chair constructor without ambiguity?

    a. Chair(int legs)

    b. Chair(int height, int legs)

    c. both of these

    d. none of these

15. Which of the following statements correctly instantiates a House object if the House class contains a single constructor with the declaration House(int bedrooms, double price)?

    a. House myHouse = new House();

    b. House myHouse = new House(3, 125000.00);

    c. House myHouse = House(4, 200,000.00);

    d. two of these

16. You explicitly call a destructor _____.

    a. when you are finished using an object

    b. when an object goes out of scope

    c. when a class is destroyed

    d. You cannot explicitly call a destructor.

17. In a program that creates five object instances of a class, the constructor executes _____ time(s) and the destructor executes _____ time(s).

    a. one; one

    b. one; five

    c. five; one

    d. five; five

18. Suppose you declare a class named `Furniture` that contains a `string` field named `woodType` and a conventionally named property with a `get` accessor. When you declare an array of 200 `Furniture` objects named `myChairs`, which of the following accesses the last `Furniture` object's wood type?

    a. `Furniture.Get(woodType[199])`

    b. `myChairs[199].WoodType()`

    c. `myChairs.WoodType[199]`

    d. `myChairs[199].WoodType`

19. A collection of methods that can be used by any class, as long as the class provides a definition to override the collection's abstract definitions, is _____.

    a. a superclass

    b. a polymorph

    c. a perimeter

    d. an interface

20. When you create a class whose members clients are likely to want to compare using the `Array.Sort()` or `Array.BinarySearch()` method, you must _____.

    a. include at least one numeric field within the class

    b. write a `CompareTo()` method for the class

    c. be careful not to override the existing `IComparable.CompareTo()` method

    d. Two of these are true.

## Exercises

Your instructor might ask you to create the programs described in these exercises either as console-based or GUI applications.

1. Create a class named `Pizza`. Data fields include a string for toppings (such as pepperoni), an integer for diameter in inches (such as 12), and a `double` for price (such as 13.99). Include properties to get and set values for each of these fields. Create a class named `TestPizza` that instantiates one `Pizza` object and demonstrates the use of the `Pizza` set and get accessors. Save this class as **TestPizza.cs**.

2. Create a class named `HousePlant`. A `HousePlant` has fields for a name (for example, "Philodendron"), a price (for example, 29.99), and a value indicating whether the plant has been fed in the last month (for example, `true`). Include properties that contain `get` and `set` accessors for each field. Create a class named `DisplayHousePlants` that instantiates three `HousePlant` objects. Demonstrate the use of each property for each object. Save the file as **DisplayHousePlants.cs**.

3. Create a class named `Circle` with fields named `radius`, `area`, and `diameter`. Include a constructor that sets the radius to 1. Also include `public` properties for each field. The `Radius` property should have `get` and `set` accessors, but `Area` and `Diameter` should be read-only. The `set` accessor for the radius should also provide values for the `diameter` and `area`. (The diameter of a circle is twice its radius; the area is pi multiplied by the square of the radius. You can use the public `Math` class property `Math.PI` for the value of pi.) Create a class named `TestCircles` whose `Main()` method declares three `Circle` objects. Assign a small radius value to one `Circle` and assign a larger radius value to another `Circle`. Do not assign a value to the radius of the third circle; instead, retain the value assigned at construction. Display the radius, diameter, and area for each `Circle`. (Display the area to two decimal places.) Save the program as **TestCircles.cs**.

4. Create a class named `Square` that contains fields for area and the length of a side and whose constructor requires a parameter for the length of one side of a `Square`. The constructor assigns its parameter to the length of the `Square`'s side field and calls a `private` method that computes the area field. Also include read-only properties to get a `Square`'s side and area. Create a class named `DemoSquares` that instantiates an array of ten `Square` objects with sides that have values of 1 through 10. Display the values for each `Square`. Save the class as **DemoSquares.cs**.

5. Create a class named `GirlScout` that contains fields for a `GirlScout`'s name, troop number, and dues owed. Include a constant `static` field that contains the last words of the `GirlScout` motto ("to obey the Girl Scout law"). Include overloaded constructors that allow you to set all three non-static `GirlScout` fields to default values or to parameter values. Also include properties for each field. Create a class named `DemoScouts` that instantiates two `GirlScout` objects and displays their values. Create one object to use the default

constructor and the other to use the constructor that requires arguments. Also display the GirlScout motto. Save the class as **DemoScouts.cs**.

6. a. Create a class named Taxpayer. Data fields for Taxpayer objects include the Social Security number (use a string for the type, but do not use dashes within the number), the yearly gross income, and the tax owed. Include a property with get and set accessors for the first two data fields, but make the tax owed a read-only property. The tax should be calculated whenever the income is set. Assume the tax is 15 % of income for incomes under $30,000 and 28 % for incomes that are $30,000 or higher. Write a program that declares an array of ten Taxpayer objects. Prompt the user for data for each object and display the ten objects. Save the program as **TaxPayerDemo.cs**.

   b. Modify the Taxpayer class so its objects are comparable to each other based on tax owed. Modify the TaxPayerDemo application so that after the ten objects are displayed, they are sorted in order by the amount of tax owed; then display the objects again. Save the program as **TaxPayerDemo2.cs**.

7. Create a class named Car with auto-implemented properties for the vehicle ID number, make, model, color, and value of a Car object. Write a DisplayFleet() method that accepts any number of Car objects, displays their values, and displays the total value of all Car objects passed to the method. Write a Main() method that declares five Car objects and assigns values to each, then calls DisplayFleet() three times—passing three, four, and five Car objects in successive calls. Save the program as **CarsDemo.cs**.

8. a. Create a class named School that contains fields for the School name and number of students enrolled and properties for each field. Also, include an IComparable.CompareTo() method so that School objects can be sorted by enrollment. Write a program that allows a user to enter information about five School objects. Display the School objects in order of enrollment size from smallest to largest School. Save the program as **SchoolsDemo.cs**.

   b. Modify the program created in Exercise 8a so that after the School objects are displayed in order, the program prompts the user to enter a minimum enrollment figure. Display all `School` objects that have an enrollment at least as large as the entered value. Save the program as **SchoolMinEnroll.cs**.

9.  a.  Create a class named `Friend`. Its auto-implemented properties include those for the `Friend`'s name, phone number, and three integers that together represent the `Friend`'s birthday—month, day, and year. Write a program that declares an array of eight `Friend` objects and prompts the user to enter data about eight friends. Display the `Friend` objects in alphabetical order by first name. Save the program as **FriendList.cs**.

    b.  Modify the program created in Exercise 9a so that after the list of `Friend` objects is displayed, the program prompts the user for a specific `Friend`'s name and the program displays the `Friend`'s birthday. Display an appropriate message if the friend the user requests is not found. Save the program as **FriendBirthday.cs**.

    c.  Modify the program in Exercise 9b so that after the requested `Friend`'s birthday displays, the program also displays a list of every `Friend` who has a birthday in the same month. Save the program as **AllFriendsInSameMonth.cs**.

10. a.  Design a `Job` class for Harold's Home Services. The class contains four data fields—`Job` description (for example, "wash windows"), time in hours to complete the `Job` (for example, 3.5), per-hour rate charged for the `Job` (for example, $25.00), and total fee for the `Job` (hourly rate times hours). Include properties to get and set each field except the total fee—that field will be read-only, and its value is calculated each time either the hourly fee or the number of hours is set. Overload the + operator so that two `Jobs` can be added. The sum of two `Jobs` is a new `Job` containing the descriptions of both original `Jobs` (joined by "and"), the sum of the time in hours for the original `Jobs`, and the average of the hourly rate for the original `Jobs`. Write a `Main()` function that demonstrates all the methods work correctly. Save the file as **DemoJobs.cs**.

    b.  Harold has realized that his method for computing the fee for combined jobs is not fair. For example, consider the following:

- His fee for painting a house is $100 per hour. If a job takes ten hours, he earns $1000.

- His fee for dog walking is $10 per hour. If a job takes 1 hour, he earns $10.

- If he combines the two jobs and works a total of 11 hours, he earns only the average rate of $55 per hour, or $605.

Devise an improved, weighted method for calculating Harold's fees for combined Jobs and include it in the overloaded operator+() method. Write a Main() function that demonstrates all the methods in the class work correctly. Save the file as **DemoJobs2.cs**.

11. a. Create a Fraction class with fields that hold a whole number, a numerator, and a denominator. In addition:

- Create properties for each field. The set accessor for the denominator should not allow a 0 value; the value defaults to 1.

- Add three constructors. One takes three parameters for a whole number, numerator, and denominator. Another accepts two parameters for the numerator and denominator; when this constructor is used, the whole number value is 0. The last constructor is parameterless; it sets the whole number and numerator to 0 and the denominator to 1. (After construction, Fractions do not have to be reduced to proper form. For example, even though 3/9 could be reduced to 1/3, your constructors do not have to perform this task.)

- Add a Reduce() method that reduces a Fraction if it is in improper form. For example, 2/4 should be reduced to 1/2.

- Add an operator+() method that adds two Fractions. To add two fractions, first eliminate any whole number part of the value. For example, 2 1/4 becomes 9/4 and 1 3/5 becomes 8/5. Find a common denominator and convert the fractions to it. For example, when adding 9/4 and 8/5, you can convert them to 45/20 and 32/20. Then you can add the numerators, giving 77/20. Finally, call the Reduce() method to reduce the result, restoring any whole number value so the fractional part of the number is less than 1. For example, 77/20 becomes 3 17/20.

- Include a function that returns a `string` that contains a `Fraction` in the usual display format—the whole number, a space, the numerator, a slash (/), and a denominator. When the whole number is 0, just the `Fraction` part of the value should be displayed (for example, 1/2 instead of 0 1/2). If the numerator is 0, just the whole number should be displayed (for example, 2 instead of 2 0/3).

Write a `Main()` method that instantiates several `Fractions` and demonstrate that all the methods work correctly. Save the program as **FractionDemo.cs**.

b. Add an `operator*()` method to the `Fraction` class created in Exercise 11a so that it correctly multiplies two `Fractions`. The result should be in proper, reduced format. Demonstrate that the method works correctly. Save the program as **FractionDemo2.cs**.

c. Create an array of four `Fractions`. Prompt the user for values for each. Display every possible combination of addition results and every possible combination of multiplication results for each `Fraction` pair (that is, each type will have 16 results). Save the program as **FractionDemo3.cs**.

 ## Debugging Exercises

Each of the following files saved in the Chapter.09 folder of your downloadable student files has syntax and/or logical errors. In each case, determine the problem and fix the program. After you correct the errors, save each file using the same filename preceded with "Fixed." For example, DebugNine1.cs will become FixedDebugNine1.cs.

    a. DebugNine1.cs

    b. DebugNine2.cs

    c. DebugNine3.cs

    d. DebugNine4.cs

 ## Up For Discussion

1. In this chapter, you learned that instance data and methods belong to objects (which are class members), but that static data and methods belong to a class as a whole. Consider the

real-life class named `StateInTheUnitedStates`. Name some real-life attributes of this class that are static attributes and instance attributes. Create another example of a real-life class and discuss what its static and instance members might be.

2. Most people's paychecks were once produced by hand, but yours probably is produced by a computer or deposited into an account electronically. Likewise, most grocery store checkers once keyed item prices into the cash register, but your groceries now are most likely scanned. Police officers who used to direct traffic at major urban intersections have been replaced by computers. What other tasks do people perform that you think would be better handled by a computer? Are there any tasks that you hope never become computerized?

3. If you are completing all the programming exercises in this book, you can see how much work goes into a full-blown professional program. How would you feel if someone copied your work without compensating you? Investigate the magnitude of software piracy in our society. What are the penalties for illegally copying software? Are there circumstances under which it is acceptable to copy a program? If a friend asked you to make a copy of a program for him, would you? What do you suggest we do about this problem, if anything?

# Introduction to Inheritance

In this chapter you will:

◎ Learn about inheritance

◎ Extend classes

◎ Use the `protected` access specifier

◎ Override base class methods

◎ Understand how a derived class object "is an" instance of the base class

◎ Learn about the `Object` class

◎ Work with base class constructors

◎ Create and use abstract classes

◎ Create and use interfaces

◎ Use extension methods

◎ Recognize inheritance in GUI applications and understand the benefits of inheritance

Understanding classes helps you organize objects in real life. Understanding inheritance helps you organize them more precisely. If you have never heard of a Braford, for example, you would have a hard time forming a picture of one in your mind. When you learn that a Braford is an animal, you gain some understanding of what it must be like. That understanding grows when you learn it is a mammal, and the understanding is almost complete when you learn it is a cow. When you learn that a Braford is a cow, you understand it has many characteristics that are common to all cows. To identify a Braford, you must learn only relatively minor details—its color or markings, for example. Most of a Braford's characteristics, however, derive from its membership in a particular hierarchy of classes: animal, mammal, and cow.

All object-oriented programming languages make use of inheritance for the same reasons—to organize the objects programs use, and to make new objects easier to understand based on your knowledge of their inherited traits. In this chapter, you will learn to make use of inheritance with your C# objects.

## Understanding Inheritance

**Inheritance** is the principle that you can apply your knowledge of a general category to more specific objects. You are familiar with the concept of inheritance from all sorts of situations. When you use the term *inheritance*, you might think of genetic inheritance. You know from biology that your blood type and eye color are the products of inherited genes. You can say that many other facts about you (your attributes) are inherited. Similarly, you often can attribute your behaviors to inheritance; for example, the way you handle money might be similar to the way your grandmother handles it, and your gait might be the same as your father's—so your methods are inherited, too.

You also might choose to own plants and animals based on their inherited attributes. You plant impatiens next to your house because they thrive in the shade; you adopt a poodle because you know poodles do not shed. Every plant and pet has slightly different characteristics, but within a species, you can count on many consistent inherited attributes and behaviors. In other words, you can reuse the knowledge you gain about general categories and apply it to more specific categories. Similarly, the classes you create in object-oriented programming languages can inherit data and methods from existing classes. When you create a class by making it inherit from another class, you are provided with data fields and methods automatically; you can reuse fields and methods that are already written and tested.

You already know how to create classes and how to instantiate objects from those classes. For example, consider the `Employee` class in Figure 10-1. The class contains two data fields, empNum and empSal, as well as properties that contain accessors for each field and a method that creates an `Employee` greeting.

```
class Employee
{
    private int empNum;
    private double empSal;
    public int EmpNum
    {
        get
        {
            return empNum;
        }
        set
        {
            empNum = value;
        }
    }
    public double EmpSal
    {
        get
        {
            return empNum;
        }
        set
        {
            empSal = value;
        }
    }
    public string GetGreeting()
    {
        string greeting = "Hello. I am employee #" + EmpNum;
        return greeting;
    }
}
```

**Figure 10-1**   An Employee class

After you create the `Employee` class, you can create specific `Employee` objects, as in the following:

```
Employee receptionist = new Employee();
Employee deliveryPerson = new Employee();
```

These `Employee` objects can eventually possess different numbers and salaries, but because they are `Employee` objects, you know that each possesses *some* number and salary.

Suppose you hire a new type of Employee who earns a commission as well as a salary. You can create a class with a name such as CommissionEmployee, and provide this class with three fields (empNum, empSal, and commissionRate), three properties (with accessors to get and set each of the three fields), and a greeting method. However, this work would duplicate much of the work that you already have done for the Employee class. The wise and efficient alternative is to create the class CommissionEmployee so it inherits all the attributes and methods of Employee. Then, you can add just the single field and property with two accessors that are additions within CommissionEmployee objects. Figure 10-2 depicts these relationships.

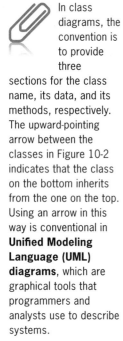

In class diagrams, the convention is to provide three sections for the class name, its data, and its methods, respectively. The upward-pointing arrow between the classes in Figure 10-2 indicates that the class on the bottom inherits from the one on the top. Using an arrow in this way is conventional in **Unified Modeling Language (UML) diagrams**, which are graphical tools that programmers and analysts use to describe systems.

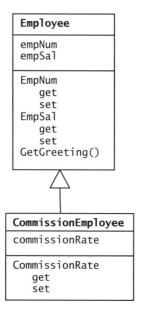

**Figure 10-2**  CommissionEmployee inherits from Employee

When you use inheritance to create the CommissionEmployee class, you acquire the following benefits:

- You save time, because you need not re-create the Employee fields, properties, and methods.

- You reduce the chance of errors, because the Employee properties and methods have already been used and tested.

- You make it easier for anyone who has used the Employee class to understand the CommissionEmployee class because such users can concentrate on the new features only.

The ability to use inheritance makes programs easier to write, easier to understand, and less prone to errors. Imagine that besides

CommissionEmployee, you want to create several other specific Employee classes (perhaps PartTimeEmployee, including a field for hours worked, or DismissedEmployee, including a reason for dismissal). By using inheritance, you can develop each new class correctly and more quickly.

## Understanding Inheritance Terminology

A class that is used as a basis for inheritance, like Employee, is called a **base class**. When you create a class that inherits from a base class (such as CommissionEmployee), it is a **derived class** or **extended class**. When presented with two classes that have a parent-child relationship, you can tell which class is the base class and which is the derived class by using the two classes in a sentence with the phrase "is a." A derived class always "is a" case or instance of the more general base class. For example, a Tree class may be a base class to an Evergreen class. Every Evergreen "is a" Tree; however, it is not true that every Tree is an Evergreen. Thus, Tree is the base class and Evergreen is the derived class. Similarly, a CommissionEmployee "is an" Employee—not always the other way around—so Employee is the base class and CommissionEmployee is derived.

You can use the terms **superclass** and **subclass** as synonyms for base class and derived class. Thus, Evergreen can be called a subclass of the Tree superclass. You also can use the terms **parent class** and **child class**. A CommissionEmployee is a child to the Employee parent. Use the pair of terms with which you are most comfortable; all of these terms will be used interchangeably in this book.

As an alternative way to discover which of two classes is the base class and which is the derived class, you can try saying the two class names together (although this technique might not work with every superclass-subclass pair). When people say their names together in the English language, they state the more specific name before the all-encompassing family name, such as "Ginny Kroening." Similarly, with classes, the order that "makes more sense" is the child-parent order. Thus, because "Evergreen Tree" makes more sense than "Tree Evergreen," you can deduce that Evergreen is the child class.

Finally, you usually can distinguish base classes from their derived classes by size. A derived class is larger than a base class, in the sense that it usually has additional fields and methods. A derived class description may look small, but any subclass contains all of its superclass's fields and methods as well as its own more specific fields and methods.

In part, the concept of class inheritance is useful because it makes class code reusable. However, you do not use inheritance simply to save work. When properly used, inheritance always involves a general-to-specific relationship.

431

It also is convenient to think of a derived class as building upon its base class by providing the "adjectives" or additional descriptive terms for the "noun." Frequently, the names of derived classes are formed in this way, as in CommissionEmployee.

Do not think of a subclass as a "subset" of another class—in other words, possessing only parts of its superclass. In fact, a derived class contains everything in the superclass, plus any new attributes and methods.

After you create the Spruce class, you might be ready to create Spruce objects. For example, you might create theTreeInMyBackYard, or you might create an array of 1000 Spruce objects for a tree farm.

A derived class can be further extended. In other words, a subclass can have a child of its own. For example, after you create a Tree class and derive Evergreen, you might derive a Spruce class from Evergreen. Similarly, a Poodle class might derive from Dog, Dog from DomesticPet, and DomesticPet from Animal. The entire list of parent classes from which a child class is derived constitutes the **ancestors** of the subclass.

Inheritance is **transitive**, which means a child inherits all the members of all its ancestors. In other words, when you declare a Spruce object, it contains all the attributes and methods of both an Evergreen and a Tree. As you work with C#, you will encounter many examples of such transitive chains of inheritance.

When you create your own transitive inheritance chains, you want to place fields and methods at their most general level. In other words, a method named Grow() rightfully belongs in a Tree class, whereas LeavesTurnColor() does not, because the method applies to only some of the Tree child classes. Similarly, a LeavesTurnColor() method would be better located in a Deciduous class than separately within the Oak or Maple child class.

---

## TWO TRUTHS **&** A LIE

### Understanding Inheritance

1. When you use inheritance to create a class, you save time because you can copy and paste fields, properties, and methods that have already been created for the original class.

2. When you use inheritance to create a class, you reduce the chance of errors because the original class's properties and methods have already been used and tested.

3. When you use inheritance to create a class, you make it easier for anyone who has used the original class to understand the new class because such users can concentrate on the new features.

The false statement is #1. When you use inheritance to create a class, you save time because you need not re-create fields, properties, and methods that have already been created for the original class. You do not copy these class members; you inherit them.

# Extending Classes

When you create a class that is an extension or child of another class, you use a single colon between the derived class name and its base class name. For example, the following class header creates a subclass-superclass relationship between CommissionEmployee and Employee.

```
class CommissionEmployee : Employee
```

Each CommissionEmployee object automatically contains the fields and methods of the base class; you then can add new fields and methods to the new derived class. Figure 10-3 shows a CommissionEmployee class.

```
class CommissionEmployee : Employee
{
    private double commissionRate;
    public double CommissionRate
    {
        get
        {
            return commissionRate;
        }
        set
        {
            commissionRate = value;
        }
    }
}
```

**Figure 10-3**  CommissionEmployee class

The CommissionEmployee class in Figure 10-3 contains three fields: empNum and empSal, inherited from Employee, and commissionRate, which is defined within the CommissionEmployee class. Similarly, the CommissionEmployee class contains three properties and a method— two properties and the method are inherited from Employee, and one property is defined within CommissionEmployee itself. When you write a program that instantiates an object using the following statement, then you can use any of the next statements to set field values for the salesperson:

```
CommissionEmployee salesperson = new CommissionEmployee();
salesperson.EmpNum = 234;
salesperson.EmpSal = Convert.ToDouble(Console.ReadLine());
salesperson.CommissionRate = 0.07;
```

The salesperson object has access to all three set accessors (two from its parent and one from its own class) because it is both a

CommissionEmployee and an Employee. Similarly, the object has access to three get accessors and the GetGreeting() method. Figure 10-4 shows a Main() method that declares Employee and CommissionEmployee objects and shows all the properties and methods that can be used with each. Figure 10-5 shows the program output.

```
using System;
public class DemoEmployees
{
    public static void Main()
    {
        Employee clerk = new Employee();
        CommissionEmployee salesperson = new CommissionEmployee();
        clerk.EmpNum = 123;
        clerk.EmpSal = 30000.00;
        salesperson.EmpNum = 234;
        salesperson.EmpSal = 20000;
        salesperson.CommissionRate = 0.07;
        Console.WriteLine("\n" + clerk.GetGreeting());
        Console.WriteLine("Clerk #{0} salary: {1} per year",
            clerk.EmpNum, clerk.EmpSal.ToString("C"));
        Console.WriteLine("\n" + salesperson.GetGreeting());
        Console.WriteLine("Salesperson #{0} salary: {1} per year",
            salesperson.EmpNum, salesperson.EmpSal.ToString("C"));
        Console.WriteLine("...plus {0} commission on all sales",
            salesperson.CommissionRate.ToString("P"));
    }
}
```

**Figure 10-4**   DemoEmployees class that declares Employee and CommissionEmployee objects

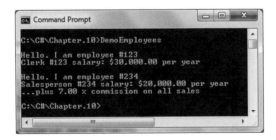

**Figure 10-5**   Output of the DemoEmployees program

Inheritance works only in one direction: A child inherits from a parent—not the other way around. If a program instantiates an Employee object as in the following statement, the Employee object does *not* have access to the CommissionEmployee properties or methods.

```
Employee clerk = new Employee();
clerk.CommissionRate = 0.1;
```

> This statement is invalid—Employee objects do not have a CommissionRate.

Employee is the parent class, and clerk is an object of the parent class. It makes sense that a parent class object does not have access to its child's data and methods. When you create the parent class, you do not know how many future child classes might be created, or what their data or methods might look like. In addition, child classes are more specific. A HeartSurgeon class and an Obstetrician class are children of a Doctor class. You do not expect all members of the general parent class Doctor to have the HeartSurgeon's RepairValve() method or the Obstetrician's DeliverBaby() method. However, HeartSurgeon and Obstetrician objects have access to the more general Doctor methods TakeBloodPressure() and BillPatients().

As with doctors, it is convenient to think of derived classes as *specialists*. That is, their fields and methods are more specialized than those of the base class.

435

Watch the video *Inheritance*.

## TWO TRUTHS & A LIE

### Extending Classes

1. The following class header indicates that Dog is a subclass of Pet:

   public class Pet : Dog

2. If class X has four fields and class Y derives from it, then class Y also contains at least four fields.

3. Inheritance works only in one direction: A child inherits from a parent—not the other way around.

The false statement is #1. The following class header indicates that Dog is a subclass of Pet:

public class Dog : Pet

# Using the **protected** Access Specifier

The Employee class in Figure 10-1 is a typical C# class in that its data fields are private and its properties and methods are public. In the chapter *Using Classes and Objects*, you learned that this scheme provides for information hiding—protecting your private data from alteration by methods outside the data's own class. When a program is a client of the Employee class (that is, it instantiates an Employee object), the client cannot alter the data in any private field directly. For example, when you write a Main() method that creates an Employee named clerk, you cannot change the Employee's empNum or empSal directly using a statement such as clerk.empNum = 2222;. Instead, you must use the public EmpNum property to set the empNum field of the clerk object.

When you use information hiding, you are assured that your data will be altered only by the properties and methods you choose and only in ways that you can control. If outside classes could alter an Employee's private fields, then the fields could be assigned values that the Employee class could not control. In such a case, the principle of information hiding would be destroyed, causing the behavior of the object to be unpredictable.

Any derived class you create, such as CommissionEmployee, inherits all the data and methods of its base class. However, even though a child of Employee has empNum and empSal fields, the CommissionEmployee methods cannot alter or use those private fields directly. If a new class could simply extend your Employee class and "get to" its data fields without "going through the proper channels," then information hiding would not be operating.

On some occasions, you do want to access parent class data from a child class. For example, suppose that the Employee class EmpSal property set accessor has been written so that no Employee's salary is ever set to less than 15,000, as follows:

```
set
{
    double MINIMUM = 15000;
    if(value < MINIMUM)
        empSal = MINIMUM;
    else
        empSal = value;
}
```

Also assume that a CommissionEmployee draws commission only and no regular salary; that is, when you set a CommissionEmployee's commissionRate field, the empSal should become 0. You would write the CommissionEmployee class CommissionRate property set accessor as follows:

```
set
{
    commissionRate = value;
    EmpSal = 0;
}
```

Using this implementation, when you create a CommissionEmployee object and set its CommissionRate, 0 is sent to the set accessor for the Employee class EmpSal property. Because the value of the salary is less than 15,000, the salary is forced to 15,000 in the Employee class set accessor, even though you want it to be 0.

A possible alternative would be to rewrite the set accessor for the CommissionRate property in the CommissionEmployee class using the field empSal instead of the property EmpSal, as follows:

```
set
{
    commissionRate = value;
    empSal = 0;
}
```

In this set accessor, you bypass the parent class's EmpSal set accessor and directly use the empSal field. However, when you include this accessor in a program and compile it, you receive an error message: "Employee.empSal is inaccessible due to its protection level". In other words, Employee.empSal is private, and no other class can access it, even a child class of Employee. So, in summary:

- Using the public set accessor in the parent class does not work because of the minimum salary requirement.

- Using the private field in the parent class does not work because it is inaccessible.

- Making the parent class field public would work, but doing so would violate the principle of information hiding.

Fortunately, there is a fourth option. The solution is to create the empSal field using the specifier protected, which provides you with an intermediate level of security between public and private access. A **protected** data field or method can be used within its own class or in any classes extended from that class, but it cannot be used by "outside" classes. In other words, protected members can be used "within the family"—by a class and its descendents.

 Some sources say that private, public, and protected are *access specifiers*, while other class designations, such as static, are *access modifiers*. However, Microsoft developers, who created C#, use the terms interchangeably in their documentation.

Figure 10-6 shows how you can declare empSal as protected within the Employee class so that it becomes legal to access it directly within the CommissionRate set accessor of the CommissionEmployee derived class. Figure 10-7 shows a program that instantiates a CommissionEmployee object, and Figure 10-8 shows the output. Notice that the CommissionEmployee's salary initially is set to 20,000 in the program, but the salary becomes 0 when the CommissionRate is set later.

```
class Employee
{
   private int empNum;
   protected double empSal;
   public int EmpNum
   {
      get
      {
         return empNum;
      }
      set
      {
         empNum = value;
      }
   }
   public double EmpSal
   {
      get
      {
         return empSal;
      }
      set
      {
         double MINIMUM = 15000;
         if(value < MINIMUM)
            empSal = MINIMUM;
         else
            empSal = value;
      }
   }
   public string GetGreeting()
   {
      string greeting = "Hello. I am employee #" + EmpNum;
      return greeting;
   }
}
class CommissionEmployee : Employee
{
   private double commissionRate;
   public double CommissionRate
   {
      get
      {
         return commissionRate;
      }
      set
      {
         commissionRate = value;
         empSal = 0;                    The protected empSal field is
      }                                 accessible in the child class.
   }
}
```

**Figure 10-6** Employee class with a protected field and CommissionEmployee class

```
using System;
public class DemoSalesperson
{
    public static void Main()
    {
        CommissionEmployee salesperson = new CommissionEmployee();
        salesperson.EmpNum = 345;
        salesperson.EmpSal = 20000;
        salesperson.CommissionRate = 0.07;
        Console.WriteLine("Salesperson #{0} makes {1} per year",
            salesperson.EmpNum,
            salesperson.EmpSal.ToString("C"));
        Console.WriteLine("...plus {0} commission on all sales",
            salesperson.CommissionRate.ToString("P"));
    }
}
```

**Figure 10-7**   The DemoSalesperson program

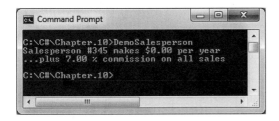

**Figure 10-8**   Output of the DemoSalesperson program

If you set the salesperson's CommissionRate first in the DemoSalesperson program, then set EmpSal to a nonzero value, empSal will not be reduced to 0. If your intention is to always create CommissionEmployees with salaries of 0, then the EmpSal property should also be overridden in the derived class.

Using the **protected** access specifier for a field can be convenient, and it also slightly improves program performance by using a field directly instead of "going through" property accessors. Also, using the **protected** access specifier is occasionally necessary. However, **protected** data members should be used sparingly. Whenever possible, the principle of information hiding should be observed, and even child classes should have to go through accessors to "get to" their parent's private data. When child classes are allowed direct access to a parent's fields, the likelihood of future errors increases.

Classes that depend on field names from parent classes are said to be **fragile** because they are prone to errors—that is, they are easy to "break."

---

**TWO TRUTHS & A LIE**

**Using the protected Access Specifier**

1. A child class does not possess the private members of its parent.

2. A child class cannot use the private members of its parent.

3. A child class can use the protected members of its parent, but outside classes cannot.

The false statement is #1. A child class possesses the private members of its parent, but cannot use them directly.

---

# Overriding Base Class Methods

When you create a derived class by extending an existing class, the new derived class contains data and methods that were defined in the original base class. Sometimes, the superclass fields, properties, and methods are not entirely appropriate for the subclass objects. Using the same method or property name to indicate different implementations is called polymorphism. The word *polymorphism* means "many forms"—it means that many forms of action take place, even though you use the same method name. The specific method executed depends on the object.

 You first learned the term *polymorphism* in Chapter 1.

Everyday cases provide many examples of polymorphism:

- Although both are musical instruments and have a `Play()` method, a guitar is played differently than a drum.

- Although both are vehicles and have an `Operate()` method, a bicycle is operated differently than a truck.

- Although both are schools and have a `SatisfyGraduationRequirements()` method, a preschool's requirements are different from those of a college.

You understand each of these methods based on the context in which it is used. In a similar way, C# understands your use of the same method name based on the type of object associated with it.

For example, suppose you have created a `Student` class as shown in Figure 10-9. `Student`s have `name`s, `credit`s for which they are enrolled, and `tuition` amounts. You can set a `Student`'s `name` and `credit`s by using the `set` accessors in the `Name` and `Credit`s properties, but you cannot set a `Student`'s `tuition` directly because there is no `set` accessor for the `Tuition` property. Instead, `tuition` is calculated based on a standard `RATE` (of $55.75) for each `credit` that the `Student` takes.

```
class Student
{
   private const double RATE = 55.75;
   private string name;
   protected int credits;
   protected double tuition;
   public string Name
   {
      get
      {
         return name;
      }
      set
      {
         name = value;
      }
   }
   public virtual int Credits
   {
      get
      {
         return credits;
      }
      set
      {
         credits = value;
         tuition = credits * RATE;
      }
   }
   public double Tuition
   {
      get
      {
         return tuition;
      }
   }
}
```

441

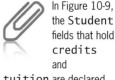 In Figure 10-9, the **Student** fields that hold **credits** and **tuition** are declared as **protected** because a child class will use them.

**Figure 10-9** The Student class

In Figure 10-9, Credits is declared to be virtual (see shading). A **virtual method** (or property) is one that can be overridden by a method with the same signature in a child class. Suppose you derive a subclass from Student called ScholarshipStudent, as shown in Figure 10-10. A ScholarshipStudent has a name, credits, and tuition, but the tuition is not calculated in the same way as it is for a Student; instead, tuition for a ScholarshipStudent should be set to 0. You want to use the Credits property to set a ScholarshipStudent's credits, but you want the property to behave differently than the parent class Student's Credits property. As a child of Student, a ScholarshipStudent possesses all the attributes, properties, and methods of a `Student`, but its `Credits` property behaves differently.

```
class ScholarshipStudent : Student
{
    override public int Credits
    {
        set
        {
            credits = value;
            tuition = 0;
        }
    }
}
```

**Figure 10-10**   The `ScholarshipStudent` class

 In C#, you can use either `new` or `override` when defining a derived class member that has the same name as a base class member. When you write a statement such as `ScholarshipStudent s1 = new ScholarshipStudent();`, you will not notice the difference. However, if you use `new` when defining the derived class `Credits` property and write a statement such as `Student s2 = new ScholarshipStudent();` (using `Student` as the type), then `s2.Credits` accesses the base class property. On the other hand, if you use `override` when defining `Credits` in the derived class, then `s2.Credits` uses the derived class property.

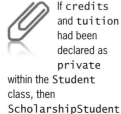 If `credits` and `tuition` had been declared as `private` within the `Student` class, then `ScholarshipStudent` would not be able to use them.

In the child `ScholarshipStudent` class in Figure 10-10, the `Credits` property is declared with the `override` modifier (see shading) because it has the same header (that is, the same signature—the same name and parameter list) as a property in its parent class. The `Credits` property overrides and **hides** its counterpart in the parent class. (You could do the same thing with methods.) If you omit `override`, the program will still operate correctly, but you will receive a warning that you are hiding an inherited member with the same name in the base class. Using the keyword `override` eliminates the warning and makes your intentions clear. When you use the `Name` property with a `ScholarshipStudent` object, a program uses the parent class property `Name`; it is not hidden. However, when you use `Credits` to set a value for a `ScholarshipStudent` object, the program uses the new, overriding property from its own class.

You are not required to override a virtual method in a derived class; a derived class can simply use the base class version. A base class member that is not hidden by the derived class is **visible** in the derived class.

Figure 10-11 shows a program that uses `Student` and `ScholarshipStudent` objects. Even though each object assigns the `Credits` property with the same number of credit hours (in the two shaded statements), the calculated `tuition` values are different because each object uses a different version of the `Credits` property. Figure 10-12 shows the execution of the program.

```
using System;
class DemoStudents
{
    public static void Main()
    {
        Student payingStudent = new Student();
        ScholarshipStudent freeStudent = new ScholarshipStudent();
        payingStudent.Name = "Megan";
        payingStudent.Credits = 15;
        freeStudent.Name = "Luke";
        freeStudent.Credits = 15;
        Console.WriteLine("{0}'s tuition is {1}",
            payingStudent.Name,
            payingStudent.Tuition.ToString("C"));
        Console.WriteLine("{0}'s tuition is {1}",
            freeStudent.Name,
            freeStudent.Tuition.ToString("C"));
    }
}
```

**Figure 10-11** The DemoStudents program

**Figure 10-12** Output of the DemoStudents program

If a base class and a derived class have methods with the same names but different parameter lists, then the derived class method does not override the base class method; instead, it overloads the base class method. For example, if a base class contains a method with the header `public void Display()`, and its child contains a method with the header `public void Display(string s)`, then the child class would have access to both methods.

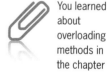

You learned about overloading methods in the chapter *Advanced Method Concepts*.

## Accessing Base Class Methods from a Derived Class

When a derived class contains a method that overrides a parent class method, you might have occasion to use the parent class version of the method within the subclass. If so, you can use the keyword **base** to access the parent class method.

For example, recall the GetGreeting() method that appears in the Employee class in Figure 10-6. If its child, CommissionEmployee, also contains a GetGreeting() method, as shown in Figure 10-13, then within the CommissionEmployee class you can call base.GetGreeting() to access the base class version of the method. Figure 10-14 shows an application that uses the method with a CommissionEmployee object. Figure 10-15 shows the output.

```
class CommissionEmployee : Employee
{
    private double commissionRate;
    public double CommissionRate
    {
        get
        {
            return commissionRate;
        }
        set
        {
            commissionRate = value;
            empSal = 0;
        }
    }
    new public string GetGreeting()
    {
        string greeting = base.GetGreeting();
        greeting += "\nI work on commission.";
        return greeting;
    }
}
```

**Figure 10-13** The CommissionEmployee class with a GetGreeting() method

```
using System;
public class DemoSalesperson2
{
    public static void Main()
    {
        CommissionEmployee salesperson = new CommissionEmployee();
        salesperson.EmpNum = 345;
        Console.WriteLine(salesperson.GetGreeting());
    }
}
```

**Figure 10-14** The DemoSalesperson2 program

**Figure 10-15** Output of the DemoSalesperson2 program

In Figure 10-13, the child class method uses the keyword new to eliminate a compiler warning. Then, within the GetGreeting() method, the parent's version is called. The returned string is stored in the greeting variable, and then an "I work on commission." statement is added to it before the complete message is returned to the calling program. By overriding the base class method in the child class, the duplicate typing to create the first part of the message was eliminated. Additionally, if the first part of the message is altered in the future, it will be altered in only one place—in the base class.

 Watch the video *Handling Methods and Inheritance*.

---

## TWO TRUTHS & A LIE

### Overriding Base Class Methods

1. When you override a parent class method in a child class, the methods have the same name.

2. When you override a parent class method in a child class, the methods have the same parameter list.

3. When you override a parent class method in a child class and then use the child class method, the parent class method executes first, followed by the child class method.

The false statement is #3. When you override a parent class method in a child class and then use the child class method, the child class method executes instead of the parent class version.

---

# Understanding How a Derived Class Object "is an" Instance of the Base Class

Every derived class object "is a" specific instance of both the derived class and the base class. In other words, myCar "is a" Car as well as a Vehicle, and myDog "is a" Dog as well as a Mammal. You can assign a

C# also makes implicit conversions when casting one data type to another. For example, in the statement `double money = 10;`, the value 10 is implicitly converted (or cast) to a double.

derived class object to an object of any of its superclass types. When you do, C# makes an **implicit conversion** from derived class to base class.

When a derived class object is assigned to its ancestor's data type, the conversion can more specifically be called an **implicit reference conversion**. This term is more accurate because it emphasizes the difference between numerical conversions and reference objects. When you assign a derived class object to a base class type, the object is treated as though it had only the characteristics defined in the base class.

For example, when a CommissionEmployee class inherits from Employee, an object of either type can be passed to a method that accepts an Employee parameter. In Figure 10-16, an Employee is passed to DisplayGreeting() in the first shaded statement, and a CommissionEmployee is passed in the second shaded statement. Each is referred to as emp within the method, and each is used correctly, as shown in Figure 10-17.

```csharp
using System;
public class DemoSalesperson3
{
    public static void Main()
    {
        Employee clerk = new Employee();
        CommissionEmployee salesperson = new CommissionEmployee();
        clerk.EmpNum = 234;
        salesperson.EmpNum = 345;
        DisplayGreeting(clerk);
        DisplayGreeting(salesperson);
    }
    internal static void DisplayGreeting(Employee emp)
    {
        Console.WriteLine("Hi there from #" + emp.EmpNum);
        Console.WriteLine(emp.GetGreeting());
    }
}
```

**Figure 10-16** The DemoSalesperson3 program

**Figure 10-17** Output of the DemoSalesperson3 program

You cannot use both **new** and **override** on the same member because they have mutually exclusive meanings. Using **new** creates a new member with the same name and causes the original member to become hidden. Using **override** extends the implementation for an inherited member.

**TWO TRUTHS & A LIE**

### Understanding How a Derived Class Object "is an" Instance of the Base Class

1. You can assign a derived class object to an object of any of its superclass types.

2. You can assign a base class object to an object of any of its derived types.

3. An implicit conversion from one type to another is an automatic conversion.

The false statement is #2. You can assign a derived class object to an object of any of its superclass types, but not the other way around.

## Using the Object Class

Every class you create in C# derives from a single class named `System.Object`. In other words, the **object** (or `Object`) class type in the `System` namespace is the ultimate base class, or **root class**, for all other types. The keyword `object` is an alias for the `System.Object` class. You can use the lowercase and uppercase versions of the class interchangeably.

The fact that `object` is an alias for `System.Object` should not surprise you. You already know, for example, that `int` is an alias for `Int32` and that `double` is an alias for `Double`.

When you create a class such as `Employee`, you usually use the header `class Employee`, which implicitly, or automatically, descends from the `Object` class. Alternatively, you could use the header `class Employee : Object` to explicitly show the name of the base class, but it would be extremely unusual to see such a format in a C# program.

Because every class descends from `Object`, every object "is an" `Object`. As proof, you can write a method that accepts an argument of type `Object`; it will accept arguments of any type. Figure 10-18 shows a program that declares three objects using classes created earlier in this chapter—a `Student`, a `ScholarshipStudent`, and an `Employee`. Even though these types possess different attributes and methods (and one type, `Employee`, has nothing in common with the other two), each type can serve as an argument to the `DisplayObjectMessage()` because each type "is an" `Object`. Figure 10-19 shows the execution of the program.

```
using System;
class DiverseObjects
{
    public static void Main()
    {
        Student payingStudent = new Student();
        ScholarshipStudent freeStudent = new ScholarshipStudent();
        Employee clerk = new Employee();
        Console.Write("Using Student: ");
        DisplayObjectMessage(payingStudent);
        Console.Write("Using ScholarshipStudent: ");
        DisplayObjectMessage(freeStudent);
        Console.Write("Using Employee: ");
        DisplayObjectMessage(clerk);
    }
    internal static void DisplayObjectMessage(Object o)
    {
        Console.WriteLine("Method successfully called");
    }
}
```

**Figure 10-18** DiverseObjects program

**Figure 10-19** Output of the DiverseObjects program

When you create any child class, it inherits all the methods of all of its ancestors. Because all classes inherit from the Object class, all classes inherit the Object class methods. The Object class contains a constructor, a destructor, and four public instance methods, as summarized in Table 10-1.

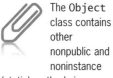

The Object class contains other nonpublic and noninstance (static) methods in addition to the four methods listed in Table 10-1. The C# documentation provides more details on these methods.

| Method | Explanation |
|---|---|
| Equals() | Determines whether two Object instances are equal |
| GetHashCode() | Gets a unique code for each object; useful in certain sorting and data management tasks |
| GetType() | Returns the type, or class, of an object |
| ToString() | Returns a String that represents the object |

**Table 10-1** The four public instance methods of the Object class

## Using the `Object` Class's `GetType()` Method

The `GetType()` method returns an object's type, or class. For example, if you have created an `Employee` object named `someWorker`, then the following statement displays `Employee`:

```
Console.WriteLine(someWorker.GetType());
```

 If an object's class is defined in a namespace, then `GetType()` returns a string composed of the namespace, a dot, and the class name.

**449**

## Using the `Object` Class's `ToString()` Method

The `Object` class methods are not very useful as they stand. For example, when you use the `Object` class's `ToString()` method with an object you create, it simply returns a string that holds the name of the class, just as `GetType()` does. That is, if `someWorker` is an `Employee`, then the following statement displays `Employee`:

```
Console.WriteLine(someWorker.ToString());
```

When you create a class such as `Employee`, you should override the `Object` class's `ToString()` method with your own, more useful version—perhaps one that returns an `Employee`'s ID number, name, or combination of the two. Of course, you could create a differently named method to do the same thing—perhaps `GetEmployeeIdentification()` or `ConvertEmployeeToString()`. However, by naming your class method `ToString()`, you make the class easier for others to understand and use. Programmers know the `ToString()` method works with every object; when they use it with your objects, you can provide a useful set of information. Additionally, many C# built-in classes use the `ToString()` method; if you have named your method conventionally, those classes will use your version because it is more helpful than the generic one.

 A class's `ToString()` method is often a useful debugging aid.

For example, you might create an `Employee` class `ToString()` method, as shown in Figure 10-20. This method assumes that `EmpNum` and `Name` are `Employee` properties with `get` accessors. The returned `string` will have a value such as "Employee: 234 Johnson".

```
public override string ToString()
{
    return(getType() + ": " + EmpNum + " " + Name);
}
```

**Figure 10-20**  An `Employee` class `ToString()` method

 You have been using overloaded versions of the `ToString()` method to format numeric output since Chapter 2.

The Equals() method compares objects for reference equality. **Reference equality** occurs when two reference type objects refer to the same object.

You first used the Equals() method to compare String objects in Chapter 2. When you use Equals() with Strings, you use the String class's Equals() method that compares String contents as opposed to String addresses. In other words, the Object class's Equals() method has already been overridden in the String class.

# Using the `Object` Class's `Equals()` Method

The `Object` class's `Equals()` method returns `true` if two `Objects` have the same memory address—that is, if one object is a reference to the other and both are literally the same object. For example, you might write the following:

```
if(oneObject.Equals(anotherObject))...
```

Like the `ToString()` method, this method might not be useful to you in its original form. For example, you might prefer to think of two `Employee` objects at unique memory addresses as equal if their ID numbers or first and last names are equal. You might want to override the `Equals()` method for any class you create if you anticipate that class clients will want to compare objects based on any of their field values.

If you overload the `Equals()` method, it should meet the following requirements by convention:

- Its header should be as follows (you can use any identifier for the `Object` parameter):

```
public override bool Equals(Object o)
```

- It should return `false` if the argument is `null`.

- It should return `true` if an object is compared to itself.

- It should return `true` only if both of the following are true:

```
oneObject.Equals(anotherObject)
anotherObject.Equals(oneObject)
```

- If `oneObject.Equals(anotherObject)` returns `true` and `oneObject.Equals(aThirdObject)` returns `true`, then `anotherObject.Equals(aThirdObject)` should also be `true`.

When you create an `Equals()` method to override the one in the `Object` class, the parameter must be an `Object`. For example, if you consider `Employee` objects equal when the `EmpNum` properties are equal, then an `Employee` class `Equals()` method might be created as follows:

```
public override bool Equals(Object e)
{
    bool equal;
    Employee temp = (Employee)e;
    if(EmpNum == temp.EmpNum)
        equal = true;
    else
        equal = false;
    return equal;
}
```

In the shaded statement in the method, the `Object` parameter is cast to an `Employee` so the `Employee`'s `EmpNum` can be compared. If you did not perform the cast and tried to make the comparison with `o.EmpNum`, the method would not compile because an `Object` does not have an `EmpNum`.

An even better alternative is to ensure that compared objects are the same type before making any other decisions. For example, the `Equals()` method in Figure 10-21 uses the `GetType()` method with both the `this` object and the parameter before proceeding. If compared objects are not the same type, then the `Equals()` method should return `false`.

```csharp
public override bool Equals(Object e)
{
    bool equal;
    if(this.GetType() != e.GetType())
        equal = false;
    else
    {
        Employee temp = (Employee)e;
        if(EmpNum == temp.EmpNum)
            equal = true;
        else
            equal = false;
    }
    return equal;
}
```

**Figure 10-21** An `Equals()` method for the `Employee` class

## Using the `Object` Class's `GetHashCode()` Method

When you override the `Equals()` method, you should also override the `GetHashCode()` method, because `Equals()` uses `GetHashCode()` and two objects considered equal should have the same hash code. A **hash code** is a number that should uniquely identify an object; you might use hash codes in some advanced C# applications. For example, Figure 10-22 shows an application that declares two `Employees` from a class in which the `GetHashCode()` method has not been overridden. The output in Figure 10-23 shows a unique number for each object. (The number, however, is meaningless to you.) If you choose to override the `GetHashCode()` method, you should write this method so it returns a unique integer for every object—an `Employee` number, for example.

 A hash code is sometimes called a "fingerprint" for an object because it uniquely identifies the object. In C#, the default implementation of the `GetHashCode()` method does not guarantee unique return values for different objects. However, if `GetHashCode()` is explicitly implemented in a derived class, it must return a unique hash code.

 In cooking, hash is a dish that is created by combining ingredients. The term *hash code* derives from the fact that the code is sometimes created by mixing some of an object's data.

452

```
using System;
public class TestHashCode
{
    public static void Main()
    {
        Employee first = new Employee();
        Employee second = new Employee();
        Console.WriteLine(first.GetHashCode());
        Console.WriteLine(second.GetHashCode());
    }
}
```

**Figure 10-22** TestHashCode program

 Although you can write an Equals() method for a class without overriding GetHashCode(), you receive a warning message. Additionally, if you overload == or != for a class, you will receive warning messages if you do not also override both the Equals() and GetHashCode() methods.

**Figure 10-23** Output of the TestHashCode program

---

**TWO TRUTHS & A LIE**

### Using the Object Class

1. The Object class contains a method named GetType() that returns an object's type, or class.

2. If you do not override the ToString() method for a class, it returns the value of all the strings within the class.

3. The Object class's Equals() method returns true if two Objects have the same memory address—that is, if one object is a reference to the other and both are literally the same object.

The false statement is #2. If you do not override the ToString() method for a class, it returns a string that holds the name of the class.

# Working with Base Class Constructors

When you create any object, you are calling a constructor that has the same name as the class itself. Consider the following example:

```
SomeClass anObject = new SomeClass();
```

When you instantiate an object that is a member of a derived class, you call both the constructor for the base class and the constructor for the extended, derived class. When you create any derived class object, the base class constructor must execute first; only then does the derived class constructor execute.

In the examples of inheritance you have seen so far in this chapter, each class contained default constructors, so their execution was transparent. However, you should realize that when you create a subclass instance, both the base and derived constructors execute. For example, consider the abbreviated `Employee` and `CommissionEmployee` classes in Figure 10-24. `Employee` contains just two fields and a constructor; `CommissionEmployee` descends from `Employee` and contains a constructor as well. The `DemoSalesperson4` program in Figure 10-25 contains just one statement; it instantiates a `CommissionEmployee`. The output in Figure 10-26 shows that this one statement causes both constructors to execute.

When you create any object, you call its constructor and the `Object` constructor because all classes are derived from `Object`. So, when you create a base class and a derived class, and instantiate a derived class object, you call three constructors: one from the `Object` class, one from the base class, and one from the derived class.

453

```
class Employee
{
    private int empNum;
    protected double empSal;
    public Employee()
    {
        Console.WriteLine("Employee constructed");
    }
}
class CommissionEmployee : Employee
{
    private double commissionRate;
    public CommissionEmployee()
    {
        Console.WriteLine("CommissionEmployee constructed");
    }
}
```

**Figure 10-24**  `Employee` and `CommissionEmployee` classes with parameterless constructors

```
using System;
public class DemoSalesperson4
{
    public static void Main()
    {
        CommissionEmployee salesperson = new CommissionEmployee();
    }
}
```

**Figure 10-25**   The DemoSalesperson4 program

**Figure 10-26**   Output of the DemoSalesperson4 program

Of course, most constructors perform many more tasks than displaying a message to inform you that they exist. When constructors initialize variables, you usually want the base class constructor to initialize the data fields that originate in the base class. The derived class constructor needs to initialize only the data fields that are specific to the derived class.

## Using Base Class Constructors That Require Arguments

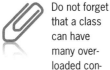

Do not forget that a class can have many overloaded constructors. As soon as you create at least one constructor for a class, you can no longer use the automatic version.

When you create a class and do not provide a constructor, C# automatically supplies one that never requires arguments. When you write your own constructor for a class, you replace the automatically supplied version. Depending on your needs, the constructor you create for a class might require arguments. When you use a class as a base class and the class has a constructor that requires arguments, you must make sure that any derived classes provide the base class constructor with what it needs.

When a base class constructor requires arguments, you must include a constructor for each derived class you create. Your derived class constructor can contain any number of statements;

however, within the header of the constructor, you must provide values for any arguments required by the base class constructor. Even if you have no other reason for creating a derived class constructor, you must write the derived class constructor so it can call its parent's constructor.

The format of the portion of the constructor header that calls a base class constructor is base(list of arguments). The keyword **base** always refers to the superclass of the class in which you use it. For example, if you create an Employee class with a constructor that requires two arguments—an integer and a string—and you create a CommissionEmployee class that is a subclass of Employee, then the following code shows a valid constructor for CommissionEmployee:

```
public CommissionEmployee() : base(1234, "XXXX")
{
      // Other statements can go here
}
```

In this example, the CommissionEmployee constructor requires no arguments, but it passes two arguments to its base class constructor. Every CommissionEmployee instantiation passes 1234 and "XXXX" to the Employee constructor. A different CommissionEmployee constructor might require arguments; then it could pass the appropriate arguments on to the base class constructor, as in the following example:

```
public CommissionEmployee(int id, string name) : base(id, name)
{
    // Other statements can go here
}
```

Although it seems as though you should be able to use the base class constructor name to call the base class constructor, C# does not allow you to do so. You must use the keyword **base**.

Yet another CommissionEmployee constructor might require that some arguments be passed to the base class constructor, and that some be used within CommissionEmployee. Consider the following example:

```
public CommissionEmployee(int id, string name, double rate) :
   base(id, name) // two parameters passed to base constructor
{
      CommissionRate = rate;
      // rate is used within child constructor
      // Other statements can go here
}
```

Watch the video *Constructors and Inheritance.*

# Creating and Using Abstract Classes

Creating classes is easier after you understand the concept of inheritance. When you create a child class, it inherits all the general attributes you need; you must create only the new, more specific attributes required by the child class. For example, a `Painter` and a `Sculptor` are more specific than an `Artist`. They inherit all the general attributes of `Artists`, but you must add the attributes and methods that are specific to `Painter` and `Sculptor`.

Another way to think about a superclass is to notice that it contains the features shared by its subclasses. The derived classes are more specific examples of the base class type; they add features to the shared, general features. Conversely, when you examine a derived class, you notice that its parent is more general. Sometimes you create a parent class to be so general that you never intend to create any specific instances of the class. For example, you might never create "just" an `Artist`; each `Artist` is more specifically a `Painter`, `Sculptor`, `Illustrator`, and so on. A class that you create only to extend from, but not to instantiate from, is an abstract class. An **abstract class** is one from which you cannot create concrete objects, but from which you can inherit. You use the keyword `abstract` when you declare an abstract class.

 Nonabstract classes from which objects *can* be instantiated are called **concrete** classes.

Abstract classes are like regular classes in that they can contain data fields and methods. The difference is that you cannot create instances of abstract classes by using the new operator. Rather, you create abstract classes simply to provide a base class from which other objects may be derived. Abstract classes usually contain abstract methods, although methods are not required. An **abstract method** has no method statements; any class derived from a class that contains an abstract method must override the abstract method by providing a body (an implementation) for it. (Alternatively, the derived class can declare the method to be abstract; in that case, the derived class's children must implement the method.)

When you create an abstract method, you provide the keyword `abstract` and the intended method type, name, and parameters, but you do not provide statements within the method; you do not even supply curly braces. When you create a derived class that inherits an abstract method from a parent, you must use the keyword **override** in the method header and provide the actions, or implementation, for the inherited method within the derived class. In other words, you are required to code a derived class method to override any empty base class methods that are inherited.

For example, suppose you want to create classes to represent different animals. You can create a generic, abstract class named `Animal` so you can provide generic data fields, such as the animal's name, only once. An `Animal` is generic, but each specific `Animal`, such as `Dog` or `Cat`, makes a unique sound. If you code an abstract `Speak()` method in the abstract `Animal` class, then you require all future `Animal` derived classes to override the `Speak()` method and provide an implementation that is specific to the derived class. Figure 10-27 shows an abstract `Animal` class that contains a data field for the name, a constructor that assigns a name, a `Name` property, and an abstract `Speak()` method.

> If you attempt to instantiate an object from an abstract class, you will receive a compiler error message.

> A method that is declared `virtual` is not required to be overridden in a child class, but a method declared `abstract` must be overridden.

```
abstract class Animal
{
    private string name;
    public Animal(string name)
    {
        this.name = name;
    }

    public string Name
    {
        get
        {
            return name;
        }
    }
    public abstract string Speak();
}
```

**Figure 10-27**   `Animal` class

458

The Animal class in Figure 10-27 is declared to be abstract. (The keyword is shaded.) You cannot place a statement such as Animal myPet = new Animal("Murphy"); within a program, because the program will not compile. Because Animal is an abstract class, no Animal objects can exist.

You create an abstract class like Animal so that you can extend it. For example, you can create Dog and Cat classes as shown in Figure 10-28. Because the Animal class contains a constructor that requires a string argument, both Dog and Cat must contain constructors that provide string arguments for their base class.

```
class Dog : Animal
{
    public Dog(string name) : base(name)
    {
    }
    public override string Speak()
    {
        return "woof";
    }
}
class Cat : Animal
{
    public Cat(string name) : base(name)
    {
    }
    public override string Speak()
    {
        return "meow";
    }
}
```

**Figure 10-28** Dog and Cat classes

 You can create an abstract class with no abstract methods, but you cannot create an abstract method outside of an abstract class.

 If a method that should be overridden in a child class has its own implementation, you declare the base class method to be virtual. If it does not have its own implementation, you declare the base class and the method to be abstract.

The Dog and Cat constructors perform no tasks other than passing out the name to the Animal constructor. The overriding Speak() methods within Dog and Cat are required because the abstract parent Animal class contains an abstract Speak() method. The keyword override (shaded) is required in the method header. You can code any statements you want within the Dog and Cat class Speak() methods, but the Speak() methods must exist.

Figure 10-29 shows a program that implements Dog and Cat objects, and Figure 10-30 shows the output. Speak() operates correctly for each animal type.

```
using System;
public class DemoAnimals
{
   public static void Main()
   {
      Dog spot = new Dog("Spot");
      Cat puff = new Cat("Puff");
      Console.WriteLine(spot.Name + " says " + spot.Speak());
      Console.WriteLine(puff.Name + " says " + puff.Speak());
   }
}
```

**Figure 10-29**  DemoAnimals program

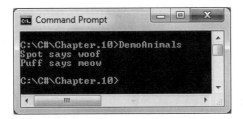

**Figure 10-30**  Output of the DemoAnimals program

Figure 10-31 shows an alternate way to create the DemoAnimals program. In this version the Dog and Cat objects are passed to a method that accepts an Animal parameter. The output is the same as in Figure 10-30. The Name property and Speak() method operate polymorphically, acting appropriately for each object type.

```
using System;
public class DemoAnimals2
{
   public static void Main()
   {
      Dog spot = new Dog("Spot");
      Cat puff = new Cat("Puff");
      DisplayAnimal(spot);
      DisplayAnimal(puff);
   }
   internal static void DisplayAnimal(Animal creature)
   {
      Console.WriteLine(creature.Name + " says " + creature.Speak());
   }
}
```

**Figure 10-31**  The DemoAnimals2 program

460

> ## TWO TRUTHS & A LIE
>
> ### Creating and Using Abstract Classes
>
> 1. An abstract class is one from which you cannot create concrete objects.
>
> 2. Unlike regular classes, abstract classes cannot contain methods.
>
> 3. When a base class contains an abstract method, its descendents must override it or declare it to be abstract.
>
> The false statement is #2. Abstract classes are like regular classes in that they can contain data fields and methods. The difference is that you cannot create instances of abstract classes by using the new operator. Rather, you create abstract classes simply to provide a base class from which other objects may be derived.

# Creating and Using Interfaces

Some object-oriented programming languages, notably C++, allow a subclass to inherit from more than one parent class. For example, you might create an Employee class that contains data fields pertaining to each employee in your organization. You also might create a Product class that holds information about each product your organization manufactures. When you create a Patent class for each product for which your company holds a patent, you might want to include product information as well as information about the employee who was responsible for the invention. In this situation, it would be convenient to inherit fields and methods from both the Product and Employee classes. The ability to inherit from more than one class is called **multiple inheritance**.

Multiple inheritance is a difficult concept, and programmers encounter many problems when they use it. For example, variables and methods in the parent classes may have identical names, creating a conflict when the child class uses one of the names. Additionally, as you already have learned, a child class constructor must call its parent class constructor. When two or more parents exist, this becomes a more complicated task: To which class should base refer when a child class has multiple parents?

For all of these reasons, multiple inheritance is prohibited in C#. However, C# does provide an alternative to multiple inheritance, known as an interface. Much like an abstract class, an **interface** is a collection of methods (and perhaps other members) that can be used by any class as long as the class provides a definition to override the interface's abstract definitions. Within an abstract class, some methods can be abstract, while others need not be. Within an interface, all methods are abstract.

You create an `interface` much as you create an `abstract` class definition, except that you use the keyword interface instead of abstract class. For example, suppose you create an `IWorkable` interface as shown in Figure 10-32. For simplicity, the `IWorkable` interface contains a single method named `Work()`.

You first learned about interfaces in the chapter titled *Using Classes and Objects* when you used the `IComparable` interface.

461

```
public interface IWorkable
{
    string Work();
}
```

**Figure 10-32**  The `IWorkable` interface

Although not required, in C# it is customary to start interface names with an uppercase "I". Other languages follow different conventions. Interface names frequently end with "able".

When any class implements `IWorkable`, it must also include a `Work()` method that returns a `string`. Figure 10-33 shows two classes that implement `IWorkable`: the `Employee` class and the `Animal` class. Because each implements `IWorkable`, each must declare a `Work()` method. The `Employee` class implements `Work()` to return the "I do my job" `string`. The abstract `Animal` class defines `Work()` as an abstract method, meaning that descendents of `Animal` must implement `Work()`.

```
class Employee : IWorkable
{
    public Employee(string name)
    {
        Name = name;
    }
    public string Name {get; set;}
    public string Work()
    {
        return "I do my job";
    }
}
abstract class Animal : IWorkable
{
    public Animal(string name)
    {
        Name = name;
    }
    public string Name {get; set;}
    public abstract string Work();
}
```

**Figure 10-33**  Employee, Animal, Cat, and Dog classes with the `IWorkable` interface (*continues*)

(continued)

```
class Dog : Animal
{
    public Dog(string name) : base(name)
    {
    }
    public override string Work()
    {
        return "I watch the house";
    }
}
class Cat : Animal
{
    public Cat(string name) : base(name)
    {
    }
    public override string Work()
    {
        return "I catch mice";
    }
}
```

**Figure 10-33**  Employee, Animal, Cat, and Dog classes with the IWorkable interface

Figure 10-33 also shows two child classes of Animal: Dog and Cat. Note how Work() is defined differently for each.

When you create a program that instantiates an Employee, a Dog, or a Cat, as in the DemoWorking program in Figure 10-34, each object type knows how to "Work()" appropriately. Figure 10-35 shows the output.

```
using System;
class DemoWorking
{
    public static void Main()
    {
        Employee bob = new Employee("Bob");
        Dog spot = new Dog("Spot");
        Cat puff = new Cat("Puff");
        Console.WriteLine(bob.Name + " says " + bob.Work());
        Console.WriteLine(spot.Name + " says " + spot.Work());
        Console.WriteLine(puff.Name + " says " + puff.Work());
    }
}
```

**Figure 10-34**  DemoWorking program

**Figure 10-35** Output of the DemoWorking program

Abstract classes and interfaces are similar in that you cannot instantiate concrete objects from either one. Abstract classes differ from interfaces in that abstract classes can contain nonabstract methods, but all methods within an interface must be abstract. A class can inherit from only one base class (whether abstract or not), but it can implement any number of interfaces. For example, if you want to create a Child that inherits from a Parent class and implements two interfaces, IWorkable and IPlayable, you would define the class name and list the base class and interfaces separated by commas:

```
class Child : Parent, IWorkable, IPlayable
```

You implement an existing interface because you want a class to be able to use a method that already exists in other applications. For example, suppose you have created a Payroll application that uses the Work() method in the interface class. Also suppose you create a new class named BusDriver. If BusDriver implements the IWorkable interface, then BusDriver objects can be used by the existing Payroll program. As another example, suppose you have written a game program that uses an IAttackable interface with methods that determine how and when an object can attack. When you create new classes such as MarsAlien, Vampire, and CivilWarSoldier, and each implements the interface, you can define how each one attacks and how each type of object can be added to the game.

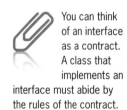

You can think of an interface as a contract. A class that implements an interface must abide by the rules of the contract.

Beginning programmers sometimes find it difficult to decide when to create an abstract base class and when to create an interface. You can follow these guidelines:

- Typically, you create an abstract class when you want to provide some data or methods that derived classes can inherit, but you want the subclasses to override some specific methods that you declare to be abstract.

- You create an interface when you want derived classes to override every method.

- Use a base class when the class you want to create "is a" subtype of another class; use an interface when the class you want to create will act like the interface.

Now that you understand how to construct your own interfaces, you will benefit from rereading the section describing the `IComparable` interface in the chapter titled *Using Classes and Objects*.

Interfaces provide you with a way to exhibit polymorphic behavior. If diverse classes implement the same interface in unique ways, then you can treat each class type in the same way using the same language. When various classes use the same interface, you know the names of the methods that are available with those classes, and C# classes adopt a more uniform functionality; this consistency helps you to understand new classes you encounter more easily. If you know, for example, the method names contained in the `IWorkable` interface, and you see that a class implements `IWorkable`, you have a head start in understanding how the class functions.

## TWO TRUTHS & A LIE

### Creating and Using Interfaces

1. An interface is a collection of methods (and perhaps other members) that can be used by any class as long as the class provides a definition to override the interface's abstract definitions.

2. Abstract classes and interfaces differ in that all methods in abstract classes must be abstract, but interfaces can contain nonabstract methods.

3. A class can inherit from only one base class, but it can implement any number of interfaces.

The false statement is #2. Abstract classes and interfaces are similar in that you cannot instantiate concrete objects from either one. However, they differ in that abstract classes can contain nonabstract methods, but all methods within an interface must be abstract.

## Using Extension Methods

When you write C# programs you constantly use classes, some that you have written yourself and many more that have been written by others. Sometimes you might wish a class had an additional method that would be useful to you. If you created the original class, you have two options:

- You could revise the existing class, including the new useful method.

- You could derive a child class from the existing class and provide it with a new method.

Sometimes, however, classes you use were created by others, and you might not be allowed to either revise or extend them. Of course, you could create an entirely new class that includes your new method, but that would duplicate a lot of the work already done when the first class was created. In these cases, the best option is to write an extension method. **Extension methods** are methods you can write to add to any type.

For example, you have used the prewritten `Int32` class throughout this book to declare integers. Suppose you work for a company that frequently uses customer account numbers, and that the company has decided to add an extra digit to each account number. For simplicity, assume all account numbers are two digits and that the new, third digit should be the rightmost digit in the sum of the first two digits. You could handle this problem by creating a class named `AccountNumber`, including a method to produce the extra digit, and redefining every instance of a customer's account number in your applications as an `AccountNumber` object. However, if you already have many applications that define the account number as an integer, you might prefer to create an extension method that extends the `Int32` class.

Figure 10-36 contains a method that extends the `Int32` class. The first parameter in an extension method specifies the type extended and must begin with the keyword `this`. For example, the first (and in this case, the only) parameter in the `AddCheckDigit()` method is `this int num`, as shown in the shaded portion of the figure. Extension methods must be static methods. Within the `AddCheckDigit()` method in Figure 10-36, the first digit is extracted from the two-digit account number by dividing by 10 and taking the resulting whole number, and the second digit is extracted by taking the remainder. Those two digits are added, and the last digit of that sum is returned from the method. For example, if 49 is passed into the method, first becomes 4, second becomes 9, and third becomes the last digit of 13, or 3. Then the original number (49) is multiplied by 10 and added to the third digit, resulting in 493.

```csharp
public static int AddCheckDigit(this int num)
{
    int first = num / 10;
    int second = num % 10;
    int third = (first + second) % 10;
    int result = num * 10 + third;
    return result;
}
```

**Figure 10-36** The `AddCheckDigit()` extension method

An extension method is static and must be stored in a static class. For example, the `DemoExtensionMethod` program in Figure 10-37 shows an application that is declared `static` in the first shaded statement and uses the extension method in the second shaded statement.

Extension methods were a new feature in C# 3.0.

465

Programmers sometimes define classes as sealed within the class header, as in `sealed class InventoryItem`. A **sealed class** cannot be extended. For example, the built-in `String` class is a sealed class.

In Chapter 2, you learned that each C# intrinsic type, such as `int`, is an alias for a class in the `System` namespace, such as `Int32`.

When organizations append extra digits to account numbers, the extra digits are called check digits. **Check digits** help assure that all the digits in account numbers and other numbers are entered correctly. Check digits are calculated using different formulas. If a digit used to calculate the check digit is incorrect, then the resulting check digit is probably incorrect as well.

The static method AddCheckDigit() is used as if it were an instance method of the Int32 class; in other words, it is attached to an Int32 object with a dot, just as instance methods are when used with objects. No arguments are passed to the AddCheckDigit() method explicitly from the DemoExtensionMethod class. The parameter in the method is implied, just as these references are always implied in instance methods. Figure 10-38 shows the execution of the program.

```csharp
using System;
static class DemoExtensionMethod
{
    public static void Main()
    {
        int acctNum = 49;
        int revisedAcctNum = acctNum.AddCheckDigit();
        Console.WriteLine("Original account number was {0}",
            acctNum);
        Console.WriteLine("Revised account number is {0}",
            revisedAcctNum);
    }
    public static int AddCheckDigit(this int num)
    {
        int first = num / 10;
        int second = num % 10;
        int third = (first + second) % 10;
        int result = num * 10 + third;
        return result;
    }
}
```

**Figure 10-37** The DemoExtensionMethod application

**Figure 10-38** Execution of the DemoExtensionMethod application

You can create extension methods for your own classes in the same way one was created for the Int32 class in this example. Just like other outside methods, and unlike ordinary class instance methods, extension methods cannot access any private members of classes they extend. Furthermore, if a class contains an instance method with the same signature as an extension method, the instance method takes priority and will be the one that executes.

# Recognizing Inheritance in GUI Applications and Recapping the Benefits of Inheritance

When you create a Windows Forms application using Visual Studio's IDE, you automatically use inheritance. Every Form you create is a descendent of the Form class. Figure 10-39 shows a just-started project in which the programmer has double-clicked the automatically generated Form to expose the code. You can see that the automatically generated Form1 class extends Form.

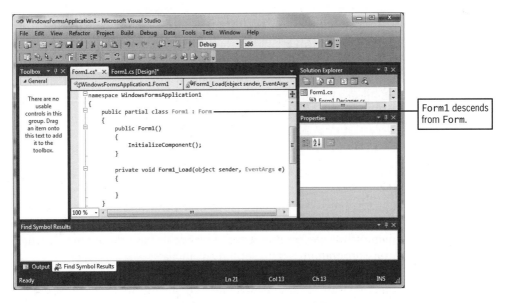

**Figure 10-39** Automatically generated Form code in the IDE

The Form class descends from the Object class like all other C# classes, but not directly. It is six generations removed from the Object class in the following line of descent:

- Object

- MarshalByRefObject

- Component

- Control

- ScrollableControl

- ContainerControl

- Form

Other GUI objects such as Labels and Buttons follow similar lengthy ancestry lines. You might guess that certain universal properties of GUI controls such as Text and Visible are inherited from ancestors. You will learn more about these hierarchies in the chapter *Using Controls*, but even though you have worked with only a few controls so far, you can understand the benefits inheritance provides.

When an automobile company designs a new car model, it does not build every component from scratch. The car might include a new feature—for example, some model contained the first air bag—but many of a new car's features are simply modifications of existing features. The manufacturer might create a larger gas tank or a more comfortable seat, but these new features still possess many of the properties of their predecessors from older models. Most features of new car models are not even modified; instead, existing components, such as air filters and windshield wipers, are included on the new model without any changes.

Similarly, you can create powerful computer programs more easily if many of their components are used either "as is" or with slight modifications. Inheritance does not enable you to write any programs that you could not write if inheritance did not exist; you *could* create every part of a program from scratch, but reusing existing classes and interfaces makes your job easier.

You already have used many "as is" classes, such as Console, Int32, and String. Using these classes made it easier to write programs than if you had to invent the classes yourself. Now that you have learned about inheritance, you can extend existing classes as well as just use them. When you create a useful, extendable base class, you and other future programmers gain several advantages:

- Derived class creators save development time because much of the code that is needed for the class already has been written.

- Derived class creators save testing time because the base class code already has been tested and probably used in a variety of situations. In other words, the base class code is reliable.

- Programmers who create or use new derived classes already understand how the base class works, so the time it takes to learn the new class features is reduced.

- When you create a derived class in C#, the base class source code is not changed. Thus, the base class maintains its integrity.

When you think about classes, you need to think about the commonalities between them, and then you can create base classes from which to inherit. You might even be rewarded professionally when you see your own superclasses extended by others in the future.

Classes that are not intended to be instantiated and that contain only `static` members are declared as `static` classes. You cannot extend `static` classes. For example, `System.Console` is a `static` class.

469

---

**TWO TRUTHS & A LIE**

### Recognizing Inheritance in GUI Applications and Recapping the Benefits of Inheritance

1. Inheritance enables you to create powerful computer programs more easily.

2. Without inheritance, you *could* create every part of a program from scratch, but reusing existing classes and interfaces makes your job easier.

3. Inheritance is frequently inefficient because base class code is seldom reliable when extended to a derived class.

The false statement is #3. Derived class creators save testing time because the base class code already has been tested and probably used in a variety of situations. In other words, the base class code is reliable.

---

# You Do It

In this section, you will create a working example of inheritance. You will create this example in four parts:

1. You will create a general Loan class that holds data pertaining to a bank loan—a loan number, a customer name, and the amount borrowed.

2. After you create the general Loan class, you will write a program to instantiate and use a Loan object.

3. You will create a more specific CarLoan derived class that inherits the attributes of the Loan class but adds information about the automobile that serves as collateral for the loan.

4. You will modify the Loan demonstration program to add a CarLoan object and demonstrate its use.

**To create the Loan class:**

1. Open a new file in your text editor, then enter the following first few lines for a Loan class. The class will contain three auto-implemented properties for the loan number, the last name of the customer, and the value of the loan.

```
class Loan
{
    public int LoanNumber {get; set;}
    public string LastName {get; set;}
    public double LoanAmount {get; set;}
}
```

2. At the top of the file, enter the following code to add a DemoLoan class that contains a Main() method. The class declares a Loan object and shows how to set each field and display the results.

```
using System;
public class DemoLoan
{
    public static void Main()
    {
        Loan aLoan = new Loan();
        aLoan.LoanNumber = 2239;
        aLoan.LastName = "Mitchell";
        aLoan.LoanAmount = 1000.00;
        Console.WriteLine("Loan #{0} for {1} is for {2}",
            aLoan.LoanNumber, aLoan.LastName,
            aLoan.LoanAmount.ToString("C2"));
    }
}
```

3. Save the file as **DemoLoan.cs**, then compile and execute the program. The output looks like Figure 10-40. There is nothing unusual about this class or how it operates; it is similar to many you saw in the last chapter before you learned about inheritance.

**Figure 10-40** Output of the DemoLoan program

# Extending a Class

Next, you will create a class named CarLoan. A CarLoan "is a" type of Loan. As such, it has all the attributes of a Loan, but it also has the year and make of the car that the customer is using as collateral for the loan. Therefore, CarLoan is a subclass of Loan.

**To create the CarLoan class that extends the Loan class:**

1.  Save the DemoLoan.cs file as **DemoCarLoan.cs**. Change the **DemoLoan** class name to **DemoCarLoan**. Begin the definition of the CarLoan class after the closing curly brace for the Loan class. CarLoan extends Loan and contains two properties that hold the year and make of the car.

    ```
    class CarLoan : Loan
    {
        public int Year {get; set;}
        public string Make {get; set;}
    }
    ```

2.  Within the Main() method of the DemoCarLoan class, just after the declaration of the Loan object, declare a CarLoan as follows:

    ```
    CarLoan aCarLoan = new CarLoan();
    ```

3.  After the three property assignments for the Loan object, insert five assignment statements for the CarLoan object.

    ```
    aCarLoan.LoanNumber = 3358;
    aCarLoan.LastName = "Jansen";
    aCarLoan.LoanAmount = 20000.00;
    aCarLoan.Make = "Ford";
    aCarLoan.Year = 2005;
    ```

4.  Following the WriteLine() statement that displays the Loan object data, insert two WriteLine() statements that display the CarLoan object's data.

    ```
    Console.WriteLine("Loan #{0} for {1} is for {2}",
        aCarLoan.LoanNumber, aCarLoan.LastName,
        aCarLoan.LoanAmount.ToString("C2"));
    Console.WriteLine(" Loan #{0} is for a {1} {2}",
        aCarLoan.LoanNumber, aCarLoan.Year,
        aCarLoan.Make);
    ```

5.  Save the program, then compile and execute it. The output looks like Figure 10-41. The CarLoan object correctly uses its own fields and properties as well as those of the parent Loan class.

**Figure 10-41**   Output of the DemoCarLoan program

## Using Base Class Members in a Derived Class

In the previous sections, you created Loan and CarLoan classes and objects. Suppose the bank adopts new rules as follows:

- No regular loan will be made for less than $5000.

- No car loan will be made for any car older than model year 2006.

- Although Loans might have larger loan numbers, CarLoans will have loan numbers that are no more than three digits. If a larger loan number is provided, the program will use only the last three digits for the loan number.

**To implement the new CarLoan rules:**

1. Open the DemoCarLoan.cs file and immediately save it as **DemoCarLoan2.cs**. Also change the class name from DemoCarLoan to **DemoCarLoan2**.

2. Within the Loan class, add a new constant that represents the minimum loan value:

   ```
   public const double MINIMUM_LOAN = 5000;
   ```

3. Add a field for the loanAmount because the LoanAmount property will need to use it:

   ```
   protected double loanAmount;
   ```

   The field is protected so that CarLoan objects will be able to access it as well as Loan objects.

4. Replace the auto-implemented property for LoanAmount in the Loan class with standard get and set accessors as follows. This change ensures that no loan is made for less than the minimum allowed value.

```
public double LoanAmount
{
    set
    {
        if(value < MINIMUM_LOAN)
            loanAmount = MINIMUM_LOAN;
        else
            loanAmount = value;
    }
    get
    {
        return loanAmount;
    }
}
```

5. Within the CarLoan class, add two new constants to hold the earliest year for which car loans will be given and the lowest allowed loan number:

```
private const int EARLIEST_YEAR = 2006;
private const int LOWEST_INVALID_NUM = 1000;
```

6. Also within the CarLoan class, add a field for the year of the car and replace the existing auto-implemented Year property with one that contains coded get and set accessors. The Year property set accessor not only sets the year field, it sets loanAmount to 0 when a car's year is less than 2006.

```
private int year;
public int Year
{
    set
    {
        if(value < EARLIEST_YEAR)
        {
            year = value;
            loanAmount = 0;
        }
        else
            year = value;
    }
    get
    {
        return year;
    }
}
```

If loanAmount was private in the parent Loan class, you would not be able to set its value in the child CarLoan class, as you do here. You could use the public property LoanAmount to set the value, but the parent class set accessor would force the value to 5000.

7. Suppose there are unique rules for issuing loan numbers for cars. Within the CarLoan class, just before the closing curly brace, change the inherited LoanNumber property to accommodate the new rules. If a car loan number is three digits or fewer, pass it on to the base class property. If not, obtain the last three digits by calculating the remainder when the loan number is divided by 1000, and pass the new number to the base class property. Add the following property after the definition of the Make property.

```
public new int LoanNumber
{
    get
    {
        return base.LoanNumber;
    }
    set
    {
        if(value < LOWEST_INVALID_NUM)
            base.LoanNumber = value;
        else
            base.LoanNumber = value % LOWEST_INVALID_NUM;
    }
}
```

A method that calls itself is a **recursive** method. Recursive methods are sometimes useful, but they require specialized code to avoid infinite loops, and are not appropriate in this case.

If you did not use the keyword base to access the LoanNumber property within the CarLoan class, you would be telling this version of the LoanNumber property to call itself. Although the program would compile, it would run continuously in an infinite loop until it ran out of memory and issued an error message.

8. Save the file. Compile it and correct any errors. When you execute the program, the output looks like Figure 10-42. Compare the output to Figure 10-41. Notice that the $1000 bank loan has been forced to $5000. Also notice that the car loan number has been shortened to three digits and the value of the loan is $0 because of the age of the car.

```
C:\C#\Chapter.10>DemoCarLoan2
Loan #2239 for Mitchell is for $5,000.00
Loan #358 for Jansen is for $0.00
   Loan #358 is for a 2005 Ford

C:\C#\Chapter.10>
```

**Figure 10-42**   Output of the DemoCarLoan2 program

9. Change the assigned values within the DemoCarLoan2 class to combinations of early and late years and valid and invalid loan numbers. After each change, save the program, compile and execute it, and confirm that the program operates as expected.

# Adding Constructors to Base and Derived Classes

When a base class contains only constructors that require parameters, then any derived classes must provide for the base class constructor. In the next steps, you will add constructors to the Loan and CarLoan classes and demonstrate that they work as expected.

**To add constructors to the classes:**

1. Open the DemoCarLoan2 program and change the class name to DemoCarLoan3. Save the file as **DemoCarLoan3.cs**.

2. In the Loan class, just after the declaration of the loanAmount field, add a constructor that requires values for all the Loan's properties:

```
public Loan(int num, string name, double amount)
{
    LoanNumber = num;
    LastName = name;
    LoanAmount = amount;
}
```

3. In the CarLoan class, just after the declaration of the year field, add a constructor that takes five parameters. It passes three of the parameters to the base class constructor and uses the other two to assign values to the properties that are unique to the child class.

```
public CarLoan(int num, string name, double amount,
    int year, string make) : base(num, name, amount)
{
    Year = year;
    Make = make;
}
```

4. In the Main() method of the DemoCarLoan3 class, remove the existing declarations for aLoan and aCarLoan and replace them with two declarations that use the arguments passed to the constructors.

```
Loan aLoan = new Loan(333, "Hanson", 7000.00);
CarLoan aCarLoan = new CarLoan(444, "Carlisle",
    30000.00, 2011, "BMW");
```

5. Remove the eight statements that assigned values to Loan and CarLoan, but retain the Console.WriteLine() statements that display the values.

6. Save the program, then compile and execute it. The output looks like Figure 10-43. Both constructors work as expected. The

CarLoan constructor has called its parent's constructor to set the necessary fields before executing its own unique statements.

**Figure 10-43**   Output of the DemoCarLoan3 program

# Chapter Summary

- The classes you create in object-oriented programming languages can inherit data and methods from existing classes. The ability to use inheritance makes programs easier to write, easier to understand, and less prone to errors. A class that is used as a basis for inheritance is called a base class, superclass, or parent class. When you create a class that inherits from a base class, it is called a derived class, extended class, subclass, or child class.

- When you create a class that is an extension or child of another class, you use a single colon between the derived class name and its base class name. The child class inherits all the methods and fields of its parent. Inheritance works only in one direction—a child inherits from a parent, but not the other way around.

- If you could use private data outside of its class, the principle of information hiding would be destroyed. On some occasions, however, you want to access parent class data from a derived class. For those occasions, you declare parent class fields using the keyword protected, which provides you with an intermediate level of security between public and private access.

- When you declare a child class method with the same name and parameter list as a method within its parent class, you override the parent class method and allow your class objects to exhibit polymorphic behavior. You can use the keyword new or override with the derived class method. When a derived class overrides a parent class method but you want to access the parent class version of the method, you can use the keyword base.

- Every derived class object "is a" specific instance of both the derived class and the base class. Therefore, you can assign a derived class object to an object of any of its base class types. When you do so, C# makes an implicit conversion from derived class to base class.

- Every class you create in C# derives from a single class named `System.Object`. Because all classes inherit from the `Object` class, all classes inherit the `Object` class methods. The `Object` class contains four `public` instance methods: `Equals()`, `GetHashCode()`, `GetType()`, and `ToString()`.

- When you instantiate an object that is a member of a subclass, you actually call the constructor for the base class and the constructor for the extended, derived class. When you create any derived class object, the base class constructor must execute first; only then does the derived class constructor execute.

- An abstract class is one from which you cannot create concrete objects, but from which you can inherit. Usually, abstract classes contain abstract methods; an abstract method has no method statements. Any class derived from a class that contains an abstract method must override the abstract method by providing a body (an implementation) for it.

- C# provides an alternative to multiple inheritance, known as an interface. Much like an abstract class, an interface is a collection of methods (and perhaps other members) that can be used by any class as long as the class provides a definition to override the interface's abstract definitions. Within an abstract class, some methods can be abstract, while others need not be. Within an interface, all methods are abstract. A class can inherit from only one abstract base class, but it can implement any number of interfaces.

- Extension methods are methods you can write to add to any type. They are static methods, but they operate like instance methods. Their parameter lists begin with the keyword `this` and the data type being extended.

- Every GUI object you create descends from ancestors. You can create powerful computer programs more easily using inheritance because it saves development and testing time.

# Key Terms

**Inheritance** is the application of your knowledge of a general category to more specific objects.

**Unified Modeling Language (UML) diagrams** are graphical tools that programmers and analysts use to describe systems.

A **base class** is a class that is used as a basis for inheritance.

A **derived class** or **extended class** is one that has inherited from a base class.

A **superclass** is a base class.

A **subclass** is a derived class.

A **parent class** is a base class.

A **child class** is a derived class.

The **ancestors** of a derived class are all the superclasses from which the subclass is derived.

**Transitive** describes the feature of inheritance in which a child inherits all the members of all its ancestors.

The keyword **protected** provides an intermediate level of security between public and private access. A protected data field or method can be used within its own class or in any classes extended from that class, but it cannot be used by "outside" classes.

**Fragile** describes classes that depend on field names from parent classes because they are prone to errors—that is, they are easy to "break."

A **virtual method** is one whose behavior is determined by the implementation in a child class.

To **hide** a parent class member is to override it in a derived class.

**Visible** describes a base class member that is not hidden by a derived class.

An **implicit conversion** occurs when a type is automatically converted to another upon assignment.

An **implicit reference conversion** occurs when a derived class object is assigned to its ancestor's data type.

The **object** (or Object) class type in the System namespace is the root base class for all other types.

A **root class** is the ultimate or first base class in a hierarchal ancestry tree.

**Reference equality** occurs when two reference type objects refer to the same object.

A **hash code** is a number that should uniquely identify an object.

The keyword **base** always refers to the superclass of the class in which you use it.

An **abstract class** is one from which you cannot create concrete objects, but from which you can inherit.

**Concrete** classes are nonabstract classes from which objects can be instantiated.

An **abstract method** has no method statements; any class derived from a class that contains an abstract method must override the abstract method by providing a body (an implementation) for it.

The keyword **override** is used in method headers when you create a derived class that inherits an abstract method from a parent.

**Multiple inheritance** is the ability to inherit from more than one class.

An **interface** is a collection of abstract methods (and perhaps other members) that can be used by any class as long as the class provides a definition to override the interface's abstract definitions.

**Extension methods** are static methods that act like instance methods. You can write extension methods to add to any type.

A **sealed class** cannot be extended.

A **check digit** is a digit calculated from a formula and appended to a number to help verify the accuracy of the other digits in the number.

**Recursive** describes a method that calls itself.

# Review Questions

1. The principle that you can apply your knowledge of a general category to more specific objects is _____.

   a. polymorphism

   b. encapsulation

   c. inheritance

   d. structure

2. Which of the following is *not* a benefit of using inheritance when creating a new class?

   a. You save time, because you need not create fields and methods that already exist in a parent class.

   b. You reduce the chance of errors, because the parent class methods have already been used and tested.

   c. You make it easier for anyone who has used the parent class to understand the new class because the programmer can concentrate on the new features.

   d. You save computer memory because when you create objects of the new class, storage is not required for parent class fields.

3. A child class is also called a(n) _____.

   a. extended class

   b. base class

   c. superclass

   d. delineated class

4. Assuming that the following classes are well named, which of the following is a parent class of House?

   a. Apartment

   b. Building

   c. Victorian

   d. myHouse

5. A derived class usually contains _____ than its parent.

   a. more fields and methods

   b. the same number of fields but fewer methods

   c. fewer fields but more methods

   d. fewer fields and methods

6. When you create a class that is an extension or child of another class, you use a(n) _____ between the derived class name and its base class name.

   a. ampersand

   b. colon

   c. dot

   d. hyphen

7. A base class named Garden contains a private field width and a property public int Width that contains get and set accessors. A child class named VegetableGarden does not contain a Width property. When you write a class in which you declare an object as follows, what statement can you use to access the VegetableGarden's width?

   VegetableGarden myGarden = new VegetableGarden();

a. `myGarden.Width`

b. `myGarden.base.Width`

c. `VegetableGarden.Width`

d. You cannot use `Width` with a `VegetableGarden` object.

8. When a parent class contains a `private` data field, the field is
_____ the child class.

   a. hidden in

   b. not a member of

   c. directly accessible in

   d. `public` in

9. When a base class and a derived class contain a method with
the same name and parameter list, and you call the method
using a derived class object, _____.

   a. you receive an error message

   b. the base class version overrides the derived class version

   c. the derived class version overrides the base class version

   d. both method versions execute

10. Which of the following is an English-language form of
polymorphism?

   a. seeing a therapist and seeing the point

   b. moving friends with a compelling story and moving
   friends to a new apartment

   c. Both of these.

   d. Neither of these.

11. When base and derived classes contain a method with the
same name and parameter list, you can use the base class
method within the derived class by using the keyword _____
before the method name.

   a. `new`

   b. `override`

   c. `base`

   d. `super`

12. In a program that declares a derived class object, you _____ assign it to an object of its base class type.

    a.  can

    b.  cannot

    c.  must

    d.  should not

13. The root base class for all other class types is _____.

    a.  `Base`

    b.  `Super`

    c.  `Parent`

    d.  `Object`

14. All of the following are `Object` class methods *except* _____.

    a.  `ToString()`

    b.  `Equals()`

    c.  `Print()`

    d.  `GetHashCode()`

15. When you create any derived class object, _____.

    a.  the base class and derived class constructors execute simultaneously

    b.  the base class constructor must execute first; then the derived class constructor executes

    c.  the derived class constructor must execute first; then the base class constructor executes

    d.  neither the base class constructor nor the derived class constructor executes

16. When a base class constructor requires arguments, then each derived class _____.

    a.  must include a constructor

    b.  must include a constructor that requires arguments

    c.  must include two or more constructors

    d.  must not include a constructor

17. When you create an abstract class, _____.

    a.  you can inherit from it

    b.  you can create concrete objects from it

    c.  Both of these are true.

    d.  None of these are true.

18. When you create an abstract method, you provide _____.

    a.  the keyword `abstract`

    b.  curly braces

    c.  method statements

    d.  all of these

19. Within an interface, _____.

    a.  no methods can be `abstract`

    b.  some methods might be `abstract`

    c.  some, but not all, methods must be `abstract`

    d.  all methods must be `abstract`

20. Abstract classes and interfaces are similar in that _____.

    a.  you can instantiate concrete objects from both

    b.  you cannot instantiate concrete objects from either one

    c.  all methods in both must be `abstract`

    d.  neither can contain nonabstract methods

## Exercises

1. Create a class named `Game`. Include auto-implemented properties for the game's name and maximum number of players. Also, include a `ToString()` `Game` method that overrides the `Object` class's `ToString()` method and returns a string that contains the name of the class (using `GetType()`), the name of the `Game`, and the number of players. Create a child class named `GameWithTimeLimit` that includes an auto-implemented integer property for the game's time limit in minutes. Write a program that instantiates an object of each class and demonstrates all the methods. Save the file as **GameDemo.cs**.

Your instructor might ask you to create the programs described in these exercises either as console-based or GUI applications.

*assignment 6.2*

2. Create a class named Tape that includes fields for length and width in inches and properties for each field. Also include a ToString() method that returns a string constructed from the return value of the object's GetType() method and the values of the length and width fields. Derive two subclasses—VideoTape and AdhesiveTape. The VideoTape class includes an integer field to hold playing time in minutes and a property for the field. The AdhesiveTape class includes an integer field that holds a stickiness factor—a value restricted to fall in the range of 1 to 10—and a property for the field. Write a program that instantiates one object of each of the three classes, and demonstrate that all of each class's methods work correctly. Be sure to use valid and invalid values when testing the numbers you can use to set the AdhesiveTape class stickiness factor. Save the file as **TapeDemo.cs**.

3. a. Create a class named Order that performs order processing of a single item that sells for $19.95 each. The class has four variable fields: order number, customer name, quantity ordered, and total price. Create a constructor that requires parameters for all the fields except total price. Include public get and set accessors for each field except the total price field; that field is calculated as quantity ordered times unit price (19.95) whenever the quantity is set, so it needs only a get accessor. Also create the following for the class:

   • An Equals() method that determines two Orders are equal if they have the same order number

   • A GetHashCode() method that returns the order number

   • A ToString() method that returns a string containing all order information

   Write an application that declares a few Order objects and sets their values, making sure to create at least two with the same order number. Display the string from the ToString() method for each order. Write a method that compares two orders at a time and displays a message if they are equal. Send the Orders you created to the method two at a time and display the results. Save the file as **OrderDemo.cs**.

   b. Using the Order class you created in Exercise 3a, write a new application that creates an array of five Orders. Prompt the user for values for each Order. Do not allow duplicate order numbers; force the user to reenter the order when a duplicate order number is entered. When five valid orders have been entered, display them all, plus a total of all orders. Save the program as **OrderDemo2.cs**.

c. Create a `ShippedOrder` class that derives from `Order`. A `ShippedOrder` has a $4.00 shipping fee (no matter how many items are ordered). Override any methods in the parent class as necessary. Write a new application that creates an array of five `ShippedOrders`. Prompt the user for values for each, and do not allow duplicate order numbers; force the user to reenter the order when a duplicate order number is entered. When five valid orders have been entered, display them all, plus a total of all orders. Save the program as **OrderDemo3.cs**.

d. Make any necessary modifications to the `ShippedOrder` class so that it can be sorted by order number. Modify the `OrderDemo3` application so the displayed orders have been sorted. Save the application as **OrderDemo4.cs**.

4. a. Create a class named `Book` that includes auto-imple-mented properties for the International Standard Book Number (ISBN), title, author, and price. (An ISBN is a unique number assigned to each published book.) Create a child class named `TextBook` that includes a grade level and a `CoffeeTableBook` child class that contains no addi-tional fields or properties. In the child classes, override the accessor that sets a `Book`'s price so that `TextBooks` must be priced between $20.00 and $80.00, inclusive, and `CoffeeTableBooks` must be priced between $35.00 and $100.00, inclusive. Write a program that creates a few objects of each type and demonstrate that all of the meth-ods and properties work correctly. Be sure to use valid and invalid values when testing the child class properties. Save the file as **BookDemo.cs**.

Hint: When a child class contains a property that accesses a property with the same name in the parent class, you must use the key-word `base` to access the parent class version of the property.

b. In the `Book` class you created in Exercise 4a, overload the `Object` class `Equals()` method to consider two `Books` equal if they have the same ISBN. Create a program that declares three `Books`; two should have the same ISBN and one should have a different one. Demonstrate that the `Equals()` method works correctly to compare the `Books`. Save the program as **BookDemo2.cs**.

c. Write an application that declares two `Book` objects and uses an extension method named `DisplayTitleAndAuthor()` with each. The method dis-plays a `Book`'s title, the word "by", and the author's name. Save the program as **BookDemo3.cs**.

5.  a.  Create a `Patient` class for the Wrightstown Hospital
        Billing Department. Include auto-implemented prop-
        erties for a patient ID number, name, age, and amount
        due to the hospital, and include any other methods
        you need. Override the `ToString()` method to return
        all the details for a patient. Write an application that
        prompts the user for data for five `Patients`. Sort them
        in patient ID number order and display them all,
        including a total amount owed. Save the program as
        **PatientDemo.cs**.

    b.  Using the `Patient` class as a base, derive an
        `InsuredPatient` class. An `InsuredPatient` contains all
        the data of a `Patient`, plus fields to hold an insurance
        company name and the percentage of the hospital bill
        the insurance company will pay. Insurance payments are
        based on the following table:

| Insurance Company | Portion of bill paid by insurance (%) |
|---|---|
| Wrightstown Mutual | 80 |
| Red Umbrella | 60 |
| All other companies | 25 |

        Create an array of five `InsuredPatient` objects. Prompt
        the user for all the patient data, plus the name of the
        insurance company; the insurance company `set` accessor
        determines the percentage paid. Override the parent class
        `ToString()` method to include the name of the insur-
        ance company, the percentage paid, and the amount due
        after the insurance has been applied to the bill. Sort all the
        records in ID number order and display them with a total
        amount due from all insured patients. Save the program as
        **PatientDemo2.cs**.

    c.  Write an application that uses an extension method for
        the `Patient` class. The method computes and returns a
        `Patient`'s quarterly insurance payment (one-fourth of the
        annual premium). The application should allow the user
        to enter data for five `Patients` and then display all the
        `Patient` data for each, including the quarterly payment.
        Save the program as **PatientDemo3.cs**.

6.  Create an abstract class called `GeometricFigure`. Each
    figure includes a height, a width, and an area. Provide
    get and set accessors for each field except area; the area is

computed and is read-only. Include an abstract method called ComputeArea() that computes the area of the GeometricFigure. Create three additional classes:

- A Rectangle is a GeometricFigure whose area is determined by multiplying width by height.

- A Square is a Rectangle in which the width and height are the same. Provide a constructor that accepts both height and width, forcing them to be equal if they are not. Provide a second constructor that accepts just one dimension and uses it for both height and width. The Square class uses the Rectangle's ComputeArea() method.

- A Triangle is a GeometricFigure whose area is determined by multiplying the width by half the height.

  Create an application that demonstrates creating objects of each class. After each is created, pass it to a method that accepts a GeometricFigure argument in which the figure's data is displayed. Change some dimensions of some of the figures and pass each to the display method again. Save the program as **ShapesDemo.cs**.

7. Create an interface named IRecoverable. It contains a single method named Recover(). Create classes named Patient, Furniture, and Football; each of these classes implements IRecoverable. Create each class's Recover() method to display an appropriate message. For example, the Patient's Recover() method might display "I am getting better." Write a program that declares an object of each of the three types and uses its Recover() method. Save the file as **RecoveringDemo.cs**.

8. Create an interface named ITurnable. It contains a single method named Turn(). Create classes named Page, Corner, Pancake, and Leaf; each of these classes implements ITurnable. Create each class's Turn() method to display an appropriate message. For example, the Page's Turn() method might display "You turn a page in a book." Write a program that declares an object of each of the four types and uses its Turn() method. Save the file as **TurningDemo.cs**.

9. Create an abstract class named Salesperson. Fields include first and last names; the Salesperson constructor requires both these values. Include properties for the fields. Include a method that returns a string that holds the Salesperson's full

name—the first and last names separated by a space. Then perform the following tasks:

- Create two child classes of Salesperson: RealEstateSalesperson and GirlScout. The RealEstateSalesperson class contains fields for total value sold in dollars and total commission earned (both of which are initialized to 0), and a commission rate field required by the class constructor. The GirlScout class includes a field to hold the number of boxes of cookies sold, which is initialized to 0. Include properties for every field.

- Create an interface named ISellable that contains two methods: SalesSpeech() and MakeSale(). In each RealEstateSalesperson and GirlScout class, implement SalesSpeech() to display an appropriate one- or two-sentence sales speech that the objects of the class could use. In the RealEstateSalesperson class, implement the MakeSale() method to accept an integer dollar value for a house, add the value to the RealEstateSalesperson's total value sold, and compute the total commission earned. In the GirlScout class, implement the MakeSale() method to accept an integer representing the number of boxes of cookies sold and add it to the total field.

- Write a program that instantiates a RealEstateSalesperson object and a GirlScout object. Demonstrate the SalesSpeech() method with each object, then use the MakeSale() method two or three times with each object. Display the final contents of each object's data fields. Save the file as **SalespersonDemo.cs**.

 *Debugging Exercises*

Each of the following files in the Chapter.10 folder of your downloadable student files has syntax and/or logical errors. In each case, determine the problem and fix the program. After you correct the errors, save each file using the same filename preceded with *Fixed*. For example, DebugTen01.cs will become FixedDebugTen01.cs.

    a.  DebugTen01.cs

    b.  DebugTen02.cs

    c.  DebugTen03.cs

    d.  DebugTen04.cs

*Up For Discussion*

1. In this chapter, you learned the difference between `public`, `private`, and `protected` class members. Why are some programmers opposed to classifying class members as `protected`? Do you agree with them?

2. Playing computer games has been shown to increase the level of dopamine in the human brain. High levels of this substance are associated with addiction to drugs. Suppose you work for a company that manufactures games and it decides to research how its games can produce more dopamine in the brains of players. Would you support the company's decision?

3. If you are completing all the programming exercises in this book, you know that it takes a lot of time to write and test programs that work. Professional programs require even more work. In the workplace, programs frequently must be completed by strict deadlines—for example, a tax-calculating program must be completed by year's end, or an advertising Web site must be completed by the launch of the product. Programmers often find themselves working into the evenings or weekends to complete rush projects at work. How would you feel about having to do this? What types of compensation would make the extra hours worthwhile for you?

# Exception Handling

In this chapter you will:

◎ Learn about exceptions, the `Exception` class, and generating `SystemExceptions`

◎ Learn about traditional and object-oriented error-handling methods

◎ Use the `Exception` class's `ToString()` method and `Message` property

◎ Catch multiple `Exception`s

◎ Use the `finally` block

◎ Handle `Exception`s thrown from outside methods

◎ Trace `Exception`s through the call stack

◎ Create your own `Exception` classes

◎ Rethrow `Exception`s

**W**hile visiting Web sites, you have probably seen an unexpected and cryptic message that announces an error and then shuts down your browser immediately. Perhaps something similar has happened to you while using a piece of application software. Certainly, if you have worked your way through all of the programming exercises in this book, you have encountered such errors while running your own programs. When a program just stops, it is aggravating, especially when you lose data you have typed and the program error message seems to indicate the program "knows" exactly what is wrong. You might grumble, "If it knows what is wrong, why does it not just fix the problem?" In this chapter, you will learn how to handle these unexpected error conditions so your programs can be more user-friendly than those that simply shut down in the face of errors.

# Understanding Exceptions

An **exception** is any error condition or unexpected behavior in an executing program. Exceptions occur because of errors in program logic or because of insufficient system resources. The programs you write can generate many types of potential exceptions, including when:

- Your program asks for user input, but the user enters invalid data.

- The program attempts to divide an integer by zero.

- You attempt to access an array with a subscript that is too large or too small.

- You calculate a value that is too large for the answer's variable type.

These errors are called exceptions because presumably they are not usual occurrences; they are "exceptional." The object-oriented techniques used to manage such errors make up the group of methods known as **exception handling**. If you do not handle an exception, the running program terminates abruptly.

In C#, all exceptions are objects that are instances of the Exception class or one of its derived classes. An exception condition generates an object that encapsulates information about the error. Like all other classes in the C# programming language, the Exception class is a descendent of the Object class. The Exception class has several descendent classes of its own, many with unusual names such as CodeDomSerializerException, SUDSParserException, and SoapException. Others have names that are more easily understood, such as IOException (for input and output errors), InvalidPrinterException (for when a user requests an invalid printer), and PathTooLongException (used when the path to a file contains more characters than a system allows). C# has more than 100 defined Exceptions; Table 11-1 lists just a few to give you an idea of the wide variety of circumstances they cover.

Managing exceptions involves an oxymoron; you must expect the unexpected.

Errors you discover when compiling a program are not exceptions; only execution-time (also called *runtime*) errors are called exceptions.

| Class | Description |
|---|---|
| System.ArgumentException | Thrown when one of the arguments provided to a method is not valid |
| System.ArithmeticException | Thrown for errors in an arithmetic, casting, or conversion operation |
| System.ArrayTypeMismatchException | Thrown when an attempt is made to store an element of the wrong type within an array |
| System.Data.OperationAbortedException | Thrown when an ongoing operation is aborted by the user |
| System.Drawing.Printing InvalidPrinterException | Thrown when you try to access a printer using printer settings that are not valid |
| System.FormatException | Thrown when the format of an argument does not meet the parameter specifications of the invoked method |
| System.IndexOutOfRangeException | Thrown when an attempt is made to access an element of an array with an index that is outside the bounds of the array; this class cannot be inherited |
| System.InvalidCastException | Thrown for an invalid casting or explicit conversion |
| System.InvalidOperationException | Thrown when a method call is invalid for the object's current state |
| System.IO.InvalidDataException | Thrown when a data stream is in an invalid format |
| System.IO.IOException | Thrown when an I/O error occurs |
| System.MemberAccessException | Thrown when an attempt to access a class member fails |
| System.NotImplementedException | Thrown when a requested method or operation is not implemented |
| System.NullReferenceException | Thrown when there is an attempt to dereference a null object reference |
| System.OperationCanceledException | Thrown in a thread upon cancellation of an operation that the thread was executing |
| System.OutOfMemoryException | Thrown when there is not enough memory to continue the execution of a program |
| System.RankException | Thrown when an array with the wrong number of dimensions is passed to a method |
| System.StackOverflowException | Thrown when the execution stack overflows because it contains too many nested method calls; this class cannot be inherited |

**Table 11-1**  Selected C# Exceptions

Table 11-1 uses the term "thrown," which is explained later in this chapter.

Most exceptions you will use derive from three classes:

- The predefined Common Language Runtime exception classes derived from SystemException

- The user-defined application exception classes you derive from ApplicationException

- The Exception class, which is the parent of SystemException and ApplicationException

## Purposely Generating a SystemException

You can deliberately generate a SystemException by forcing a program to contain an error. As an example, in every programming language, it is illegal to divide an integer by zero because the operation is mathematically undefined. Consider the simple MilesPerGallon program in Figure 11-1, which prompts a user for two values and divides the first by the second. If the user enters nonzero integers, the program runs correctly and without incident. However, if the user enters 0 when prompted to enter gallons, division by 0 takes place and an error is generated. Figure 11-2 shows two executions of the program.

```
using System;
public class MilesPerGallon
{
    public static void Main()
    {
        int milesDriven;
        int gallonsOfGas;
        int mpg;
        Console.Write("Enter miles driven ");
        milesDriven = Convert.ToInt32(Console.ReadLine());
        Console.Write("Enter gallons of gas purchased ");
        gallonsOfGas = Convert.ToInt32(Console.ReadLine());
        mpg = milesDriven / gallonsOfGas;
        Console.WriteLine("You got {0} miles per gallon", mpg);
    }
}
```

**Figure 11-1** MilesPerGallon program

Microsoft previously advised that you should create your own custom exceptions from the ApplicationException class. They have revised their thinking because in practice, they have not found the approach to be of significant value. For updates, visit *http:// msdn.microsoft.com*.

When you divide a floating-point value by 0 in C#, no exception occurs. Instead, C# assigns the special value Infinity to the result. Because floats and doubles are imprecise, dividing them by 0.000000...to an infinite number of decimal places approaches infinity mathematically.

493

494

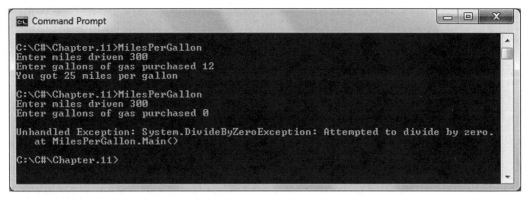

**Figure 11-2** Two executions of `MilesPerGallon` program

When the user enters a 0 for gallons in the `MilesPerGallon` program, a dialog box reports that the application has stopped working and needs to close. Because this error is intentional for demonstration purposes, you can ignore the message by clicking Close program.

In the first execution of the `MilesPerGallon` program in Figure 11-2, the user entered two usable integers, and division was carried out successfully. However, in the second execution, the user entered 0 for gallons of gas, and the error message indicates that an unhandled exception named `System.DivideByZeroException` was created. The message gives further information ("Attempted to divide by zero."), and shows the method where the exception occurred—in `MilesPerGallon.Main()`.

The `DivideByZeroException` object was generated automatically by C#. It is an instance of the `DivideByZeroException` class that has four ancestors. It is a child of the `ArithmeticException` class, which descends from the `SystemException` class. The `SystemException` class derives from the `Exception` class, which is a child of the `Object` class.

Just because an exception occurs and an `Exception` object is created, you do not necessarily have to deal with it. In the `MilesPerGallon` class, you simply let the offending program terminate; that is why the error message in Figure 11-2 indicates that the `Exception` is "Unhandled." However, the termination of the program is abrupt and unforgiving. When a program divides two numbers, or even performs a more trivial task like playing a game, the user might be annoyed if the program ends abruptly. If the program is used for air-traffic control or to monitor a patient's vital statistics during surgery, an abrupt conclusion could be disastrous. Object-oriented error-handling techniques provide more elegant solutions than simply shutting down.

Programs that can handle exceptions appropriately are said to be more fault tolerant and robust than those that do not. **Fault-tolerant** applications are designed so that they continue to operate, possibly at a reduced level, when some part of the system fails. **Robustness** represents the degree to which a system is resilient to stress, maintaining correct functioning.

Watch the video *System Exceptions.*

With exception handling, a program can continue after dealing with a problem. This is especially important in mission-critical applications. The term **mission critical** refers to any process that is crucial to an organization.

---

**TWO TRUTHS & A LIE**

**Understanding Exceptions**

1. An exception is any error condition or unexpected behavior in an executing program.

2. In C#, all exceptions are objects that are members of the Exception class or one of its derived classes.

3. In C#, when an exception occurs and an Exception object is created, you must employ a specific set of exception-handling techniques in order to manage the problem.

The false statement is #3. Just because an exception occurs and an Exception object is created, you do not necessarily have to deal with it.

---

# Understanding Traditional and Object-Oriented Error-Handling Methods

Programmers had to deal with error conditions long before object-oriented methods were conceived. For example, dividing by zero is an avoidable error for which programmers always have had to plan. If you simply check a variable's value with an if statement before attempting to divide it into another number, you can prevent the creation of an Exception object. For example, the following code uses a traditional if statement to check a variable to prevent division by zero.

```
if(gallonsOfGas != 0)
    mpg = milesDriven / gallonsOfGas;
else
    mpg = 0;
```

This code successfully prevents division by zero, but it does not really "handle an exception" because no Exception class object is created. The example code illustrates a perfectly legal and reasonable method of preventing division by zero, and it represents the most efficient method of handling the error if you think it will be a frequent problem. Because a program that contains this code does not have to instantiate an Exception object every time the user enters a 0 for the value of gallonsOfGas, the program saves time and computer memory. (Programmers say this program has little "overhead.") On the other hand, if you think dividing by zero will be infrequent—that is, the

The creators of C# define "infrequent" as an event that happens less than 30% of the time. That is, if you think an error will occur in less than 30% of all program executions, create an Exception; if you think the error will occur more often, use traditional error checking. Of course, your boss or instructor might prefer a different percentage.

Exception handling is critical in operations that are prone to failure. For example, after you open a file, it might not exit, or when you attempt to connect to a remote server, the connection might be down.

*exception* to the rule—then the decision will execute many times when it is not needed. In other words, if a user enters 0 for `gallonsOfGas` in only one case out of 1000, then the `if` statement is executed unnecessarily 999 times. In that case, it is more efficient to eliminate the `if` test and instantiate an `Exception` object when needed.

When a program's main logic is interrupted by a series of `if` statements and decisions that might detect errors, the program can become more complicated and difficult to understand. The object-oriented approach to error handling separates a program's main tasks from code that deals with rare exceptions.

Programmers use the phrase "sunny day case" to describe a scenario in which everything goes well and no errors occur.

## Understanding Object-Oriented Exception-Handling Methods

In object-oriented terminology, you "try" a procedure that may not complete correctly. A method that detects an error condition or `Exception` "throws" an `Exception`, and the block of code that processes the error "catches" the `Exception`.

When you write a block of code in which something can go wrong, you can place the code in a **try block**, which consists of the following elements:

- The keyword `try`

- A pair of curly braces containing statements that might cause `Exceptions`

You must code at least one `catch` block or `finally` block immediately following a `try` block. (You will learn about `finally` blocks later in this chapter.) Each **catch block** can "catch" one type of `Exception`. You create a `catch` block by typing the following elements:

- The keyword `catch`

- Parentheses containing an `Exception` type, and optionally, a name for an instance of the `Exception` type

- A pair of curly braces containing statements that deal with the error condition

Figure 11-3 shows the general format of a `try...catch pair`. The placeholder `XxxException` in the `catch` block represents the `Exception` class or any of its more specific subclasses. The placeholder `XxxException` is the data type of the `anExceptionInstance` object. A `catch` block looks a lot like a method named `catch()`, which takes an argument that is an instance of `XxxException`. However, it is not a method; it can catch only one object, it has no return type, and you cannot call it directly.

As XxxException implies, Exception classes typically are created using Exception as the second half of the name, as in SystemException and ApplicationException. The compiler does not require this naming convention, but the convention does make Exception descendents easier to identify.

```
try
{
    // Any number of statements;
    // some might cause an Exception
}
catch(XxxException anExceptionInstance)
{
    // Do something about it
}
// Statements here execute whether there was an Exception or not
```

**Figure 11-3**   General form of a try...catch pair

Any one of the statements you place within the try block in Figure 11-3 might throw an Exception. If an Exception occurs during the execution of the try block, the statements in the catch block will execute. If no Exception occurs within the try block, then the catch block will not execute. Either way, the statements following the catch block execute normally.

Some programmers refer to a catch block as a catch clause.

For example, Figure 11-4 contains a program in which the statements that prompt for, accept, and use gallonsOfGas are encased in a try block. Figure 11-5 shows two executions of the program. In the first execution, a usable value is entered for gallonsOfGas and the program operates normally, bypassing the catch block. In the second execution, however, the user enters 0 for gallonsOfGas. When division is attempted, an Exception object is automatically created and thrown. The catch block catches the Exception, where it becomes known as e. (The shaded arrow in Figure 11-4 indicates the throw and catch.) The statements in the catch block set mpg to 0 and display a message. Whether the catch block executes or not, the final WriteLine() statement that follows the catch block's closing curly brace executes.

498

```
using System;
public class MilesPerGallon2
{
    public static void Main()
    {
        int milesDriven;
        int gallonsOfGas;
        int mpg;
        try
        {
            Console.Write("Enter miles driven ");
            milesDriven = Convert.ToInt32(Console.ReadLine());
            Console.Write("Enter gallons of gas purchased ");
            gallonsOfGas = Convert.ToInt32(Console.ReadLine());
            mpg = milesDriven / gallonsOfGas;

        }
        catch (Exception e)
        {
            mpg = 0;
            Console.WriteLine("You attempted to divide by zero!");
        }
        Console.WriteLine("You got {0} miles per gallon", mpg);
    }
}
```

**Figure 11-4**   MilesPerGallon2 program

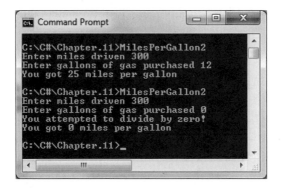

**Figure 11-5**   Two executions of MilesPerGallon2 program

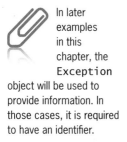

In later examples in this chapter, the Exception object will be used to provide information. In those cases, it is required to have an identifier.

When you compile the program in Figure 11-4, you receive a warning that e is declared but never used. You can declare a variable to hold the thrown Exception, but you do not want to use it in this example, so you can safely ignore the warning. If you do not want to use the caught Exception object within a catch block, then you do not have to provide an instance name for it. For example, in Figure 11-4, the catch clause could begin as follows:
catch(Exception)

In the application in Figure 11-4, the source of the exception and the catch block reside in the same method. Later in this chapter, you will learn that exceptions and their corresponding catch blocks frequently reside in separate methods.

Watch the video *Throwing and Catching Exceptions.*

In the MilesPerGallon2 program, you could catch a more specific DivideByZeroException object instead of catching an Exception object. You will employ this technique later in the chapter. If you are working on a professional project, Microsoft recommends that you never use the general Exception class in a catch block.

---

### TWO TRUTHS & A LIE

#### Understanding Traditional and Object-Oriented Error-Handling Methods

1. Before object-oriented methods were conceived, programmers had no way of handling unexpected conditions.

2. Using object-oriented techniques, when you write a block of code in which something can go wrong, you can place the code in a try block.

3. If a catch block executes, then an Exception must have been thrown.

The false statement is #1. Programmers had to deal with error conditions long before object-oriented methods were conceived.

---

## Using the Exception Class's ToString() Method and Message Property

When the MilesPerGallon2 program displays the error message ("You attempted to divide by zero!"), you actually cannot confirm from the message that division by zero was the source of the error. In reality, any Exception generated within the try block of the program would be caught by the catch block in the method because the argument in the catch block is an Exception.

Instead of writing your own message, you can use the ToString() method that every Exception inherits from the Object class. The Exception class overrides ToString() to provide a descriptive error message so a user can receive precise information about the nature of any Exception that is thrown. For example, Figure 11-6 shows a MilesPerGallon3 program. The only changes from theMilesPerGallon2 program are shaded: the name of the class and the message that is displayed when an Exception is thrown.

You learned about overriding the Object class ToString() method in the chapter titled *Introduction to Inheritance.*

In this example, the `ToString()` method is used with the caught `Exception e`. Figure 11-7 shows an execution of the program in which the user enters 0 for `gallonsOfGas`.

```
using System;
public class MilesPerGallon3
{
    public static void Main()
    {
        int milesDriven;
        int gallonsOfGas;
        int mpg;
        try
        {
            Console.Write("Enter miles driven ");
            milesDriven = Convert.ToInt32(Console.ReadLine());
            Console.Write("Enter gallons of gas purchased ");
            gallonsOfGas = Convert.ToInt32(Console.ReadLine());
            mpg = milesDriven / gallonsOfGas;
        }
        catch(Exception e)
        {
            mpg = 0;
            Console.WriteLine(e.ToString());
        }
        Console.WriteLine("You got {0} miles per gallon", mpg);
    }
}
```

**Figure 11-6** `MilesPerGallon3` program

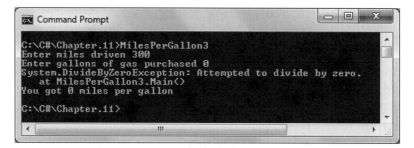

**Figure 11-7** Execution of `MilesPerGallon3` program

The error message displayed in Figure 11-7 ("System.DivideByZeroException: Attempted to divide by zero.") is the same message that appeared in Figure 11-2 when you provided no exception handling. Therefore, you can assume that the operating

system uses the same ToString() method you can use when displaying information about an Exception. In the program in which you
provided no exception handling, execution simply stopped; in this
one, execution continues and the final output statement is displayed
whether the user's input was usable or not. Programmers would say
this new version of the program ended more "elegantly."

The Exception class also contains a read-only property named
Message that contains useful information about an Exception.
For example, the program in Figure 11-8 contains just two shaded
changes from the MilesPerGallon3 program: the class name and
the use of the Message property in the statement that displays the
error message in the catch block. The program produces the output
shown in Figure 11-9. The value of e.Message is a string that is
identical to the second part of the value returned by the ToString()
method. You can guess that the DivideByZeroException class's
ToString() method used in MilesPerGallon3 constructs its string
from two parts: the return value of the getType() method (that
indicates the name of the class) and the return value from the
Message property.

```csharp
using System;
public class MilesPerGallon4
{
    public static void Main()
    {
        int milesDriven;
        int gallonsOfGas;
        int mpg;
        try
        {
            Console.Write("Enter miles driven ");
            milesDriven = Convert.ToInt32(Console.ReadLine());
            Console.Write("Enter gallons of gas purchased ");
            gallonsOfGas = Convert.ToInt32(Console.ReadLine());
            mpg = milesDriven / gallonsOfGas;
        }
        catch(Exception e)
        {
            mpg = 0;
            Console.WriteLine(e.Message);
        }
        Console.WriteLine("You got {0} miles per gallon", mpg);
    }
}
```

**Figure 11-8** MilesPerGallon4 program

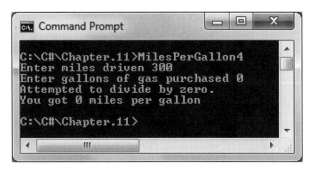

**Figure 11-9**  Execution of MilesPerGallon4 program

---

## TWO TRUTHS & A LIE

### Using the Exception Class's ToString() Method and Message Property

1. Any Exception generated within a try block in a program will be caught by a catch block that has an Exception type argument.

2. The Exception class overrides the Object class Description() method to provide a descriptive error message so a user can receive precise information about the nature of any Exception that is thrown.

3. The Exception class contains a property named Message that contains useful information about an Exception.

The false statement is #2. The Exception class overrides the Object class ToString() method to provide a descriptive error message so a user can receive precise information about the nature of any Exception that is thrown.

---

## Catching Multiple Exceptions

The set of catch blocks should cover all possible exceptions that the code in the try block might encounter. If an exception is thrown without a matching catch block, the program will terminate abruptly.

You can place as many statements as you need within a try block, and you can include as many catch blocks as you want to handle different Exception types. When a try block contains more than one statement, only the first error-generating statement throws an Exception. As soon as the Exception occurs, the logic transfers to the catch block, which leaves the rest of the statements in the try block unexecuted.

When an Exception is thrown and multiple catch blocks are present, the catch blocks are examined in sequence until a match is found. The matching catch block then executes, and each remaining catch block is bypassed.

For example, consider the program in Figure 11-10. The Main() method in the TwoErrors class potentially throws two types of Exceptions— a DivideByZeroException and an IndexOutOfRangeException. (An IndexOutOfRangeException occurs when an array subscript is not within the allowed range. In the TwoErrors program, the array has only three elements, but 13 is used as a subscript.)

The TwoErrors class declares three integers and an integer array with three elements. In the Main() method, the try block executes, and at the first statement within the try block, an Exception occurs because the denom in the division problem is zero. The try block is abandoned and control transfers to the first catch block. Integer division by zero causes a DivideByZeroException, and because the first catch block receives that type of Exception, the message "In first catch block" appears along with the Message value of the Exception. In this example, the second try statement is never attempted, and the second catch block is skipped. Figure 11-11 shows the output.

```
using System;
public class TwoErrors
{
    public static void Main()
    {
        int num = 13, denom = 0, result;
        int[] array = {22, 33, 44};
        try
        {
            result = num / denom;
            result = array[num];
        }
        catch(DivideByZeroException error)
        {
            Console.WriteLine("In first catch block: ");
            Console.WriteLine(error.Message);
        }
        catch(IndexOutOfRangeException error)
        {
            Console.WriteLine("In second catch block: ");
            Console.WriteLine(error.Message);
        }
    }
}
```

**Figure 11-10**  TwoErrors program with two catch blocks

**Figure 11-11**    Output of TwoErrors program

If you reverse the two statements within the try block in the TwoErrors program, the process changes. If you use the try block in Figure 11-12, division by zero does not take place because the invalid array access throws an Exception first.

```
using System;
public class TwoErrors2
{
   public static void Main()
   {
      int num = 13, denom = 0, result;
      int[] array = {22, 33, 44};
      try
      {
         result = array[num];
         result = num / denom;
      }
      catch(DivideByZeroException error)
      {
         Console.WriteLine("In first catch block: ");
         Console.WriteLine(error.Message);
      }
      catch (IndexOutOfRangeException error)
      {
         Console.WriteLine("In second catch block: ");
         Console.WriteLine(error.Message);
      }
   }
}
```

**Figure 11-12**    The TwoErrors2 program

The first statement within the try block in Figure 11-12 attempts to access element 13 of a three-element array, so the program throws an IndexOutOfRangeException. The try block is abandoned, and the first catch block is examined and found unsuitable because the Exception is of the wrong type—it is not a DivideByZeroException object. The program logic proceeds to the second catch block, whose IndexOutOfRangeException argument type is a match for the thrown Exception. The message "In second catch block" and the Exception's Message value are therefore displayed. Figure 11-13 shows the output.

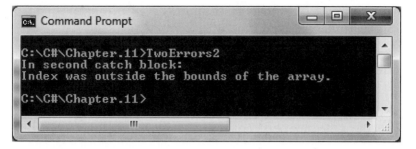

```
Command Prompt

C:\C#\Chapter.11>TwoErrors2
In second catch block:
Index was outside the bounds of the array.

C:\C#\Chapter.11>
```

**Figure 11-13** Output of TwoErrors2 program

Sometimes you want to execute the same code, no matter which Exception type occurs. For example, in each version of the TwoErrors program, each of the two catch blocks displays a unique message. Instead, you might want both the DivideByZeroException catch block and the IndexOutOfRangeException catch block to use the thrown Exception's Message field. Because DivideByZeroExceptions and IndexOutOfRangeExceptions both are subclasses of Exception, you can rewrite the TwoErrors class as shown in Figure 11-14 and include only one Exception catch block that catches any type of Exception.

```csharp
using System;
public class TwoErrors3
{
    public static void Main()
    {
        int num = 13, denom = 0, result;
        int[] array = {22, 33, 44};
        try
        {
            result = array[num];
            result = num / denom;
        }
        catch(Exception error)
        {
            Console.WriteLine(error.Message);
        }
    }
}
```

As an alternative to using a single catch block for multiple Exception types that require the same action, as in Figure 11-14, you could create the class to have separate catch blocks, each of which calls the same method that contains the action.

**Figure 11-14** TwoErrors3 class with one catch block

As stated earlier, Microsoft recommends that a catch block should not handle general Exceptions. They say that if you cannot predict all possible causes of an exception and ensure that malicious code cannot exploit the resulting application state, you should allow the application to terminate instead of handling the exception.

The catch block in Figure 11-14 accepts a more generic Exception type than either of the potentially error-causing try statements throw, so the generic catch block can act as a "catch-all" block. That is, when either a division arithmetic error or an array error occurs, the thrown error is "promoted" to an Exception error in the catch block. Through inheritance, DivideByZeroExceptions and IndexOutOfRangeExceptions are Exceptions.

Although a block of code can throw any number of Exception types, many developers believe that it is poor style for a block or method to throw more than three or four types. If it does, one of the following conditions might be true:

- Perhaps the code block or method is trying to accomplish too many diverse tasks and should be broken up into smaller blocks or methods.

- Perhaps the Exception types thrown are too specific and should be generalized, as they are in the TwoErrors3 program in Figure 11-14.

When you list multiple catch blocks following a try block, you must be careful that some catch blocks do not become unreachable. **Unreachable** blocks contain statements that can never execute under any circumstances because the program logic "can't get there." For example, if successive catch blocks catch an Exception and a DivideByZeroException, then even DivideByZeroExceptions will be caught by the Exception catch. The DivideByZeroException catch block is unreachable because the more general Exception catch block is in its way, and therefore the class will not compile.

Programmers also call unreachable code **dead code**.

## TWO TRUTHS & A LIE

### Catching Multiple Exceptions

1. If you try more than one statement in a block, each error-generating statement throws an Exception.

2. You can write catch blocks that catch multiple Exception types.

3. When you list multiple catch blocks following a try block, you must be careful that some catch blocks do not become unreachable.

The false statement is #1. If you try more than one statement in a block, only the first error-generating statement throws an Exception.

# Using the finally Block

When you have actions to perform at the end of a `try...catch` sequence, you can use a **finally block**, which executes whether the `try` block identifies any `Exception`s or not. Typically, you use the `finally` block to perform clean-up tasks that must occur, regardless of whether any errors occurred or were caught. Figure 11-15 shows the format of a `try...catch` sequence that uses a `finally` block.

```
try
{
    // Statements that might cause an Exception
}
catch(SomeException anExceptionInstance)
{
    // What to do about it
}
finally
{
    // Statements here execute
    // whether an Exception occurred or not
}
```

**Figure 11-15** General form of a `try...catch` block with a `finally` block

At first glance, it seems as though the `finally` block serves no purpose. When a `try` block works without error, control passes to the statements that come after the `catch` block. Additionally, if the `try` code fails and throws an `Exception` that is caught, then the `catch` block executes and control again passes to any statements that are coded after the `catch` block. Therefore, it seems as though the statements after the `catch` block always execute, so there is no need to place any statements within a special `finally` block. However, statements after the `catch` block might never execute for at least two reasons:

- An `Exception` for which you did not plan might occur.

- The `try` or `catch` block might contain a statement that terminates the application.

The possibility exists that a `try` block might throw an `Exception` for which you did not provide a `catch`. After all, `Exception`s occur all the time without your handling them, as you saw in the first `MilesPerGallon` program at the beginning of this chapter. In case of an unhandled `Exception`, program execution stops immediately, sending the error to the operating system for handling and abandoning the current method. Likewise, if the `try` block contains an exit statement, execution stops immediately. When you include a `finally` block, you are assured that its enclosed statements will execute before the program is abandoned, even if the method concludes prematurely.

 You can terminate an application with a statement such as `Environment.Exit(0);`. The `Environment.Exit()` method is part of the `System` namespace. It terminates a program and passes the argument (which can be any integer) to the operating system. You also might exit a `catch` block with a `break` statement or a `return` statement. You encountered `break` statements when you learned about the `switch` statement and you learned about `return` statements when you studied methods.

For example, the finally block is used frequently with file input and output to ensure that open files are closed. You will learn more about writing to and reading from data files in a later chapter. For now, however, consider the format shown in Figure 11-16, which represents part of the logic for a typical file-handling program. The catch block was written to catch an IOException, which is the type of exception automatically generated if there is a problem opening a file, reading data from a file, or writing to a file.

```
try
{
    // Open the file
    // Read the file
    // Place the file data in an array
    // Calculate an average from the data
    // Display the average
}
catch(IOException e)
{
    // Issue an error message
    // Exit
}
finally
{
    // If the file is open, close it
}
```

**Figure 11-16**   Format of code that tries reading a file and handles an Exception

If an application might throw several types of exceptions, you can try some code, catch the possible exception, try some more code, catch the possible exception, and so on. Usually, however, the superior approach is to try all the statements that might throw exceptions, then include all the needed catch blocks and an optional finally block. This is the approach shown in Figure 11-16, and it usually results in logic that is easier to follow.

The pseudocode in Figure 11-16 handles any file problems. However, because the application uses an array (see the statement "Place the file data in an array") and performs division (see the statement "Calculate an average..."), an uncaught Exception could occur even though the file opened successfully. In such an event, you would want to close the file before proceeding. By using the finally block, you ensure that the file is closed, because the code in the finally block executes before the uncaught exception returns control to the operating system. The code in the finally block executes no matter which of the following outcomes of the try block occurs:

- The try ends normally.

- The try ends abnormally and the catch executes.

- The try ends abnormally and the catch does not execute. For example, an Exception might cause the method to abandon prematurely—perhaps the array is not large enough to hold the data, or calculating the average results in division by 0. These

Exceptions do not allow the try block to finish, nor do they cause the catch block to execute.

You often can avoid using a finally block, but you would need repetitious code. For example, instead of using the finally block in the pseudocode in Figure 11-16, you could insert the statement "If the file is open, close it" as both the last statement in the try block and the second-to-last statement in the catch block, just before the program exits. However, writing code just once in a finally block is clearer and less prone to error.

 Java and C++ provide try and catch blocks. Java also provides a finally block, but C++ does not.

509

 Many well-designed programs that try code do not include catch blocks; instead, they contain only try-finally pairs. The finally block is used to release resources that other applications might be waiting for, such as database connections.

---

## TWO TRUTHS & A LIE

### Using the finally Block

1. When a finally block follows a try block, it executes whether the try block identifies any Exceptions or not.

2. Typically, you use a finally block to perform clean-up tasks that must occur after an Exception has been thrown and caught.

3. Statements that follow a try...catch pair might never execute because an unplanned Exception might occur, or the try or catch block might contain a statement that quits the application.

The false statement is #2. Typically, you use a finally block to perform clean-up tasks that must occur, regardless of whether any errors occurred or were caught.

---

# Handling Exceptions Thrown from Outside Methods

An advantage of using object-oriented exception-handling techniques is the ability to deal with Exceptions appropriately as you decide how to handle them. When methods from other classes throw Exceptions, the methods do not have to catch them; instead, your calling program can catch them, and you can decide what to do.

For example, suppose you prompt a user to enter a value at the console and then call the Convert.ToInt32() method to convert the input to an integer with a statement such as the following:

```
int answer = Convert.ToInt32(Console.ReadLine());
```

If the user enters a noninteger value, a FormatException is generated from the Convert.ToInt32() method, but it is not caught and handled there. Instead, your program can catch the exception and you can take appropriate action for your specific application. For example, you might want to force the user to reenter a value, but a different program might force the value to a default value or display an error message and terminate the program. This flexibility is an advantage when you need to create specific reactions to thrown Exceptions. In many cases, you want a method to check for errors, but you do not want to require the method to handle an error if it finds one. Just as a police officer can deal with a speeding driver differently depending on circumstances, you can react to Exceptions specifically for your current purposes.

When you design classes containing methods that have statements that might throw Exceptions, you most frequently should create the methods so they throw the Exception, but do not handle it. Handling an Exception should be left to the client—the program that uses your class—so the Exception can be handled in an appropriate way for the application.

For example, consider the very brief PriceList class in Figure 11-17. The class contains a list of prices and a single method that displays one price based on a parameter subscript value. Because the DisplayPrice() method uses an array, an IndexOutOfRangeException might be thrown. However, the DisplayPrice() method does not handle the potential Exception.

```
class PriceList
{
   private static double[] price = {15.99, 27.88, 34.56, 45.89};
   public static void DisplayPrice(int item)
   {
      Console.WriteLine("The price is " +
         price[item].ToString("C"));
   }
}
```

**Figure 11-17** The PriceList class

Figure 11-18 shows an application that uses the DisplayPrice() method. It calls the method in a try block and handles an IndexOutOfRangeException by displaying a price of $0. Figure 11-19 shows the output when a user enters an invalid item number.

```
using System;
public class PriceListApplication1
{
    public static void Main()
    {
        int item;
        try
        {
            Console.Write("Enter an item number >> ");
            item = Convert.ToInt32(Console.ReadLine());
            PriceList.DisplayPrice(item);
        }
        catch(IndexOutOfRangeException e)
        {
            Console.WriteLine(e.Message + " The price is $0");
        }
    }
}
```

**Figure 11-18**  The PriceListApplication1 program

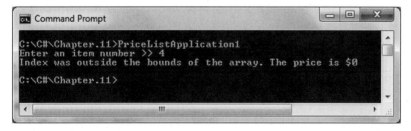

**Figure 11-19**  Output of PriceListApplication1 program when user enters invalid item number

Figure 11-20 shows a different application that uses the same PriceList class, but handles the exception differently. In this case, the programmer wanted the user to keep responding until a correct entry was made. If an IndexOutOfRangeException is thrown from the try block, the try block is abandoned, isGoodItem is not set to true, and the catch block executes. Because isGoodItem remains false, the while loop continues to execute. Only when the first three statements in the try block are successful does the last statement execute, changing isGoodItem to true and ending the loop repetitions. Because the DisplayPrice() method in the PriceList class was written to throw an Exception but not handle it, the programmer of PriceListApplication2 could handle the Exception in a totally different manner from the way it was handled in PriceListApplication1. Figure 11-21 shows a typical execution of this program.

```
using System;
public class PriceListApplication2
{
    public static void Main()
    {
        int item = 0;
        bool isGoodItem = false;
        while(!isGoodItem)
        {
            try
            {
                Console.Write("Enter an item number >> "");
                item = Convert.ToInt32(Console.ReadLine());
                PriceList.DisplayPrice(item);
                isGoodItem = true;
            }
            catch(IndexOutOfRangeException e)
            {
                Console.WriteLine("You must enter a number less " +
                    "than 4");
                Console.WriteLine("Please reenter item number ");
            }
        }
        Console.WriteLine("Thank you");
    }
}
```

**Figure 11-20**   The `PriceListApplication2` program

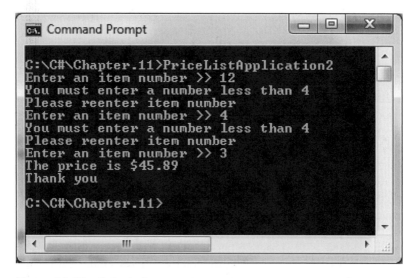

**Figure 11-21**   Output of `PriceListApplication2` program when user enters invalid item number several times

## TWO TRUTHS & A LIE

### Handling Exceptions Thrown from Outside Methods

1. When methods from other classes throw Exceptions, the methods do not have to catch them; instead, your calling program can catch them, and you can decide what to do.

2. Often, you do not want a method to handle its own Exception; in many cases, you want the method to check for errors, but you do not want to require a method to handle an error if it finds one.

3. When you design classes containing methods that have statements that might throw Exceptions, you should make sure your class handles each Exception appropriately.

The false statement is #3. When you design classes containing methods that have statements that might throw Exceptions, you most frequently should create the methods so they throw the Exception, but not handle it.

# Tracing Exceptions Through the Call Stack

When one method calls another, the computer's operating system must keep track of where the method call came from, and program control must return to the calling method when the called method is complete. For example, if MethodA() calls MethodB(), the operating system has to "remember" to return to MethodA() when MethodB() ends. Similarly, if MethodB() calls MethodC(), then while MethodC() is executing, the computer needs to "remember" that it will return to MethodB() and eventually to MethodA(). The memory location where the computer stores the list of locations to which the system must return is known as the **call stack**.

If a method throws an Exception and does not catch it, then the Exception is thrown to the next method "up" the call stack; in other words, it is thrown to the method that called the offending method. Consider this sequence of events:

1. MethodA() calls MethodB().

2. MethodB() calls MethodC().

3. MethodC() throws an Exception.

4. C# looks first for a catch block in MethodC().

5. If none exist, then C# looks for the same thing in MethodB().

6. If MethodB() does not have a catch block for the Exception, then C# looks to MethodA().

7. If MethodA() does not catch the Exception, then the program terminates and the operating system displays an error message.

This system of passing an Exception through the chain of calling methods is called **propagating the exception**. It has great advantages because it allows your methods to handle Exceptions more appropriately. However, a program that uses several classes makes it difficult for the programmer to locate the original source of an Exception.

You already have used the Message property to obtain information about an Exception. Another useful Exception property is the StackTrace property. When you catch an Exception, you can display the value of StackTrace to provide a list of methods in the call stack so you can determine the location of the Exception.

The StackTrace property can be a useful debugging tool. When your program stops abruptly, it is helpful to discover the method in which the Exception occurred. Often, you do not want to display a StackTrace property in a finished program; the typical user has no interest in the cryptic messages that would appear. However, while you are developing a program, using StackTrace can help you diagnose your program's problems.

## A Case Study: Using StackTrace

As an example of when StackTrace can be useful, consider the Tax class in Figure 11-22. Suppose your company has created or purchased this class to make it easy to calculate tax rates on products sold. For simplicity, assume that only two tax rates are in effect— 6% for sales of $20 or less and 7% for sales over $20. The Tax class would be useful for anyone who wrote a program involving product sales, except for one flaw: in the shaded statement, the subscript is erroneously set to 2 instead of 1 for the higher tax rate. If this subscript is used with the taxRate array in the next statement, it will be out of bounds.

```
class Tax
{
    private static double[] taxRate = {0.06, 0.07};
    private static double CUTOFF = 20.00;
    public static double DetermineTaxRate(double price)
    {
        int subscript;
        double rate;
        if(price <= CUTOFF)
            subscript = 0;
        else
            subscript = 2;
        rate = taxRate[subscript];
        return rate;
    }
}
```

**Don't Do It**
This mistake is
intentional.

**515**

**Figure 11-22**   The Tax class

Assume your company has also created a revised `PriceList`
class, as shown in Figure 11-23. This class is similar to the one in
Figure 11-17, except that it includes a tax calculation and calls the
`DetermineTaxRate()` method in the shaded statement.

```
class PriceList
{
    private static double[] price = {15.99, 27.88, 34.56, 45.89};
    public static void DisplayPrice(int item)
    {
        double tax;
        double total;
        double pr;
        pr = price[item];
        tax = pr * Tax.DetermineTaxRate(pr);
        total = pr + tax;
        Console.WriteLine("The total price is " +
            total.ToString("C"));
    }
}
```

**Figure 11-23**   `PriceList` class that includes call to the Tax class method `DetermineTaxRate()`

Suppose you write the application shown in Figure 11-24. Your
application is similar to the price list applications earlier in this
chapter, including a call to `PriceList.DisplayPrice()`. As in
`PriceListApplication1` and `PriceListApplication2`, your new

program tries the data entry and display statement and then catches an exception. When you run the program using what you know to be a good item number, as in Figure 11-25, you are surprised to see the shaded "Error!" message you have coded in the `catch` block. In the earlier examples that used `PriceList.DisplayPrice()`, using an item number 1 would have resulted in a successful program execution.

When you compile the program in Figure 11-24, you receive a warning that variable e is declared but never used. If you omit the name e from the catch block, the application will execute identically.

```
using System;
public class PriceListApplication3
{
    public static void Main()
    {
        int item;
        try
        {
            Console.Write("Enter an item number >> ");
            item = Convert.ToInt32(Console.ReadLine());
            PriceList.DisplayPrice(item);
        }
        catch(Exception e)
        {
            Console.WriteLine("Error!");
        }
    }
}
```

**Figure 11-24** `PriceListApplication3` class

**Figure 11-25** Execution of `PriceListApplication3` program when user enters 1 for item number

When the statement to display e.Message is added to the price list program, a warning that e is never used no longer appears when the program is compiled.

To attempt to discover what caused the "Error!" message, you can replace the statement that writes it as follows:

```
Console.WriteLine(e.Message);
```

However, when you execute the program with this modification, you receive the output in Figure 11-26, indicating that the index is out of the bounds of the array. You are puzzled because you know 1 is a valid item number for the price array, and it should not be considered out of bounds.

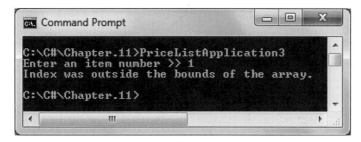

**Figure 11-26** Execution of modified price list application in which
`e.Message` is displayed in the `catch` block

Finally, you decide to replace the `WriteLine()` argument in the `catch`
block statement with a `StackTrace` call, as follows:

```
Console.WriteLine(e.StackTrace);
```

The output is shown in Figure 11-27. You can see from the list of methods
that the error in your application came from `PriceList.DisplayPrice()`,
which in turn came from `Tax.DetermineTaxRate()`. You might have not
even considered that the `Tax` class could have been the source of the problem. If you work in a small organization, you can look at the code yourself
and fix it. If you work in a larger organization or you purchased the class
from an outside vendor, you can contact the programmer who created the
class for assistance.

**Figure 11-27** Execution of modified price list application in which
`e.StackTrace` is displayed in the `catch` block

The classes in this example were small to help you easily follow the
discussion. However, a full-blown application might have many more
classes that contain many more methods, and so using `StackTrace`
would become increasingly beneficial.

Watch the
video *Tracing
Exceptions
Through the
Call Stack.*

You might find it useful to locate `StackTrace` calls strategically throughout
a program while testing it, and then remove them or comment them out when
the program is complete.

518

## Creating Your Own Exception Classes

C# provides more than 100 categories of Exceptions that you can throw in your programs. However, C#'s creators could not predict every condition that might be an Exception in the programs you write. For example, you might want to declare an Exception when your bank balance is negative or when an outside party attempts to access your e-mail account. Most organizations have specific rules for exceptional data, such as "an employee number must not exceed three digits" or "an hourly salary must not be less than the legal minimum wage." Of course, you can handle these potential error situations with if statements, but you also can create your own Exceptions.

The C# documentation recommends that you create all Exception messages to be grammatically correct, complete sentences ending in a period.

To create your own Exception that you can throw, you can extend the ApplicationException class, which is a subclass of Exception, or you can extend Exception. As you saw earlier in the chapter, Microsoft's advice on this matter has changed over time. Although you might see extensions of ApplicationException in classes written by others, the current advice is simply to derive your own classes from Exception. Either approach will produce workable programs.

Figure 11-28 shows a NegativeBalanceException class that extends Exception. This class passes an appropriate string message to its parent's constructor. If you create an Exception and display its

Message property, you will see the message "Error in the application."
When the NegativeBalanceException constructor passes the string
"Bank balance is negative." to its parent's constructor, the Message
property will hold this more descriptive message.

```
class NegativeBalanceException : Exception
{
   private static string msg = "Bank balance is negative. ";
   public NegativeBalanceException() : base(msg)
   {
   }
}
```

**Figure 11-28**   The NegativeBalanceException class

When you create a BankAccount class like the one shown in
Figure 11-29, you can create the Balance property set accessor to
throw a NegativeBalanceException when a client attempts to set the
balance to be negative.

```
class BankAccount
{
   private double balance;
   public int AccountNum {get; set;}
   public double Balance
   {
      get
      {
         return balance;
      }
      set
      {
         if(value < 0)
         {
            NegativeBalanceException nbe =
               new NegativeBalanceException();
            throw(nbe);
         }
         balance = value;
      }
   }
}
```

**Figure 11-29**   The BankAccount class

Instead of creating the nbe object in the Balance property in Figure 11-29, you could code the following statement, which creates and throws an anonymous NegativeBalanceException in a single step:
throw(new NegativeBalanceException());

Figure 11-30 shows a program that attempts to set a BankAccount balance to a negative value in the shaded statement. When the BankAccount class's Balance set accessor throws the NegativeBalanceException, the catch block in the TryBankAccount program executes, displaying both the NegativeBalanceException Message and the value of StackTrace. Figure 11-31 shows the output.

```csharp
using System;
public class TryBankAccount
{
    public static void Main()
    {
    BankAccount acct = new BankAccount();
    try
    {
        acct.AccountNum = 1234;
        acct.Balance = -1000;
    }
    catch(NegativeBalanceException e)
    {
        Console.WriteLine(e.Message);
        Console.WriteLine(e.StackTrace);
    }
    }
}
```

**Figure 11-30**  The TryBankAccount program

In Figure 11-31, notice that the set accessor for the Balance property is known internally as set_Balance. You can guess that the set accessor for the AccountNum property is known as set_AccountNum.

**Figure 11-31**  Output of TryBankAccount program

📎 **Exceptions** can be particularly useful when you throw them from constructors. Constructors do not have a return type, so they have no other way to send information back to the calling method.

📎 The **StackTrace** begins at the point where an **Exception** is thrown, not where it is created. This consideration makes a difference when you create an **Exception** and throw it from two different methods.

In C#, you cannot throw an object unless it is an **Exception** or a descendent of the **Exception** class. In other words, you cannot throw a **double** or a **BankAccount**. However, you can throw any type of **Exception** at any time, not just **Exceptions** of your own creation. For example, within any program you can code any of the following:

```
throw(new ApplicationException());
throw(new IndexOutOfRangeException());
throw(new Exception());
```

Of course, you should not throw an **IndexOutOfRangeException** when you encounter division by 0 or data of an incorrect type; you should use it only when an index (subscript) is too high or too low. However, if a built-in **Exception** type is appropriate and suits your needs, you should use it. You should not create an excessive number of special **Exception** types for your classes, especially if the C# development environment already contains an **Exception** that accurately describes the error. Extra **Exception** types add a level of complexity for other programmers who will use your classes. Nevertheless, when appropriate, creating a specialized **Exception** class is an elegant way for you to take care of error situations. **Exceptions** allow you to separate your error code from the usual, nonexceptional sequence of events and allow for errors to be passed up the stack and traced.

## TWO TRUTHS & A LIE

### Creating Your Own **Exception** Classes

1. To create your own **Exception** that you can throw, you can extend the **ApplicationException** class or the **Exception** class.

2. In C#, you can throw any object you create if it is appropriate for the application.

3. You can throw any type of **Exception** at any time—both those that are already created as part of C# and those of your own creation.

The false statement is #2. In C#, you cannot throw an object unless it is an **Exception** or a descendent of the **Exception** class.

# Rethrowing an Exception

When you write a method that catches an Exception, your method does not have to handle the Exception. Instead, you might choose to **rethrow the Exception** to the method that called your method. Then you can let the calling method handle the problem. Within a catch block, you can rethrow the Exception that was caught by using the keyword throw with no object after it. For example, Figure 11-32 shows a class that contains four methods. In this program, the following sequence of events takes place:

1. The Main() method calls MethodA().

2. MethodA() calls MethodB().

3. MethodB() calls MethodC().

4. MethodC() throws an Exception.

5. When MethodB() catches the Exception, it does not handle the Exception; instead, it throws the Exception back to MethodA().

6. MethodA() catches the Exception, but does not handle it either. Instead, MethodA() throws the Exception back to the Main() method.

7. The Exception is caught in the Main() method, where the message that was created in MethodC() is finally displayed.

Figure 11-33 shows the execution of the program.

```
using System;
public class ReThrowDemo
{
   public static void Main()
   {
      try
      {
         Console.WriteLine("Trying in Main() method");
         MethodA();
      }
      catch(Exception ae)
      {
         Console.WriteLine("Caught in Main() method --\n    {0}",
            ae.Message);
      }
      Console.WriteLine("Main() method is done");
   }
```

**Figure 11-32** The ReThrowDemo program *(continues)*

*(continued)*

```
    public static void MethodA()
    {
        try
        {
            Console.WriteLine("Trying in method A");
            MethodB();
        }
        catch(Exception)
        {
            Console.WriteLine("Caught in method A");
            throw;
        }
    }
    public static void MethodB()
    {
        try
        {
            Console.WriteLine("Trying in method B");
            MethodC();
        }
        catch(Exception)
        {
            Console.WriteLine("Caught in method B");
            throw;
        }
    }
    public static void MethodC()
    {
        Console.WriteLine("In method C");
        throw(new Exception("This came from method C"));
    }
}
```

**Figure 11-32** The ReThrowDemo program

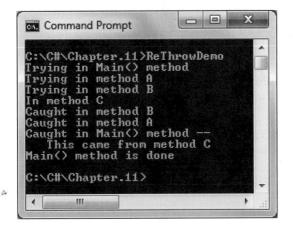

**Figure 11-33** Execution of the ReThrowDemo program

If you name the Exception argument to the catch block in Figure 11-32 (for example, catch(Exception e)), then you should use that identifier in the throw statement at the end of the block (for example, throw e;).

**TWO TRUTHS & A LIE**

**Rethrowing an Exception**

1. When you write a method that catches an Exception, your method must handle the Exception.

2. When a method catches an Exception, you can rethrow it to a method that called the method.

3. Within a catch block, you can rethrow a caught Exception by using the keyword throw with no object after it.

The false statement is #1. When you write a method that catches an Exception, your method does not have to handle the Exception.

# You Do It

## Purposely Causing Exceptions

C# generates SystemExceptions automatically under many circumstances. In the next steps, you will purposely generate a SystemException by executing a program that provides multiple opportunities for Exceptions.

**To create a program that purposely generates Exceptions:**

1.  Open a new file in your text editor and type the following program, which allows you to generate several different Exceptions.

```
using System;
public class ExceptionsOnPurpose
{
    public static void Main()
    {
        int answer;
        int result;
        int zero = 0;
        Console.Write("Enter an integer >> ");
        answer = Convert.ToInt32(Console.ReadLine());
        result = answer / zero;
        Console.WriteLine("The answer is " + answer);
    }
}
```

 You would never write a program that purposely divides by zero; you do so here to demonstrate C#'s Exception-generating capabilities.

2. The variable zero cannot be defined as a constant; if it is, the program will not compile. As a variable, the compiler "trusts" that a legitimate value will be provided for it before division occurs (although in this case, the trust was not warranted). Save the program as **ExceptionsOnPurpose.cs**. Compile the program.

3. Execute the program several times using different values and observe the results. Two windows appear with each execution. The first reports that Windows is collecting more information about the problem. This window is soon replaced with the one shown in Figure 11-34, which repeats that ExceptionsOnPurpose.exe has stopped working. If you were executing a professional application, you might be notified of a solution. Because you created this exception on purpose, just click the **Close program** button.

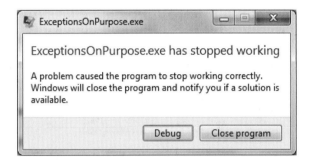

**Figure 11-34**  Error report window generated by an unhandled Exception

Figure 11-35 shows three executions of the program during which the user typed the following:

- **seven**—This generates a System.FormatException, which occurs when the program tries to convert the input value to an integer, because letters are not allowed in integers.

- **7.7**—This also generates a System.FormatException because the decimal point is not allowed in an integer.

- **7**—This does not generate a System.FormatException, but instead causes a System.DivideByZero exception when the result is calculated.

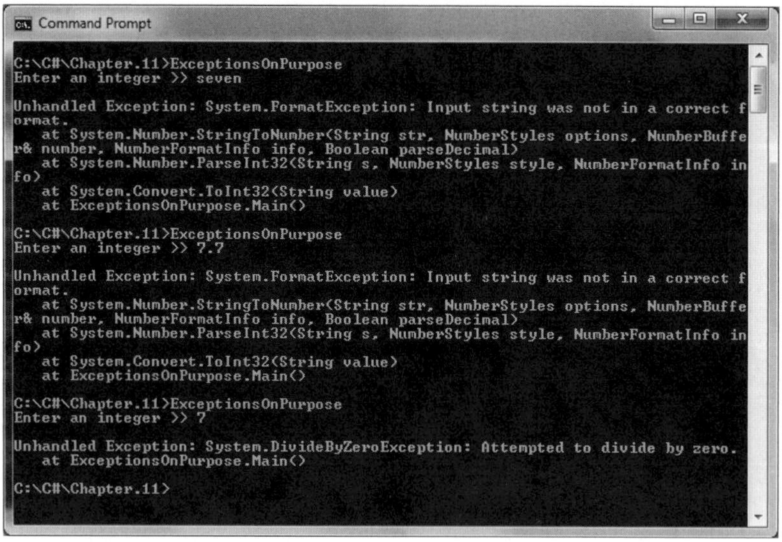

**Figure 11-35** Error messages generated by successive executions of ExceptionsOnPurpose program

## Handling Exceptions

You can handle Exceptions by placing them in a try block and then catching any Exceptions that are thrown from it.

**To add a try... catch block to your application:**

1. Open the ExceptionsOnPurpose.cs file if it is not still open. Change the class name to **ExceptionsOnPurpose2** and immediately save the file as **ExceptionsOnPurpose2.cs**.

2. In the Main() method, after the three variable declarations, enclose the next three statements in a try block as follows:

```
try
{
    Console.Write("Enter an integer >> ");
    answer = Convert.ToInt32(Console.ReadLine());
    result = answer / zero;
}
```

3. Following the try block (but before the statement that displays the answer), add a catch block that catches any thrown Exception and displays its Message property:

```
catch(Exception e)
{
    Console.WriteLine(e.Message);
}
```

4. Save the program and compile it. You should receive a compiler error that indicates that answer is an unassigned local variable. This error occurs at the last line of the program where answer is displayed. In the first version of this program, no such message appeared. However, now that the assignment to answer is within the try block, the compiler understands that an Exception might be thrown before a valid value is assigned to answer. To eliminate this problem, initialize answer at its declaration:

```
int answer = 0;
```

5. Compile and execute the program again. Figure 11-36 shows three executions. The values typed by the user are the same as in Figure 11-35. However, the results are different in several significant ways:

   - No error message window appears (as in Figure 11-34).

   - The error messages displayed are cleaner and "friendlier" than the automatically generated versions in Figure 11-35.

   - The program ends normally in each case, with the answer value displayed in a user-friendly manner.

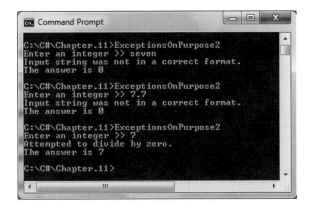

**Figure 11-36** Error messages generated by successive executions of ExceptionsOnPurpose2 program

# Catching Various Exception Types

When you want appropriate actions to occur for various Exceptions, you can provide multiple catch blocks.

**To provide multiple catch blocks for the ExceptionsOnPurpose program:**

1. Open the ExceptionsOnPurpose2.cs file if it is not still open. Change the class name to **ExceptionsOnPurpose3** and immediately save the file as **ExceptionsOnPurpose3.cs**.

2. Replace the existing generic `catch` block with two `catch` blocks. (The statement that displays the answer still follows these `catch` blocks.) The first catches any `FormatException` and displays a short message. The second catches a `DivideByZeroException` and displays a much longer message.

```
catch(FormatException e)
{
    Console.WriteLine("You did not enter an integer");
}
catch(DivideByZeroException e)
{
    Console.WriteLine("This is not your fault.");
    Console.WriteLine("You entered the integer correctly.");
    Console.WriteLine("The program divides by zero.");
}
```

3. Save the program and compile it. When you execute the program and enter an invalid integer, the first `catch` block executes. When you enter an integer so that the program can proceed to the statement that divides by 0, the second `catch` block executes. Figure 11-37 shows two typical executions of the program.

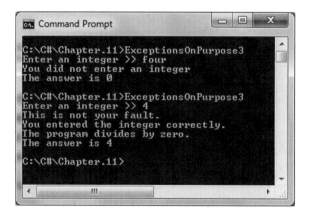

**Figure 11-37** Error messages generated by successive executions of `ExceptionsOnPurpose3` program

# Chapter Summary

- An exception is any error condition or unexpected behavior in an executing program. In C#, all exceptions are objects that are instances of the Exception class or one of its derived classes. Most exceptions you will use are derived from three classes: SystemException, ApplicationException, and their parent Exception. You can purposely generate a SystemException by forcing a program to contain an error. Although you are not required to handle Exceptions, you can use object-oriented techniques to provide elegant error-handling solutions.

- When you think an error will occur frequently, the most efficient approach is to handle the error in the traditional way, with if statements. If an error will occur infrequently, instantiating an Exception object when needed is more efficient. In object-oriented terminology, you "try" a procedure that may not complete correctly. A method that detects an error condition or Exception "throws" an Exception, and the block of code that processes the error "catches" the Exception. You must include at least one catch block or finally block immediately following a try block.

- Every Exception object contains a ToString() method and a Message property that contains useful information about the Exception.

- You can place as many statements as you need within a try block, and you can catch as many different Exceptions as you want. If you try more than one statement, only the first error-generating statement will throw an Exception. When multiple catch blocks are present, they are examined in sequence until a match is found for the Exception that occurred. When you list multiple catch blocks after a try block, you must be careful about their order, or some catch blocks might become unreachable.

- When you have actions to perform at the end of a try...catch sequence, you can use a finally block.

- When methods throw Exceptions, the methods do not have to catch them; instead, the program that calls a method that throws an Exception can catch it and determine what to do. For the best software design, you should create your classes to throw any Exceptions so that various application programs can catch them and handle them appropriately.

- If a method throws an Exception and does not catch it, then the Exception is thrown to the method that called the offending method. When you catch an Exception, you can display the value of the StackTrace property, which provides a list of methods in the call stack, allowing you to determine the location of the Exception.

- To create your own Exception that you can throw, you can extend the ApplicationException class or the Exception class. The current advice is to extend Exception.

- When you write a method that catches an Exception, your method does not have to handle the Exception. Instead, you might choose to rethrow the Exception to the method that called your method and let that method handle it.

## Key Terms

An **exception** is any error condition or unexpected behavior in an executing program.

**Exception handling** is the set of object-oriented techniques used to manage unexpected errors in an executing program.

**Fault-tolerant** applications are designed so that they continue to operate, possibly at a reduced level, when some part of the system fails.

**Robustness** represents the degree to which a system is resilient to stress, maintaining correct functioning even in the presence of errors.

The term **mission critical** refers to any process that is crucial to an organization.

A **try block** contains code that might create exceptions you want to handle.

A **catch block** can catch one type of Exception.

**Unreachable** blocks contain statements that can never execute under any circumstances because the program logic "can't get there."

**Dead code** is unreachable code.

A **finally block** can follow a try block; code within one executes whether the try block identifies any Exceptions or not.

The **call stack** is the memory location where the computer stores the list of locations to which the system must return after method calls.

**Propagating an exception** is the act of transmitting it unchanged through the call stack.

To **rethrow an Exception** is to throw a caught Exception instead of handling it.

# Review Questions

1. Any error condition or unexpected behavior in an executing program is known as an _____.

   a. exception

   b. anomaly

   c. exclusion

   d. omission

2. Which of the following is *not* treated as a C# `Exception`?

   a. Your program asks the user to input a number, but the user enters a character.

   b. You attempt to execute a C# program, but the C# compiler has not been installed.

   c. You attempt to access an array with a subscript that is too large.

   d. You calculate a value that is too large for the answer's variable type.

3. Most exceptions you will use derive from three classes: _____.

   a. `Object`, `ObjectException`, and `ObjectApplicationException`

   b. `Exception`, `SystemException`, and `ApplicationException`

   c. `FormatException`, `ApplicationException`, and `IOException`

   d. `SystemException`, `IOException`, and `FormatException`

4. `Exceptions` can be _____.

   a. generated automatically by C#

   b. created by a program

   c. both of these

   d. none of these

5. When a program creates an `Exception`, you _____ .

   a. must handle it

   b. can handle it

   c. must not handle it

   d. none of these; programs cannot create `Exceptions`

6. Without using object-oriented techniques, _____ .

   a. there are no error situations

   b. you cannot manage error situations

   c. you can manage error situations, but with great difficulty

   d. you can manage error situations

7. In object-oriented terminology, you _____ a procedure that may not complete correctly.

   a. circumvent

   b. attempt

   c. catch

   d. try

8. In object-oriented terminology, a method that detects an error condition _____ an `Exception`.

   a. throws

   b. catches

   c. tries

   d. unearths

9. When you write a block of code in which something can go wrong, and you want to throw an `Exception` if it does, you place the code in a _____ block.

   a. `catch`

   b. `blind`

   c. `system`

   d. `try`

10. A catch block executes when its try block _____.

   a. completes

   b. throws any Exception

   c. throws an Exception of an acceptable type

   d. completes without throwing anything

11. Which of the following catch blocks will catch any Exception?

   a. `catch(Any e) {}`

   b. `catch(Exception e) {}`

   c. `catch(e) {}`

   d. All of the above will catch any Exception.

12. Which of the following is valid within a catch block with the header `catch(Exception error)`?

   a. `Console.WriteLine(error.ToString());`

   b. `Console.WriteLine(error.Message);`

   c. `return(error.ToString());`

   d. two of these

13. You can place _____ statement(s) within a try block.

   a. zero

   b. one

   c. two

   d. any number of

14. How many catch blocks might follow a try block within the same method?

   a. only one

   b. any number as long as it is greater than zero

   c. any number as long as it is greater than one

   d. any number, including zero or one

15. Consider the following `try` block. If x is 15, what is the value of a when this code completes?

```
try
{
    a = 99;
    if(x > 10)
        throw(new Exception());
    a = 0;
    ++a;
}
```

   a.  0

   b.  1

   c.  99

   d.  undefined

16. Consider the following `catch` blocks. The variable b has been initialized to 0. If a `DivideByZeroException` occurs in a `try` block just before this `catch` block, what is the value of b when this code completes?

```
catch(DivideByZeroException e)
{
    ++b;
}
catch(Exception e)
{
    ++b;
}
```

   a.  0

   b.  1

   c.  2

   d.  3

17. Consider the following `catch` blocks. The variable c has been initialized to 0. If an `IndexOutOfRangeException` occurs in a `try` block just before this `catch` block, what is the value of c when this code completes?

```
catch(IndexOutOfRangeException e)
{
    ++c;
}
catch(Exception e)
{
    ++c;
}
```

```
finally
{
    ++c;
}
```

a. 0

b. 1

c. 2

d. 3

18. If your program throws an `IndexOutOfRangeException` and the only available `catch` block catches an `Exception`, _____.

    a. an `IndexOutOfRangeException` catch block is generated automatically

    b. the `Exception` catch block executes

    c. the `Exception` catch block is bypassed

    d. the `IndexOutOfRangeException` is thrown to the operating system

19. When you design your own classes that might cause `Exceptions`, and other classes will use your classes as clients, you should usually create your methods to _____.

    a. neither throw nor handle `Exceptions`

    b. throw `Exceptions` but not handle them

    c. handle `Exceptions` but not throw them

    d. both throw and handle `Exceptions`

20. When you create an `Exception` of your own, you should extend the _____ class.

    a. `SystemException`

    b. `PersonalException`

    c. `OverloadedException`

    d. `Exception`

# Exercises

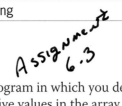

Assignment 6.3

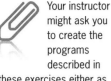

Your instructor might ask you to create the programs described in these exercises either as console-based or GUI applications.

1. Write a program in which you declare an array of five integers and store five values in the array. Write a `try` block in which you place a loop that attempts to access each element of the array, incrementing a subscript from 0 to 10. Create a `catch` block that catches the eventual `IndexOutOfRangeException`; within the block, display "Now you've gone too far." on the screen. Save the file as **GoTooFar.cs**.

2. a. The `Convert.ToInt32()` method requires a string argument that can be converted to an `int`. Write a program in which you prompt the user for a stock number and quantity ordered. Accept the strings the user enters and convert them to integers. Catch the `Exception` that is thrown when the user enters noninteger data for either field. Within the `catch` block, display an error message and set both the stock number and quantity values to 0. Save the file as **PlacingOrder.cs**.

   b. Modify the `PlacingOrder` application so that data entry is performed in a `DataEntry()` function that accepts a string parameter to use as a prompt. The function prompts the user, reads a value from the keyboard, attempts to convert it to an integer, and then returns the integer. If an `Exception` is encountered, the function should return 0. Save the file as **PlacingOrder2.cs**.

3. `ArgumentException` is an existing class that derives from `Exception`; you use it when one or more of a method's arguments do not fall within an expected range. Create a class named `CarInsurance` containing variables that can hold a driver's age and state of residence. Within the class, create a method that accepts the two input values and calculates a premium. The premium base price is $100 for residents of Illinois (IL) and $50 for residents of Wisconsin (WI). Additionally, each driver pays $3 times the value of 100 minus his or her age. If the driver is younger than 16, older than 80, or not a resident of Illinois or Wisconsin, throw an `ArgumentException` from the method. In the `Main()` method of the `CarInsurance` class, try code that prompts the user for each value. If the user does not enter a numeric value for age, catch a `FormatException` and display an error message. Call the method that calculates the premium and catch the potential `ArgumentException` object. Save the file as **CarInsurance.cs**.

4. The Math class contains a static method named Sqrt() that accepts a double and returns the parameter's square root. Write a program that declares two doubles: number and sqrt. Accept an input value for number from the user. Handle the FormatException that is thrown if the input value cannot be converted to a double by displaying the message "The input should be a number." and setting the sqrt variable to 0. If no FormatException is thrown, test the input number's value. If it is negative, throw a new ApplicationException to which you pass the message "Number can't be negative." and again set sqrt to 0. If number is not negative, pass it to the Math.Sqrt() method, returning the square root to the sqrt variable. As the last program statement, display the value of sqrt. Save the file as **FindSquareRoot.cs**.

5. a. Create an Employee class with two fields: iDNum and hourlyWage. The Employee constructor requires values for both fields. Upon construction, throw an ArgumentException if the hourlyWage is less than 6.00 or more than 50.00. Write a program that establishes, one at a time, at least three Employees with hourlyWages that are above, below, and within the allowed range. Immediately after each instantiation attempt, handle any thrown Exceptions by displaying an error message. Save the file as **EmployeeExceptionDemo.cs**.

   b. Using the Employee class created in Exercise 5a, write an application that creates an array of five Employees. Prompt the user for values for each field for each Employee. If the user enters improper or invalid data, handle any exceptions that are thrown by setting the Employee's ID number to 999 and the Employee's pay rate to the $6.00 minimum. At the end of the program, display all the entered, and possibly corrected, records. Save the file as **EmployeeExceptionDemo2.cs**.

6. a. The Peterman Publishing Company has decided that no published book should cost more than 10 cents per page. Create a BookException class whose constructor requires three arguments: a string Book title, a double price, and an int number of pages. Create an error message that is passed to the Exception class constructor for the Message property when a Book does not meet the price-to-pages ratio. For example, an error message might be:

   ```
   For Goodnight Moon, ratio is invalid.
   ...price is $12.99 for 25 pages.
   ```

Create a Book class that contains fields for title, author, price, and number of pages. Include properties for each field. Throw a BookException if a client program tries to construct a Book object for which the price is more than 10 cents per page. Create a program that creates at least four Book objects—some where the ratio is acceptable and others where it is not. Catch any thrown exceptions and display the BookException Message. Save the file as **BookExceptionDemo.cs**.

b. Using the Book class created in Exercise 6a, write an application that creates an array of five Books. Prompt the user for values for each Book. To handle any exceptions that are thrown because of improper or invalid data entered by the user, set the Book's price to the maximum 10 cents per page. At the end of the program, display all the entered, and possibly corrected, records. Save the file as **BookExceptionDemo2.cs**.

7. Create a GUI application that prompts a user to enter an integer. When the user clicks a button, try to convert the user's entry to an integer and display a message indicating whether the user was successful. Save the project as **ExceptionHandlingDemoGUI**.

8. In Chapter 6, you created a game named GuessAWord in which a player guesses letters to try to replicate a hidden word. Now modify the program to throw and catch an exception when the user enters a guess that is not a letter of the alphabet. Create a NonLetterException class that descends from Exception. The Message string for your new class should indicate the nonletter character that caused the Exception's creation. When a NonLetterException is thrown and caught, the message should be displayed. Save the file as **GuessAWordWithExceptionHandling.cs**.

*Debugging Exercises*

Each of the following files in the Chapter.11 folder of your download-able student files has syntax and/or logical errors. In each case, determine the problem and fix the program. After you correct the errors, save each file using the same filename preceded with *Fixed*. For example, DebugEleven1.cs will become FixedDebugEleven1.cs.

    a.  DebugEleven1.cs

    b.  DebugEleven2.cs

    c.  DebugEleven3.cs

    d.  DebugEleven4.cs

 *Up For Discussion*

1.    What do the terms *syntactic sugar* and *syntactic salt* mean? From your knowledge of the C# programming language, list as many syntactic sugar and salt features as you can.

2.    Have you ever been victimized by a computer error? For example, were you ever incorrectly denied credit, billed for something you did not purchase, or assigned an incorrect grade in a course? How did you resolve the problem? On the Web, find the most outrageous story you can involving a computer error.

3.    Search the Web for information about educational video games in which historical simulations are presented in an effort to teach students about history. For example, Civilization IV is a game in which players control a society as it progresses through time. Do you believe such games are useful to history students? Does the knowledge gained warrant the hours it takes to master the games? Do the makers of the games have any obligations to present history factually? Do they have a right to penalize players who choose options of which the game writers disapprove (such as using nuclear weapons or allowing slavery)? Do game creators have the right to create characters who possess negative stereotypical traits—for example, a person of a specific nationality portrayed as being stupid, weak, or evil? Would you like to take a history course that uses such games?

# Using Controls

In this chapter you will:

◎ Learn about Controls

◎ Examine the IDE's automatically generated code

◎ Set a Control's Font

◎ Create a Form that contains LinkLabels

◎ Add color to a Form

◎ Add CheckBox and RadioButton objects to a Form

◎ Add a PictureBox to a Form

◎ Add ListBox, ComboBox, and CheckedListBox items to a Form

◎ Add a MonthCalendar and DateTimePicker to a Form

◎ Work with a Form's layout

◎ Add a MenuStrip to a Form

◎ Learn to use other controls

Throughout this book, you have created both console and GUI applications. Your GUI applications have used only a few Controls—Forms, Labels, TextBoxes, and Buttons.

When using programs or visiting Internet sites, you have encountered and used many other interactive **widgets**—elements of graphical interfaces that allow you to interact with programs—such as scroll bars, check boxes, and radio buttons. C# has many classes that represent these GUI objects, and the Visual Studio IDE makes it easy to add them to your programs. In this chapter, you will learn to incorporate some of the most common and useful widgets into your programs. Additionally, you will see how these components work in general so you can use other widgets that are not covered in this book or that become available to programmers in future releases of C#.

If you have been creating mostly console applications while learning the concepts in this book, you might want to review the chapter *Using GUI Objects and The Visual Studio IDE*. That chapter provides instruction in the basic procedures used to create GUI applications, and it also describes Visual Studio Help.

541

## Understanding Controls

When you design a Form, you can place Buttons and other controls on the Form surface. The **Control** class provides the definitions for these GUI objects. Control objects such as Forms and Buttons, like all other objects in C#, ultimately derive from the Object class. Figure 12-1 shows where the Control class fits into the inheritance hierarchy.

```
System.Object
    System.MarshalByRefObject
        System.ComponentModel.Component
            System.Windows.Forms.Control
                26 Derived classes
```

**Figure 12-1**  Control class inheritance hierarchy

GUI components are referred to as *widgets*, which some sources claim is a combination of the terms *window* and *gadgets*. Originally, "widget" comes from the 1924 play "Beggar on Horseback," by George Kaufman and Marc Connelly. In the play, a young composer gets engaged to the daughter of a rich businessman, and foresees spending his life doing pointless work in a bureaucratic big business that manufactures widgets, which represent a useless item whose purpose is never explained.

Figure 12-1 shows that all Controls are Objects, of course. They are also all MarshalByRefObjects. (A MarshalByRefObject is one you can instantiate on a remote computer so that you can manipulate a reference to the object rather than a local copy of the object.) Controls also descend from Component. (The **Component** class provides containment and cleanup for other objects—inheriting from Component allows Controls to be contained in objects such as Forms, and provides for disposal of Controls when they are destroyed. The Control class adds visual representation to Components.) The Control class implements very basic functionality required by classes that appear to the user—in other words, the GUI objects the user sees on the screen. This class handles user input through the keyboard and pointing devices as well as message routing and security. It defines the bounds of a Control by determining its position and size.

Table 12-1 shows the 26 direct descendents of Control and some commonly used descendents of those classes. It does not show all the descendents that exist; rather, it shows only the descendents covered previously or in this chapter. For example, the ButtonBase class is the parent of Button, a class you have used throughout this book. In this chapter, you will use two other ButtonBase children—CheckBox and RadioButton. This chapter cannot cover every Control that has been invented; however, after you learn to use some Controls, you will find that others work in much the same way. You also can read more about them in the Visual Studio Help documentation.

| Class | Commonly used descendents |
| --- | --- |
| Microsoft.WindowsCE.Forms.DocumentList | |
| System.Windows.Forms.AxHost | |
| System.Windows.Forms.ButtonBase | Button, CheckBox, RadioButton |
| System.Windows.Forms.DataGrid | |
| System.Windows.Forms.DataGridView | |
| System.Windows.Forms.DateTimePicker | |
| System.Windows.Forms.GroupBox | |
| System.Windows.Forms.Integration.ElementHost | |
| System.Windows.Forms.Label | LinkLabel |
| System.Windows.Forms.ListControl | ListBox, ComboBox, CheckedListBox |
| System.Windows.Forms.ListView | |
| System.Windows.Forms.MdiClient | |
| System.Windows.Forms.MonthCalendar | |
| System.Windows.Forms.PictureBox | |
| System.Windows.Forms.PrintPreviewControl | |
| System.Windows.Forms.ProgressBar | |
| System.Windows.Forms.ScrollableControl | |
| System.Windows.Forms.ScrollBar | |
| System.Windows.Forms.Splitter | |
| System.Windows.Forms.StatusBar | |
| System.Windows.Forms.TabControl | |
| System.Windows.Forms.TextBoxBase | TextBox |
| System.Windows.Forms.ToolBar | |
| System.Windows.Forms.TrackBar | |
| System.Windows.Forms.TreeView | |
| System.Windows.Forms.WebBrowserBase | |

**Table 12-1**  Classes derived from System.Windows.Forms.Control

Because Controls are all relatives, they share many of the same attributes. Each Control has more than 80 public properties and 20 protected properties. For example, each Control has a Font and a ForeColor that dictate how its text is displayed, and each Control has a Width and Height. Table 12-2 shows just some of the public properties associated with Controls in general; reading through them will give you an idea of the Control attributes that you can change.

| Property | Description |
| --- | --- |
| AllowDrop | Gets or sets a value indicating whether the control can accept data that the user drags onto it |
| Anchor | Gets or sets the edges of the container to which a control is bound and determines how a control is resized with its parent |
| BackColor | Gets or sets the background color for the control |
| BackgroundImage | Gets or sets the background image displayed in the control |
| Bottom | Gets the distance, in pixels, between the bottom edge of the control and the top edge of its container's client area |
| Bounds | Gets or sets the size and location of the control, including its nonclient elements, in pixels, relative to the parent control |
| CanFocus | Gets a value indicating whether the control can receive focus |
| CanSelect | Gets a value indicating whether the control can be selected |
| Capture | Gets or sets a value indicating whether the control has captured the mouse |
| Container | Gets the IContainer that contains the Component (inherited from Component) |
| ContainsFocus | Gets a value indicating whether the control or one of its child controls currently has the input focus |
| Cursor | Gets or sets the cursor that is displayed when the mouse pointer is over the control |
| Disposing | Gets a value indicating whether the base Control class is in the process of disposing |
| Dock | Gets or sets which control borders are docked to their parent control and determines how a control is resized with its parent |
| Enabled | Gets or sets a value indicating whether the control can respond to user interaction |
| Focused | Gets a value indicating whether the control has input focus |
| Font | Gets or sets the font of the text displayed by the control |
| ForeColor | Gets or sets the foreground color of the control |

**Table 12-2**  Selected public Control properties *(continues)*

*(continued)*

| Property | Description |
|----------|-------------|
| HasChildren | Gets a value indicating whether the control contains one or more child controls |
| Height | Gets or sets the height of the control |
| IsDisposed | Gets a value indicating whether the control has been disposed of |
| Left | Gets or sets the distance, in pixels, between the left edge of the control and the left edge of its container's client area |
| Location | Gets or sets the coordinates of the upper-left corner of the control relative to the upper-left corner of its container |
| Margin | Gets or sets the space between controls |
| ModifierKeys | Gets a value indicating which of the modifier keys (Shift, Ctrl, and Alt) is in a pressed state |
| MouseButtons | Gets a value indicating which of the mouse buttons is in a pressed state |
| MousePosition | Gets the position of the mouse cursor in screen coordinates |
| Name | Gets or sets the name of the control |
| Parent | Gets or sets the parent container of the control |
| Right | Gets the distance, in pixels, between the right edge of the control and the left edge of its container's client area |
| Size | Gets or sets the height and width of the control |
| TabIndex | Gets or sets the tab order of the control within its container |
| TabStop | Gets or sets a value indicating whether the user can give focus to the control using the Tab key |
| Text | Gets or sets the text associated with this control |
| Top | Gets or sets the distance, in pixels, between the top edge of the control and the top edge of its container's client area |
| TopLevelControl | Gets the parent control that is not parented by another Windows Forms control; typically, this is the outermost Form in which the control is contained |
| Visible | Gets or sets a value indicating whether the control and all its parent controls are displayed |
| Width | Gets or sets the width of the control |

**Table 12-2**   Selected public Control properties

The description of each property in Table 12-2 indicates whether the property is read-only; such properties only get values and do not set them.

You have altered Label, TextBox, and Button properties such as Text and Visible using the Properties window in Visual Studio. All the other Controls you learn about in this chapter can be manipulated in the same way.

A project can contain multiple Forms, each with its own Controls. You will learn how to add more Forms to a project in the You Do It exercises later in this chapter.

---

## TWO TRUTHS & A LIE

### Understanding Controls

1. The Control class implements basic functionality required by GUI objects that a user sees on the screen.

2. Most Controls have Font and ForeColor properties.

3. Every Control has Width and Height properties.

The false statement is #2. Every Control has Font and ForeColor properties.

---

# Examining the IDE's Automatically Generated Code

Figure 12-2 shows a Form created in the IDE. The following actions have been performed:

1. A new Windows Forms project has been started and given the name FormWithALabelAndAButton.

2. A Label has been dragged onto Form1. Using the Properties window in the IDE, the Label's Text property has been changed to "Click the button", and its Font has been changed to Georgia, Bold, and size 16.

3. A Button has been dragged onto Form1. The Button's Text property has been changed to "OK" and its Name has been changed to okButton.

**Figure 12-2** Form generated by FormWithALabelAndAButton program

Within the Form1.Designer.cs file in Visual Studio, two lines of code are generated as follows:

```
private System.Windows.Forms.Label label1;
private System.Windows.Forms.Button okButton;
```

These lines appear under a gray box that contains *Windows Form Designer generated code*, and they declare the `Label` and `Button` objects using the default identifier `label1` and the programmer-created identifier `okButton`.

You can expand the code generated by the Form Designer by clicking the + in the **method node** to the left of the gray box that contains *Windows Form Designer generated code*, or you can double-click the gray box. As partially shown in Figure 12-3, more than 30 statements are generated.

In Figure 12-3, every instance of `this` means "this Form."

**Figure 12-3** Some of the code in the `InitializeComponent()` method for FormWithALabelAndAButton

So much code is automatically generated by Visual Studio that it can be hard to find what you want. To locate a line of code, click Edit on the main menu in the IDE, point to Find and Replace, point to Quick Find, type a key phrase to search for, and click the Find Next button. (Instead of using the menu, you also can type Ctrl+F to get the Find dialog box.)

Do not be intimidated by the amount of code automatically generated by the IDE. Based on what you have learned so far in this book, you can easily make sense of most of it.

- After the `InitializeComponent()` method header and opening brace, the next two statements call the constructor for each object the programmer dragged onto the `Form`:

```
this.label1 = new System.Windows.Forms.Label();
this.okButton = new System.Windows.Forms.Button();
```

- The next statement is a method call as follows:

```
this.SuspendLayout();
```

  `SuspendLayout()` is a method that prevents conflicts when you are placing `Control`s on a form. Its counterparts are `ResumeLayout()` and `PerformLayout()`, which appear at the bottom of the method. If you remove these method calls from small applications, you will not notice the difference. However, in large applications, suspending the layout logic while you adjust the appearance of components improves performance.

- Comments that start with forward slashes serve to separate the `label1` code from other code in the method. Following the `label1` comment lines, seven statements set properties of the `Label` as follows:

```
this.label1.AutoSize = true;
this.label1.Font = new System.Drawing.Font("Georgia",
    15.75F, System.Drawing.FontStyle.Bold,
    System.Drawing.GraphicsUnit.Point, ((byte)(0)));
this.label1.Location = new System.Drawing.Point(33, 41);
this.label1.Name = "label1";
this.label1.Size = new System.Drawing.Size(182, 25);
this.label1.TabIndex = 0;
this.label1.Text = "Click the button";
```

  You can see that the `Font`, `Location`, `Name`, `Size`, and `Text` have been assigned values based on the programmer's choices in the IDE. The `TabIndex` for `label1` is 0 by default; `TabIndex` values determine the order in which `Control`s receive focus when the user presses the Tab key. This property is typically more useful for selectable items like `Button`s.

- Although not visible in Figure 12-3, the next set of statements defines the properties of the `Button` on the `Form`. Notice that the

TabIndex for the Button is set to 1 because it was dragged onto the Form after the Label. Additional Controls would receive consecutive TabIndex values.

```
this.okButton.Location = new System.Drawing.Point(101, 94);
this.okButton.Name = "okButton";
this.okButton.Size = new System.Drawing.Size(50, 23);
this.okButton.TabIndex = 1;
this.okButton.Text = "OK";
this.okButton.UseVisualStyleBackColor = true;
```

- The InitializeComponent() method ends with statements that set the properties of the Form, such as its drawing size and text, and that add the Label and Button to the Form:

```
// Form1
//
this.AutoScaleDimensions = new System.Drawing.SizeF(6F, 13F);
this.AutoScaleMode = System.Windows.Forms.AutoScaleMode.Font;
this.ClientSize = new System.Drawing.Size(284, 262);
this.Controls.Add(this.okButton);
this.Controls.Add(this.label1);
this.Name = "Form1";
this.Text = "Form1";
this.ResumeLayout(false);
this.PerformLayout();
```

Although the property settings for the Label and Button include identifiers for the Controls (for example, this.label1.Name or this.okButton.Text), the property settings for the Form itself use only the reference this. That is because the statements are part of the Form1 class.

In this chapter, you will learn about several additional Controls. When designing a Form, you usually will use the drag-and-drop design features in the IDE instead of typing code statements. However, this chapter also teaches you about the code behind these actions so you can troubleshoot problems in projects and write usable statements when necessary.

Watch the video *Examining the IDE Code.*

---

## TWO TRUTHS & A LIE

### Examining the IDE's Automatically Generated Code

1. By using the Visual Studio Designer, you save time and eliminate many chances for error.

2. When you use the Visual Studio IDE to drag a Label onto a Form, no constructor call is needed for the Label.

3. You can use the Visual Studio IDE to set properties for a Label such as Font, Location, Size, and Text.

The false statement is #2. When you use the Visual Studio IDE to drag a Label onto a Form, you do not have to write a constructor call, but one is generated for you.

# Setting a Control's Font

You use the **Font** class to change the appearance of printed text on
your Forms. When designing a Label, Button, or other Control on a
Form, it is easiest to select a Font from the Properties list. After you
place a Control on a Form in the IDE, you can select the ellipsis (three
dots) that follows the current Font property name in the Properties
list. (See Figure 12-4.) This selection displays a Font window in
which you can choose a Font name, size, style, and other effects.
(See Figure 12-5.)

**Figure 12-4**   Clicking the ellipsis following the Font property

**Figure 12-5**   The Font window

However, if you wanted to change a Font later in a program—for
example, after a user clicks a button—you might want to create your
own instance of the Font class. As another example, suppose you
want to create multiple controls that use the same Font. In that case,
it makes sense to declare a named instance of the Font class. For
example, you can declare the following Font:

```
System.Drawing.Font bigFont = new
    System.Drawing.Font("Courier New", 16.5f);
```

In Chapter 2, you learned to use an *f* following a floating-point constant to indicate the float type. Recall that a numeric constant with digits to the right of the decimal point is a **double** by default.

This version of the Font constructor requires two arguments—a string and a float. The string you pass to the Font constructor is the name of the font. If you use a font name that does not exist in your system, the font defaults to Microsoft Sans Serif. The second value is a float that represents the font size. Notice that you must use an *F* (or an *f*) following the Font size value constant when it contains a decimal point to ensure that the constant will be recognized as a float and not a double. (If you use an int as the font size, you do not need the *f* because the int will automatically be cast to a float.) An alternative would be to instantiate a float constant or variable and use its name as an argument to the Font constructor.

After a Font object named bigFont is instantiated, you can code statements similar to the following:

```
this.label1.Font = bigFont;
this.okButton.Font = bigFont;
```

If you want to change the properties of several objects at once in the IDE, you can drag your mouse around them to create a temporary group, and then change the property for all of them with one entry in the Properties list.

The Font class includes a number of overloaded constructors.

You also can create a Font using three arguments, adding a FontStyle, as in the following example:

```
Font aFancyFont = new Font("Arial", 24, FontStyle.Italic);
```

Table 12-3 lists the available FontStyles. You can combine multiple styles using the pipe (|), which is also called the **logical OR operator**. For example, the following code creates a Font that is bold and underlined:

```
Font boldAndUnderlined = new Font("Helvetica",
    10, FontStyle.Bold | FontStyle.Underline);
```

| Member Name | Description |
| --- | --- |
| Bold | Bold text |
| Italic | Italic text |
| Regular | Normal text |
| Strikeout | Text with a line through the middle |
| Underline | Underlined text |

**Table 12-3** FontStyle enumeration

Instead of instantiating a named Font object, you can create and assign an anonymous Font in one step. In other words, you do not provide an identifier for the Font, as in this example:

```
this.label1.Font = new
    System.Drawing.Font("Courier New", 12.5F);
```

 If you do not provide an identifier for a Font, you cannot reuse it. You will have to create it again to use it with additional Controls.

---

## TWO TRUTHS & A LIE

### Setting a Control's Font

1. You use the Font class to change the appearance of printed text on Controls in your Forms.

2. When designing a Control on a Form, you must select a Font from the Properties list in the IDE.

3. The Font class includes several overloaded constructors.

The false statement is #2. When designing a Label or other Control on a Form, it is easiest to select a Font from the Properties list, but you also can create your own instance of the Font class.

---

## Using a LinkLabel

A **LinkLabel** is similar to a Label; it is a child of Label. Therefore, you can use it like a Label, but it provides the additional capability to link the user to other sources, such as Web pages or files. Table 12-4 summarizes the properties and lists the default event method for a LinkLabel. The **default event** for a Control is:

- The method whose shell is automatically created when you double-click the Control while designing a project in the IDE

- The method that you are most likely to alter when you use the Control

- The event that users most likely expect to generate when they encounter the Control in a working application

With many Controls, including a LinkLabel, a mouse click by the user triggers the default event. When designing a program, you can double-click a Control in the IDE to generate a method shell, and then write any necessary statements within the shell.

| Property or Method | Description |
|---|---|
| ActiveLinkColor | The color of the link when it is clicked |
| LinkColor | The original color of links before they have been visited; usually blue by default |
| LinkVisited | If true, the link's color is changed to the VisitedLinkColor |
| VisitedLinkColor | The color of a link after it has been visited; usually purple by default |
| LinkClicked() | Default event that is generated when the link is clicked by the user |

**Table 12-4** Commonly used LinkLabel properties and default event

 You can create a program so that a user generates an event by clicking many types of objects. For example, for a Label named label1, you could write statements in a label1_Click() method. However, users do not usually expect to click Labels; they do expect to click LinkLabels.

 The default event for many Controls, such as Buttons and LinkLabels, occurs when the user clicks the Control. However, the default event for a Form is the Load() method. In other words, if you double-click a Form in the IDE, you generate this method. In it, you can place statements that execute as soon as a Form is loaded.

When you create a LinkLabel, it appears as underlined text. The text is blue by default, but you can change the color in the LinkLabel Properties list in the IDE. When you pass the mouse pointer over a LinkLabel, the pointer changes to a hand; you have seen similar behavior while using hyperlinks in Web pages. When a user clicks a LinkLabel, it generates a click event, just as clicking a Button does. When a click event is fired from a LinkLabel, a LinkClicked() method is executed, similar to how clicking a Button can execute a Click() method.

 When you double-click a Label, the automatically generated method name ends with Click(), but when you double-click a LinkLabel, the corresponding method ends with Clicked().

Figure 12-6 shows a Form onto which two LinkLabels have been dragged from the Toolbox in the IDE. The Text properties of the LinkLabels have been changed to "Course Technology Website" and "Read Our Policy".

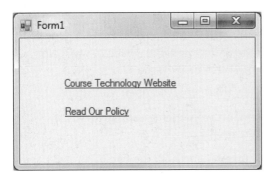

**Figure 12-6** A Form with two LinkLabels

If you double-click a LinkLabel in the IDE, a method shell is created for you in the format xxx_LinkClicked(), where xxx is the value of the Name property assigned to the LinkLabel. (This corresponds to what happens when you double-click a Button in the IDE.) For example, Figure 12-7 shows the two generated methods for the Form in Figure 12-6 when the default LinkLabel identifiers linkLabel1 and linkLabel2 are used. In Figure 12-7, all the code was automatically generated except for the two shaded lines. The programmer added those lines to indicate which actions should occur when a user clicks the corresponding LinkLabel in a running application.

```csharp
public partial class Form1 : Form
{
    public Form1()
    {
        InitializeComponent();
    }

    private void linkLabel1_LinkClicked(object sender,
        LinkLabelLinkClickedEventArgs e)
    {
        System.Diagnostics.Process.Start("IExplore",
            "http://www.course.com");
    }

    private void linkLabel2_LinkClicked(object sender,
        LinkLabelLinkClickedEventArgs e)
    {
        System.Diagnostics.Process.Start
            (@"C:\C#\Chapter.12\Policy.txt");
    }
}
```

**Figure 12-7** Two LinkClicked() methods

In each of the LinkClicked() methods in Figure 12-7, the programmer has added a call to System.Diagnostics.Process.Start (). This method allows you to run other programs within an application. The Start() method has two overloaded versions:

- When you use one string argument, you open the named file.

- When you use two arguments, you open an application and provide its needed arguments.

In the linkLabel1_LinkClicked() method, the two arguments open Internet Explorer ("IExplore") and pass it the address of the Course Technology Web site. If an Internet connection is active, control transfers to the Web site.

In the linkLabel2_LinkClicked() method, only one argument is provided. It opens a file stored on the local disk. The correct application opens based on the default application for the file. For example, Notepad is the default application for a file with a .txt extension. Alternatively, you could code the following, which explicitly names Notepad as the application:

```
System.Diagnostics.Process.Start("Notepad",
    @"C:\C#\Chapter.12\Policy.txt");
```

 In the linkLabel2_LinkClicked() method, an at sign (@) appears in front of the filename to be opened. This symbol indicates that all characters in the string should be interpreted literally. Therefore, the backslashes in the path are not interpreted as escape sequence characters.

The LinkVisited property can be set to true when you determine that a user has clicked a link, as shown in Figure 12-8. This setting indicates that the link should be displayed in a different color so the user can see the link has been visited. By default, the visited link color is purple, but you can change this setting in the Properties list for the LinkLabel.

```
private void linkLabel1_LinkClicked(object sender,
    LinkLabelLinkClickedEventArgs e)
{
    System.Diagnostics.Process.Start("IExplore",
        "http://www.course.com");
    linkLabel1.LinkVisited = true;
}
```

**Figure 12-8** Setting the LinkVisited property

## TWO TRUTHS & A LIE

### Using a LinkLabel

1. A `LinkLabel` is a child class of `Label` and it provides the additional capability to link the user to other sources.

2. The default event for a `Control` is the method whose shell is automatically created when you double-click the `Control` while designing a project in the IDE. Users most likely expect to generate this event when they encounter the `Control` in a working application.

3. When you create a `LinkLabel`, it appears as italicized underlined text, and when you pass the mouse pointer over a `LinkLabel`, the pointer changes to an hourglass.

The false statement is #3. When you create a `LinkLabel`, it appears as underlined text, and when you pass the mouse pointer over a `LinkLabel`, the pointer changes to a hand.

## Adding Color to a Form

The **Color** class contains a wide variety of predefined `Colors` that you can use with your `Controls` (see Table 12-5).

 C# also allows you to create custom colors. If no color in Table 12-5 suits your needs, search for "custom color" in the Visual Studio Help to obtain more information.

| | | | |
|---|---|---|---|
| AliceBlue | BurlyWood | DarkGray | DarkTurquoise |
| AntiqueWhite | CadetBlue | DarkGreen | DarkViolet |
| Aqua | Chartreuse | DarkKhaki | DeepPink |
| Aquamarine | Chocolate | DarkMagenta | DeepSkyBlue |
| Azure | Coral | DarkOliveGreen | DimGray |
| Beige | CornflowerBlue | DarkOrange | DodgerBlue |
| Bisque | Cornsilk | DarkOrchid | Firebrick |
| Black | Crimson | DarkRed | FloralWhite |
| BlanchedAlmond | Cyan | DarkSalmon | ForestGreen |
| Blue | DarkBlue | DarkSeaGreen | Fuchsia |
| BlueViolet | DarkCyan | DarkSlateBlue | Gainsboro |
| Brown | DarkGoldenrod | DarkSlateGray | GhostWhite |

**Table 12-5** Color properties *(continues)*

*(continued)*

| | | | |
|---|---|---|---|
| Gold | LightSkyBlue | OldLace | SeaShell |
| Goldenrod | LightSlateGray | Olive | Sienna |
| Gray | LightSteelBlue | OliveDrab | Silver |
| Green | LightYellow | Orange | SkyBlue |
| GreenYellow | Lime | OrangeRed | SlateBlue |
| Honeydew | LimeGreen | Orchid | SlateGray |
| HotPink | Linen | PaleGoldenrod | Snow |
| IndianRed | Magenta | PaleGreen | SpringGreen |
| Indigo | Maroon | PaleTurquoise | SteelBlue |
| Ivory | MediumAquamarine | PaleVioletRed | Tan |
| Khaki | MediumBlue | PapayaWhip | Teal |
| Lavender | MediumOrchid | PeachPuff | Thistle |
| LavenderBlush | MediumPurple | Peru | Tomato |
| LawnGreen | MediumSeaGreen | Pink | Transparent |
| LemonChiffon | MediumSlateBlue | Plum | Turquoise |
| LightBlue | MediumSpringGreen | PowderBlue | Violet |
| LightCoral | MediumTurquoise | Purple | Wheat |
| LightCyan | MediumVioletRed | Red | White |
| LightGoldenrodYellow | MidnightBlue | RosyBrown | WhiteSmoke |
| LightGray | MintCream | RoyalBlue | Yellow |
| LightGreen | MistyRose | SaddleBrown | YellowGreen |
| LightPink | Moccasin | Salmon | |
| LightSalmon | NavajoWhite | SandyBrown | |
| LightSeaGreen | Navy | SeaGreen | |

**Table 12-5**  Color properties

If you add using System. Drawing; at the top of your file, you can eliminate the references in the preceding lines and refer to the colors simply as Color.Blue and Color.Gold.

When you are designing a Form, you can choose colors from a list next to the BackColor and ForeColor properties in the IDE's Properties list. The statements created will be similar to the following:

```
this.label1.BackColor = System.Drawing.Color.Blue;
this.label1.ForeColor = System.Drawing.Color.Gold;
```

For professional-looking results when you prepare a resume or most other business documents, business executives recommend that you only use one or two fonts and colors, even though your word-processing program allows many such selections. The same is true when you design interactive GUI applications. Although many fonts and colors are available, you probably should stick with a few choices in a single project.

---

**TWO TRUTHS & A LIE**

### Adding Color to a Form

1. Because the choice of colors in C# is limited, you are required to create custom colors for many GUI applications.

2. When you are designing a Form, color choices appear in a list next to the BackColor and ForeColor properties in the IDE's Properties list.

3. The complete name of the color pink in C# is System.Drawing.Color.Pink.

The false statement is #1. The Color class contains a wide variety of predefined Colors that you can use with your controls.

---

# Using CheckBox and RadioButton Objects

**CheckBox** and RadioButton widgets allow users to select an option by clicking a small square or circle beside a label. Like Button, both classes descend from ButtonBase. When a Form contains multiple CheckBoxes, any number of them can be checked or unchecked at the same time. **RadioButtons** differ in that only one RadioButton in a group can be selected at a time—selecting any RadioButton automatically deselects the others.

Table 12-6 contains commonly used CheckBox and RadioButton properties and the default event for which a method shell is generated when you double-click a CheckBox or RadioButton in the IDE.

If you precede a letter with an ampersand (&) in the Text property value of a ButtonBase object, that letter acts as an access key. For example, if a Button's text is defined as &Press, then typing Alt+P has the same effect as clicking the Button. Access keys are also called hot keys.

You can place multiple groups of RadioButtons on a Form by using a GroupBox or Panel. You will learn more about GroupBoxes and Panels later in this chapter.

| Property or Method | Description |
|---|---|
| Checked | Indicates whether the CheckBox or RadioButton is checked |
| Text | The text displayed to the right of the CheckBox or RadioButton |
| CheckedChanged() | Default event that is generated when the Checked property changes |

**Table 12-6**  Commonly used CheckBox and RadioButton properties and default event

Figure 12-9 shows an example of a Form that contains several Labels, four CheckBox objects, and three RadioButton objects. It makes sense for the pizza topping choices to be displayed using CheckBoxes because a user might select multiple toppings. However, options for delivery, pick-up, and dining in the restaurant are mutually exclusive, so they are presented using RadioButton objects.

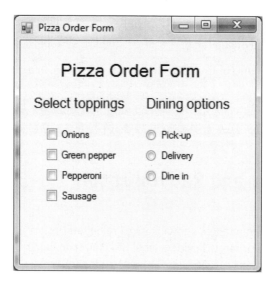

**Figure 12-9** A Form with Labels, CheckBoxes, and RadioButtons

When you add CheckBox and RadioButton objects to a form, they automatically are named using the same conventions you have seen with Buttons and Labels. That is, the first CheckBox without an explicitly assigned name is checkBox1 by default, the second is named checkBox2, and so on. Using the Properties list, you can assign more meaningful names such as sausageCheckBox and pepperoniCheckBox. Naming objects appropriately makes your code more understandable to others, and makes your programming job easier.

The Checked property is a read/write property. That is, you can assign a value to it as well as access its value.

Both CheckBox and RadioButton objects have a Checked property whose value is true or false. For example, if you create a CheckBox named sausageCheckBox and you want to add $1.00 to a pizzaPrice value when the user checks the box, you can write the following:

```
if(sausageCheckBox.Checked)
    pizzaPrice = pizzaPrice + 1.00;
```

The default method that executes when a user clicks either a CheckBox or RadioButton is xxx_CheckedChanged(), where xxx represents the name of the invoking object. For example, suppose the total price of a pizza should be altered based on a user's CheckBox selections. In this example, the base price for a pizza is $12.00, and $1.25 is added for each selected topping. You can declare constants for the BASE_PRICE and TOPPING_PRICE of a pizza and declare a variable that is initialized to the pizza base price as follows:

```
private const double BASE_PRICE = 12.00;
private const double TOPPING_PRICE = 1.25;
private double price = BASE_PRICE;
```

Figure 12-10 shows some of the code you would add to the Form.cs file for the application. The sausageCheckBox_CheckedChanged() method changes the pizza price. The shaded statements in the method were written by a programmer; the unshaded statements were generated by the IDE. If a change occurs because the sausageCheckBox was checked, then the TOPPING_PRICE is added to the price. If the change to the checkBox was to uncheck it, the TOPPING_PRICE is subtracted from the price. Either way, the Text property of a Label named outputLabel is changed to reflect the new price. Figure 12-11 shows the Form after the user has checked a box and then unchecked it.

```
private void sausageCheckBox_CheckedChanged(object sender, EventArgs e)
{
    if (sausageCheckBox.Checked)
        price += TOPPING_PRICE;
    else
        price -= TOPPING_PRICE;
    outputLabel.Text = "Total is " + price.ToString("C");
}
```

**Figure 12-10** The sausageCheckBox_CheckedChanged() method

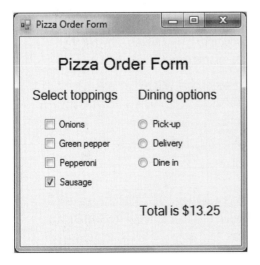 

**Figure 12-11** Typical execution of PizzaOrder program after code is added for CheckBoxes

The entire pizza-order application can be found in the downloadable student files.

In a similar fashion, you can add appropriate code for RadioButton objects. For example, assume that a $2.00 delivery charge is in effect, but there is no extra charge for customers who pick up a pizza or dine in. The code for deliverRadioButton_CheckedChanged() appears in Figure 12-12. When the user selects the deliverRadioButton, $2.00 is added to the total. When the user selects either of the other RadioButtons, the deliverRadioButton becomes unchecked and the $2.00 charge is removed from the total.

```
private void deliverRadioButton_CheckedChanged(object sender, EventArgs e)
{
    const double DELIVERY_CHARGE = 2.00;
    if (deliverRadioButton.Checked)
        price += DELIVERY_CHARGE;
    else
        price -= DELIVERY_CHARGE;
    outputLabel.Text = "Total is " + price.ToString("C");
}
```

**Figure 12-12** The deliverRadioButton_CheckedChanged() method

Watch the video CheckBoxes and RadioButtons.

When an application starts, sometimes you want a specific CheckBox or RadioButton to be selected by default. If so, you can set the Control's Checked property to true in the Properties list in the IDE.

## TWO TRUTHS & A LIE

### Using CheckBox and RadioButton Objects

1. CheckBox objects are GUI widgets that the user can click to select or deselect an option; when a Form contains multiple CheckBoxes, any number of them can be checked or unchecked at the same time.

2. RadioButtons are similar to CheckBoxes, except that when they are placed on a Form, only one RadioButton can be selected at a time—selecting any RadioButton automatically deselects the others.

3. The default event for a CheckBox is CheckBoxChanged(), and the default event for a RadioButton is RadioButtonChanged().

The false statement is #3. The default event for both CheckBox and RadioButton objects is CheckedChanged().

# Adding a PictureBox to a Form

A **PictureBox** is a Control in which you can display graphics from a bitmap, icon, JPEG, GIF, or other image file type. Just as with a Button or a Label, you can easily drag a PictureBox Control onto a Form in the Visual Studio IDE. Table 12-7 shows the common properties and default event for a PictureBox.

| Property or Method | Description |
|---|---|
| Image | Sets the image that appears in the PictureBox |
| SizeMode | Controls the size and position of the image in the PictureBox; values are Normal, StretchImage (which resizes the image to fit the PictureBox), AutoSize (which resizes the PictureBox to fit the image), and CenterImage (which centers the image in the PictureBox) |
| Click() | Default event that is generated when the user clicks the PictureBox |

**Table 12-7**   Commonly used PictureBox properties and default event

Figure 12-13 shows a new project in the IDE. The following tasks have been completed:

- A project was started.

- The Form Text property was changed to "Save Money".

- The Form BackColor property was changed to White.

- A Label was dragged onto the Form, and its Text and Font were changed.

- A PictureBox was dragged onto the Form.

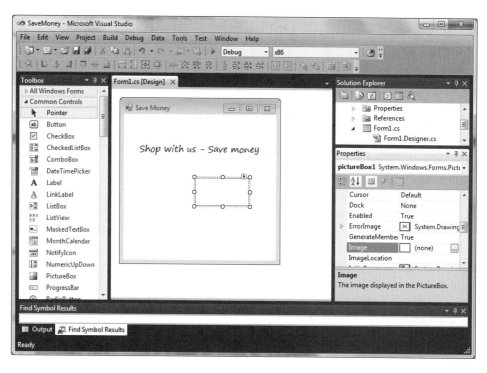

**Figure 12-13**    The IDE with a `Form` that contains a `PictureBox`

In Figure 12-13, in the Properties list at the right of the screen, the `Image` property is set to *none*. If you click the button with the ellipsis, a Select Resource window appears, as shown on the left in Figure 12-14. When you click the Import button, you can browse for stored images. When you select one, you see a preview in the Select Resource window, as shown on the right in Figure 12-14.

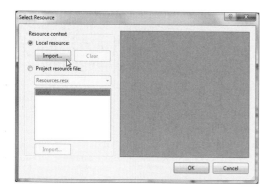 

**Figure 12-14**    Select Resource window before and after image is selected

562

After you click OK, the image appears in the PictureBox, as in Figure 12-15. (You can resize the PictureBox so the image displays clearly.)

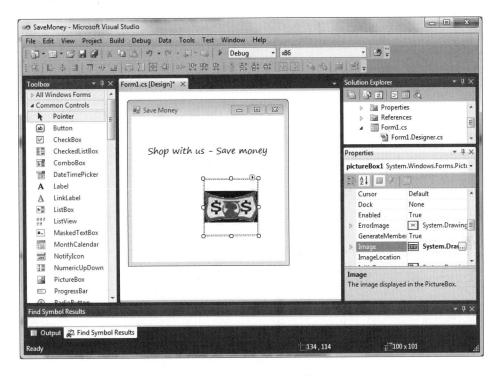

**Figure 12-15** The SaveMoney project with an inserted image

If you examine the generated code, you can find the statements that instantiate a PictureBox (named pictureBox1 by default) and statements that set its properties, such as Size and Location.

## TWO TRUTHS & A LIE

### Adding a PictureBox to a Form

1. A PictureBox is a Control in which you can display graphics from a bitmap, icon, JPEG, GIF, or other image file type.

2. The default event for a PictureBox is LoadImage().

3. The Image property of a PictureBox holds the name of a file where a picture is stored.

The false statement is #2. The default event for a PictureBox is Click().

# Adding ListBox, CheckedListBox, and ComboBox Controls to a Form

ListBox, CheckedListBox, and ComboBox objects all allow users to select choices from a list. The three classes descend from ListControl. Of course, they are also Controls and so inherit properties such as Text and BackColor from the Control class. Other properties are more specific to list-type objects. Table 12-8 describes some commonly used ListBox properties.

| Property or Method | Description |
| --- | --- |
| Items | The collection of items in the ListBox; frequently, these are strings, but they can also be other types of objects |
| MultiColumn | Indicates whether display can be in multiple columns |
| SelectedIndex | Returns the index of the selected item. If no item has been selected, the value is $-1$. Otherwise, it is a value from 0 through $n - 1$, where $n$ is the number of items in the ListBox. |
| SelectedIndices | Returns a collection of all the selected indices (when SelectionMode is more than One) |
| SelectedItem | Returns a reference to the selected item |
| SelectedItems | Returns a collection of the selected items (when SelectionMode is more than One) |
| SelectionMode | Determines how many items can be selected (see Table 12-9) |
| Sorted | Sorts the items when set to true |
| SelectedIndexChanged() | Default event that is generated when the selected index changes |

**Table 12-8**    Commonly used ListBox properties and default event

Figure 12-16 shows a typical ListBox on a Form. The **ListBox** Control enables you to display a list of items that the user can select by clicking. After you drag a ListBox onto a Form, you can select its Items property and type a list into a String Collection Editor, as shown on the right in Figure 12-16.

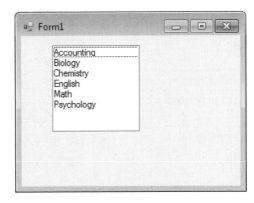

**Figure 12-16** The String Collection Editor filling a ListBox and the completed ListBox on a Form

Assuming the Name property of the ListBox is majorListBox, the following code is generated in the InitializeComponent() method when you fill the String Collection Editor with the strings in Figure 12-16:

```
this.majorListBox.Items.AddRange(new object[] {
    "Accounting",
    "Biology",
    "Chemistry",
    "English",
    "Math",
    "Psychology"});
```

Objects added to a ListBox are not required to be strings. For example, you could add a collection of Employee or Student objects. The value returned by each added object's ToString() method is displayed in the ListBox. After the user selects an object, you can cast the ListBox's SelectedItem to the appropriate type and access the object's other properties. The Chapter.12 folder of your student files contains a project named AddRangeObjectsDemo that illustrates this technique.

With a ListBox, you allow the user to make a single selection or multiple selections by setting the SelectionMode property appropriately. For example, when the SelectionMode property is set to One, the user can make only a single selection from the ListBox. When the SelectionMode is set to MultiExtended, pressing Shift and clicking the mouse or pressing Shift and one of the arrow keys (up, down, left, or right) extends the selection to span from the previously selected item to the current item. Pressing Ctrl and clicking the mouse selects or deselects an item in the list. Table 12-9 lists the possible SelectionMode values.

 When the SelectionMode property is set to SelectionMode.MultiSimple, click the mouse or press the spacebar to select or deselect an item in the list.

| Member Name | Description |
| --- | --- |
| MultiExtended | Multiple items can be selected, and the user can press the Shift, Ctrl, and arrow keys to make selections |
| MultiSimple | Multiple items can be selected |
| None | No items can be selected |
| One | Only one item can be selected |

**Table 12-9**　SelectionMode enumeration list

For example, within a Form's Load() method (the one that executes when a Form is first loaded), you could add the following:

```
this.majorListBox.SelectionMode =
    System.Windows.Forms.SelectionMode.MultiExtended;
```

As the example in Figure 12-17 shows, when you size a ListBox so that all the items cannot be displayed at the same time, a scroll bar is provided automatically on the side. The ListBox also provides the Boolean MultiColumn property, which you can set to display items in columns instead of a straight vertical list. This approach allows the control to display more items and avoids the need for the user to scroll down to an item. See Figure 12-18.

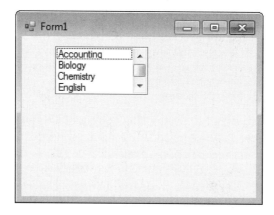

**Figure 12-17**　A ListBox with a scroll bar

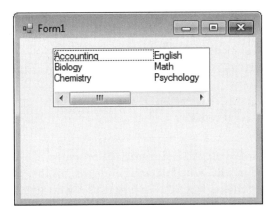

**Figure 12-18** A multicolumn `ListBox`

The `SelectedItem` property of a `ListBox` contains a reference to the item a user has selected. For example, you can modify a label's `Text` property in the `majorListBox_SelectedIndexChanged()` method with a statement such as the following:

```
private void majorListBox_SelectedIndexChanged
    (object sender, EventArgs e)
{
    majorLabel.Text = "You selected " + majorListBox.SelectedItem;
}
```

The `SelectedItem` is appended to the label. Figure 12-19 shows a typical result.

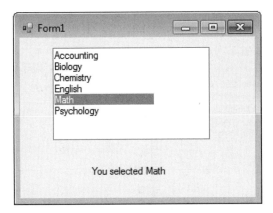

**Figure 12-19** `MajorListDemo` application after user has chosen *Math*

The `Items.Count` property of a `ListBox` object holds the number of items in the `ListBox`. The `GetSelected()` method accepts an integer

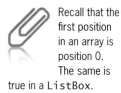

Recall that the first position in an array is position 0. The same is true in a ListBox.

argument representing the position of an item in the list. The method returns true if an item is selected and false if it is not. Therefore, code like the following could be used to count the number of selections a user makes from majorListBox:

```
int count = 0;
for(int x = 0; x < majorListBox.Items.Count; ++x)
    if(majorListBox.GetSelected(x))
        ++count;
```

Alternatively, you can use a ListBox's SelectedItems property; it contains the items selected in a list. The following code assigns the number of selections a user makes from the majorListBox to count:

```
count = majorListBox.SelectedItems.Count;
```

The SetSelected() method can be used to set a ListBox item to be automatically selected. For example, the following statement causes the first item in majorListBox to be the selected one:

```
majorListBox.SetSelected(0, true);
```

A **ComboBox** is similar to a ListBox, except that it displays an additional editing field to allow the user to select from the list or to enter new text. The default ComboBox displays an editing field with a hidden list box. The application in Figure 12-20 contains a ComboBox for selecting an airline. A **CheckedListBox** is also similar to a ListBox, with check boxes appearing to the left of each desired item. The application in Figure 12-20 uses a CheckedListBox for flight options.

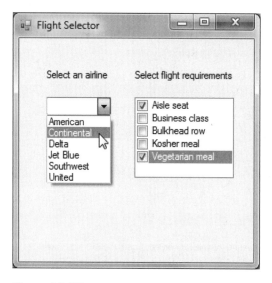

**Figure 12-20** FlightDemo application after user has made some selections

569

# Adding MonthCalendar and DateTimePicker Controls to a Form

The **MonthCalendar** and **DateTimePicker** Controls allow you to retrieve date and time information. Figure 12-21 shows a MonthCalendar that has been placed on a Form. The current date is contained in a rectangle by default, and the date that the user clicked is shaded. Controls at the top of the calendar allow the user to go forward or back one month at a time. Table 12-10 describes common MonthCalendar properties and the default event.

**Figure 12-21**  Typical execution of MonthCalendarDemo

| Property or Method | Description |
|---|---|
| MaxDate | Sets the last day that can be selected (the default is 12/31/9998) |
| MaxSelectionCount | Sets the maximum number of dates that can be selected at once (the default is 7) |
| MinDate | Sets the first day that can be selected (the default is 1/1/1753) |
| MonthlyBoldedDates | An array of dates that appear in boldface in the calendar (for example, holidays) |
| SelectionEnd | The last of a range of dates selected by the user |
| SelectionRange | The dates selected by the user |
| SelectionStart | The first of a range of dates selected by the user |
| ShowToday | If true, the date displays in text at the bottom of the calendar |
| ShowTodayCircle | If true, today's date is circled (the "circle" appears as a square) |
| DateChanged() | Default event that is generated when the user selects a date |

**Table 12-10** Commonly used MonthCalendar properties and default event

If you set the MinDate value to the MonthCalendar's TodayDate property, the user cannot select a date before the date you select. For example, you cannot make appointments or schedule deliveries to happen in the past, so you might code the following:

`monthCalendar1.MinDate = monthCalendar1.TodayDate;`

Conversely, you might want to prevent users from selecting a date in the future—for example, if the user is entering the date he placed an outstanding order. In that case, you could code a statement similar to the following:

`monthCalendar1.MaxDate = monthCalendar1.TodayDate;`

The format in which dates are displayed depends on the operating system's regional settings. For example, using United Kingdom settings, the short string format would use the day first, followed by the month, as in 16/02/2012. The examples in the list above assume United States settings.

The AddDays() method accepts a double argument because you can add fractional days to SelectionStart and SelectionEnd.

You can use several useful methods with the SelectionStart and SelectionEnd properties of MonthCalendar, including the following:

- ToShortDateString(), which displays the date in the format 2/16/2012

- ToLongDateString(), which displays the date in the format Thursday, February 16, 2012

- AddDays(), which takes a double argument and adds a specified number of days to the date

- AddMonths(), which takes an int argument and adds a specified number of months to the date

- AddYears(), which takes an int argument and adds a specified number of years to the date

SelectionStart and SelectionEnd are structures of the DateTime type. The chapter *Files and Streams* contains additional information about using DateTime objects to determine when files were created, modified, or accessed.

Many business and financial applications use AddDays(), AddMonths(), and AddYears() to calculate dates for events, such as payment for a bill (perhaps due in ten days from an order) or scheduling a salesperson's call-back to a customer (perhaps two months after initial contact). The default event for MonthCalendar is DateChanged(). For example, Figure 12-22 shows a method that executes when the user clicks a MonthCalendar named calendar. A string is created from the literal text "You selected" and the start of the user's selection is converted to a short string. The message is placed on a Label that has been named messageLabel. Figure 12-23 shows the output when the user selects March 29, 2011. The date that is ten days in the future is correctly calculated as April 8.

```
private void calendar_DateChanged(object sender, DateRangeEventArgs e)
{
    const int DAYS_TO_ADD = 10;
    string newDate = "You selected " +
        calendar.SelectionStart.ToShortDateString();
    messageLabel.Text = newDate + "\nTen days ahead is " +
        calendar.SelectionStart.AddDays(DAYS_TO_ADD).ToShortDateString();
}
```

**Figure 12-22** MonthCalendarDemo application calendar_DateChanged() method

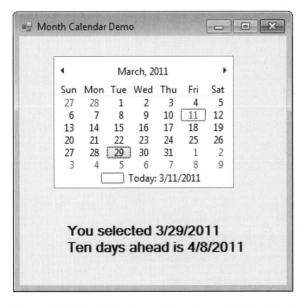

**Figure 12-23** Typical execution of MonthCalendarDemo

The DateTimePicker Control displays a month calendar when the down arrow is selected. For example, Figure 12-24 shows a DateTimePicker before and after the user clicks the down arrow.

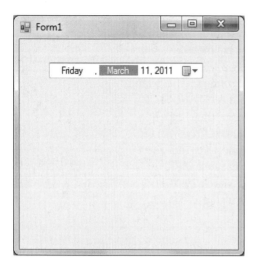

**Figure 12-24** The DateTimePicker Control

When you use the CustomFormat property, the date displayed in a DateTimePicker Control is more customizable than the one in a MonthCalendar. Table 12-11 describes some commonly used DateTimePicker properties and the default event.

| Property or Method | Description |
| --- | --- |
| CalendarForeColor | Sets the calendar text color |
| CalendarMonthBackground | Sets the calendar background color |
| CustomFormat | A string value that uses codes to set a custom date and time format. For example, to display the date and time as 02/16/2011 12:00 PM - Wednesday, set this property to "MM'/'dd'/'yyyy hh':'mm tt - dddd". See the C# documentation for a complete set of format string characters. |
| Format | Sets the format for the date or time. Options are Long (for example, Wednesday, February 16, 2011), Short (2/16/2011), and Time (for example, 3:15:01 PM). You can also create a CustomFormat. |
| Value | The data selected by the user |
| ValueChanged() | Default event that is generated when the Value property changes |

**Table 12-11** Commonly used DateTimePicker properties and default event

## Working with a Form's Layout

When you place `Controls` on a `Form` in the IDE, you can drag them to any location to achieve the effect you want.

When you drag multiple `Controls` onto a `Form`, blue **snap lines** appear and help you align new `Controls` with others already in place. Figure 12-25 shows two snap lines that you can use to align a second label below the first one. Snap lines also appear when you place a control closer to the edge of a container than is recommended.

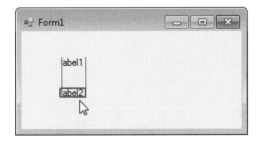

**Figure 12-25** Snap lines in the Visual Studio Designer

You also can use the `Location` property in a `Control`'s Properties list to specify a location. With either technique, code like the following is generated:

```
this.label1.Location = new System.Drawing.Point(23, 19);
```

Several other properties can help you to manage the appearance of a `Form` (or other `ContainerControl`). For example, setting the **Anchor**

**property** causes a Control to remain at a fixed distance from the side of a container when the user resizes it. Figure 12-26 shows the Properties window for a Label that has been placed on a Form. The Anchor property has a drop-down window that lets you select or deselect the sides to which the label should be anchored. For most Controls, the default setting for Anchor is Top, Left.

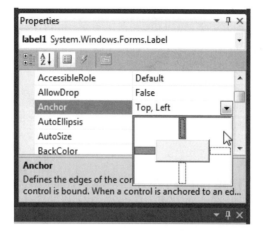

**Figure 12-26** Selecting an Anchor property

Figure 12-27 shows a Form with two Labels. On the Form, label1 has been anchored to the top left and label2 has been anchored to the bottom right. The left side of the figure shows the Form as it first appears to the user, and the right side shows the Form after the user has resized it. Notice that in the resized Form, label1 is still the same distance from the top left as it originally was, and label2 is still the same distance from the bottom right as it originally was. Anchoring is useful when users expect a specific control to always be in the same general location in a container.

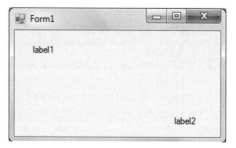

**Figure 12-27** A Form with two Labels anchored to opposite corners

Setting the **Dock property** attaches a Control to the side of a container so that the Control stretches when the container's size is adjusted. Figure 12-28 shows the drop-down Dock Properties window for a Button. You can select any region in the window. Figure 12-29 shows a Button docked to the bottom of a Form before and after the Form has been resized.

**Figure 12-28**  The Dock Properties window

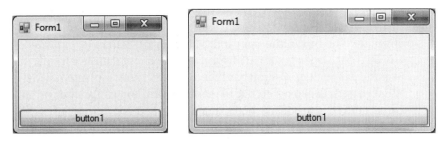

**Figure 12-29**  A Form with a docked Button

A Form has a **Padding property** that specifies the distance between docked Controls and the edges of the Form. The Padding property has four values—one for each side of the Form (left, top, right, and bottom). They are set to 0 by default. Figure 12-30 shows the docked button from Figure 12-29 when the padding values have been set to 0, 0, 30, 10. The Button is three times further from the right edge of the Form than it is from the bottom.

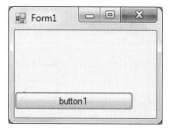

**Figure 12-30**   A docked button on a Form with padding

A Form also has a **MinimumSize property** and a **MaximumSize property**. Each has two values—Width and Height. If you set these properties, the user cannot make the Form smaller or larger than you have specified. If you do not want the user to be able to adjust a Form's size at all, set the MinimumSize and MaximumSize properties to be equal.

## Understanding GroupBoxes and Panels

Many types of ContainerControls are available to hold Controls. For example, you can use a **GroupBox** or **Panel** to group related Controls on a Form. When you move a GroupBox or Panel, all its Controls are moved as a group. To create either of these Controls, you drag it from the Toolbox in the IDE, and then drag the Controls you want on top of it. GroupBoxes can display a caption, but Panels cannot. Panels can include a scroll bar that the user can manipulate to view Controls; GroupBoxes do not have scroll bars. You can anchor or dock Controls inside a GroupBox or Panel, and you can anchor or dock a GroupBox or Panel inside a Form. Doing this provides Control groups that can be arranged easily.

If you place several GroupBox Controls on a Form and several RadioButtons in each GroupBox, then a user can select one RadioButton from each GroupBox instead of being able to select just one RadioButton on a Form. In other words, each GroupBox operates independently.

---

**TWO TRUTHS & A LIE**

### Working with a Form's Layout

1. Setting the Anchor property causes a Control to remain at a fixed distance from the side of a container when the user resizes it.

2. Setting the Dock property attaches a Control to the side of a container so that the Control's size does not change when the container's size is adjusted.

3. A Form has a Padding property that specifies the distance between docked Controls and the edges of the Form.

The false statement is #2. Setting the Dock property attaches a Control to the side of a container so that the Control stretches when the container's size is adjusted.

---

## Adding a MenuStrip to a Form

Many programs you use in a Windows environment contain a **menu strip**, which is a horizontal list of general options that appears under the title bar of a Form or Window. When you click an item in a menu strip, you might initiate an action. More frequently, you see a list box that contains more specific options. Each of these might initiate an action or lead to another menu. For example, the Visual Studio IDE contains a horizontal main menu strip that begins with the options File, Edit, and View. You have used word-processing, spreadsheet, and game programs with similar menus.

If you do not see a MenuStrip in your Toolbox, click the Menus & Toolbars group to expose it.

You can add a **MenuStrip** Control object to any Form you create. Using the Visual Studio IDE, you can add a MenuStrip to a Form by dragging it from the Toolbox onto the Form. This creates a menu bar horizontally across the top of the Form, just below the title bar. The strip extends across the width of the Form and contains a "Type Here" text box. When you click the text box, you can enter a menu item. New text boxes appear below and to the right of the first one, as shown in Figure 12-31. Each time you add a menu item, new boxes are created so you can see where your next options will go.

You can click the MenuStrip icon at the bottom of the design screen to view and change the properties for the MenuStrip. For example, you might want to change the Font or BackColor for the MenuStrip.

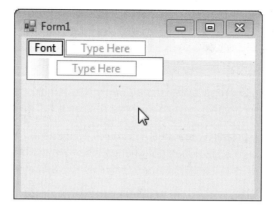

**Figure 12-31** Form with MenuStrip

The left side of Figure 12-32 shows a MenuStrip in which the programmer has typed *Font,* and beneath it, *Large* and *Small.* New boxes are available to the right of Font and beneath Small. The right side of the figure shows that the programmer continued by entering *Color* and three choices beneath it.

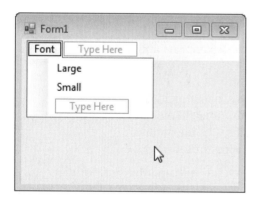
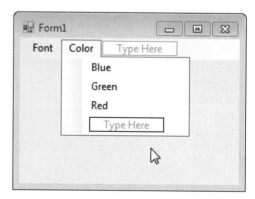

**Figure 12-32** Form that contains MenuStrip as the programmer makes entries

If possible, your main menu selections should be single words. That way, a user will not mistakenly think that a single menu item represents multiple items.

If you create each main menu item with an ampersand (&) in front of a unique letter, then the user can press Alt and the letter to activate the menu choice, besides clicking it with the mouse. For example, if two choices were Green and Gray, you might want to type &Green and G&ray so the user could type Alt+G to select Green and Alt+R to select Gray.

When you double-click an entry in the MenuStrip, a Click() method is generated. For example, if you click *Large* under Font in a menu, the method generated is largeToolStripMenuItem_Click(), as follows:

```
private void largeToolStripMenuItem_Click
    (object sender, EventArgs e)
{
}
```

As with all the other controls you have learned about, you can write any code statements you want within the method. For example, suppose a Label named helloLabel has been dragged onto the Form. If choosing the *Large* menu option should result in a larger font for the label, you might code the method as follows:

```
private void largeToolStripMenuItem_Click
    (object sender, EventArgs e)
{
    helloLabel.Font = new Font("Courier New", 34);
}
```

With the addition of this method, the Form operates as shown in Figure 12-33. If the Label appears in a small font and the user clicks the *Large* menu option, the font changes.

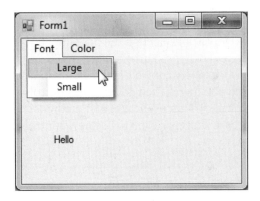
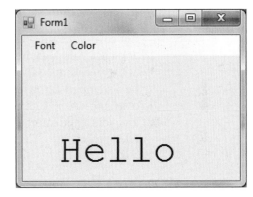

**Figure 12-33** Executing the MenuStripDemo program

You can work with the other menu items in this program in an exercise at the end of this chapter.

Users expect menu options to appear in conventional order. For example, users expect the far-left option on the main menu to be File, and they expect the Exit option to appear under File. Similarly, if an application contains a Help option, users expect to find it at the right side of the main menu. You should follow these conventions when designing your own main menus.

Watch the video *Using a MenuStrip*.

---

## TWO TRUTHS & A LIE

### Adding a MenuStrip to a Form

1. When you click an item in a menu strip, the most common result is to initiate an action.

2. When you drag a MenuStrip Control object onto a Form using the Visual Studio IDE, the MenuStrip is added horizontally across the top of the Form, just below the title bar.

3. The default event for MenuStrip is Click().

The false statement is #1. When you click an item in a menu strip, you might initiate an action. More frequently, you see a list box that contains more specific options.

---

## Using Other Controls

If you examine the Visual Studio IDE or search through the Visual Studio documentation, you will find many other Controls that are not covered in this chapter. If you click Project on the main menu and click Add New Item, you can add extra Forms, Files, Controls, and other elements to your project. New controls and containers will be developed in the future, and you might even design new controls of your own. Still, all controls will contain properties and methods, and your solid foundation in C# will prepare you to use new controls effectively.

## You Do It

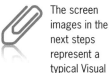

The screen images in the next steps represent a typical Visual Studio environment. Based on options you selected in your installation, your screen might look different.

### Adding Labels to a Form and Changing their Properties

In the next steps, you will begin to create an application for Bailey's Bed and Breakfast. The main Form allows the user to select one of two suites and discover the amenities and price associated with each choice. You will start by placing two Labels on a Form and setting several of their properties.

**To create a Form with Labels:**

1. Open Microsoft Visual Studio. Select **New Project** and **Windows Forms Application**. Near the bottom of the New Project window, click in the **Name** text box and replace the default name with **BedAndBreakfast**. Make sure the Location field contains the folder where you want to store the project. See Figure 12-34.

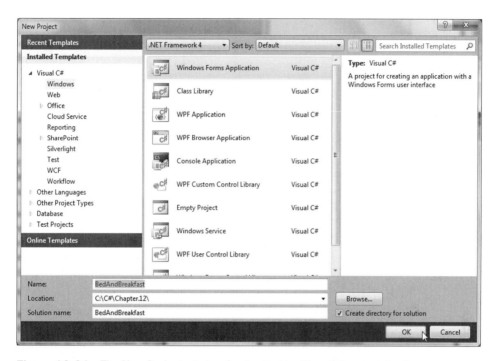

**Figure 12-34** The New Project window for the BedAndBreakfast application

2. Click **OK**. The design screen opens. The blank Form in the center of the screen has an empty title bar. Click the Form. The lower-right corner of the screen contains a Properties window that lists the Form's properties. (If you do not see the Properties window, you can click **View** on the main menu, then click **Properties Window**. Another option is to type **Ctrl+W** and then type **P**.) In the Properties list, click the **Name** property and change the Name of the Form to **BaileysForm**. Click the **Text** property and change it to **Bailey's Bed and Breakfast**.

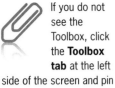

582

If you do not see the Toolbox, click the **Toolbox tab** at the left side of the screen and pin it to the screen by clicking the pushpin. Alternatively, you can select **View** from the main menu, and then click **Toolbox**.

3. From the Toolbox at the left of the screen, drag a Label onto the Form. Change the Name of label1 to **welcomeLabel** and change the Text property to **Welcome to Bailey's**. Drag and resize the Label so it is close to the position of the Label in Figure 12-35. (If you prefer to set the Label's Location property manually in the Properties list, the Location should be **60, 30**.)

**Figure 12-35**  A Label placed on the Form in the BedAndBreakfast project

4. Locate the Font property in the Properties list. Currently, it lists the default font: Microsoft Sans Serif, 8.25 pt. Notice the ellipsis (three dots) at the right of the Font property name. (You might have to click in the Property to see the button.) Click the ellipsis to display the Font dialog box. Make selections to change the font to **Microsoft Sans Serif, 18 point**, and **Bold**. Click **OK**. When you enlarge the Font for the Label, it is too close to the right edge of the Form. Drag the Label to change its Location property to approximately **20, 30**, or type the new Location value in the Properties window.

5. Drag a second Label onto the Form beneath the first one, and then set its Name property to rateLabel and its Text property to **Check our rates**. Change its Location to approximately **80, 80** and its Font to **Microsoft Sans Serif, 12 point, Regular**.

6. Save the project, then click **Debug** on the menu bar and click **Start Without Debugging**, or press **Ctrl+F5**. The Form appears, as shown in Figure 12-36.

**Figure 12-36** The BedAndBreakfast Form with two Labels

7. Dismiss the Form by clicking the **Close** button in its upper-right corner.

## Examining the Code Generated by the IDE

In the next steps, you will examine the code generated by the IDE for at least two reasons:

- To gain an understanding of the types of statements created by the IDE.

- To lose any intimidation you might have about the code that is generated. You will recognize many of the C# statements from what you have already learned in this book.

**To examine the generated code:**

1. Click **View** on the menu bar and then click **Code** (or press **F7**) to view the code. As shown in Figure 12-37, you see several using statements, the BedAndBreakfast namespace header, the BaileysForm class header, and the constructor for BaileysForm that calls the InitializeComponent() method.

584

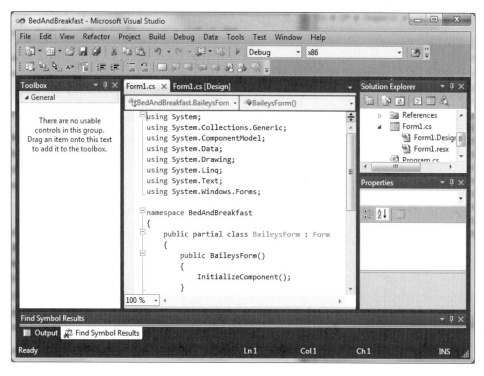

**Figure 12-37** The Form1.cs code

**2.** In the Solution Explorer at the right side of the screen, double-click the **Form1.Designer.cs** filename. Scroll to the gray rectangle that contains **Windows Form Designer generated code** and click the node to its left to expose the hidden code. (You can drag the bottom and side borders of the code window to expose more of the code, or you can scroll to see all of it.) As Figure 12-38 shows, welcomeLabel, rateLabel, and BaileysForm have been declared and assigned the attributes you provided for them.

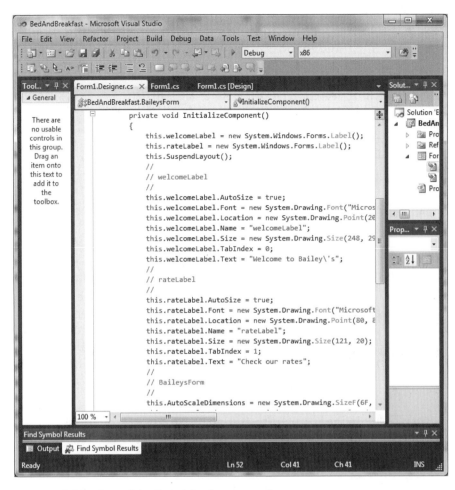

**Figure 12-38** Part of the Form1.Designer.cs code

3. Next, change the `BackColor` property of the Bailey's Bed and Breakfast `Form`. Click the **Form** or click the list box of components at the top of the Properties window and select **BaileysForm**. In the Properties list, click the **BackColor** property to see its list of choices. Choose the **Custom** tab and select **Yellow** in the third row of available colors. Click the **Form**, notice the color change, and then view the code in the Form1.Designer.cs file. Locate the statement that changes the `BackColor` of the `Form` to `Yellow`. As you continue to design Forms, periodically check the code to confirm your changes and better learn C#.

4. Save the project.

5. If you want to take a break at this point, close Visual Studio.

## Adding CheckBoxes to a Form

In the next steps, you will add two CheckBoxes to the BedAndBreakfast Form. These controls allow the user to select an available room and view information about it.

**To add CheckBoxes to a Form:**

1. Open the BedAndBreakfast project in Visual Studio, if it is not still open on your screen.

2. In the Design view of the Bed and Breakfast project in the Visual Studio IDE, drag a CheckBox onto the Form below the "Check our rates" Label. (See Figure 12-39 for its approximate placement.) Change the Text property of the CheckBox to **BelleAire Suite**. Change the Name of the property to **belleAireCheckBox**. Drag a second CheckBox onto the Form beneath the first one. Change its Text property to **Lincoln Room** and its Name to **lincolnCheckBox**.

**Figure 12-39** BedAndBreakfast Form with two CheckBoxes

3. Next, you will create two new Forms: one that appears when the user selects the BelleAire CheckBox and one that appears when the user selects the Lincoln CheckBox. Click **Project** on the menu bar, then click **Add New Item**. In the Add New Item window, click **Windows Form**. (You might have to scroll down to get to Windows Form.) In the Name text box at the bottom of the window, type **BelleAireForm**. See Figure 12-40.

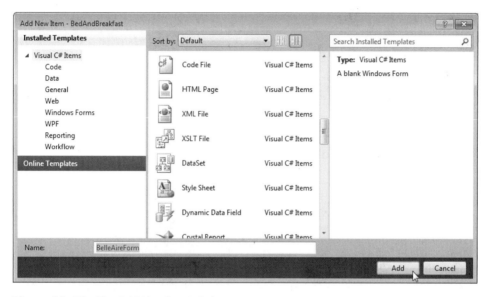

**Figure 12-40**　The Add New Item window

4. Click the **Add** button. A new Form is added to the project, and its Name and Text (title bar) properties contain *BelleAireForm*. Save the project (and continue to do so periodically).

5. Change the BackColor property of the Form to Yellow to match the color of BaileysForm.

6. Drag a Label onto the Form, using Figure 12-41 as a guide to approximate its placement. Change the Name of the Label to **belleAireDescriptionLabel**. Change the Text property of the Label to contain the following: **The BelleAire suite has two bedrooms, two baths, and a private balcony**. Click the arrow on the text property to type the long label message on two lines. Adjust the size and position of the Label, if necessary, to resemble Figure 12-41. Drag a second Label onto the Form, name it **belleAirePriceLabel**, and type the price as the Text property: **$199.95 per night**.

**Figure 12-41**  BelleAireForm with two Labels

7. Select the **Pointer** tool from the Toolbox at the left of the screen. Drag it to encompass both Labels. In the Properties list, select the **Font** property to change the Font for both Controls at once. Choose a pleasing Font. Figure 12-42 shows **9-point Bold Papyrus**; you might choose a different font. Adjust the positions of the Labels if necessary to achieve a pleasing effect.

**Figure 12-42**  Font changed for the Labels

8. Click the **Form1.cs[Design]** tab at the top of the Designer screen to view the Bailey's Bed and Breakfast Form. Double-click the **BelleAire Suite CheckBox**. The program code (the method shell for the default event of a CheckBox) appears in the IDE main window. Within the belleAireCheckBox_CheckedChanged() method, add an if statement that determines whether the BelleAire CheckBox is checked. If it is checked, create a new instance of BelleAireForm and display it.

```
private void belleAireCheckBox_CheckedChanged(object sender,
    EventArgs e)
{
    if (belleAireCheckBox.Checked)
    {
        BelleAireForm belleAireForm = new BelleAireForm();
        belleAireForm.ShowDialog();
    }
}
```

When a new Frame (or other Windows class) is instantiated, it is not visible by default. ShowDialog() shows the window and disables all other windows in the application. The user must dismiss the new Frame before proceeding. A secondary window that takes control of a program is a **modal window**; the user must deal with this window before proceeding.

9. Save and then execute the program by selecting **Debug** from the main menu, then **Start Without Debugging**. The main Bed and Breakfast Form appears. Click the **BelleAire Suite CheckBox**. The BelleAire Form appears. Dismiss the Form. Click the **Lincoln Room CheckBox**. Nothing happens because you have not yet written event code for this CheckBox. When you uncheck and then check the **BelleAire Suite CheckBox** again, the BelleAire form reappears. Dismiss the BelleAire Form.

10. When you dismiss the BelleAire Form, the BelleAire CheckBox remains checked. To see it appear as unchecked after its Form is dismissed, dismiss the program's main form (Bailey's Bed and Breakfast) and add a third statement within the if block in the CheckedChanged() message as follows:

```
belleAireCheckBox.Checked = false;
```

That way, whenever the CheckedChanged() method executes because the belleAireCheckBox was checked, it will become unchecked.

**11.** Save the project, then execute it again. When you select the BelleAire CheckBox, view the Form, and dismiss it, the CheckBox appears unchecked and is ready to check again. Dismiss the BedAndBreakfast Form.

**12.** Click **Project** on the menu bar and then click **Add New Item**. Click **Windows Form** and enter its Name: **LincolnForm**. When the new Form appears, its Name and Text properties will have been set to **LincolnForm**. Change the Text property to **Lincoln Room**. Then add two Labels to the Form and provide appropriate Name properties for them. Change the Text on the first Label to **Return to the 1850s in this lovely room with private bath**. The second should be **$110.00 per night**. Change the Form's BackColor property to **White**. Change the Font to match the Font on the BelleAire Form. See Figure 12-43.

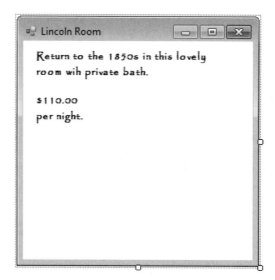

**Figure 12-43** The LincolnForm

13. From the Toolbox, drag a `PictureBox` onto the `Form`. Select its **Image** property. A dialog box allows you to browse for an image. Find the AbeLincoln file in the Chapter.12 folder of your downloadable student files and select **Import**. Adjust the size of the `Form` and the sizes and positions of the labels and picture box so that everything looks attractive on the `Form`. See Figure 12-44.

The AbeLincoln file was obtained at *www.free-graphics.com*. You can visit the site and download other images to use in your own applications. You should also search the Web for "free clip art" and similar phrases.

591

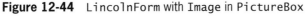

**Figure 12-44**   `LincolnForm` with Image in `PictureBox`

14. In the Solution Explorer, double-click **Form1.cs** or click the **Form1.cs[Design]** tab at the top of the design screen. On the Bed and Breakfast `Form`, double-click the Lincoln Room `CheckBox`, and add the following `if` statement to the `lincolnCheckBox_CheckedChanged()` method:

```
private void lincolnCheckBox_CheckedChanged(object sender,
    EventArgs e)
{
    if (lincolnCheckBox.Checked)
    {
        LincolnForm lincolnForm = new LincolnForm();
        lincolnForm.ShowDialog();
        lincolnCheckBox.Checked = false;
    }
}
```

15. Save the project and then execute it. When the Bed and Breakfast `Form` appears, click either `CheckBox`—the appropriate informational `Form` appears. Close it and then click the other `CheckBox`. Again, the appropriate `Form` appears.

16. Close all forms.

## Adding RadioButtons to a Form

Next you will add more Controls to the Bed and Breakfast Form. You generally use RadioButtons when a user must select from mutually exclusive options.

**To add RadioButtons to the project:**

1. Open the BedAndBreakfast project if it is not still open. In the Design view of the main Form, add a Button to the Form, using Figure 12-45 as a general guide to locations. Change the Button's Name property to **mealButton** and the Button's Text to **Click for meal options**.

**Figure 12-45** BedAndBreakfast Form with an added Button

2. From the main menu, select **Project**, click **Add New Item**, and click **Windows Form**. Name the Form **BreakfastOptionForm** and click **Add**. On the new Form, make the following changes:

   • Set the Form's BackColor to **Yellow**.

   • Drag a Label onto the Form. Name it appropriately and set its Text to **Select your breakfast option**.

   • Drag three RadioButtons onto the Form. Set their respective Text properties to **Continental**, **Full**, and **Deluxe**. Set their respective Names to **contButton**, **fullButton**, and **deluxeButton**.

   • Drag a Label onto the Form, then set its Text to **Price:** and its Name to **priceLabel**. Make the Font property a little larger than for the other Form components.

See Figure 12-46 for approximate placement of all these Controls.

**Figure 12-46** Developing the `BreakfastOptionForm`

3. Double-click the title bar of the `BreakfastOptionForm` to generate a method named `BreakfastOptionForm_Load()`. Within this method, you can type statements that execute each time the `Form` is created. Add the following statements within the `BreakfastOptionForm` class, which declare three constants representing prices for different breakfast options. Within the `BreakfastOptionForm_Load()` method, set the `priceLabel` `Text` to the lowest price by default when the `Form` loads.

```
public partial class BreakfastOptionForm : Form
{
    private const double CONT_BREAKFAST_PRICE = 6.00;
    private const double FULL_BREAKFAST_PRICE = 9.95;
    private const double DELUXE_BREAKFAST_PRICE = 16.50;
    public BreakfastOptionForm()
    {
        InitializeComponent();
    }
    private void BreakfastOptionForm_Load
        (object sender, EventArgs e)
    {
        priceLabel.Text = "Price: " +
            CONT_BREAKFAST_PRICE.ToString("C");
    }
}
```

593

4. Return to the Design view for the `BreakfastOptionForm`
and double-click the **Continental breakfast RadioButton**.
When you see the generated `CheckedChanged()` method, add
a statement that sets `priceLabel` to the continental breakfast
price when the user makes that selection:

```
private void contButton _CheckedChanged
   (object sender, EventArgs e)
{
   priceLabel.Text = "Price: " +
      CONT_BREAKFAST_PRICE.ToString("C");
}
```

5. Return to the Design view for the `BreakfastOptionForm`,
double-click the **Full breakfast RadioButton**, and add a statement to the generated method that sets the `priceLabel` to the
full breakfast price when the user makes that selection:

```
private void fullButton_CheckedChanged
   (object sender, EventArgs e)
{
   priceLabel.Text = "Price: " +
      FULL_BREAKFAST_PRICE.ToString("C");
}
```

6. Return to the Design view for the `BreakfastOptionForm`,
double-click the **Deluxe breakfast RadioButton**, and add a
statement to the generated method that sets the `priceLabel`
to the deluxe breakfast price when the user makes that
selection:

```
private void deluxeButton_CheckedChanged
   (object sender, EventArgs e)
{
   priceLabel.Text = "Price: " +
      DELUXE_BREAKFAST_PRICE.ToString("C");
}
```

7. In the Solution Explorer, double-click the **Form1.cs file**
to view the original `Form`. Double-click the **Click for meal
options Button**. When the `Click()` method is generated, add
the following code so that the `BreakfastOptionForm` is loaded
when a user clicks the `Button`.

```
private void mealButton_Click(object sender,
   EventArgs e)
{
   BreakfastOptionForm breakfastForm = new
      BreakfastOptionForm();
   breakfastForm.ShowDialog();
}
```

8. Save the project and execute it. When the BedAndBreakfast Form appears, confirm that the BelleAire Suite and Lincoln Room CheckBoxes still work correctly, displaying their information Forms when they are clicked. Then click the **Click for meal options Button**. By default, the Continental breakfast option is chosen, as shown in Figure 12-47, so the price is $6.00. Click the other RadioButton options to confirm that each correctly changes the breakfast price.

**Figure 12-47** The BreakfastOptionForm with Continental breakfast RadioButton selected

9. Dismiss all the Forms and close Visual Studio.

## Chapter Summary

- The Control class provides definitions for GUI objects such as Forms and Buttons. There are 26 direct descendents of Control and additional descendents of those classes. Each Control has more than 80 public properties and 20 protected ones. For example, each Control has a Font and a ForeColor that dictate how its text is displayed, and each Control has a Width and Height.

- When you design GUI applications using the Visual Studio IDE, much of the code is automatically generated.

- You use the Font class to change the appearance of printed text on your Forms. When designing a Label, Button, or other Control on a Form, it is easiest to select a Font from the Properties list. The Font class includes a number of overloaded constructors.

- A LinkLabel is similar to a Label; it is a child of Label, but it provides the additional capability to link the user to other sources, such as Web pages or files.

- The Color class contains a wide variety of predefined Colors that you can use with your Controls.

- CheckBox objects are GUI widgets the user can click to select or deselect an option. When a Form contains multiple CheckBoxes, any number of them can be checked or unchecked at the same time. RadioButtons are similar to CheckBoxes, except that when they are placed on a Form, only one RadioButton can be selected at a time—selecting any RadioButton automatically deselects the others. CheckBox and RadioButton objects both have a Checked property whose value is true or false.

- A PictureBox is a Control in which you can display graphics from a bitmap, icon, JPEG, GIF, or other image file type. Just as with a Button or a Label, you can easily add a PictureBox by dragging its Control onto the Form in the Visual Studio IDE.

- ListBox, ComboBox, and CheckedListBox objects descend from ListControl. The ListBox Control enables you to display a list of items that the user can select by clicking. With a ListBox, you allow the user to make a single selection or multiple selections by setting the SelectionMode property appropriately. A ComboBox is similar to a ListBox, except that it displays an additional editing field to allow the user to select from the list or to enter new text. A CheckedListBox is also similar to a ListBox, with check boxes appearing to the left of each desired item.

- The MonthCalendar and DateTimePicker Controls allow you to retrieve date and time information.

- When you place Controls on a Form in the IDE, you can drag them to any location to achieve the effect you want. When you drag multiple Controls onto a Form, blue snap lines appear and help you align new Controls with others already in place. You also can use the Location property in the Properties list to specify a location. Anchor, Dock, and Padding properties help you determine a Control's size and position in the Form. A Form also has a MinimumSize property and a MaximumSize property. Each has two values—Width and Height. Many types of ContainerControls are available to hold Controls. For example, you can use a GroupBox or Panel to group related Controls on a Form. When you move a GroupBox or Panel, all its Controls are moved as a group.

- Many programs you use in a Windows environment contain a menu strip, which is a horizontal list of general options that appears under the title bar of a Form or Window. When you click an item in a menu strip, you might initiate an action. More frequently, you see a list box that contains more specific options. Each of these might initiate an action or lead to another menu. You can add a `MenuStrip Control` object to any `Form` you create.

- If you examine the Visual Studio IDE or search through the Visual Studio documentation, you will find many other `Controls` you can use. If you click Project on the main menu and click Add New Item, you can add extra `Forms`, `Files`, `Controls`, and other elements to a project.

# Key Terms

**Widgets** are interactive controls such as labels, scroll bars, check boxes, and radio buttons.

The **Control** class provides the definitions for GUI objects.

The **Component** class provides containment and cleanup for other objects.

In Visual Studio, a **method node** is a small box that appears to the left of code; you use it to expand or collapse code.

The **Font** class is used to change the appearance of printed text on `Forms`.

The **logical OR operator** is the pipe (|).

A **LinkLabel** is similar to a `Label`, but it provides the additional capability to link the user to other sources, such as Web pages or files.

The **default event** for a `Control` is the one generated when you double-click the `Control` while designing it in the IDE. The default event is the method you are most likely to alter when you use the `Control`, as well as the event that users most likely expect to generate when they encounter the `Control` in a working application.

The **Color** class contains a wide variety of predefined colors to use with `Controls`.

**CheckBox** objects are GUI widgets the user can click to select or deselect an option. When a `Form` contains multiple `CheckBoxes`, any number of them can be checked or unchecked at the same time.

**RadioButtons** are similar to `CheckBoxes`, except that when they are placed on a `Form`, only one `RadioButton` can be selected at a time—selecting any `RadioButton` automatically deselects the others.

A **PictureBox** is a `Control` in which you can display graphics from a bitmap, icon, JPEG, GIF, or other image file type.

The **ListBox** `Control` enables you to display a list of items that the user can select by clicking.

A **ComboBox** is similar to a `ListBox`, except that it displays an additional editing field that allows a user to select from the list or enter new text.

A **CheckedListBox** is also similar to a `ListBox`, with check boxes appearing to the left of each desired item.

The **MonthCalendar** and **DateTimePicker** Controls allow you to retrieve date and time information.

**Snap lines** appear in a design environment to help you align new Controls with others already in place.

The **Anchor property** for a Control causes it to remain at a fixed distance from the side of a container when the user resizes it.

The **Dock property** for a Control attaches it to the side of a container so that the Control stretches when the container's size is adjusted.

The **Padding property** of a Control specifies the distance between a docked Control and the edges of its container.

The **MinimumSize property** and **MaximumSize property** of a Control define the limits of the sizes to which users can adjust the Control. Each property has two values: `Width` and `Height`.

A **GroupBox** or **Panel** can be used to group related Controls on a Form.

A **menu strip** is a horizontal list of general options that appears under the title bar of a Form or `Window`.

A **MenuStrip** Control is an object on a Form that contains a menu strip.

A **modal window** is a secondary window that takes control from a primary window. A user must deal with a modal window before proceeding.

## Review Questions

1. Labels, Buttons, and CheckBoxes are all _____.

   a. GUI objects

   b. Controls

   c. widgets

   d. all of these

2. All Control objects descend from _____.

   a. Form

   b. Component

   c. ButtonBase

   d. all of these

3. Which of the following is most like a RadioButton?

   a. ListControl

   b. CheckedListBox

   c. PictureBox

   d. Button

4. Which of the following is not a commonly used Control property?

   a. BackColor

   b. Language

   c. Location

   d. Size

5. The Control you frequently use to provide descriptive text for another Control object is a _____.

   a. Form

   b. Label

   c. CheckBox

   d. MessageBox

6. Which of the following creates a Label named firstLabel?

   a. firstLabel = new firstLabel();

   b. Label = new firstLabel();

   c. Label firstLabel = new Label();

   d. Label firstLabel = Label();

7. The property that determines what the user reads on a Label is the _____ property.

   a. Text

   b. Label

   c. Phrase

   d. Setting

8. Which of the following correctly creates a Font?

    a. Font myFont = new Font("Arial", 14F, FontStyle.Bold);

    b. Font myFont = new Font("Courier", 13.6);

    c. myFont = Font new Font("TimesRoman", FontStyle.Italic);

    d. Font myFont = Font(20, "Helvetica", Underlined);

9. The default event for a Control is the one that _____.

    a. occurs automatically whether a user manipulates the Control or not

    b. is generated when you double-click the Control while designing it in the IDE

    c. requires no parameters

    d. occurs when a user clicks the Control with a mouse

10. Assume you have created a Label named myLabel. Which of the following sets myLabel's background color to green?

    a. myLabel = BackColor.System.Drawing.Color.Green;

    b. myLabel.BackColor = System.Drawing.Color.Green;

    c. myLabel.Green = System.DrawingColor;

    d. myLabel.Background = new Color.Green;

11. A difference between CheckBox and RadioButton objects is _____.

    a. RadioButtons descend from ButtonBase; CheckBoxes do not

    b. only one RadioButton can be selected at a time

    c. only one CheckBox can appear on a Form at a time

    d. RadioButtons cannot be placed in a GroupBox; CheckBoxes can

12. The Checked property of a RadioButton can hold the values _____.

    a. true and false

    b. Checked and Unchecked

    c. 0 and 1

    d. Yes, No, and Undetermined

13. The `Control` in which you can display a bitmap or JPEG image is a(n) _____.

   a. `DisplayModule`

   b. `ImageHolder`

   c. `BitmapControl`

   d. `PictureBox`

14. `ListBox`, `ComboBox`, and `CheckedListBox` objects descend from the same family: _____.

   a. `ListControl`

   b. `List`

   c. `ButtonBase`

   d. `ListBase`

15. Which of the following properties is associated with a `ListBox` but not a `Button`?

   a. `BackColor`

   b. `SelectedItem`

   c. `Location`

   d. `IsSelected`

16. With a `ListBox` you can allow the user to choose _____.

   a. only a single option

   b. multiple selections

   c. either of these

   d. none of these

17. You can add items to a `ListBox` by using the _____ method.

   a. `AddList()`

   b. `Append()`

   c. `List()`

   d. `AddRange()`

18. A `ListBox`'s `SelectedItem` property contains _____.

 a. the position of the currently selected item

 b. the value of the currently selected item

 c. a Boolean value indicating whether an item is currently selected

 d. a count of the number of currently selected items

19. When you create a `ListBox`, by default its `SelectionMode` is _____.

 a. `Simple`

 b. `MultiExtended`

 c. `One`

 d. `false`

20. A horizontal list of general options that appears under the title bar of a `Form` or `Window` is a _____.

 a. task bar

 b. subtitle bar

 c. menu strip

 d. list box

## Exercises

1. Create a `Form` that contains two `Button`s, one labeled Stop and one labeled Go. Add a `Label` telling the user to click a button. When the user clicks Stop, change the `BackColor` of the `Form` to Red; when the user clicks Go, change the `BackColor` of the `Form` to Green. Save the project as **StopGo**.

2. Create a `Form` that contains at least five `Button` objects, each labeled with a color. When the user clicks a `Button`, change the `BackColor` of the `Form` appropriately. Save the project as **FiveColors**.

3. Create a `Form` that contains at least five `RadioButton` objects, each labeled with a color. When the user clicks a `RadioButton`, change the `BackColor` of the `Form` appropriately. Save the project as **FiveColors2**.

4. Create a `Form` for a video store that contains a `ListBox` with the titles of at least eight videos available to rent. Provide directions that tell users they can choose as many videos as they want by holding down the Ctrl key while making selections. When the user clicks a `Button` to indicate the choices are final, display the total rental price, which is $2.50 per video. If the user selects or deselects items and clicks the button again, make sure the total is updated correctly. Save the project as **Video**.

5. Create a `Form` with two `ListBoxes`—one contains at least four `Font` names and the other contains at least four `Font` sizes. Let the first item in each list be the default selection if the user fails to make a selection. Allow only one selection per `ListBox`. After the user clicks a `Button`, display "Hello" in the selected `Font` and size. Save the project as **FontSelector**.

6. Create a `Form` for a car rental company. Allow the user to choose a car style (compact, standard, or luxury) and a number of days (1 through 7). After the user makes selections, display the total rental charge, which is $19.95 per day for a compact car, $24.95 per day for a standard car, and $39 per day for a luxury car. Use the `Controls` that you think are best for each function. Label items appropriately and use fonts and colors to achieve an attractive design. Save the project as **CarRental**.

7. Create a `Form` for a restaurant. Allow the user to choose one item from at least three options in each of the following categories—appetizer, entrée, and dessert. Assign a different price to each selection and display the total when the user clicks a `Button`. Use the `Controls` that you think are best for each function. Label items appropriately and use fonts and colors to achieve an attractive design. Save the project as **Restaurant**.

8. Create a `Form` for an automobile dealer. Include options for at least three car models. After users make a selection, proceed to a new `Form` that contains information about the selected model. Use the `Controls` that you decide are best for each function. Label items on the `Form` appropriately and use fonts and colors to achieve an attractive design. Save the project as **CarDealer**.

9. Create a spreadsheet and then include a few numbers in it that represent an annual budget, or use the AnnualBudget. xls file in the Chapter.12 folder of the downloadable student files. Create a `Form` that includes two `LinkLabels`. One opens the spreadsheet for viewing, and the other visits your favorite

Web site. Include Labels on the Form to explain each link. Save the project as **AnnualBudget**.

10. Create a Form for Nina's Cookie Source. Allow the user to select from at least three types of cookies, each with a different price per dozen. Allow the user to select 1/2, 1, 2, or 3 dozen cookies. Adjust the final displayed price as the user chooses cookie types and quantities. Also allow the user to select an order date from a MonthCalendar. Assuming that shipping takes three days, display the estimated arrival date for the order. Include as many labels as necessary so the user understands how to use the Form. Save the project as **NinasCookieSource**.

11. Using the MenuStripDemo project in the Chapter.12 folder of your downloadable student files (see Figure 12-33), add appropriate functionality to the currently unprogrammed menu options (Small in the Font menu and the three options in the Color menu). Add at least three other menu options to the program, either vertically, horizontally, or both. Save the modified project as **MenuStripDemo2**.

12. Create a game called "Let's Make a Deal" in which three prizes of varying value are assigned randomly to three "doors" that you can implement as Buttons. For example, the prizes might be a new car, a big-screen TV, and a live goat. The player chooses a Button, and then one of the two other prizes is revealed; the one revealed is never the most desirable prize. The user then has the option of changing the original selection to the remaining unseen choice. For example, consider these two game scenarios:

- Suppose the new car is randomly assigned to the first button. If the user chooses the first button, reveal either of the other two prizes and ask the user if he wants to change his selection.

- Suppose the car is assigned to the first button, but the user chooses the second button. Reveal the third prize so that the car's location is still hidden, and then ask the user whether he wants to change the selection.

Save the project as **LetsMakeADeal**.

## Debugging Exercises

Each of the following projects in the Chapter.12 folder of your downloadable student files has syntax and/or logical errors. In each case, determine the problem and fix the program. After you correct the errors, save each project using the same name preceded with *Fixed*. For example, DebugTwelve1 will become FixedDebugTwelve1.

Immediately save the four project folders with their new names before starting to correct their errors.

      a.  DebugTwelve1

      b.  DebugTwelve2

      c.  DebugTwelve3

      d.  DebugTwelve4

 ## Up For Discussion

1.  Making exciting, entertaining, professional-looking GUI applications becomes easier once you learn to include graphics images, as you did when you learned about PictureBox objects in this chapter. You can copy graphics images from many locations on the Web. Should there be any restrictions on what graphics you use? Does it make a difference if you are writing programs for your own enjoyment, as opposed to putting them on the Web where others can see them? Should restrictions be different for using photographs versus using drawings? Does it matter if the photographs contain recognizable people? Would you impose any restrictions on images posted to your organization's Web site?

2.  Should you be allowed to store computer games on your computer at work? If so, should you be allowed to play the games at work? If so, should there be any restrictions on when you can play them?

3.  Suppose you discover a way to breach security in a Web site so that visitors might access information that belongs to the company. Should you be allowed to publish your findings? Should you notify the organization? Should the organization pay you a reward for discovering the breach? If they do, would this encourage you to search for more potential security violations? Suppose the newly available information on the Web site is relatively innocuous—for example, office telephone numbers of company executives. Suppose it is not—for example, home telephone numbers for the same executives. Does this make a difference?

# Handling Events

In this chapter you will:

◎   Learn about event handling

◎   Learn about delegates

◎   Declare your own events and handlers and use the built-in `EventHandler`

◎   Handle `Control` component events

◎   Handle mouse and keyboard events

◎   Manage multiple `Control`s

◎   Learn how to continue your exploration of `Control`s and events

Throughout this book, you have learned how to create interactive GUI programs in which a user can manipulate a variety of Controls. You have worked with several Controls that respond to a user-initiated event, such as a mouse click, and you have provided actions for Control default events. In this chapter, you will expand your understanding of the event-handling process. You will learn more about the object that triggers an event and the object that captures and responds to that event. You also will learn about delegates—objects that act as intermediaries in transferring messages from senders to receivers. You will create delegates and manage interactive events. You will learn to manage multiple events for a single Control and to manage multiple Controls for a project.

# Event Handling

In C#, an **event** is a reaction to an occurrence in a program; an event transpires when something interesting happens to an object. When you create a class, you decide exactly what is considered "interesting." For example, when you create a Form, you might decide to respond to a user clicking a Button but ignore a user who clicks a Label—clicking the Label is not "interesting" to the Form. A program uses an event to notify a client when something happens to an object. Events are used frequently in GUI programs—for example, a program is notified when the user clicks a Button or chooses an option from a ListBox. In addition, you can use events with ordinary classes that do not represent GUI controls. When an object's client might want to know about any changes that occur in the object, events enable the object to signal the client.

The actions that occur during the execution of a program occur **at runtime**. The expression *at runtime* is used to distinguish execution-time activities from those that occur during development time and compile time. Events are runtime occurrences.

You have learned that when a user interacts with a GUI object, an event is generated that causes the program to perform a task. GUI programs are **event driven**—an event such as a button click "drives" the program to perform a task. Programmers also say that an action like a button click **raises an event**, **fires an event**, or **triggers an event**. A method that performs a task in response to an event is an **event handler**.

For example, Figure 13-1 shows a Form that contains a Label and a Button. The following changes are the only ones that have been made to the default Form in the IDE:

- The Size property of the Form has been adjusted to 500, 120.

- A Label has been dragged onto the Form, its Name property has been set to helloLabel, its Text property has been set to "Hello", and its Font has been increased to 9.

- A Button has been dragged onto the Form, its Name property has been set to changeButton, and its Text property has been set to "Change Label".

**Figure 13-1** A Form with a Label and a Button

If you double-click the button on the form in the IDE, you generate the following empty method in the program code:

```
private void changeButton_Click(object sender, EventArgs e)
{
}
```

The changeButton_Click() method is an event handler. Conventionally, event handlers are named using the identifier of the Control (in this case, changeButton), an underscore, and the name of the event type (in this case, Click). You can create your own methods to handle events and provide any names for them, but the names should follow these conventions.

Suppose that when a user clicks the button, you want the text on the label to change from "Hello" to "Goodbye". You can write the following code within the event handler:

```
private void changeButton_Click(object sender, EventArgs e)
{
    helloLabel.Text = "Goodbye";
}
```

Then, when you run the application and click the button, the output appears as shown in Figure 13-2.

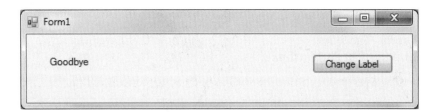

**Figure 13-2** Output of EventDemo application after user clicks button

The event-handler method is also known as an **event receiver**. The control that generates an event is an **event sender**. The first parameter in the list for the event receiver method is an object named sender; it is a reference to the object that generated the event. For example, if you code the event handler as follows, the output appears as in Figure 13-3.

```
private void changeButton_Click(object sender, EventArgs e)
{
    helloLabel.Text = sender.ToString();
}
```

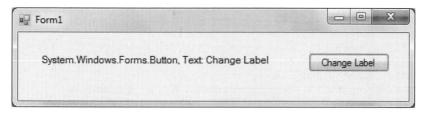

**Figure 13-3** EventDemo application modified to display sender information

The label in Figure 13-3 shows that the sender of the event is an instance of System.Windows.Forms.Button, whose Text property is "Change Label".

The second parameter in the event-handler parameter list is a reference to an event arguments object of type EventArgs; in this method, the EventArgs argument is named e. **EventArgs** is a C# class designed for holding event information. If you change the code in the event handler to the following, then run the program and click the button, you see the output in Figure 13-4.

```
private void changeButton_Click(object sender, EventArgs e)
{
    helloLabel.Text = e.ToString();
}
```

**Figure 13-4** EventDemo application modified to display EventArgs information

In Figure 13-4, you can see that the e object is a MouseEventArgs object. That makes sense, because the user used the mouse to click the Button.

When you open the Designer.cs file in the IDE, you can examine all the code generated for the application that creates the Form shown in Figure 13-4. Expanding the Windows Form Designer-generated code lets you see comments as well as statements that set the Controls' properties. For example, the code generated for changeButton appears in Figure 13-5. You can recognize that such features as the button's Location, Name, and Size have been set.

```
//
// changeButton
//
this.changeButton.Location = new System.Drawing.Point(359, 24);
this.changeButton.Name = "changeButton";
this.changeButton.Size = new System.Drawing.Size(101, 23);
this.changeButton.TabIndex = 1;
this.changeButton.Text = "Change Label";
this.changeButton.UseVisualStyleBackColor = true;
this.changeButton.Click += new
    System.EventHandler(this.changeButton_Click);
```

**Figure 13-5**   Code involving changeButton generated by Visual Studio

The code generated in Design mode in the IDE is not meant to be altered by typing. You should modify Control properties through the Properties window in the IDE, not by typing in the Designer.cs file.

Connecting an event to its resulting actions is called **event wiring**.

The most unusual statement in the section of changeButton code is shaded in Figure 13-5. This statement concerns the **Click event**, which is generated when changeButton is clicked by a user. The statement is necessary because changeButton does not automatically "know" what method will handle its events—C# and all other .NET languages allow you to choose your own names for event-handling methods for events generated by GUI objects. In other words, the event-handling method is not required to be named changeButton_Click(). You *could* create your program so that when the user clicks the button, the event-handling method is named calculatePayroll(), changeLabel(), or any other identifier for a method you could then write. Of course, you do not want to make such a change; using the name changeButton_Click() for the method that executes when changeButton is clicked is the clearest approach. The shaded statement indicates that, for this program, the method named changeButton_Click() is the receiver for changeButton's Click event. Programmers say the shaded method creates a delegate, or more specifically, a composed delegate. The delegate's type is EventHandler, and it takes a reference to the changeButton_Click() method. That method is the one that will react when a user clicks the button. You will learn about delegates in the next two sections of this chapter.

---

**TWO TRUTHS & A LIE**

**Event Handling**

1. An action such as a key press or button click raises an event.

2. A method that performs a task in response to an event is an event handler.

3. The control that generates an event is an event receiver.

The false statement is #3. The control that generates an event is an event sender.

---

# Understanding Delegates

A **delegate** is an object that contains a reference to a method; object-oriented programmers would say that a delegate encapsulates a method. In government, a delegate is a representative that you authorize to make choices for you. For example, you select a delegate to a presidential nominating convention. When human delegates arrive at a convention, they are free to make last-minute choices based on current conditions. Similarly, C# delegates provide a way for a program to take alternative courses that are not determined until runtime. When you write a method, you do not always know which actions will occur at runtime, so you give your delegates authority to run the correct methods.

 In Chapter 1, you learned that encapsulation is a basic feature of object-oriented programming. Recall that encapsulation is the technique of packaging an object's attributes and methods into a cohesive unit that can then be used as an undivided entity.

After you have instantiated a C# delegate, you can pass this object to a method, which then can call the method referenced within the delegate. In other words, a delegate provides a way to pass a reference to a method as an argument to another method. For example, if `del` is a delegate that contains a reference to the method `M1()`, you can pass `del` to a new method named `MyMethod()`. Alternatively, you could create a delegate named `del` that contains a reference to a method named `M2()` and then pass this version to `MyMethod()`. When you write `MyMethod()`, you do not have to know whether it will call `M1()` or `M2()`; you only need to know that it will call whatever method is referenced within `del`.

 A C# delegate is similar to a function pointer in C++. A function pointer is a variable that holds a method's memory address. In the C++ programming language, you pass a method's address to another method using a pointer variable. Java does not allow function pointers because they are dangerous— if the program alters the address, you might inadvertently execute the wrong method. C# provides a compromise between the dangers of C++ pointers and the Java ban on passing functions. Delegates allow flexible method calls, but they remain secure because you cannot alter the method addresses.

You declare a delegate using the keyword delegate, followed by an ordinary method declaration that includes a return type, method name, and argument list. For example, by entering the following statement, you can declare a delegate named GreetingDelegate(), which accepts a string argument and returns nothing:

```
delegate void GreetingDelegate(string s);
```

The GreetingDelegate can encapsulate any method as long as it has a void return type and a single string parameter. Any delegate can encapsulate any method that has the same return type and parameter list as the delegate. If you declare the delegate and then write a method with the same return type and parameter list, you can assign an instance of the delegate to represent it. For example, the following Hello() method is a void method that takes a string parameter:

```
public static void Hello(string s)
{
    Console.WriteLine("Hello, {0}!", s);
}
```

Because the Hello() method matches the GreetingDelegate definition, you can assign a reference to the Hello() method to a new instance of GreetingDelegate, as follows:

```
GreetingDelegate myDel = new GreetingDelegate(Hello);
```

Once the reference to the Hello() method is encapsulated in the delegate myDel, each of the following statements will result in the same output: "Hello, Kim!".

```
Hello("Kim");
myDel("Kim");
```

In this example, the ability to use the delegate myDel does not seem to provide any benefits over using a regular method call to Hello(). If you have a program in which you pass the delegate to a method, however, the method becomes more flexible; you gain the ability to send a reference to an appropriate method you want to execute at the time.

For example, Figure 13-6 shows a Greeting class that contains Hello() and Goodbye() methods. The Main() method declares two delegates named firstDel and secondDel. One is instantiated using the Hello() method, and the other is instantiated using the Goodbye() method. When the Main() method calls GreetMethod() two times, it passes a different method and string each time. Figure 13-7 shows the output.

```
using System;
delegate void GreetingDelegate(string s);
class Greeting
{
    public static void Hello(string s)
    {
        Console.WriteLine("Hello, {0}!", s);
    }
    public static void Goodbye(string s)
    {
        Console.WriteLine("Goodbye, {0}!", s);
    }
    public static void Main()
    {
        GreetingDelegate firstDel, secondDel;
        firstDel = new GreetingDelegate(Hello);
        secondDel = new GreetingDelegate(Goodbye);
        GreetMethod(firstDel, "Cathy");
        GreetMethod(secondDel, "Bob");
    }
    public static void GreetMethod
        (GreetingDelegate gd, string name)
    {
        Console.WriteLine("The greeting is:");
        gd(name);
    }
}
```

**Figure 13-6** The Greeting program

**Figure 13-7** Output of the Greeting program

## Creating Composed Delegates

You can assign one delegate to another using the = operator. You also can use the + and += operators to combine delegates into a **composed delegate** that calls the delegates from which it is built. As an example, assume that you declare three delegates named del1,

613

A composed delegate is a collection of delegates. The += and −= operators add and remove items from the collection.

del2, and del3, and that you assign a reference to the method M1() to del1 and a reference to method M2() to del2. When the statement del3 = del1 + del2; executes, del3 becomes a delegate that executes both M1() and M2(), in that order. Only delegates with the same parameter list can be composed, and the delegates used must have a void return type. Additionally, you can use the - and -= operators to remove a delegate from a composed delegate.

Figure 13-8 shows a program that contains a composed delegate. This program contains only two changes from the Greeting program in Figure 13-6: the class name (Greeting2) and the shaded statement that creates the composed delegate. The delegate firstDel now executes two methods, Hello() and Goodbye(), whereas secondDel still executes only Goodbye(). Figure 13-9 shows the output; "Cathy" is used with two methods, but "Bob" is used with only one.

```
using System;
delegate void GreetingDelegate(string s);
class Greeting2
{
    public static void Hello(string s)
    {
        Console.WriteLine("Hello, {0}!", s);
    }
    public static void Goodbye(string s)
    {
        Console.WriteLine("Goodbye, {0}!", s);
    }
    public static void Main()
    {
        GreetingDelegate firstDel, secondDel;
        firstDel = new GreetingDelegate(Hello);
        secondDel = new GreetingDelegate(Goodbye);
        firstDel += secondDel;
        GreetMethod(firstDel, "Cathy");
        GreetMethod(secondDel, "Bob");
    }
    public static void GreetMethod
        (GreetingDelegate gd, string name)
    {
        Console.WriteLine("The greeting is:");
        gd(name);
    }
}
```

**Figure 13-8** The Greeting2 program

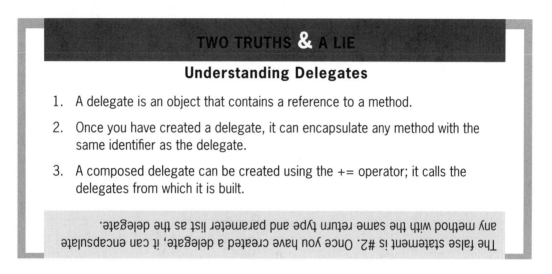

**Figure 13-9** Output of the Greeting2 program

Watch the video *Event Handling*.

## TWO TRUTHS & A LIE

### Understanding Delegates

1. A delegate is an object that contains a reference to a method.

2. Once you have created a delegate, it can encapsulate any method with the same identifier as the delegate.

3. A composed delegate can be created using the += operator; it calls the delegates from which it is built.

The false statement is #2. Once you have created a delegate, it can encapsulate any method with the same return type and parameter list as the delegate.

## Declaring Your Own Events and Handlers and Using the Built-in EventHandler

To declare your own event, you use a delegate. An event provides a way for the clients of a class to dictate methods that should execute when an event occurs. The clients identify methods to execute by associating the delegate with the method that should execute when the event occurs. Just like the event handlers that are automatically created in the IDE, each of your own event handler delegates requires two arguments: the object where the event was initiated (the sender) and an EventArgs argument. You can create an EventArgs object that contains event information, or you can use the EventArgs class static field named Empty, which represents an event that contains no event data. In other words, using the EventArgs.Empty field simply tells the client that an event has occurred, without specifying details.

The value of EventArgs .Empty is a read-only instance of EventArgs. You can pass it to a method that accepts an EventArgs parameter.

For example, you can declare a **delegate** event handler named ChangedEventHandler, as follows:

```
public delegate void ChangedEventHandler
    (object sender, EventArgs e);
```

The identifier ChangedEventHandler can be any legal identifier you choose. This delegate defines the set of arguments that will be passed to the method that handles the event. The delegate ChangedEventHandler can be used in a client program that handles events.

For example, Figure 13-10 contains the ChangedEventHandler delegate and a simple Student class that is similar to many classes you already have created. The Student class contains just two data fields and will generate an event when the data in either field changes.

```
public delegate void ChangedEventHandler
    (object sender, EventArgs e);
class Student
{
    private int idNum;
    private double gpa;
    public event ChangedEventHandler Changed;
    public int IdNum
    {
        get
        {
            return idNum;
        }
        set
        {
            idNum = value;
            OnChanged(EventArgs.Empty);
        }
    }
    public double Gpa
    {
        get
        {
            return gpa;
        }
        set
        {
            gpa = value;
            OnChanged(EventArgs.Empty);
        }
    }
    private void OnChanged(EventArgs e)
    {
        Changed(this, e);
    }
}
```

**Figure 13-10** The Student class

The class in Figure 13-10 contains fields that will hold an ID number and grade point average (GPA) for a Student. The first shaded statement in the figure defines a third Student class attribute—an event named Changed. The declaration for an event looks like a field, but instead of being an int or a double, it is a ChangedEventHandler.

**617**

The Student class event (Changed) looks like an ordinary field. However, you cannot assign values to the event as easily as you can to ordinary data fields. You can take only two actions on an event: You can compose a new delegate onto it using the += operator, and you can remove a delegate from it using the -= operator. For example, to add StudentChanged to the Changed event of a Student object named stu, you would write the following:

```
stu.Changed += new ChangedEventHandler(StudentChanged);
```

In the Student class, each set accessor assigns a value to the appropriate class instance field. However, when either the idNum or the gpa changes, the method in the Student class named OnChanged() is also called, using EventArgs.Empty as the argument. The OnChanged() method calls Changed() using two arguments: a reference to the Student object that was changed and the empty EventArgs object. Calling Changed() is also known as **invoking the event**.

If no client has wired a delegate to the event, the Changed field will be null, rather than referring to the delegate that should be called when the event is invoked. Therefore, programmers often check for null before invoking the event, as in the following example:

```
if(Changed != null)
    Changed(this, e);
```

For simplicity, the example in Figure 13-10 does not bother checking for null.

Figure 13-11 shows an EventListener class that listens for Student events. This class contains a Student object that is assigned a value using the parameter to the EventListener class constructor. The StudentChanged() method is added to the Student's event delegate using the += operator. The StudentChanged() method is the event-handler method that executes in response to a Changed event; it displays a message and Student data.

```
class EventListener
{
    private Student stu;
    public EventListener(Student student)
    {
        stu = student;
        stu.Changed += new ChangedEventHandler
            (StudentChanged);
    }
    private void StudentChanged(object sender, EventArgs e)
    {
        Console.WriteLine("The student has changed.");
        Console.WriteLine("    ID# {0}   GPA {1}",
            stu.IdNum, stu.Gpa);
    }
}
```

**Figure 13-11**   The EventListener class

Figure 13-12 shows a program that demonstrates the Student and EventListener classes. The program contains a single Main() method, which declares one Student and registers the program to listen for events from the Student class. Then three assignments are made. Because this program is registered to listen for events from the Student, each change in a data field triggers an event. That is, each assignment not only changes the value of the data field, it also executes the StudentChanged() method that displays two lines of explanation. In Figure 13-13, the program output shows that an event occurs three times—once when the ID becomes 2345 (and the GPA is still 0), again when the ID becomes 4567 (and the GPA still has not changed), and a third time when the GPA becomes 3.2.

```
using System;
class DemoStudentEvent
{
    public static void Main()
    {
        Student oneStu = new Student();
        EventListener listener = new EventListener(oneStu);
        oneStu.IdNum = 2345;
        oneStu.IdNum = 4567;
        oneStu.Gpa = 3.2;
    }
}
```

**Figure 13-12**   The DemoStudentEvent program

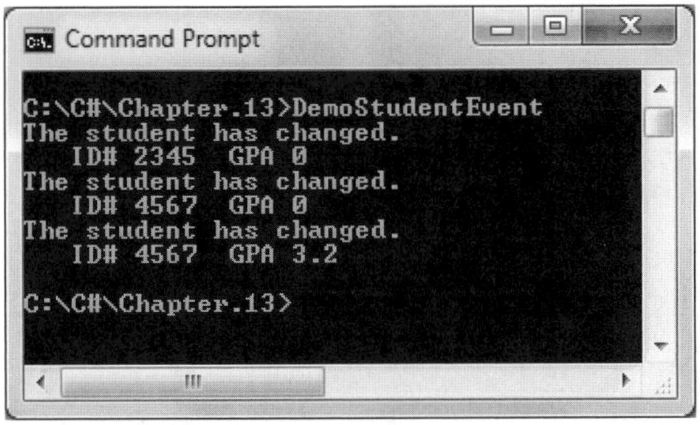

**Figure 13-13**  Output of the DemoStudentEvent program

## Using the Built-in EventHandler

The C# language allows you to create events using any delegate type. However, the .NET Framework provides guidelines you should follow if you are developing a class that others will use. These guidelines indicate that the delegate type for an event should take exactly two parameters: a parameter indicating the source of the event, and an EventArgs parameter that encapsulates any additional information about the event. For events that do not use additional information, the .NET Framework has already defined an appropriate delegate type named **EventHandler**.

Figure 13-14 shows all the code necessary to demonstrate an EventHandler. Note the following changes from the classes used in the DemoStudentEvent program:

- No delegate is declared explicitly in the Student class.

- In the first statement with shading in the Student class, the event is associated with the built-in delegate EventHandler.

- In the second statement with shading, which appears in the EventListener class, the delegate composition uses EventHandler.

```
using System;
class Student
{
    private int idNum;
    private double gpa;
    public event EventHandler Changed;
    public int IdNum
    {
        get
        {
            return idNum;
        }
```

**Figure 13-14**  The Student, EventListener, and DemoStudentEvent2 classes *(continues)*

619

620

*(continued)*

```
      set
      {
         idNum = value;
         OnChanged(EventArgs.Empty);
      }
   }
   public double Gpa
   {
      get
      {
         return gpa;
      }
      set
      {
         gpa = value;
         OnChanged(EventArgs.Empty);
      }
   }
   private void OnChanged(EventArgs e)
   {
      Changed(this, e);
   }
}
class EventListener
{
   private Student stu;
   public EventListener(Student student)
   {
      stu = student;
      stu.Changed += new EventHandler(StudentChanged);
   }
   private void StudentChanged(object sender, EventArgs e)
   {
      Console.WriteLine("The student has changed.");
      Console.WriteLine("   ID# {0}   GPA {1}",
        stu.IdNum, stu.Gpa);
   }
}
class DemoStudentEvent2
{
   public static void Main()
   {
      Student oneStu = new Student();
      EventListener listener = new EventListener(oneStu);
      oneStu.IdNum = 2345;
      oneStu.IdNum = 4567;
      oneStu.Gpa = 3.2;
   }
}
```

**Figure 13-14** The Student, EventListener, and DemoStudentEvent2 classes

When you compile and execute the program in Figure 13-14, the output is identical to that shown in Figure 13-13.

---

**TWO TRUTHS & A LIE**

### Declaring Your Own Events and Handlers and Using the Built-in EventHandler

1. When an event occurs, any delegate that a client has given or passed to the event is invoked.

2. Built-in event handler delegates have two arguments, but those you create yourself have only one.

3. You can take only two actions on an event field: composing a new delegate onto the field using the += operator, and removing a delegate from the field using the -= operator.

The false statement is #2. Every event handler delegate requires two arguments—the object where the event was initiated (the sender) and an EventArgs argument.

---

# Handling Control Component Events

Handling events requires understanding several difficult concepts. Fortunately, you most frequently will want to handle events in GUI environments when the user will manipulate Controls, and the good news is that these events have already been defined for you. When you want to handle events generated by GUI Controls, you use the same techniques as when you handle events that are not generated by Controls. The major difference is that when you create your own classes, like Student, you must define both the data fields and events you want to manage. However, existing Control components, like Buttons and ListBoxes, already contain fields and public properties, like Text, as well as events with names, like Click. Table 13-1 lists just some of the more commonly used Control events.

 You can consult the Visual Studio Help feature to discover additional Control events as well as more specific events assigned to individual Control child classes.

| Event | Description |
|---|---|
| BackColorChanged | Occurs when the value of the BackColor property has changed |
| Click | Occurs when a control is clicked |
| ControlAdded | Occurs when a new control is added |
| ControlRemoved | Occurs when a control is removed |
| CursorChanged | Occurs when the Cursor property value has changed |
| DragDrop | Occurs when a drag-and-drop operation is completed |
| DragEnter | Occurs when an object is dragged into a control's bounds |
| DragLeave | Occurs when an object has been dragged into and out of a control's bounds |
| DragOver | Occurs when an object has been dragged over a control's bounds |
| EnabledChanged | Occurs when the Enabled property value has changed |
| Enter | Occurs when a control is entered |
| FontChanged | Occurs when the Font property value has changed |
| ForeColorChanged | Occurs when the ForeColor property value has changed |
| GotFocus | Occurs when a control receives focus |
| HelpRequested | Occurs when a user requests help for a control |
| KeyDown | Occurs when a key is pressed while a control has focus; event is followed immediately by KeyPress |
| KeyPress | Occurs when a key is pressed while a control has focus; event occurs just after KeyDown |
| KeyUp | Occurs when a key is released while a control has focus |
| Leave | Occurs when a control is left |
| LocationChanged | Occurs when the Location property value has changed |
| LostFocus | Occurs when a control loses focus |
| MouseDown | Occurs when the mouse pointer hovers over a control and a mouse button is pressed |
| MouseEnter | Occurs when the mouse pointer enters a control |
| MouseHover | Occurs when the mouse pointer hovers over a control |
| MouseLeave | Occurs when the mouse pointer leaves a control |
| MouseMove | Occurs when the mouse pointer moves over a control |
| MouseUp | Occurs when the mouse pointer hovers over a control and a mouse button is released |
| MouseWheel | Occurs when the mouse wheel moves while a control has focus |
| Move | Occurs when a control is moved |
| Resize | Occurs when a control is resized |
| TextChanged | Occurs when the Text property value has changed |
| VisibleChanged | Occurs when the Visible property value has changed |

**Table 13-1**   Some Control class public instance events

You have already used the IDE to create some event-handling methods. These methods have been the default events generated when you double-click a Control in the IDE. For example, you have created a Click() method for a Button and a LinkClicked() method for a LinkLabel. A Form can contain any number of Controls that might have events associated with them. Additionally, a single Control might be able to raise any number of events. For example, besides creating a Button's default Click event, you might want to define various actions when the user's mouse rolls over the button. Table 13-1 lists only a few of the many events available with Controls; any Control could conceivably raise many of those events.

Suppose you want to create a project that takes a different set of actions when the mouse is over a Button than when the mouse is clicked. Figure 13-15 shows a project that has been started in the IDE. The following actions have been taken:

- The Form was resized to 225, 150.

- A Button was dragged onto the Form and its Text was set to "Click me".

- A Label was added to the Form, its Text was set to "Hello", and its Font was increased.

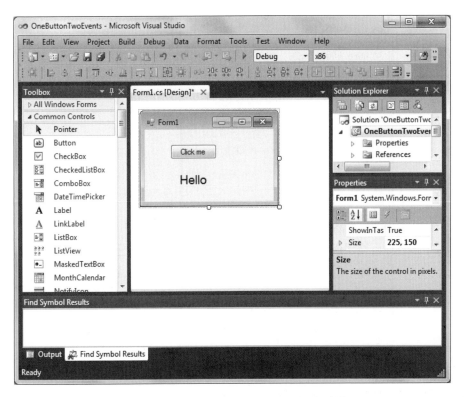

**Figure 13-15**  Start of OneButtonTwoEvents project in the IDE

When you double-click the Button on the Form in the IDE, you generate the shell of a Click() method into which you can type a command to change the Label's text and color, as follows:

```
private void button1_Click(object sender, EventArgs e)
{
    label1.Text = "Button was clicked";
    label1.BackColor = Color.CornflowerBlue;
}
```

 Color.CornflowerBlue is one of C#'s predefined Color properties. A complete list appears in Table 12-5 in Chapter 12.

With the Button selected on the design Form, you can click the Events icon in the Properties window at the right side of the screen. The Events icon looks like a lightning bolt. Figure 13-16 shows that the Properties window displays events instead of properties and that the Click event has an associated method.

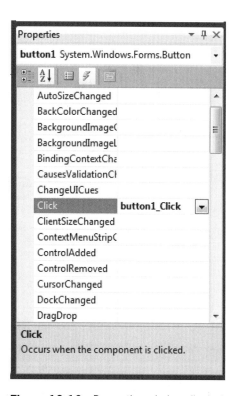

**Figure 13-16**  Properties window displaying events

If you scroll through the Events listed in the Properties window, you can see a wide variety of Event choices. If you scroll down to MouseEnter and double-click, you can view the code for an event handler in the Form1.cs file as follows:

When you are viewing events in the Properties window, you can return to the list of properties by clicking the Properties icon. This icon is to the immediate left of the Events icon.

```
private void button1_MouseEnter(object sender, EventArgs e)
{
}
```

You can type any statements you want within this method. For example:

```
private void button1_MouseEnter(object sender, EventArgs e)
{
   label1.Text = "Go ahead";
   button1.BackColor = Color.Red;
}
```

When you run the program with the two new methods, two different events can occur:

- When you enter the button with the mouse (that is, pass the mouse over it), the Label's Text changes to "Go ahead" and the button turns red, as shown on the left in Figure 13-17.

- After the button is clicked, the Label's Text changes again and the Label becomes blue, as shown on the right in Figure 13-17.

 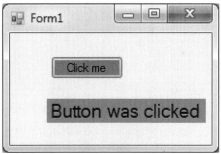

**Figure 13-17** OneButtonTwoEvents program when mouse enters button and after button is clicked

If you examine the code generated by the Windows Form Designer, you will find the following two statements:

```
this.button1.Click += new System.EventHandler
   (this.button1_Click);
this.button1.MouseEnter += new System.EventHandler
   (this.button1_MouseEnter);
```

These EventHandler statements are similar to those in the Student class in Figure 13-14. The Click and MouseEnter delegates have been set to handle events appropriately for this application. You could

Watch the video *Handling Control Component Events*.

have used the IDE to create these events just by selecting them from the Properties list and writing the action statements you want. The IDE saves you time by automatically entering the needed statement correctly. However, by knowing how to manually create a GUI program that contains events, you gain a greater understanding of how event handling works. This knowledge helps you troubleshoot problems and helps you create your own new events and handlers when necessary.

---

## TWO TRUTHS & A LIE

### Handling Control Component Events

1. The default methods generated when you double-click a Control in the IDE are known as procedures.

2. A Form can contain any number of Controls that might have events associated with them, and a single Control might be able to raise any number of events.

3. You can type any statements you want within an automatically generated event method.

The false statement is #1. The default methods generated when you double-click a Control in the IDE are known as event handlers.

---

# Handling Mouse and Keyboard Events

Users can interact with GUI applications in multiple ways. Certainly the most common tactics are to use a mouse or to type on a keyboard. Mouse and keyboard events are similar in that every mouse or key event-handling method must have two parameters: an object representing the sender and an object that holds information about the event.

## Handling Mouse Events

Mouse events include all the actions a user takes with a mouse, including clicking, pointing, and dragging. Mouse events can be handled for any Control through an object of the class MouseEventArgs. The delegate used to create mouse event handlers is MouseEventHandler. Depending on the event, the type of the second parameter in the event-handling method is EventArgs or

MouseEventArgs. Table 13-2 describes several common mouse events, and Table 13-3 lists some properties of the MouseEventArgs class.

The MouseEventArgs class descends from EventArgs.

| Mouse event | Description | Event argument type |
|---|---|---|
| MouseClick | Occurs when the user clicks the mouse within the Control's boundaries | MouseEventArgs |
| MouseDoubleClick | Occurs when the user double-clicks the mouse within the Control's boundaries | MouseEventArgs |
| MouseEnter | Occurs when the mouse cursor enters the Control's boundaries | EventArgs |
| MouseLeave | Occurs when the mouse cursor leaves the Control's boundaries | EventArgs |
| MouseDown | Occurs when a mouse button is pressed while the mouse is within the Control's boundaries | MouseEventArgs |
| MouseHover | Occurs when the mouse cursor is within the Control's boundaries | MouseEventArgs |
| MouseMove | Occurs when the mouse is moved while within the Control's boundaries | MouseEventArgs |
| MouseUp | Occurs when a mouse button is released while the mouse is within the Control's boundaries | MouseEventArgs |

**Table 13-2**    Common mouse events

A MouseDown event can occur without a corresponding MouseUp if the user presses the mouse but switches focus to another control or application before releasing the mouse button.

| MouseEventArgs property | Description |
|---|---|
| Button | Specifies which mouse button triggered the event; the value can be Left, Right, Middle, or none |
| Clicks | Specifies the number of times the mouse was clicked |
| X | The x-coordinate where the event occurred on the control that generated the event |
| Y | The y-coordinate where the event occurred on the control that generated the event |

**Table 13-3**    Properties of the MouseEventArgs class

MouseClick and Click are separate events. The Click event takes an EventArgs parameter, but MouseClick takes a MouseEventArgs parameter. For example, if you define a Click event, you do not have the MouseEventArgs class properties.

Figure 13-18 contains a Form with a single Label named clickLocationLabel that changes as the user continues to click the mouse on it. The figure shows how the Label changes in response to a series of user clicks. Initially, the Label is empty (that is, the default Text property has been deleted and not replaced), but the following code was added to the Form.cs file:

```
private void Form1_MouseClick(object sender, MouseEventArgs e)
{
    clickLocationLabel.Text += "\nClicked at " + e.X +
        ", " + e.Y;
}
```

Every time the mouse is clicked on the Form, the Label is appended with a new line that contains "Clicked at" and the x- and y-coordinate position where the click occurred on the Form.

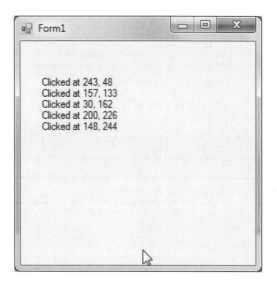

**Figure 13-18** A Form that responds to clicks

When the programmer selects the MouseClick() event for Form1 from the Event list in the IDE, the following code is generated in the Designer.cs file. This code instantiates the MouseClick delegate.

```
this.MouseClick += new System.Windows.Forms.MouseEventHandler
    (this.Form1_MouseClick);
```

## Handling Keyboard Events

Keyboard events, also known as **key events**, occur when a user presses and releases keyboard keys. Table 13-4 lists some common keyboard events. Similar to the way mouse events work, every keyboard event-handling method must have two parameters. Depending on the event, the delegate used to create the keyboard event handler is either `KeyEventHandler` or `KeyPressEventHandler`, and the type of the second parameter is `KeyEventArgs` or `KeyPressEventArgs`.

| Keyboard event | Description | Event argument type |
|---|---|---|
| KeyDown | Occurs when a key is first pressed | KeyEventArgs |
| KeyUp | Occurs when a key is released | KeyEventArgs |
| KeyPress | Occurs when a key is pressed | KeyPressEventArgs |

**Table 13-4**   Keyboard events

Table 13-5 describes `KeyEventArgs` properties, and Table 13-6 describes `KeyPressEventArgs` properties. An important difference is that `KeyEventArgs` objects include data about helper keys or modifier keys that are pressed with another key. For example, if you need to distinguish between a user pressing *A* and pressing *Alt+A* in your application, then you must use a keyboard event that uses an argument of type `KeyEventArgs`.

| Property | Description |
|---|---|
| Alt | Indicates whether the Alt key was pressed |
| Control | Indicates whether the Control (Ctrl) key was pressed |
| Shift | Indicates whether the Shift key was pressed |
| KeyCode | Returns the code for the key |
| KeyData | Returns the key code along with any modifier key |
| KeyValue | Returns a numeric representation of the key (this number is known as the Windows virtual key code) |

**Table 13-5**   Some properties of `KeyEventArgs` class

| Property | Description |
|---|---|
| KeyChar | Returns the ASCII character for the key pressed |

**Table 13-6**   A property of `KeyPressEventArgs` class

For example, suppose you create a `Form` with an empty `Label`, like the first `Form` in the series in Figure 13-20. From the Properties window for the `Form`, you can double-click the `KeyUp` event to generate the shell for a method named `Form1_KeyUp()`. Suppose you then insert the statements into the method in the Form1.cs file, as shown in Figure 13-19. When the user runs the program and presses and releases a keyboard key, the Label is filled with information about the key. Figure 13-20 shows four executions of this modified program. During the first execution, the user typed *a*. You can see on the form that the KeyCode is "A" (not "a"), but you also can see that the user did not press the Shift key.

```
private void Form1_KeyUp(object sender, KeyEventArgs e)
{
    label1.Text += "Key Code " + e.KeyCode;
    label1.Text += "\nAlt " + e.Alt;
    label1.Text += "\nShift " + e.Shift;
    label1.Text += "\nControl " + e.Control;
    label1.Text += "\nKey Data " + e.KeyData;
    label1.Text += "\nKey Value " + e.KeyValue + "\n\n";
}
```

**Figure 13-19** KeyUp() method

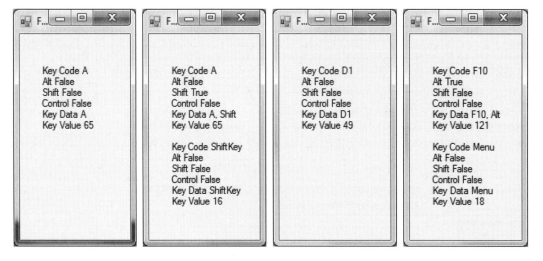

**Figure 13-20** Four executions of KeyDemo program

In the second execution in Figure 13-20, the user held down Shift, pressed *a*, and then released the Shift key. This causes two separate KeyUp events. The first has KeyCode "A" with Shift true, and the second has KeyCode ShiftKey. Notice that the Key values generated after typing *A* and Shift are different.

In the third execution in Figure 13-20, the user pressed the number 1, whose code is D1.

In the final execution, the user pressed Alt+F10 and released the F10 key first. When you view the Form1.Designer.cs file for the KeyDemo program, you see the following automatically created statement, which defines the composed delegate:

```
this.KeyUp += new System.Windows.Forms.KeyEventHandler
    (this.Form1_KeyUp);
```

---

**TWO TRUTHS & A LIE**

### Handling Mouse and Keyboard Events

1. The delegate used to create mouse event handlers is MouseEventHandler.

2. Keyboard events, also known as key events, occur when a user presses and releases keyboard keys.

3. Unlike mouse events, every keyboard event-handling method must be parameterless.

The false statement is #3. Like mouse events, every keyboard event-handling method must have two parameters: an object representing the sender and an object that holds information about the event.

---

# Managing Multiple Controls

When Forms contain multiple Controls, you often want one to have focus. You also might want several actions to have a single, shared consequence. For example, you might want the same action to occur whether the user clicks a button or presses the Enter key, or you might want multiple buttons to generate the same event when they are clicked.

## Defining Focus

When users encounter multiple GUI Controls on a Form, usually one Control has **focus**. For example, when a Button has focus, a user expects that clicking the button or pressing the Enter key will raise an event.

TabStop is a Boolean property of a Control that identifies whether the Control will serve as a stopping place—that is, a place that will receive focus—in a sequence of Tab key presses. The default value for TabStop for a Button is true, but the default value for a Label is false

 Setting two or more Controls' TabIndex values to 0 does not cause an error. Only one Control will receive focus, however.

because Labels are not expected to be part of a tabbing sequence. TabIndex is a numeric property that indicates the order in which the Control will receive focus when the user presses the Tab key. Programmers typically use small numbers for TabIndex values, beginning with 0. When a Control's TabStop value is true and the Control has the lowest TabIndex of a Form's Controls, it receives focus when the Form is initialized.

Figure 13-21 shows a Form that contains three Buttons and a Label. Each Button has been associated with a Click() event such as the following:

```
private void button1_Click(object sender, EventArgs e)
{
    buttonInfoLabel.Text = "Button 1 selected";
}
```

Each Button has been assigned a TabIndex value in ascending order. When the application starts, the first Button (labeled "1") has focus. Whether the user clicks that button or presses Enter, the message appears as shown on the left in Figure 13-21. In the next part of the figure, the user has pressed Tab and Enter to select button2, so it has focus and the Label's Text property has changed. Alternatively, the user could have clicked button2 to achieve the same result. The user could then select either of the other Buttons by clicking them as usual, or by pressing Tab until the desired button has focus and then pressing Enter.

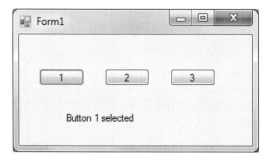 

**Figure 13-21** The FocusDemo application

## Handling Multiple Events with a Single Handler

When a Form contains multiple Controls, you can create a separate event handler for each Control. However, you can also associate the same event handler with multiple Controls. For example, suppose you create a Form that contains three Buttons and a Label. The buttons have been labeled "A", "B", and "3". Further suppose you want to display one message when the user clicks a letter button and a different message when the user clicks a number button. In the IDE, you can double-click the first Button and create an associated method such as the following:

```
private void button1_Click(object sender, EventArgs e)
{
    buttonInfoLabel.Text += "You clicked a letter button";
}
```

If you click the second button so its properties are displayed in the IDE's Properties list, you can click the Events icon to see a list of events associated with the second button. In Figure 13-22, no Click event has been chosen yet, but a list box is available. This list contains all the existing events that have the correct signature to be the event handler for the event. The list shows that the button1_Click() handler can also handle a button2_Click event, so you can select it. When you run the program, clicking either button produces the output shown in Figure 13-23. When you run the program and click the third button, no message is displayed.

 If you run the application in Figure 13-23 and click a letter button, the label changes. If you subsequently click the "3" button, nothing happens because no event has been associated with the third button, so the Label's Text property remains "You clicked a letter button". Most likely, you would want to associate an event with the "3" button to modify the Label's Text to "You clicked a number button".

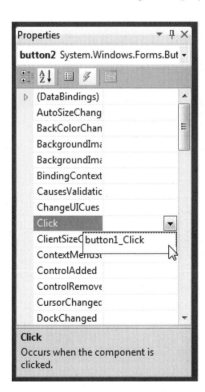

**Figure 13-22** Event properties for button2

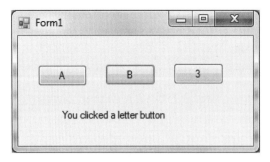

**Figure 13-23** Output of `SingleHandler` program after either letter button is clicked

When two or more `Control`s generate the same event, many programmers prefer to generalize the event method name. For example, if `button1` and `button2` call the same method when clicked, it makes sense to name the event method `letterButton_Click()` instead of `button1_Click()`.

Watch the video *Managing Multiple Controls*.

Perhaps you have shopped online at a site that offers multiple ways to "buy now." For example, you might click a grocery cart icon, choose "Place order now" from a menu, or click a button. Often, "Place order now" buttons are displayed at several locations on the page. If you want to encourage a user's behavior, you should provide multiple ways to accommodate it.

## TWO TRUTHS & A LIE

### Managing Multiple Controls

1.  The `Control` `TabStop` property can be set to true or false; it identifies whether the `Control` will serve as a stopping place in a sequence of Tab key presses.

2.  On a `Form` with multiple `Control`s, one `Control` must have a `TabIndex` value of 0.

3.  When a `Form` contains multiple `Control`s, you can associate the same event with all of them.

The false statement is #2. `TabIndex` is a numeric property that indicates the order in which the `Control` will receive focus when the user presses the Tab key. Programmers typically use small numbers for `TabIndex` values, beginning with 0. However, you might choose not to use any `TabIndex` values, or if you do, you might choose not to start with 0.

# Continuing to Learn about `Controls` and Events

If you examine the Visual Studio IDE, you will discover many additional `Controls` that contain hundreds of properties and events. No single book or programming course can demonstrate all of them for you. However, if you understand good programming principles and the syntax and structure of C# programs, learning about each new C# feature becomes progressively easier. When you encounter a new control in the IDE, you probably can use it without understanding all the code generated in the background, but when you do understand the background, your knowledge of C# is more complete.

Continue to explore the Help facility in the Visual Studio IDE. Particularly, read the brief tutorials there. Also, you should search the Internet for C# discussion groups. C# is a new, dynamic language, and programmers pose many questions to each other online. Reading these discussions can provide you with valuable information and suggest new approaches to resolving problems.

# You Do It

## Creating Delegates

To demonstrate how delegates work, you will create two delegate instances in the next steps and assign different method references to them.

**To demonstrate delegates:**

1. Open a new file in your text editor. Type the necessary `using` statement, then create a delegate that encapsulates a `void` method that accepts a `double` argument:

```
using System;
delegate void DiscountDelegate(ref double saleAmount);
```

2. Begin creating a `Discount` class that contains a `StandardDiscount()` method. The method accepts a reference parameter that represents an amount of a sale. If the sale amount is at least $1000.00, a discount of 5% is calculated and subtracted from the sale amount. If the sale amount is not at least $1000, nothing is subtracted.

```
class Discount
{
    public static void StandardDiscount
       (ref double saleAmount)
    {
       const double DISCOUNT_RATE = 0.05;
       const double CUTOFF = 1000.00;
       double discount;
       if(saleAmount >= CUTOFF)
          discount = saleAmount * DISCOUNT_RATE;
       else
          discount = 0;
       saleAmount -= discount;
    }
```

3. Add a PreferredDiscount() method. The method also accepts a reference parameter that represents the amount of a sale and calculates a discount of 10% on every sale.

```
public static void PreferredDiscount(ref double saleAmount)
{
    const double SPECIAL_DISCOUNT = 0.10;
    double discount = saleAmount * SPECIAL_DISCOUNT;
    saleAmount -= discount;
}
```

4. Start a Main() method that declares variables whose values (a sale amount and a code) will be supplied by the user. Declare two DiscountDelegate objects named firstDel and secondDel. Assign a reference to the StandardDiscount() method to one DiscountDelegate object and a reference to the PreferredDiscount() method to the other DiscountDelegate object.

```
public static void Main()
{
    double saleAmount;
    char code;
    DiscountDelegate firstDel, secondDel;
    firstDel = new DiscountDelegate(StandardDiscount);
    secondDel = new DiscountDelegate(PreferredDiscount);
```

5. Continue the Main() method with prompts to the user to enter a sale amount and a code indicating whether the standard or preferred discount should apply. Then, depending on the code, use the appropriate delegate to calculate the correct new value for saleAmount. Display the value and add closing curly braces for the Main() method and the class.

```
            Console.Write("Enter amount of sale ");
            saleAmount = Convert.ToDouble(Console.ReadLine());
            Console.Write("Enter S for standard discount, " +
                "or P for preferred discount ");
            code = Convert.ToChar(Console.ReadLine());
            if(code == 'S')
                firstDel(ref saleAmount);
            else
                secondDel(ref saleAmount);
            Console.WriteLine("New sale amount is {0}",
                saleAmount.ToString("C2"));
        }
    }
```

6. Save the file as **DiscountDelegateDemo.cs**, then compile and execute it. Figure 13-24 shows the results when the program is executed several times.

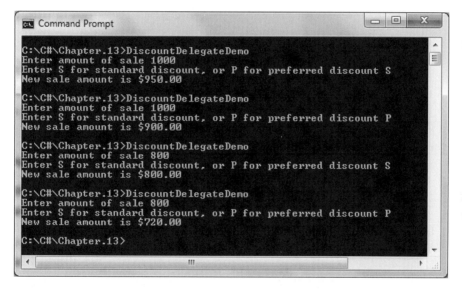

**Figure 13-24** Sample executions of DiscountDelegateDemo program

## Creating a Composed Delegate

When you compose delegates, you can invoke multiple method calls using a single statement. In the next steps, you will create a composed delegate to demonstrate how composition works.

**To create a composed delegate:**

1. Open the **DiscountDelegateDemo.cs** file in your text editor. Immediately save it as **DiscountDelegateDemo2.cs**.

2. Within the `Main()` method, add a third `DiscountDelegate` object to the statement that declares the two existing versions, as follows:

```
DiscountDelegate firstDel, secondDel, thirdDel;
```

3. After the statements that assign values to the existing `DiscountDelegate` objects, add statements that assign the `firstDel` object to `thirdDel` and then add `secondDel` to it through composition.

```
thirdDel = firstDel;
thirdDel += secondDel;
```

4. Change the prompt for the code, as follows, to reflect three options. The standard and preferred discounts remain the same, but the extreme discount (supposedly for special customers) provides both types of discounts, first subtracting 5% for any sale equal to or greater than $1000, and then providing a discount of 10% more.

```
Console.Write("Enter S for standard discount, " +
   "P for preferred discount, " +
   "\nor X for eXtreme discount ");
```

5. Change the `if` statement so that if the user does not enter *S* or *P*, then the extreme discount applies.

```
if(code == 'S')
   firstDel(ref saleAmount);
else
   if(code == 'P')
      secondDel(ref saleAmount);
   else
      thirdDel(ref saleAmount);
```

6. Save the program, then compile and execute it. For reference, Figure 13-25 shows the complete program. Figure 13-26 shows the output when the program is executed several times. When the user enters a sale amount of $1000 and an *S*, a 5% discount is applied. When the user enters a *P* for the same amount, a 10% discount is applied. When the user enters *X* with the same amount, a 5% discount is applied, followed by a 10% discount, which produces a net result of a 14.5% discount.

```
using System;
delegate void DiscountDelegate(ref double saleAmount);
class Discount
{
    public static void StandardDiscount(ref double saleAmount)
    {
        const double DISCOUNT_RATE = 0.05;
        const double CUTOFF = 1000.00;
        double discount;
        if(saleAmount >= CUTOFF)
            discount = saleAmount * DISCOUNT_RATE;
        else
            discount = 0;
        saleAmount -= discount;
    }
    public static void PreferredDiscount(ref double saleAmount)
    {
        const double SPECIAL_DISCOUNT = 0.10;
        double discount = saleAmount * SPECIAL_DISCOUNT;
        saleAmount -= discount;
    }
    public static void Main()
    {
        double saleAmount;
        char code;
        DiscountDelegate firstDel, secondDel, thirdDel;
        firstDel = new DiscountDelegate(StandardDiscount);
        secondDel = new DiscountDelegate(PreferredDiscount);
        thirdDel = firstDel;
        thirdDel += secondDel;
        Console.Write("Enter amount of sale ");
        saleAmount = Convert.ToDouble(Console.ReadLine());
        Console.Write("Enter S for standard discount, " +
            "P for preferred discount, " +
            "\nor X for eXtreme discount ");
        code = Convert.ToChar(Console.ReadLine());
        if(code == 'S')
            firstDel(ref saleAmount);
        else
            if(code == 'P')
                secondDel(ref saleAmount);
            else
                thirdDel(ref saleAmount);
        Console.WriteLine("New sale amount is {0}",
            saleAmount.ToString("C2"));
    }
}
```

Figure 13-25   DiscountDelegateDemo2 program

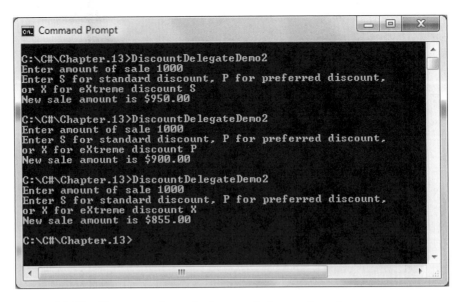

**Figure 13-26** Three executions of `DiscountDelegateDemo2` program

For `static` methods like `StandardDiscount` and `PreferredDiscount`, a `delegate` object encapsulates the method to be called. When creating a class that contains instance methods, you create `delegate` objects that encapsulate both an instance of the class and a method of the instance. You will create this type of `delegate` in the next section.

## Creating a Delegate that Encapsulates Instance Methods

In the next set of steps, you will create a simple `BankAccount` class that is similar to many classes you already have created. The `BankAccount` class will contain just two data fields: an account number and a balance. It also will contain methods to make withdrawals and deposits. An event will be generated after any withdrawal or deposit.

**To create the BankAccount class:**

1. Open a new file in your text editor. Type the `using System;` statement, then begin a class named `BankAccount`. The class contains an account number, a balance, and an event that executes when an account's balance is adjusted.

```
using System;
class BankAccount
{
    private int acctNum;
    private double balance;
    public event EventHandler BalanceAdjusted;
```

2. Add a constructor that accepts an account number parameter and initializes the balance to 0.

```
public BankAccount(int acct)
{
    acctNum = acct;
    balance = 0;
}
```

3. Add read-only properties for both the account number and the account balance.

```
public int AcctNum
{
    get
    {
        return acctNum;
    }
}
public double Balance
{
    get
    {
        return balance;
    }
}
```

4. Add two methods. One makes account deposits by adding the parameter to the account balance, and the other makes withdrawals by subtracting the parameter value from the bank balance. Each uses the OnBalanceAdjusted event handler that reacts to all deposit and withdrawal events by displaying the new balance.

```
public void MakeDeposit(double amt)
{
    balance += amt;
    OnBalanceAdjusted(EventArgs.Empty);
}
public void MakeWithdrawal(double amt)
{
    balance -= amt;
    OnBalanceAdjusted(EventArgs.Empty);
}
```

5. Add the OnBalanceAdjusted() method that accepts an EventArgs parameter and calls BalanceAdjusted(), passing it references to the newly adjusted BankAccount object and the EventArgs object. Include a closing curly brace for the class.

```
public void OnBalanceAdjusted(EventArgs e)
{
    BalanceAdjusted(this, e);
}
}
```

 Earlier in the chapter, you learned that calling a method such as OnBalanceAdjusted() is also known as invoking the event.

6. Save the file as **DemoBankEvent.cs**.

## Creating an Event Listener

When you write an application that declares a BankAccount, you might want the client program to listen for BankAccount events. To do so, you create an EventListener class.

**To create an EventListener class:**

1. After the closing curly brace of the BankAccount class, type the following EventListener class that contains a BankAccount object. When the EventListener constructor executes, the BankAccount field is initialized with the constructor parameter. Using the += operator, add the BankAccountBalanceAdjusted() method to the event delegate. Next, write the BankAccountBalanceAdjusted() method to display a message and information about the BankAccount.

```
class EventListener
{
    private BankAccount acct;
    public EventListener(BankAccount account)
    {
        acct = account;
        acct.BalanceAdjusted += new EventHandler
          (BankAccountBalanceAdjusted);
    }
    private void BankAccountBalanceAdjusted(object sender,
        EventArgs e)
    {
        Console.WriteLine
            ("The account balance has been adjusted.");
        Console.WriteLine(" Account# {0} balance {1}",
            acct.AcctNum, acct.Balance.ToString("C2"));
    }
}
```

2. Create a class to test the BankAccount and EventListener classes. Below the closing curly brace for the EventListener class, start a DemoBankAccountEvent class that contains a Main() method. Declare an integer to hold the number of transactions that will occur in the demonstration program. Also declare two variables: One can hold a code that indicates whether a transaction is a deposit or withdrawal, and one is the amount of the transaction.

```
class DemoBankAccountEvent
{
    public static void Main()
    {
        const int TRANSACTIONS = 5;
        char code;
        double amt;
```

3. Declare a `BankAccount` object that is assigned an arbitrary account number, and declare an `EventListener` object so this program is registered to listen for events from the `BankAccount`. Each change in the `BankAccount` balance will not only change the balance data field, it will execute the `BankAccountBalanceAdjusted()` method that displays two lines of explanation.

```
BankAccount acct = new BankAccount(334455);
EventListener listener = new EventListener (acct);
```

4. Add a loop that executes five times (the value of `TRANSACTIONS`). On each iteration, prompt the user to indicate whether the current transaction is a deposit or withdrawal and to enter the transaction amount. Call the `MakeDeposit()` or `MakeWithdrawal()` method accordingly. At the end of the `for` loop, add a closing curly brace for the `Main()` method and another one for the class.

```
for(int x = 0; x < TRANSACTIONS; ++x)
{
    Console.Write
        ("Enter D for deposit or W for withdrawal ");
    code = Convert.ToChar(Console.ReadLine());
    Console.Write("Enter dollar amount ");
    amt = Convert.ToDouble(Console.ReadLine());
    if(code == 'D')
        acct.MakeDeposit(amt);
    else
        acct.MakeWithdrawal(amt);
}
}
}
```

5. Save the file, then compile and execute it. For reference, Figure 13-27 shows a typical execution in which five transactions modify the account. The output shows that an event occurs five times—twice for deposits and three times for withdrawals.

644

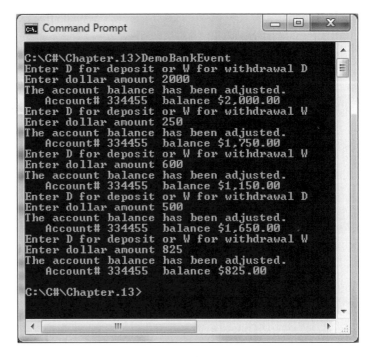

**Figure 13-27** Typical execution of DemoBankEvent program

## Using TabIndex

In the next steps, you will create a Form in the Visual Studio IDE and add four Buttons so you can demonstrate how to manipulate their TabIndex properties.

**To demonstrate TabIndex:**

1. Open the Visual Studio IDE and start a new project. Define it to be a **Windows Forms Application** named **ManyButtons**.

2. Change the Size of the Form to **350, 130**. Change the Text property of Form1 to **Many Buttons**.

3. Drag four Buttons onto the Form and place them so that they are similar to the layout shown in Figure 13-28. Change the Name properties of the buttons to redButton, whiteButton, blueButton, and favoriteButton. Change the Text on the Buttons to **Red**, **White**, **Blue**, and **My favorite color**, respectively. Adjust the size of the last button so its longer Text is fully displayed.

**Figure 13-28** Four `Buttons` on the Many Buttons `Form`

4. Examine the Properties list for the Red button. The `TabIndex` is 0. Examine the properties for the White, Blue, and My favorite color buttons. The IDE has set their `TabIndex` values to 1, 2, and 3, respectively.

5. Click the **Save All** button and then run the program. When the `Form` appears, the Red button has focus. Press the **Tab** key, and notice that focus changes to the White button. When you press **Tab** again, focus changes to the Blue button. Press **Tab** several more times and observe that the focus rotates among the four `Buttons`.

6. Dismiss the `Form`.

7. Change the `TabIndex` property of the Blue button to **0**, and change the `TabIndex` of the Red button to **2**. (The `TabIndex` of the White button remains 1 and the `TabIndex` of the My favorite color button remains 3.) Save the program again and then run it. This time, the Blue button begins with focus. When you press Tab, the order in which the `Buttons` receive focus is Blue, then White, then Red, then My favorite color. (Clicking the `Buttons` or pressing Enter raises no event because you have not assigned events to the `Buttons`.)

8. Change the `TabIndex` property for the Red button back to **0** and the `TabIndex` property for the Blue button back to **2**. Click the **Save All** button.

## Associating One Method with Multiple Events

In the next steps, you will add three methods to the Many Buttons `Form` and cause one of the methods to execute each time the user clicks one of the four `Buttons`.

646

At first glance, you might think this refers to the Button that is clicked. However, if you examine the redButton_Click() code in the Form1.cs file in the IDE, you will discover that the method is part of the Form1 class. Therefore, this.BackColor refers to the Form's BackColor property.

When you double-click a component on a Form in Design View, you move to the default method code. Clicking the component, however, causes the correct set of properties to appear in the Properties list.

**To associate methods with the application's events:**

1. If it is not still open, open the **ManyButtons** project in the Visual Studio IDE.

2. Double-click the **Red** button on the Form to view the code for the shell of a redButton_Click() method. Between the method's curly braces, insert a statement that will change the Form's background color to red as follows:

   ```
   this.BackColor = Color.Red;
   ```

3. Select the **Form1.cs [Design]** tab and then double-click the **White** button. Add the following code to the whiteButton_Click() method that is generated:

   ```
   this.BackColor = Color.White;
   ```

4. On the Form, double-click the **Blue** button. In its Click() method, add the following statement:

   ```
   this.BackColor = Color.Blue;
   ```

5. On the form, click the **My favorite color** button. In its Properties list, click the **Events** button (the lightning bolt). Select the Click event. From the list box next to the Click event, select one of the three events to correspond to your favorite color of the three.

6. Click the **Save All** button and then execute the program. As you click Buttons, the Form's background color changes appropriately.

7. Dismiss the form and exit Visual Studio.

## Chapter Summary

- Programs use events to notify clients when something happens to an object. GUI programs are event driven—an event such as a button click "drives" the program to perform a task. Programmers also say a button click raises an event, fires an event, or triggers an event. A method that performs a task in response to an event is an event handler. The Click event is the event generated when a button is clicked.

- A delegate is an object that contains a reference to a method. C# delegates provide a way for a program to take alternative courses that are not predetermined; a delegate provides a way to pass a reference to a method as an argument to another method. You can assign one delegate to another using the = operator. You also can use the + and += operators to combine delegates into a composed delegate that calls the delegates from which it is built.

- To declare your own event, you use a delegate. A client identifies methods to execute by associating the delegate with the method that should execute when the event occurs. The .NET Framework provides guidelines that the delegate type for an event should take exactly two parameters: a parameter indicating the source of the event, and an EventArgs parameter that encapsulates any additional information about the event. For events that do not use additional information, the .NET Framework has already defined an appropriate type named EventHandler.

- When you use existing Control components like Buttons and ListBoxes, they contain fields and public properties like Text as well as events with names like Click. A Form can contain any number of Controls that might have events associated with them. Additionally, a single control might be able to raise any number of events.

- Every mouse or keyboard event-handling method must have two parameters: an object representing the sender and an object that holds event information. Mouse events include all the actions a user takes with a mouse, including clicking, pointing, and dragging. Mouse events can be handled for any Control through an object of the class MouseEventArgs. The delegate used to create mouse event handlers is MouseEventHandler. Depending on the mouse event, the type of the second parameter is EventArgs or MouseEventArgs. Keyboard events, also known as key events, occur when a user presses and releases keyboard keys. Depending on the key event, the type of the second parameter is KeyEventArgs or KeyPressEventArgs.

- When users encounter multiple GUI Controls on a Form, usually one Control has focus. That is, if the user presses Enter, the Control will raise an event. When a Form contains multiple Controls, you can create a separate event for each Control. However, you can also associate the same event with multiple Controls.

- When you encounter a new control in the IDE, you probably can use it without understanding all the code generated in the background. However, when you do understand the background, your knowledge of C# is more complete.

648

## Key Terms

An **event** is a reaction to an occurrence in a program.

**"At runtime"** describes actions that occur during a program's execution.

**Event-driven** programs contain code that causes an event such as a button click to drive the program to perform a task.

A button click **raises an event**, **fires an event**, or **triggers an event**.

An **event handler** is a method that performs a task in response to an event.

An **event receiver** is another name for an event handler.

An **event sender** is the control that generates an event.

**EventArgs** is a C# class designed for holding event information.

The **Click event** is the event generated when a Control is clicked.

**Event wiring** is the act of connecting an event to its resulting actions.

A **delegate** is an object that contains a reference to a method.

A **composed delegate** calls the delegates from which it is built.

**Invoking the event** occurs when you call an event method.

**EventHandler** is an appropriate type for events that do not use any information besides the source of the event and the EventArgs parameter.

**Key events** are keyboard events that occur when a user presses and releases keyboard keys.

When a Control has **focus** and the user presses Enter, the Control will raise an event.

## Review Questions

1. In C#, events are _____.

   a. triggered by actions

   b. handled by catch blocks

   c. Boolean objects

   d. only used in GUI programs

2. A delegate is an object that contains a reference to a(n) _____.

   a. object

   b. class

   c. method

   d. Control

3. C# delegates provide a way for a program to _____.

   a. take alternative courses that are not determined until runtime

   b. include multiple methods

   c. include methods from other classes

   d. include multiple Controls that use the same method

4. Which of the following correctly declares a delegate type?

   a. void aDelegate(int num);

   b. delegate void aDelegate(num);

   c. delegate void aDelegate(int num);

   d. delegate aDelegate(int num);

5. If you have declared a delegate instance, you can assign it a reference to a method as long as the method has the same _____ as the delegate.

   a. return type

   b. identifier

   c. parameter list

   d. two of the above

6. You can combine two delegates to create a(n) _____ delegate.

   a. assembled

   b. classified

   c. artificial

   d. composed

7. To combine two delegates using the + operator, the `delegate` objects must _____.

   a. have the same parameter list

   b. have the same return type

   c. both of these

   d. neither of these

8. In C#, a(n) _____ is triggered when specific changes to an object occur.

   a. delegate

   b. event

   c. notification

   d. instantiation

9. An event handler delegate requires _____ argument(s).

   a. zero

   b. one

   c. two

   d. at least one

10. In an event-handler method, the sender is the _____.

   a. delegate associated with the event

   b. method called by the event

   c. object where the event was initiated

   d. class containing the method that the event invokes

11. The `EventArgs` class contains a static field named _____.

   a. `Empty`

   b. `Text`

   c. `Location`

   d. `Source`

12. When creating events, you can use a predefined delegate type named _____ that is automatically provided by the .NET Framework.

    a. `EventArgs`

    b. `EventHandler`

    c. `EventType`

    d. `Event`

13. Which of the following is not a predefined `Control` event?

    a. `MouseEnter`

    b. `Click`

    c. `Destroy`

    d. `TextChanged`

14. A single `Control` can raise _____ event(s).

    a. one

    b. two

    c. five

    d. any number of

15. When you create `Forms` with `Controls` that raise events, an advantage to creating the code by hand over using the Visual Studio IDE is _____.

    a. you are less likely to make typing errors

    b. you save a lot of repetitious typing

    c. you are less likely to forget to set a property

    d. you gain a clearer understanding of the C# language

16. When a `Form` contains three `Controls` and one has focus, you can raise an event by _____.

    a. clicking any `Control`

    b. pressing Enter

    c. either of these

    d. none of these

17. The `TabStop` property of a `Control` is a(n) _____.

    a. integer value indicating the tab order

    b. Boolean value indicating whether the `Control` has a position in the tab sequence

    c. string value indicating the name of the method executed when the `Control` raises an event

    d. `delegate` name indicating the event raised when the user tabs to the `Control`

18. The `TabIndex` property of a `Control` is a(n) _____.

    a. integer value indicating the tab order

    b. Boolean value indicating whether the `Control` has a position in the tab sequence

    c. string value indicating the name of the method executed when the `Control` raises an event

    d. `delegate` name indicating the event raised when the user tabs to the `Control`

19. The `Control` that causes an event is the _____ argument to an event method.

    a. first

    b. second

    c. third

    d. fourth

20. Which of the following is true?

    a. A single event can be generated from multiple `Control`s.

    b. Multiple events can be generated from a single `Control`.

    c. Both of the above are true.

    d. None of the above are true.

# Exercises

1. Create a Form that contains three Labels that hold famous quotes of your choice. When the program starts, the background color of the Form and each Label should be black. When the user passes a mouse over a Label, change its BackColor to white, revealing the text of the quote. Save the project as **DisplayQuotes**.

2. Create a Form with a list of three LinkLabels that link to any three Web sites you choose. When a user clicks a LinkLabel, link to that site. When a user's mouse hovers over a LinkLabel, display a brief message that explains the site's purpose. After a user clicks a link, move it to the top of the list and move the other two links down, making sure to retain the correct explanation with each link. Save the project as **RecentlyVisitedSites**.

3. Create a Form with a ListBox that lists at least four sports teams of your choice. When the user places the mouse over the ListBox, display a Label that contains single-game ticket prices for each team. The Label disappears when the user's mouse leaves the ListBox area. When the user clicks a team name in the ListBox, display another Label that contains the correct ticket price. Also change the BackColor of the Form to the selected team's color. Save the project as **TeamSelector**.

4. Locate an animated .gif file on the Web or use the one stored in the Chapter.13 folder of your downloadable student files. Create a Form that contains a PictureBox. Display three different messages on a Label—one when the user's mouse is over the PictureBox, one when the mouse is not over the PictureBox, and one when the user clicks the PictureBox. Save the project as **Animated**.

5. The Sunshine Subdivision allows residents to select siding for their new homes, but only specific trim colors are allowed with each siding color. Create a Form for Sunshine Subdivision that allows a user to choose one of three siding colors from a ListBox—white, gray, or blue. When the user selects a siding

654

Hint: You can remove the entire contents of a `ListBox` using the `Items.Clear()` method, as in `this.listBox2.Items.Clear();`.

color, the program should display a second `ListBox` that contains only the following choices:

- White siding—black, red, green, or dark blue trim

- Gray siding—black or white trim

- Blue siding—white or dark blue trim

After the user selects a trim color, the program should display a congratulatory message on a `Label` indicating that the choice is a good one. The trim `ListBox` also becomes invisible. If the user makes a new selection from the siding `ListBox`, the congratulatory message is invisible until the user selects a complementary trim.

Save the project as **SunshineSubdivision**.

6. Create a `Form` that contains a guessing game with five `RadioButtons` numbered 1 through 5. Randomly choose one of the `RadioButtons` as the winning button. When the user clicks a `RadioButton`, display a message indicating whether the user is right.

   Add a `Label` to the `Form` that provides a hint. When the user's mouse hovers over the label, notify the user of one `RadioButton` that is incorrect. After the user makes a selection, disable all the `RadioButtons`. Save the project as **GuessANumber**.

You can create a random number that is at least `min` but less than `max` using the following statements:

```
Random ranNumberGenerator = new Random();
int randomNumber;
randomNumber = ranNumberGenerator.Next(min, max);
```

7. Create a `Form` that contains two randomly generated arrays, each containing 100 numbers. Include two `Buttons` labeled "1" and "2". Starting with position 0 in each array, ask the user to guess which of the two arrays contains the higher number and to click one of the two buttons to indicate the guess. After each button click, the program displays the values of the two compared numbers, as well as running counts of the number of correct and incorrect guesses. After the user makes a guess, disable the `Buttons` while the user views the results. After clicking a Next `Button`, the user can make another guess using the next two array values. If the user makes more than 100 guesses, the program should reset the array subscript to 0 so the comparisons start over, but continue to keep a running score. Save the project as **PickLarger**.

*Debugging Exercises*

Each of the following files or projects in the Chapter.13 folder of your downloadable student files has syntax and/or logical errors. In each case, determine the problem and fix the program. After you correct the errors, save each file or project using the same filename preceded with *Fixed*. For example, the file DebugThirteen1.cs will become FixedDebugThirteen1.cs and the project folder for DebugThirteen3 will become FixedDebugThirteen3.

 Immediately save the two project folders with their new names before starting to correct their errors.

655

    a. DebugThirteen1.cs

    b. DebugThirteen2.cs

    c. DebugThirteen3.cs

    d. DebugThirteen4.cs

 *Up For Discussion*

1. Programming is a job that can be done from a remote location. For example, as a professional programmer, you might be able to work from home. Does this appeal to you? What are the advantages and disadvantages? If you have other programmers working for you, would you allow them to work from home? Would you require any "face time"—that is, time in the office with you or other workers?

2. Programming is a job that can be done from a remote location. For example, your organization might contract with programmers who live in another country where wages are considerably lower than in the United States. Do you have any objections to employers using these workers? If so, what are they? If not, what objections might others have?

3. Suppose your organization hires programmers to work in another country. Suppose you also discover that working conditions there are not the same as in your country. For example, the buildings in which the workers do their jobs might not be subject to the same standards for ventilation and fire codes as the building where you work. Is your company under any obligation to change the working conditions?

4. Would you ever participate in a computer dating site? Would you go on a date with someone you met over the Web? What precautions would you take before such a date?

# Files and Streams

In this chapter you will:

◎ Learn about computer files and the `File` and `Directory` classes

◎ Understand data organization within a file

◎ Understand streams

◎ Write to and read from a sequential access text file

◎ Search a sequential access text file

◎ Understand serialization and deserialization

In the early chapters of this book, you learned that using variables to store values in computer memory provides programs with flexibility; a program that uses variables to replace constants can manipulate different values each time the program executes. However, when data values in a program are stored in memory, they are lost when the program ends. To retain data values for future use, you must store them in files. In this chapter, you will learn to create and manage files in C#.

# Computer Files and the `File` and `Directory` Classes

When data items are stored in a computer system, they can be stored for varying periods of time—temporarily or permanently.

Temporary storage is usually called computer memory or **random access memory** (RAM). When you write a C# program that stores a value in a variable, you are using temporary storage; the value you store is lost when the program ends or the computer loses power. This type of storage is **volatile**.

Permanent storage, on the other hand, is not lost when a computer loses power; it is **nonvolatile**. When you write a program and save it to a disk, you are using permanent storage.

A **computer file** is a collection of data stored on a nonvolatile device in a computer system. Files exist on **permanent storage devices**, such as hard disks, USB drives, reels of magnetic tape, and optical discs, which include CDs and DVDs.

You can categorize files by the way they store data:

- **Text files** contain data that can be read in a text editor because the data has been encoded using a scheme such as ASCII or Unicode. Text files might include facts and figures used by business programs; when they do, they are also called **data files**. The C# source programs you have written are stored in text files.

- **Binary files** contain data that has not been encoded as text. Their contents are in binary format, which means that you cannot understand them by viewing them in a text editor. Examples include images, music, and the compiled program files with an .exe extension that you have created using this book.

Although their contents vary, files have many common characteristics, as follows:

- Each has a name. The name often includes a dot and a file extension that describes the type of the file. For example, .txt is a plain text file, .dat is a data file, and .jpg is an image file in Joint Pictures Expert Group format.

When discussing computer storage, *temporary* and *permanent* refer to volatility, not length of time. For example, a *temporary* variable might exist for several hours in a large program or one that the user forgets to end, but a *permanent* piece of data might be saved and then deleted within a few seconds.

- Each file has a specific time of creation and a time it was last modified.

- Each file occupies space on a section of a storage device; that is, each file has a size. Sizes are measured in bytes. A **byte** is a small unit of storage; for example, in a simple text file, a byte holds only one character. Because a byte is so small, file sizes usually are expressed in **kilobytes** (thousands of bytes), **megabytes** (millions of bytes), or **gigabytes** (billions of bytes).

When you use data, you never directly use the copy that is stored in a file. Instead, you use a copy that is in memory. Especially when data items are stored on a hard disk, their locations might not be clear to you—data just seems to be "in the computer." However, when you work with stored data, you must transfer copies from the storage device into memory. When you copy data from a file on a storage device into RAM, you **read from the file**. When you store data in a computer file on a persistent storage device, you **write to the file**. This means you copy data from RAM to the file.

Computer files are the electronic equivalent of paper documents stored in file cabinets. In a physical file cabinet, the easiest way to store a document is to toss it into a drawer without a folder. When storing computer files, this is the equivalent of placing a file in the main or **root directory** of your storage device. However, for better organization, most office clerks place documents in folders; most computer users also organize their files into **folders** or **directories**. Users also can place folders within folders to form a hierarchy. The combination of the disk drive plus the complete hierarchy of directories in which a file resides is its **path**. For example, in the Windows operating system, the following line would be the complete path for a file named Data.txt on the C drive in a folder named Chapter.14 within the C# folder:

`C:\C#\Chapter.14\Data.txt`

C# provides built-in classes named `File` and `Directory` that contain methods to help you manipulate files and their directories, respectively.

## Using the `File` and `Directory` Classes

The **`File` class** contains methods that allow you to access information about files. Some of the methods are listed in Table 14-1.

Because you can erase data from files, some programmers prefer the term *persistent* storage to permanent storage. In other words, you can remove data from a file stored on a device such as a disk drive, so it is not technically permanent. However, the data remains in the file even when the computer loses power, so, unlike RAM, the data persists, or perseveres.

The terms *directory* and *folder* are used synonymously to mean an entity that is used to organize files. *Directory* is the more general term; the term *folder* came into use in graphical systems. For example, Microsoft began calling directories *folders* with the introduction of Windows 95.

| Method | Description |
|---|---|
| Create() | Creates a file |
| CreateText() | Creates a text file |
| Delete() | Deletes a file |
| Exists() | Returns true if the specified file exists |
| GetCreationTime() | Returns a DateTime object specifying when a file was created |
| GetLastAccessTime() | Returns a DateTime object specifying when a file was last accessed |
| GetLastWriteTime() | Returns a DateTime object specifying when a file was last modified |
| Move() | Moves a file to the specified location |

**Table 14-1**    Selected File class methods

DateTime is a structure that contains data about a date and time. In the chapter *Using Controls*, you used the data from DateTime structures with MonthCalendar and DateTimePicker GUI objects. DateTime values can be expressed using Coordinated Universal Time (UTC), which is the internationally recognized name for Greenwich Mean Time (GMT). By default, DateTime values are expressed using the local time set on your computer. The property DateTime.Now returns the current local time. The property DateTime.UtcNow returns the current UTC time.

The File class is contained in the System.IO namespace. So, to use the File class, you can use its fully qualified name, System.IO.File, or you can add the statement using System.IO; at the top of your file. Figure 14-1 shows a program that includes the using statement and demonstrates several File class methods. The program prompts the user for a filename and then tests the file's existence. If the file exists, the creation time, last access time, and last write time are displayed. If the file does not exist, a message is displayed. Figure 14-2 shows two executions of the program. In the first execution, the user enters a filename that is not found. In the second execution, the file is found and the three significant dates are displayed.

The System.IO.FileInfo class also allows you to access information about a file. See the Microsoft documentation at *http://msdn.microsoft.com* for more information.

```
using System;
using System.IO;
public class FileStatistics
{
    public static void Main()
    {
        string fileName;
        Console.Write("Enter a filename >> ");
        fileName = Console.ReadLine();
```

**Figure 14-1**    The FileStatistics program *(continues)*

*(continued)*

```
        if(File.Exists(fileName))
        {
            Console.WriteLine("File exists");
            Console.WriteLine("File was created " +
                File.GetCreationTime(fileName));
            Console.WriteLine("File was last accessed " +
                File.GetLastAccessTime(fileName));
            Console.WriteLine("File was last written to " +
                File.GetLastWriteTime(fileName));
        }
        else
        {
            Console.WriteLine("File does not exist");
        }
    }
}
```

**Figure 14-1** The FileStatistics program

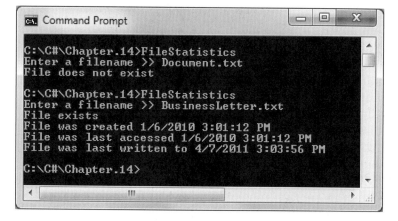

**Figure 14-2** Two typical executions of the FileStatistics program

In the FileStatistics program in Figure 14-1, the file must be in the same directory as the program that is running.

The **Directory class** provides you with information about directories or folders. Table 14-2 lists some available methods in the Directory class.

| Method | Description |
|---|---|
| CreateDirectory() | Creates a directory |
| Delete() | Deletes a directory |
| Exists() | Returns true if the specified directory exists |
| GetCreationTime() | Returns a DateTime object specifying when a directory was created |
| GetDirectories() | Returns a string array that contains the names of the subdirectories in the specified directory |
| GetFiles() | Returns a string array that contains the names of the files in the specified directory |
| GetLastAccessTime() | Returns a DateTime object specifying when a directory was last accessed |
| GetLastWriteTime() | Returns a DateTime object specifying when a directory was last modified |
| Move() | Moves a directory to the specified location |

**Table 14-2**   Selected Directory class methods

Figure 14-3 contains a program that prompts a user for a directory and then displays a list of the files stored within it. Figure 14-4 shows two typical executions of the program.

```
using System;
using System.IO;
public class DirectoryInformation
{
    public static void Main()
    {
        string directoryName;
        string[] listOfFiles;
        Console.Write("Enter a folder >> ");
        directoryName = Console.ReadLine();
        if(Directory.Exists(directoryName))
        {
            Console.WriteLine("Directory exists, " +
                "and it contains the following: ");
            listOfFiles = Directory.GetFiles(directoryName);
            for(int x = 0; x < listOfFiles.Length; ++x)
                Console.WriteLine("   {0}", listOfFiles[x]);
        }
        else
        {
            Console.WriteLine("Directory does not exist");
        }
    }
}
```

**Figure 14-3**   The DirectoryInformation program

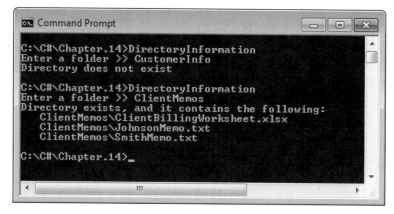

Watch the video *File Handling.*

**Figure 14-4** Two typical executions of the DirectoryInformation program

---

## TWO TRUTHS & A LIE

### Computer Files and the File and Directory Classes

1. Temporary storage is nonvolatile; permanent storage is volatile.

2. When you write to a file, you copy data from RAM to a permanent storage device.

3. Most computer users organize their files into directories; the complete hierarchy of directories in which a file resides is its path.

The false statement is #1. Temporary storage is volatile; permanent storage is nonvolatile.

---

## Understanding Data Organization Within a File

Most businesses generate and use large quantities of data every day. You can store data in variables within a program, but this type of storage is temporary. When the application ends, the variables no longer exist, and the data is lost. Variables are stored in the computer's main or primary memory (RAM). When you need to retain data for any significant amount of time, you must save the data on a permanent, secondary storage device.

Businesses store data in a relationship known as the **data hierarchy**, as shown in Figure 14-5. The smallest useful piece of data to most people is the character. A **character** is any one of the letters, numbers, or other special symbols (such as punctuation marks) that comprise data. Characters are made up of bits (the zeros and ones that represent computer circuitry), but people who use data do not care whether the internal representation for an 'A' is 01000001 or 10111110; rather, they are concerned with the meaning of 'A'. For example, it might represent a grade in a course, a person's initial, or a company code.

C# uses Unicode to represent its characters. You first learned about Unicode in Chapter 1.

In computer terminology, a character can be any group of bits, and it does not necessarily represent a letter or number. Some of these do not correspond to characters in natural language; for example, some "characters" produce a sound or control your display. You also have used the '\n' character to start a new line.

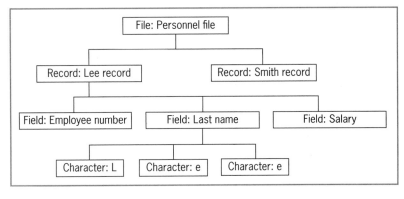

Figure 14-5   Data hierarchy

You can think of a character as a unit of information instead of data with a particular appearance. For example, the mathematical character pi (π) and the Greek letter pi look the same, but have two different Unicode values.

The set of all the characters used to represent data on a particular computer is that computer's **character set**.

When businesses use data, they group characters into fields. A **field** is a character or group of characters that has some meaning. For example, the characters T, o, and m might represent your first name. Other data fields might represent items such as last name, Social Security number, zip code, and salary.

Fields are grouped together to form records. A **record** is a collection of fields that contain data about an entity. For example, a person's first and last names, Social Security number, zip code, and salary represent that person's record. When programming in C#, you have created many classes, such as an Employee class or a Student class. You can think of the data typically stored in each of these classes as a record. These classes contain individual variables that represent data fields. A business's data records usually represent a person, item, sales transaction, or some other concrete object or event.

The field used to uniquely identify each record in a sequential file is the **key field**. Frequently, records are sorted based on the key field.

When records are not used in sequence, the file is used as a random access file, which means that records can be accessed in any order.

Frequently, business data is stored in databases. You will learn about databases in the next chapter.

Records are grouped to create files. **Data files** consist of related records, such as a company's personnel file that contains one record for each company employee. Some files have only a few records; perhaps your professor maintains a file for your class with 25 records—one record for each student. Other files contain thousands or even millions of records. For example, a large insurance company maintains a file of policyholders, and a mail-order catalog company maintains a file of available items. A data file is a **sequential access file** when each record is read in order of its position in the file. Usually, the records are stored in order based on the value in some field; for example, employees might be stored in Social Security number order, or inventory items might be stored in item number order.

Before an application can use a data file, it must open the file. A C# application **opens a file** by creating an object and associating a stream of bytes with that object. When you finish using a file, the program should **close the file**—that is, make the file no longer available to your application. Failing to close an input file (a file from which you are reading data) usually does not result in serious consequences; the data still exists in the file. However, if you fail to close an output file (a file to which you are writing data), the data might become inaccessible. You should always close every file you open, and you should close the file as soon as you no longer need it. Leaving a file open for no reason uses computer resources, and your computer's performance will suffer. Also, particularly within a network, another program might be waiting to use the file.

Failing to close an input file for which only one client is allowed access at a time can present consequences for another application. For example, if your program leaves the company's inventory file open after adding a new item, the program that fills orders for customers might fail to work correctly.

## TWO TRUTHS & A LIE

### Understanding Data Organization Within a File

1. A field is a character or group of characters that has some meaning.

2. A record is a collection of data files that contain information about an entity.

3. A sequential access data file frequently contains records stored in order based on the value in some field.

The false statement is #2. A record is a collection of fields that contain data about an entity. Data files consist of related records.

# Understanding Streams

Whereas people view files as a series of records, with each record containing data fields, C# views files as just a series of bytes. When you perform an input operation in an application, you can picture bytes flowing into your program from an input device through a **stream**, which functions as a pipeline or channel. When you perform output, some bytes flow out of your application through another stream to an output device, as shown in Figure 14-6. A stream is an object, and like all objects, streams have data and methods. The methods allow you to perform actions such as opening, closing, and flushing (clearing) the stream.

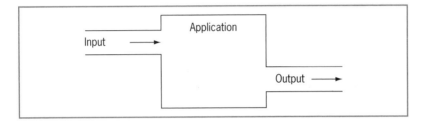

**Figure 14-6** File streams

When you produce screen output and accept keyboard input, you use the Console class, which provides access to several standard streams:

- Console.In refers to the standard input stream object, which accepts data from the keyboard.

- Console.Out refers to the standard output stream object, which allows a program to produce output on the screen.

- Console.Error refers to the standard error stream object, which allows a program to write error messages to the screen.

You have been using Console.Out and its WriteLine() and Write() methods throughout this book. However, you may not have realized it because you do not need to refer explicitly to Out, so you have been writing the instruction as Console.WriteLine(). Likewise, you have used Console.In with the ReadLine() and Read() methods.

Most streams flow in only one direction; each stream is either an input or output stream. You might open several streams at once within an application. For example, an application that reads a data disk and separates valid records from invalid ones might require three streams. The data arrives via an input stream, and as the program checks the data for invalid values, one output stream writes some records to a file of valid records, and another output stream writes other records to a file of invalid records.

When you read from or write to a file, you use a file processing class instead of `Console`. Many file processing classes are available in C#, including:

- `StreamReader`, for text input from a file

- `StreamWriter`, for text output to a file

- `FileStream` (which is used alone and with both `StreamReader` and `StreamWriter`), for both input from and output to a file

> `StreamReader` and `StreamWriter` inherit from `TextReader` and `TextWriter`, respectively. `Console.In` and `Console.Out` are properties of `TextReader` and `TextWriter`, respectively.

When you write a program that stores data in a file, you create a `FileStream` object that you can use to open a file, read data from it, write data to it, and close it. Table 14-3 lists some `FileStream` properties.

| Property | Description |
|----------|-------------|
| CanRead | Gets a value indicating whether current `FileStream` supports reading |
| CanSeek | Gets a value indicating whether current `FileStream` supports seeking |
| CanWrite | Gets a value indicating whether current `FileStream` supports writing |
| Length | Gets the length of the `FileStream` in bytes |
| Name | Gets the name of the `FileStream` |
| Position | Gets or sets the current position of the `FileStream` |

**Table 14-3**    Selected `FileStream` properties

The `FileStream` class has 15 overloaded constructors. One that is used frequently includes the filename (which might include the complete path), mode, and type of access. For example, you might construct a `FileStream` object using the following statement:

```
FileStream outFile = new FileStream("SomeText.txt",
    FileMode.Create, FileAccess.Write);
```

> Another of `FileStream`'s overloaded constructors requires only a filename and mode. If you use this version and the mode is set to `Append`, then the default access is `Write`; otherwise, the access is set to `ReadWrite`.

In this example, the filename is "SomeText.txt". Because no path is indicated, the file is assumed to be in the current directory. The mode is Create, which means a new file will be created even if one with the same name already exists. The access is Write, which means you can write data to the file, but not read from it. Table 14-4 describes the available file modes, and Table 14-5 describes the access types.

| Member | Description |
| --- | --- |
| Append | Opens the file if it exists and seeks the end of the file to append new data |
| Create | Creates a new file; if the file already exists, it is overwritten |
| CreateNew | Creates a new file; if the file already exists, an IOException is thrown |
| Open | Opens an existing file; if the file does not exist, a System.IO.FileNotFoundException is thrown |
| OpenOrCreate | Opens an existing file; if the file does not exist, it is created |
| Truncate | Opens an existing file; once opened, the file is truncated so its size is zero bytes |

**Table 14-4**    FileMode enumeration

| Member | Description |
| --- | --- |
| Read | Data can be read from the file. |
| ReadWrite | Data can be read from and written to the file. |
| Write | Data can be written to the file. |

**Table 14-5**    FileAccess enumeration

You can use a FileStream object as an argument to the StreamWriter constructor. Then you use WriteLine() or Write() with the StreamWriter object in much the same way you use it with Console.Out. For example, Figure 14-7 shows an application in which a FileStream object named outFile is created, then associated with a StreamWriter named writer in the first shaded line. The writer object then uses WriteLine() to send a string to the FileStream file instead of sending it to the Console. Figure 14-8 shows a typical execution of the program, and Figure 14-9 shows the file as it appears in Notepad.

Although the WriteSomeText application uses Console.ReadLine() to accept user input, you could also create a GUI Form to accept input. You will create an application that writes to and reads from files using a GUI environment in the "You Do It" exercises at the end of this chapter.

```
using System;
using System.IO;
public class WriteSomeText
{
    public static void Main()
    {
        FileStream outFile = new
            FileStream("SomeText.txt", FileMode.Create,
                FileAccess.Write);
        StreamWriter writer = new StreamWriter(outFile);
        Console.Write("Enter some text >> ");
        string text = Console.ReadLine();
        writer.WriteLine(text);
        // Error occurs if the next two statements are reversed
        writer.Close();
        outFile.Close();
    }
}
```

**Figure 14-7**   WriteSomeText program

**Figure 14-8**   Typical execution of WriteSomeText program

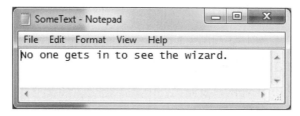

**Figure 14-9**   File created by WriteSomeText program

 In most applications that use files, you will want to place all the statements that open, write to, read from, and close files in a try block and then catch any IOExceptions that are thrown. Exception handling is eliminated from many examples in this chapter so that you can concentrate on the details of handling files without extra statements. In the "You Do It" section at the end of this chapter, you will add exception handling to an application.

The classes BinaryReader and BinaryWriter exist for working with binary files, which can store any of the 256 combinations of bits in any byte instead of just those combinations that form readable text. For example, photographs and music are stored in binary files.

The classes XmlTextReader and XmlTextWriter exist for working with XML files. **XML** is an abbreviation of eXtensible Markup Language, which is a standard for exchanging data over the Internet.

---

**TWO TRUTHS & A LIE**

### Understanding Streams

1. When a file is opened in C#, an object is created and a stream is associated with that object.

2. Most streams flow in only one direction; each stream is either an input or output stream.

3. You can open one stream at a time within a C# application.

The false statement is #3. You might open several streams at once within an application.

---

# Writing to and Reading From a Sequential Access Text File

Although people think of data files as consisting of records that contain fields, C# uses files only as streams of bytes. Therefore, when you write a program to store a data file, or write a program to retrieve data from an already-created file, you must dictate the form in which the program will handle the file. Additionally, whether you are writing data to a file or reading data from one, you create a FileStream object.

## Writing Data to a Sequential Access Text File

For example, suppose you want to store Employee data in a file. Assume an Employee contains an ID number, a name, and a salary. You could write stand-alone data for each of the three types to a file, or you could create an Employee class that is similar to many you have seen throughout this book. Figure 14-10 shows a typical Employee class that contains three fields and properties for each.

```
class Employee
{
    public int EmpNum {get; set;}
    public string Name {get; set;}
    public double Salary {get; set;}
}
```

**Figure 14-10** An Employee class

A comma is a commonly used delimiter, but a delimiter can be any character that is not needed as part of the data in a file. A file that contains comma-separated values is often called a **CSV file**. When commas are needed as part of the data, sometimes either the Tab character, the pipe character (|), or a comma within quotes is used as a delimiter.

To store Employee data to a persistent storage device, you declare a FileStream object. For example:

```
FileStream outFile = new FileStream(FILENAME,
        FileMode.Create, FileAccess.Write);
```

The object is then passed to the constructor of a StreamWriter object. For example:

```
StreamWriter writer = new StreamWriter(outFile);
```

You can then use the writer object's WriteLine() method to write Employee data to the output stream. When you write Employee data to a file, the fields should be separated by a delimiter. A **delimiter** is a character used to specify the boundary between data items in text files. Without a delimiter, the process of separating and interpreting data fields on a storage device is more difficult. For example, suppose you define a delimiter as follows:

```
const string DELIM = ",";
```

Then, when you write data to a file, you can separate the fields with a comma using a statement such as the following:

```
writer.WriteLine(emp.EmpNum + DELIM + emp.Name + DELIM + emp.Salary);
```

Because WriteLine() is used for writing data to the file, the automatically appended carriage return becomes the *record delimiter*.

A block of text within a string that represents an entity or field is a **token**.

Figure 14-11 contains a complete program that opens a file and continuously prompts the user for Employee data. When all three fields have been entered for an employee, the fields are written to the file, separated by commas. When the user enters the sentinel value 999 for an Employee ID number, the data entry loop ends and the file is closed. Figure 14-12 shows a typical execution, and Figure 14-13 shows the contents of the sequential data file that is created.

```
using System;
using System.IO;
public class WriteSequentialFile
{
   public static void Main()
   {
      const int END = 999;
      const string DELIM = ",";
      const string FILENAME = "EmployeeData.txt";
      Employee emp = new Employee();
      FileStream outFile = new FileStream(FILENAME,
         FileMode.Create, FileAccess.Write);
      StreamWriter writer = new StreamWriter(outFile);
      Console.Write("Enter employee number or " + END +
         " to quit >> ");
      emp.EmpNum = Convert.ToInt32(Console.ReadLine());
      while(emp.EmpNum != END)
      {
         Console.Write("Enter last name >> ");
         emp.Name = Console.ReadLine();
         Console.Write("Enter salary >> ");
         emp.Salary = Convert.ToDouble(Console.ReadLine());
         writer.WriteLine(emp.EmpNum + DELIM + emp.Name +
            DELIM + emp.Salary);
         Console.Write("Enter next employee number or " +
            END + " to quit >> ");
         emp.EmpNum = Convert.ToInt32(Console.ReadLine());
      }
      writer.Close();
      outFile.Close();
   }
}
```

**Figure 14-11** `WriteSequentialFile` class

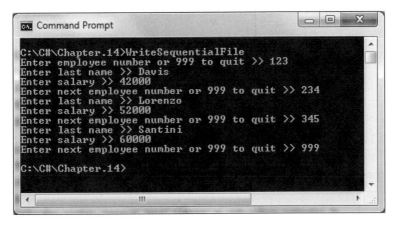

**Figure 14-12** Typical execution of `WriteSequentialFile` program

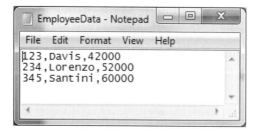

**Figure 14-13** Contents of file created by `WriteSequentialFile` program

 In the `WriteSequentialFile` class, the delimiter is defined to be a `string` instead of a `char` to force the composed argument to `WriteLine()` to be a `string`. If the first data field sent to `WriteLine()` was a `string`, then DELIM could have been declared as a `char`.

 In the `WriteSequentialFile` program in Figure 14-11, the constant END is defined to be 999 so it can be used to check for the sentinel value. You first learned to use named constants in Chapter 2. Defining a named constant eliminates using a magic number in a program. The term **magic number** refers to the bad programming practice of hard-coding numbers (unnamed, literal constants) in code without explanation. In most cases, this makes programs harder to read, understand, and maintain.

## Reading from a Sequential Access Text File

A program that reads from a sequential access data file contains many similar components to one that writes to a file. For example, a `FileStream` object is created, as in a program that writes a file. However, the access must be `FileAccess.Read` (or `ReadWrite`), as in the following statement:

```
FileStream inFile = new FileStream(FILENAME,
    FileMode.Open, FileAccess.Read);
```

Then, as when data is being written, the `FileStream` object is passed to a `StreamReader` object's constructor, as in the following statement:

```
StreamReader reader = new StreamReader(inFile);
```

Using `ReadLine()` assumes a carriage return is the record delimiter, which is true, for example, if the records were created using `WriteLine()`.

After the `StreamReader` has been defined, the `ReadLine()` method can be used to retrieve one line at a time from the data file. For example, the following statement gets one line of data from the file and stores it in a string named `recordIn`:

```
string recordIn = reader.ReadLine();
```

If the value of `recordIn` is `null`, then no more data exists in the file. Therefore, a loop that begins `while(recordIn != null)` can be used to control the data entry loop.

After a record (line of data) is read in, the `Split()` method can be used to separate the data fields into an array of strings. The `Split()` method is a member of the `String` class; it takes a character parameter and separates a string into substrings at each occurrence of the character delimiter. For example, the following code splits `recordIn` into the `fields` array at each `DELIM` occurrence. Then the three array elements can be stored as an `int`, `string`, and `double`, respectively.

```
string[] fields;
fields = recordIn.Split(DELIM);
emp.EmpNum = Convert.ToInt32(fields[0]);
emp.Name = fields[1];
emp.Salary = Convert.ToDouble(fields[2]);
```

Figure 14-14 contains a complete `ReadSequentialFile` application that uses the data file created in Figure 14-12. The records stored in the EmployeeData.txt file are read in one at a time, split into their `Employee` record components, and displayed. Figure 14-15 shows the output.

```
using System;
using System.IO;
public class ReadSequentialFile
{
    public static void Main()
    {
        const char DELIM = ',';
        const string FILENAME = "EmployeeData.txt";
        Employee emp = new Employee();
        FileStream inFile = new FileStream(FILENAME,
            FileMode.Open, FileAccess.Read);
        StreamReader reader = new StreamReader(inFile);
        string recordIn;
        string[] fields;
        Console.WriteLine("\n{0,-5}{1,-12}{2,8}\n",
            "Num", "Name", "Salary");
        recordIn = reader.ReadLine();
        while(recordIn != null)
        {
            fields = recordIn.Split(DELIM);
            emp.EmpNum = Convert.ToInt32(fields[0]);
```

**Figure 14-14** ReadSequentialFile program *(continues)*

*(continued)*

```
            emp.Name = fields[1];
            emp.Salary = Convert.ToDouble(fields[2]);
            Console.WriteLine("{0,-5}{1,-12}{2,8}",
                emp.EmpNum, emp.Name, emp.Salary.ToString("C"));
            recordIn = reader.ReadLine();
        }
        reader.Close();
        inFile.Close();
    }
}
```

**Figure 14-14** ReadSequentialFile program

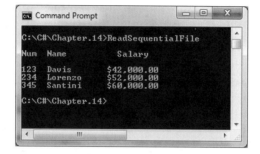

Watch the video *Sequential Access Files.*

**Figure 14-15** Output of ReadSequentialFile program

---

## TWO TRUTHS **&** A LIE

### Writing to and Reading From a Sequential Access Text File

1. Although people think of data files as consisting of records that contain fields, C# uses files only as streams of bytes.

2. A comma is the default C# delimiter.

3. The Split() method can be used to separate data fields into an array of strings based on the placement of the designated delimiter.

The false statement is #2. A delimiter is any character used to specify the boundary between characters in text files. Although a comma is commonly used for this purpose, there is no default C# delimiter, and any character could be used.

# Searching a Sequential Text File

When you read data from a sequential text file, as in the ReadSequentialFile program in Figure 14-14, the program starts at the beginning of the file and reads each record in turn until all the records have been read. Subsequent records are read in order because a file's **file position pointer** holds the byte number of the next byte to be read. For example, if each record in a file is 32 bytes long, then the file position pointer holds 0, 32, 64, and so on in sequence during the execution of the program.

Sometimes it is necessary to process a file multiple times from the beginning during a program's execution. For example, suppose you want to continue to prompt a user for a minimum salary and then search through a file for Employees who make at least that salary. You can compare the user's entered minimum with each salary in the data file and list those employees who meet the requirement. However, after one list is produced, the file pointer is at the end of the file and no more records can be read. To reread the file, you could close it and reopen it, but that requires unnecessary overhead. Instead, you can just reposition the file pointer using the Seek() method and the SeekOrigin enumeration. For example, the following statement repositions the pointer of a file named inFile to 0 bytes away from the Begin position of the file:

```
inFile.Seek(0, SeekOrigin.Begin);
```

Table 14-6 lists the values in the SeekOrigin enumeration that you can use.

| Member | Description |
| --- | --- |
| Begin | Specifies the beginning of a stream |
| Current | Specifies the current position of a stream |
| End | Specifies the end of a stream |

**Table 14-6**　The SeekOrigin enumeration

Figure 14-16 contains a program that repeatedly searches a file to produce lists of employees who meet a minimum salary requirement. The shaded portions of the program represent differences from the ReadSequentialFile application in Figure 14-14. In this program, each time the user enters a minimum salary that does not equal 999, the file position pointer is set to the beginning of the file, and then each record is read and compared to the minimum. Figure 14-17 shows a typical execution of the program.

```
using System;
using System.IO;
public class FindEmployees
{
    public static void Main()
    {
        const char DELIM = ',';
        const int END = 999;
        const string FILENAME = "EmployeeData.txt";
        Employee emp = new Employee();
        FileStream inFile = new FileStream(FILENAME,
            FileMode.Open, FileAccess.Read);
        StreamReader reader = new StreamReader(inFile);
        string recordIn;
        string[] fields;
        double minSalary;
        Console.Write("Enter minimum salary to find or " +
            END + " to quit >> ");
        minSalary = Convert.ToDouble(Console.ReadLine());
        while(minSalary != END)
        {
            Console.WriteLine("\n{0,-5}{1,-12}{2,8}\n",
                "Num", "Name", "Salary");
            inFile.Seek(0, SeekOrigin.Begin);
            recordIn = reader.ReadLine();
            while(recordIn != null)
            {
                fields = recordIn.Split(DELIM);
                emp.EmpNum = Convert.ToInt32(fields[0]);
                emp.Name = fields[1];
                emp.Salary = Convert.ToDouble(fields[2]);
                if(emp.Salary >= minSalary)
                    Console.WriteLine("{0,-5}{1,-12}{2,8}",
                        emp.EmpNum, emp.Name,
                            emp.Salary.ToString("C"));
                recordIn = reader.ReadLine();
            }
            Console.Write("\nEnter minimum salary to find or " +
                END + " to quit >> ");
            minSalary = Convert.ToDouble(Console.ReadLine());
        }
        reader.Close();  // Error occurs if
        inFile.Close(); //these two statements are reversed
    }
}
```

**Figure 14-16**  FindEmployees program

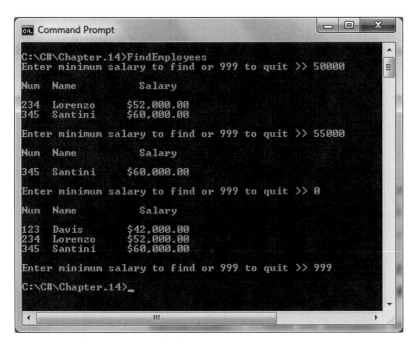

 The program in Figure 14-16 is intended to demonstrate using the Seek() method. In a business setting, you might prefer to not leave a file open in one application if other users might be waiting for it. As an alternative, you could load all the records into an array and then search the array for desired records. Problems also exist with this approach because you would have to overestimate the number of records in the file to create an array large enough to hold them.

**Figure 14-17** Typical execution of FindEmployees program

 When you seek beyond the length of the file, you do not cause an error. Instead, the file size grows. In Microsoft Windows NT and later, any data added to the end of a file is set to zero. In Microsoft Windows 98 or earlier, any data added to the end of the file is not set to zero. This means that previously deleted data might become visible to the stream.

## TWO TRUTHS & A LIE

### Searching a Sequential Text File

1. When you read data from a sequential file, the program starts at the beginning of the file and reads each record in turn until all the records have been read.

2. When you read from a sequential file, its file position pointer holds the number of the record to be read.

3. To reread a file, you can close it and reopen it, or you can reposition the file pointer to the beginning of the file.

The false statement is #2. When you read from a sequential file, its file position pointer holds the byte number of the next byte to be read.

# Understanding Serialization and Deserialization

Writing to a text file allows you to store data for later use. However, writing to a text file does present two disadvantages:

- Data in a text file is easily readable in a text editor such as Notepad. Although this feature is useful to developers when they test programs, it is not a very secure way to store data.

- When a record in a data file contains many fields, it is cumbersome to convert each field to text and combine the fields with delimiters before storing the record on a disk. Similarly, when you read a text file, it is somewhat unwieldy to eliminate the delimiters, split the text into tokens, and convert each token to the proper data type. Writing an entire object to a file at once would be more convenient.

C# provides a technique called serialization that can be used for writing objects to and reading objects from data files. **Serialization** is the process of converting objects into streams of bytes. **Deserialization** is the reverse process; it converts streams of bytes back into objects.

 Attributes provide a method of associating information with C# code. They are always contained in square brackets. The C# documentation at *http://msdn.microsoft.com* provides more details.

To create a class that can be serialized, you mark it with the [Serializable] attribute, as shown in the shaded statement in Figure 14-18. The Employee class in the figure is identical to the one in Figure 14-10 except for the [Serializable] attribute.

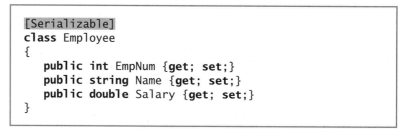

```
[Serializable]
class Employee
{
    public int EmpNum {get; set;}
    public string Name {get; set;}
    public double Salary {get; set;}
}
```

**Figure 14-18** Serializable Employee class

In a class marked with the [Serializable] attribute, every instance variable must also be serializable. By default, all C# simple data types are serializable, including strings. However, if your class contains fields that are more complex data types, you must check the declaration of those classes to ensure they are serializable. By default, array objects are serializable. However, if the array contains references to other objects, such as Dates or Students, those objects must be serializable.

If you want to be able to write class objects to a file, you can implement the ISerializable interface instead of marking a class with the [Serializable] attribute. When you use this approach, you must write a method named GetObjectData(). Marking the class with the attribute is simpler.

Two namespaces are included in programs that employ serialization:

- System.Runtime.Serialization.Formatters.Binary;

- System.Runtime.Serialization;

When you create a program that writes objects to files, you declare an instance of the BinaryFormatter class with a statement such as the following:

BinaryFormatter bFormatter = new BinaryFormatter();

Then, after you fill a class object with data, you can write it to the output file stream named outFile with a statement such as the following:

bFormatter.Serialize(outFile, objectFilledWithData);

The Serialize() method takes two arguments—a reference to the output file and a reference to a serializable object that might contain any number of data fields. The entire object is written to the data file with this single statement.

Similarly, when you read an object from a data file, you use a statement like the following:

objectInstance = (TypeOfObject)bFormatter.Deserialize(inFile);

This statement uses the Deserialize() method with a BinaryFormatter object to read in one object from the file. The object is cast to the appropriate type and can be assigned to an instance of the object. Then you can access individual fields. An entire object is read with this single statement, no matter how many data fields it contains.

Figure 14-19 shows a program that writes Employee class objects to a file and later reads them from the file into the program. After the FileStream is declared for an output file, a BinaryFormatter is declared in the first shaded statement. The user enters an ID number, name, and salary for an Employee, and the completed object is written to a file in the second shaded statement. When the user enters 999, the output file is closed.

```csharp
using System;
using System.IO;
using System.Runtime.Serialization.Formatters.Binary;
using System.Runtime.Serialization;
public class SerializableDemonstration
{
    public static void Main()
    {
        const int END = 999;
        const string FILENAME = "Data.ser";
        Employee emp = new Employee();
        FileStream outFile = new FileStream(FILENAME,
            FileMode.Create, FileAccess.Write);
        BinaryFormatter bFormatter = new BinaryFormatter();
        Console.Write("Enter employee number or " + END +
            " to quit >> ");
        emp.EmpNum = Convert.ToInt32(Console.ReadLine());
        while(emp.EmpNum != END)
        {
            Console.Write("Enter last name >> ");
            emp.Name = Console.ReadLine();
            Console.Write("Enter salary >> ");
            emp.Salary = Convert.ToDouble(Console.ReadLine());
            bFormatter.Serialize(outFile, emp);
            Console.Write("Enter employee number or " + END +
                " to quit >> ");
            emp.EmpNum = Convert.ToInt32(Console.ReadLine());
        }
        outFile.Close();
        FileStream inFile = new FileStream(FILENAME,
            FileMode.Open, FileAccess.Read);
        Console.WriteLine("\n{0,-5}{1,-12}{2,8}\n",
            "Num", "Name", "Salary");
        while(inFile.Position < inFile.Length)
        {
            emp = (Employee)bFormatter.Deserialize(inFile);
            Console.WriteLine("{0,-5}{1,-12}{2,8}",
                emp.EmpNum, emp.Name, emp.Salary.ToString("C"));
        }
        inFile.Close();
    }
}
```

**Figure 14-19** SerializableDemonstration program

After the output file closes in the SerializableDemonstration program in Figure 14-19, it is reopened for reading. A loop is executed while the Position property of the input file is less than its Length property. In other words, the loop executes while there is more data in the file. The last shaded statement in the figure deserializes data from the file and casts it to an `Employee` object, where the individual fields can be accessed. Figure 14-20 shows a typical execution of the program.

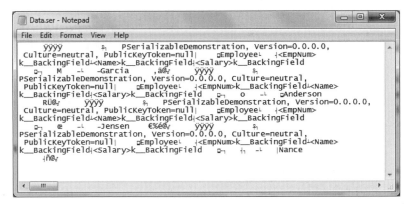

**Figure 14-20**    Typical execution of `SerializableDemonstration` program

The file created by the `SerializableDemonstration` program is not as easy to read as the text file created by the `WriteSequentialFile` program discussed earlier in the chapter (in Figure 14-13). Figure 14-21 shows the file contents displayed in Notepad (with some newline characters inserted so the output can fit on this page). If you examine the file carefully, you can discern the string names and some `Employee` class information, but the rest of the file is not easy to read.

Watch the video
*Understanding
Serialization
and
Deserialization.*

**Figure 14-21**    Data file created using `SerializableDemonstration` program

> ## TWO TRUTHS & A LIE
>
> ### Understanding Serialization and Deserialization
>
> 1. An advantage of writing data to a text file is that the data is easily readable in a text editor such as Notepad.
>
> 2. Serialization is the process of converting objects into streams of bytes. Deserialization is the reverse process; it converts streams of bytes back into objects.
>
> 3. By default, all C# classes are serializable.

The false statement is #3. By default, all C# simple data types are serializable, including strings. However, if your class contains fields that are more complex data types, you must check the declaration of those classes to ensure they are serializable.

## You Do It

### Creating a File

In the next steps, you will create a file that contains a list of names.

**To create a file:**

1. Open a new file in your editor and write the first lines needed for a program that creates a file of names.

```
using System;
using System.IO;
public class CreateNameFile
{
```

2. Start a `Main()` method that declares a `FileStream` you can use to create a file named Names.txt that is open for writing. Also create a `StreamWriter` to which you associate the file.

```
public static void Main()
{
    FileStream file = new FileStream("Names.txt",
        FileMode.Create, FileAccess.Write);
    StreamWriter writer = new StreamWriter(file);
```

3. Add an array of names as follows. Each name is ten characters long.

```
string[] names = {"Anthony   ",
                  "Belle     ",
                  "Carolyn   ",
                  "David     ",
                  "Edwin     ",
                  "Frannie   ",
                  "Gina      ",
                  "Hannah    ",
                  "Inez      ",
                  "Juan      "};
```

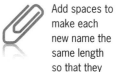 Add spaces to make each new name the same length so that they can demonstrate the Seek() method in a later exercise.

683

4. Declare a variable to use as an array subscript, then write each name to the output file.

```
int x;
for(x = 0; x < names.Length; ++x)
   writer.WriteLine(names[x]);
```

5. Close the StreamWriter and the FileStream. Also add two closing curly braces—one for the Main() method and one for the class.

```
      writer.Close();
      file.Close();
   }
}
```

6. Save the file as **CreateNameFile.cs**. Compile and execute it. Using My Computer or Windows Explorer, open the newly created **Names.txt** file in a text editor. The file contents appear in Figure 14-22.

**Figure 14-22** File created by CreateNameFile program

# Reading from a File

In the next steps, you will read the text from the file created by the CreateNameFile program.

**To read text from a file:**

1. Start a new file in your text editor as follows:

```
using System;
using System.IO;
public class ReadNameFile
{
```

2. Start a Main() method that declares a FileStream that uses the same filename as the one created by the CreateNameFile program. Declare the file mode to be Open and the access to be Read. Declare a StreamReader with which to associate the file. Also declare an integer that counts the names read and a string that holds the names.

```
public static void Main()
{
    FileStream file = new FileStream("Names.txt",
        FileMode.Open, FileAccess.Read);
    StreamReader reader = new StreamReader(file);
    int count = 1;
    string name;
```

3. Display a heading and read the first line from the file. While a name is not null, display a count and a name, and increment the count.

```
Console.WriteLine("Displaying all names");
name = reader.ReadLine();
while(name != null)
{
    Console.WriteLine("" + count + " " + name);
    name = reader.ReadLine();
    ++count;
}
```

4. Close the StreamReader and the File, and add closing curly braces for the method and the class.

```
        reader.Close();
        file.Close();
    }
}
```

5. Save the file as **ReadNameFile.cs**. Compile and execute it. The output appears in Figure 14-23.

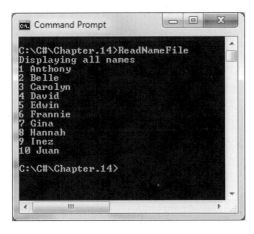

**Figure 14-23** Output produced by ReadNameFile program

## Using the Seek() Method

In the next steps, you will use the Seek() method to reposition a file pointer so you can access a file from any location. The user will be prompted to enter a number representing a starting point to list the names in the Names.txt file. Names from that point forward will be listed, and then the user will be prompted for another selection.

**To demonstrate the Seek() method:**

1. Open a new file in your editor and start a program that will demonstrate how to access certain names from the Names.txt file. You created this file in the CreateNameFile application.

```csharp
using System;
using System.IO;
public class AccessSomeNames
{
    public static void Main()
    {
        FileStream file = new FileStream("Names.txt",
            FileMode.Open, FileAccess.Read);
        StreamReader reader = new StreamReader(file);
```

2. Declare a constant named END that represents an input value that allows the user to exit the program. Then declare other variables that the program will use.

```csharp
const int END = 999;
int count = 0;
int num;
int size;
string name;
```

3. Read a line from the input file. While names are available, continue to read and count them. Then compute the size of each name by dividing the file length by the number of strings stored in it.

```
name = reader.ReadLine();
while(name != null)
{
    ++count;
    name = reader.ReadLine();
}
size = (int)file.Length / count;
```

4. Prompt the user for the number of the first record to read, and read the value from the Console.

```
Console.Write("\nWith which number do you want to start? >> ");
num = Convert.ToInt32(Console.ReadLine());
```

5. As long as the user does not enter the sentinel END value, display the number and then use the Seek() method to position the file pointer at the correct file location. Because users enter numbers starting with 1, you calculate the file position by first subtracting 1 from the user's entry. For example, when a user enters 1 as the number of the first record to view, the file should start at position 0. The calculated record number is then multiplied by the size of each name in the file. For example, if each name is 12 bytes long, then the calculated starting position should be 0, 12, 24, 36, or some other multiple of the record size. Read and write the name at the calculated location. Then, in a loop, read and write all the remaining names until the end of the file. Finally, prompt the user for the next starting value for a new list and inform the user how to quit the application.

```
while(num != END)
{
    Console.WriteLine("Starting with name " + num +": ");
    file.Seek((num - 1) * size, SeekOrigin.Begin);
    name = reader.ReadLine();
    Console.WriteLine(" " + name);
    while(name != null)
    {
        name = reader.ReadLine();
        Console.WriteLine("  " + name);
    }
    Console.WriteLine("\nWith which number do you " +
        "want to start?");
    Console.Write("   (Enter " + END + " to quit) >> ");
    num = Convert.ToInt32(Console.ReadLine());
}
```

6. Close the `StreamReader` and `File` objects, and add closing braces for the method and the class.

```
        reader.Close();
        file.Close();
    }
}
```

7. Save the file as **AccessSomeNames.cs**. Compile and execute it. Figure 14-24 shows a typical execution during which the user displays three sets of names starting at a different point each time.

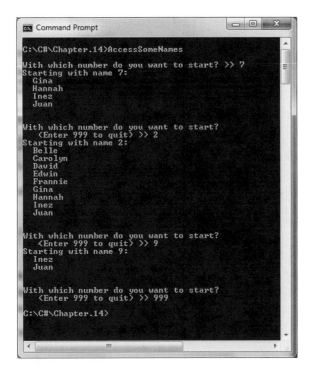

**Figure 14-24**  Typical execution of AccessSomeNames program

# Creating a Text File in a GUI Environment

The file writing and reading examples in this chapter have used console applications so that you could concentrate on the features of files in the simplest environment. However, you can write and read files in GUI environments as well. In the next steps, you will create two applications. The first allows a user to enter invoice records using a Form and to store them in a file. The second application allows a user to view stored records using a Form.

**To write a GUI application that creates a file:**

1. Open the Visual Studio IDE and start a new Windows Forms Application project named **EnterInvoices**.

2. Create a Form like the one shown in Figure 14-25 by making the following changes:

   • Change the Text property of the Form to **Invoice Data**.

   • Drag a Label onto the Form and change its Text property to **Enter invoice data**. Increase the Label's Font to **12**.

   • Drag three more Labels onto the Form and change their Text properties to **Invoice number**, **Last name**, and **Amount**, respectively.

   • Drag three TextBoxes onto the Form next to the three descriptive Labels. Change the Name properties of the three TextBoxes to **invoiceBox**, **nameBox**, and **amountBox**, respectively.

   • Drag a Button onto the Form, change its Name to **enterButton**, and change its Text to **Enter record**. If necessary, resize **enterButton** so all of its text is visible.

**Figure 14-25** Designing the EnterInvoices Form

3. View the code for the Form. At the start of the class, before the Form1() constructor, add the shaded code shown in Figure 14-26. The new code contains statements that perform the following:

   • Declare a delimiter that will be used to separate records in the output file.

- Declare a path and filename. You can change the path if you want to store the file in a different location on your system.

- Declare variables for the number, name, and amount of each invoice.

- Open the file and associate it with a `StreamWriter`.

```
namespace EnterInvoices
{
    public partial class Form1 : Form
    {
        const string DELIM = ",";
        const string FILENAME =
            @"C:\C#\Chapter.14\Invoices.txt";
        int num;
        string name;
        double amount;
        static FileStream outFile = new
            FileStream(FILENAME, FileMode.Create,
            FileAccess.Write);
        StreamWriter writer = new StreamWriter(outFile);
        public Form1()
        {
            InitializeComponent();
        }
```

**Figure 14-26**  Partial code for `EnterInvoices` program with typed statements shaded

 Remember that placing an at sign (@) in front of a filename indicates that all characters in the string should be interpreted literally. This means that the backslashes in the path will not be interpreted as escape sequence characters.

4. At the top of the file, with the other `using` statements, add the following so that the `FileStream` can be declared:

   `using System.IO;`

5. Click **Save All** (and continue to do so periodically as you work). Return to Design view and double-click the **Enter record** button. As shown in the shaded portions of Figure 14-27, add statements within the method to accept data from each of the three `TextBox`es and convert each field to the appropriate type. Then write each field to a text file, separated by delimiting commas. Finally, clear the `TextBox` fields to be ready for the user to enter a new set of data.

```
private void enterButton_Click(object sender, EventArgs e)
{
    num = Convert.ToInt32(invoiceBox.Text);
    name = nameBox.Text;
    amount = Convert.ToDouble(amountBox.Text);
    writer.WriteLine(num + DELIM + name + DELIM + amount);
    invoiceBox.Clear();
    nameBox.Clear();
    amountBox.Clear();
}
```

**Figure 14-27**   Code for enterButton_Click() method of EnterInvoices program

6.  Locate the Dispose() method, which executes when the user clicks the Close button to dismiss the Form. A quick way to locate the method in the Visual Studio IDE is to select **Edit** from the main menu, click **Find and Replace**, click **Quick Find**, and type **Dispose** in the Find What: box. (The Look in: setting can be either Entire Solution or Current Project.) The method appears on the screen. Add two statements to close writer and outFile, as shown in the shaded statements in Figure 14-28.

```
protected override void Dispose(bool disposing)
{
    writer.Close();
    outFile.Close();
    if (disposing && (components != null))
    {
        components.Dispose();
    }
    base.Dispose(disposing);
}
```

**Figure 14-28**   The Dispose() method in the EnterInvoices program

7.  Click **Save All**. Execute the program. When the Form appears, enter data in each TextBox and then click the **Enter record** button when you finish. The TextBoxes clear in preparation for you to enter another record. Enter at least three records before dismissing the Form. Figure 14-29 shows data entry in progress.

**Figure 14-29**  Entering data in the `EnterInvoices` application

# Reading Data from a Text File into a `Form`

In the next steps, you will create a `Form` that you can use to read records from a `File`.

**To read data into a `Form`:**

1. Open a new Windows project in Visual Studio and name it **ViewInvoices**.

2. Create a `Form` like the one shown in Figure 14-30 by making the following changes:

   • Change the `Text` of `Form1` to **Invoice Data**.

   • Add four `Label`s with the text, font size, and approximate locations shown in Figure 14-30. (You can click the down arrow next to the `Text` property of a component to get a box into which you can type multiline text.)

   • Add a `Button` with the `Text` **View records**. Resize the `Button` if necessary. Name the `Button` `viewButton`.

   • Add three `TextBox`es. Name them **invoiceBox**, **nameBox**, and **amountBox**, respectively.

**Figure 14-30**    The `ViewInvoices` Form

3. In the IDE, double-click the **View records** `Button` to view the code.

4. Add the shaded statements shown in Figure 14-31. They include:

- A `using System.IO` statement

- Constants for the file delimiter character and the filename (Change the path for your file if necessary.)

- A `string` into which records can be read, and an array of `strings` into which to separate the string read in

- A `FileStream` and `StreamReader` to handle the input file

- Within the `viewButton_Click()` method, statements to read in a line from the file and split it into three components

If you used a different path for the Invoices.txt file in the `EnterInvoices` program, then change this file's path accordingly.

```
using System;
using System.Collections.Generic;
using System.ComponentModel;
using System.Data;
using System.Drawing;
using System.Text;
using System.Windows.Forms;
using System.IO;
```

**Figure 14-31**    Partial code for the `ViewInvoices` application *(continues)*

*(continued)*

```
namespace ViewInvoices
{
    public partial class Form1 : Form
    {
        const char DELIM = ',';
        const string FILENAME = @"C:\C#\Chapter.14\Invoices.txt";
        string recordIn;
        string[] fields;
        static FileStream file = new FileStream(FILENAME,
            FileMode.Open, FileAccess.Read);
        StreamReader reader = new StreamReader(file);
        public Form1()
        {
            InitializeComponent();
        }

        private void viewButton_Click(object sender, EventArgs e)
        {
            recordIn = reader.ReadLine();
            fields = recordIn.Split(DELIM);
            invoiceBox.Text = fields[0];
            nameBox.Text = fields[1];
            amountBox.Text = fields[2];
        }
    }
}
```

**Figure 14-31** Partial code for the ViewInvoices application

5. Add two Close() statements to the Dispose() method in the Form1Designer.cs file, as shown in Figure 14-32.

```
protected override void Dispose(bool disposing)
{
    reader.Close();
    file.Close();
    if (disposing && (components != null))
    {
        components.Dispose();
    }
    base.Dispose(disposing);
}
```

**Figure 14-32** The Dispose() method for the ViewInvoices program

**6.** Save the project and then execute it. When the Form appears, click the Button to view records. You see the data for the first record you entered when you ran the EnterInvoices application; your Form should look like the one in Figure 14-33. Click the Button again to display the next record.

**Figure 14-33**   Typical execution of ViewInvoices program

**7.** Continue to click the Button to view each record. After you view the last record you entered, click the Button again. An unhandled exception is generated, as shown in Figure 14-34, because you attempted to read data past the end of the input file.

**Figure 14-34**   Error message window displayed after user attempts to read past the end of the file

**8.** Click the **Details** button in the UnhandledException window to view details of the error. Figure 14-35 shows that a System.NullReferenceException was thrown and not handled.

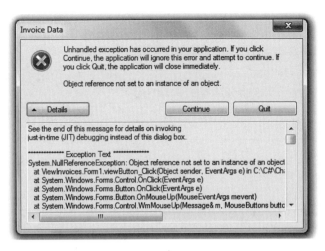

**Figure 14-35** Details displayed by unhandled exception window

9. Click **Quit** to close the unhandled exception window.

10. To remedy the unhandled `NullReferenceException` problem, you could take any number of actions. Depending on the application, you might want to do one or more of the following:

   - Display a message.
   - Disallow any more button clicks.
   - End the program.
   - Reposition the file pointer to the file's beginning so the user can view the records again.

   For this example, you will take the first two actions: display a message and disallow further button clicks. Return to Visual Studio and locate the code for the `viewButton_Click()` method. Add a `try...catch` block, as shown in Figure 14-36. Place all the record-handling code in a `try` block, and if a `NullReferenceException` is thrown, change the `Text` in `label1` and disable the View records `Button`.

```
private void viewButton_Click(object sender, EventArgs e)
{
    try
    {
        recordIn = reader.ReadLine();
        fields = recordIn.Split(DELIM);
        invoiceBox.Text = fields[0];
        nameBox.Text = fields[1];
        amountBox.Text = fields[2];
    }
```

**Figure 14-36** The `viewButton_Click()` method modified to handle an exception *(continues)*

*(continued)*

```
catch (NullReferenceException)
{
    label1.Text = "You have viewed\nall the records";
    viewButton1.Enabled = false;
}
}
```

**Figure 14-36** The `viewButton_Click()` method modified to handle an exception

11. Save the project and then execute it. This time, after you have viewed all the available records, the last record remains on the Form, an appropriate message is displayed, and the button is disabled, as shown in Figure 14-37.

**Figure 14-37** `ViewInvoices` Form after user has viewed last record

12. Dismiss the Form. Close Visual Studio.

# Chapter Summary

- Computer memory or random access memory (RAM) is temporary and volatile. Permanent storage is nonvolatile. A computer file is a collection of information stored on a nonvolatile, permanent storage device in a computer system. When you store data in a computer file on a persistent storage device, you write to the file.

When you copy data from a file on a storage device into RAM, you read from the file. Computer users organize their files into folders or directories. The File class contains methods that allow you to access information about files. The Directory class provides you with information about directories or folders.

- A character can be any one of the letters, numbers, or other special symbols (such as punctuation marks) that comprise data. A field is a group of characters that has some meaning. Fields are grouped together to form records. A record is a collection of fields that contain data about an entity. Records are grouped to create files. A data file is a sequential access file when each record is read in order of its position in the file. Usually, the records are stored in order based on the value in some field. Before an application can use a data file, it must open the file by creating an object and associating a stream of bytes with that object. When you close a file, it is no longer available to your application.

- Bytes flow into and out of applications through streams. When you use the Console class, you have access to several standard streams: Console.In, Console.Out, and Console.Error. When you read from or write to a file, you use a file processing class instead of Console. Many file processing classes are available in C#, including StreamReader for text input from a file, StreamWriter for text output to a file, and FileStream for both input and output. The FileStream class has 15 overloaded constructors.

- You can use a StreamWriter object to write objects to a file using the WriteLine() method. Fields should be separated by a delimiter, which is a character used to specify the boundary between data items in text files. Data can be read from a file using a StreamReader object and the ReadLine() method. If the value of the returned string from ReadLine() is null, then no more data exists in the file. After a record (line of data) is read in, the String class Split() method can be used to separate the data fields into an array of strings.

- When you read data from a sequential file, subsequent records are read in order because a file's position pointer holds the byte number of the next byte to be read. To reread a file, you could close it and reopen it, or you can just reposition the file pointer using the Seek() method and the SeekOrigin enumeration.

- Serialization is the process of converting objects into streams of bytes. Deserialization is the reverse process; it converts streams of bytes back into objects. To create a class that can be serialized, you mark it with the [Serializable] attribute. A serializable object can be written to or read from a data file with a single statement.

# Key Terms

**Random access memory** (RAM) is temporary storage in a computer.

**Volatile** describes storage in which data is lost when power is interrupted.

**Nonvolatile** storage is permanent storage; it is not lost when a computer loses power.

A **computer file** is a collection of information stored on a nonvolatile device in a computer system.

**Permanent storage devices**, such as hard disks, USB drives, reels of magnetic tape, and optical discs, are used to store files.

**Text files** contain data that can be read in a text editor because the data has been encoded using a scheme such as ASCII or Unicode.

**Data files** contain facts and figures.

**Binary files** contain data that has been encoded in binary format.

A **byte** is a small unit of storage; in a simple text file, a byte holds only one character.

A **kilobyte** is approximately one thousand bytes.

A **megabyte** is approximately one million bytes.

A **gigabyte** is approximately one billion bytes.

To **read from a file** is to copy data from a file on a storage device into RAM.

To **write to a file** is to store data in a computer file on a permanent storage device.

**Persistent** storage is nonvolatile storage.

The **root directory** is the main directory of a storage device.

**Folders** or **directories** are structures used to organize files on a storage device.

A **path** is composed of the disk drive in which a file resides plus the complete hierarchy of directories.

The **File class** contains methods that allow you to access information about files.

The **Directory class** provides information about directories or folders.

The **data hierarchy** is the relationship of characters, fields, records, and files.

A **character** is any one of the letters, numbers, or other special symbols (such as punctuation marks) that comprise data.

A **character set** is the group of all the characters used to represent data on a particular computer.

A **field** is a character or group of characters that has some meaning.

A **record** is a collection of fields that contain data about an entity.

**Data files** consist of related records.

A **sequential access file** is a data file in which each record is read in order based on its position in the file; usually the records are stored in order based on the value in some field.

The **key field** is the field used to control the order of records in a sequential file.

**Opening a file** involves creating an object and associating a stream of bytes with it.

**Closing a file** means it is no longer available to an application.

A **stream** is a pipeline or channel through which bytes are input from and output to a file.

Programmers say `FileStream` **exposes** a stream around a file.

**XML** is an abbreviation of eXtensible Markup Language, which is a standard for exchanging data over the Internet.

A **delimiter** is a character used to specify the boundary between characters in text files.

A **CSV file** is one that contains comma-separated values.

A **token** is a block of text within a string that represents an entity or field.

The term **magic number** refers to the bad programming practice of hard-coding numbers in code without explanation.

A file's **file position pointer** holds the byte number of the next byte to be read.

**Serialization** is the process of converting objects into streams of bytes.

**Deserialization** is the process of converting streams of bytes back into objects.

# Review Questions

1. Random access memory is _____.

   a. persistent

   b. volatile

   c. permanent

   d. sequential

2. A collection of data stored on a nonvolatile device in a computer system is a(n) _____.

   a. application

   b. computer file

   c. operating system

   d. memory map

3. Which of the following is not permanent storage?

   a. RAM

   b. a hard disk

   c. a USB drive

   d. all of these

4. When you store data in a computer file on a persistent storage device, you are _____.

   a. reading

   b. directing

   c. writing

   d. rooting

5. Which of the following is not a `File` class method?

   a. `Create()`

   b. `Delete()`

   c. `Exists()`

   d. `End()`

6. In the data hierarchy, a group of characters that has some meaning, such as a last name or ID number, is a _____.

   a. byte

   b. field

   c. file

   d. record

7. When each record in a file is stored in order based on the value in some field, the file is a(n) _____ file.

   a. random access

   b. application

   c. formatted

   d. sequential

8. A channel through which data flows between a program and storage is a _____.

   a. path

   b. folder

   c. stream

   d. directory

9. Which of the following is not part of a FileStream constructor?

   a. the file size

   b. the file mode

   c. the filename

   d. the type of access

10. When a file's mode is Create, a new file will be created _____.

   a. even if one with the same name already exists

   b. only if one with the same name does not already exist

   c. only if one with the same name already exists

   d. only if the access is Read

11. Which of the following is not a `FileStream` property?

    a. `CanRead`

    b. `CanExist`

    c. `CanSeek`

    d. `CanWrite`

12. Which of the following is not a file `Access` enumeration?

    a. `Read`

    b. `Write`

    c. `WriteRead`

    d. `ReadWrite`

13. A character used to specify the boundary between data items in text files is a _____.

    a. sentinel

    b. stopgap

    c. delimiter

    d. margin

14. Which character can be used to specify a boundary between characters in text files?

    a. a comma

    b. a semicolon

    c. either of these

    d. neither of these

15. After a `StreamReader` has been created, the `ReadLine()` method can be used to _____.

    a. retrieve one line at a time from the file

    b. retrieve one character at a time from the file

    c. store one line at a time in a file

    d. split a `string` into tokens

16. The argument to the `String` class `Split()` method is
    _____.

    a. `void`

    b. the number of fields into which to split a record

    c. the character that identifies a new field in a `string`

    d. a `string` that can be split into tokens

17. The `String` class `Split()` method stores its results in
    _____.

    a. a `string`

    b. an array of `strings`

    c. an appropriate data type for each token

    d. an array of bytes

18. A file's _____ holds the byte number of the next byte to
    be read.

    a. index indicator

    b. position pointer

    c. header file

    d. key field

19. The process of converting objects into streams of bytes is
    _____.

    a. extrication

    b. splitting

    c. mapping

    d. serialization

20. Which of the following is serializable?

    a. an `int`

    b. an array of `ints`

    c. a `string`

    d. all of the above

# Exercises

1. Create a program that allows a user to continually enter directory names until the user types "end". If the directory name exists, display a list of the files in it; otherwise, display a message indicating the directory does not exist. If the directory exists and files are listed, prompt the user to enter one of the filenames. If the file exists, display its creation date and time; otherwise, display a message indicating the file does not exist. Save the program as **TestFileAndDirectory.cs**. Create as many test directories and files as necessary to test your program. Figure 14-38 shows a typical execution.

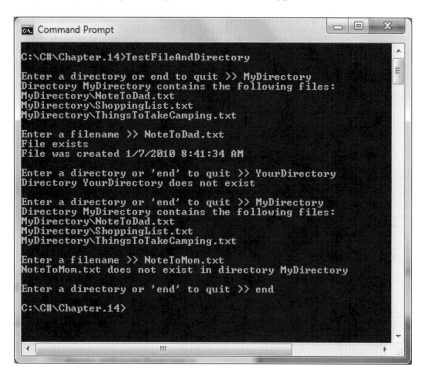

**Figure 14-38** Typical execution of `TestFileAndDirectory` program

2. Create a file that contains your favorite movie quote. Use a text editor such as Notepad, and save the file as **Quote.txt**. Copy the file contents and paste them into a word-processing program such as Word. Save the file as **Quote.docx**. Write an application that displays the sizes of the two files as well as the ratio of their sizes to each other. To discover a file's size, you can create a `System.IO.FileInfo` object using a

statement such as the following, where FILE_NAME is a string that contains the name of the file:

```
FileInfo wordInfo = new FileInfo(FILE_NAME);
```

Save the file as **FileComparison.cs**.

3. Using Visual Studio, create a Form like the one shown in Figure 14-39. Specify a directory on your system, and when the Form loads, list the files the directory contains in a CheckedListBox. Allow the user to click a file's check box and display the file's creation date and time. (Each time the user checks a new filename, display its creation date in place of the original selection.) Save the project as **TestFileAndDirectory2**. Create as many files as necessary to test your program. Figure 14-39 shows a typical execution.

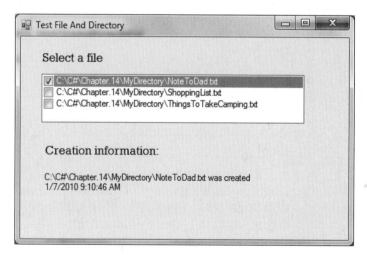

**Figure 14-39** Typical execution of TestFileAndDirectory2 program

4. a. Create a Friend class in which you can store your friends' first and last names, phone numbers, and the month and day of your friends' birthdays. Write a program that prompts you to enter friends' data and saves each record to a file. Save the program as **WriteFriendRecords.cs**.

   b. Create a program that reads the file created in Exercise 4a and displays each friend's data to the screen. Save the program as **ReadFriendRecords.cs**.

   c. Create a program that prompts you for a birth month, reads the file created in Exercise 4a, and displays data for each friend who has a birthday in the specified month. Save the program as **FriendBirthdayReminder.cs**.

5. a. In the Visual Studio IDE, design a Form that allows a user to select options for the background color and size and to give the Form a title. The Form should look like the one shown in Figure 14-40. Change each feature of the Form as the user makes selections. After the user clicks the "Save form settings" Button, save the color, size, and title as strings to a file and disable the button. Save the project as **CustomizeAForm**.

**Figure 14-40**   Form in CustomizeAForm project

b. Design a Form like the one in Figure 14-40, except include a Button to retrieve the Form settings. When the user clicks the "Retrieve form settings" Button, read the settings from the file saved in the CustomizeAForm project, and set the Form's color, size, and title to the values that were saved previously. Save the project as **RetrieveCustomizedForm**.

6. Using the Visual Studio IDE, create a Form that contains a game in which the computer randomly selects one of three letters (A, B, or C) ten times, and the user tries to guess which letter was selected. At the start of the game, read in the previous high score from a data file. (Create this file to hold "0" the first time the game is played.) Display the previous high score on the Form to show the player the score to try to beat. As the player makes each guess, show the player's guess and the computer's choice, and award a point if the player correctly guesses the computer's choice. Keep a running count of the number of correct guesses. After ten random

selections and guesses, disable the game controls and create a file that holds the new high score, which might be the same as before the game or a new higher number. When the player begins a new game, the high score will be displayed on the Form as the new score to beat. Save the project as **HighScore**.

## Debugging Exercises

Each of the following files in the Chapter.14 folder of your downloadable student files has syntax and/or logical errors. In each case, determine the problem and fix the program. After you correct the errors, save each file using the same filename preceded with *Fixed*. For example, save DebugFourteen1.cs as **FixedDebugFourteen1.cs**.

    a.   DebugFourteen1.cs

    b.   DebugFourteen2.cs

    c.   DebugFourteen3.cs

    d.   DebugFourteen4.cs

## Up For Discussion

1.   In Exercise 2 earlier in this chapter, what did you discover about the size difference between files that hold the same contents but were created using different software (such as Word and Notepad)? Why do you think the file sizes are so different, even though the files contain the same data?

2.   Suppose your employer asks you to write a program that lists all the company's employees, their salaries, and their ages. You are provided with the company personnel file to use as input. You decide to take the file home so you can create the program over the weekend. Is this acceptable? What if the file contained only employees' names and departments, but not more sensitive data such as salaries and ages?

# Using LINQ to Access Data in C# Programs

In this chapter you will:

◎ Understand relational database fundamentals

◎ Create databases and table descriptions

◎ Create SQL queries

◎ Create an Access database

◎ Understand implicitly typed variables

◎ Understand LINQ

◎ Retrieve data from an Access database in C#

◎ Use LINQ queries with an Access database table

◎ Use LINQ operators to sort and group data

Businesses run by using data. Most businesses would be damaged severely if their data was lost—for example, customers could not be contacted, employees could not be paid, and orders could not be shipped. Well-run businesses do not just possess a lot of data; the data must be organized to be useful. When a business's data is structured in a useful manner, the business can improve its performance. For example, salespeople can track which customers prefer specific products or services, and administrators can identify which employees are the most productive. Businesses can determine which products and services produce the most profit and which should be dropped. Relational databases provide a means to accomplish all these tasks.

In this chapter, you will learn about databases. You also will learn about LINQ, which is a Visual Studio tool for accessing data stored in databases and other collections, and you will learn how to incorporate LINQ into your C# programs. This chapter is only a brief introduction to these topics. You can buy entire books on database construction and theory and the details of LINQ. This chapter covers only the fundamentals of each topic so you can begin to appreciate how your C# programs have the potential to satisfy important business data needs.

LINQ is pronounced "link."

A **collection** is any data structure that holds objects of the same type. Data structures include arrays, lists, queues, and directories. You will learn about other data structures as you continue to study C#.

## Understanding Relational Database Fundamentals

When you store data items for use within computer systems, they are often stored in what is known as a data hierarchy, where the smallest usable unit of data is the character, often a letter or number. Characters are grouped together to form fields, such as firstName, lastName, and socialSecurityNumber. Related fields are often grouped together to form records—groups of fields that go together because they represent attributes of some entity, such as an employee, customer, inventory item, or bank account. Files are composed of related records; for example, a file might contain a record for each employee in a company or each account at a bank.

The term *data hierarchy* was introduced in the chapter *Files and Streams*.

Most organizations store many files that contain the data they need to operate their businesses. For example, businesses often need to maintain files that contain data about employees, customers, inventory items, and orders. Many organizations use database software to organize the information in these files. A **database** holds a file, or more frequently, a group of files that an organization needs to support its applications. In a database, the files often are called **tables** because you can arrange their contents in rows and columns. Real-life examples of database-like tables abound. For example, consider the listings

Arrays (stored in memory) and tables (stored in databases) are similar in that both contain rows and columns. When an array has multiple columns, all must have the same data type. The same is not true for tables stored in databases.

Sometimes, one record or row is also called an entity; however, many definitions of "entity" exist in database texts. One column (field) can also be called an attribute.

in a telephone book. Each listing in a city directory might contain four columns, as shown in Figure 15-1—last name, first name, street address, and phone number. Although your local phone directory might not store its data in the rigid columnar format shown in the figure, it could. You can see that each column represents a field and that each row represents one record. You can picture a table within a database in the same way.

| Last name | First name | Address | Phone |
|-----------|------------|---------|-------|
| Abbott | William | 123 Oak Lane | 490-8920 |
| Ackerman | Kimberly | 467 Elm Drive | 787-2781 |
| Adams | Stanley | 8120 Pine Street | 787-0129 |
| Adams | Violet | 347 Oak Lane | 490-8912 |
| Adams | William | 12 Second Street | 490-3667 |

**Figure 15-1** A telephone book table

Figure 15-1 includes five records, each representing a unique person. It is relatively easy to scan this short list of names to find a person's phone number; of course, telephone books contain many more records. Some telephone book users, such as telemarketers or even the phone company, might prefer to use a book in which the records are organized in telephone-number order. Others, such as door-to-door salespeople, might prefer a telephone book in which the records are organized in street-address order. Most people, however, prefer a telephone book in which the records are organized as shown, in alphabetical order by last name. Computerized databases can sort records in various orders based on the contents of different columns, offering greater flexibility and convenience for different users.

Unless you are reading a telephone book for a very small town, a last name alone often is not sufficient to identify a person. In the example in Figure 15-1, three people have the last name Adams. For these records, you need to examine the first name before you can determine the correct phone number. In a large city, many people might have the same first and last names; in that case, you might also need to examine the street address to identify a person. As with the telephone book, most computerized database tables require a way to identify each record uniquely, even if it means using multiple columns. A value that uniquely identifies a record is called a **primary key**, or a **key** for short. Key fields often are defined as a single column, but as with the telephone book, keys can be constructed from multiple columns. A key constructed from multiple columns is a **compound key**, also known as a **composite key**.

Telephone books are republished periodically because changes have occurred—new people have moved into the city and become telephone customers, and others have left, canceled service, or changed phone numbers. With computerized database tables, you also need to add, delete, and modify records, although usually far more frequently than phone books are published.

As with telephone books, computerized database tables frequently contain thousands of records, or rows, and each row might contain entries in dozens of columns. Handling and organizing all the data contained in an organization's tables requires sophisticated software. **Database management software**, also known as a **database management system (DBMS)**, is a set of programs that allows users to:

- Create table descriptions.

- Identify keys.

- Add, delete, and update records within a table.

- Arrange records within a table so they are sorted by different fields.

- Write questions that select specific records from a table for viewing.

- Write questions that combine information from multiple tables. This is possible because the database management software establishes and maintains relationships between the columns in the tables. A group of database tables from which you can make these connections is a **relational database**.

- Create reports that allow users to easily interpret your data, and create forms that allow users to view and enter data using an easy-to-manage interactive screen.

- Keep data secure by employing sophisticated security measures.

If you have used different word-processing or spreadsheet programs, you know that each version works a little differently, although each carries out the same types of tasks. Like other computer programs, each database management software package operates differently; however, with each, you need to perform the same types of tasks.

Another key provision of some DBMS software is the ability to view data relationships graphically.

Watch the video *Relational Databases*.

712

# Creating Databases and Table Descriptions

When you save a table description, many database management programs suggest a default, generic name such as Table1. Usually, a more descriptive name is more useful as you continue to create objects.

Beginning table names with the "tbl" prefix is part of the **Leszynski naming convention (LNC)**. This convention is most popular with Microsoft Access users and Visual Basic programmers. This format is just a convention, and is not required by any database. Your instructor or supervisor might approve of a different convention.

Creating a useful database requires a lot of planning and analysis. You must decide what data will be stored, how that data will be divided between tables, and how the tables will interrelate. Before you create any tables, you must create the database itself. With most database software packages, creating the database that will hold the tables requires nothing more than providing a name for the database and indicating the physical location, perhaps a hard disk drive, where the database will be stored. When you save a table, one convention recommends you use a name that begins with the prefix "tbl"—for example, tblCustomers. Your databases often become filled with a variety of objects—tables, forms that users can use for data entry, reports that organize the data for viewing, queries that select subsets of data for viewing, and so on. Using naming conventions, such as beginning each table name with a prefix that identifies it as a table, helps you to keep track of the various objects in your system.

Before you can enter any data into a database table, you must design the table. At minimum, this involves two tasks:

- You must decide what columns your table needs, and provide names for them.

- You must provide a data type for each column.

For example, assume you are designing a customer database table. Figure 15-2 shows some column names and data types you might use.

| Column | Data type |
| --- | --- |
| customerID | Text |
| lastName | Text |
| firstName | Text |
| streetAddress | Text |
| balanceOwed | Numeric |

**Figure 15-2** Customer table description

The table description in Figure 15-2 uses just two data types—text and numeric. Text columns can hold any type of characters, including letters, digits, and punctuation. Numeric columns can hold numbers only. Depending on the database management software you use, you might have many more sophisticated data types at your disposal. For example, some database software divides the numeric data type into several subcategories such as integers (whole number only) and double-precision numbers (numbers that contain decimals). Other options might include special categories for currency numbers (representing dollars and cents), dates, and Boolean columns (representing true or false). At the least, all database software recognizes the distinction between text and numeric data.

 Unassigned variables within computer programs might be empty (containing a null value), or might contain unknown or garbage values. Similarly, columns in database tables might also contain null or unknown values. When a field in a database contains a null value, it does not mean that the field holds a 0 or a space; it means that no data has been entered for the field at all. Although "null" and "empty" are used synonymously by many database developers, the terms have slightly different meanings to some programming professionals, such as Visual Basic programmers.

The table description in Figure 15-2 uses one-word column names and camel casing, in the same way that variable names have been defined throughout this book. Many database software packages do not require that data column names be single words without embedded spaces, but many database table designers prefer single-word names because they resemble variable names in programs. In addition, when you write programs that access a database table, the single-word field names can be used "as is," without special syntax to indicate the names that represent a single field. As a further advantage, when you use a single word to label each database column, it is easier to understand whether just one column is being referenced, or several.

Many database management software packages allow you to add a narrative description of each data column in a table. This allows you

 A table description closely resembles the list of variables that you have used with every program throughout this book.

 It is important to think carefully about the original design of a database. After the database has been created and data has been entered, it could be difficult and time consuming to make changes to the structure.

 Throughout this book, you have been aware of the distinction that computers make between text and numeric data. Because of the way computers handle data, every type of software observes this distinction. This book has consistently used the term "string" to describe text fields. The term "text" is used in this chapter only because popular database packages use it.

714

to make comments that become part of the table. These comments do not affect the way the table operates; they simply serve as documentation for those who are reading a table description. For example, you might want to make a note that `customerID` should consist of five digits, or that `balanceOwed` should not exceed a given limit. Some software allows you to specify that values for a certain column are required; in such cases, the user cannot create a record without providing data for these columns. In addition, you might be able to indicate column value limits—high and low numbers between which the column contents must fall.

## Identifying Primary Keys

In some database software packages, such as Microsoft Access, you indicate a primary key simply by selecting a column name and clicking a button that is labeled with a key icon.

In most tables you create for a database, you want to identify a column, or possibly a combination of columns, as the table's key column or field, also called the primary key. The primary key in a table is the column that makes each record different from all others. For example, in the customer table in Figure 15-2, the logical choice for a primary key is the `customerID` column—each customer record that is entered into the customer table has a unique value in this column. Many customers might have the same first name or last name (or both), and multiple customers also might have the same street address or balance due. However, each customer possesses a unique ID number.

Other typical examples of primary keys include:

- A student ID number in a table that contains college student information

- A part number in a table that contains inventory items

- A Social Security number in a table that contains employee information

A primary key should be immutable, meaning that a value does not change during normal operation.

In each of these examples, the primary key uniquely identifies the row. For example, each student has a unique ID number assigned by the college. Other columns in a student table would not be adequate keys, because many students have the same last name, first name, hometown, or major. Even if a database table contains only one employee named Smith, for example, or only one employee with the job title of Salesperson, those fields are still not good primary key candidates because more Smiths and salespeople could be added later. Analyzing existing data is not a foolproof way to select a good key; you must also consider likely future data.

It is no coincidence that each of the listed examples of a key is a number, such as a student ID number or item number. Often, assigning a number to each row in a table is the simplest and most efficient method of obtaining a useful key. However, a table's key could be a text field.

Sometimes, several columns could serve as the key. For example, if an employee record contains both a company-assigned employee ID and a Social Security number, then both columns are candidate keys. After you choose a primary key from among candidate keys, the remaining candidate keys become alternate keys.

The primary key is important for several reasons:

- You can configure your database software to prevent multiple records from containing the same value in this column, thus avoiding data-entry errors.

- For some applications, you might want to sort your records in this order before displaying or printing them.

- You use this column when setting up relationships between this table and others that will become part of the same database.

In addition, you need to understand the concept of the primary key when you normalize a database. **Normalization** is the process of designing and creating a set of database tables that satisfies users' needs and avoids many potential problems such as data redundancies and anomalies. **Data redundancy** is the unnecessary repetition of data. An **anomaly** is an irregularity in a database's design that causes problems and inconveniences. To keep the examples in this chapter simple, only single database tables are used. However, as you grow proficient in database use and constructions, you will want to create databases with relationships among multiple tables, which requires a more thorough understanding of normalization.

As an example of data redundancy, consider a table of names and addresses in which many addresses are in the same zip code. Instead of storing the same city and state name with each record, it is more efficient to store only the zip code with each record, and then to associate the table with another table that contains a list of zip codes and the corresponding cities and states.

715

Anomalies take many forms. For example, an anomaly occurs when the same data is stored in multiple locations. If a database contains a table of in-stock items and their prices, and another table contains customer orders, including items and prices, then any price changes must be made in multiple locations, increasing the chance for error.

Usually, after you have identified the necessary fields and their data types and identified the primary key, you are ready to save your table description and begin to enter data.

## Understanding Database Structure Notation

A shorthand way to describe a table is to use the table name followed by parentheses that contain all the field names, with the primary key underlined. Thus, when a table is named tblStudents and contains columns named idNumber, lastName, firstName, and gradePointAverage, and idNumber is the key, you can reference the table using the following notation:

```
tblStudents(idNumber, lastName, firstName, gradePointAverage)
```

Although this shorthand notation does not provide information about data types or range limits on values, it does provide a quick overview of the table's structure.

Some database designers insert an asterisk after the key instead of underlining it.

The key does not have to be the first attribute listed in a table reference, but frequently it is.

---

### TWO TRUTHS & A LIE

### Creating Databases and Table Descriptions

1. Databases are often filled with multiple objects such as tables, forms, and queries.

2. The primary key in a table is the record that appears first in a sorted list.

3. Data redundancy is the unnecessary repetition of data.

The false statement is #2. The primary key in a table is the column that makes each record different from all others.

---

## Creating SQL Queries

Data tables often contain hundreds or thousands of rows; making sense out of that much information is a daunting task. Frequently, you want to cull subsets of data from a table you have created. For example, you might want to view only those customers with an address in a specific state, only inventory items whose quantity in stock has fallen below the normal reorder point, or only employees who participate in an insurance plan. Besides limiting records, you might also want to limit the columns that you view. For example, student records might contain dozens of fields, but a school administrator might only be interested in looking at names and grade point averages (GPAs). The questions that cause the database software to extract the appropriate records from a table and specify the fields to be viewed are called queries; a **query** is simply a request using syntax that the database software can understand.

Depending on the software you use, you might create a query by filling in blanks (using a language called **query by example**) or by writing statements similar to those in many programming languages. The most common language that database administrators use to access data in their tables is **Structured Query Language**, or **SQL**. The basic form of the SQL command that retrieves selected records from a table is **SELECT-FROM-WHERE**. The SELECT-FROM-WHERE SQL statement:

- *Selects* the columns you want to view

- *From* a specific table

- *Where* one or more conditions are met

"SQL" frequently is pronounced "sequel," but several SQL product Web sites insist that the official pronunciation is "S-Q-L." Similarly, some people pronounce GUI as "gooey" and others insist that it should be "G-U-I." In general, a preferred pronunciation evolves in an organization. The **TLA**, which is a three-letter abbreviation for *three-letter abbreviation*, is the most popular type of abbreviation in technical terminology.

For example, suppose a customer table named `tblCustomer` contains data about your business customers and that the structure of the table is `tblCustomer(custId, lastName, state)`. Then, a statement such as:

`SELECT custId, lastName FROM tblCustomer WHERE state = "WI"`

would display a new table that contains two columns—`custId` and `lastName`—and only as many rows as needed to hold customers whose state column contains "WI". Besides using = to mean "equal to," you can use the comparison conditions > (greater than), < (less than), >= (greater than or equal to), and <= (less than or equal to). As you have already learned from working with programming variables throughout this book, text field values are always contained within quotes, whereas numeric values are not.

To select all fields for each record in a table, you can use the asterisk as a wildcard; a **wildcard** is a symbol that means "any" or "all." For example, `SELECT * FROM tblCustomer WHERE state = "WI"` would select all columns for every customer whose state is "WI", not just specifically named columns. To select all customers from a table, you can omit the WHERE clause in a SELECT-FROM-WHERE statement. In other words, `SELECT * FROM tblCustomer` selects all columns for all customers.

You learned about making selections in computer programs much earlier in this book, and you have probably noticed that SELECT-FROM-WHERE statements serve the same purpose as programming decisions. As with decision statements in programs, SQL allows you to create compound conditions using AND or OR operators. In addition, you can precede any condition with a NOT operator to achieve a negative result. In summary, Figure 15-3 shows a database table named `tblInventory` with the following structure:

`tblInventory(itemNumber, description, quantityInStock, price)`

The table contains five records. Figure 15-4 lists several typical SQL SELECT statements you might use with `tblInventory`, and explains each.

Conventionally, SQL keywords such as SELECT appear entirely in uppercase; this book follows that convention.

In database management systems, a particular way of looking at a database is sometimes called a **view**. Typically, a view arranges records in some order and makes only certain fields visible. The different views provided by database software are virtual; that is, they do not affect the physical organization of the database.

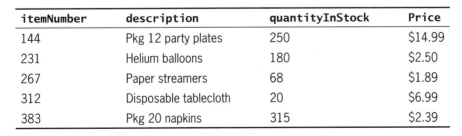

| itemNumber | description | quantityInStock | Price |
|---|---|---|---|
| 144 | Pkg 12 party plates | 250 | $14.99 |
| 231 | Helium balloons | 180 | $2.50 |
| 267 | Paper streamers | 68 | $1.89 |
| 312 | Disposable tablecloth | 20 | $6.99 |
| 383 | Pkg 20 napkins | 315 | $2.39 |

**Figure 15-3**   The `tblInventory` table

| SQL Statement | Explanation |
|---|---|
| SELECT itemNumber, price FROM tblInventory | Shows only the item number and price for all five records. |
| SELECT * FROM tblInventory WHERE price > 5.00 | Shows all fields from only those records in which price is greater than $5.00—items 144 and 312. |
| SELECT itemNumber FROM tblInventory WHERE quantityInStock > 200 AND price > 10.00 | Shows item number 144—the only record that has a quantity greater than 200 as well as a price greater than $10.00. |
| SELECT description, price FROM tblInventory WHERE description = "Pkg 20 napkins" OR itemNumber < 200 | Shows the description and price fields for the package of 12 party plates and the package of 20 napkins. Each selected record only needs to satisfy one of the two criteria. |
| SELECT itemNumber FROM tblInventory WHERE NOT price < 14.00 | Shows the item number for the only record in which the price is not less than $14.00—item 144. |

**Figure 15-4** Sample SQL statements and explanations

## TWO TRUTHS & A LIE

### Creating SQL Queries

1. A query is a question that causes database software to extract appropriate fields and records from a table.

2. The most common language that database administrators use to access data in their tables is Structured Query Language, or SQL.

3. The basic form of the SQL command that retrieves selected records from a table is RETRIEVE-FROM-SELECTION.

The false statement is # 3. The basic form of the SQL command that retrieves selected records from a table is SELECT-FROM-WHERE.

## Creating an Access Database

**Microsoft Office Access** is a relational database that is part of some versions of the Microsoft Office system. It combines the relational Microsoft Jet Database Engine with a GUI user interface and other tools. Access is not the only database on the market, but it is convenient for many users because it comes packaged with some versions of Microsoft Office. Using Access correctly and efficiently can take some time to learn; at most colleges, you can take at least a two-semester course to learn Access thoroughly. This section introduces you to Access as an example of a typical database.

Access was the name of an earlier failed Microsoft communications program. The corporation reused the name when it developed its database software in 1992.

Figure 15-5 shows the environment in which a database table is designed in Access. Suppose Cartman College wants to keep track of some student data in a database. To keep the example simple, suppose the college wants to store only an ID number, first and last names, and a GPA for each student. In Access, a database developer can type field names for the data that will be stored and can assign an appropriate data type for each. In Figure 15-5, a `tblStudents` table is defined, including fields for `ID`, `LastName`, `FirstName`, and `GradePointAverage`.

Other popular database packages include Microsoft SQL, MySQL, Borland Paradox, FileMaker Pro, Lotus Approach, Oracle XE, and Sun StarBase.

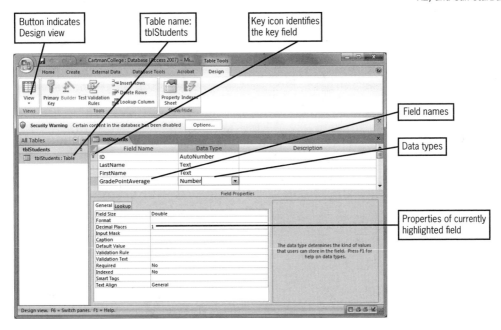

**Figure 15-5** The Design view of the `tblStudents` table in Access

Figure 15-5 shows that the ID field type was chosen to be `AutoNumber`, which means Access will automatically assign consecutive numbers to each new record as it is entered. Figure 15-5 also shows Microsoft Access 2007, which was the latest available version of Access when this book was in production. If you are using a different version, your screen might look slightly different.

After a table's design has been completed, a user can enter data into the table. Figure 15-6 shows the **tblStudents** table in Access's Datasheet view, in which a user can type data like it would be typed into a spreadsheet. The column headings in the datasheet are provided automatically based on the names that were selected in the Design view.

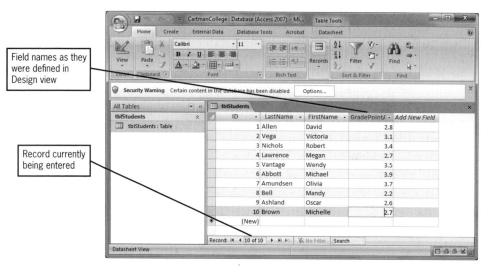

**Figure 15-6** The Datasheet view of the **tblStudents** table in Access

In a database actually used by a college, many more fields would be stored for each student and additional tables would be created for courses, faculty, and so on. However, this small database provides enough data to demonstrate using C# to access the stored data.

## TWO TRUTHS & A LIE

### Creating an Access Database

1. Microsoft Office Access is a relational database that is part of the Microsoft Office system.

2. Access is the only popular commercial database that can be used with C#.

3. In Access, a user designs tables by choosing fields and data types; then the user can enter data into the tables.

The false statement is #2. Access is not the only database on the market, and is not the only one that can be accessed in C#, but it is convenient for many users because it comes packaged with Microsoft Office.

# Understanding Implicitly Typed Variables

An **implicitly typed variable** has a data type that is inferred from the expression used to initialize the variable. To create an implicitly typed variable, you use a variable declaration with **var** as the data type. When you use an implicitly typed variable, the C# compiler decides on a data type for you. This process is called **type inference**—an object's set of allowed properties and methods is not fixed when the code is written, but is determined when the program executes.

For example, in the following statement, money is implicitly typed as a double because the value assigned to the variable is a double:

```
var money = 1.99;
```

Because money is a double, you can, for example, perform arithmetic with it. If the declaration had been var money = "a dollar ninety-nine";, then money would be a string and you could not perform arithmetic with it. The statement var money = 1.99; has exactly the same meaning as the following:

```
double money = 1.99;
```

Other examples of assigning values to implicitly typed variables include the following:

- var age = 30; has the same meaning as int age = 30;

- var name = "Roxy"; has the same meaning as
  string name = "Roxy";

- var book = new Book() has the same meaning as
  Book book = new Book();

- var emp = new Employee(101, "Smith", 15.00); has the same meaning as Employee emp = new Employee(101, "Smith", 15.00);

You have already learned that you can use the foreach statement to process array elements. For example, the following code displays each double in the payRate array:

```
double[] payRate = {6.00, 7.35, 8.12, 12.45, 22.22};
foreach(double money in payRate)
    Console.WriteLine("{0}", money.ToString("C"));
```

In this example, money is declared as a double and is used as the **iteration variable**—the variable that is used to hold each successive value in the array. Alternatively, you can declare the iteration variable in a foreach statement to be an implicitly typed local variable.

Using var to create implicitly typed variables is also called **duck typing** because it fits the phrase, "If it walks like a duck and quacks like a duck, I would call it a duck." The phrase is attributed to an American writer and poet, James Whitcomb Riley, who lived from 1849 to 1916.

Although each of these uses of var is a valid C# statement, you should not use var simply to avoid declaring a data type for an item. The var keyword should be used only in specific situations, such as with LINQ statements.

In this case, the iteration variable's type is inferred from the collection type it uses. For example, the same results can be achieved with the following:

```
double[] payRate = {6.00, 7.35, 8.12, 12.45, 22.22};
foreach(var money in payRate)
    Console.WriteLine("{0}", money.ToString("C"));
```

In this example, money is implied to be a double because payRate is an array of doubles. In Figure 15-7, the implicitly typed variable n is an int because numbers is an int array. Figure 15-8 shows the program's output.

```
using System;
public class ImplicitVariableDemo
{
    public static void Main()
    {
        int[] numbers = { 6, 4, 2, 1, 8, 3, 7, 5, 2, 0 };
        Console.WriteLine("Numbers List");
        foreach (var n in numbers)
            Console.Write("{0} ", n);
        Console.WriteLine();
    }
}
```

**Figure 15-7** The ImplicitVariableDemo class

**Figure 15-8** Output of the ImplicitVariableDemo program

Unlike C#, Visual Basic is considered to be a weakly typed language. If you run a VB program in Visual Studio 2008, you have the option of declaring Option Strict, which means that types will be checked.

When you declare a variable, usually you want to assign a data type. One advantage of a modern programming language like C# is that it is **strongly typed**. When a language is strongly typed, severe restrictions are placed on what data types can be mixed. Strong typing prevents certain errors—for example, the loss of data that might occur if you inadvertently assigned a double to an integer. You will use implicitly typed variables frequently in LINQ statements, which help you access data stored in a database.

723

# Understanding LINQ

As you have studied C#, you have become comfortable with the ideas of objects and classes. However, businesses operate using data that frequently is stored in relational databases. Applications that tried to bridge the gap between modern languages and traditional databases have been difficult to build and maintain. To reduce the complexity of accessing and integrating data that is stored in databases and other collections, Microsoft Corporation developed the **LINQ** (Language INtegrated Query) Project to provide queries that can be used in C# and Visual Basic.

In older versions of C#, you could access database data by passing an SQL string to a database object (and you still *can* do so). For example, if you want to select all the fields in records in a table named `tblStudents` for which the field `GradePointAverage` is greater than 3.0, you could create a string such as `"SELECT * from tblStudents WHERE GradePointAverage > 3.00"` and pass it to an object of type `OleDbCommand`, which is a built-in type used to access databases. (The "Ole" stands for "Object linking and embedding.") You also would be required to type a few other statements that performed tasks like establishing a connection to the database and opening the database, and the select command would then select all the fields for all the records in the table that met the GPA criterion. The drawback to using a string command is that C# does not provide any syntax checking for characters stored within a string. For example, if you misspelled SELECT or GradePointAverage, the compiler would not issue an error message, but the program would fail when you executed it. Obviously, allowing any spelling is a beneficial feature when you want to store people's names or addresses, but it is a shortcoming when you want to issue a correct command.

LINQ was created to help solve these problems. LINQ provides a set of general-purpose standard operators that allow queries to be constructed using syntax that is easy to understand. This syntax is similar to SQL's, and the compiler can check it for errors. The operators defined in LINQ can be used to query arrays, enumerable classes, XML, relational databases, and other sources. This chapter concentrates on arrays and databases, but the LINQ queries you learn can be used with many types of data.

Some keywords in the LINQ vocabulary include the following:

- **select** indicates what to select.

- **from** indicates the collection or sequence from which data will be drawn.

- **where** indicates conditions for selecting records.

It is no accident that these are the same words you learned about in the discussion of SQL earlier in this chapter.

Figure 15-9 shows an example of LINQ in action. In the first shaded section, an implicitly typed collection, highNums, is constructed from each variable x in the numbers array where the value of x is greater than 3. The foreach loop uses the sequence that is a subset of the original array to display all the records that meet the selection criteria—that is, all the integers greater than 3. Figure 15-10 shows the output.

The operator where is a **restriction operator**, or one that places a restriction on which data is added to a collection. The operator select is a **projection operator**, or one that projects, or sends off, specific data from a collection.

```
using System;
using System.Linq;
public class LinqDemo1
{
  public static void Main()
  {
    int[] numbers = { 6, 4, 2, 1, 8, 3, 7, 5, 2, 0 };
    const int CUTOFF = 3;
    var highNums =
        from x in numbers
        where x > CUTOFF
        select x;

    Console.WriteLine("Numbers > " + CUTOFF);
    foreach (var n in highNums)
    {
        Console.Write("{0}  ", n);
    }
    Console.WriteLine();
  }
}
```

**Figure 15-9**   LinqDemo1 program

**Figure 15-10**   Output of the LinqDemo1 application

You can use LINQ with more complicated sequences, such as an array of objects. Figure 15-11 shows a Student class that is similar to many you have seen throughout this book. The class contains three auto-implemented properties and a constructor that requires three parameters. Figure 15-12 provides an example of how LINQ can select specific Students from an array. Figure 15-13 shows this output.

```
class Student
{
    public Student(int num, string name, double avg)
    {
        IdNumber = num;
        Name = name;
        GradePointAverage = avg;
    }
    public int IdNumber {get; set;}
    public string Name {get; set;}
    public double GradePointAverage {get; set;}
}
```

**Figure 15-11**   Student class

```
using System;
using System.Linq;
public class LinqDemo2
{
    public static void Main()
    {
        Student[] stus = { new Student(1,  "Jones",    3.1),
                           new Student(2,  "Kimball",  2.9),
                           new Student(5,  "Oliver",   2.6),
                           new Student(6,  "Mitchell", 3.0),
                           new Student(8,  "Lee",      4.0),
                           new Student(10, "Cooper",   3.5)  };
        const double CUTOFF = 3.0;
        var goodStudents =
            from s in stus
            where s.GradePointAverage > CUTOFF
            select s;

        Console.WriteLine("Students with GPA > " + CUTOFF);
        foreach (var s in goodStudents)
        {
            Console.WriteLine("{0,3} {1,-8} {2,5}", s.IdNumber,
                s.Name, s.GradePointAverage.ToString("F1"));
        }
    }
}
```

**Figure 15-12**   LinqDemo2 program

Figure 15-13  Output of the LinqDemo2 program

Although LINQ statements work well to select specific records from an array, you could have used traditional C# statements to achieve the same results. However, few businesses can operate with all their data hard coded and stored in arrays within programs. The true power of LINQ becomes available when you can access an external database.

Watch the video *An Introduction to LINQ*.

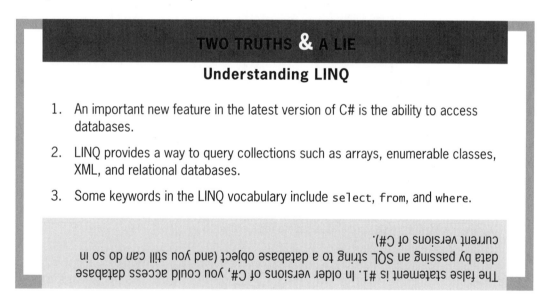

TWO TRUTHS **&** A LIE

### Understanding LINQ

1. An important new feature in the latest version of C# is the ability to access databases.

2. LINQ provides a way to query collections such as arrays, enumerable classes, XML, and relational databases.

3. Some keywords in the LINQ vocabulary include select, from, and where.

The false statement is #1. In older versions of C#, you could access database data by passing an SQL string to a database object (and you still can do so in current versions of C#).

# Retrieving Data from an Access Database in C#

As with many features of C#, you can write code to access a database table by hand, but you save time and reduce the chance for error by using the built-in tools of the Visual Studio IDE.

Adding a database to a Windows Forms project requires making only a few menu selections and browsing for a stored database. (In the "You Do It" section later in this chapter, you can walk through instructions that add a database to your project.) To add a database table to a Windows Forms project, you can perform two sets of tasks:

- You drag a `DataGridView` object from the IDE's Toolbox onto a `Form`. As Figure 15-14 shows, a dialog box appears from which you can select a project data source. (If you inadvertently dismiss the `DataGridView` Tasks dialog box before selecting a data source, you can select Data Source from the Properties list and make the same selections.)

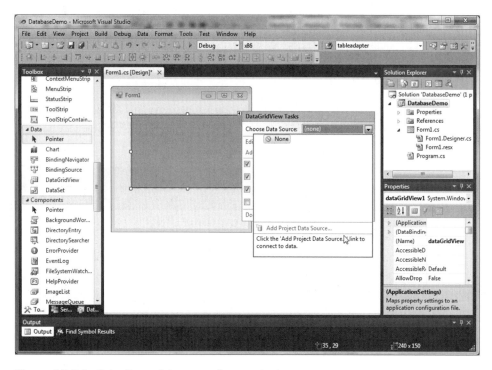

**Figure 15-14** Selecting a data source for a project

- You make a few choices and browse for the database file to add to the project. After a few more choices, the empty grid appears (see Figure 15-15). The Solution Explorer window at the right side of the screen shows that the CartmanCollegeDatabase has been added to the project. Also note at the bottom of the screen that three objects have been created:

  - `cartmanCollegeDataSet`—A **dataset** is a temporary set of data stored in your project. In other words, changes made to this dataset in the program will not automatically alter the original database.

  - `tblStudentsBindingSource`—A **BindingSource** object establishes a link from a database to your program.

  - `tblStudentsTableAdapter`—A **table adapter** passes data back and forth between the dataset and the `BindingSource`.

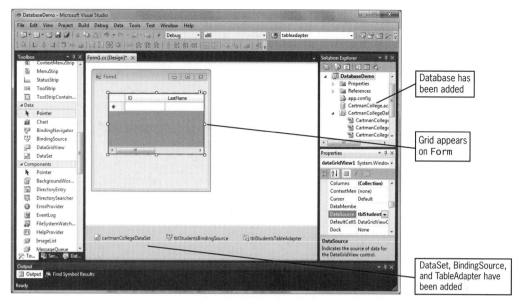

**Figure 15-15** Database file has been added to the project

After the database table has been added to the project, you can execute the program shown on the left in Figure 15-16. The data from the database appears in the grid, and scroll bars appear so that you can navigate to see the rows and columns that do not fit. If you want to see more columns and rows at a time when the program executes again, you can close the Form, return to the IDE, and resize the Form and DataGridView (see the right side in Figure 15-16).

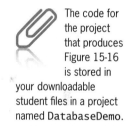

The code for the project that produces Figure 15-16 is stored in your downloadable student files in a project named DatabaseDemo.

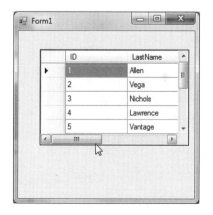

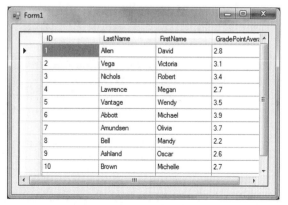

**Figure 15-16** Execution of the DatabaseDemo project

When you view the code behind the Form in Figure 15-16, you can see that one comment and one statement have been added to the Form1_Load() method, the method that executes when a Windows application starts and the main form is initialized. Figure 15-17 shows the method.

```
private void Form1_Load(object sender, EventArgs e)
{
    // TODO: This line of code loads data
    // into the 'cartmanCollegeDataSet.tblStudents' table.
    // You can move, or remove it, as needed.

    this.tblStudentsTableAdapter.Fill
        (this.cartmanCollegeDataSet.tblStudents);
}
```

The line breaks in Figure 15-17 have been altered from the way they appear in Visual Studio to better fit this page.

**Figure 15-17** Form1_Load() method with automatically generated code after CartmanCollege database is added to the Form

If you search the code for the project, you will find more than a dozen references to cartmanCollegeDataSet. All this code was automatically generated when you added the data to the project and added the table to the Form, saving you many chances for error.

The comment in the Form1_Load() method indicates that you can move the Fill() method statement or delete it. The Fill() method fills the table adapter with the data from tblStudents in the cartmanCollegeDataSet. You do not have to load the data into the viewing grid when the Form loads. For example, you could add a button to the Form and move the Fill() statement to the button's Click() method. Then, when the Form loads, no data would be visible, but after the user clicks the button, the data fills the table.

## TWO TRUTHS & A LIE

### Retrieving Data from an Access Database in C#

1. A dataset is another name for a database that your project accesses and alters.

2. A BindingSource object establishes a link from a database to a program.

3. A table adapter passes data back and forth between a dataset and the BindingSource.

The false statement is #1. A dataset is a temporary set of data stored in a project.

# Using LINQ Queries with an Access Database Table

You are not required to use the data grid to view database records. You also are not required to view all the records in the database table or to view all the fields for each record. Instead, you can use a LINQ query to select a collection of data from a table when specific criteria are met. For example, Figure 15-18 shows a showButton_Click() method that could be used to fill a list box with only the last names of students who have a GPA greater than 3.0. The shaded code in the figure is quite similar to the shaded code used with the array in Figure 15-12. Instead of using Console.WriteLine() to display students, this method adds them to a ListBox named outputListBox.

```
private void showButton_Click(object sender, EventArgs e)
{
    const double CUTOFF = 3.0;
    this.tblStudentsTableAdapter.Fill
      (this.cartmanCollegeDataSet.tblStudents);
    var goodStudents =
        from s in this.cartmanCollegeDataSet.tblStudents
        where s.GradePointAverage > CUTOFF
        select s;
    foreach (var s in goodStudents)
        outputListBox.Items.Add(s.LastName);
}
```

**Figure 15-18**  The showButton_Click() method that uses a ListBox to display the last names of students with high GPAs

 The method in Figure 15-18 is part of the project named DatabaseDemo2, which is available in your downloadable student files.

 The from-where-select combination is a single statement. Conventionally, its parts are written on separate lines for clarity, but that is not required. However, be careful not to use a semicolon until the entire statement is complete.

In the example in Figure 15-18, goodStudents is an implicitly typed collection of students with high GPAs. In this case, goodStudents is the following type (where DatabaseDemo2 is the name of the current project):

System.Data.EnumerableRowCollection<DatabaseDemo2.
    CartmanCollegeDataSet.tblStudentsRow>

This means that goodStudents is a collection of rows from the tblStudents database table. However, it is easier to use var and to have the type inferred than to use this lengthy type name.

Assume that you start a C# Windows Forms project and take the following steps:

- Add the CartmanCollege database tblStudents table to the project.

- Delete the automatically added grid from the Form.

- Drag a button onto the Form. Change its Text property to "Show students with high GPA" and its Name property to showButton.

- Drag a ListBox onto the Form and change its Name property to outputListBox.

- Add the showButton_Click() method from Figure 15-18.

Figure 15-19 shows the results when you execute the program and click the button. Although ten student records are stored in the table, the figure lists only the last names of the five students who have GPA values over 3.0. You can confirm that these are the correct students by referring back to the complete listing in Figure 15-6.

**Figure 15-19** Execution of the program containing the method in Figure 15-18

In the method in Figure 15-18, goodStudents is a collection of student records gathered from the tblStudents table in the CartmanCollege database, as indicated in the from clause. The where clause specifies the condition for selection—a GPA greater than CUTOFF. The select clause indicates what to select—a record. The foreach statement that follows the shaded portion of the method selects each record in the collection, and adds its LastName field to the ListBox.

As an alternative to the code in Figure 15-18, instead of creating a collection of records, you could create a collection of last names. Figure 15-20 shows an example, in which only last names are selected to be added to the collection (see the first shaded expression in the figure). That is, in this example goodStudents is a collection of strings, and not a collection of records. When each s is added to the

ListBox in the second shaded expression, a string is added. In the example in Figure 15-18, you selected records and output each one's last name. In this example, you select last names and output each one. The results are identical to those shown in Figure 15-19.

```
var goodStudents =
    from s in this.cartmanCollegeDataSet.tblStudents
    where s.GradePointAverage > CUTOFF
    select s.LastName;
foreach (var s in goodStudents)
    outputListBox.Items.Add(s);
```

**Figure 15-20** Collecting strings from a database table

Figure 15-21 contains a showButton_Click() method from a different application in which a constant GPA cutoff is not used. Instead, the user can enter a cutoff GPA value into a TextBox that has been named gpaTextBox (see the first shaded expression). In this example, a student's GPA must be greater than the user-supplied value to qualify for the list. The last name, a comma, and the first name of each qualifying student (see the last shaded expression in Figure 15-21) are shown in the ListBox. Figure 15-22 shows a typical execution.

```
private void showButton_Click(object sender, EventArgs e)
{
    double minGpa = Convert.ToDouble(gpaTextBox.Text);
    this.tblStudentsTableAdapter.Fill
      (this.cartmanCollegeDataSet.tblStudents);
    var goodStudents =
        from s in this.cartmanCollegeDataSet.tblStudents
        where s.GradePointAverage > minGpa
        select s;
    foreach (var s in goodStudents)
        outputListBox.Items.Add(s.LastName + ", " + s.FirstName);
}
```

**Figure 15-21** The showButton_Click() method that displays students with a minimum GPA entered by the user

 The method in Figure 15-21 is part of the project named DatabaseDemo3, which is available in your downloadable student files. In the example in Figure 15-21, instead of using a showButton_Click() method, you might prefer to add the code to a gpaTextBox_TextChanged() method so that it executes each time the user enters a new value as a minimum GPA, instead of when the user clicks a button. You might also prefer to add some error checking in case the user enters a non-numeric value. Error checking was omitted from this example to keep it short.

When you execute an application that contains the method in Figure 15-21, the list of items in the ListBox is appended each time the user clicks the Button. In other words, if a user clicks the button twice without changing the selection criterion, the ListBox contains a second set of the same records. To prevent the list from growing and to see only the students who meet the current criteria, add the following statement near the beginning of the Click() method:

```
outputListBox.Items.Clear();
```

With the inclusion of this statement, the ListBox is emptied before each new group is added to it.

**Figure 15-22** Typical execution of an application containing the showButton_Click() method in Figure 15-21

Many other options are available when you use LINQ expressions. For example, you can use AND and OR expressions in your LINQ statements. The following code selects all students with GPAs between 2.5 and 3.0:

```
var someStudents =
    from s in this.cartmanCollegeDataSet.tblStudents
    where s.GradePointAverage > 2.5 && s.GradePointAverage < 3.0
    select s;
```

With text values, you can use StartsWith(), EndsWith(), and Contains(). For example, the following code selects all students whose first name starts with "M".

```
var someStudents =
    from s in this.cartmanCollegeDataSet.tblStudents
    where s.FirstName.StartsWith("M")
    select s;
```

You can use several **aggregate operators**, or operators that produce statistics for groups of data. The aggregate operators include Average(), Count(), Sum(), Max(), and Min(). For example, the method in Figure 15-23 assembles a collection of GradePointAverage values named gpas. Then several aggregate operators are applied to the collection and the results are assigned to Labels. Figure 15-24 shows the output when this method is used with tblStudents. You can confirm the accuracy of these statistics by referring to the complete dataset in Figure 15-6.

```
private void showButton_Click(object sender, EventArgs e)
{
    var gpas =
        from s in this.cartmanCollegeDataSet.tblStudents
            select s.GradePointAverage;
    countLabel.Text = "Count is " + gpas.Count();
    minLabel.Text = "Lowest GPA is " + gpas.Min();
    maxLabel.Text = "Highest GPA is " + gpas.Max();
    avgLabel.Text = "Average of all GPAs is " + gpas.Average();
}
```

**Figure 15-23** Method that uses some aggregate operators

 The method in Figure 15-23 is part of the project named DatabaseDemo4, which is available in your downloadable student files.

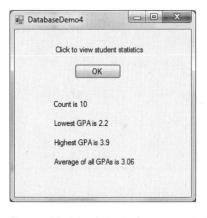

**Figure 15-24** Output of program that uses the method in Figure 15-23

> ## TWO TRUTHS & A LIE
>
> ### Using LINQ Queries with an Access Database Table
>
> Consider this code:
>
> ```
> var emps =
>     from e in this.abcDataSet.tblEmployees
>     where e.YearsOnJob < 10
>     select e.IdNumber;
> ```
>
> 1. emps is an implicitly typed collection of ID numbers.
>
> 2. emps is a collection of rows from tblEmployees in the abcDataSet.
>
> 3. The only data added to emps comes from records in which YearsOnJob is less than 10.
>
> The false statement is #2. In this code, emps is a collection of fields (IdNumbers). Most likely, this means it is a collection of strings or integers—it depends on how IdNumber has been defined in the tblEmployees table.

## Using LINQ Operators to Sort and Group Data

You can use the **orderby operator** to sort a collection of data based on a field or fields. For example, the method in Figure 15-25 produces the output in Figure 15-26. The shaded statement causes the list of students to be ordered by GPA.

```
private void showButton_Click(object sender, EventArgs e)
{
    outputListBox.Items.Add("GPA    LastName");
    var students =
        from s in this.cartmanCollegeDataSet.tblStudents
        orderby s.GradePointAverage
        select s;
    foreach (var s in students)
        outputListBox.Items.Add(" " + s.GradePointAverage + "    " +
            s.LastName);
}
```

**Figure 15-25** Method that uses orderby

 The method in Figure 15-25 is part of the project named DatabaseDemo5, which is available in your downloadable student files.

**Figure 15-26**  Output of project that uses the method in Figure 15-25

The default order for sorting is ascending—that is, from lowest to highest. You can explicitly indicate an ascending sort by using the following phrase:

```
orderby s.GradePointAverage ascending
```

To view the students in the reverse order, from the highest GPA to the lowest, you would write the following:

```
orderby s.GradePointAverage descending
```

You can use compound conditions for ordering. For example, the following would sort students by last name, and then by first name when last names are the same:

```
orderby s.LastName, s.FirstName
```

Data items also can be grouped; the **group operator** groups data by specified criteria. For example, Figure 15-27 shows a Click() method that groups students by the integer part of the GradePointAverage field. In other words, all students with GPAs between 2 and 3 are in one group, and students with GPAs between 3 and 4 are in another group. (Additional groups would be formed if students had higher or lower GPAs.) The example in Figure 15-27 uses nested foreach loops. In the outer loop, which executes one time for each group, the group Key is displayed as a heading. The Key is not required to be the key field in the database table, although it might be; the Key is the value used to determine the groups, which in this case is determined by the integer part of the GPA. In the inner foreach loop in Figure 15-27, the GPA and last name for each record in the group are added to the ListBox. Figure 15-28 shows the results.

```
private void showButton_Click(object sender, EventArgs e)
{
   var stus = from s in cartmanCollegeDataSet.tblStudents
      group s by (int)s.GradePointAverage;

   foreach (var groupByGpa in stus)
   {
      outputListBox.Items.Add("GPA: " + groupByGpa.Key);
      foreach (var s in groupByGpa)
         outputListBox.Items.Add("   " + s.GradePointAverage +
            "   " + s.LastName);
   }
}
```

**Figure 15-27**   A method that groups records

 The method in Figure 15-27 is part of the project named DatabaseDemo6, which is available in your downloadable student files.

**Figure 15-28**   Output of application that contains the method in Figure 15-27

When you use the group operator, the number of possible values in the criterion determines the number of possible groups. For example, if a company has five departments and you group employees with an expression such as the following, you form five groups:

```
group e by e.Department
```

However, if you use a Boolean expression in the by clause, then only two groups are possible because the by expression has only two possible values—true or false:

```
group e by e.Department == 1
```

That is, every e is part of the group for which e.Department == 1 is true, or the group for which e.Department == 1 is false.

A query body must end with a `select` clause or a `group` clause. Therefore, if you combine `orderby` and `group`, `orderby` must come first and `group` must come last. For example, to view the students in each GPA category in alphabetical order by last name, you would write the following:

```
var stus = from s in cartmanCollegeDataSet.tblStudents
    orderby s.LastName
    group s by (int)s.GradePointAverage;
```

739

Many more LINQ operations are available than can be covered in this chapter. More than 50 operators are available, and they can be combined in practically an infinite number of ways. For example, you can insert and delete records from a database. Additionally, a key feature of normalized relational databases is the ability to make relationships between tables. LINQ allows you to join multiple object collections together using a relatively simple syntax that is familiar to those who already know SQL. As you learn more about databases, C#, and LINQ, you will discover many possibilities and learn to create useful applications that access data and provide business clients with powerful ways to view and use their information.

For more good ideas on working with LINQ, see "101 LINQ Samples" at *http://msdn. microsoft.com/en-us/ vcsharp/aa336746.aspx.*

Watch the video *Using LINQ with a Database.*

---

## TWO TRUTHS & A LIE

### Using LINQ Operators to Sort and Group Data

Consider the following code:

```
var emps =
    from e in this.abcDataSet.tblEmployees
        orderby e.LastName
        group e by e.Department;
```

1. In the collection `emps`, Brown in Department 1 would come before Adams in Department 3.

2. In the collection `emps`, Graham in Department 4 would come before Lee in Department 7.

3. In the collection `emps`, Kimball in Department 5 would come before Thompson in Department 3.

The false statement is #3. Each lower-numbered department group would precede any higher-numbered group. Within the groups, the employees would be in alphabetical order.

# You Do It

## Adding a Dataset to a Project

In the next steps, you will add a previously created database table to a C# project and retrieve data from the table so you can display it in a Form.

**To add a dataset to a project:**

1. Your downloadable student files contain a Microsoft Office Access Database file named **HonestRalphsUsedCars**. If Access is installed on your computer, you can open the database file by double-clicking its name. When Access opens, double-click **tblCars : Table** under All Tables. (See Figure 15-29.) Examine the data in the table. The fields are ID, ModelYear, Make, Price, and Color. Ten records have been entered into the table. When you finish examining the records, close Access.

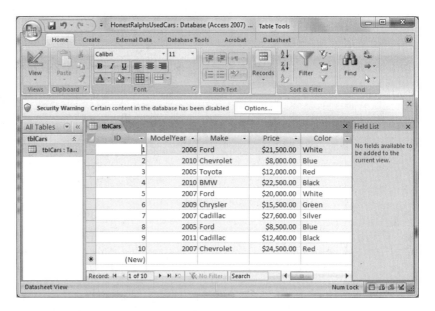

**Figure 15-29**  HonestRalphsUsedCars tblCars table in Access

2. Open Visual Studio and start a new Windows Forms Application named **AccessCars**. Change the Text property of the Form to **Honest Ralph's Used Cars**.

3. From the Toolbox at the left of the IDE, drag a DataGridView object onto the Form. Set its Location

property to **20, 20**. Select its `DataSource` property and select **Add Project Data Source**. In the Choose a Data Source Type dialog box, select **Database** and then click **Next**. In the Choose a Database Model dialog box, select **Dataset** and then click **Next**.

4. In the Choose Your Data Connection dialog box, click **New Connection**. In the Choose Data Source dialog box, select **Microsoft Access Database file** as the Data Source, click **Continue**, and then, in the Add Connection dialog box, click **Browse** to find the file to use. Select **HonestRalphsUsedCars.accdb** from the folder where the file is stored. Then click **OK** and **Next**. A dialog box opens and asks if you want to copy the file into your project. Click **Yes**.

5. In the Save the Connection String dialog box, check **Yes** to save the connection, and click **Next**. In the next window that appears, select both **Tables** and **Views**. Then click the **Finish** button.

6. In the Solution Explorer, confirm that the `HonestRalphsUsedCars` database has been added to the project. Also confirm that the DataSet, BindingSource, and Table-Adapter objects have been created. See Figure 15-30.

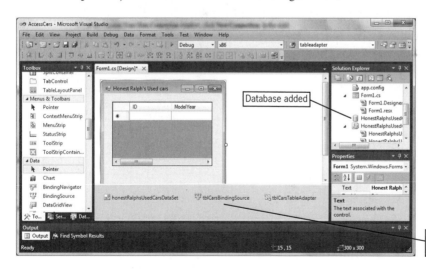

**Figure 15-30** Database added to project

7. Save the project, then click **Debug** and **Start Without Debugging**. The data appears in the table grid, as shown in Figure 15-31. Scroll down and to the right to view all the data. When you finish, dismiss the Form.

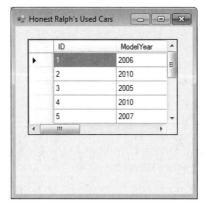

**Figure 15-31** Honest Ralph's Used Cars data as it appears in the grid

8. In Design view, reposition the grid and widen both the table and the grid so you will be able to see all the records' fields when the program executes. Save the project, then click **Debug** and **Start Without Debugging**. The data appears in the table grid, as shown in Figure 15-32. Use the vertical scroll bar to view the hidden records at the bottom of the list.

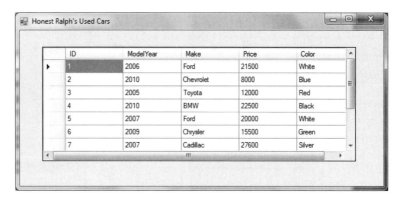

**Figure 15-32** Honest Ralph's Used Cars data as it appears in a wider grid

9. Dismiss the Form. In the IDE, double-click the Form title bar. The Form1_Load() method appears as follows. (Note that the comment has been divided into three lines and the Fill() method has been divided into two lines so the code fits better on this page.)

```
private void Form1_Load(object sender, EventArgs e)
{
    // TODO: This line of code loads data into the
    // 'honestRalphsUsedCarsDataSet.tblCars' table.
    // You can move, or remove it, as needed.

    this.tblCarsTableAdapter.Fill
        (this.honestRalphsUsedCarsDataSet.tblCars);
}
```

10. Return to Design view. Drag a `Button` onto the `Form`. Change
its `Name` property to **recordsButton** and its `Text` property
to **View records**. Double-click the `Button` to generate a
`recordsButton_Click()` method and view its code. Cut the
`Fill()` method call from the `Form1_Load()` method and
paste it into the `recordsButton_Click()` method. Save the
project and then execute the program again. This time the
grid is empty. When you click the button, the grid fills with
data. After viewing the data, dismiss the form.

## Querying a Dataset

In the next steps, you will write LINQ queries that demonstrate how
to access subsets of the data stored in the `tblCars` table.

**To query a dataset:**

1. In Visual Studio, in the `AccessCars` project, go to Form1.
cs[Design] view. Delete the data grid from the `Form`. Drag a
`Label` and a `ListBox` onto the `Form`, as shown in Figure 15-33.
Change the `Label`'s `Text` to **Inexpensive Cars**. Change the
`ListBox` name to **inexpensiveCarsBox**. Reduce the width of
the `Form` appropriately.

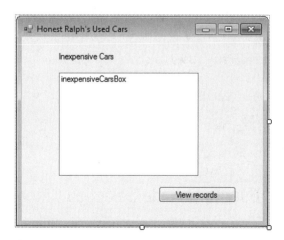

**Figure 15-33** Adding a `Label` and `ListBox` to the
AccessCars project

2. Double-click the button on the Form and revise the recordsButton_Click() method, as shown in the shaded portions of Figure 15-34. The LINQ code selects all the records in the table in which Price is less than 20000 and then adds the ID number, model year, and make of those cars to the ListBox.

```
private void recordsButton_Click(object sender, EventArgs e)
{
    const int HIGHPRICE = 20000;
    this.tblCarsTableAdapter.Fill
        (this.honestRalphsUsedCarsDataSet.tblCars);
    var inexpensiveCars =
        from c in this.honestRalphsUsedCarsDataSet.tblCars
        where c.Price < HIGHPRICE
        select c;
    foreach (var c in inexpensiveCars)
        inexpensiveCarsBox.Items.Add
            (c.ID + " - " + c.ModelYear + " " + c.Make);
}
```

**Figure 15-34** The recordsButton_Click() method

3. Save and execute the project. When the Form appears, click the Button. The output looks like Figure 15-35. Five cars appear in the list.

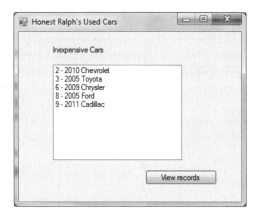

**Figure 15-35** Execution of AccessCars project

4. Dismiss the Form.

## Allowing the User to Provide Selection Criteria

In the next steps, you will provide a TextBox to make the application more flexible. Instead of listing cars priced under $20,000, the user will be able to enter a cutoff price.

**To provide selection criteria for the user:**

1.  In the Form1.cs Design view, rearrange the existing components and add a new `Label` and `TextBox`, as shown in Figure 15-36. Name the `TextBox` **priceTextBox**.

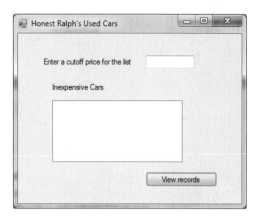

**Figure 15-36** Form with `Label` and `TextBox` for data entry

2.  Modify the `recordsButton_Click()` method, as shown in the shaded sections of Figure 15-37. Delete the declaration of the constant `HIGHPRICE` and replace it with a statement that accepts entered text from the `TextBox` and converts it to an `int`. Change the selection criterion from less than the constant `HIGHPRICE` to less than or equal to the value entered by the user. Also, add the price to the output in the `ListBox`, which will make it easier for you to confirm that the correct cars were selected for the `inexpensiveCars` collection.

```
private void recordsButton_Click(object sender, EventArgs e)
{
    int highPrice = Convert.ToInt32(priceTextBox.Text);
    this.tblCarsTableAdapter.Fill
        (this.honestRalphsUsedCarsDataSet.tblCars);
    var inexpensiveCars =
        from c in this.honestRalphsUsedCarsDataSet.tblCars
        where c.Price <= highPrice
        select c;
    foreach (var c in inexpensiveCars)
        inexpensiveCarsBox.Items.Add
            (c.ID + " - " + c.ModelYear + " " + c.Make +
                " $" + c.Price);
}
```

**Figure 15-37** The `recordsButton_Click()` method that allows user data entry

**3.** Save and execute the program. Depending on the value you type into the TextBox, the output will look similar to Figure 15-38.

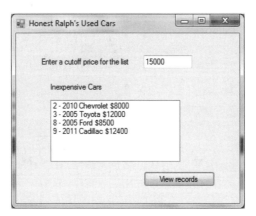

**Figure 15-38** Typical execution of application that contains the method in Figure 15-37

**4.** If you click the button more than once in the current project, the ListBox list is appended rather than replaced. To remedy the problem, dismiss the Form and return to the code. Add the following statement near the beginning of the recordsButton_Click() method, before any items are added to the inexpensiveCarsBox:

```
inexpensiveCarsBox.Items.Clear();
```

**5.** Save and run the application again. If you enter different values and click the Button multiple times, now the list of cars is replaced with each new selection.

**6.** Dismiss the Form and run the application again, entering a low value such as $3500 for the maximum price in the search. When you click the Button, the ListBox is empty, as it should be, because no cars in the table are priced below that value. However, providing no feedback can confuse or frustrate a user, who might think the application is not working properly. To remedy the problem, you can add a message that appears when no cars meet the search criterion. Just before the closing curly brace of the recordsButton_Click() method, add the following:

```
if (inexpensiveCars.Count() == 0)
{
    inexpensiveCarsBox.Items.Add("Sorry - there are no cars");
    inexpensiveCarsBox.Items.Add
        ("less than or equal to $" + highPrice);
}
```

This code uses the `Count()` aggregate operator to determine the number of records in the `inexpensiveCars` collection. When the count is 0, the user sees an appropriate message.

7. Save and execute the program. When the entered price is too low, the user sees a message confirming that the program works, but that no records meet the search criterion. See Figure 15-39.

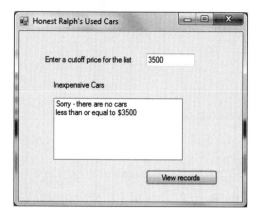

**Figure 15-39** Output of `AccessCars` application when no cars meet the selection criterion

## Grouping Data

In the next steps, you will group output records to make them easier for users to view and inspect.

1. Open a new Visual Studio C# project named **CarsGroupByMake**.

2. As shown in Figure 15-40, change the `Form`'s `Text` property to **Honest Ralph's Used Cars**. Add a `Button` to the `Form`, change its `Name` to **carsButton**, and change its `Text` property to **View Cars**. Add a `ListBox` to the `Form` and change its name to **carsList**.

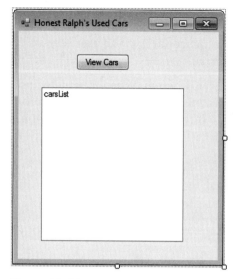

**Figure 15-40** Form design for `CarsGroupByMake` project

3. Add `HonestRalphsUsedCars.accdb` to the project.

4. Double-click the `Button` and add the following LINQ query within the automatically generated `Click()` method:

```
var cars =
    from c in this.honestRalphsUsedCarsDataSet.tblCars
    group c by c.Make;
```

This statement groups the cars by the value in each `Make` field.

5. Following the LINQ query, add a nested `foreach` loop that displays a car make for each group and lists the year and price for each car within each group.

```
foreach (var group in cars)
{
    carsList.Items.Add("Make: " + group.Key);
    foreach( var c in group)
        carsList.Items.Add("      " + c.ModelYear + " $"
            + c.Price);
}
```

6. Save and execute the project. Click the `Button` on the `Form`. The output appears as shown in Figure 15-41. The year and price for each of the ten cars in the table is displayed. Each car is grouped with others of the same make, and each group is preceded by a heading that shows the make.

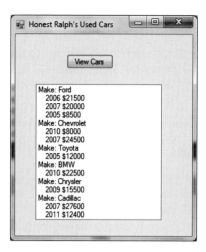

**Figure 15-41**   Output of `CarsGroupByMake` project

7. In Figure 15-41, the order in which cars are listed in each group is inconsistent. For example, the Chevrolets are listed from newest to oldest but the Cadillacs are listed from oldest to newest. To consistently display the cars in each group in order from newest to oldest, insert an `orderby` clause in the LINQ query as follows:

```
var cars =
    from c in this.honestRalphsUsedCarsDataSet.tblCars
    orderby c.ModelYear descending
    group c by c.Make;
```

8. Save the project and execute it again. When you click the `Button`, the output appears as shown in Figure 15-42. The cars are listed in order by model year within each group.

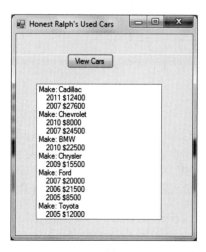

**Figure 15-42**   Output of `CarsGroupByMake` project ordered by `ModelYear`

9. The output in Figure 15-42 contains only ten cars in only six different groupings by make. However, if there were more cars, it might be difficult to locate a specific car. To show the `Make` groups in alphabetical order, add a condition to the sort order specified in the LINQ query, as follows:

```
var cars =
    from c in this.honestRalphsUsedCarsDataSet.tblCars
    orderby c.Make, c.ModelYear descending
    group c by c.Make;
```

10. Save and execute the program. When you click the `Button` on the `Form`, the output appears as shown in Figure 15-43. Each make is listed in alphabetical order and each car is listed in descending model-year order within its `Make` group.

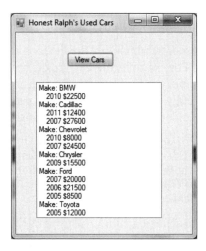

**Figure 15-43** Output of `CarsGroupByMake` project ordered by `ModelYear` within alphabetized `Make`

11. Dismiss the `Form` and exit Visual Studio.

## Chapter Summary

- A database holds a group of files that an organization needs to support its applications. In a database, the files often are called tables because you can arrange their contents in rows and columns. A value that uniquely identifies a record is called a primary key, or a key for short. Database management software, or a database management system, is a set of programs that allows users to create table descriptions; identify keys; add, delete, and update records within a table; arrange records within a table so they are sorted by different fields; write questions that select specific records from a table for viewing; and perform other tasks.

- Creating a useful database requires a lot of planning and analysis. You must decide what data will be stored, how that data will be divided between tables, and how the tables will interrelate. For each table you must decide what columns are needed, provide names for them, and enter data. In most tables you create for a database, you want to identify a primary key, which is the column that makes each record different from all others. A shorthand way to describe a table is to use the table name followed by parentheses that contain all the field names, with the primary key underlined.

- A query is a request to retrieve information from a database using syntax that the database software can understand. The most common language that database administrators use to access data in their tables is Structured Query Language, or SQL. The basic form of the SQL command that retrieves selected records from a table is SELECT-FROM-WHERE.

- Microsoft Office Access is a relational database that is part of the Microsoft Office system. In Access, a database developer can type field names for the data that will be stored and can assign an appropriate data type for each. After a table's design has been completed, a user can enter data into the table.

- An implicitly typed variable has a data type that is inferred from the expression used to initialize the variable. When you use an implicitly typed variable, an object's set of allowed properties and methods is not fixed when the code is written, but is determined when the program executes. Implicitly typed variables are used frequently in LINQ statements, which access data stored in a database.

- The LINQ (Language INtegrated Query) Project provides a set of general-purpose standard operators that allow queries to be constructed using syntax that is easy to understand. This syntax is similar to SQL's, and the compiler can check it for errors. The operators defined in LINQ can be used to query arrays, enumerable classes, XML, relational databases, and other sources. Some keywords in the LINQ vocabulary include `select`, `from`, and `where`.

- To add a database table to a Windows Forms project, you can add a data source to your project and drag a table onto your form. The table's data is bound to the form, and you are supplied with a grid in which you can view the data.

- You can use a LINQ query to select a collection of data from a table when specific criteria are met. You can use AND and OR expressions to limit criteria in your LINQ statements. With text values, you can use StartsWith(), EndsWith(), and Contains(). You can use several aggregate operators, or operators that produce statistics for groups of data, including Average(), Count(), Sum(), Max(), and Min().

- You can use the orderby operator to sort a collection of data based on a field or fields. Data items also can be grouped. A query body must end with a select clause or a group clause.

# Key Terms

A **collection** is any data structure that holds objects of the same type.

A **database** holds a group of files that an organization needs to support its applications.

**Tables** are database files. They are called *tables* because their contents are arranged in rows and columns.

A **primary key**, or **key** for short, is a value that uniquely identifies a record.

A **compound key** or **composite key** is constructed from multiple columns.

**Database management software**, also known as a **database management system (DBMS)**, is a set of programs that allows users to create table descriptions; identify keys; add, delete, and update records within a table; arrange records within a table so they are sorted by different fields; write questions that select specific records from a table for viewing; write questions that combine information from multiple tables; create reports; and keep data secure.

A **relational database** is one in which you can establish and maintain relationships between columns in the tables.

The **Leszynski naming convention (LNC)** is a convention for naming database elements that is popular with Microsoft Access users and Visual Basic programmers.

**Normalization** is the process of designing and creating a set of database tables that satisfies users' needs and avoids many potential problems such as data redundancies and anomalies.

**Data redundancy** is the unnecessary repetition of data.

An **anomaly** is an irregularity in the design of a database that causes problems and inconveniences.

A **query** is a request to retrieve information from a database using syntax that the database software can understand.

**Query by example** is a language that allows you to query relational databases by filling in blanks.

**Structured Query Language**, or **SQL**, is the most common language that database administrators use to access data in their tables.

**SELECT-FROM-WHERE** is the basic form of the SQL command that retrieves selected records from a table.

**TLA** is a three-letter abbreviation for *three-letter abbreviation*; it is the most popular type of abbreviation in technical terminology.

A **view** is a particular way of looking at a database in database management systems.

A **wildcard** is a symbol that means "any" or "all."

**Microsoft Office Access** is a relational database that is part of the Microsoft Office system.

An **implicitly typed variable** has a data type that is inferred from the expression used to initialize the variable.

The **var** data type creates an implicitly typed variable.

**Type inference** is the process of implicitly typing a variable; it is also called **duck typing**.

An **iteration variable** is used to hold each successive value in an array.

When a language is **strongly typed**, severe restrictions are placed on what data types can be mixed.

The **LINQ** (Language INtegrated Query) Project provides a set of general-purpose standard operators that allow queries to be constructed in C# using syntax that is easy to understand. This syntax is similar to SQL's, and the compiler can check it for errors.

The LINQ keyword **select** indicates what to select from a collection.

The LINQ keyword **from** indicates the collection or sequence from which data will be drawn.

The LINQ keyword **where** indicates conditions for selecting records.

A **restriction operator** places a restriction on which data is added to a collection.

A **projection operator** is one that projects, or sends off, specific data from a collection.

A **dataset** is a temporary set of data stored in a project.

A **BindingSource** object establishes a link from a database to a program.

A **table adapter** passes data back and forth between a dataset and the BindingSource.

**Aggregate operators** are operators that produce statistics for groups of data.

The **orderby operator** sorts a collection of data based on a field or fields.

The **group operator** groups data by specified criteria.

# Review Questions

1. Files in a database often are called _____.

    a. records

    b. tables

    c. catalogs

    d. registers

2. A value that uniquely identifies a record is a(n) _____.

    a. source

    b. ID

    c. key

    d. prime

3. Database management software is a set of programs that allows users to do all of the following except _____.

    a. add, delete, and update records within a table

    b. sort records in a table

    c. verify that all entered data is correct

    d. write queries

4. When you design a database table, you must do all of the following except _____.

    a. decide how many columns the table needs

    b. decide how many rows the table needs

    c. provide names for the columns

    d. provide a data type for each column

5. Which of the following would not be a good candidate for a primary key?

    a. the number of seats on a bus in a table that stores data about a city's fleet of buses

    b. a bus pass number in a table of a city's bus service customers

    c. a bus driver's ID number in a table that stores data about bus drivers

    d. a bus route number in a table that stores bus route data

6. Normalization _____.

    a. is the process of entering data into database tables

    b. is a design process that reduces redundancy and anomalies in databases

    c. is a flaw in database design that results in the repetition of data

    d. is a flaw in database design that causes anomalies

7. Which of the following do you know based on this database notation?

    `tblProducts(itemNum, description, price, quantity)`

    a. The table name is `Products`.

    b. `itemNum` is the key field.

    c. No two descriptions hold the same value.

    d. `price` is a numeric field.

8. A question asked using syntax that database software can understand is a(n) _____.

    a. query

    b. anomaly

    c. request

    d. redundancy

9. The basic form of the SQL command that retrieves selected records from a table is _____.

    a. QUERY-BY-EXAMPLE

    b. SELECT-FROM-WHERE

    c. RETRIEVE-FROM-SOURCE

    d. STRUCTURED-QUERY-LIST

10. Based on the following SQL statement, you know that _____ will be displayed.

    `SELECT itemNum, price FROM tblProducts WHERE quantity <= 0`

    a. two rows

    b. two columns

    c. more than two columns

    d. more than two rows

11. Microsoft Office Access is _____.

    a. a spreadsheet as well as a database

    b. no longer used by professional information specialists

    c. part of Visual Studio

    d. a typical database program

12. Which of the following is not true of implicitly typed variables?

    a. Their data types are inferred from the expression used to initialize the variable.

    b. They are declared using var as the data type.

    c. They use a process called type inference.

    d. They use a process called static typing.

13. Which of the following is true?

    a. `var product = new Product();` has the same meaning as `Product product = new Product();`.

    b. `var x = 3;` has the same meaning as `double x = 3.0;`.

    c. `var a = 17;` has the same meaning as `var b = 17;`.

    d. `var Item();` has the same meaning as `var item = Item();`.

14. C# is _____.

    a. strongly typed, like Visual Basic

    b. strongly typed, unlike Visual Basic

    c. weakly typed, like Visual Basic

    d. weakly typed, unlike Visual Basic

15. In _____ you can access database data.

    a. C# 3.0

    b. older versions of C#

    c. both of the above

    d. none of the above

16. The operators defined in LINQ can be used to query _____.

    a. arrays

    b. relational databases

    c. both of these

    d. none of the above

17. Consider the following code. In this example, `nums` is _____.

```
var nums =
    from n in numbers
    where n > 5
    select n;
```

    a. an array of integers

    b. a database

    c. an implicitly typed collection

    d. a single record in the collection `numbers`

18. Consider the following code. In this example, `numbers` is a(n) _____.

```
var nums =
    from n in numbers
    where n > 5
    select n;
```

a. array of integers

b. record in a database

c. database

d. implicitly typed collection

19. Consider the following code. In this example, `x` is a _____.

```
var cheapProducts =
    from p in this.abcCompany.tblProducts
    where p.Price < MAX
    select p.Description;
foreach (var x in cheapProducts)
    outputListBox.Items.Add(x);
```

a. row in `tblProducts`

b. column in `tblProducts`

c. price

d. description

20. Which of the following is not true of LINQ?

a. `Average()` is an aggregate operator.

b. `Max()` is an aggregate operator.

c. You can use the `orderby` operator to sort data.

d. You can use the `groupby` operator to group data.

## Exercises

1. Create a program that holds an array of ten integers. Prompt the user for and accept a value for each integer. Use LINQ statements to sort the integers in descending order and display them. Save the program as **LinqIntegersDemo.cs**.

2. Create a program that holds an array of eight integers. Prompt the user for and accept a value for each integer. Use LINQ

statements to group the integers into two groups (even and
odd), and then display each group. Figure 15-44 shows a typical execution. Save the program as **EvenAndOdd.cs**.

**Figure 15-44** Typical execution of EvenAndOdd program

3. Create a program that contains an array of 12 strings. Prompt
the user to enter a minimum string length, and use LINQ
statements to display all the strings that are at least as long
as the value entered by the user. If no strings meet the criterion, display an appropriate message. Save the program as
**LongWords.cs**.

4. Create a program that contains an array of 20 words of your
choice. Use LINQ statements to display separate lists: One
shows words that begin with letters in the first half of the
alphabet (A through M), and the other list shows words that
begin with letters in the second half (N through Z). Display
a count of the number of words in each group. Save the program as **SplitAlphabet.cs**.

5. Create a Book class that contains Title, Author, and Price properties and a constructor that requires data for all three. Create a
program that declares an array of at least eight Books and stores
appropriate data. Prompt the user for an author and display all
the books written by that author, or display an appropriate message if no such books exist. Save the program as **BookQuery.cs**.

6. Create a Book class that contains Title, Author, and Price
properties and a constructor that requires data for all three.
Create a program that declares an array of at least eight Books
and stores appropriate data. Display the Book titles and prices
alphabetically by title and grouped by author. For an example,
see Figure 15-45. Save the program as **BookQuery2.cs**.

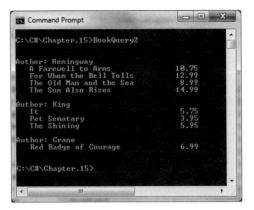

Figure 15-45   Typical execution of BookQuery program

7. Create an application that displays statistics about a database table when a user clicks various buttons. Using the HonestRalphsUsedCars database in your downloadable student files, display a count of the records, the most expensive car, and the least expensive car. Figure 15-46 shows the program before the user has clicked any buttons and after the user has clicked one of the buttons. Save the project as **CarStatistics**.

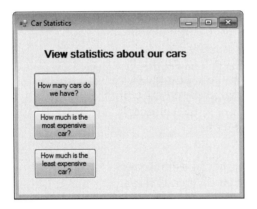
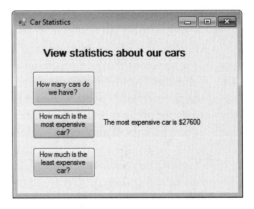

Figure 15-46   Typical execution of CarStatistics program before and after the user has clicked a button

8. Create an application that allows a user to display cars of different makes. Use the HonestRalphsUsedCars database in your downloadable student files. Your application should contain four check boxes labeled "Ford", "Chevrolet", "Cadillac", and "All". The user should be able to click any combination of check boxes to see the color, year, make, and price for each car with the desired make. For example, when the user clicks

"Cadillac" and "Chevrolet", only those cars are displayed. Save the project as **CarFinderByMake**.

9. Create an application in which all of the cars in a database are displayed in a checked list box. When the user makes a selection, the car's price is displayed, as shown in Figure 15-47. Use the HonestRalphsUsedCars database in your downloadable student files. Save the project as **CarPriceFinder**.

**Figure 15-47**   Execution of `CarPriceFinder` project

10. Create an application in which the user can select movies to view by entering part of the title or part of the director's name. The user clicks a radio button to choose which type of criterion is used. Then the user can enter all or part of the title's name or director's name into a TextBox. Allow the user to find matches regardless of case. See Figure 15-48 for a typical execution. Use the Movies database in your downloadable student files. Save the project as **MovieFinder**.

**Figure 15-48**   Typical execution of `MovieFinder` project

11. Create an application in which the user can enter a year to split a list of movies into those released before the indicated year and those released in the indicated year or afterward. Labels above each list should reflect the user's chosen cut-off year. Each list should be in order by release year. See Figure 15-49 for a typical execution. Use the Movies database in your downloadable student files. Save the project as **MovieFinder2**.

**Figure 15-49** Typical execution of `MovieFinder2` project

## Debugging Exercises

Each of the following files in the Chapter.15 folder of your downloadable student files has syntax and/or logical errors. In each case, determine the problem and fix the program. After you correct the errors, save each file using the same filename preceded with *Fixed*. For example, save DebugFifteen1.cs as **FixedDebugFifteen1.cs**.

    a. DebugFifteen1.cs

    b. DebugFifteen2.cs

    c. DebugFifteen3.cs

    d. DebugFifteen4.cs

## Up For Discussion

1. In this chapter, a phone book was mentioned as an example of a database you use frequently. Name some other examples.

2. Suppose you have authority to browse your company's database. The company keeps information on each employee's past jobs, health insurance claims, and any criminal records. Also suppose that you want to ask one of your co-workers out on a date. Should you use the database to obtain information about the person? If so, are there any limits on the data you should use? If not, should you be allowed to pay a private detective to discover similar data?

3. The FBI's National Crime Information Center (NCIC) is a computerized database of criminal justice information, including data on criminal histories, fugitives, stolen property, and missing persons. The NCIC is available to law enforcement and other criminal justice agencies 24 hours a day. Inevitably, such large systems contain some inaccuracies, and various studies have indicated that perhaps less than half the records in this database are complete, accurate, and unambiguous. Do you approve of the NCIC or object to it? Would you change your mind if the system had no inaccuracies? Is there a level of inaccuracy you would find acceptable to realize the benefits such a system provides?

4. What type of data might be useful to a community in the wake of a natural disaster? Who should pay for the expense of gathering, storing, and maintaining this data?

# Operator Precedence And Associativity

When an expression contains multiple operators, their **precedence** controls the order in which the individual operators are evaluated. For example, multiplication has a higher precedence than addition, so the expression 2 + 3 * 4 evaluates as 14 because the value of 3 * 4 is calculated before adding 2. Table A-1 summarizes all operators in order of precedence from highest to lowest.

When you use two operators with the same precedence, the **associativity** of the operators controls the order in which the operations are performed:

- Except for the assignment and conditional operators, all binary operators (those that take two arguments) are **left-associative**, meaning that operations are performed from left to right. For example, 5 + 6 + 7 is evaluated first as 5 + 6, or 11; then 7 is added, bringing the value to 18.

- The assignment operators and the conditional operator (?:) are **right-associative**, meaning that operations are performed from right to left. For example, x = y = z is evaluated as y = z first, and then x is set to the result.

- All unary operators (those that take one argument) are right-associative. If b is 5, the value of −++b is determined by evaluating ++b first (6), then taking its negative value (−6).

You can control precedence and associativity by using parentheses. For example, a + b * c first multiplies b by c and then adds the result to a. The expression (a + b) * c, however, forces the sum of a and b to be calculated first; then the result is multiplied by c.

| Category | Operators | Associativity |
|---|---|---|
| Primary | x.y f(x) a[x] x++ x− − new | left type of checked unchecked |
| Unary | + − ! ~ ++x − −x (T)x | right |
| Multiplicative | * / % | left |
| Additive | + − | left |
| Shift | << >> | right |
| Relational | < > <= >= is as | left and type testing |
| Equality | == != | left |
| Logical AND | & | left |
| Logical XOR | ^ | left |
| Logical OR | \| | left |
| Conditional AND | && | left |
| Conditional OR | \|\| | left |
| Conditional | ?: | right |
| Assignment | = *= /= %= += = | |
|  | <<= >>= &= ^= \|= | right |

**Table A-1**   Operator precedence

# Key Terms

The **precedence** of operators controls the order in which individual operators are evaluated in an expression.

The **associativity** of operators controls the order in which operations of equal precedence are performed in an expression.

With **left-associative** operators, operations are performed from left to right.

With **right-associative** operators, operations are performed from right to left.

# Understanding Numbering Systems and Computer Codes

The numbering system with which you are most familiar is the **decimal numbering system**, which is based on ten digits: 0 through 9. When you use the decimal system to express positive whole numbers, no other symbols are available; if you want to express a value larger than 9, you must resort to using multiple digits from the same pool of ten, placing them in columns.

When you use the decimal system, you analyze a multicolumn number by mentally assigning place values to each column. The value of the rightmost column is 1, the value of the next column to the left is 10, the next column is 100, and so on, multiplying the column value by 10 as you move to the left. There is no limit to the number of columns you can use; you simply keep adding columns to the left as you need to express higher values. For example, Figure B-1 shows how the value 305 is represented in the decimal system. You simply sum the value of the digit in each column after it has been multiplied by the value of its column.

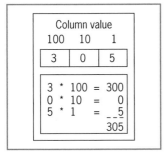

**Figure B-1**   Representing 305 in the decimal system

The **binary numbering system** works in the same way as the decimal numbering system, except that it uses only two digits: 0 and 1. When you use the binary system, if you want to express a value greater than 1, you must resort to using multiple columns, because no single symbol is available that represents any value other than 0 or 1. However, instead of each new column to the left being 10 times greater than the previous column, when you use the binary system, each new column is only two times the value of the previous column. For example, Figure B-2 shows how the numbers 9 and 305 are represented in the binary system. Notice that in both binary numbers and the decimal system, it is perfectly acceptable—and often necessary—to create numbers with 0 in one or more columns. As with the decimal system, the binary system has no limit to the number of columns; you can use as many as it takes to express a value.

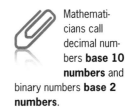

Mathematicians call decimal numbers **base 10 numbers** and binary numbers **base 2 numbers**.

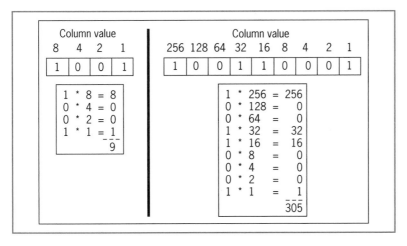

**Figure B-2**   Representing decimal values 9 and 305 in the binary system

A computer stores every piece of data it ever uses as a set of 0s and 1s. Each 0 or 1 is known as a **bit**, which is short for binary digit. Every computer uses 0s and 1s because all values in a computer are stored as electronic signals that are either on or off. This two-state system is most easily represented using just two digits.

Computers use a set of binary digits to represent stored characters. If computers used only one binary digit to represent characters, then only two different characters could be represented, because the single bit could be only 0 or 1. If computers used only two digits, then only four characters could be represented—the four codes 00, 01, 10, and 11, which in decimal values are 0, 1, 2, and 3, respectively. Many computers use sets of eight binary digits to represent each character they store, because using eight binary digits provides 256 different combinations. One combination can represent an "A", another a "B", still others "a" and "b", and so on. Two hundred fifty-six combinations are enough so that each capital letter, small letter, digit, and punctuation mark used in English has its own code; even a space has a code. For example, in some computers 01000001 represents the character "A". The binary number 01000001 has a decimal value of 65, but this numeric value is not important to ordinary computer users; it is simply a code that stands for "A". The code that uses 01000001 to mean "A" is the **American Standard Code for Information Interchange**, or **ASCII**.

A set of eight bits is called a **byte**. Half a byte, or four bits, is a **nibble**. You will learn more about bytes later in this appendix.

The ASCII code is not the only computer code; it is typical, and is the one used in most personal computers. The **Extended Binary Coded Decimal Interchange Code**, or **EBCDIC**, is an eight-bit code that is used in IBM mainframe computers. In these computers, the principle is the same—every character is stored as a series of binary digits. However, the actual values used are different. For example, in EBCDIC, an "A" is 11000001, or 193. **Unicode** is another code used by languages such as Java and C#; with this code, 16 bits are used to represent each character. The character "A" in Unicode has the same decimal value (65) as the ASCII "A", but it is stored as 0000000001000001. Using 16 bits provides many more possible combinations than using only eight bits—65,536 to be exact. Unicode has enough available codes for all English letters and digits and for characters from many international alphabets.

Most of the values not included in Table B-1 have a purpose. For example, the decimal value 7 represents a bell—a dinging sound your computer can make, often used to notify you of an error or some other unusual condition.

Ordinary computer users seldom think about the numeric codes behind the letters, numbers, and punctuation marks they enter from their keyboards or see displayed on a monitor. However, they see the consequence of the values behind letters when they see data sorted in alphabetical order. When you sort a list of names, "Andrea" comes before "Brian", and "Caroline" comes after "Brian" because the numeric code for "A" is lower than the code for "B", and the numeric code for "C" is higher than the code for "B", no matter whether you are using ASCII, EBCDIC, or Unicode.

Each binary number in Table B-1 is shown containing two sets of four digits; this convention makes the long eight-digit numbers easier to read.

Table B-1 shows the decimal and binary values behind the most commonly used characters in the ASCII character set—the letters, numbers, and punctuation marks you can enter from your keyboard using a single key press.

| Decimal number | Binary number | ASCII character | Decimal number | Binary number | ASCII character |
|---|---|---|---|---|---|
| 32 | 0010 0000 | Space | 55 | 0011 0111 | 7 |
| 33 | 0010 0001 | ! Exclamation point | 56 | 0011 1000 | 8 |
| 34 | 0010 0010 | " Quotation mark, or double quote | 57 | 0011 1001 | 9 |
| 35 | 0010 0011 | # Number sign, also called an octothorpe or a pound sign | 58 | 0011 1010 | : Colon |
| 36 | 0010 0100 | $ Dollar sign | 59 | 0011 1011 | ; Semicolon |
| 37 | 0010 0101 | % Percent | 60 | 0011 1100 | < Less-than sign |
| 38 | 0010 0110 | & Ampersand | 61 | 0011 1101 | = Equal sign |
| 39 | 0010 0111 | ' Apostrophe, single quote | 62 | 0011 1110 | > Greater-than sign |
| 40 | 0010 1000 | ( Left parenthesis | 63 | 0011 1111 | ? Question mark |
| 41 | 0010 1001 | ) Right parenthesis | 64 | 0100 0000 | @ At sign |
| 42 | 0010 1010 | * Asterisk | 65 | 0100 0001 | A |
| 43 | 0010 1011 | + Plus sign | 66 | 0100 0010 | B |
| 44 | 0010 1100 | , Comma | 67 | 0100 0011 | C |
| 45 | 0010 1101 | - Hyphen or minus sign | 68 | 0100 0100 | D |
| 46 | 0010 1110 | . Period or decimal point | 69 | 0100 0101 | E |
| 47 | 0010 1111 | / Slash or front slash | 70 | 0100 0110 | F |
| 48 | 0011 0000 | 0 | 71 | 0100 0111 | G |
| 49 | 0011 0001 | 1 | 72 | 0100 1000 | H |
| 50 | 0011 0010 | 2 | 73 | 0100 1001 | I |
| 51 | 0011 0011 | 3 | 74 | 0100 1010 | J |
| 52 | 0011 0100 | 4 | 75 | 0100 1011 | K |
| 53 | 0011 0101 | 5 | 76 | 0100 1100 | L |
| 54 | 0011 0110 | 6 | 77 | 0100 1101 | M |
|  |  |  | 78 | 0100 1110 | N |

**Table B-1**    Decimal and binary values for common ASCII characters (*continues*)

(continued)

| Decimal number | Binary number | ASCII character | Decimal number | Binary number | ASCII character |
| --- | --- | --- | --- | --- | --- |
| 79 | 0100 1111 | O | 103 | 0110 0111 | g |
| 80 | 0101 0000 | P | 104 | 0110 1000 | h |
| 81 | 0101 0001 | Q | 105 | 0110 1001 | i |
| 82 | 0101 0010 | R | 106 | 0110 1010 | j |
| 83 | 0101 0011 | S | 107 | 0110 1011 | k |
| 84 | 0101 0100 | T | 108 | 0110 1100 | l |
| 85 | 0101 0101 | U | 109 | 0110 1101 | m |
| 86 | 0101 0110 | V | 110 | 0110 1110 | n |
| 87 | 0101 0111 | W | 111 | 0110 1111 | o |
| 88 | 0101 1000 | X | 112 | 0111 0000 | p |
| 89 | 0101 1001 | Y | 113 | 0111 0001 | q |
| 90 | 0101 1010 | Z | 114 | 0111 0010 | r |
| 91 | 0101 1011 | [ Opening or left bracket | 115 | 0111 0011 | s |
| 92 | 0101 1100 | \ Backslash | 116 | 0111 0100 | t |
| 93 | 0101 1101 | ] Closing or right bracket | 117 | 0111 0101 | u |
| 94 | 0101 1110 | ^ Caret | 118 | 0111 0110 | v |
| 95 | 0101 1111 | _ Underline or underscore | 119 | 0111 0111 | w |
| 96 | 0110 0000 | ` Grave accent | 120 | 0111 1000 | x |
| 97 | 0110 0001 | a | 121 | 0111 1001 | y |
| 98 | 0110 0010 | b | 122 | 0111 1010 | z |
| 99 | 0110 0011 | c | 123 | 0111 1011 | { Opening or left brace |
| 100 | 0110 0100 | d | 124 | 0111 1100 | \| Vertical line or pipe |
| 101 | 0110 0101 | e | 125 | 0111 1101 | } Closing or right brace |
| 102 | 0110 0110 | f | 126 | 0111 1110 | ~ Tilde |

**Table B-1**   Decimal and binary values for common ASCII characters

# The Hexadecimal System

The **hexadecimal numbering system** is a **base 16 system** because it uses 16 digits. As shown in Table B-2, the digits are 0 through 9 and A through F. Computer professionals often use the hexadecimal system to express addresses and instructions as they are stored in computer memory because hexadecimal provides convenient shorthand expressions for groups of binary values. In Table B-2, each hexadecimal value represents one of the 16 possible combinations of four-digit binary values. Therefore, instead of referencing memory contents as a 16-digit binary value, for example, programmers can use a 4-digit hexadecimal value.

| Decimal value | Hexadecimal value | Binary value (shown using four digits) |
|---|---|---|
| 0 | 0 | 0000 |
| 1 | 1 | 0001 |
| 2 | 2 | 0010 |
| 3 | 3 | 0011 |
| 4 | 4 | 0100 |
| 5 | 5 | 0101 |
| 6 | 6 | 0110 |
| 7 | 7 | 0111 |
| 8 | 8 | 1000 |
| 9 | 9 | 1001 |
| 10 | A | 1010 |
| 11 | B | 1011 |
| 12 | C | 1100 |
| 13 | D | 1101 |
| 14 | E | 1110 |
| 15 | F | 1111 |

**Table B-2**   Values in the decimal and hexadecimal systems

In the hexadecimal system, each column is 16 times the value of the column to its right. Therefore, column values from right to left are 1, 16, 256, 4096, and so on. Figure B-3 shows how 171 and 305 are expressed in hexadecimal.

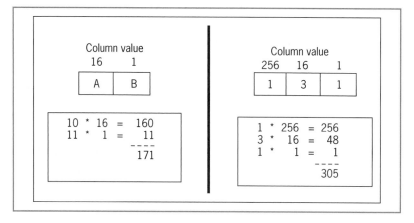

**Figure B-3** Representing decimal values 171 and 305 in the hexadecimal system

# Measuring Storage

In computer systems, both internal memory and external storage are measured in bits and bytes. Eight bits make a byte, and a byte frequently holds a single character (in ASCII or EBCDIC) or half a character (in Unicode). Because a byte is such a small unit of storage, the size of memory and files is often expressed in thousands or millions of bytes. Table B-3 describes some commonly used terms for storage measurement.

| Term | Abbreviation | Number of bytes using binary system | Number of bytes using decimal system | Example |
|------|-------------|------------------------------------|--------------------------------------|---------|
| Kilobyte | KB or kB | 1024 | one thousand | This appendix occupies about 85 kilobytes on a hard disk. |
| Megabyte | MB | 1,048,576 (1024 × 1024 kilobytes) | one million | One megabyte can hold an average book in text format. A 3½-inch diskette you might have used a few years ago held 1.44 megabytes. |
| Gigabyte | GB | 1,073,741,824 (1,024 megabytes) | one billion | The hard drive on a fairly new laptop computer might be 160 gigabytes. An hour of HDTV video is about 4 gigabytes. |
| Terabyte | TB | 1024 gigabytes | one trillion | The entire Library of Congress can be stored in 10 terabytes. |

**Table B-3** Commonly used terms for computer storage *(continues)*

*(continued)*

| Term | Abbreviation | Number of bytes using binary system | Number of bytes using decimal system | Example |
|------|--------------|-------------------------------------|--------------------------------------|---------|
| Petabyte | PB | 1024 terabytes | one quadrillion | Popular Web sites, such as YouTube and Google, have 20 to 30 petabytes of activity per month. |
| Exabyte | EB | 1024 petabytes | one quintillion | A popular expression claims that all words ever spoken by humans could be stored in text form in 5 exabytes. |
| Zettabyte | ZB | 1024 exabytes | one sextillion | A popular expression claims that all words ever spoken by humans could be stored in audio form in 42 zettabytes. |
| Yottabyte | YB | 1024 zettabytes | one septillion (a 1 followed by 24 zeros) | All data accessible on the Internet and in corporate networks is estimated to be 1 yottabyte. |

**Table B-3**  Commonly used terms for computer storage

In the metric system, "kilo" means 1000. However, in Table B-3, notice that a kilobyte is 1024 bytes. The discrepancy occurs because everything stored in a computer is based on the binary system, so multiples of two are used in most measurements. If you multiply 2 by itself 10 times, the result is 1024, which is a little over 1000. Similarly, a gigabyte is 1,073,741,624 bytes, which is more than a billion.

Confusion arises because many hard-drive manufacturers use the decimal system instead of the binary system to describe storage. For example, if you buy a hard drive that holds 10 gigabytes, it actually holds exactly 10 billion bytes. However, in the binary system, 10 GB is 10,737,418,240 bytes, so when you check your hard drive's capacity, your computer will report that you do not quite have 10 GB, but only 9.31 GB.

# Key Terms

The **decimal numbering system** is a numeric system that uses ten digits, 0 through 9, arranged in columns to represent numbers.

The **binary numbering system** is a numbering system that uses two digits, 0 and 1, arranged in columns to represent numbers.

**Base 10 numbers** are decimal system numbers.

**Base 2 numbers** are binary system numbers.

A **bit** is a binary digit.

The **American Standard Code for Information Interchange (ASCII)** is an eight-bit code that represents characters.

A **byte** is eight bits.

A **nibble** is four bits.

The **Extended Binary Coded Decimal Interchange Code (EBCDIC)** is an eight-bit code used in IBM mainframe computers.

**Unicode** is a 16-bit code used with languages such as C# and Java.

The **hexadecimal numbering system** is a number system that uses 16 digits, 0 through 9 and A through F, arranged in columns to represent numbers.

The **base 16 system** is the hexadecimal system.

# Using The IDE Editor

The Visual C# Code Editor is like a word processor for writing source code. Just as a word-processing program provides support for spelling and grammar, the C# Code Editor helps ensure that your C# syntax is free of spelling and grammar errors. This support can be grouped into several categories that are described in this appendix.

## IntelliSense

**IntelliSense** is Microsoft's name for the set of features designed to minimize the time you spend looking for help and to help you enter code more accurately and efficiently. The IntelliSense features provide basic information about C# language keywords, .NET Framework types, and method signatures as you type them in the editor. The information is displayed in ToolTips, list boxes, and Smart Tags. Features of IntelliSense include:

- Providing completion lists
- Providing quick information
- Providing parameter information
- Adding using statements

### Providing Completion Lists

As you enter source code in the editor, IntelliSense displays a list box that contains all the C# keywords, .NET Framework classes, and names you have defined in your program that fit the current circumstances. This feature is called **completion mode**. For example, Figure C-1 shows a list box that makes suggestions based on what the programmer has typed in the Code Editor. If you find a match in the list box for the name you intend to type, you can select the item. Alternatively, you can press the Tab key to have IntelliSense finish entering the name or keyword for you.

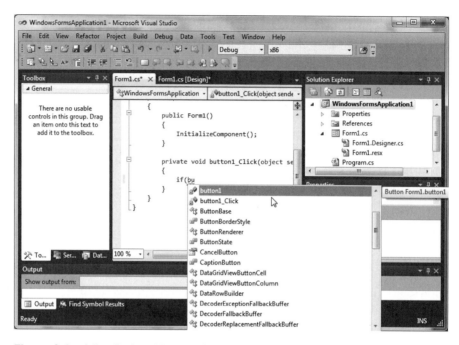

**Figure C-1**  A list displayed by IntelliSense

IntelliSense also supports a **suggestion mode**. In this mode, IntelliSense does not automatically complete identifiers, which makes it easier for you to type variable or method names without the completion list appearing. You can toggle between completion mode and suggestion mode by pressing CTRL+ALT+SPACEBAR, or by pointing to IntelliSense on the Edit menu and clicking Toggle Completion Mode.

Similarly, when you enter a .NET Framework type or an identifier of a specific type into the Code Editor, and then type the dot operator (.), IntelliSense displays a list box that contains the members of that type. When you do not know what method or property you want for an object, typing its identifier and a dot can direct you to the appropriate choice. This technique sometimes teaches you about features you did not even realize were available.

## Providing Quick Information

When you hover the cursor over a .NET Framework type, IntelliSense displays a Quick Info ToolTip that contains basic documentation about that type.

## Providing Parameter Information

When you enter a method name in the Code Editor and then type an opening parenthesis, IntelliSense displays a Parameter Info ToolTip that shows the method's parameter list. If the method is overloaded, multiple method signatures are displayed and you can scroll through them.

## Adding `using` Statements

If you attempt to create an instance of a .NET Framework class without a sufficiently qualified name, IntelliSense displays a Smart Tag after the unresolved identifier. When you click the Smart Tag, IntelliSense displays a list of `using` statements to help you resolve the identifier. When you select a statement from the list, IntelliSense adds the `using` directive to the top of your source code file, and you can continue to write code at your current location.

# Code Snippets

**Code snippets** are small units of commonly used C# source code that you can enter accurately and quickly with only a couple of keystrokes. To access the code snippet menu, right-click in the Code Editor. You can browse from the many snippets provided with Visual C#, and you can also create your own.

# Wavy Underlines

Wavy underlines give you instant feedback about errors in your code as you type. A red wavy underline identifies a syntax error, such as a missing semicolon or mismatched braces. A green wavy underline identifies a potential compiler warning, and blue identifies an Edit and Continue issue. In Figure C-2, two wavy underlines appear (under `button1` and the closing curly brace that follows it) because the code in the last statement is not yet complete.

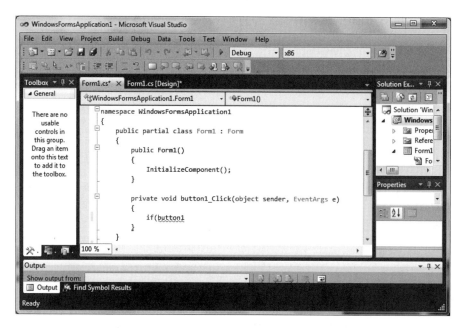

**Figure C-2**  Wavy underlines in Code Editor

# Readability Aids

The editor assigns different colors to various categories of identifiers in a C# source code file to make the code easier to read. For example, C# keywords are bright blue, classes are blue-green, and comments are green.

# Key Terms

**IntelliSense** is Microsoft's name for the set of features designed to minimize the time you spend looking for help and to help you enter code more accurately and efficiently.

**Completion mode** is an IDE editing mode in which suggestions are automatically provided for your code based on context.

**Suggestion mode** is an IDE editing mode in which completion mode is turned off.

**Code snippets** are small units of commonly used C# source code that you can enter accurately and quickly with only a couple of keystrokes.

# Glossary

## A

**abstract class** a class from which you cannot create concrete objects, but from which you can inherit. Contrast with *concrete*.

**abstract method** a method that contains no statements; any class derived from a class that contains an abstract method must override the abstract method by providing a body (an implementation) for it.

**access modifier** a keyword that defines the circumstances under which a method or class can be accessed; `public` access is the most liberal type of access.

**accessibility** describes limits set for a method as to whether and how other methods can use it.

**accessors** methods in properties that specify how a class's fields are accessed. See *get accessors* and *set accessors*.

**accumulated** describes totals that are added into a final sum by processing individual records one at a time in a loop.

**actual parameters** arguments within a method call.

**add and assign operator (+=)** an operator that adds the operand on the right to the operand on the left and

assigns it to the operand on the left in one step.

**aggregate operators** in LINQ, operators that produce statistics for groups of data.

**alias** an alternative name or pseudonym.

**ambiguous** describes overloaded methods between which the compiler cannot distinguish.

**American Standard Code for Information Interchange (ASCII)** an eight-bit code that represents characters.

**ancestors** all the superclasses from which a subclass is derived.

**Anchor property** an attribute that causes a `Control` to remain at a fixed distance from the side of a container when the user resizes it.

**AND operator** an operator that determines whether two expressions are both true; it is written using two ampersands (&&). Also called the *conditional AND operator*. Contrast with *Boolean logical AND operator*.

**anomaly** an irregularity in a database's design that causes problems and inconveniences.

**applicable methods** the collection of potential methods that could be used by a method call.

**application classes** classes that contain a Main() method and are executable programs.

**application files** files that store software instructions; program files. Contrast with *data files*.

**application software** programs that allow users to complete tasks, in contrast with system software that the computer needs to complete tasks.

**argument** the expression passed to a method.

**array** a list of data items that all have the same data type and the same name, but are distinguished from each other by a subscript or index.

**array element** one object in an array.

**assembly** a group of code modules compiled together to create an executable program.

**assignment** a statement that provides a variable with a value.

**assignment operator** the equal sign (=); any value to the right of the assignment operator is assigned to, or taken on by, the variable to the left.

**associativity** specifies the order in which a sequence of operations with the same precedence are evaluated.

**at runtime** a phrase that means "during the time a program is running."

**attributes of an object** the characteristics of an object.

**auto-implemented property** a property in which the code within the accessors is created automatically. The only action in the set accessor is to assign a value to the associated field, and the only action in the get accessor is to return the associated field value.

**automatic properties** auto-implemented properties.

# B

**backing field** a field that has a property coded for it.

**base** a keyword that refers to the superclass of the class in which you use it.

**base 2 numbers** binary system numbers.

**base 10 numbers** decimal system numbers.

**base 16 system** a mathematical system that uses 16 symbols to represent numbers; hexadecimal.

**base class** a class that is used as a basis for inheritance.

**behaviors of an object** the methods associated with an object.

**betterness rules** the rules that determine the best overloaded method to execute based on the arguments in a method call.

**binary files** files that can store any of the 256 combinations of bits in any byte instead of just those combinations that form readable text.

**binary numbering system** a numbering system that uses two digits, 0 and 1, arranged in columns to represent numbers.

**binary operators** operators that use two arguments: one value to the left of the operator and another value to the right of it.

**BinarySearch() method** a member of the System.Array class that finds a requested value in a sorted array.

**BindingSource** an object that establishes a link from a database to a program.

**bit** a binary digit.

**bitwise operators** operators that are used to manipulate the individual bits of values.

**black box** any device you can use without knowing how it works internally.

**block** a collection of one or more statements contained within a pair of curly braces.

**block comments** comments that start with a forward slash and an asterisk (/*) and end with an asterisk and a forward slash (*/). Block comments can appear on a line by themselves, on a line before executable code, or after executable code. They can also extend across as many lines as needed. Compare with *line comments*.

**bool** a data type that holds a Boolean value.

**Boolean logical AND operator** an operator that determines whether two expressions are both true; it is written using a single ampersand (&). Unlike the conditional AND operator, it does not use short-circuit evaluation.

**Boolean logical inclusive OR operator** an operator that determines whether at least one of two conditions is true; it is written using a single pipe (|). Unlike the conditional OR operator, it does not use short-circuit evaluation.

**Boolean variable** a variable that can hold only one of two values—true or false.

**break** a keyword that optionally terminates a switch structure at the end of each case.

**Button** a clickable object that allows a user to interact with a GUI program.

**byte** an integral data type that can hold an unsigned numeric value from 0 through 255.

# C

**C# programming language** a computer programming language developed as an object-oriented and component-oriented language. It exists as part of Visual Studio 2010, a package used for developing applications for the Windows family of operating systems.

**call** to invoke a method.

**call stack** the memory location where the computer stores the list of locations to which the system must return after method calls.

**called** describes a method that has been invoked.

**called method** a method that has been invoked by another method.

**calling method** a method that calls another method.

**camel casing** a style of creating identifiers in which the first letter is not capitalized, but each new word is. Contrast with *Pascal casing*.

**case** a keyword in a switch structure that is followed by one of the possible values that might equal the switch expression.

**case label** identifies a course of action in a switch structure.

**catch block** a block of code that can catch one type of Exception.

**char** an integral data type that can store a character such as 'A', '4', or '$'.

**character** any one of the letters, numbers, or other special symbols (such as punctuation marks) that comprise data.

**character set** the group of all the characters used to represent data on a particular computer.

**check digit** a digit calculated from a formula and appended to a number to help verify the accuracy of the other digits in the number.

**CheckBox** a GUI widget that a user can click to select or deselect an option. When a Form contains multiple CheckBoxes, any number of them can be checked or unchecked at the same time.

**CheckedListBox** a `Control` similar to a `ListBox`, with check boxes appearing to the left of each desired item.

**child class** a derived class; a subclass; a class that has inherited from a base class.

**class** a category of objects or a type of object.

**class access modifier** describes access to a class.

**class client** a program or class that instantiates objects of another prewritten class. Also called a *class user*.

**class definition** the first class line that describes a class; it contains an optional access modifier, the keyword `class`, and any legal identifier for the name of the class.

**class header** the first class line that describes a class; it contains an optional access modifier, the keyword `class`, and any legal identifier for the name of the class.

**class user** a program or class that instantiates objects of another prewritten class. Also called a *class client*.

**click event** an action fired when a user clicks a button in a GUI environment.

**Click event** the event generated when a `Control` is clicked.

**client** a method that uses another method.

**closing a file** the process of making a file no longer available to an application.

**code bloat** a term that describes unnecessarily long or repetitive program statements.

**code refactoring** the process of changing a program's internal structure without changing the way the program works.

**code snippets** small units of commonly used C# source code that you can enter accurately and quickly with only a couple of keystrokes.

**Color** a class that contains a wide variety of predefined colors to use with `Controls`.

**collection** any data structure that holds objects of the same type.

**ComboBox** a `Control` similar to a `ListBox`, except that it displays an additional editing field that allows a user to select from the list or enter new text.

**command line** the line on which you type a command in a system that uses a text interface.

**command prompt** a request for input that appears at the beginning of the command line.

**comment out** to turn a statement into a comment so that the compiler will not execute its command.

**Compare() method** a method that compares two values. In the `String` class, it is a method that requires two `string` arguments. When it returns 0, the two `strings` are equivalent; when it returns a positive number, the first `string` is greater than the second; and when it returns a negative value, the first `string` is less than the second.

**CompareTo()** a method that compares objects. In the `String` class, a method that is used with a `string` and a dot before the method name, with another `string` as an argument. When the method returns 0, the two `strings` are equivalent; when it returns a positive number, the first `string` is greater than the second; and when it returns a negative value, the first `string` is less than the second. In the `IComparable` interface, a method that compares one object to another and returns an integer.

**comparison operator(==)** an operator that compares two items; an expression containing a comparison operator has a Boolean value.

**compiler** a computer program that translates high-level language statements into machine code.

**completion mode** an IDE editing mode in which suggestions are automatically provided for your code based on context.

**Component** a class that provides containment and cleanup for other objects.

**composed delegate** a delegate that calls the delegates from which it is built.

**composite key** a key constructed from multiple columns; a compound key.

**composition** the technique of using an object within another object.

**compound key** a key constructed from multiple columns; a composite key.

**computer file** a collection of information stored on a nonvolatile device in a computer system.

**computer simulations** programs that attempt to mimic real-world activities to foster a better understanding of them.

**concatenate** to join strings together in a chain.

**concrete** nonabstract; describes classes from which objects can be instantiated.

**conditional AND operator** an operator that determines whether two expressions are both true; it is written using two ampersands (&&). Also called the *AND operator*. Contrast with *Boolean logical AND operator*.

**conditional operator** a ternary operator that is used as an abbreviated version of the if-else statement; it requires three expressions separated by a question mark and a colon.

**conditional OR operator** an operator that determines whether at least one of two conditions is true; it is written using two pipes (||). Also called the *OR operator*. Contrast with *Boolean logical inclusive OR operator*.

**Console.ReadLine()** a method that accepts user input from the keyboard.

**constant** describes a data item when it cannot be changed after a program is compiled—in other words, when it cannot vary.

**constructor** a method that instantiates (creates an instance of) an object.

**constructor initializer** a clause that indicates another instance of a class constructor should be executed before any statements in the current constructor body.

**contextual keywords** identifiers that act like keywords in specific circumstances.

**Control class** a class that provides the definitions for GUI objects.

**control statement** the part of a structure that determines whether the subsequent block of statements executes.

**Controls** GUI components such as text fields, buttons, and check boxes that users can manipulate to interact with a program.

**counted loop** a definite loop.

**CSV file** a file that contains comma-separated values.

**culture** a set of rules that determines how culturally dependent values such as money and dates are formatted.

# D

**data files** files that contain facts and figures; persistent collections of related records. Contrast with *program files* and *application files*.

**data hierarchy** the relationship of characters, fields, records, and files.

**data redundancy** the unnecessary repetition of data.

**data type** a description of the format and size of a data item as well as the operations that can be performed on it.

**database** a collection of files that an organization needs to support its applications.

**database management software** a set of programs that allows users to create table descriptions; identify keys; add, delete, and update records within a table; arrange records within a table so they are sorted by different fields; write questions that select specific records from a table for viewing; write questions that combine information from multiple tables; create reports; and keep data secure.

**dataset** a temporary set of data stored in a project.

**DateTimePicker** a Control that retrieves date and time information.

**dead code** statements that can never execute under any circumstances because the program logic "can't get there." Also see *unreachable code*.

**debugging** the process of removing all syntax and logical errors from a program.

**decimal** a floating-point data type that has a greater precision and a smaller range than a float or double, which makes it suitable for financial and monetary calculations.

**decimal numbering system** the system that uses ten digits, 0 through 9, arranged in columns to represent numbers.

**decision structure** a unit of program logic that involves choosing between alternative courses of action based on some value.

**decrement operator (--)** an operator that reduces a variable's value by 1; there is a prefix and a postfix version.

**decrementing** the act of decreasing the value of a variable, often by 1.

**default** a keyword that optionally is used prior to any action that should occur if the test expression in a case structure does not match any case.

**default constructor** a constructor that requires no parameters; the automatically supplied parameterless constructor for a class is a default constructor, but you can also create a default constructor.

**default event** for a Control, the event or method generated when you double-click it while designing it in the IDE. It is the method you are most likely to alter when you use the Control, as well as the event that users most likely expect to generate when they encounter the Control in a working application.

**default value of an object** the value initialized with a default constructor.

**definite loop** a loop in which the number of iterations is predetermined. Also a *counted loop*. Contrast with *indefinite loop*.

**delegate** an object that contains a reference to a method.

**delimiter** a character used to specify the boundary between characters in text files.

**derived class** a subclass; a class that has inherited from a base class.

**deserialization** the process of converting streams of bytes back into objects.

**destructor** a method that contains the actions performed when an instance of a class is destroyed.

**DialogResult** an enumeration that contains a user's potential MessageBox button selections.

**directories** structures used to organize files on a storage device; folders.

**Directory class** a class that provides information about directories or folders.

**dismiss** to get rid of a component, frequently by pressing its Close button, but in some cases by making some other selection.

**do loop** a type of posttest loop; a loop that is tested at the bottom of the loop after one repetition has occurred.

**Dock property** an attribute that attaches a Control to the side of a container so that the Control stretches when the container's size is adjusted.

**double** a data type that can hold a floating-point number with 15 or 16 significant digits of accuracy.

**dual-alternative decisions** decisions that have two possible outcomes.

**duck typing** the process of implicitly typing a variable.

**dynamic typing** the process of implicitly typing a variable.

# E

**empty body** a block that has no statements in it.

**encapsulation** the technique of packaging an object's attributes and methods into a cohesive unit that can be used as an undivided entity.

**enum** an enumeration; a programmer-defined type that declares a set of constants.

**enumeration** a list of values in which names are substituted for numeric values.

**Equals()** a method that determines equivalency. In the String class, it is the method that determines if two strings have the same value; it requires two string arguments that you place within its parentheses, separated by a comma.

**error list tab** a portion of the Visual Studio IDE that displays compiler errors.

**escape sequence** a single character composed of two symbols beginning with a backslash.

**event** an object generated when a user interacts with a GUI object, causing the program to perform a task.

**EventArgs** a C# class designed for holding event information.

**event-driven programs** programs that contain code that causes an event such as a button click to perform a task.

**event handler** a method that performs a task in response to an event; an event receiver.

**EventHandler** a class for events that do not use any information besides the source of the event and the EventArgs parameter.

**event receiver** a method that performs a task in response to an event; an event handler.

**event sender** the control that generates an event.

**event wiring** the act of connecting an event to its resulting actions.

**exception** an error condition or unexpected behavior in an executing program.

**exception handling** the set of object-oriented techniques used to manage unexpected errors.

**explicit cast** purposefully assigns a value to a different data type; it involves placing the desired result type in parentheses followed by the variable or constant to be cast.

**explicitly** purposefully. Contrast with *implicitly*.

**exposes** associates a `FileStream` with a file.

**Extended Binary Coded Decimal Interchange Code (EBCDIC)** an eight-bit code that is used in IBM mainframe computers.

**extended class** a derived class; a child class; a subclass; a class that has inherited from a base class.

**extension methods** static methods that act like instance methods. You can write extension methods to add to any type.

# F

**fault-tolerant** describes applications that are designed so that they continue to operate, possibly at a reduced level, when some part of the system fails.

**field** in a class, an instance variable. In a file or database, a character or group of characters that has some meaning.

**File class** a class that contains methods that allow you to access information about files.

**file position pointer** a variable that holds the byte number of the next byte to be read from a file.

**finally block** a block of code that optionally follows a `try` block; the code within a `finally` block executes whether

the preceding `try` block identifies any `Exceptions` or not.

**fires an event** causes an event to occur. Also see *raises an event* and *triggers an event*.

**float** a data type that can hold a floating-point number with as many as seven significant digits of accuracy.

**floating-point** describes a number that contains decimal positions.

**flowchart** a tool that helps programmers plan a program's logic by writing program steps in diagram form, as a series of shapes connected by arrows.

**focus** the state of a GUI component when the user's attention is drawn to it visually. When a component has focus, you can execute its action by pressing the Enter key.

**folders** structures used to organize files on a storage device; directories.

**Font** a class used to change the appearance of printed text on `Forms`.

**for loop** a loop that contains the starting value for the loop control variable, the test condition that controls loop entry, and the expression that alters the loop control variable, all in one statement.

**foreach statement** a statement used to cycle through every array element without using a subscript.

**Form Designer** a portion of the Visual Studio IDE in which you visually design applications.

**formal parameter** a parameter within a method header that accepts a value.

**format specifier** one of nine built-in format characters in a format string that defines the most commonly used numeric format types.

**format string** a string of characters that contains one or more placeholders for variable values.

**Forms** a GUI interface for collecting, displaying, and delivering information.

**fragile** describes classes that depend on field names from parent classes because they are prone to errors—that is, they are easy to "break."

**from** a LINQ keyword that indicates the collection or sequence from which data will be drawn.

## G

**garbage** an unknown memory value.

**get accessors** methods in properties that allow retrieval of a field value by using a property name.

**getter** another term for a class property's get accessor.

**gigabyte** approximately a billion bytes.

**governing type** in a `switch` statement, the type that is established by the `switch` expression. The governing type can be `sbyte`, `byte`, `short`, `ushort`, `int`, `uint`, `long`, `ulong`, `char`, `string`, or `enum`.

**graphical user interface (GUI)** an interface that employs graphical images the user manipulates. GUI objects include the buttons, check boxes, and toolbars you are used to controlling with a mouse when you interact with Windows-type programs.

**group operator** in LINQ, the operator that groups data by specified criteria.

**GroupBox** a `Control` that can be used to group other `Control`s on a `Form`; similar to a `Panel` but it has a `Title` property.

## H

**hardware** the physical devices associated with a computer.

**has-a relationship** the relationship created using composition, so called because one class "has an" instance of another.

**hash code** a number that should uniquely identify an object.

**hexadecimal** a mathematical system that uses 16 symbols to represent numbers; base 16.

**hides** overrides so as to make invisible.

**high-level programming language** a language that allows you to use a vocabulary of reasonable terms such as "read," "write," or "add" instead of the sequence of on/off switches that perform these tasks.

## I

**IComparable interface** an interface that contains the definition for the `CompareTo()` method.

**identifier** the name of a program component such as a variable, class, or method.

**if statement** a program statement used to make a single-alternative decision.

**if-else statement** a statement that performs a dual-alternative decision.

**immutable** unchangeable.

**implementation hiding** the technique of keeping the details of a method's operations hidden.

**implicit cast** the automatic transformation that occurs when a value is assigned to a type with higher precedence.

787

**implicit conversion** the conversion that occurs when a type is automatically changed to another upon assignment.

**implicit parameter** an undeclared parameter that gets its value automatically.

**implicit reference conversion** the type of conversion that occurs when a derived class object is assigned to its ancestor's data type.

**implicitly** automatically. Contrast with *explicitly*.

**implicitly typed variable** a variable that has a data type that is inferred from the expression used to initialize the variable.

**incrementing** the act of increasing the value of a variable, often by 1.

**indefinite loop** a loop in which the number of iterations is not predetermined. Contrast with *definite loop*.

**index** an integer contained within square brackets that indicates the position of one of an array's elements. Also see *subscript*.

**infinite loop** a loop that (theoretically) never ends.

**information hiding** a feature found in all object-oriented languages, in which a class's data is private and changed or manipulated only by its own methods.

**inheritance** the ability to extend a class so as to create a more specific class that contains all the attributes and methods of a more general class; the extended class usually contains new attributes or methods as well.

**initialization** an assignment made when a variable is declared.

**initializer list** the list of values provided for an array.

**inner loop** the loop in a pair of nested loops that is entirely contained within another loop.

**instance methods** methods that are used with object instantiations.

**instance of a class** an object; a tangible example of a class.

**instance variables** data components of a class that exist separately for each instantiation. Also called *fields*.

**instantiation** a created object.

`int` an integral data type that can hold a signed numeric value in four bytes.

**integers** whole numbers.

**integral data types** data types that store whole numbers; the nine integral types are `byte`, `sbyte`, `short`, `ushort`, `int`, `uint`, `long`, `ulong`, and `char`.

**Integrated Development Environment (IDE)** a program development environment that allows you to select options from menus or by clicking buttons. An IDE provides such helpful features as color coding and automatic statement completion.

**IntelliSense** Microsoft's name for the set of features designed to minimize the time you spend looking for help and to help you enter code more accurately and efficiently.

**interactive program** a program that allows user input.

**interface** a collection of abstract methods (and perhaps other members) that can be used by any class as long as the class provides a definition to override the interface's abstract definitions. The interaction between a method and an object.

**intermediate language (IL)** the language into which source code statements are compiled.

`internal` a class access modifier that means access is limited to the assembly to which the class belongs.

**internal access** a level of method accessibility that limits method access to the containing program.

**intrinsic types** basic, built-in data types; C# provides 15 intrinsic types.

**invoke** to call a method.

**invoking object** the object referenced by `this` in an instance method.

**invoking the event** calling an event method.

**iteration** one execution of any loop.

**iteration variable** a temporary variable that holds each array value in turn in a `foreach` statement.

## J

**jagged array** a one-dimensional array in which each element is another array.

**jump statement** a statement that causes program logic to "jump" out of the normal flow in a control structure. Jump statements include `break` and `continue`.

**just in time (JIT)** the C# compiler that translates intermediate code into executable code.

## K

**K & R style** a way of writing code so that the opening curly brace of a structure is on the same line as the control statement; it is named for Brian Kernighan and Dennis Ritchie, who wrote the first book on the C programming language

**key** a value that uniquely identifies a record.

**key events** keyboard events that occur when a user presses and releases keyboard keys.

**key field** the field used to control the order of records in a sequential file.

**keywords** predefined and reserved identifiers that have special meaning to the compiler.

**kilobyte** approximately a thousand bytes.

## L

**Label** a `Control` object that typically provides descriptive text for another `Control` object or displays other text information on a `Form`.

**left-associative** describes operators whose operations are performed from left to right.

**Length property** a member of the `System.Array` class that automatically holds an array's length.

**Leszynski naming convention (LNC)** a convention for naming database elements that is most popular with Microsoft Access users and Visual Basic programmers.

**lexically** alphabetically.

**line comments** comments that start with two forward slashes (//) and continue to the end of the current line. Line comments can appear on a line by themselves, or at the end of a line following executable code. Compare with *block comments*.

**LinkLabel** a `Control` that is similar to a `Label`, but that provides the additional capability to link the user to other sources, such as Web pages or files.

**LINQ (Language INtegrated Query)** a set of general-purpose standard query operators that allow queries to be constructed in C# using easy-to-understand syntax. LINQ is similar to SQL, and the compiler can check it for errors.

**ListBox** a `Control` that enables you to display a list of items that the user can select by clicking.

**literal constant** a value that is taken literally at each use.

**literal string** a series of characters that is used exactly as entered.

**local variable** a variable that is declared in the current method.

**logic** the sequence of statements and methods that produce the desired results in a computer program.

**logical AND operator** the ampersand (&).

**logical OR operator** the pipe (|).

**long** an integral data type that can hold a signed numeric value in eight bytes.

**loop** a structure that allows repeated execution of a block of statements.

**loop body** the block of statements executed in a loop.

**loop control variable** a variable that determines whether loop execution will continue on each iteration.

# M

**machine language** the most basic circuitry-level language.

**magic number** a hard-coded number.

**main menu** in the Visual Studio IDE, the list of choices that run horizontally across the top of the screen; it includes a File menu from which you open, close, and save projects.

**mandatory parameters** method parameters for which an argument is required in every method call.

**matrix** a name frequently used by mathematicians when referring to an array. Also see *table*.

**MaximumSize property** an attribute of a `Form` that has two values: `Width` and `Height`.

**megabyte** approximately a million bytes.

**menu strip** a horizontal list of general options that appears under the title bar of a `Form` or `Window`.

**MenuStrip** a control that creates a menu strip.

**MessageBox** a GUI object that can contain text, buttons, and icons that inform and instruct a user.

**method** an encapsulated series of statements that carry out a task.

**method body** all the instructions contained within a pair of curly braces ({ }) following a method header.

**method declaration** a method header or definition; it precedes a method and includes a return type, identifier, and an optional parameter list.

**method definition** a method header or declaration; it precedes a method and includes a return type, identifier, and an optional parameter list.

**method header** the first line of a method, which includes the method name and information about what will pass into and be returned from a method.

**method node** in Visual Studio, a small box that appears to the left of code; you use it to expand or collapse code.

**method's type** a method's `return` type.

**Microsoft Office Access** a relational database that is part of the Microsoft Office software suite.

**MinimumSize property** an attribute of a `Form` that has two values: `Width` and `Height`.

**mission critical** describes any process that is crucial to an organization.

**modal dialog box** a dialog box that prevents a program from further progress until the user dismisses it.

**modal window** a secondary window that takes control from a primary window. The user must deal with a modal window before proceeding.

**MonthCalendar** a `Control` that retrieves date and time information.

**multidimensional arrays** arrays that require multiple subscripts to access the array elements.

**multifile assembly** a group of files containing methods that work together to create an application.

**multiple inheritance** the ability to inherit from more than one class.

# N

**named constant** an identifier whose contents cannot change.

**namespace** a scheme that provides a way to group similar classes.

**nested** `if` a statement in which one decision structure is contained within another.

**nested method calls** method calls placed inside other method calls.

**new** a keyword used to create objects; also known as the `new` operator.

**node** In the Visual Studio IDE, a box that appears on a vertical tree to the left of a list or a section of code and that can be expanded or condensed.

**nonapplication classes** classes that do not contain a `Main()` method and therefore are not runnable programs; they provide support for other classes.

**nonstatic** describes a method that requires an object reference.

**nonvolatile** the type of computer storage that is permanent; it is not lost when a computer loses power.

**normalization** the process of designing and creating a set of database tables that satisfies the users' needs and avoids many potential problems such as data redundancies and anomalies.

**NOT operator (!)** an operator that negates the result of any Boolean expression.

# O

**object (or Object)** a class type in the `System` namespace that is the ultimate base class for all other types.

**object initializer** a clause that allows you to assign values to any accessible members or properties of a class at the time of instantiation without calling a constructor with parameters.

**object-oriented approach** an approach to a problem that involves defining the objects needed to accomplish a task and developing classes that describe the objects so that each maintains its own data and carries out tasks when another object requests them.

**object-oriented programming (OOP)** a programming technique that features objects, classes, encapsulation, interfaces, polymorphism, and inheritance.

**objects** program elements that are instances of a class.

**one-dimensional array** an array whose elements you can access using a single subscript. Also see *single-dimensional array*.

**opening a file** the process of creating an object and associating a stream of bytes with it.

**operands** the values that operators use in expressions.

**operator precedence** rules that determine the order in which parts of a mathematical expression are evaluated. Also called *order of operation*.

**optional parameter** a parameter to a method for which a default value is automatically supplied if you do not explicitly send one as an argument; a parameter is optional when it is given a value in the method declaration.

**OR operator** an operator that determines whether at least one of two conditions is true; it is written using two pipes (||). Also called the *conditional OR operator*. Contrast with *Boolean logical inclusive OR operator*.

**order of operation** rules that determine the order in which parts of a mathematical expression are evaluated. Also called *operator precedence*.

**orderby operator** in LINQ, the operator that sorts a collection of data based on a field or fields.

**out of scope** describes a variable that is not usable because it has ceased to exist.

**outer loop** the loop in a pair of nested loops that contains another loop.

**output parameter** a parameter to a method that receives the argument's address; it is not required to have an initial value. Contrast with *value parameter* and *reference parameter*.

**overload resolution** the process of determining which of multiple applicable methods is the best match for a method call.

**overloading** using one term to indicate diverse meanings. When you overload a C# method, you write multiple methods with the same name but different parameter lists.

**override** a keyword used in method headers when you create a derived class that inherits an abstract method from a parent.

**overrides** the action that occurs when a method takes precedence over another method, hiding the original version.

# P

**Padding property** an attribute of a Form that specifies the distance between docked Controls and the edges of the Form.

**Panel** a Control that can be used to group other Controls on a Form; similar to a GroupBox, but it does not have a Title property.

**parallel array** an array that has the same number of elements as another array and holds corresponding data.

**parameter array** a local array declared within a method header.

**parameter to a method** an object or reference that is declared in a method definition.

**parameterless constructor** a constructor that takes no parameters; one that is called using no arguments.

**params** a keyword used to declare a local array in a method so the method can receive any number of arguments.

**parent class** a base class; a superclass; a class that is used as a basis for inheritance.

**Pascal casing** a style of creating identifiers in which the first letter of all new words in a variable name, even the first one, is capitalized. Contrast with *camel casing*.

**passed by reference** describes how data is passed to a method when the method receives the memory address of the argument passed to it.

**path** the disk drive in which a file resides plus the complete hierarchy of directories.

**permanent storage devices** hardware such as hard disks, USB drives, and compact discs, that are used to store files.

**persistent** describes storage that is nonvolatile.

**PictureBox** a Control in which you can display graphics from a bitmap, icon, JPEG, GIF, or other image file type.

**placeholder** in a format string, it consists of a pair of curly braces containing a number that indicates the desired variable's position in a list that follows the string.

**polymorphism** the ability to create methods that act appropriately depending on the context.

**postfix increment operator** an operator that evaluates a variable and then adds 1 to it. This operator is represented by a ++ after a variable.

**posttest loop** a loop in which the loop control variable is tested after the loop body executes. Contrast with *pretest loop*.

**precision specifier** a specifier that controls the number of significant digits or zeros to the right of the decimal point in a format string.

**prefix increment operator** an operator that increases the variable's value by 1 and then evaluates it. This operator is represented by a ++ before a variable.

**pretest loop** a loop in which the loop control variable is tested before the loop body executes. Contrast with *posttest loop*.

**primary key** a value that uniquely identifies a record; the term is often used in databases.

**private** an access modifier that indicates other classes may not use the method or variable that it modifies. When used as a class access modifier, it means access is limited to another class to which the class belongs.

**private access** a level of method accessibility that limits method access to the containing class.

**procedural program** a program created by writing a series of steps or operations to manipulate values.

**procedures** compartmentalized program units that accomplish tasks. See also *method*.

**program** a set of instructions that you write to tell a computer what to do.

**program comments** nonexecuting statements that document a program.

**program files** files that store software instructions; application files. Contrast with *data files*.

**projection operator** in LINQ, an operator that projects, or sends off, specific data from a collection.

**prompt** an instruction to the user to enter data.

**propagating an exception** the act of transmitting an exception object unchanged through the call stack.

**Properties window** a portion of the Visual Studio IDE that allows you to configure properties and events on controls in your user interface.

**property** a member of a class that provides access to a field of a class; properties define how fields will be set and retrieved. The value of an object.

**protected** a keyword that provides an intermediate level of security between `public` and `private` access. A `protected` data field or method can be used within its own class or in any classes extended from that class, but it cannot be used by "outside" classes. As a class access modifier, it means access to the class is limited to the class and to any classes derived from the class.

**protected access** a level of method accessibility that limits method access to the containing class or types derived from the containing class.

**pseudocode** a tool that helps programmers plan a program's logic by writing plain English statements.

**public** an access modifier that indicates other classes may use the method or variable that it modifies. As a class access modifier, it means access to the class is not limited.

**public access** a level of method accessibility that allows unlimited access to a method.

## Q

**query** a question that retrieves information from a database using syntax that the database software can understand.

**query by example** the process of using database software to create a query by filling in blanks.

## R

**RadioButtons** GUI widgets, similar to `CheckBoxes`, except that when they are placed on a `Form`, only one `RadioButton` can be selected at a time—selecting any `RadioButton` automatically deselects the others.

**raises an event** causes an event to occur. Also see *fires an event* and *triggers an event*.

**random access memory (RAM)** temporary storage in a computer.

**range check** a series of statements that determine whether a value falls within a specified range.

**range match** a process that determines whether a value falls between a pair of limiting values.

**read from the file** to copy data from a file on a storage device into RAM.

**read-only property** a property that has only a get accessor, and not a set accessor.

**record** a collection of fields that contain data about an entity.

**rectangular array** an array in which each row has the same number of columns.

**recursive** describes a method that calls itself.

**reference equality** the type of equality that occurs when two reference type objects refer to the same object.

**reference parameter** a parameter to a method that receives the argument's address; it is required to have an initial value. Contrast with *value parameter* and *output parameter*.

**reference type** a data type that holds a memory address. Contrast with *value types*.

**relational database** a database in which you can establish and maintain relationships between columns in the tables.

**restriction operator** in LINQ, an operator that places a restriction on which data is added to a collection.

**rethrow an Exception** to throw a caught Exception instead of handling it.

**return statement** a method statement that causes a value to be sent back from a method to its calling method.

**return type** the type of value a method will return to any other method that calls it.

**Reverse() method** a member of the System.Array class that reverses the order of items in an array.

**right-associative** describes operators whose operations are performed from right to left.

**robustness** describes the degree to which a system is resilient to stress, maintaining correct functioning even in the presence of errors.

**root class** the ultimate or first base class in a hierarchical ancestry tree.

**root directory** the main directory of a storage device.

# S

**sbyte** an integral data type that can hold a signed numeric value from −128 through 127.

**scientific notation** a numeric expression format that includes an *E* (for exponent) and that specifies a number of implied decimal places.

**scope** the area where a variable or constant is known and can be used.

**sealed class** a class that cannot be extended.

**select** a LINQ keyword that indicates what to select from a collection.

**SELECT-FROM-WHERE** the basic form of the SQL command that retrieves selected records from a table.

**self-documenting** describes a program element that is self-explanatory.

**semantic errors** the type of logical errors that occur when you use a correct word in the wrong context.

**sentinel value** a value that a user must supply to stop a loop.

**sequence structure** a unit of program logic in which one step follows another unconditionally.

**sequential access file** a data file in which each record is stored in order based on the value in some field.

**sequential search** a search that is conducted by examining a list item by item in sequence.

**serialization** the process of converting objects into streams of bytes.

**set accessors** methods in properties that allow use of the assignment operator with a property name.

**setter** another term for a class property's set accessor.

**short** an integral data type that can hold a signed numeric value in two bytes.

**short-circuit evaluation** the C# feature in which parts of an AND or OR expression are evaluated only as far as necessary to determine whether the entire expression is true or false.

**side effect** an unintended consequence of an operation.

**signature** a method's name and parameter list.

**significant digits** specifies the mathematical accuracy of a value.

**simple type** describes one of the following in C#: byte, sbyte, short, ushort, int, uint, long, ulong, float, double, decimal, char, and bool.

**single-dimensional array** an array whose elements you can access using a single subscript. Also see *one-dimensional array*.

**snap lines** lines that appear in a design environment to help you align new `Controls` with others already in place.

**software** computer programs.

**Solution Explorer** a portion of the Visual Studio IDE that allows you to view and manage project files and settings.

**Sort() method** a member of the `System.Array` class that arranges array items in ascending order.

**source code** the statements you write when you create a program.

**standard numeric format strings** strings of characters expressed within double quotation marks that indicate a format for output.

**StartsWith() method** a `string` method that returns `true` if its first `string` parameter starts with the characters contained in the second `string` parameter.

**state of an object** the collective value of all an object's attributes at any point in time.

**static** a keyword that indicates that a method will be executed through a class and not by an object.

**step value** the amount by which a loop control variable is altered on each iteration, especially in a `for` loop.

**stream** a pipeline or channel through which bytes are input from and output to a file.

**string** a data type that can hold a series of characters.

**strongly typed** describes a language in which severe restrictions are placed on what data types can be mixed.

**Structured Query Language (SQL)** the most common language that database administrators use to access data in their tables.

**subclass** a derived class; a child class; a class that has inherited from a base class.

**subscript** an integer contained within square brackets that indicates the position of one of an array's elements. Also see *index*.

**Substring() method** a method that can be used to extract a portion of a string from a starting point for a specific length.

**suggestion mode** an IDE editing mode in which completion mode is turned off.

**superclass** a base class; a parent class; a class that is the basis for inheritance.

**switch** a keyword that starts a `switch` structure.

**switch expression** a condition in a `switch` statement enclosed in parentheses.

**switch structure** a structure that tests a single variable against a series of exact matches.

**syntax** the set of grammar rules in a programming language.

**syntax error** an error that occurs when a programming language is used incorrectly.

**System namespace** a scheme built into the C# compiler that holds commonly used classes.

**System.Array** a built-in class that defines fields and methods that belong to every array.

# T

**table** a name frequently used by mathematicians when referring to an array. Also see *matrix*.

**tables** database files, so called because their contents are arranged in rows and columns.

**ternary** describes an operator that requires three arguments.

**TextBoxes** controls through which a user can enter input data in a GUI application.

**text files** files that contain data that can be read in a text editor because the data has been encoded using a scheme such as ASCII or Unicode.

**this reference** the reference to an object that is implicitly passed to an instance method of its class.

**TLA** a three-letter abbreviation for *three-letter abbreviation*; it is the most popular type of abbreviation in technical terminology.

**token** a block of text within a string that represents an entity or field.

**Toolbox tab** a portion of the Visual Studio IDE that contains controls you can drag onto a Form so that you can develop programs visually, using a mouse.

**transitive** inheriting all the members of one's ancestors.

**triggers an event** causes an event to occur. Also see *fires an event* and *raises an event*.

**truth tables** diagrams used in mathematics and logic to help describe the truth of an entire expression based on the truth of its parts.

**try block** a block that contains code that might create exceptions you want to handle.

**two-dimensional arrays** multidimensional arrays that have two or more columns of values for each row.

**type inference** the process of implicitly typing a variable.

**type precedence** a hierarchy of data types used to determine the unifying type in arithmetic expressions containing dissimilar data types.

## U

**uint** an integral data type that can hold an unsigned numeric value in four bytes.

**ulong** an integral data type that can hold an unsigned numeric value in eight bytes.

**unary operators** operators used with one operand.

**Unicode** a 16-bit coding scheme for characters.

**Unified Modeling Language (UML) diagrams** graphical tools that programmers and analysts use to describe systems.

**unifying type** the type chosen for an arithmetic result when operands are of dissimilar types.

**unreachable code** statements that can never execute under any circumstances because the program logic "can't get there." Also see *dead code*.

**ushort** an integral data type that can hold an unsigned numeric value in two bytes.

**using clause, or using directive** code that declares a namespace.

## V

**value parameter** a parameter to a method that receives a copy of the value passed to it. Contrast with *reference parameter* and *output parameter*.

**value types** data types that hold a value; they are predefined types such as int, double, and char. Contrast with *reference type*.

**var** a data type that creates an implicitly typed variable.

**variable** a named location in computer memory that can hold different values at different points in time.

**variable declaration** the statement that names a variable; it includes the data type that the variable will store, an identifier that is the variable's name, an optional assignment operator and assigned value when you want a variable to contain an initial value, and an ending semicolon.

**verbatim identifier** an identifier with an @ prefix.

**view** a particular way of looking at a database in database management systems.

**virtual method** a method whose behavior is determined by the implementation in a child class.

**visible** describes a class member that has not been hidden.

**void** a keyword that indicates that a method does not return any value when called.

**volatile** the type of computer storage that is lost when power is lost.

# W

**where** a LINQ keyword that indicates conditions for selecting records.

**while loop** a structure that executes a body of statements continuously while some condition continues to be true; it uses the keyword **while**.

**whitespace** any combination of spaces, tabs, and carriage returns (blank lines) in a program.

**widgets** interactive controls such as labels, scroll bars, check boxes, and radio buttons.

**wildcard** a symbol that means "any" or "all."

**write to a file** to store data in a computer file on a permanent storage device.

**Write() method** a method that displays a line of output on the screen, but the cursor does not advance to a new line; it remains on the same line as the output.

**WriteLine() method** a method that displays a line of output on the screen, positions the cursor on the next line, and waits for additional output.

# X

**XML** an abbreviation of eXtensible Markup Language, which is a standard for exchanging data over the Internet.

**XML-documentation format comments** comments that use a special set of tags within angle brackets to create documentation within a program.

# Index

# D